W9-CYS-400

 Routledge
Taylor & Francis Group

www.routledgesw.com

Melinda Lewis, The University of Kansas, Series Editor

An authentic breakthrough in social work education . . .

New Directions in Social Work is an innovative, integrated series of texts, website, and interactive case studies for generalist courses in the Social Work curriculum at both undergraduate and graduate levels. Instructors will find everything they need to build a comprehensive course that allows students to meet course outcomes, with these unique features:

- All texts, interactive cases, and test materials are **linked to the 2015 Educational Policy and Accreditation Standards (EPAS) from the Council on Social Work Education (CSWE).**

- **One web portal with easy access** for instructors and students from any computer—no codes, no CDs, no restrictions. Go to www.routledgesw.com and discover.

- **The Series is flexible and can be easily adapted for use in online distance-learning courses as well as hybrid and bricks-and-mortar courses.**

- Each text and the website can be used **individually** or as an **entire Series** to meet the needs of any social work program.

TITLES IN THE SERIES

The Practice of Generalist Social Work

Fourth Edition
by Julie Birkenmaier, Saint Louis University
Marla Berg-Weger, Saint Louis University

In this book and companion custom website, you will find:

- Complete coverage of the range of social work generalist practice within the framework of planned change, encompassing engagement, assessment, intervention, evaluation, and termination—for work with individuals, families, groups, organizations, and communities. This edition features expanded coverage of practice with individuals, families, groups, organizations, and communities.

- Consistent and in-depth use of key theoretical perspectives and case examples to demonstrate essential knowledge, values, and skills for generalist social work practice. But the text does not overwhelm the student reader with a plethora of nuances of intervention and other skills that will occur in a variety of practice settings and roles. *Instead, this book presents clearly the core competencies for general social work practice.*

- Six *unique,* in-depth, interactive, easy-to-access cases, which students can easily reach from *any* computer, provide a "learning by doing" format unavailable with any other text(s). Your students will have an advantage unlike any other they will experience in their social work education. Go to www.routledgesw.com/ cases to see each of these cases on the free website.

- In addition, *four* streaming videos relate to competencies and skills discussed in the book at the three client system levels—individuals and families, groups, and communities. The videos depict social workers demonstrating skills discussed in the chapters and offer instructors numerous possibilities for classroom instruction. In the video for the case, "Brickville," a social worker combines individual and family practice skills with multicultural community engagement as he works with an African American family about to be displaced by redevelopment and facing multiple stressors. Go to http://routledgesw.com//sanchez/engage/video, http://routledgesw.com//riverton/engage/video, and http://routledgesw.com//washburn/engage/video, and http://routledgesw.com//brickville/engage/video to see *each* of these videos that are included within *each* of the web-based cases.

- At least ten exercises at the end of each chapter provide you with the means to ensure that your students can *demonstrate their mastery* of the theoretical frameworks, skills, and core competencies of generalist social work practice as presented *not just* in the text, but in the free web-based cases as well. Instructors can choose from among the approximately five exercises that relate to relevant practice issues, and five that relate specifically to one of the online cases.

- A wealth of instructor-only resources also available at www.routledgesw. com/practice provide: full-text readings that link to the concepts presented in each of the chapters; a complete bank of objective and essay-type test items, all linked to current CSWE EPAS standards; PowerPoint presentations to help students master key concepts; a sample syllabus; annotated links to a treasure trove of social work assets on the Internet and teaching tips on how to use them in your practice sequence of courses.

- A clear focus on generalist social work practice, informed by the authors' decades of real-world practice experience, at *all* levels of engagement and intervention.

The Practice of Generalist Social Work

Fourth Edition

Julie Birkenmaier
Saint Louis University

Marla Berg-Weger
Saint Louis University

Routledge
Taylor & Francis Group

NEW YORK AND LONDON

Fourth edition published 2017
by Routledge
711 Third Avenue, New York, NY 10017

and by Routledge
2 Park Square, Milton Park, Abingdon, Oxon OX14 4RN

Routledge is an imprint of the Taylor & Francis Group, an informa business

First edition published by Mcgraw-Hill College 2005
Third edition published by Routledge 2014

Library of Congress Cataloging in Publication Data
A catalog record for this book has been requested

ISBN: 978–1–138–67603–9 (hbk)
ISBN: 978–1–138–67604–6 (pbk)
ISBN: 978–1–315–39490–9 (ebk)

Typeset in Stone Serif
by RefineCatch Limited, Bungay, Suffolk

Printed and bound in the United States of America by Sheridan

BRIEF CONTENTS

DETAILED CONTENTS

PREFACE

MAJOR CHANGES TO THE FOURTH EDITION

Like the previous editions, this new edition of *The Practice of Generalist Social Work* provides detailed coverage of the knowledge, skills, values, competencies, and behaviors needed for contemporary generalist social work practice. Using a strengths-based perspective, students are given a comprehensive overview of the major areas relevant for social work practice, including: theoretical frameworks, values and ethics, expanded coverage of communication skills for all client systems and examples of their use, and extensive coverage of practice with clients through all phases of the change process. *The Practice of Generalist Social Work* offers a comprehensive discussion of practice with individuals, families, groups, communities, and organizations within the concepts of planned change, encompassing engagement, assessment, intervention, evaluation, and termination and follow-up. Students have the opportunity to learn about generalist practice through in-depth case studies, examples, and exercises integrated throughout the text. This edition provides all the material necessary and relevant for a two- or three-course sequence.

This fourth edition is fully updated to the 2015 EPAS, with connections made between specific competencies and chapter content. This edition also provides additional examples of the application of theory and knowledge through case studies for all client levels, particularly in practice with individuals, families, and groups. For example, many chapters now open with a case and refer back to the case throughout to provide additional connections between content and real-life practice. Additional values and ethics material and cultural competency and humility content provide additional guidance for contemporary practice. Each chapter also now incorporates a link to a Grand Challenge of Social Work, from the American Academy of Social Work and Social Welfare, which facilitates a connection between the profession and the most significant societal challenges of today. The Quick Guides within the text offer students guidance for their field experience and practice after graduation. New Quick Guides in this edition provide students with brief guidelines for community practice.

In sum, this new edition provides expanded resources that contain up-to-date individual, family, group, community, and organizational guidance for the beginning practitioner. New end-of-chapter exercises connect with the wealth of case-based information available at www.routledgesw.com/ and facilitate a dynamic, experiential introduction to social work for your students.

Available with this edition are the following resources:

- Updated companion readings that are linked to key concepts in each chapter, along with questions to encourage further thought and discussion.

- Six interactive fictional cases with accompanying exercises that bring to life the concepts covered in the book, readings, and classroom discussions.

- A bank of exam questions (both objective and open-ended).

- PowerPoint presentations, which can serve as a starting point for class discussions.

- Sample syllabi demonstrating how the text and website, when used together through the course, satisfy the 2015 Educational Policy and Accreditation Standards (EPAS) from the Council on Social Work Education (CSWE).

- Quick Guides from the books offered online for students to print and take into the field for guidance.

- Updated annotated links to websites and other online resources, such as videos and podcasts.

ORGANIZATION OF THE BOOK

The following paragraphs serve to briefly introduce each of the chapters included in this book with emphasis on the updated content. All chapters have updated and specific connections to 2015 CSWE EPAS, and expanded end-of-chapter exercises that use online resources.

Chapter 1

Understanding Social Work Practice provides an overview of social work practice by grounding students in the purpose of social work; social work competencies; types of client grouping; and the practice framework of engagement, assessment, intervention, termination, and evaluation. A discussion of the ethics that guide social work practice, licensure of social work, client populations that social workers work with, and the tensions in social work provides students with real-world information about the profession. Students are also introduced to major theoretical perspectives for social work practice, including the ecosystems, social justice, human rights, strengths, and postmodern perspectives. In this fourth edition, connections made to the Grand Challenges for Social Work are introduced.

Chapter 2

In contrast to a straightforward overview of values and ethics, **Applying Values and Ethics to Practice** provides a brief history of social work ethics and the NASW *Code of Ethics* (2008), then contrasts the *Code of Ethics* with the International Federation of Social Workers' Ethical Statement, and also discusses the limits of ethical codes. A discussion of the intersection of ethics and the law gives students information about the interplay between the two, followed by a discussion of ethical dilemmas and processes for resolving them. Extensive discussion about common practice dilemmas gives students exposure to situations that they may encounter in practice, followed by an emphasis on risk management. Expanded coverage of ethics violations and state sanctions round out the discussion. New content in Chapter 2 includes expanded examples of value conflict, and discussion of the Grand Challenge of Social Work to "Create Social Responses to a Changing Environment."

Chapter 3

Individual Engagement: Relationship Skills for Practice at All Levels provides students with the characteristics of core relationships qualities, as well as a description of the specific skills for dialogue with clients at all system levels, including coverage of common communication pitfalls. As the helping relationship includes the dimension of power, the chapter provides extensive coverage of sources of power within relationships and provides guidance on the use of power through a case study of "Power in Client Lives: Jasmine Johnson." Practical questions guide students toward active listening. Students are also provided with strategies and skills for promoting social justice and human rights within helping relationships. New content in this fourth edition includes discussion of the Grand Challenge of Social Work to "Close the Health Gap."

Chapter 4

Social Work Practice with Individuals: Assessment and Planning includes a focus on the assessment and planning process within the global environment in which practicing social workers live. The chapter begins with a discussion of the history of assessment and moves to an overview of theoretical approaches to social work practice, both classic and contemporary (strengths, narrative, and solution-focused). The application of evidence-based practice approaches is highlighted. The need for practice knowledge and behaviors in the area of diversity within the assessment and planning phases emphasizes the need for cultural humility and competence. The chapter introduces the concepts of compassion satisfaction, intersectionality, and the cultural genogram and includes an exercise to address culture change from the student perspective. The chapter concludes with a discussion of the relevant skills and practice behaviors in the assessment and planning phases of the social work intervention process, including skills needed for strengths-based, narrative, and solution-focused approaches, documentation, and self-care for the social worker. This edition offers content on narrative and solution-focused approaches, documentation, self-care, and suicide risk assessment with vulnerable populations with more examples on applications of knowledge and theory. A discussion of the Grand Challenge of Social Work to "Eradicate Social Isolation" is brought to life with an exercise.

Chapter 5

Social Work Practice with Individuals: Intervention, Termination, and Evaluation introduces students to key areas of social work practice that will impact virtually every dimension of their professional lives. With an emphasis on theoretical perspectives, students learn to apply various intervention, termination, evaluation, and follow-up skills and behaviors. Traditional and contemporary social work roles are highlighted and discussed. Documentation and record-keeping for social work interventions is explained. Interventions with individuals are also framed within an empowerment practice approach. Framed within theoretical perspectives for understanding diversity, students are offered an overview of the skills required to be a culturally competent social work practitioner. New features in Chapter 5 include additional content on connecting the change process to the client's identified goals, therapeutic use of self, managing countertransference, being a social work professional, self-care, and the use of supervision. A Grand Challenge of Social Work, to "Advance Long and Productive Lives," is addressed through discussion, reading, and an exercise.

Chapter 6

Social Work Practice with Families: Engagement, Assessment, and Planning begins with a history of social work practice with families, grounded within a systems framework. Theoretical perspectives, including narrative and solution-focused, are discussed within the context of the engagement, assessment, and planning phases of interventions with families with emphasis on empowerment. Students encounter a broad range of family constellations as they read about contemporary family social work. Practice behaviors and skills are presented for achieving engagement and assessment with families and documentation strategies are included. This newest version of Chapter 6 offers more examples relating to the engagement, assessment, and planning with families. To "Ensure Healthy Development for All Youth" is the Grand Challenge of Social Work that is the focus in this chapter.

Chapter 7

Social Work Practice with Families: Intervention, Termination, and Evaluation conceptualizes generalist social work practice interventions with families. Continuing with the theoretical perspectives discussed in Chapter 6, this chapter develops interventions with families using strengths and empowerment, narrative, and solution-focused approaches. Skills and behaviors for intervening, terminating, evaluating, following up, and documenting family-focused interventions are discussed in detail. New to this edition is more in-depth content on evaluation of family interventions. The Grand Challenge for Social Work, "Ending Gender-Based Violence," is the focus of this chapter with a reading and an exercise.

Chapter 8

Social Work Practice with Groups: Engagement, Assessment, and Planning provides students with up-to-date perspectives on social work practice with groups. The chapter opens with an overview of the role of groups within our communities and profession followed by a historical and contemporary perspective on the use of groups for change. The dimensions of group practice are presented within the framework of theoretical perspectives (i.e., narrative and solution-focused). Planning for group interventions, including the engagement and assessment of group members, is emphasized from a practice perspective along with the importance of cultural competence in the group setting. With this edition, Chapter 8 now includes expanded content and examples on group-level social work skills and behaviors. To "End Homelessness" is the Grand Challenge of Social Work that is highlighted in this chapter.

Chapter 9

Social Work Practice with Groups: Intervention, Termination, and Evaluation emphasizes the development and implementation of interventions with various types of groups. Continuing the framing of skills and techniques within theoretical perspectives, the use of evidence-based interventions with groups is introduced using the strengths, narrative, and solution-focused frameworks. Models for group intervention are described, along with an in-depth examination of the roles, skills, and practice behaviors required for carrying out a group-level intervention. Termination, evaluation, and follow-up of group interventions are also covered. New to Chapter 9 is additional content on group dynamics and leadership. A Grand Challenge of Social Work that emphasizes how to "Harness Technology for Social Good" is discussed.

Chapter 10

Social Work Practice with Communities: Engagement, Assessment, and Planning introduces students to the concept of community. The chapter defines and discusses types and functions of communities. Students learn about various theoretical perspectives, including contemporary perspectives for community practice. Engagement and assessment concepts, including community-based analysis, evidence-based practice, and community needs assessments, are extensively discussed. Examples of types of needs assessments, surveys used in needs assessments, and needs assessment summaries provide additional practice guidance. Community practice skills are thoroughly covered, as are the implications of global interdependence for community practice in the United States. This edition contains new Quick Guides on running focus groups and community forums, as well as content on interprofessional engagement and community planning. Discussion of the Grand Challenge for Social Work, "Building Financial Capability for All" is also new for this edition.

Chapter 11

Social Work Practice with Communities: Intervention, Termination, and Evaluation builds on the engagement and assessment content of Chapter 10 to present strategies and techniques for community practice. Using the insights gained about practice at the individual, family, and group levels, this chapter expands the students' awareness of social work practice with communities through a discussion of today's trends and skills for intervention, including community social and economic development, and community organizing. Included in this discussion is coverage of international community practice. Examples of public and private efforts to promote evidence-based community practice assist students in applying the material. Additional guidance on advocacy efforts and asset-based development are presented. Students also learn the knowledge and skills needed for termination and evaluation of community practice. The fourth edition offers discussion of the Grand Challenge for Social Work to "Reduce Extreme Economic Inequality" and content on follow-up as part of the change process with communities.

Chapter 12

Social Work Practice with Organizations: Engagement, Assessment, and Planning covers a challenging client system for beginning practitioners—the organization. Students learn a wealth of practical and theoretical aspects of organizations, including a discussion about the purpose and structure of organizations, power relations within organizations, and social work within host organizational settings. The chapter provides discussion about the elements of an internal assessment of organizations, including organizational culture and external assessments as well. Material about organizational policy advocacy and nonprofit partnerships help guide practice. Examples of organizational engagement and assessment provide students with contemporary illustrations of key content in Chapter 12. New content in the fourth edition includes discussion of the Grand Challenge for Social Work to "Promote Smart Decarceration" and planning with organizations. A new exhibit displays the organizational hierarchy to help students understand how organizations are often structured.

Chapter 13

Social Work Practice with Organizations: Intervention, Termination, and Evaluation uses the foundation built in Chapter 12 to discuss approaches, perspectives, and models for intervening with organizations. This chapter provides extensive coverage of the relationship between theoretical perspectives and organizational change, as well as a practical framework for thinking about generating change and the needed knowledge for a social work generalist in this endeavor. Termination and evaluation of change efforts within organizations, including a discussion about the role of the generalist practitioner in this process, help students see their potential role in a change effort with organizations. Content about the challenges of implementing organizational change, and persuasion skills to assist in these efforts, provide direction for the practitioner. In this edition, Chapter 13 has expanded content that includes discussion of the Grand Challenge for Social Work to "Achieve Equal Opportunity and Justice" as well as content on follow-up with organizations.

INTERACTIVE CASES

The website www.routledgesw.com/cases presents six unique, in-depth, interactive, fictional cases with dynamic characters and real-life situations that students can easily access from any computer. They provide a "learning by doing" format unavailable with any other text. Your students will have an advantage unlike any other they will experience in their social work training. Each of the interactive cases uses text, graphics, and video to help students learn about engagement, assessment, intervention, evaluation, and termination at multiple levels of social work practice. The "My Notebook" feature allows students to take and save notes, type in written responses to tasks, and share their work with classmates and instructors by email. These interactive cases allow you to integrate the readings and classroom discussions:

The Sanchez Family: Systems, Strengths, and Stressors   The ten individuals in this extended Latino family have numerous strengths but are faced with a variety of challenges. Students will have the opportunity to experience the phases of the social work intervention, grapple with ethical dilemmas, and identify strategies for addressing issues of diversity.

Riverton: A Community Conundrum   Riverton is a small Midwest city in which the social worker lives and works. The social worker identifies an issue that presents her community with a challenge. Students and instructors can work together to develop strategies for engaging, assessing, and intervening with the citizens of the social worker's neighborhood.

Carla Washburn: Loss, Aging, and Social Support   Students will get to know Carla Washburn, an older African American woman who finds herself living alone after the loss of her grandson and in considerable pain from a recent accident. In this case, less complex than the Sanchez Family, students will apply their growing knowledge of gerontology and exercise the skills of culturally competent practice.

RAINN: Rape Abuse and Incest National Network   The RAINN Online Hotline links callers to local Rape Crisis Centers and hospitals, as well as other services. In addition, rape crisis telephone hotlines have played an important role in extending services to those in communities in which services are not available. Students will learn how and why this national hotline was developed; they will evaluate both qualitative and quantitative data to assess how the program can better achieve its goals.

Hudson City: An Urban Community Affected by Disaster   Hudson City has just been devastated by Hurricane Diane, a category 4 hurricane with wind speeds of 140 miles per hour. Students will take up the role of a social worker who also resides in the community, who has been tasked with finding workable solutions to a variety of problems with diverse clients systems. Students will learn about disaster response and how to focus on many clients at once.

Brickville: Families and Communities Consider Transitions   Brickville is a low-income community faced with a development proposal that would dramatically change the community. Students will take the role of a social worker who lives in the community and works for a community development corporation. Students will learn about community development and approaches that can be used to empower community members.

This book takes full advantage of the interactive element as a unique learning opportunity by including exercises that require students to go to the Web and use the cases. To maximize the learning experience, you may want to start the course by asking your students to explore each case by activating each button. The more the students are familiar with the presentation of information and the locations of the individual case files, the Case Study Tools, and the questions and tasks contained within each phase of the case, the better they will be able to integrate the text with the online practice component.

IN SUM

When presented as separate issues, all of the aforementioned developmental topics can seem overwhelming to students, particularly when they realize they have to keep at hand all their knowledge when working with clients. However, all of these topics, as well as other topics that are discussed, are set in a framework that will help students to think about the types of problems their clients might be likely to face at different phases in life. Students will also learn that organizing their knowledge about these areas into a theoretical context that "makes sense" to them will help them to manage the seemingly endless stream of information at their disposal. Ultimately, then, students will become more and more proficient at applying concepts to client problems. Meanwhile, students can enjoy the process of learning about them.

Being an effective social worker means being able to understand the complexities of human behavior, the societies and cultures in which we live, and the interplay between them. Being an effective social worker also means having a solid grounding in various disciplines, such as psychology, sociology, and human biology. It means possessing a well-rounded education and an ability to apply this knowledge to the myriad client problems and situations that students will face in the profession. This edition is intended to help students understand this complexity in the field and to help them gain the knowledge and critical thinking skills they will need to practice social work.

ACKNOWLEDGMENTS

We would like to thank the many colleagues who helped to make this book and previous editions possible. To Alice Lieberman, we are grateful for your innovation and vision that has resulted in this series and the web-based supplements that bring the material alive. We appreciate the camaraderie and support of the authors of the other books in this series—Rosemary Chapin, Anissa Rogers, Judy Kryzik, and Jerry Finn. A special thank you to Anissa Rogers, Shannon Cooper-Sadlo, Andrea Seper, and Megan Armentrout whose creativity makes the exercises, test questions, and PowerPoint slides enticing and easy to use. A special thanks to Shannon Cooper-Sadlo for sharing her practice wisdom and exercises. We want to thank the group who participated in the production of the video vignettes: actors John Abram, Patti Rosenthal, Beverly Sporleder, Sabrina Tyuse, Kristi Sobbe, Myrtis Spencer, Phil Minden, Katie Terrell, and Shannon Cooper-Sadlo and videographers, Tom Meuser and Elizabeth Yaeger. A special thanks goes to Megan Armentrout, graduate student assistant, for her extensive assistance with this edition and supplemental materials. Thanks also goes to social work graduate student assistant Dan Stewart for his assistance. We also want to thank:

Joan Allen, Arizona State University
Nancy Barker, Nassau Community College
Robin Bonifas, Arizona State University
Sally Booth, Rivier University
Heidi Brocious, University of Alaska Fairbanks
May Guenin, Mary Baldwin College
Kur Miller, Lancaster Bible College

Paul Sachdev, Memorial University
Mary Thomas, Mary Baldwin College
Gary Whitford, St. Cloud State University
Jeffrey Wylie, Murray State University

for their reviews of the book as it was evolving. Finally, we are most appreciative to the staff of Routledge for their support and encouragement for making this book a reality. It takes a village.

ABOUT THE AUTHORS

Julie Birkenmaier is a Professor in the School of Social Work at Saint Louis University, Missouri. Dr. Birkenmaier's practice experience includes community organizing, community development, and nonprofit administration. Her research and writing focuses on financial capability, financial credit, community development, and asset development. With colleagues, she co-wrote *Financial capability and asset-building in vulnerable households*. She also co-edited *Financial Capability and Asset Development: Research, Education, Policy and Practice*. With Marla Berg-Weger, she co-authored the textbook, *The Practicum Companion for Social Work: Integrating Class and Field Work* (4th edition).

Marla Berg-Weger is a Professor in the School of Social Work at Saint Louis University, Missouri and Executive Director of the Geriatric Education Center. Dr. Berg-Weger holds social work degrees at the bachelor's, master's, and doctoral levels. Her social work practice experience includes public social welfare services, intimate partner violence services, mental health, medical social work, and gerontological social work. Her research and writing focuses on gerontological social work and social work practice. She is the author of *Social Work and Social Welfare: An Invitation* (4th edition). With Julie Birkenmaier, she co-authored the textbook, *The Practicum Companion for Social Work: Integrating Class and Field Work* (4th edition). She is the Past President of the Association of Gerontology in Social Work and currently serves as the Managing Editor of the *Journal of Gerontological Social Work* and is a fellow in the Gerontological Society of America.

CHAPTER 1

Understanding Social Work Practice

Debbie, Joan, Marcy, and Kate felt as if the whole cosmos had just opened up for them. As a group, they had already shared their experiences with intimate partner violence. Their social worker had explained how they could use their stories to help educate children in schools about violence at home. They found their collective power liberating.

Chan, an 11-year-old orphaned child in Southeast Asia, hung on every word the community development worker uttered. The worker spoke of Chan's human rights in his workplace. Chan had never imagined that he had any rights.

Jamie was very relieved after the hospital social worker provided information about potential rehabilitation centers for his father, who was struggling with physical and mental health issues. Jamie's family could not care for their father at home, and Jamie now knew how his father would receive care during his recovery.

At their annual meeting, the neighborhood association expressed gratitude for their community social worker's work. Her efforts, along with her colleagues', helped neighbors connect to job opportunities, involved teens in working for a new community park, and secured additional city funding for the neighborhood.

Key Questions for Chapter 1

1. How can I prepare to engage, assess, intervene, evaluate, and follow-up with clients? [EPAS 6–9]
2. How do you define the practice of social work? [EPAS 1]
3. How does theory relate to social work practice? [EPAS 6–9]

WELCOME TO THE WORLD OF SOCIAL work practice. This world is sometimes exhilarating, sometimes frustrating, and sometimes heartbreaking. It is nearly always challenging, offers a deep sense of purpose, and once you have entered it, you may find it impossible to imagine doing any other kind of work.

This chapter examines the social work profession and the development of its mission. It explores different ways of thinking about social work practice, types of client groupings and processes, professional tensions within social work, the way the profession has dealt with theory, and contemporary practice commitments. The brief vignettes you have just read describe only a few of the many types of social work practice and clients. The chapter also describes the collective focus of the profession on societal challenges.

PURPOSE OF SOCIAL WORK

What is social work trying to accomplish? The primary mission of social work, according to the National Association of Social Workers' (NASW) *Code of Ethics* (2008), is "to enhance human well-being and help meet the basic human needs of all people, with particular attention to the needs and empowerment of people who are vulnerable, oppressed, and living in poverty." This mission can be narrowly applied to a particular type of system (e.g., mental health, corrections, and child welfare). Alternatively, the mission can be applied to a specific method (e.g., behavioral or cognitive change), a particular problem-solving process, or the elimination of a problem-focus (e.g., through the strengths perspective). The mission can also be applied to establishing and achieving goals, such as adaptation, sobriety, or re-entering society after incarceration. These endpoints are real examples of social work purpose embedded in the deeper and broader mission. The *Code of Ethics* expresses the purpose of social work broadly, leaving much open to interpretation.

PRACTICING SOCIAL WORK

Social work is a complex and multifaceted profession, with practitioners in virtually every setting from health clinics to housing programs. Social workers engage in a wide variety of activities. **Social work practice** is a licensed profession shaped by competencies and behaviors, client populations, settings, practice frameworks, professional history, and its purpose.

Social work practice can be conceptualized in several different ways, including: (1) a type of practice or range of practice settings, (2) a set of activities, (3) a set of roles, (4) a set of competencies and practice behaviors, (5) types of client grouping, (6) practice frameworks, (7) a profession that is licensed by states, and (8) purpose (as mentioned earlier). Self-knowledge is also a critical component of effective practice. These concepts are described in this chapter.

Undergraduate and foundational graduate work in generalist social work practice prepares students to work with a range of systems, from direct, one-to-one practice to group-level practice to local and global community development work and work in international settings. Graduate concentrations in advanced social work practice focus on more specialized practice, such as social work within a medical setting, family therapy, or the administration of social service organizations. The range of generalist and advanced practice settings includes psychiatric facilities, schools, community organizations, family service organizations, legislatures, correctional settings, and a host of others.

Social work practice activities are often associated with particular agencies and their functions in the community. Examples of these include: (1) advocating for policy change regarding the rights of older adults to services from an area agency on aging; (2) facilitating an empowerment group in a domestic violence program, such as the group in which Debbie, Joan, Marcy, and Kate belong; (3) mentoring students in a neighborhood school; (4) developing a psycho-educational group in a mental health agency; (5) supporting families in an emergency housing shelter; (6) implementing human rights policies in another culture by learning a new language and traveling to another part of the world to assist children like Chan; (7) advocating with public officials, companies, and corporations; (8) working with a group of adolescents; and (9) fundraising from government and foundation sources to assist in the empowerment of disadvantaged neighborhoods.

© Lisa F. Young

Generalist social work practice emphasizes the role of the social worker and the relationship between social worker and client. In the helping process, the generalist social worker, in direct practice with individuals, may take on the role of **case manager** (i.e., assisting clients to assess for, arrange, and coordinate needed goods and services); **counselor** (i.e., providing suggestions to assist clients to reach their goals); **broker** (i.e., referring clients to appropriate needed goods and services); **mediator** (i.e., assisting two parties to mutually resolve a dispute); **educator** (i.e., providing relevant information to clients); and **client advocate** (i.e., working with or on behalf of a client to obtain goods and services). Theoretical perspectives drive the definitions of role relationships. Chapter 5 discusses these roles in detail. Social worker functions specify the nature of the interaction between a social worker and the client. These roles are fluid; they can change from interaction to interaction and even within interactions. The roles define responsibilities for both the client and the social worker. Social work practice involves a wide variety of roles because social work deals with the breadth of human experience.

SOCIAL WORK COMPETENCIES

Generalist social work practitioners bring a set of competencies and behaviors to serve clients. The Council on Social Work Education's Educational Policy and Accreditation Standards (EPAS) defines these competencies, or the "ability to integrate and apply social work knowledge, values, and skills to practice situations in a purposeful, intentional, and professional manner to promote human and community well-being" (Council on Social Work Education (CSWE), 2015, p. 6), to guide social work education and, therefore, to influence social work practice. The nine competencies define practice elements and address the practice structure of engagement, assessment, intervention, and termination and evaluation. Each competency consists of several descriptive behaviors that social workers should be able to demonstrate effectively in practice settings. These competencies encompass knowledge, values, and skills and are the attributes social workers bring to the interaction with the client system of individuals, families, groups, organizations, and communities.

Knowledge, Values, and Skills [EPAS 1]

Knowledge, values, and skills are the core of social work education and training. These elements can be considered the tools that a practitioner brings to the work. They reflect personal attributes acquired by the social worker. Each is necessary for effective service delivery.

Knowledge Professional **knowledge** is made up of facts and research findings as well as less concrete elements such as intuitional and cultural awareness. Practicing social workers need to have "biopsychosocial" knowledge; that is, they need to know facts, histories, theories, and trends about human development, policy, research, and practice. Theories of human behavior and the social environment are central to generalist social work practice. Familiarity with these theories enables social workers to understand normal (or expected) behavior for an adolescent under stress or the likely dynamics in an agency when the administration initiates a policy change. The profession has agreed on the knowledge areas needed by social workers, and the knowledge is attainable through study, discussion, research experimentation, and related activities. According to the EPAS competencies, social workers should know the history of social work, the value base and ethical standards of the profession, and the history and current structures of social policies and services (CSWE, 2015). Through lifelong learning, social workers continually need to update their knowledge to ensure that they are relevant and effective. Through their professional experience, social workers gain first-hand knowledge, or "practice wisdom." This form of practice knowledge may elude traditional empirical measurement, an ongoing challenge both in the field and in social work education. This practice wisdom integrates what is learned "on the job" with knowledge from other sources, such as prior education and continuing education. Practice wisdom is an invaluable part of social work practice.

Culture and spirituality are also critical to professional practice. Social workers must understand the broad ways a culture's structure and values may create or enhance privilege and power for certain groups in society. This understanding can eliminate the influence of personal biases and values when working with diverse clients (Cross, 2013). **Cultural competence** refers to the "capacity to function effectively as a helper in the context of cultural differences" (Cross, 2013, p. 3). Diversity in practice also includes the notion of spirituality. Spirituality is an integral part of many cultures and gives practitioners access to knowledge about important dimensions of their clients. For example, recognizing a Navajo child's spiritual affirmation of harmony may help a social worker understand the child's reluctance to engage in aggressive competition in school. In some areas of practice, such as end of life, social workers use a model that combines two major areas of knowledge – a "biopsychosocial-spiritual" model to serve the needs of clients as whole persons (Hodgson, Lamson, & Kolobova, 2016).

Values Social work has always strongly identified itself as a profession of **values**, which are strongly held beliefs about preferred conditions of life. Key professional social work values include (1) the inherent worth of people, (2) the need for open and honest communication to build relationships, and (3) respect for the unique characteristics of diverse populations. Though the National Association of Social Workers (NASW) *Code of Ethics* (2008) clearly articulates the social work profes-sional values, you may hear spirited discussion about how best to implement these values in practice. Values and ethics present many challenges to social workers; they often look different in complicated practice contexts than they do in isolation. The National Association of Social Workers' (NASW) *Code of Ethics* (NASW, 2008) plays a significant role in sorting out complex situations in which values and ethical

The full NASW *Code of Ethics* is available in English and Spanish here:

http://www.socialworkers.org/pubs/code/code.asp

NASW has also published a series of publications that articulate standards for social work in various practice settings (e.g., school social work) and with various populations (e.g., family caregivers of older adults). These publications provide guidance to practitioners about the basic standards to which their organizations, as well as themselves as practitioners, should aspire to meet. See the listing of standards publications here:

http://www.socialworkers.org/practice/

conflicts arise. While values guide professional thinking about behavior and judgments about conduct, ethics are the rules, or prescriptions, for behavior that reflect those values. For example, the ethical principle that social workers should actively prevent any person from harm stems from the cardinal social work value that all human life is important. Conflicting ethical principles lead to dilemmas, as when the act of trying to prevent harm to one person may put another person at risk. The National Association of Social Workers developed a *Code of Ethics* to clarify the principles of ethical practice. Values provide critical criteria for the ways in which the profession shapes itself and for its professional rules of conduct.

Skills   The third element the social worker brings to her or his work with clients is **skills,** or the implementation of relevant knowledge, theoretical perspectives, and values. Social workers need a wide range of skills, from traditional communication skills and individual assessment skills, to skills in working with families, groups, communities, and organizations. Subsequent chapters discuss the range of social work skills with an emphasis on the EPAS competencies (CSWE, 2015).

Types of Client Groupings

Social work practice competencies may be viewed within the context of client groupings: work with individuals, couples, families of all types, groups, communities, and organizations, both domestically and internationally. These client groups often overlap, as when a social worker engages in group work within community practice, or in community work to assist families. These groupings define the constellation of the service beneficiaries involved in the interaction. Recent expansion of global awareness has resulted in the inclusion of international and global social work, extending the arena in which social work practice is both relevant and critical.

- *Individual work, family work, or casework:* This face-to-face focus spans all fields of practice, populations, and settings. Casework may include working with an adolescent struggling with sexuality issues, with a mother concerned about her child's development, with an older adult facing an inability to care for himself, or with a 5-year-old who does not pay attention in school. The nature of the work is heavily influenced by the agency's purpose, the practice perspective, the personal characteristics of the client (individual or family), and the social worker's skills and theoretical perspective. Cultural context, social and political influences, and current community concerns also affect client relationships.
- *Group work:* Social workers frequently practice with groups. The focus of group work may be on helping group members make individual changes, helping the group as a whole make changes, or helping the group make changes in the environment. Group-level social work practice is a shared experience that embodies the profession's emphasis on relationships. Group work can be a powerful tool for change. It is one of the most distinctive practices of the profession.
- *Community practice:* The method of practice known as community practice usually involves a common locality, such as a city neighborhood, small town, or rural area. Beyond locality, however, *community* also refers to a common concern, interest, or identification. For example, you might consider yourself to be a part of a community of gay men or Jewish women or people of Irish descent. Social work practice has historical roots in community practice and aims to actively involve community members in the solutions to their self-defined concerns.
- *International work:* An emerging focus of practice is international social work. International social work is a broad concept that can include: (1) a worldview, (2) a domestic practice and/or action informed by knowledge of international issues, (3) participation in international professional associations, and (4) social and economic development and human rights (Healy & Link, 2012).

EXHIBIT 1.2

Types of client groupings

The social work profession increasingly brings a global, transnational perspective to local issues, such as employment, homelessness, and health.

A number of cultural assumptions about social work skill development underlie organizational schemes based on client groupings. For example, many U.S. social workers agree that one-to-one practice work is the natural starting place for social work practice, and other types of practice refer back to one-to-one methods. However, in family- or community-centered cultures, this assumption may not fit. For example, a social worker providing mental health services may be accustomed to seeing clients individually. However, it may be more culturally appropriate to work with a Latino client's entire family, rather than just the individual client, in order to best assist the client (Falicov, 2013). Although the distinctions between types of groupings continue to be a useful way of thinking about social work, generalist practice emphasizes an integration of knowledge and skills across all system levels and sizes.

Practice Framework

The practice framework views social work practice in relation to the progression of the work. The most commonly used practice framework describes the activities of the social worker and the client as they proceed together through relatively standard phases. Although these phases are described here in a linear fashion, the social worker and client frequently loop back and forth between phases as necessary. The phases described next are more fully discussed relative to clients in Chapters 3–13.

Engagement   The process of building a relationship among the social worker, the client, and the client's environment is called **engagement**. Successful engagement involves establishing a degree of trust and a sense that the work ahead will be helpful to the client and professionally rewarding and satisfying for the social worker. Engaging a client requires not only effective communication and relationship skills with individuals but also the formation of significant collaborative connections with the client's environment and with the relevant service systems. For example, your client, Lara, has asked you to help negotiate and advocate within the school system for her child who has a disability. You carefully develop a relationship with Lara so that you may understand her issues and experiences. You engage with Lara's network (in this case, the school system) to learn about the school system's constraints and challenges in order to effectively facilitate a more productive relationship between Lara and the school. [EPAS 6]

Successful engagement is essential to effective work with clients. Engagement may fail for a variety of reasons; for instance, the client may lose the sense of investment in the process if he or she does not feel meaningfully connected to the work, or critical contacts in the client network may feel that their role is neither appreciated nor fully understood. In Lara's case, if the school staff thinks you do not understand the challenges they face, they may be less willing to work on improving their relationship with your client.

Assessment and Planning   In an **assessment**, the social worker recognizes the parameters of the practice situation and the way in which they affect the client. Client goals are central to the assessment process and to planning for an intervention. Through mutual exploration of the client issues, the client and social worker decide how best to address the client's goals. Assessment focuses on the analysis of the major purpose for work; the aspects of the client environment that can offer support for a solution; the client knowledge, skills, and values that can be applied to the situation; and ways in which the client can meet her or his goals. [EPAS 7]

Planning is an integral part of the change process. A plan describes how the social worker and client will work toward achieving the client's goals. Developing a plan requires the client and social worker to assess or evaluate options, resources, barriers, client preferences, and agreed-upon goals, along with established methods of achieving those goals. The plan should also take into consideration the

A social worker engages in a child welfare assessment.

© Lisa F. Young

less-than-obvious or unexpected outcomes of reaching a goal. For example, a social worker may help foster parents adopt a child. Another child in the family may have accepted the temporary nature of the foster care arrangement and may now feel threatened by the permanency of adoption. The complexity of human emotion can arise in unexpected places and times in social work practice.

The social worker's theoretical perspective guides the selection of assessment styles and planning approaches. The overall agency mission also plays an important, perhaps defining, role in the activity. For example, assessments conducted in foster care agencies may vary, but they are all likely to focus on children and parenting, rather than on vocational development or personal growth counseling.

Intervention   The next stage, **intervention**, refers to the action—the execution of the work that will enable the client and the practitioner to accomplish the goals agreed upon in the assessment. Intervention is the joint activity of the client and the social worker. Generalist practice interventions vary widely, from helping an older adult tenants' union organize a rent strike to helping a family receiving Medicaid benefits obtain health care for a sick child. In some cases, an intervention may involve the social worker listening to and reflecting on the client's situation, helping the client think about that situation and her or his role in it, and facilitating an opportunity to create a different, preferable situation. The social worker's theoretical and/or practice orientation influences the intervention process. In some practice models, the social worker actively determines the client's best interests and initiates action to achieve a specific outcome. In other models, planning and intervention is a more collaborative process, with the social worker and client sharing responsibility for deciding upon and carrying out the best course of action. As with other aspects of practice, the type, level, and focus of the intervention vary widely. [**EPAS 8**]

Termination   Ending a relationship with a client, or **termination**, is a long-standing area of focus for social workers. The profession is committed to facilitating appropriate and effective termination with clients and follow-up when needed. In general, the termination process includes reviewing the work and accomplishments, discussing the development of the working relationship, and planning to sustain the changes that have been achieved. To many social workers, termination is one of the most difficult and most important aspects of the work. Those who want to focus more on the future sometimes call this stage "consolidation" or "graduation." [**EPAS 9**]

Evaluation   Although many social workers are pressed for time to complete other tasks, making the effort to perform an **evaluation** helps to determine the effectiveness of the practice intervention. The social work *Code of Ethics* (NASW, 2008) mandates that social workers engage in and utilize research to improve practice. Engaging in research can include program evaluation and research on individual practitioner effectiveness. CSWE accreditation guidelines require social work educators prepare practitioners to "engage in practice-informed research and research-informed practice" (CSWE, 2015; EPAS 4). At the same time, the profession has put increasing emphasis on evidence-based practice, defined as "an educational and practice paradigm that includes a series of predetermined steps aimed at helping practitioners and agency administrators identify, select, and implement efficacious interventions for clients" (Jensen & Howard, 2013, p. 1). Evidence-based practice facilitates the integration of research findings, client values and preferences, practitioner knowledge and expertise, and other factors to make practice, policy, and research decisions.

Research on practice may involve evaluation tools that assess the progress of a program and may encourage individual social workers to reflect on the quality of their work. Practitioner research findings, as well as research from scholars, can be useful for effective client advocacy. For example, if you want to advocate for persons who are homeless by demonstrating that existing services are inadequate or not directed effectively, you need to understand the size and scope of the homeless population and previous research findings about effective services for homeless populations. You can also discuss your own practitioner-generated research findings.

There are many kinds of evaluation, including quantitative, qualitative, subjective, objective, formative (conducted during the work), summative (conducted at the end of the work), self-report, reflection, and standardized tests. The prevailing trend within the various funding and accountability arrangements associated with social work practice is to require more evaluative activity, both to demonstrate effectiveness and to justify continued or increased financial support for practice initiatives and policy programs.

Licensure of Social Work

One of the many ways to view social work is as a helping profession licensed and regulated by states to protect the public. All fifty states, the District of Columbia, Puerto Rico, the Virgin Islands, and ten Canadian provinces regulate the social work profession. Regulation protects the public by establishing: (1) the qualifications that a professional must possess, (2) a means of holding professionals accountable, and (3) a system for the public to lodge complaints against incompetent or unethical practitioners and to have them investigated and adjudicated. Today, there are almost 400,000 licensed social workers practicing in the United States and Canada (Randall & DeAngelis, 2013).

There are four types of social work licensure: bachelor of social work (BSW, usually earned upon graduation); master of social work (MSW, one type earned upon graduation and a second type, independent, earned after two years of supervised general experience); and clinical (earned after two years of supervised clinical experience). Most jurisdictions license social workers at two or more of these categories. While they vary from jurisdiction to jurisdiction, general requirements for licensure include earning a specific level of education; gaining experience under the supervision of a practicing social worker; and demonstrating knowledge and minimum competence by passing an exam, providing references, and displaying evidence of good moral character. Some locales require more than two years of supervised clinical experience, proof of a minimum number of hours in a clinical field placement, or proof of specific clinical coursework. After licensure, many states require that licensed social workers complete ongoing professional continuing education units (CEUs) through professional workshops or conferences that provide skills training for new situations, new populations, and new ways of thinking about the work (Randall & DeAngelis, 2013).

Social workers seeking continuing education (CE) credit have a variety of online and face-to-face options. Below are some examples of resources for social work CE:

From NASW: www.socialworkers.org

From NASW California: www.socialworkweb.com/nasw/

From the Saint Louis University School of Social Work: www.slu.edu/college-for-public-health-and-social-justice/careers/social-work-continuing-education

EXHIBIT 1.3

Continuing Education

Professional Tensions in Social Work

Social work is a profession with a wide range of theories, practice areas, skills, and settings. Like many professions, tensions exist among these differences. Almost since its inception, the social work profession has faced a set of tensions, the most significant of which are those that strongly shape the identity of the social work profession and the way in which social workers practice. These include:

- whether to promote a clinical or nonclinical approach to working with clients;

- the extent to which social workers should exercise social control or promote social change;

- the extent to which social workers should promote change or accept their clients;

- the struggle between encouraging clients to adjust to their circumstances or to challenge their circumstances;

- whether social workers promote their professional, expert position or share power with clients; and

- the extent of the profession's adjustment to globalization.

Clinical and Nonclinical Approaches   In a social work context, the word clinical has many meanings. It can signify a medically based private practice model that involves diagnosis and managed care, or it may be associated with cold, calculated, stiff, or impersonal interchanges by a social work professional.

In this book, **clinical work** refers to social work with individuals, groups, and/ or families that is not only direct practice, or direct work (face-to-face), but that is also designed to change behaviors, solve problems, or resolve emotional or psychological issues (Grant, 2013). For example, clinical work can include intervening individually with a young woman to address her self-harming behavior, facilitating a series of groups for children who have experienced the death of a parent, or assisting a family to redefine the communication patterns among three generations. Clinical work can extend into many practice arenas, such as physical and mental health, substance abuse treatment, school social work, gerontological social work, and some child welfare work. Some states explicitly define clinical work and require those who wish to practice it to earn a master's degree. For example, West Virginia has separate levels of licensure for new MSW graduates, MSWs with over two years' experience, and MSW clinical social workers with over two years of experience (West Virginia Board of Social Work Examiners, n.d.). The state requires additional or different credentials to work in some areas (e.g., an addictions certificate for substance abuse work).

Nonclinical (indirect) **work** usually refers to work that addresses the client's environment. Nonclinical or indirect practice addresses social problems in community, organizational, institutional, and societal systems. Nonclinical practice social workers achieve social change through neighborhood organizing, community planning, locality development, public education, policy development, administration, and social action. Nonclinical work can also include social work that is political or focused on social reform efforts. These efforts may involve policy practice in which the social worker endeavors to improve institutional responses or advocates for or against certain laws, policies, and social structures relating to various dimensions of diversity, such as class, gender, ability, and cultural ethnicity. Policy practice focuses on ensuring that policies are responsive to client needs and rights. Nonclinical work focuses less on the internal dynamics of an individual's experience and more on opportunity and change in the environment.

While tension can exist between clinical and nonclinical work, thoughtful and principled efforts can connect the two approaches. For example, clinical social workers can identify and communicate client needs to administrators and other nonclinical social workers, so that policy practice efforts are appropriately channeled to the most significant client needs. In another example, clinical social workers could be involved in and refer clients to neighborhood organizing efforts to make social connections with others concerned about similar topics. The following discussion considers some dimensions of this tension.

Developmental Socialization and Resocialization   The late Harry Specht, a social work policy educator, distinguished between "developmental socialization" and "resocialization" (Specht, 1990). Specht defined **developmental socialization** as the attempt, through providing support, information, and opportunities, to help people enhance their environments by making the most of their roles. Developmental socialization also involves confronting obstacles such as abuse or oppression that impede people's attempts to make the most of their roles. Developmental socialization is the natural domain of social work and is nonclinical. In contrast, Specht defined **resocialization** as the attempt to help people with issues related to feelings and inner perceptions that relate primarily to the self. Specht purported that psychotherapeutic approaches associated with psychology and psychiatry, rather than social work, should deal with such issues. Significantly, Specht argued that social work had been seduced from its original mission by clinical psychotherapy, which many people characterize as a higher-status activity. As an advocate for an emphasis on the social environment, rather than inner psychological life, Specht called for social work to build its professional core in public services and institutions and to replace all its clinical training with adult education, community work, and group work. His last major co-written publication was tellingly called *Unfaithful Angels: How Social Work Has Abandoned Its Mission* (Specht & Courtney, 1994).

Many social workers are committed to the kind of work that Specht rejects as inappropriate. These practitioners view social work as providing useful perspectives for dealing with clinical, interactional, interpersonal, and sometimes intrapersonal issues. Many practitioners view these perspectives as appropriate tools in the realms of individual counseling, family intervention, and a host of other areas that might be called clinical or therapeutic. Controversy regarding social work's appropriate domain has been prevalent since the early days of the profession. In more recent times, some social workers committed to environmental or structural intervention have seen the movement to license social workers as a negative outgrowth of the move into professionalism, which in this context usually means individual psychotherapy and, often, private-pay practice. Clinical practitioners, however, embody values, ethical principles, and practices consistent with social work's mission to improve human well-being, promote social justice, and promote wellness over pathology (Grant, 2013).

The perceived polarity between clinical and nonclinical practice is a challenge in contemporary social work. The *Code of Ethics* (NASW, 2008) requires social workers to engage in work that supports socially equitable allocations of opportunity. The effort to support equitable allocations is inherently environmental and political. When clinical practice focuses entirely on individual issues and ignores or excludes nonclinical advocacy and power analysis work inherent in the pursuit of social justice, it comes into conflict with the *Code*. The proximity of some clinical practice settings (such as mental health and substance abuse) to health care delivery and its requirements for individualized, decontextualized labels of pathology sometimes discourages or diverts social workers from entering into social justice pursuits.

Integrating Approaches for Clinical and Indirect Practice   One way to reconcile the conflict between an individual, clinical focus and a nonclinical, or macro, environmental focus is to integrate the two approaches. For example, Gitterman and Germain (2008) argue that social work professionals must be prepared to work with all types of clients, as situations require. Many methods and skills are common across all clients. Historical loyalties to both the individual and to macro advocacy pursuits are a strength of the profession. The Educational Policy and Accreditation Standards (EPAS) (CSWE, 2015) for social work education underscore social work's commitment to competencies and behaviors that require mastery of knowledge, skills, and values across all clients.

There are many contemporary, complementary efforts to connect clinical practice with social justice issues. One approach expands the definition of clinical work to include a wide variety of practice with individuals and families ("micro practice") (i.e., case management, advocacy, teamwork, mediation, and prevention roles, therapeutic, and counseling roles (Hahn & Scanlon, 2016)). In this approach, the clinician reflects on her or his own privilege, which in turn addresses the worker's accountability to clients, an important component of a social justice approach. Newer areas of contemporary practice, such as environmental social work, also propel social workers to connect individual work with work at a systems level (Dominelli, 2014).

Social workers can also integrate approaches through the use of theoretical perspectives and alternate methods that guide social workers through interactions with clients. For example, a generalist, empowerment perspective locates social work practice at the intersection of private troubles and public issues; it is both clinical and indirect. According to the empowerment perspective, social work employs an integrated view of humans in the context of their physical and social environments. Social workers using the empowerment perspective seek to promote a mutually beneficial interaction between individuals and society (Parsons & East, 2013). Narrative approaches (discussed in more detail in Chapters 4–7) illustrate how the integration of clinical practice and nonclinical pursuit of social justice occurs. A narrative approach to working with clients focuses on empowerment, collaboration, and viewing problems in social context. A narrative-oriented practitioner addresses societal injustices in the client intervention (Kelley, 2013). The social worker views the issues individuals and families bring to the work in the context of the social and power relations in the client's experience. Although narrative approaches developed in family therapy work, they have also been applied to work at the individual, group, and community levels (Kelley, 2013).

Social construction blurs the distinction between clinical and nonclinical work. Social construction emphasizes the power of agency, the ability to affect one's own circumstances. In this view, people shape their environments, which in turn (or recursively) influence them. For example, you are a member of a community, and you respond to other members of that community. However, you also participate in creating your community, a process that goes beyond simply reacting to various individuals. From this perspective, social work involves helping the client create a new and empowering identity (Dybicz, 2015). By focusing on the client as a participant in the creation of the environment, this approach blurs the distinction between clinical work with the person and nonclinical work with the environment. Another highly integrative model, deconstruction, bridges individual, clinical work and environmental practice concerns (Fook & Pease, 2016). In this conceptualization, the social worker moves from helping the client conquer the internal ramifications of the problem (such as clinical depression) to helping the client connect with others who are experiencing and resisting the same kind of oppression. For example, consider Georgia's story.

Georgia is a 25-year-old woman from the southern United States. She came to a large city in the Midwest to see a different part of the country. Very early in her stay, she met and fell in love with Tom, a native Midwesterner. Georgia and Tom developed a serious relationship, and when Georgia discovered that she was pregnant, she moved into Tom's apartment. From then on, things did not go well for Georgia. Tom began to resent her interest in the coming birth, and at times, he was verbally abusive, insulting her southern background and degrading every personal aspect he could find wrong with her. He became physically rough with her when they had any difference of opinion. Eventually, he began to shove her into the wall, slap her, and kick at her belly. Georgia was disillusioned and frightened both for her own safety and for the safety of her child. She could not understand how she had failed Tom, what she had done to become so disgusting to him, or how she had become so hard for him to be around. When Georgia finally believed she could no longer manage the situation, she contacted a local women's shelter. She was devastated. By this time, Tom's treatment had convinced her that she was worthless and unlovable. Georgia was at a very low point and was fearful for her future.

Over time, Georgia's social worker helped Georgia see that Tom's battering was not a function of Georgia's personality or unworthiness but rather of his own trauma and choices. Tom, not Georgia, was responsible for Tom's abusive behavior. With support, Georgia began to regain her sense of worth and resilience and to feel stronger about her own capacities. She began to explore how our society condones men expressing themselves through violence. She met with other women at the shelter and joined in their resistance to societal violence, advocating for education in the schools and providing personal testimonies to groups of women.

This work empowered Georgia because it enabled her to take control of her emotions while meaningfully addressing an environmental issue. Georgia's experience with her social worker is an example of an integrated approach that addresses both clinical issues and social justice concerns. The approach transformed Georgia's inner psychological turmoil into political action; it facilitated Georgia's role in influencing her environment. In this way, the work shifted from an individual clinical focus to a nonclinical, integrated political focus without sacrificing either.

Social Control and Social Change   Social work is part of the society that it tries to change. An authoritative sanction for social control is authorized by some of the regulatory bodies in which social workers practice, such as child protection, criminal justice, and mental health. In some circumstances, this control appears to be at odds with the profession's commitment to social change. For example, reporting a parent for suspected neglect could be viewed at odds with encouraging the same parent to advocate to change policy to make their employment pay better, which would allow more time for parenting. The two functions—control and change—are not inherently irreconcilable, but the ways in which they play out in their respective practice arenas tend to make them appear incompatible at times.

Change and Acceptance   Another tension involves how much the goal of social work is to implement change—either individual or environmental—or to help a client accept their status as "good enough." The particular circumstances and settings associated with each situation strongly influence the best approach. This tension is so contextually influenced that it may never be fully put to rest as long as individuals continue to evaluate social contexts based on their own idiosyncrasies.

For example, many practitioners might support a female client who feels angry, distressed, and overburdened in a marital relationship and who struggles with the sociological realities of contemporary families. These realities might include the expectations of partners, employers, and society at large that most mothers, even those working full time outside the home, should assume more responsibility than fathers for child care and home life. In this situation, the social worker might want to offer support to bolster the client's existing coping mechanisms rather than facilitating a change within the client.

The social worker, who may empathize with the client, could offer suggestions for child care respite, recreation, or self-care that would help mitigate the client's sense of injustice in the arrangement but that would not lead to a significant or structural change, while other clients and practitioners might respond differently. They may be unwilling to wait until parenting and homemaking become more equitable in society but may instead demand or at least work for substantial change, both within the marriage and in the larger society, as well as in the client's life. The possible stances that either clients or practitioners take are not necessarily polarized. They can be thought of as situated on a continuum, meaning that both the client and social worker may wish for large-scale social change, and both may believe that they personally need to make peace with the current reality of an individual situation.

The question becomes, are their respective positions compatible enough that they can agree on the goal of the work? If the social worker believes strongly that the client needs to change the situation, but the client wants to learn to accept the situation, setting mutually agreeable goals will be a challenge. There may be situations in which the tension between change and acceptance involves significant concern for the personal safety of an adult. The response to such a situation may not be clear. You may suggest that, to overcome this stress, the client can engage in interpersonal work to change her situation rather than overt activism. The tension between change and acceptance is difficult, in part because of the differences of opinion about what is tolerable and in part because of the political ramifications of inequitable relationships.

Experts and Shared Power   The relationship between expertise and shared power has recently created a tension within the social work profession. The history and development of both educational and professional systems in U.S. culture have revolved around the idea of expertise, or expert knowledge. Social workers are educated and socialized in professional programs to become respected members of a profession in which others share the same or similar expertise. The relatively recent introduction of the idea of shared power has challenged claims of expert power. In shared power, the individual is the expert on her or his life, culture, dreams, experience, and goals. This perspective mandates that social work practitioners assume power only over the limited activities in which they are trained while the client retains the power to direct the work. For example, if you are working in a college setting as an advocate for an African American student who has experienced discrimination in housing options on campus, you may claim expertise on the advocacy process, but your client would retain control over those issues on which you focus and the goals of the advocacy. In this way, you and your client would share power.

For some, shifting your views of your expertise and interest in sharing power may not come easily. In the United States, we are socialized to value expertise, thus, we may interpret our own value and contributions through the lens of expertise. Given the competition that can develop between complex specialization, on the one hand, and client empowerment, on the other, this tension is likely to persist. Some clients may want social workers to be the expert on their lives and relationships in the same way people want their dentist to be an expert on dental care.

Social workers have spent decades trying to scientifically demonstrate the effectiveness of their interventions and have fought for professional prestige through this "expert" label. However, social workers have come to recognize that the only expert on the experience of any particular relationship, oppression, or event is the person who has lived it, and social workers can honor that person's wisdom by sharing power within the professional relationship. In the contemporary world, many strong client voices in the realm of human service interchanges, situations, and relationships have made it known that adopting the "expert" role is not necessarily helpful, because oftentimes it obscures their own ownership or participation in the work. Social workers see firsthand how service systems that rely on expertise can come across as humiliating, insulting, or patronizing and thus inspire disillusionment and anger in the people they are intended to serve, such as people with disabilities, women, and people of color. The development of many contemporary social work perspectives that attempt to reduce the centrality of expertise and to substitute an enhanced commitment to partnership, or shared power, reflects this reality.

Minimization of Distance   Theoretical perspectives like the strengths perspective, nearly all feminist approaches, and empowerment approaches (covered in detail in later chapters) make a conscious effort to minimize the rigid boundaries of expertise between social worker and client. They view the client as the expert on her or his life and the social worker as skilled in various arenas that will help the client reach a client-defined destination. In contrast to more social worker-centered approaches in which interactions often take place in agency offices, this focus on the client places social worker–client interactions in clients' homes or in public facilities like coffee shops, houses of worship, and community centers. It also promotes an egalitarian relationship in which the client's right to enter into a relationship of shared power is recognized. The relationship recognizes, values, and uses the assets of both the client and the worker.

These theoretical perspectives support and conceptualize shared power as an allocation of shared responsibility according to each participant's particular strengths. This view does not require equality of responsibility but recognizes that skill levels differ and emphasizes the worth of all contributions. Social workers are responsible for maintaining professional ethics, and clients are responsible for making changes in their lives. For example, in a situation of client substance abuse, social workers would ask questions like, "How does your drinking affect your children?" rather than making a statement such as, "You need to quit drinking." This discourages hierarchies in the client–worker relationship and encourages a sense of joint investment in both the process and the results.

Global Citizenship and the Local Community   The tension between local and global investments of effort is more relevant for social work practitioners now than ever before. Traditionally, U.S. social workers have carried out most of their activities in local or neighborhood contexts and have regarded global developments as remote. The social and cultural history, geography, and resource wealth of the United States have contributed to national and professional insularity. When U.S. residents describe other places using devaluing language like "third world" or "underdeveloped," they reflect the U.S. tendency toward ethnocentrism based almost exclusively on U.S.-defined dimensions of prosperity in any given culture. Traditional Western markers are primarily limited to economic assets that are important for all people but that are not the totality of life for any person.

Globalization is a process comprised of complex of economic, social, and technological processes that have resulted in the formation of a single world community in which we are all citizens. As a result, national ties have been weakened (Steger, 2009, p. 9). The essence of globalization is the flow of information, ideas, knowledge, technology, capital, labor, artifacts, and cultural norms and values across national borders. Social problems such as homelessness, neglect and exploitation of children, poverty, violence, health and aging issues, and epidemic infections are worldwide issues that impact all nations. Global events like terrorism and wars have a direct and compelling influence on the environment and practice of social work at home and require workers to develop new skills and new perspectives (Sowers & Rowe, 2009; Steger, 2009).

The process of globalization highlights U.S. economic dominance. For example, the availability of Coca-Cola in Bangkok and the presence of Pizza Hut in Manila signal U.S. economic stature in many world markets. The outsourcing of many U.S. jobs to countries in which much cheaper labor can be located has resulted in changing patterns of employment domestically as well as labor exploitation abroad. Outsourcing labor has helped many U.S. and other Western-based companies to thrive. These dimensions of globalization are part of the reality of expanding international trade (Payne & Askeland, 2008).

Factors Promoting Globalization   International financial institutions, such as the World Bank, the International Monetary Fund (IMF), and the World Trade

Organization (WTO), have promoted and facilitated globalization. These organizations were originally instituted to promote economic stability and growth and to help individual countries emerge from economic crises, but critics charge that the strategies they have adopted to achieve these objectives have been problematic and counterproductive. Some question their policies, which critics charge have disproportionately benefited wealthy people around the world, failed to address concerns about the environment and social justice, and led to human rights abuses. Critics argue that globalization agreements and efforts disregard opportunities to improve people's standard of living through creating employment, improving health, or expanding educational or social services for the poor and that they fail to promote progressive land reform. They charge that decision-making within these international financial institutions lacks transparency and often reflects the interests of wealthier countries (Head, 2008; World Health Organization, 2012).

One example is the WTO, which has been the primary proponent of free trade policies. Although WTO free trade policies were ostensibly designed to encourage the development of market economies, they often require receiving nations to accept particular conditions aimed at fostering trade and economic growth, including privatization of resources; restrictions on imports and exports; and cutbacks in many social programs such as health, education, and housing and income assistance. In many cases, these conditions have effectively abolished welfare entitlement programs and social safety nets, debilitated local economies, altered or eliminated substantial aspects of indigenous ways of life, and eroded the autonomy of national governments. In their place, large multinational corporations have been free to build enormous for-profit industries, with little regard to environmental or other concerns. Globalization policies have been associated with a substantial increase in worldwide poverty, violence, HIV/AIDS cases, drug addiction, and economic stratification (to name a few) as well as the exploitation of the land and other important environmental resources (Payne & Askeland, 2008).

Social Work Response to Globalization   Globalization provides both challenges and opportunities for social work. The social work profession is developing global models of understanding. For example, social workers in domestic settings are working with diverse populations, including immigrants and refugees in this country, and gaining knowledge of non-Western ideas and perceptions. Rather than focus on strictly clinical work, social workers in international settings may be called upon to help eradicate economic inequality and poverty (Payne & Askeland, 2008). Social workers can advocate for the social dimensions of globalization to help improve such global issues as poverty, environmental degradation, unemployment, and human rights (Hong & Song, 2010).

Individual practitioners can incorporate globalization into their work by making a commitment to reciprocity, interdependence, human rights, and social justice. That commitment involves following global events and understanding the ways in which events that occur within the U.S. impact individuals outside our borders. The implications of globalization for social work practice are likely to increase in number and impact, and social workers must be involved in strengthening local structures, such as nonprofit organizations to ensure civil rights (Hong & Song, 2010). Ironically, increased localization has been one important response to globalization (Payne & Askeland, 2008). Social work, therefore, must focus on both global and local perspectives in order to discourage artificial local/global polarity by making meaningful connections between global inequities and domestic social justice issues (Hong & Song, 2010). At the same time, social workers must initiate educational and political initiatives to ensure respect for human rights, democratic decision-making, environmental protection, and meaningful benefits to local populations.

Perspectives on Conceptualizations of the Social Work Profession   Although each of these conceptualizations provides a useful way of thinking about social work practice, each also has its limitations. To best serve the interests of the client, social workers should be flexible in their application of different models. For example, knowledge, values, and skills can overlap, and overfocusing on one dimension, such as factual knowledge, may lead a practitioner to apply that dimension without adequate consideration of other dimensions. A goal of social work education is to foster the competent integration of many kinds of knowledge, values, and skills. The reality of practice is that there is a great deal of overlap between the background, values, and skills needed for various types of practice.

Generalist social work practice requires proficiency at all levels of client groupings. Levels are more similar than they are different; work at any level is grounded in the practitioner's consistent set of values, theoretical perspectives, and goals. Similarly, a social worker does not abandon engagement skills (i.e., become "all business") because she or he has moved on to the assessment phase. Like all relationships, the professional connection between social worker and client must be attended to, nurtured, and encouraged to grow throughout their work together, or it will wither. Likewise, assessment occurs throughout the course of the work. The phases of helping are highly connected, with special emphasis on one phase at a time. The tensions discussed in social work, while useful, may fall short of describing the full, day-to-day realities of social work practice within specific practice settings and with specific populations. Therefore, while the structure of phases of helping is helpful, flexibility in their application is important.

Importance of Self-Knowledge   To practice competently, social workers must have a clear understanding of themselves and their own biases. For example, do you find that you respond differently to people who are living in poverty than you do to people who are socioeconomically middle class? To become more culturally competent, you can explore the reasons for this difference; perhaps you learned as a child that "poor people" are somehow less worthy than affluent people or that they are not hardworking. Your family and/or the wider culture may have supported these views. To uncover your possible socioeconomic biases, consider the following questions: How does this view clash with the view that people living in poverty are resilient in the face of debilitating exploitation? How do you act on your view in your practice? Are you less empathic, energetic, or invested when you work with people living in poverty? Are you less likely to advocate or seek out resources for them? Do you have an opinion about a client that is a "truth" in your mind, or do you treat it as one interpretation out of many?

Our experiences, motivations, values, attitudes, and other factors shape our practice decisions, sometimes without our realizing it. Social workers need to continually explore how they prioritize their values and the patterns they develop in making decisions and exhibiting practice behaviors. This exploration may include recognizing idiosyncratic approaches, quick responses, and typical reactions. Are you patient and likely to stand by your client, even when things do not go well? Are you quick to assume someone is judging you or wants to bring you harm? Are you likely to blow off steam or sulk when you are rebuffed? Do you assume that you are competent to deal with any crisis? Are you inclined to address an interpersonal problem privately and quietly? Are you likely to "sound off" in a meeting? All of us have our own idiosyncratic ways of dealing with relationships, stresses, and social interactions. Social workers must recognize these behavioral patterns, understand how they impact their work, and identify those responses that, if changed, would help them to develop a higher degree of competency and skill.

Culture profoundly influences social work practitioner biases. For example, culture may impact practitioner beliefs and attitudes about a situation in which an adolescent's choice of vocation (such as becoming a nurse) may clash with the family's ideas about suitable professions for a male. In another example, cultural bias may influence a practitioner's belief that, in social relationships, participants are equal and all should speak out honestly about tension in the relationship. These two examples are part of mainstream U.S. culture and are cultural variants that are not necessarily shared by all people and therefore do not represent a universal truth. Emphasis on individual drive and ambition, nurturing professions for women, as well as equality and forthrightness, are Western beliefs, and may clash with other cultures. In another example, an Asian client, who is twenty years older than a practitioner, may relate in very formal terms with the practitioner and appear reluctant to share details about her family life, even though she has been referred for parent support and family information is needed. Rather than labeling her "resistant" or "closed," the practitioner can recognize her own potential bias in the perspective she applies about such relationships. She can recognize the lack of fit between her perspective and the client perspective.

The emphasis on our own biases and assumptions closely relates to how our values influence our ideas of ethical practices. These constructs are critical to social work practice. The next chapter deals more explicitly with values and ethical frameworks in social work practice.

QUICK GUIDE 1   CLIENT POPULATIONS

Social workers work with many different types of client populations including the following:

- LGBTQ youth, adults, and older adults
- A range of religions (such as Jehovah's Witnesses, Jews, Catholics, Mormons, and Muslims)
- People with disabilities (physical, emotional, behavioral, developmental)
- Ethnic minorities (such as Native Americans, Hispanics, African Americans, Asian Americans, and Pacific Islanders)
- Immigrants
- Refugees
- Older adults
- Active military and veterans and their families
- Rural populations
- People in poverty
- Children, adolescents, and youth

Explore your self-knowledge about diversity
- What is my race, ethnicity, religious affiliation, and socioeconomic status?
- How does my background impact my knowledge about this client's background?
- How does my culture define "family"? How do other cultures define it?
- Do I assume that my culture is the norm?
- To what degree do I understand the ideas of cultures other than my own?
- To what degree is my language respectful of other cultures?
- Do I think that I will be less empathic or energetic when working with persons in certain populations?
- Do I acknowledge that cultural differences exist?
- Do I recognize the thought patterns of other groups as equally valid as mine?
- What is diverse within my culture? What diversity exists between my culture and others?

Questions to ponder about building cultural competency
- How might my biases impact my practice?
- Do I think that I will be less likely to advocate for or seek out resources for particular types of clients?
- Do I think that I will advocate for effective services that differ by culture?
- Do I stereotype clients from specific groups?
- Am I aware that some clients may not relate closely to their cultural group?
- Am I aware of various natural support systems that may differ from my own (e.g., folk healers and religious leaders)? Do I understand how to utilize natural support systems in practice?
- Do I know how to respectfully obtain personal and family background information from clients to determine their ethnic/community sense of identity, rather than making assumptions?
- Will I look for work environments that positively impact my cultural competence?

Source: Lum, 2011; Mason, 1995; NASW, 2007

THEORETICAL PERSPECTIVES FOR SOCIAL WORK PRACTICE

Social work has a history of adopting, adapting, formulating, and integrating various theoretical perspectives. A **theory** is an explanation, supported by a body of empirically based evidence and involving clear principles and propositions that provide a predictive framework, of some event or phenomenon. Theories enable social workers to see clients and social problems from many points of view, to anticipate outcomes of different interventions, and to apply results to future situations (Floersch, 2013). Theories can bring order and coherence to practice situations so that social worker and client can base activities on a logical assessment of the fit between a client's situation and the assertions of the theory. Theories about the social world evolve and adjust to fit new ideas or to accommodate new evidence that adds to or contradicts theories. Consequently, some theories are discarded when they are no longer acceptable to the professional community (for example, theories asserting that some races are superior to others) or when they are refuted by reliable research. Other theories evolve, such as contemporary interpretations of Freud's 19th-century psychoanalytic theory.

A **perspective** is a view or lens through which to observe and interpret the world. A perspective is generally less structured than a theory but is similar in that it is often based on values and beliefs about the nature of the world. For example, if a social worker believes people are generally good, that perspective will guide her practice and interpretations of client situations. In that way, theory and perspective are similar. In social work practice and in this book, the terms theory and perspective are often used interchangeably and may also be called theoretical perspectives.

Biology, ecology, sociology, anthropology, psychology, and many of the humanities and human service professions have made important contributions to social work theory and practice approaches. More recently, social work scholars have expanded the development of the profession's own understandings of practice to posit theories specific to the provision of social work services. Some of these theories focus on psychosocial systems, problem solving, ecological/ecosystems, and empowerment, as they represent uniquely social work emphases on the interface between a person and her or his environment.

This book focuses on five central practice perspectives: (1) the ecosystems perspective; (2) the social justice perspective; (3) the human rights perspective; (4) the strengths perspective; and (5) postmodern perspective approaches, including critical social construction, narrative theory, and solution-focused interventions. Other perspectives are included in subsequent chapters as they relate to specific levels of practice. Some perspectives have a longstanding history within social work education and practice (such as social justice), and others are more contemporary (such as postmodern approaches).

Ecosystems Perspective

Drawing on systems theory and ecology, the **ecosystems perspective** is an often-used framework for generalist practice. This perspective examines the exchanges between individuals, families, groups, and communities and their environment. Systems theory uses constructs to organize complex activity in the social environment, while ecology seeks to explain how people adapt to and influence their environment. Taken together, these two concepts describe the functioning and adaptation of human systems in a dynamic interchange with each other. Interactions or transactions between people and their environment help explain how people influence their environment, and vice versa. The ecosystems perspective is very useful for social work practice because it encourages matching people as much as possible with their environments. This ideal can lead the social worker providing direct services with individuals, families, and groups to mobilize and draw on personal and environmental resources for effective coping. Striving to increase the fit between human needs and environment can also lead the social worker to influence the client's social and physical environment to better address human needs. Influencing the environment can include working to influence organizations to develop more responsive policies and programs, as well as working to influence legislation, regulation, and the implementation of laws (Gitterman & Germain, 2013).

Social Justice Perspective

Social justice refers to the manner in which society distributes resources among its members, including material goods and social benefits, rights, and protections. Although there are various theories of what constitutes a socially just distribution of wealth, the social work profession generally accepts an egalitarian focus concerned with the fair distribution of both material and nonmaterial resources and equal access for all people (Reichert, 2011). From this perspective, developing or distributing social and natural resources based on political or social power rather than on social justice or human need is unacceptable (Libal & Harding, 2015). The social justice perspective has important implications for social workers and their practice as it requires a response to the injustice that is status quo in our society.

The National Association of Social Workers' *Code of Ethics* (NASW, 2008) requires social workers to invest a significant amount of time and effort in championing individual, group, and community rights, working toward more effective institutional responses, and influencing major social policy shifts. Social work is, therefore, a political profession. Social workers identify individual, family, group, and community needs and seek to address areas of injustice. For example, if a social worker is working at the community level with a group of older adults who have been wrongfully denied access to services or government support programs, it is the social worker's responsibility to use community resources to confront that injustice.

The social worker may address the issue at the individual level, or, if the problem rests in policy or procedures, at the group level.

Human Rights Perspective

The United Nations describes **human rights** as rights that are inherent in our nature and without which we cannot live a full life. Human rights and fundamental freedoms allow us to completely develop and use our human qualities, our intelligence, our talents, and our conscience and to satisfy our spiritual and other needs. They are basic for humankind's demand for a life in which the inherent dignity and worth of each human being receives respect and protection (Lundy, 2011; United Nations Office of the High Commission for Human Rights, 2006).

The principle of human rights offers a powerful and comprehensive framework for social work practice that not only recognizes the needs but also strives to satisfy those needs (Lundy, 2011). The human rights perspective provides a moral grounding for social work practice and reflects an ongoing commitment to the belief that all people should have basic rights and access to the broad benefits of their societies. Many social workers evaluate their practice based on its contribution to an environment in which universal human rights are honored.

Contemporary perspectives on human rights emphasize common social understandings rather than rigid assertions about specific human rights. They view human rights as socially constructed, reflecting differing contexts, ideas, and cultures (Gregg, 2012). Ife (2012) likewise suggests that human rights discourse should de-emphasize legalistic, Western views of entitlements in favor of a dialogue that better reflects the world's peoples. This dialogue should center on exploring the global meaning of human existence, recognizing our interdependence and safeguarding our survival now and in the future. This focus is consistent with social work's emphasis on community, quality of relationship, and concern for the future of the world's inhabitants. It also recognizes the dynamic nature of living one's principles, such as those inherent in human rights, as they continuously evolve to remain meaningful.

Human rights occupies a central place in social work practice and can provide a focal point in the evolution of people's understanding of their place on the planet. As dynamic principles that help guide international relations as well as community-based practice, human rights are a vital focus for work with people. The social work profession can build upon global efforts to make human rights a central discourse and to explore the relevance of human rights in our everyday work (Healy & Link, 2012).

The Strengths Perspective

An increasingly widespread approach in social work practice, the **strengths perspective** explicitly emphasizes affirming and working with the client strengths and the

1. Everyone is free, and we should all be treated in the same way.
2. Everyone is equal, despite differences in characteristics such as skin color, sex, religion, and language.
3. Everyone has the right to life and to live in freedom and safety.
4. No one has the right to treat you as a slave, nor should you make anyone your slave.
5. No one has the right to hurt you or to torture you.
6. Everyone has the right to be treated equally by the law.
7. The law is the same for everyone, and it should be applied in the same way for all.
8. Everyone has the right to ask for legal help when their rights are not respected.
9. No one has the right to imprison you unjustly or to expel you from your own country.
10. Everyone has the right to a fair and public trial.
11. Everyone should be considered innocent until proven guilty.
12. Everyone has the right to ask for help.
13. No one can enter your home, open your letters, or bother you or your family without a good reason.
14. Everyone has the right to travel as they wish.
15. Everyone has the right to go to another country and to ask for protection if they are being persecuted or are in danger of being persecuted.
16. Everyone has the right to belong to a country. No one has the right to prevent you from belonging to another country if you wish to.
17. Everyone has the right to marry and have a family.
18. Everyone has the right to own property and possessions.
19. Everyone has the right to practice and observe all aspects of their own religion and change their religion if they want to.
20. Everyone has the right to say what they think and to give and receive information.
21. Everyone has the right to take part in meetings and to join associations in a peaceful way.
22. Everyone has the right to help choose and take part in the government of their country.
23. Everyone has the right to social security and to opportunities to develop their skills.
24. Everyone has the right to work for a fair wage in a safe environment and to join a trade union.
25. Everyone has the right to rest and leisure.
26. Everyone has the right to an adequate standard of living and to medical help if they are ill.
27. Everyone has the right to go to school.
28. Everyone has the right to share in their community's cultural life.
29. Everyone must respect the 'social order' necessary for all these rights to be available.
30. Everyone must respect the rights of others, the community, and public property.
31. No one has the right to take away any of the rights in this declaration.

Source: Human Rights Education Association (n.d.).

EXHIBIT 1.4

A Summary of the Universal Declaration of Human Rights

resources available in their environments. Like human rights practice, the strengths perspective stresses basic dignity and the client's ability to overcome challenging obstacles (Kim, 2013).

Saleebey (2013) identified six key principles for the strengths perspective (pp. 17–21):

1. *Every individual, group, family, and community has strengths:* Social workers must view clients as competent and possessing skills and strengths that may not be initially visible. Social workers should also explore useful resources in client families and communities.

2. *Trauma and abuse, illness, and struggle are challenging, but they may also present opportunities:* Clients can not only overcome difficult situations but also learn new skills and develop positive protective factors. Individuals exposed to a variety of trauma are not always helpless victims or damaged beyond repair.

3. *Assume that you do not know the upper limits of clients' capacity to grow and change and take individual, group, and community aspirations seriously.* Too often, professional "experts" hinder their clients' potential for growth by viewing client-identified goals as unrealistic. Instead, social workers need to set high expectations for their clients so that the clients believe they can fully recover and that they can achieve their goals.

4. *We best serve clients by collaborating with them.* Playing the role of expert or professional with all the answers does not allow social workers to appreciate their clients' strengths and resources. The strengths perspective emphasizes collaboration between the social worker and the client.

5. *Every environment is full of resources.* Every community, regardless of how impoverished or disadvantaged, has something to offer in terms of knowledge, support, mentorship, and resources.

6. *Caring, caretaking, and context.* The strengths perspective recognizes the importance of community and the inclusion of all its members in society and working for social justice. This principle is premised on the idea that caring for each other is a basic form of civic participation.

Although these key principles may evolve, the strengths perspective focuses on clients' personal assets along with their environmental resources rather than on their pathology and limitations. Strengths-based social work interventions center on helping the client achieve his or her goals, affirming and developing values and commitments, and making and finding membership in or as a community. The strengths perspective does not preclude the need to validate the suffering and pain of the client (i.e., the physical, emotional, or existential) nor the seriousness of the situation or distress. Rather, the strengths perspective seeks to acknowledge clients' expertise regarding their own lives and to focus on their resilience and capacities to survive and to confront seemingly overwhelming obstacles.

Postmodern Perspective and the Social Construction Approach

Any contemporary perspective that questions the way in which knowledge is attained and valued and distinguishes belief from truth comes under the broad heading of **postmodernism**. Postmodern approaches invite examination of the cultural assumptions that underlie many arrangements of power and politics, and they tend to be critical of assumptions or theories that claim absolute or authoritative truth. To illustrate, the contention that "all people in the United States can get ahead if they work hard enough; therefore, all poor people are lazy" is an example of an assumption or belief asserted as truth. Postmodernism invites people to challenge the truth of such claims (Logan, 2013).

Social Construction   A useful postmodern perspective for understanding the social realities of the people social workers serve, **social construction** suggests that people construct reality based on their experiences in the social world, which occur within the context of a particular culture, society, history, and language. Social workers who practice from this perspective view social realities not as a product of an objective external world, or the result of the individual mind, but as beliefs formed through social interchanges (usually starting with the family) that regulate learning to make sense of things and, often, to form judgments. For example, when children experience people as good-hearted and the world as a kind place throughout their youth, this social experience informs their adult belief that the world is a relatively decent place. On the other hand, when their social experiences tell them that the world is full of evil, hurtful people, their view of reality is often very different. This observation of how people decide the nature of their world is meaningful for social workers, particularly when they work with clients whose experiences differ from their own (Lee & Greene, 2009).

Recognizing that a person's reality is based on her or his perceptions and experiences in the social world and that there can be more than one reality because each person perceives the world differently and has different experiences is one way to implement postmodernism and social construction. Social workers who practice from these perspectives work with clients' realities, rather than their own. For example, if a client appears to have little ambition to financially support herself or to participate in civic life, an understanding of the reality of the client's culture and environment may help you to understand why. Perhaps institutionalized racism leaves your client bitter and nonparticipatory, with little vision of what her life might be. Recognition of this postmodern principle of multiple realities may expand one's practice to advocate for or take up the causes of people who have little power. In practice, postmodernism and social construction approaches require acknowledgment of the practitioner's boundaries and allow practitioners to enter the world of the client.

Deconstruction   Constructionist thinking opens the way to explore particular beliefs, such as that the world is a kind place, through the process **deconstruction**, of taking apart those beliefs to examine how they developed. Through the process of deconstruction, you can explore the factors that spawned these beliefs. The following is an example of both social construction and deconstruction.

For many years in the 20th century, it was an accepted "reality" that adults with severe disabilities were neither capable of negotiating nor entitled to engage in adult relationships, particularly sexual ones. Institutions and community-based facilities worked diligently to prevent relationships and sometimes even kept couples with disabilities from being together alone in the same room. That particular social understanding and sense of reality contributed to the infamous practice of eugenics, which sought to prevent the reproduction of people deemed genetically deficient (See Exhibit 1.5). As advocates for the rights of persons with disabilities began to deconstruct and debunk the assumptions of the social construction that supported this callous practice, eugenics became less acceptable.

Although these assumptions are by no means extinct, they are situated in a specific economic, historical, and cultural setting that is no longer dominant. The concept of contextual setting, or **social location**, refers to the time, place, and prevailing ideas or discourse that influence standards, particularly about what is considered "right." All ideas emerge from a context that includes attitudes or beliefs, and ideas must be recognized as contextual rather than as absolute, moral truths (Kelley, 2013). Consider, for example, a new social worker who is judged and silenced if she or he counters the so-called truth regarding transgendered persons and, based on human rights or social justice concerns, objects to certain social restrictions. Consider what beliefs or customs are so strongly held in your own community or agency that deviance from them has significant professional or personal consequences and is interpreted as a moral failing.

Questions that expose the attitudes and beliefs underlying ideas often have the effect of creating opportunities for people. Using social construction, social workers are likely to question arrangements that bring people harm and to be suspicious or wary of presumed expertise that denies people their own experience. For example, a social worker may advocate for an older adult whose physician is dismissing his acute medical distress. The social worker, with support from a supervisor or others, may even need to challenge the adequacy of the client's medical care. In this way, the social worker refutes the idea that any particular set of assumptions or positions

EXHIBIT 1.5 *Eugenics Assumptions*	• People with severe disabilities are like children who should not enter into adult relationships. • People with severe disabilities are not adequate as human beings and should not have children. • People with severe disabilities are not entitled to define their own needs or desires. • People with severe disabilities do not have the capacity for love.

cannot be challenged and operates on the idea that all beliefs, ideas, and arrangements can be respectfully questioned.

Narrative Theory   Narrative and solution-focused interventions are consistent with postmodernism (Kelley, 2013). Narrative theory guides practitioners to utilize "stories" to understand the lived experience of clients. **Narrative theory** is a therapeutic theory founded on the notion that people's sense of their identity consists of interacting narratives. A social worker using narrative theory would take a conversational approach to unearth the cultural discourses about identity and power that have shaped the client. This approach involves helping clients make sense of the meanings they attach to events in their lives. A narrative is the thread that binds together disparate events. Narrative approaches view problems as separate from people, and people possess the qualities and skills needed to change their relationship with the problem(s) they are facing in life (Madigan, 2010).

Solution-Focused Approach   In contrast to a narrative approach, a **solution-focused approach** invites clients to explore and determine the concrete change they desire in their lives and the resources and strengths they possess to make the change occur (Yee Lee, 2013). Using a solution-focused approach, clients identify a specific goal they believe will make their lives better and attach specific strengths to a plan to reach that goal. Often clients are asked to think about an exception, times in which the challenge did not exist, and to identify the conditions under which the challenge did not exist as indicators of potential ways to address the problem. For example, if a child is struggling to focus in school, a discussion of the exceptions to this situation, or conditions under which the child has been able to focus on schoolwork, may shed light on possible solutions. Is the child able to focus early in the school day? When seated with specific classmates or away from specific classmates?

Critical Social Construction   The *critical* in **critical social construction** is derived from a contemporary analysis of power, which recognizes that any social group can shape its beliefs to its own benefit at the expense of other groups. The critical dimension then allows the social worker to question power arrangements, especially if many people's voices have been silenced or "subjugated" (Hartman, 1994). Those who were able to arrange systems like slavery had the power to privilege themselves while oppressing others. In these conditions, privileged groups not only benefit from but also perpetuate their privilege by using their power to assert their beliefs, which come to be regarded as truth. Although many groups today who benefit from privilege would not consciously choose such advantage if presented with a choice, such groups as whites, heterosexuals, Christians, and those who are able bodied, benefit from privilege in many parts of the U.S. (Diller, 2015).

Social workers can use critical social construction to analyze power relations and the dominant beliefs that result. For example, social workers can discuss power

QUICK GUIDE 2   SUMMARY OF APPROACHES IN SOCIAL WORK PRACTICE

Ecosystems perspective: Examines the exchanges between individuals, families, groups, and communities and their environment.

Social justice perspective: Focuses on the manner in which society distributes resources among its members, including material goods and social benefits, rights, and protections.

Human rights perspective: Reflects an ongoing commitment to the belief that all people should have basic rights and access to the broad benefits of their societies.

Strengths perspective: Affirms and works with the strengths found both in people seeking help and in their environments.

Postmodern approaches: Examine the cultural assumptions that underlie many of the arrangements of power and politics and are critical of assumptions or theories that claim absolute or authoritative truth.

> *Critical social construction:* As people construct reality based on their experiences in the social world, this approach examines power relations and the dominant beliefs that result.
>
> *Narrative theory:* Through telling "stories," this approach helps clients make sense of the meanings they give to events in their lives.
>
> *Solution-focused interventions:* This approach explores and determines the concrete change desired in client lives and the resources and strengths clients possess to make the change occur.

relations with clients who are nonwhite, nonheterosexual, or non-Christian or persons with disabilities about their less powerful position in society and the way in which this shapes their experiences. Power and dominant beliefs often negatively impact nonprivileged groups with whom social workers often work. This book will address the repercussions of this critical analysis for social work practice.

Complementary Aspects of the Theoretical Perspectives

Each of the five perspectives—ecosystems, social justice, human rights, the strengths perspective, and the postmodern perspectives (critical social construction, narrative theory, and solution-focused interventions)—offers the social worker unique and complex challenges. In many respects, the different perspectives complement each other. The strengths perspective, for example, may bring social justice to people who have experienced inequities. Human rights, in turn, may be seen as the moral grounding for undertaking justice-oriented work. Constructionist ideas regarding the influence of historical and cultural standpoints on power relations and beliefs allow the social worker to question accepted ideas and approaches that marginalize people and characterize them as pathological or undeserving. Taken together these perspectives provide a comprehensive and compelling approach to social work.

STRAIGHT TALK ABOUT TRANSLATING PERSPECTIVES INTO PRACTICE

Students and social work educators have often questioned the relevance of theoretical perspectives to actual practice situations. Some of the frameworks and perspectives may seem abstract or far removed from clients. On the other hand, when perspectives reflect and honor the experience of people and fit the situation, they can be a critical guide to social work practice. For example, the strengths perspective may direct social workers to focus on the support networks and cleanup efforts of a struggling, poverty-stricken neighborhood, emphasizing the client system's capabilities and assets, rather than the dilapidated housing, trash, and abandoned cars that line the streets. While applying frameworks and perspectives and integrating theory and practice can be challenging, it can help guide and serve as a foundation for social work practice.

Social Work Profession's Focus on Societal Problems

As a profession, social work has historically had strong influence to address social problems, such as poverty, child labor, and mental illness. Led by the American Academy of Social Work & Social Welfare (AASWSW), the Grand Challenges for Social Work is a recent initiative to spur social progress on significant social problems using social work's science and knowledge base. In this way, social work can meet the challenges of individuals, families, groups, and communities in individual and coordinated efforts locally and regionally, as well as in society as a whole through coordinated, focused efforts. The Grand Challenges are areas of foci for the social work profession that collectively serve as an agenda for the profession that promote individual and family well-being, a stronger social fabric, and a just society (American Academy of Social Work & Social Welfare, 2016).

The twelve Grand Challenges are the following (American Academy of Social Work & Social Welfare, 2016):

1. *Ensure healthy development for all youth:* Prevent mental, emotional, and behavioral problems in youth to help youth grow into healthy and productive adults.
2. *Close the health gap:* Use evidence-based social strategies to ensure access to health care and prevent ill health effects from discrimination, poverty, and dangerous environments.
3. *Stop family violence:* Use proven interventions to prevent and identify abuse, and help families break the cycle of violence.
4. *Advance long and productive lives:* Facilitate engagement in education and productive activities throughout life to promote better health, financial security, and a vital society.
5. *Eradicate social isolation:* Promote deep social connections and community for all.

6. *End homelessness:* Develop service innovations and technologies and create policy that advances affordable housing and income security.

7. *Create social responses to a changing environment:* Forge new partnerships with communities and catalyze innovations to address the environmental challenges of climate change and urban development that affect all, but especially marginalized, communities.

8. *Harness technology for social good:* Use new technologies to more quickly address growing societal needs.

9. *Promote smart decarceration:* Develop an evidence-based strategy to reduce the prison population and ensure a just approach to public safety.

10. *Reduce extreme economic inequality:* Promote education, wages, tax benefits, and changes in labor practices.

11. *Building financial capability for all:* Promote adoption of social policies that improve lifelong income and savings, expand workforce training, and expand access to financial literacy and services.

12. *Achieve equal opportunity and justice:* Engage in practice and policy efforts to address racial and social injustices, dismantle inequality, and embrace diversity of the population.

These twelve challenges will be interwoven throughout this book to provide examples and ideas about the ways in which the profession of social work can provide knowledge and skills to address social problems.

CONCLUSION

Social work practice is defined in the following ways: (1) by type of practice or range of practice settings, (2) as a set of activities, (3) as a set of roles, (4) as a set of competencies and practice behaviors, (5) by types of client grouping, (6) by practice frameworks, (7) as a licensed profession, (8) by purpose, and (9) by the tensions experienced in the profession. Self-knowledge is also a critical component of effective social work practice.

Exploring social work practice through this array of dimensions allows for many interpretations of situations and various foci of attention, some of which will be discussed in subsequent chapters. An understanding of the tensions social workers experience can help you put the ongoing concerns within the profession in context.

This chapter also introduced five explicit theoretical perspectives that guide social workers to empower and liberate people who have lived their lives at society's margins. Although translating these approaches into ethical, effective social work competencies is a challenge in practice, it is one that sustains professional growth. Chapter 2 will delve further into the role these values and ethics play in social work practice. Further chapters will also explore the twelve Grand Challenges for social work that serve as a professional agenda on which social work will bring knowledge and skills.

MAIN POINTS

- Social work practice can be conceptualized in at least nine different ways, including as a type of practice or range of practice settings, a type of professional activity, a set of roles, and a licensed profession.

- Tensions that persist in contemporary practice include those between social control and social change, acceptance and change, clinical and nonclinical perspectives, experts and shared power, and global citizenship and the local community.

- Effective social work practice requires questioning your own assumptions and understanding how they impact your work.

- Theoretical perspectives play a significant role in guiding practice activities. The five perspectives, or frames, presented in this book are the ecosystem perspective; the social justice perspective; the human rights perspective; the strengths perspective; and postmodern approaches, which includes narrative and solution-focused approaches and critical social constructionism.

- The ecosystems perspective provides a frame for generalist practice and examines the fit between individuals and their environment.

- The social justice perspective addresses the manner in which resources are allocated.

- Guided by the United Nations' Universal Declaration of Human Rights, the human rights perspective is a frame that emphasizes the conviction that all people have civil, political, social, economic, and cultural rights simply because they are human beings.

- The strengths perspective is a practice approach that highlights and works with individual, family, group, and community resilience and assets, honoring the client's goals and dreams, and asserts that all communities possess resources.

- Critical social constructionism is a contemporary, postmodern frame based on the assertion that social truths are agreed-upon beliefs shaped in a common history and culture and perpetuated through assumptions, language, and stories. It also notes the power arrangements responsible for the prevalence of such truths.

- Applying theoretical perspectives to practice is challenging but necessary for effective social work to maintain its mission, integrity, and consistency.

The twelve Grand Challenges serve as a collective agenda for social work's professional efforts to address society's most pressing social problems.

EXERCISES

a. Case Exercises

1. Go to www.routledgesw.com/cases and explore the Sanchez family interactive case study by reviewing the introduction and the tasks of each of the four phases. Click on the "Start this Case" button (under the "Engage" tab) and complete Tasks #1, #2, and #3.

2. After completing Exercise #1, imagine you are working with the Sanchez family as a social worker employed by the U.S. Bureau of Citizenship and Immigration Service. You are assigned to Celia and Hector Sanchez as they receive their permanent resident cards, or "green cards," which authorize them to live and work legally in the U.S. Your role is to help them understand their new rights and responsibilities. What knowledge, values, and skills do you think would be particularly important for your work with the couple? Identify at least one *specific* area of knowledge, one value, and one skill. What challenges might result from emphasizing one (i.e., knowledge, value, or skill) over the other two?

3. After completing Exercises #1 and #2, consider the social justice issues involved in the family's permanent resident status and the ways in which these issues are related to human rights. Respond to the following:
   a. From your knowledge of human rights and the Sanchez family, identify two human rights that apply particularly to Hector and Celia as immigrants.
   b. How might you expect that having a green card would impact the family?

4. Consider the consequences of different social work practice discourses and respond to the following:
   a. Describe the ways in which a social work discourse of strengths differs from a discourse of pathology when applied to the Sanchez family.
   b. Describe how a strengths-based social worker would approach the family. How would you describe the professional relationship? How would you describe the focus of the work? Be as specific as possible.

5. Go to www.routledgesw.com/cases. Click on the Sanchez family, then "Start This Case," then review the case file for Emilia Sanchez (including Client History, Client Concerns, and Goals for the Client). Click on "Mapping this Case" under "Case Study Tools." Explore Emilia's relationship with her relatives by reviewing the family genogram. Also review Emilia's ecomap and interaction matrix (under "Case Study Tools"). Answer Emilia's critical thinking questions.

6. After completing Exercise #5, consider the following case, which occurs prior to the time depicted on the website:

   You are employed as a hospital social worker and have been assigned to Emilia Sanchez. Emilia is 24 years old and has just given birth to Joey. She used crack cocaine during her pregnancy, and Joey tested positive for the drug. A child protection social worker assigned to the case believes that Joey will likely be taken into the custody of the state and probably placed with Celia and Hector, who have already indicated their willingness to take him as a foster child. As Emilia's social worker, your specific responsibility is to work with her on a plan to address her substance abuse and to adjust to Joey's placement in foster care with her parents. The nursing staff has informed you that she has just had an angry outburst and is now quietly sullen. You are currently heading to her hospital room.

   a. What do you notice about your own responses to the information you have received about Emilia? How will they influence your attitude about her? How will your attitude influence your work with her?

   b. What are you thinking as you walk to her room to meet with her? What emotions, if any, are you bringing with you?

   c. From the information you have at this point, what areas of strengths can you see in Emilia?

   d. Balancing the safety of the child with the rights of the parent, would you suggest that Emilia interact with Joey while he is in foster care? If so, under what circumstances?

   e. You anticipate that Emilia will be morose when you first meet with her. What will you say to her? If she later expresses anger at the situation, what might you say? What might be the next step in this situation?

7. Go to www.routledgesw.com/cases. Click on the Sanchez family. Go to the "Assess" menu, then click on "My Values." Take the Values and Ethics assessment.

b. Other exercises:

8. Write a two-paragraph reflection journal entry to answer the question, "Why do I want to be in the helping profession?"

9. Reflect on three of your concerns about being an effective helper. How can those also be strengths? (For example, Concern: "I am afraid that I will become too attached to my clients." Strength: "I am capable of developing strong relationships.")

10. Imagine a scenario in which a friend or family member is expressing doubts that social work is really a profession; for example, she says, "a person without a college degree can be a social worker." Write a 1–2-page paper summarizing the reasons that social work can be considered a profession, using the main points from this chapter.

Applying Values and Ethics to Practice

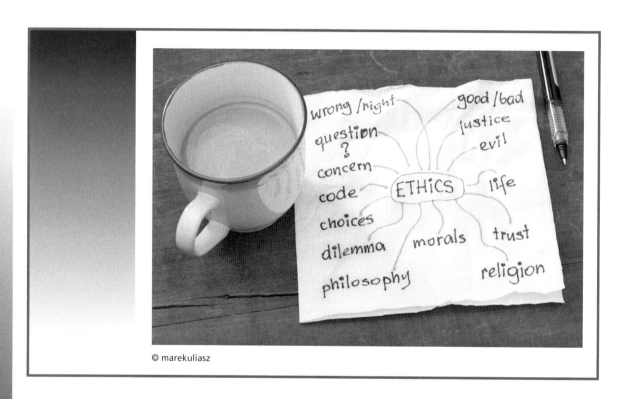

© marekuliasz

Deeply earnest and thoughtful people stand on shaky footing with the public.
Johann Wolfgang von Goethe (1749–1832)

Key Questions for Chapter 2

1. How can I identify as a professional social worker and conduct myself accordingly? [EPAS 1]
2. How can I apply social work ethical principles to guide my professional practice? [EPAS 1]
3. How can I apply critical thinking to inform and communicate professional judgments? [EPAS 1]
4. How can I advance human rights and social and economic justice through my professional practice? [EPAS 2]

CONSIDER THE DEGREE TO WHICH YOU AGREE WITH the following statements related to social work practice. Your response to these statements may shed light on your values:

- People who choose to smoke cigarettes or cigars, chew tobacco, or drink excessive amounts of alcohol are responsible for resolving and paying for their own health care since the risks of these behaviors are widely known.

- Under some conditions, physical discipline of children is acceptable.

- Children who are sexually abused should never be returned to the residence of the person who abused them.

- Social workers who agree to an agency's terms of employment do not have the right to criticize the agency's practices.

- Most homeless people want to live on the streets.

- Under particular circumstances, suicide is an acceptable strategy.

- World citizens who are working at gainful employment deserve to be free from hunger.

- HIV-positive people should be tattooed on the heel so potential sexual partners can take precautions.

- Perpetrators and victims of crime are equally deserving of social work services.

Social work is a value-laden profession. While social workers may not agree about all values, adherence to professional social work values is central to the practice of social work and facilitates identification as a professional social worker.

Values are best defined as beliefs, while **ethics** are the rules of conduct that embody those beliefs. This chapter focuses on the way that social work values shape professional ethics—specifically, ethical codes and their application to practice, the relationship between ethics and the law, and the ways social workers manage ethical conflicts and dilemmas.

A BRIEF HISTORY OF SOCIAL WORK ETHICS

When social work first became a profession in 1908, social workers were more concerned about their clients' morals than about the conduct of individual social workers (Reamer, 2013b). In the first two decades of the 20th century, the emphasis of social reform shifted to address social problems, such as those related to health, employment, and poverty (Reamer, 2013a). In the late 1940s and early 1950s, social workers made several attempts to develop an official, written code of conduct that articulated the current, collective thinking of the profession. In 1947, the American Association of Social Workers (one of seven organizations that joined to become the National Association of Social Workers) adopted the profession's first formal code that established guidelines and standards for its ethical conduct (Reamer, 2013b). The National Association of Social Workers adopted its first formal code of ethics in 1960 (Reamer, 2013a).

The second wave of ethical development occurred in the late 1970s and early 1980s. Advances in biotechnology, such as organ and bone marrow transplants, changed the medical profession. These advances were especially influential in sensitizing social workers and other human service workers to the importance of their values and the relationship between their values and their professional decisions. New concerns about decision-making developed: Who should make certain decisions? Who should be involved in decisions? For example, who decides whether a dying relative is taken off life support? Which decisions were acceptable? Was it acceptable to abort a fetus diagnosed with a severe developmental disability? Other societal changes, such as developments in computer technology, globalized ecopolitics, and growing interest in human rights, also shaped and intensified the concern for values in ethical practice (Reamer, 2013a).

Recently, social work ethics have been concerned with risk management. Ethical standards guide conduct to manage liability risk and avoid professional malpractice. A body of literature has arisen around risk-management strategies that protect clients and prevent ethics problems (Reamer, 2013c). Over time, social work has developed standards to guide workers, prioritize ethical principles, affirm its values, and distinguish social workers' responsibilities. The *Code of Ethics* (NASW, 2008) reflects the profession's official views on appropriate conduct with clients, with one another, with organizations, and with society at large.

PROFESSIONAL CODES OF ETHICS [EPAS 1]

The social work *Code of Ethics* (2008) is a comprehensive code of ethical standards and guidelines that serves to: (1) affirm social work as a legitimate profession, (2) provide guidance for practice circumstances, and (3) explicate the standards to which the public may hold the profession accountable. The *Code of Ethics* provides social work practitioners with a useful structure for today's increasingly complex

EXHIBIT 2.1

Specialized Ethical Codes

Subgroups of the social work profession, such as those working with specific populations, have developed their own ethical codes. These subgroups include (Reamer, 2013a):

- National Association for Black Social Workers
- Clinical Social Work Federation
- International Federation of Social Workers (IFSW)
- Canadian Association of Social Workers

practice situations. Subgroups of social workers have also developed their own ethical codes (as seen in Exhibit 2.1).

The *Code of Ethics* is the official code of the social work profession in the United States. This chapter will review the *Code of Ethics,* discuss the *Code* as a tool of practice, and highlight the most recent International Federation of Social Workers (IFSW) code.

The NASW *Code of Ethics*

The six core values in the preamble form the basis of the *Code of Ethics* (see Exhibit 2.2). These core values represent a mix of the worker's activities, skills, principles, character, and attitudes. The ethical standards cover and are organized according to the following six relationship categories or standards:

1. Social workers' ethical responsibilities to clients
2. Social workers' ethical responsibilities to colleagues

EXHIBIT 2.2

The Foundation of the Social Work Perspective

CORE VALUES	ETHICAL PRINCIPLES
Service	Social workers' primary goal is to help people in need and to address social problems.
Social justice	Social workers challenge social injustice.
Dignity and worth of the person	Social workers respect the inherent dignity and worth of the person.
Importance of human relationships	Social workers recognize the central importance of human relationships.
Integrity	Social workers behave in a trustworthy manner.
Competence	Social workers practice within their areas of competence and develop and enhance their professional expertise.

<table>
<tr><td>

EXHIBIT 2.3

Sample of the NASW Code of Ethics

</td><td>

6. SOCIAL WORKERS' ETHICAL RESPONSIBILITIES TO THE BROADER SOCIETY

6.01 Social Welfare

Social workers should promote the general welfare of society, from local to global levels, and the development of people, their communities, and their environments. Social workers should advocate for living conditions conducive to the fulfillment of basic human needs and should promote social, economic, political, and cultural values and institutions that are compatible with the realization of social justice.

6.02 Public Participation

Social workers should facilitate informed participation by the public in shaping social policies and institutions.

6.03 Public Emergencies

Social workers should provide appropriate professional services in public emergencies to the greatest extent possible.

6.04 Social and Political Action

Social workers should engage in social and political action that seeks to ensure that all people have equal access to the resources, employment, services, and opportunities they require to meet their basic human needs and to develop fully. Social workers should be aware of the impact of the political arena on practice and should advocate for changes in policy and legislation to improve social conditions in order to meet basic human needs and promote social justice.

Source: NASW, 2008

</td></tr>
</table>

3.   Social workers' ethical responsibilities in practice settings
4.   Social workers' ethical responsibilities as professionals
5.   Social workers' ethical responsibilities to the social work profession
6.   Social workers' ethical responsibilities to the broader society

Within each of these categories the *Code of Ethics* contains from 2 (Category 5) to 16 standards (Category 1), along with varying substandards, a total of 155 standards. These substandards explain the appropriate conduct for social workers (see Exhibit 2.3 for a sample of the *Code of Ethics*). Social workers may deviate from these expected norms when appropriate ethical justification is available (Barsky, 2010).

International Federation of Social Workers' Ethical Statement [EPAS 2]

The International Federation of Social Workers (IFSW), a worldwide professional organization of social work organizations and individuals, documents its position on ethical practice in a statement that reflects concerns that are similar, but not identical to, those articulated in the NASW *Code of Ethics*. The International Federation of Social Workers and the International Association of Schools of Social Work jointly approved the IFSW document, *Ethics in Social Work: Statement of Principles ("Statement of Principles")*, in 2001. This document contains a more explicit and pervasive emphasis on human rights than the *Code of Ethics*, for example (IFSW & IASW, 2012, para. 3):

> *Definition of Social Work: The social work profession promotes social change, problem solving in human relationships, and the empowerment and liberation of people to enhance well-being. Utilising theories of human behaviour and social systems, social work intervenes at the points where people interact with their environments. Principles of human rights and social justice are fundamental to social work.*

As a federation, IFSW assumes that member organizations, including the National Association of Social Workers (NASW), adhere to the standards in the *Statement of Principles*. Therefore, a comparison of the *Code of Ethics* and the *Statement of Principles* reveals that they both contain essentially the same principles but have different emphases for U.S. and international ethical practice. The *Statement of Principles* highlights seven international conventions that form "common standards of achievement and recognise rights that are accepted by the global community" (IFSW & IASW, 2012, para. 4). These include the Universal Declaration of Human Rights (1948); the International Covenant on Civil and Political Rights (1965); and the International Covenant on Economic, Social, and Cultural Rights (1965) as well as some conventions that the U.S. has not yet ratified.

The next two sections in the IFSW statement, on human rights and social justice (see Exhibit 2.4), are equivalent to the first two principles in the *Code of Ethics* (refer back to Exhibit 2.2). These address social work's commitment to human rights and human dignity. Although the values in these statements are similar to those in the *Code of Ethics*, the Universal Declaration of Human Rights, which is central to the IFSW statement, includes emphases on a global (rather than national) perspective and on the importance of economic, social, and cultural rights for all people.

Limits of Ethical Codes

Although the *Code of Ethics* (NASW, 2008) offers helpful guidance to social work practitioners wrestling with difficult situations, the *Code* is often difficult to apply because it offers general statements, can be hard to interpret, and may offer unrealistic guidance given a social worker's specific situation (Strom-Gottfried, 2008). As examples in this chapter will show, issues of context, risk taking and creativity, and diversity can also challenge ethical codes.

EXHIBIT 2.4

Ethics in Social Work, Statement of Principles

Human rights and human dignity: Social work is based on respect for the inherent worth and dignity of all people, and the rights that follow from this. Social workers should uphold and defend each person's physical, psychological, emotional, and spiritual integrity and well-being. This means:

1. *Respecting the right to self-determination:* social workers should respect people's rights to make their own choices and decisions, irrespective of their values and life choices, providing this does not threaten the rights and interests of others.
2. *Promoting the right to participation:* social workers should promote the full involvement and participation of people using their services in ways that enable them to be empowered in all aspects of decisions and actions affecting their lives.
3. *Treating each person as a whole:* social workers should be concerned with the whole person, within the family and the community, and should seek to recognise all aspects of a person's life.
4. *Identifying and developing strengths:* social workers should focus on the strengths of all individuals, groups and communities and thus promote their empowerment.

Social justice: Social workers have a responsibility to promote social justice, in relation to society generally, and in relation to the people with whom they work. This means:

1. *Challenging negative discrimination:* social workers have a responsibility to challenge negative discrimination on the basis of irrelevant characteristics such as ability, age, culture, gender or sex, marital status, political opinions, skin color or other physical characteristics, sexual orientation, or spiritual beliefs.
2. *Recognizing diversity:* social workers should recognize and respect the racial and cultural diversity of societies in which they practice, taking account of individual, family, group, and community differences.
3. *Distributing resources equitably:* social workers should ensure that resources at their disposal are distributed fairly, according to need.
4. *Challenging unjust policies and practices:* social workers have a duty to bring to the attention of policy makers, politicians, and the general public situations where resources are inadequate or where policies and practices are unfair or harmful.
5. *Working in solidarity:* social workers have an obligation to challenge social conditions that contribute to social exclusion, stigmatization or subjugation, and to work towards an inclusive society.

Source: IFSW & IASSW, 2012

The Role of Context Social workers make ethical decisions within a practice context, and that context may shape the decision-making process in subtle ways. For example, if, without realizing it, a social worker attributes negative qualities to David, a client, because of missed appointments: the social worker may believe that David does not want services, is unable to take full advantage of scarce resources, or that David does not deserve these resources. If the social worker is in a position to choose which clients have access to a limited service, she or he may disqualify David without further reflection. On the one hand, it may appear that the social worker is using good judgment in seeking to maximize the effectiveness of the scarce service. On the other hand, the decision reflects a decision-making process that is not transparent and that is influenced by one possibly inaccurate interpretation of David's behavior. For example, if the social worker took into account that David missed appointments because he lacked reliable transportation, had an unstable home life, or had a child with medical need, the decision-making process may have resulted in a different outcome. Judgments such as these, which may be based on inaccurate or incomplete information, present an ethical question relating to the professional discretion and impartial judgment that the *Code of Ethics* requires. Therefore, an ethical code provides decontextualized guidance. Social workers following an ethical code must still exercise judgment based on the specific circumstances of each situation.

Professionals must be aware of how their perspectives and judgments influence their ethical decision-making (Barsky, 2010). Social workers frequently come to the conclusion that the resolution of an ethical question depends on many factors, in recognition of the importance of the surrounding circumstances, social location, and current pressures (Harrington & Dolgoff, 2008). Ethical decision-making also benefits from consultation with knowledgeable colleagues (Reamer, 2013b). In some settings, social workers find it helpful to initiate an in-depth conversation with their colleagues regarding their thinking, the implications of varying choices, and an analysis of their values. In other settings, committees review cases with ethical questions and the group makes a decision.

Risk Taking and Creativity   Another pitfall inherent in the rigid interpretation of ethical rules is the potential for oversimplification. Social workers may rely solely on the *Code of Ethics* rather than using their own creativity and professional judgment. Using critical thinking to inform professional judgment is a valuable component of social work practice that sometimes requires the social worker to take risks (Strom-Gottfried, 2008). There is rarely one correct answer to an ethical dilemma. Social workers must have a tolerance for ambiguity and must determine how to apply ethical principles in practice (Dolgoff, Harrington, & Lowenberg, 2012). **[EPAS 1]**

The following case vignette illustrates this idea:

A school social worker named Cora, in strict adherence to the ethical principle of practicing only within her area of competency (Code, Standard 4.01a), at first declined to see a young African American student from a family struggling with poverty who was experiencing substance abuse. Cora felt competent to work with adolescents with developmental issues, but she was not educated to treat those struggling with substance abuse, so she decided it would be unethical to work with the student. The student was in need of assistance, was ready to work on the problem, and had no other obvious or realistic options for services in her rural community. The student's substance use issue was intertwined with other challenges related to growing up in difficult circumstances, and developmental issues were involved. When the student asked her to reconsider, Cora decided to discuss the matter with a colleague. The colleague reminded Cora that she had skills and experience that would directly benefit the student. For example, she knew about adolescent development, had strong relationship skills with adolescents, and was committed to a hopeful, resilience-based perspective. Cora's colleague also advised that she might find a resource in her former supervisor, who was a certified substance abuse counselor. Cora contacted her former supervisor, who recommended available training and the supervision of a clinician who also was a certified substance abuse counselor.

Substance abuse in school populations is a common and potentially life-changing issue for youth. Cora was able to negotiate with the school administration for time and reimbursement to obtain training that would allow her to better serve her clients and the school population in general. Because Cora was creative and willing to explore options in response to important needs, her client(s) were likely to receive competent services from an experienced worker who sought both training and supervision. There is some risk in Cora's assumption of the role of providing substance abuse treatment; however, taking on the issue is more closely aligned with social work's values than denying help to the student.

Strict and nonreflective adherence to a standard code can help preserve the current social order, which may be in direct conflict with the profession's commitment to confront social injustice and oppression (MacDonald, 2016). Since the student's family in the example was limited financially and belonged to an ethnic population that experienced oppression, the student would likely face more barriers to receiving needed services than students in families without these characteristics. The student's access to needed resources would be constricted, a situation of social injustice. Cora's commitment to responding to the student's need and providing services embodies social work's obligation to confront injustices.

While Cora made a decision using the *Code of Ethics,* colleague advice, and critical thinking, not everyone will agree that her solution was the best one. For example, advocates for diversity empowerment might view Cora's effort as perpetuating social injustice because the situation involves nonwhite people receiving substandard services from a worker without the appropriate credentials. While there may be different, well-informed opinions about the best course of action in a situation, a too-narrow interpretation of the *Code of Ethics* that precludes critical thinking and creativity should be avoided. Resolving issues like Cora's is seldom easy; it is not hard to overlook worthwhile concerns, such as the competency of the worker in a particular area. Practitioners are encouraged to consider the *Code of Ethics* and to talk to colleagues to fully explore issues. This decision-making process contributes to the ongoing development of the profession's larger ethical stance.

Diversity A postmodern recognition of diversity and multiple realities raises another concern about the use of codes. Universal codes meant to apply to everyone in all situations can fail to address the contexts of individual social workers and their clients or fail to recognize differences among people and cultures. For example, the ethical mandate for confidentiality, which refers to the social worker's obligation to keep information about clients from becoming public in any way, is often regarded as absolutely critical in maintaining a professional relationship. However, universally applying confidentiality as an ethical mandate may present an obstacle in cultures less individualistic than that in the U.S., in which the community may be both the reference point and a rich source of resources that may assist individual clients. In such communities, maintaining confidentiality can be experienced as secretive, alienating, divisive, and harmful. For example, some Latino families may not be receptive to individual work with a social worker but may instead become engaged and respond to family systems work (Diller, 2015).

Briskman and Noble (1999) suggest that social work needs an ethical model that is more affirming of difference. One possibility is to develop multiple codes, grounded in client-centered service delivery plans. For example, the authors cite an organization that works to prevent and treat sexual assault in Melbourne, Australia, that shapes its code according to the perspective that sexual assault is a violation of human rights (p. 64). This is an example of a specific code tailored to the organization's commitments to a particular client population. Another way to recognize difference is to develop constituency-based codes founded on specific concerns, such as tolerance for sexual orientation in schools. In this case, norms would develop with specific reference to the issues raised by gay, lesbian, bisexual, transgendered, and questioning groups. The development of specialized codes for different groups departs from the universal application of U.S. and Canadian codes.

In some cases, a bicultural code of practice may work best. For example, the Aotearoa New Zealand Association of Social Work (ANZASW) currently uses a Bicultural Code that reflects an effort to deal justly with its native Maori people through recognition of the independence guaranteed to them in a treaty negotiated in 1840. The historical emphasis on the Maori people's independence has led New Zealander social workers to recognize the contemporary demands that this principle places on their work with Maori people. This code is based on the IFSW code and explicitly requires a bicultural focus for all of New Zealand's social workers. See Exhibit 2.5 for an excerpt from the ANZASW *Code of Ethics*.

Despite these challenges, the NASW *Code of Ethics* provides a valuable structure for the social work profession. The *Code* articulates expectations and provides overall guidance about conduct so that social workers have clear expectations and can identify points of departure from the norms. The *Code of Ethics* is value-based and is consistent with social work history. While it has limitations, it is framed in consideration of experiences outside of the mainstream. As such, the *Code of Ethics* addresses growing concerns for recognition and affirmation of diverse peoples worldwide. Codes are evolving documents that reflect the consensus of the

EXHIBIT 2.5

Sample
Bicultural
Code of Ethics

In New Zealand, the Treaty of Waitangi, negotiated in 1840 between the occupying British and the native Maori chiefs, recognized the native Maori people as Tangata Whanua and guaranteed their right to independence. This treaty is an integral part of contemporary ethics in New Zealand social work, and it reflects an active commitment to the promotion of indigenous identity. The following is an excerpt from the Code of Ethics of the Aotearoa New Zealand Association of Social Workers.

1 Responsibility for Te Tiriti o Waitangi-based Society

1.1 In all relationships with Tangata Whenua, members make ethical decisions and stand by these, in accordance with this Code.

1.2 Te Tiriti o Waitangi is a required subject in the education of members both upon entry into social work and ongoing. This includes a knowledge and understanding of their own ethnicity and the Tangata Whenusa and Tauiwi histories of Aotearoa New Zealand.

1.3 Ideally, members will work with agencies and organisations whose policies, procedures and practice are based in Te Tiritio Waitangi, and actively and constructively promote change in those agencies and organisations that operate from a mono-cultural base.

1.4 Appropriate social work requires members to seek to understand differing Tangata Whenua perspectives. Members and social service agencies and organisations respect these differences and at all times avoid imposing mono-cultural values and concepts on Tangata Whenua.

1.5 Mono-cultural control over power and resources must be relinquished so that Tangata Whenua can achieve Tino Rangatiratanga. Members relinquish control over their discretionary power and those resources available, so far as that is appropriate within the realities of their workplace.

1.6 Members actively promote the rights of Tangata Whenua to utilize Tangata Whenua social work modes of practice and ensure the protection of the integrity of Tangata Whenua in a manner which is culturally appropriate.

1.7 Members accept the responsibility of their status and are actively anti-racist in their practice.

Source: Aotearoa New Zealand Association of Social Workers (ANZAWS), 2007

profession at the time of adoption, a consensus that can change as contexts change (see, for example, Exhibit 2.6). Social workers are encouraged to be involved in professional dialogue about the *Code* through professional organizations and to contribute to its evolution.

ETHICS AND THE LAW

International, federal, state, and local laws have a significant impact on social work practice, and their constant changes create a complex, sometimes bewildering

The first NASW *Code of Ethics*, adopted in 1960, was only one page long, with fourteen brief declarations such as "to give appropriate service in public emergencies." In 1979, the NASW adopted a second *Code*, which included six sections of brief principles and a preamble. This Code was revised twice and eventually contained around eighty principles. For example, statements about solicitation of referrals, fees for referral, and dual relationships were added.

EXHIBIT 2.6

Changes to the NASW Code of Ethics

   The NASW approved a third Code in 1996, which included four major sections: a preamble, the purpose of the NASW *Code of Ethics*, Ethical Principles, and Ethical Standards. There were many changes from the previous Code, including the addition of a mission statement, a section on the uses of codes, a list of social work values and principles, and almost twice the amount of practice standards as the 1979 Code. This third Code also contained standards about confidentiality limits, avoiding conflict of interest, and emphasizing social justice and social change (Brill, 1998; Reamer, 2013a). The 2008 version of the Code includes standards regarding cultural competence and social diversity, respect, discrimination, and social and political action (NASW, 2008).

climate in which to practice (Strom-Gottfried, 2008). Ethics and the law are related and sometimes overlap, yet there are clear distinctions between the two. The following discussion highlights parallels and distinctions between social work ethics and the law, as well as the potential for, and benefit of, collaboration between social workers and lawyers.

Parallels between Ethics and the Law

Many parallels exist between social work ethics and the laws that impact practitioners. For example, social workers who breach client confidentiality may be accused of violating the *Code of Ethics* (Section 1.12). In many states, clients could initiate a complaint with the state licensing board that a social worker has violated the *Code of Ethics*. State licensing boards can impose sanctions or require various forms of corrective action, such as license suspension or revocation (Reamer, 2013c). NASW can also sanction social workers through an ethics committee process and can impose a range of penalties such as suspension from NASW, mandated supervision or consultation, censure, publishing the names of those sanctioned in organizational outlets, and others (Reamer, 2013c). While NASW's process is professional rather than legal, sanctions can still harm a social worker's career.

Conflicts between Ethics and the Law

Social workers may experience practice situations in which there is an overt conflict between ethical practice and the law. The next section considers two legal duties:

the duty to report and the duty to protect. Both of these legal mandates support ethical practice in most contexts and create conflicts in others.

Duty to Report: Child Protection   Social workers operating in the arena of child protection frequently find themselves in a contentious environment. Like many types of helping professionals, social workers have a legal duty to report their suspicions of child abuse or neglect to child protection authorities or law enforcement.

A common sequence of events leading to a report of suspected child abuse or neglect begins with a child telling a teacher, school nurse, or another school-related adult that she or he has been abused or neglected. Alternatively, a nurse or doctor may suspect abuse or neglect based on physical signs. In either situation, the professional reports these allegations to the proper authorities. A child protection worker then investigates the charges, often interviewing the parents/guardians as well as the child, and determines whether the charges are substantiated and further action is required. The person making the referral may be convinced that the child is being abused or neglected, but she or he may also suspect that the abuse or neglect is going to be difficult to substantiate. In such a case, reporting the abuse might place the child at much greater risk, because the parent/guardian will learn about the accusation and may become angry and take out the anger on the child. Where there

A discussion of abuse or neglect can elicit strong emotions.

© Mark Bowden

is no obvious way to protect the child, the referring professional may be tempted not to obey the reporting law.

A similar situation may occur if the social worker is cynical about the adequacy, timeliness, or effectiveness of the response of child protection agencies. For example, a social worker who must wait an unreasonably long time for a response from a child protection agency due to inadequate department staffing may be reluctant to report again.

Social workers may encounter other practice situations in which compliance with the law may create more harm than good. For example, consider a social worker who is working with a pregnant 15-year-old client to discuss her options. In a discussion with the client, the social worker discovers that the client knows who the father of the baby is and that the father is terribly frightened about his family's possible reaction to the pregnancy. The client is under 18 and legally a child; therefore, the pregnancy may become a matter of child abuse and, by law, must be reported. However, the social worker views the reporting possibility as nonproductive. Since the client claims that the sexual activity was consensual, reporting will not assist the client. Reporting will possibly alienate the baby's father, who is also under 18 and who might otherwise participate in the decision-making process. Finally, reporting could put the baby's father at risk of a violent reaction from his family.

Duty to Report: Adult Protection   All states have reporting laws designed to protect older adults from abuse, neglect, and exploitation. However, each state has its own definition of reportable acts and its own designations of who is responsible for reporting and what entity is responsible for accepting and investigating the report (Barsky, 2010). Social workers may experience similar challenges between the law and ethical duties in situations involving suspected abuse of older adults. For example, a social worker may encounter evidence that her client, Betty, who is an older adult, was financially exploited by her daughter at least once. The daughter handles Betty's bills, and the social worker encountered evidence that she once paid one of her smaller bills with Betty's money. The social worker may wonder whether it's worth reporting financial exploitation if it only happened once (as far as she knows), and Betty relies on her daughter for many other tasks that enables her to maintain independent living. Reporting could put this vital relationship at risk as well as risk Betty's ability to live in her home.

Duty to Protect: Threats of Violence   Social workers also have an ethical obligation to protect people from serious, foreseeable, and imminent harm (Barsky, 2010). This ethical and legal responsibility emerged from a court case resulting from a tragic situation. In 1969, Tatiana Tarasoff, a young student at the University of California at Berkeley, had a casual dating relationship with a graduate student from India. He apparently did not understand dating customs in the U.S. and consequently was despondent that Tatiana was simultaneously dating several men. Depressed, he went to a psychologist at the University Health Services and told the psychologist that he intended to kill Tatiana with a gun. The psychologist wrote a letter to the campus police and asked that the graduate student be detained in a psychiatric hospital. The police interviewed the young man but did not feel there was evidence to prove that he was dangerous. The police required him to promise that he would not contact Tatiana. When Tatiana returned from a summer visit abroad, the man stalked her and stabbed her to death. Tatiana's family sued the campus police, the University Health Services, and the Regents of the University of California for failing to warn them that their daughter's life was in danger. The trial court dismissed the case because although there was precedence for notifying the victim, there was no precedence for warning a third party (which, in this situation, would have been Tatiana's parents). The appeals court supported the dismissal, and an appeal was taken to the California Supreme Court, which overturned the dismissal, citing the therapist's responsibility to warn people who have been threatened as Tatiana had been. This case, *Tarasoff I* of 1974, is often called the Duty to Warn decision.

This ruling opened the way for the family to sue the police and the therapist. A massive outcry from members of both police and treatment-related groups led the California Supreme Court to hear the case again. The 1976 court decision, *Tarasoff II,* stressed that, when a therapist has determined that her or his client presents serious danger of violence to another, the therapist must "use reasonable care to protect the intended victim against such danger." The court's position was that the therapist might have to take any of several steps to ensure the safety of the person threatened by the client, and the emphasis was on the Duty to Protect rather than the warning emphasized in *Tarasoff I.* Although the Tarasoff decisions were based on the work of a clinical psychologist, social workers and other human service professionals are subject to the same legal precedents in most states.

Social workers must now carefully consider any threats of violence they learn about in the course of practice. For example, if a client with a history of violence threatens to "belt" his girlfriend after her discharge from a hospital, the social worker is obligated to assess the seriousness of the threat. Additionally, social workers must protect themselves and their employers against legal charges. A situation of this type is complex, and social workers must respond with several considerations in mind, including their employer's policies, the legal obligation of Duty to Protect, and the *Code of Ethics.* In the case of the *Tarasoff* decisions, the courts, not the ethics board of the profession, defined the parameters of responsibility.

Conflicts Working with Individuals, Families, Groups, Organizations, and Communities   Practice situations at various client system levels can involve the legal system. U.S. society has become increasingly litigious, and social workers may encounter practice situations with legal questions in policy practice, research, and community and direct practice (Barksy, 2010). For example, a social worker may encounter ethical challenges at the policy level if a new law requires adoption workers to provide the "adoption triad" (i.e., birth parents, adoptive parents, and adopted children) with access to all information about the adoption. If a birth mother was guaranteed confidentiality at the time of the adoption, she, along with her social worker, may be distraught by this sudden breach of the document that she signed, which she considered a binding legal agreement that would be in effect permanently. Another example is a social worker faced with maintaining a city zoning ordinance against a group home for those leaving prison, an establishment that she believes is critically needed in the community. Social workers working at the community level can experience ethical challenges in supporting community initiatives. For example, a community group may work toward an ordinance that would discourage individuals who are not documented from residing in the community. A social worker working with this group would face the ethical dilemma about whether to support the group's self-determination to exclude others from the community.

Collaboration between Ethics and the Law

In the best scenarios, the law and social work professions can work together to empower people whose legal and social rights are frequently violated. There are many examples of this kind of collaboration in joint law and social work degree programs. For example, collaborations occur in legal clinics for refugee and immigrant peoples and in family law and social work partnerships. In the U.S., the law drives much of the complex social welfare system, as well as the structures for shaping income and benefits distribution. A joint effort between the professions of social work and the law, based on common goals, can benefit a great number of people, with each profession enhancing and enriching the work of the other.

The law also places external pressure on all of the helping professions to hold one another accountable within their professions. The law protects the general public from the possibility that helping professionals can collude to cover up or obscure unethical conduct within their profession. Although the incidence of covering up unethical behavior is relatively low, all professionals may be tempted to minimize the seriousness of any offense raised. In more recent years, child abuse allegations and convictions involving priests from the Roman Catholic Church and the abuse of developmentally disabled individuals in state care in New York state have served as tragic reminders of the potential dangers the unethical behavior of people in helping professions pose to vulnerable populations.

DILEMMAS AND CRITICAL PROCESSES

The complex context of real client situations often highlights the potential for competition between social work values and/or between ethical standards in a given situation. This complexity can make it difficult to identify the appropriate ethical decision. The next section addresses the distinction between ethical conflicts and dilemmas, the idea of an ethical screen, various models for resolving dilemmas, and some examples of common dilemmas in social work practice.

The Distinction between Value Conflicts and Ethical Dilemmas

Value conflicts occur when an individual's personal values clash with those of another person or system. In contrast, ethical dilemmas occur when a social worker must choose between two or more relevant, but contradictory, ethical directives. An ethical dilemma exists when there is no clear single response that satisfies all ethical directives in a situation (Dolgoff et al., 2012).

Many practice situations involve clashes of values that are not ethical dilemmas. For example, a social worker may learn that a married client is having an affair. While the social worker may not agree with the client's choices, the situation does not meet the criteria for an ethical dilemma. However, a social worker who learns that a client is having an affair and using prostitutes, who may pose a health risk to other people because of an HIV status, may struggle with contrasting ethical and legal obligations to maintain confidentiality and notify client partners of harm. In another example, clients may demonstrate racism toward their social worker, who would then struggle with weighing an ethical mandate against abandoning clients with client self-determination and other ethical obligations. Another situation involving an ethical dilemma is when a relative of a suicidal person asks a social worker to help their relative, but the person has not sought services.

In all of these circumstances, no one response is clearly the correct, ethical way to handle the situation. Social workers must grapple with their ethical and legal mandates, consult with colleagues, and engage in other activities to arrive at a decision. The next section discusses structures to assist with the decision-making process.

The Ethical Principles Screen [EPAS 1]

A useful tool in considering ethical priorities is the ethical principles screen (Dolgoff et al., 2012). This screen assists in the decision-making process by highlighting the relative significance of values and the likely results of particular decisions. The elements in the screen, listed in Quick Guide 3, are reflected and prioritized in professional social work values, and are rank ordered so that Principle 1 has the highest priority and Principle 7 has the lowest. The screen is constructed to reflect socially constructed priorities that involve values.

The following scenario demonstrates the use of the ethical principle screen. A social worker believes that a child on her caseload is at risk because his father regularly beats him. This case clearly reflects Principle 1 regarding threats of bodily harm. A competing concern is a violation of confidentiality and the continuing trust of the child that is threatened if the abuse is reported. Thus, the case also involves Principle 6. To resolve the dilemma, the social worker identifies the ethical principles involved:

QUICK GUIDE 3   ELEMENTS OF THE ETHICAL PRINCIPLES SCREEN

- **Principle 1:** *Protection of life:* This principle refers to guarding against death, starvation, violence, neglect, and any other event or phenomenon that endangers a person's life.
- **Principle 2:** *Social justice:* This principle reflects a commitment to equal and fair access to services and basic treatment.
- **Principle 3:** *Self-determination, autonomy, and freedom:* This principle affirms the notion of self-determination and supports people's right to make free choices regarding their lives.
- **Principle 4:** *Least harm:* This principle supports the idea of protecting people from harm; when harm seems likely in any event, it asserts that people have the right to experience the least amount possible.
- **Principle 5:** *Quality of life:* This principle confirms that people, families, and communities all have the right to define and pursue the quality of life they desire.
- **Principle 6:** *Privacy and confidentiality:* This principle supports the right of people to be protected from having their personal information made public. Maintaining confidentiality means the social worker must not share client circumstances, struggles, or decisions without the client's explicit (generally written and signed) permission. Information revealing any identifying characteristics (such as name and physical description) must also be kept confidential.
- **Principle 7:** *Truthfulness and full disclosure:* This principle directs social workers to tell clients the full truth of any information pertaining to them and explain whatever is needed to ensure understanding.

Source: Dolgoff, Harrington, & Loewenberg, 2012

the protection of life versus confidentiality. The social worker then ranks the priority of these principles using the ethical priorities screen. In this situation, the life of the child is a more urgent and compelling guiding principle than the desire to maintain silence so that the child will continue to trust the social worker.

While not all social workers would agree with the prioritizations in the ethical screen in this situation, the screen offers a tool for decision-making. However, the principles address very broad concepts that are subject to interpretation, and their relative evaluation in the real practice world often requires critical thinking skills. The next section explores other models for resolving ethical dilemmas.

Models for Resolution of Ethical Dilemmas

Different models for resolving ethical dilemmas structure decision-making in other ways, reflecting a different ordering of social work values. Here are two examples.

Reamer (2013b) suggests that social workers follow several steps to enhance the quality of their ethical decision-making:

1. Identify the ethical issues, including the social work values and duties that conflict.

2. Identify the individuals, groups, and organizations that are likely to be affected by the ethical decision.
3. Tentatively identify all possible courses of action and the participants involved in each, along with the possible benefits and risks for each.
4. Thoroughly examine the reasons in favor of and opposed to each possible course of action.
5. Consult with colleagues and appropriate experts (i.e., professional colleagues, supervisors, agency administrators, and attorneys).
6. Make the decision and document the decision-making process.
7. Monitor and evaluate the decision.

Strom-Gottfried (2008) adds several options for addressing ethical dilemmas, including researching the literature, relevant laws, and policies; consulting formally with established committees; obtaining supervision; and consulting peers. Strom-Gottfried (2003) also suggests the following strategies for solving ethical dilemmas:

1. Consider the "worst case scenario" of each option.
2. Consider the principles of least harm, justice, and fairness.
3. Consider clinical and ethical implications.
4. Consider the process.
5. Consider barriers to acting on the principal identified power relationships.

Both Reamer's and Strom-Gottfried's approaches help analyze the issues involved in any particular dilemma. While Reamer's model is more methodical than Strom-Gottfried's because it prescribes a specific sequence of analysis, the Strom-Gottfried model allows for a creative strategy that can accommodate the specifics of the client's situation. Like codes of ethics, neither can produce an infallible result, and flexibility is needed in applying models to the specifics of the individual context.

Representative Examples of Practice Dilemmas

Of the many potential dilemmas, three types are common in social work: dual relationships, professional versus private tensions, and struggles between paternalism and client self-determination.

Dual Relationships   Relationships between social workers and clients that exist in addition to and distinct from their professional contacts create dual relationships. Such relationships often only become public in extreme circumstances, such as when the worker has a sexual relationship with the client. Sexual relationships, although an egregious affront to the profession, are fairly easy to resolve because ethical guidelines clearly prohibit such relationships.

Nonsexual dual relationships pose another set of questions. For example, consider the situation of Lara, a new social worker.

Lara works in a local community health center with young adults who have had brushes with the law. Her responsibility is to support their integration into the community's work-study program that the center sponsors. Lara finds her work interesting and rewarding, and she particularly enjoys working with one client, Joe, who is progressing in the program. Lara's 20-year-old sister recently called her to tell her about her new boyfriend. Lara realized that her sister's new boyfriend is her client, Joe.

This dual relationship presents a conflict between personal values and professional responsibilities. There are many reasons for Lara to maintain the current situation. Lara enjoys her job, values her work with Joe, and does not want to resign. On the other hand, Lara also wants to participate in her family gatherings, which are likely to include her sister's new boyfriend. The *Code of Ethics,* however, cautions against dual relationships. Because of the ethical mandate about confidentiality, Lara is not free to tell her family that Joe is a client, or to reveal anything about his situation.

Specifically, Section 1.06c of the *Code of Ethics* stresses that social workers should not engage in dual relationships with clients or former clients in which there is a risk of exploitation or potential harm to the client. Reamer (2013b) classifies dual relationships as unethical when they

- interfere with the social worker's exercise of professional discretion;

- interfere with the social worker's exercise of impartial judgment;

- exploit clients, colleagues, or third parties to further the social worker's personal interests; or

- harm clients, colleagues, or third parties.

In this scenario, the dual relationship Lara has with Joe has the potential to affect her professional discretion and impartial judgment. For example, if Lara discovers personal information about Joe that suggests he might not be a viable candidate for marriage, Lara may experience difficulty conducting herself in a professional manner.

In some situations, the social worker may have justification for a dual relationship with a client. For example, in rural areas, dual relationships may be very difficult to avoid, given the small number of service providers (Dolgoff et al., 2012). In a rural area, clients may work for or with a member of a social worker's family, share the same faith community as the social worker, or be behind the social worker in the checkout line at the local grocery store. In a world characterized by expanding notions of community and multicultural experiences, social workers may find that they are asked to maintain relationships with others in several domains and to perform multiple roles. For example, in some cultures, social workers would risk insulting a family by refusing an invitation to a family dinner party.

Some social workers disagree that rigid boundaries are necessary or desirable. Zur and Lazarus (2002) maintain that some aspects of dual relationships—such as greater connectedness and an increase in the client's self-determination—can actually benefit rather than harm the client. They discuss a specific framework that separates the idea of exploitation into manageable components to determine whether a certain aspect is potentially beneficial or hurtful in any particular relationship. A continuum, displayed in Exhibit 2.7, allows the social worker to explore the areas and degrees to which a specific relationship's dimension (for example, a social relationship with a client) might benefit or harm a client.

Applying this to the situation described earlier, Lara might evaluate the risk of exploiting Joe rather than empowering him if she were to continue working with him. Lara might also consider the likelihood of increasing Joe's vulnerability through her knowledge of his past struggles. Some variables, such as control of resources, might not be applicable—unless, of course, Lara favored Joe as a potential brother-in-law by allocating an unfair share of resources, such as work stipends. Lara may be at high risk of clouding the professional relationship by working with him while he is dating her sister. Lara will need to evaluate whether the level of risk is too high to continue working with him.

A second framework that includes the idea of "boundary crossing" as different from "boundary violation" (Zur & Lazarus, 2002, p. 6) allows the social worker to decide if the dual relationship occurs naturally (with no intention of the social worker) or is contrived (arranged by the social worker for her or his own purposes). The framework also allows the social worker to examine whether the relationship is exploitive (for the worker's benefit), essential (for survival in the community), or enhancing (beneficial to the client). Returning to Lara's situation, although her relationship with Joe is naturally occurring (she did not arrange for the relationship),

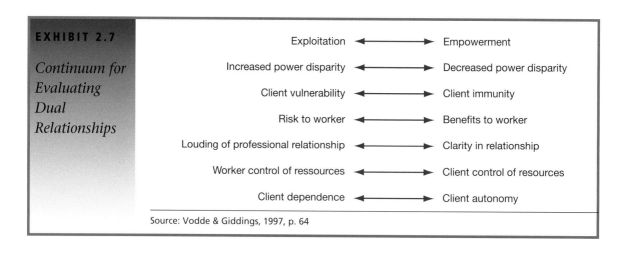

EXHIBIT 2.7

Continuum for Evaluating Dual Relationships

Exploitation ←→ Empowerment

Increased power disparity ←→ Decreased power disparity

Client vulnerability ←→ Client immunity

Risk to worker ←→ Benefits to worker

Louding of professional relationship ←→ Clarity in relationship

Worker control of ressources ←→ Client control of resources

Client dependence ←→ Client autonomy

Source: Vodde & Giddings, 1997, p. 64

the dual relationship is neither essential for the community's well-being nor empowering for Joe. The dual relationship has the potential to be exploitive. This framework can be helpful in situations in which dual relationships are impossible to avoid; it uses the specific content of the case rather than applying a one-size-fits-all model that simply prohibits all dual relationships.

Responsibility to the Larger Society and Client Well-Being   Relationships that involve child or older adult abuse, neglect, or exploitation or intimate partner violence were once considered private family issues outside the jurisdiction of the law or of any public sector interest. Through the legal and social welfare systems, the larger society has wrestled with the question of whether certain events are private matters or public issues that impact society. While social workers often tend to value the private experience of families to recognize and acknowledge clients' perspectives on their experiences, social workers are also sometimes obligated to intervene with the client's family environment. The dilemma in this situation arises when the social worker values both the client's right to privacy and the potential benefit to the community of making the family issues public in order to prevent or treat others in the same situation.

For example, a social worker might struggle with his or her obligation to encourage a survivor of rape to report the incident to the police (Dombo, 2011). Survivors are reluctant to pursue legal recourse for many reasons. These may include: (1) wanting to heal and to avoid dredging up the past through legal proceedings; (2) fear of rejection if their experiences are made public; and (3) fear of re-traumatization if authorities imply that the survivor is the guilty party. For these and other reasons, rape is often underreported. Many social workers encourage reporting, so the crime is logged and appropriate resources can be devoted to the issue for the individual involved, and others who may be in the same situation in the future, and to possibly devote resources and attention to prevention of the problem. The benefit to society of reporting the crime must be balanced with the experiences and wishes of individuals who have been raped. Attempting to force a person to report an experience of rape to the authorities may jeopardize the individual's mental and physical well-being. Striking a balance between promoting the public's general welfare and honoring the wishes of individuals is very challenging in practice, and requires the application of critical thinking and practice experience. When making decisions between a responsibility to the larger society and the responsibility to individual clients, social workers must consider the following questions: Which issues are public, and which are clearly private? Is violence against people an individual event or a violation of a larger social order as well? Does violence affect the entire community? Does a social worker have the right to raise a public issue that could exploit the client's pain?

Paternalism and Client Self-Determination   Long a cornerstone of social work, self-determination is the right of a client to make choices and exercise control over her or his life. In the *Code of Ethics,* self-determination is listed in Section 1.02, second only to a general commitment to clients. In contrast, **paternalism** occurs when a social worker, believing she or he has a better understanding than the client of what is in the client's best interests, interferes with a client's self-determination. Reamer (2013b) identifies three different forms of paternalism: (1) withholding information from clients "for their own good" (for example, not communicating a medical prognosis or the extent of injury in an accident); (2) deliberately lying to clients (for example, assuring a distraught family member that a dying client will improve); and (3) intervening to prevent clients' behavior by controlling their physical placement (for example, facilitating involuntary hospitalizations). A social worker who provides too much assistance to clients who avoid developing their own problem-solving skills, who gives too many suggestions, or who interacts in a controlling manner is taking a paternalistic approach. For example, a social worker who contacts a resource for a client when the client is capable of making the contact is acting in a paternalistic manner.

Questions about the rights and responsibilities social workers have to interfere in client situations have been debated since the profession began. In some situations involving abuse, neglect, and exploitation, the law dictates social worker rights and responsibilities. However, social workers are sometimes asked to make an ethical decision concerning client self-determination without such a clear-cut guide, such as intervening with a client who is disorderly or who does not adhere to social norms in public. Another example is whether a client should be forced to conform to mainstream standards of cleanliness in a residential setting or whether a social worker must facilitate the involuntary hospitalization of a person with a mental illness who is not able to adequately attend to her or his self-care. In such a case, someone must make a judgment about the standards of "adequate." In another example, some social workers may struggle with the question of whether to intervene with clients who are eating in an unhealthy manner that exacerbates an existing health condition. Situations in which social workers question whether to intervene involve social control and social change and raise broader issues about the degree to which U.S. society tolerates eccentricities or even mere differences. Social workers are obliged to "promote the well-being of clients" (Section 1.01 of the *Code of Ethics)* and must make decisions about the balance between responsible care-taking and excessive interference with client self-determination.

A subtler variation of this dilemma occurs when the social worker urges clients to engage in an activity that the worker values. Reamer (2013b) has called this "pseudopaternalism" because the paternalistic interference does not arise out of professional values but from personal self-interest, even if the social worker has good intentions. For example, most social workers would agree that it is consistent with the profession's values to encourage a young person to achieve the highest level of education possible. At the same time, most social workers also personally value education. If a social worker encourages an adolescent with great academic potential to achieve scholastically beyond the goals of her or his family, the social worker could be acting paternalistically if the client is not interested in such achievement, and would rather attend job training. The social worker could be imposing her or his dreams and goals on the client. In contrast, accepting the adolescent's limited view of life may not be upholding the social worker's commitment to promote an individual's well-being. In another example, a social worker could encourage a community to enact a community-wide recycling program when the community is not interested in recycling currently. The social worker could again be imposing his or her values about environmentalism on the client—in this case, the community. The issue of client self-determination versus paternalism occurs frequently in social work practice; social workers must be constantly aware of this dilemma and make decisions based on critical thinking.

STRAIGHT TALK ABOUT EXPECTATIONS AND STANDARDS IN A LITIGIOUS WORLD

Many issues concerning ethics and values are complicated by context and are difficult to resolve in real practice situations. Social workers must consider values and ethics thoughtfully throughout their practice career. The following sections consider ethical social work practice in terms of postmodernism and in the context of a professional environment where professionals must be concerned with lawsuits. While different from one another, social workers must navigate social work practice with consideration of both postmodernism and a litigious environment.

Thoughtful Practice in a Postmodern World

The current substance of professional ethical inquiry tends to focus on ethics enforcement and risk management (Reamer, 2013a). Rather than serious client issues, such as poverty, or the collective responsibilities of the social work profession, the *Code of Ethics* and most ethical inquiries focus on the individual conduct of the practitioner. Social workers, however, can explore other dimensions to enrich the professional discourse about ethical practice. For example, Walz and Ritchie (2000) suggest that Gandhian principles, based on the work of Mahatma Gandhi, the nonviolent leader of the independence movement in British-ruled India, could make a valuable contribution to Western thinking about ethical issues in social work practice. These principles include service, social justice, nonviolence, prioritizing the disadvantaged, and the notion of the heart as the unifier of all things. Social workers interested in expanding the notion of ethical practice might examine the degree to which their practice is consistent with nonviolence, maintaining material simplicity, or prioritizing the needs of the disadvantaged. For example, a school social worker may experience tension with decisions about how much time to devote working with children struggling with similar issues – identity questions, sexuality struggles and others – but come from families with a range of resources.

Should the social worker devote more resources to the children from families experiencing poverty, as compared to students from middle-class families, because they have more barriers to success?

Risk Management in a Litigious World

Some situations require social workers to be concrete and decisive about their actions. U.S. society is increasingly litigious, particularly in the helping professions. State regulating bodies obligate licensed social workers to uphold the *Code of Ethics,* even if practitioners question certain aspects and/or challenge the *Code of Ethics* to encourage change. Though litigation in social work is relatively uncommon, social workers do face risks of censure and lawsuits charging malpractice or negligence. The profession holds social workers accountable for upholding the *Code of Ethics* through the NASW ethics complaints process. The courts and state licensing boards also hold social workers accountable for their professional actions. In a very small number of cases, social workers are also indicted on criminal charges about ethical misconduct (such as an allegation of fraudulent billing) (Reamer, 2013c). In a study of the actions of 27 state regulatory boards against 874 certified and licensed social workers, Boland-Prom (2009) found that the most frequent violations were dual relationships, license-related problems, problems with basic practice, crimes, and practice below specific standards of care. State regulatory boards typically sanctioned social workers with letters of reprimand, revoked certificates or licenses, imposed probation or instituted the supervision of practice, and accepted the social workers' surrender of their licenses. In an examination of 781 ethics violations, Strom-Gottfried (2000) discovered that boundary violations, and especially sexual relationships, composed the greatest number of ethics violations (254). "Poor practice" (160) was the second most common violation, and "Competence" (86) was the third, with "Record keeping," "Honesty," "Breach of confidentiality," "Informed consent," "Collegial violations," "Billing," and "Conflicts of interest" accounting for the remainder violations. In addition, the areas that pose key risks for social work more recently also include client rights, use of digital and electronic technology, documentation, defamation of character, record storage and retention, supervision and consultation, client referral, fraud, termination of services, and practitioner impairment and misconduct (Reamer, 2013c).

When wrestling with decisions that have an ethical component, social workers are encouraged to take advantage of the knowledge and experiences of other competent and concerned social workers through supervision. Strategic thinking and planning with another professional, particularly one with more experience in recognizing various perspectives and aspects of the situation, can be an invaluable decision-making aid. Further, receiving input on practice through regular social work supervision can assist in the prevention of inadvertent ethical violations.

Social work practice occurs within a context of reflective, contextual practice, in which values are explored and rules about them are challenged, and within the

One of the most pressing challenges for today's society, particularly in marginalized communities, is environmental change. Identified by the American Academy of Social Work and Social Welfare Grand Challenges for Social Work Initiative as one of the most challenging social problems facing our society, Kemp and Palinkas (2016) discuss environmental factors as a key social work concern.

Due to climate change and increasing urbanization, the world is facing such environmental challenges as prolonged drought, pollution, rising sea levels, and natural disasters. These challenges threaten human health and well-being because of their destabilizing effects on communities and particularly negatively impact people with low income or social status. The vulnerable are affected through disrupted employment and income instability, food insecurity, and ecological degradation in their living environments.

Social work is well positioned to strategize and implement interventions to prevent and address the human and social dimensions of environmental challenges. Social work can be involved in disaster preparedness and responses, and those dislocated can be provided with resources and support. Social workers can also work at the macro level to increase the capacity of local communities to prevent and respond to local aspects, as well as advocate to change policy so that further attention is given to the social and human aspects of environmental challenges.

Social workers are required in the NASW *Code of Ethics* to give "attention to environmental forces that create, contribute to, and address problems in living" (NASW, 2008, preamble, para. 1). Social work's person-in-environment perspective requires attention to the human and social implications of increasing social and economic inequality, increased density, and inadequate infrastructure and services. To familiarize yourself with the issues related to environmental changes, visit the Grand Challenges website and read Working Paper No. 5, *Strengthening the Social Response to the Human Impacts of Environmental Change* (Kemp & Palinkas, 2016) at: http://aaswsw.org/wp-content/uploads/2015/12/WP5-with-cover.pdf. (See also Exercise #a1 for additional exploration of this Grand Challenge.)

litigious structure of absolute rights and wrongs of ethical violations. The ability of social workers to transition from a postmodern perspective to one in which the legal and professional obligations are clear requires that social workers be "bilingual" in a sense. Social workers must be aware of the expectations of the law and of the profession and must maintain a personal obligation to engage in critical thinking.

CONCLUSION

This chapter has examined many of the moral rules and values that govern social work practice. Consistent with the postmodern ideas of challenging taken-for-granted precepts, the chapter has encouraged social workers to explore the implications of the profession's values and ethics.

As social workers gain skills in ethical decision-making, they increasingly recognize ethical dilemmas and become more skilled at making ethical decisions. Although social workers strengthen the profession through active questioning of the values and ethics principles, social workers must also understand contemporary concerns about ethical violations and the need for critical thinking about societal expectations.

MAIN POINTS

- Ethical codes are useful in providing standards of professional conduct, but they may also restrict creativity when dealing with different contexts and multiple realities.

- Social workers have an ethical responsibility to contemplate, challenge, and work to change the profession's ethical awareness.

- Social work ethics and the law do not always coincide, although they have parallels and offer the potential for interdisciplinary collaboration. Ethics and law can conflict when legal duties, such as the duty to report, come into question in certain contexts.

- Ethical dilemmas arise out of competing values—for example, dilemmas involving dual relationships, privacy versus public issues, and paternalism versus self-determination.

- Social workers need to develop sophistication in risk management practices that protect them from ethical violations by learning from others' experiences and familiarizing themselves with basic legal mandates.

EXERCISES

a. Case Exercises

1. To appreciate the ethical issues the environmental challenges can pose for social workers, review the Riverton case at www.routledgesw.com/caseStudies and respond to the following items:
   a. Which of the environmental challenges identified in Working Paper No. 5 are present in the Riverton case information?
   b. What is your assessment of Riverton's problems related to the challenges?
   c. Select one of the Riverton's challenges. Use the tools on the Routledge website to develop an assessment and intervention plan for working with your selected Riverton challenge.

2. Go to www.routledgesw.com/cases and select the Sanchez family case. Review the client histories of Celia and Hector Sanchez. Imagine that you are a social worker employed by Our Lady of Guadalupe Church, where the Sanchez family are parishioners. You have noticed that, when Celia comes to pick up commodities, she talks about the desperation of her family. When asked about food stamps (SNAP benefits), she replies that her husband will not allow her to enroll in the program. She thinks it would be a good idea and is considering enrolling despite her husband's wishes, if she can think of a way to do it. You have helped other families access the program, even when one member does not wish to enroll. Should you encourage Celia to use your assistance to enroll? What social work values are involved in this situation? Is it an ethical dilemma? How might you resolve the situation? What might be the implications?

3. Go to www.routledgesw.com/cases and select and become familiar with the Riverton case. Under the "Engage" tab, answer Critical Thinking Question #1.

4. Go to www.routledgesw.com/cases and select and become familiar with the Riverton case. Under the "Assess" tab, take the Values and Ethics Assessment (under the "My Values" option).

5. Go to www.routledgesw.com/cases and select and become familiar with the RAINN case. Under the "Engage" tab, answer Critical Thinking Question #2. Also consider the following question: The RAINN website combines services and fundraising. Using the NASW *Code of Ethics* as a guide, do you believe it is ethical to combine these activities on the same website? Explain.

6. Go to www.routledgesw.com/cases and select and become familiar with the Hudson City case. Under the "Engage" tab, answer the Critical Thinking Questions.

7. Go to the www.routledgesw.com/cases and select and become familiar with the Brickville case. Under the "Assess" tab, "My Values" option, take the Values and Ethics Assessment.

b. Other Exercises

8. You are a social worker in a psychiatric hospital setting. While most patients are discharged from the hospital setting after only a few days, some patients are able to stay for longer periods of time. Due to the mandate from insurance companies to discharge patients as soon as possible, discharge planning begins when patients are admitted.

   Your client, Bea, was admitted for psychiatric symptoms and is terrified to leave the hospital after a stay of over three weeks. Your responsibility is to locate long-term housing and outpatient care for her in the community. As you meet with her one morning, you find her tearfully pleading with you to be allowed to stay longer, as she does not feel able to live independently. You are not sure that she is ready either, although the medical staff states that she is ready for discharge. You feel caught between the demands of your organization and the wishes of Bea.

a. What three primary values does your thinking about Bea's situation represent?

b. Is this an ethical dilemma? Justify your answer.

c. In what section of the *Code of Ethics* would you look for guidance?

d. Apply one strategy for resolving ethical dilemmas discussed in the chapter to Bea's situation.

e. How will you go about resolving this situation?

f. Compare your response with other students. Do different strategies lead to different resolutions?

9. After reading the following scenarios, consider these questions:

a. What is the ethical issue?

b. What are the values of the client system?

c. Are they in conflict with your values? Societal values?

d. What strategy would you use to resolve the situation?

e. What would you do?

After answering these questions, discuss findings with classmates.

Scenario A: In a public setting over lunch, one of your co-workers begins speaking disparagingly about a client who she finds challenging. The co-worker does not use the client's full name.

Scenario B: You are new to the area in which you have taken a job. Your new client, a hairdresser, offers to cut your hair.

Scenario C: You are seeing a couple for marriage counseling. Both parties report that they are committed to remaining in the marriage. While you are out socially, you see the wife holding hands with someone other than her husband.

Scenario D: While out with friends at a restaurant, you notice one of your clients is sitting at the next table.

Scenario E: You are working with a teenage girl in a youth shelter. She reveals to you that she was raped by her neighbor, who is involved with gangs and drugs. She reports that she told her father, and they agreed not to press charges due to fear of retaliation.

Scenario F: Your client of six months reveals that he/she has begun to experience romantic feelings for you.

Scenario G: One of your clients reports symptoms of a mental illness to you. She reports that she wanders around her neighborhood at night in the winter without appropriate clothing, is hearing voices, and refuses to take her medication or go to the hospital. You are concerned about her safety.

Scenario H: You are working with a family in a family preservation program. In the home, the teenage daughter is violent toward her mother. During an altercation, the mother hits the daughter, presumably in self-defense, leaving a mark.

Scenario I: You are leaving the agency for another position. On your last day, a client brings you a goodbye gift and asks if you will still call her.

Scenario J: You receive an emergency call from your client. He reports to you that he just got fired from his job. He states, "I am not going to let him get away with this. He is going to be sorry. He has not seen the last of me." You know that this client has access to firearms and a history of assault.

Scenario K: You receive a call from the spouse of your client. He wants to discuss his wife's case with you. The wife's chart does not contain a release of information.

Scenario L: One of your adolescent clients invites you to his graduation and family party.

Scenario M: A client's insurance benefits have ended, but you feel she needs continued care.

Scenario N: You are working with a teenage client. She reports to you that she is having sex with her boyfriend when her parents are not at home. She asks you not to tell her parents and says that if you do she will feel as though you have betrayed her trust.

10. In a journal entry, reflect on a time when you faced a situation that challenged your personal values. What did you do? Why? How did you decide what to do? What were the results of your decision? If you could relive the situation, would you handle it differently?

11. In a journal entry, reflect on a time when you observed a person doing something that was unethical according to the NASW *Code of Ethics*. Describe the situation and the part(s) of the *Code* it violated. What did you do? Why? How did you decide what to do? What were the results of your decision? If you could relive the situation, would you handle it differently?

Individual Engagement: Relationship Skills for Practice at All Levels

What do I need out of a relationship? What can I give in a relationship? I am no different than any of you out there today. I have the same heart, I have the same feelings, I have the same aches and pains and the same hopes and dreams that you do. I have suffered disappointment in relationships, as have you. I have been hurt too, but through all of this I have grown . . . .

Resa Hayes, disability activist (Mackelprang & Salsgiver, 2015, p. 330)

Key Questions for Chapter 3

1. How can I prepare for action with all clients? [EPAS 6]
2. What are the key interpersonal skills and techniques that I need to know to work with any client? [EPAS 6]
3. What communication mistakes can I avoid? [EPAS 6]
4. How do I utilize a social justice and human rights perspective when working with clients? [EPAS 3]

Cynthia nervously awaits her first client, a young teen who has had her first brush with the law. As the client enters the room, Cynthia nervously puts out her hand for a handshake, makes eye contact, smiles, and greets her. The client ignores her hand, does not make eye contact, sits down in a chair, and crosses her arms across her chest. Cynthia is not sure what to do next.

THE ABILITY TO CREATE A RELATIONSHIP is at the very heart of social work practice. The idea of building relationships is part of what attracts many people to social work in the first place, and it can be an abiding component that sustains a social worker's commitment. Social work scholars and practitioners have long recognized relationships as a crucial element of the profession's work with all types of clients. Relationship building, or **engagement**, is the first step in the professional helping process and leads to the other steps of assessment, intervention, and evaluation.

When you think of relationships, you may first think of the one-to-one partnerships that characterize much of direct social work practice. These relationships, however, rarely stand alone. They are usually enhanced by other connections in the client system, such as teachers, landlords, therapists, case managers, clergy, friends, family, and anyone helping the client to reach her or his goals. Relationships are as critical in group, family, organization, and community development work as they are in interventions with individuals. At the community and global levels, relationship skills necessary for working with individuals are the basis for working with groups, community members, coalition partners, funders, and organizations.

This chapter explores aspects of engagement—the process of building relationships across direct and indirect practice settings—and its critical role in the overall success of social work practice. The first section examines the importance of listening to ascertain the situation and perspective of the client system (i.e., individual, family, group, community, and organization). It introduces interviewing skills and approaches that can help your client share with you and help you to enlist the assistance of others. This section also discusses skill combinations that can help you establish productive connections with your clients. Later sections in the chapter consider the engagement process from strengths-based, social justice, and human rights perspectives.

LISTENING TO THE CLIENT'S SITUATION AND PERSPECTIVE [EPAS 3 AND 6]

Regardless of your agency's focus or your theoretical perspective, the most important moments of a social work relationship often occur at the beginning, when you listen to the client in order to learn the client's situation and perspective. The length and type of listening you do will vary depending on the agency and practice setting. For example, some agencies expect social workers to complete a comprehensive psychosocial history detailing a client's whole life, which may seem to focus more on the past than on the present, while other agencies prefer a more present-focused assessment. Quick Guide 4 provides questions to consider as you first listen to the client.

QUICK GUIDE 4   LISTENING TO A CLIENT

The following questions can help guide the engagement process. As you listen to a client, ask yourself the following questions:

- What brings the client here today?
- How does the client describe the situation that brings them to your agency, and what meaning does that situation have for them?
- What might life look like when the client's situation improves?
- What strengths, talents, and resources can you identify in the client?
- What does the client expect of me?
- What does the client hope to gain from working with me?
- What can we accomplish together?

These initial considerations are helpful in establishing the respect and connection that lead to a successful working relationship. Strive to demonstrate genuine curiosity in your questioning and to show interest in the client in all of your interactions with the client. When you seek to understand the client's situation and perspective with an open mind, you are less likely to ask questions designed to confirm what you already think. Have you ever been frustrated when someone assumed they understood your thoughts or your situation because they knew someone else with a similar experience or because they had simply already formed opinions about people in your situation? It is difficult to hear your client's story from her or his point of view if you draw conclusions mid-conversation based on your own prior information or experience. The ability to listen carefully is a critical social work skill because you want to understand the client's situation as she or he has experienced it, not according to your own expectations.

Relationship and listening skills are essential to work with clients, client family members, community members, and staff. For example, suppose that you have forged a connection with a client after listening to her situation and perspective, conveying professional warmth and acceptance, demonstrating confidence and hope, and working with her to set tasks and goals. One of those tasks is to help her locate and secure housing that better suits her needs, and in completing this task, you encounter a reluctant landlord. In this type of situation, you might perceive the scenario only in the client's terms—that is, you might be inclined to criticize the landlord for being unwilling to rent to your client. For this reason, in your initial contacts with the landlord, you should use the same relationship approach and listening skills that you used with your client. Avoid stereotyping the landlord by entering the conversation with an open mind. Do not assume that your past experience with landlords means you know about the rental business. Being open minded may enable you to hear the landlord's assessment of the current situation and even a solution that you might not have thought about on your own. Approaching the landlord with an adversarial approach will make it more difficult to be persuasive. Trying to understand the diffi-culties the landlord faces maintaining rental properties in a profitable manner will help gain an alliance with the landlord, and a solution to the situation may be more possible than approaching the landlord with a closed mind.

Social workers are often so invested in clients' rights that they may be tempted to leap to unfounded conclusions about a perceived adversary. In some cases, that "adversary" may be the only person who can help the client; therefore, the social worker must put effort into developing an effective relationship. The social worker's role is to be fair, articulate, and open with all parties concerned.

Core Relationship Qualities

In a seminal work that still applies to social work practice, psychologist Carl Rogers (1957) defined unconditional positive regard and empathy as the characteristics key to forming and maintaining effective professional relationships. Later, helping professions added genuineness and warmth (described next) as essential relationship qualities. These core attitudes or conditions are the basis for caring, and help the social worker form a positive, nonpossessive (noninvasive) relationship with a client.

Warmth   A social worker demonstrates **warmth** when he or she expresses sincere interest in the comfort of the client. Examples of warmth include compassionate facial expressions, soothing tone of voice, and appropriate pacing of verbal interactions. Social workers also exhibit warmth when they extend courtesies, such as making sure the client is physically comfortable, offering them a beverage, making eye contact, and using well-timed, appropriate humor (Shebib, 2015). In your work, consider ethnic and cultural considerations about the expression of warmth and adjust the amount of warmth you demonstrate to coincide with the comfort level of the client.

Empathy   A core condition for all helping relationships, **empathy** is the "act of perceiving, understanding, experiencing, and responding to the emotional state and ideas of another person" (Barker, 2014, p. 139). Social workers must develop a capacity for working with feelings, even intense feelings, without displaying emotion, changing the subject, offering quick solutions, or moving the dialogue to an intellectual level. Suspending judgment by controlling personal biases, assump-tions, and reactions is a first step toward adopting an empathetic attitude. A practi-tioner who is empathetic is willing to learn about the emotional world of another without actually experiencing that person's feelings. For example, if a client has experienced a death in the family, rather than making assumptions about how the client feels, an empathetic social worker might attempt to understand the nature and intensity of the client's feelings to facilitate engagement. The client could be grief-stricken, relieved, or satisfied at some sense of justice being served if the family member was abusive to the client. Empathy is important in all professional relation-ships, not just those involving clients. For example, a social worker might express empathy by attempting to understand her colleague's feelings about significant challenges he has experienced in his work. When responding with empathy, it is helpful to state the feelings back to the person into your own words, so the person is clear that you have understood them. You will learn more about this later in the chapter.

Genuineness   Social workers who are genuine provide information that is timely, helpful, and accurate, and avoid hidden agendas or playing emotional games with clients (Shebib, 2015). **Genuineness**, the quality of being honest and sincere, is essential to the development of an effective working relationship. When you are genuine, you avoid pretense, acknowledge your limitations, and provide only sincere reassurances (Barker, 2014). Being authentic and reliable encourages trust, which is the core of a helping relationship.

Unconditional Positive Regard   Each human being is a person "of worth whose rights and dignity are to be respected without reservation" (Barker, 2014, p. 391). As such, social workers must approach clients with **unconditional positive regard**, nonjudgmental acceptance regardless of whether a social worker approves of individual or collective client actions.

While these qualities are necessary to the formation of a positive relationship, they do not guarantee a positive client response. Clients will sometimes reject even a social worker's best efforts. For example, a client may interpret empathy as manipulation or may misread genuineness as fake. Accepting these possibilities can help social workers avoid developing unrealistic expectations.

Specific Skills for the Dialogue with Clients

Communication is complex, and oral communication skills are important to professional practice. This section will address approaches and skills that can be effective in purposeful communication with clients. These include both nonverbal and verbal communication skills that facilitate professional relationships with clients. Consistent with the strengths approach, the discussion here emphasizes skills that facilitate dialogue with clients (Saleebey, 2013) rather than interviewing skills.

Preparing to Listen   When you convey interest in communication with clients in order to promote the exploration of ideas and client challenges, you are attentive to the client. **Attending** involves verbal and nonverbal components, described later in this chapter (Barker, 2014).

In order to have a professional conversation in the best interest of the client, ensure that any psychological or physical needs you may have do not interfere with your ability to listen to the client. Attending requires that you fully disengage from interactions with others before engaging with a client and that you mentally prepare yourself to avoid reacting to the client, either verbally or nonverbally, in a way that conveys judgment or impatience.

Certain nonverbal behaviors can help facilitate dialogue. See Exhibit 3.1 for nonverbal behavior guidelines. These are general guidelines; you will need to adjust your nonverbal behaviors to match each client's comfort level. In most cases, you will want to sit relatively close to the client. When the client is not seated or standing (i.e., the client is in a hospital bed), you will usually want to minimize the height differential by sitting on a low chair positioned to empower the client to control the amount of eye and facial contact.

Culturally competent social workers use verbal and nonverbal behaviors consistent with their clients' cultural expectations (NASW, 2015). It may be necessary to modify these general guidelines, depending on the culture of the client.

- Turn your shoulders and legs toward the client.
- Sit with an open body position, with uncrossed arms and legs.
- Lean slightly toward the client.
- Smile and nod your head to provide positive reinforcement.
- Maintain eye contact, within the comfort and cultural norms of the client.
- Use responsive facial expressions.
- Speak in a warm, pleasant tone.
- Give brief, encouraging comments.
- Avoid the presence of large objects and heavy furniture between you and the client.

EXHIBIT 3.1

Nonverbal Behavior Guidelines

Professional working with a client at eye level

© Yuri Arcurs

The degree of eye contact you maintain with the client can be powerful and may be highly variable. In most cases, you will make strong intermittent contact to indicate interest and connection. For clients of almost any culture, eye contact that is too constant and intense may be acutely uncomfortable; to some clients, even minimal amounts may seem intrusive. Individualizing your eye contact to maintain client comfort is an important practice skill.

Another important aspect of client interaction is dress. In general, your dress will be guided by the policies of your agency. Some agencies ask their staff to dress formally; some require "business casual" (i.e., professional but less formal than traditional business wear); and some ask staff to match their client's style of dress, which may be informal. Clothes that are relatively modest in nature help ensure that the interaction focuses on the client, rather than on the social worker. Social workers' schedules vary, depending on the nature of the work. If meeting clients outside of the office, social workers must exercise some flexibility because they can exert less control over the environment in which the interaction takes place. In settings outside of offices, such as in client homes, community centers, and public locations, social workers must maintain professional verbal and nonverbal communication and work to minimize distractions.

Cultural Competence Considerations Your preparation for dialogue with a client will include consideration of elements of culture or style—both yours and your client's—to which you need to attend. Suggestions from your supervisor (or another experienced worker), peer consultation, and a general assessment of the community and agency cultures in which you work will be helpful. Weigh whether your dress, posture, and language are appropriate to the person with whom you are working and the setting in which that work takes place. In general, aim to communicate respect for your client and for the nature of your work together. For example, in most practice contexts it would not be appropriate to wear jeans to a courtroom appearance or to use informal language with the judge. Conversely, you might dress more informally in making an outreach home visit to a client and family or while engaging in community organizing or community outreach. Continually be aware of the customs and contexts of the client system with which you are working and strive to match the nonverbal behaviors of the client.

Specific Interviewing Skills

Interviews are "purposeful conversations between social workers and clients . . ." (De Jong, 2013, para. 1). Social workers use the core relationship qualities and specific skills already discussed in this chapter for interviews, in addition to those discussed next.

Discovery-Oriented Questions Your role as a social worker is to hear the client's situation and perspective in the way in which she or he wants to tell it, without making assumptions and filling in gaps yourself. **Discovery-oriented questions** invite your client to convey her or his purposes in communicating with you and to express goals for your relationship. These questions help you get to know the client, and they can put the client at ease. The discovery-oriented process may involve waiting a minute after you make welcoming introductions to allow your client an opportunity to begin. If she or he does not take that cue, you can invite her or him with such phrases as "Where would you like to begin?" or "Please tell me what brings you here today?" Some clients may be prepared for a much more directive stance on your part, so you may need gently to encourage their ownership of the dialogue.

Silence   As you dialogue with a client, allow for moments of silence. Silence can be interpreted in many ways, and some people feel more comfortable with silence than others. Exhibit 3.2 describes the possible meanings of silence. During moments of silence, you can remain attentive through eye contact; psychological and nonverbal

---

Silence can mean many things. Six of the most common meanings are listed here:

EXHIBIT 3.2

Meanings of Silence

1. *The client is thinking:* Some clients need more time than others to gather and organize their thoughts. Allowing time for this helps clients feel empowered and worthy of the social worker's patience.
2. *The client is confused:* Your questions may be unclear, or your client may be unsure what you expect from her. If you suspect this may be the case, ask whether the client is confused and would like you to repeat your question or explanation.
3. *The client is experiencing uncomfortable thoughts and/or feelings:* Silence gives the client time to process pain or anxiety and to consider proceeding further in the discussion. If you think the client is silent because of powerful emotions, you may wish to provide empathy. A statement, such as "I sense that your daughter's life provokes some strong feelings," provides support for the client and conveys understanding.
4. *The client is working to develop trust with you:* Silence provides clients with a sense of dignity and control over their lives, a way to avoid rejection, and a way to maintain control over the conversation. To move the relationship toward more openness, you could proceed slowly with a discussion of less personal matters, or you might choose to raise the issue of trust directly.
5. *The client is a quiet person:* You might utilize open-ended questions to draw out the client, or, in a supportive manner, discuss her or his silence directly in terms of your working relationship. Consider using other methods for the discussion, as some clients are more expressive when combining an activity with a discussion, when journaling, or when expressing themselves through the arts.
6. *The client has achieved closure:* If you think this may explain the client's silence, you can ask the client if there is anything else to discuss at the moment.

focus on the client (i.e., avoid shifting your body, checking your watch, or other means of communicating discomfort); and minimizing external and internal distraction. You can encourage silence during your dialogue to allow for self-reflection and to slow the pace of the conversation. Silence can also lead clients to answer their own questions and to discover their own next steps toward a resolution (Shebib, 2015). At times, the social worker may wish to break a silence in order to discern its meaning or to shift to another topic. For example, the social worker could say, "I notice that you have been silent for several minutes. If you are comfortable talking about it, I hope you can share what you are thinking about or feeling."

The situation or context determines the appropriate length of silence between the social worker and the client. If, for example, a client is giving extensive thought to a question a social worker has asked, a long silence may be appropriate. Long silences may be less appropriate in settings where the social worker only has a few minutes with each client, such as some hospital or school settings, or when a client is clearly suicidal or homicidal. Ultimately, professional judgment must be the guide to interpreting and responding to silence.

> **Example:**
>
> Social Worker: *You mentioned that your daughter was really angry with you the other morning, and you had a fight before she left for school. What was the argument about?*
>
> Client: *Well, I think she and I. . . . (lapses into silence for a minute). (The client begins to cry).*
>
> Social Worker: (After a few minutes). *This argument really upset you.*

Following Responses   A **following response** gives clients immediate feedback that their message has been heard and understood. This immediate feedback can be conveyed through paraphrasing, summarizing (discussed next), conveying empathy, and showing attentiveness through short verbal statements and questions such as "Go on," "I see," and "Can you tell me more?" (Barker, 2014). Following responses should provide only enough response to encourage the client to continue speaking. A more complete response may interrupt the client's direction and distract the client from fully sharing her or his situation and/or perspective.

Paraphrasing   When you express an idea of the relevant points of a client's statement in your own words, you **paraphrase.** When a social worker paraphrases, clients are assured that the social worker heard and understood them accurately. Paraphrasing can also help clients clarify their own thoughts (Barker, 2014). After paraphrasing, you can invite the client to correct you if you are mistaken. An invitation to correct can communicate both that you care enough about them to want to accurately understand their situation and perspective and that you recognize that you may have the wrong understanding of the specific issues at hand. When you paraphrase, do so without judgment, without adding meaning or changing the meaning of the client's statement, and without attempting to solve any issues (Shebib, 2015).

Example:

Client: *I don't really get what is going on. I mean, I put food on the table, keep a roof over our heads, and try to keep her going to school. I don't understand what her problem is!*

Social Worker: *You are working really hard to provide for her, and cannot understand what your daughter is talking about.*

Client: *Yeah! She is skipping school, running off, and now I am in trouble!*

Social Worker: *In other words, she is not grateful for everything you are doing for her. In fact, she is getting you in hot water with the law.*

To avoid monotony, social workers can use a variety of lead-ins for paraphrasing, such as:

As I understand it . . . .
It sounds a little like . . . .
As I hear it . . . .
The picture I am seeing is . . . .

Clarifying   Clarification helps you to understand the uniqueness of the client's message rather than generalizing or framing it in a way that matches your own perceptions. **Clarifying** increases the accuracy of your assessment while communicating a respect for the complexity of the client. Clarifying is closely related to paraphrasing, but when clarifying, the social worker directly asks for client feedback in order to illuminate a point. Clarifying could be used at the end of a paraphrase. For example, the worker might say, "What I understand you to be saying is . . . Is that right?" Clarification may be needed at any point in the planned change process, especially to clarify each other's intent, interpretations, and meanings. For example, a client may demonstrate giddiness or tearfulness, which could indicate joy or be a sign of regret, loss, or confusion.

Example:

Client: *The last time she ran off, she told me that she was never coming back, and that she hated me. Can you believe that?*

Social Worker: *Did I get this right? You are saying that she refuses to ever come back home?*

Client: *Yeah. What does she think, that she can live at a friend's house forever?*

Summarizing   A summary can provide closure and consensus either after a segment of the session is complete or at the conclusion of the whole session. A summary is a way of confirming your understanding of the client's message thus far and checking the validity of your assumptions. **Summarizing**, or providing a concise statement of main points, can also help to establish organization for the entirety of your work together as well as frame a particular interaction or series of interactions. In situations in which the issues evoke significant client emotion, or in which the work is directed at some complex task, summing up the interaction can demonstrate manageability and hopefulness. Summing up can provide both you and your client with a snapshot of the topics discussed thus far, which can help to clarify the future direction of the dialogue. Summarizing can also help focus a conversation that wanders off topic.

Examples:

Social Worker to Colleague: *So far, we have talked about your job responsibilities and my responsibilities and how they overlap. We have discussed this vaguely in prior staff meetings, but no one has really picked up on the idea that this is a problem because we are wasting some time. Do you agree with this?*

Social Worker to Client: *Let me try to sum up our discussion so far. Your daughter has run away many times and now refuses to come home. As far as you can tell, you have not done anything to cause her to run away and skip school. No one at the school believes that you are trying to fix the problem. Is that a fair summary so far?*

Social Worker to Client: *You have been working to get this street fair organized, but you are really in need of some people from the business community to get involved in the organizing and recruiting phase. Do you agree?*

Direct or Closed-Ended Questions   When you want to encourage the client to provide factual information in a concise manner in order to glean specifics about behaviors or events, such as their frequency, duration, and intensity, you may wish to ask **direct or closed-ended questions**. This type of question can be answered "yes" or "no" or with a numerical answer. While such questions do not encourage clients to open up and share, they are useful in situations in which precise information is needed. These situations include times when you need specific information to confirm the status of a situation or when dangerous conduct or some imminent threat of harm must be dealt with directly in order to ensure safety. An example of a situation in which you would seek concrete information is one in which a client is expressing the intention of hurting her- or himself or someone else and you need to know if the client has a real plan to engage in the dangerous behavior (for example, suicide) and the means to carry out the plan (Shebib, 2015).

Example:

Client: *I have not eaten in quite a while.*

Social Worker: *How many days has it been since you have eaten?*

Community Member: *We had a community organizer working on health care in this neighborhood a while back.*

Social Worker: *How many years did the organizer work in this neighborhood?*

Open-Ended Questions   At the beginning of a dialogue, **open-ended questions**, which are designed to elicit extensive answers, help to encourage clients to share their experiences and perceptions in the manner most comfortable to them, and in the way that makes the most sense to them (Barker, 2014).

> **Examples:**
> Client: *My brother and I always fight after school.*
> Social Worker: *What are your fights like?*
> Community Member: *We are trying to push the drug dealers out of our community.*
> Social Worker: *How do the drug dealers affect the neighborhood?*

Indirect Questions   Questions phrased as sentences are called **indirect questions**. Indirect questions allow clients the freedom to choose whether or not to respond as well as provide flexibility in the type of response. In a conversation, mixing direct and indirect questions can help clients feel less pressured and can avoid monotony in the types of questions asked.

> **Examples:**
> Client: *I would like to save some money to buy a house some day.*
> Social Worker: *I wonder how you would be able to save money, given all of your responsibilities.*
> Client: *My teacher is picking on me! She punishes me for things that other kids get away with!*
> Social Worker: *Wow! That sounds really upsetting. It must be so hard to try to get your work done in class while you are worrying about your teacher looking over your shoulder all of the time.*

Empathic Communication   To demonstrate empathy, social workers identify the feelings a client is expressing and communicate their understanding of those feelings to the client. **Empathic communications** help clients identify and label their feelings and provide the support to process feelings that might seem overwhelming. Social workers need to be familiar with a range of feelings, and to become skilled at accepting feelings at face value, rather than placing judgments on feelings or demonstrating disapproval about client feelings (Shebib, 2015). Social workers also must be aware of their own emotional state at the start of a relationship and be aware of the potential impact of her or his emotional state on the interaction with the client (Shulman, 2015).

Three types of empathy are: (a) **basic empathy**, in which the social worker mirrors clients' statements; (b) **inferred empathy**, in which the social worker makes guesses about feelings based on clues in clients' statements; and (c) **invitational empathy**, in which the social worker encourages clients to talk about their feelings.

Invitational empathy provides an opening for clients to talk about feelings, without demanding that they do so (Shebib, 2015).

Example of basic empathy:

Client: *I am ready to kill my daughter. This whole thing is very embarrassing. I have not done anything wrong!*

Social Worker: *So you are angry with your daughter for putting you in this situation where you have to defend yourself.*

Example of inferred empathy:

Client: *My husband tells me that I am no good and beats me all the time. But last week, he started beating my daughter, too!*

Social Worker: *This is a really tough situation. I suspect that you might have been scared of what he might do to her.*

Example of invitational empathy:

Client: *My son died in a fire last week.*

Social Worker: *Oh, I am so sorry for your loss. A lot of people in your situation might feel like they are in shock about their sudden loss.*

Empathetic communication can be challenging for beginning social workers working with older clients, who have had different types of life experiences. For example, if a client, the mother of several children, asks her young social worker whether she has any children, the social worker may be tempted to respond defensively, perhaps bringing up her training or suggesting that they are not here to talk about her background, but instead about the mother's situation. In this situation, the social worker might practice inferred empathy and consider the possibility that the client is asking because she may be wondering about the social worker's ability to understand her situation. A response like, "No, I do not have any children. Are you wondering whether I am going to be able to understand what it is like for you to raise your children? I am wondering that, too, and I think it will be helpful for you to explain it to me so I can better understand," might help to uncover the true concern underlying the question (Shulman, 2015).

Avoiding Communication Pitfalls

Communication is an art and a skill. When dialoguing with clients, social workers should be wary of communication errors. Some of the more common errors that occur in social work are described in this section.

Jargon   Social workers, like most professionals, have their own **jargon**, or verbal shortcuts, to describe their activities, which clients may not understand. Jargon can include abbreviations like DJO ("Deputy Juvenile Officer"), distinctive words ("intake process," "ecomap"), and routines ("level one"). Keep your communication with clients as free from jargon as possible (Shebib, 2015).

Examples of jargon:

Social Worker: *After the intake process, you will be on level one for a week. Then your DJO will assess you and decide whether you can go to level two or you need to go back to court.*

Rather than:

Social Worker: *After I've gathered all of the needed information from you, we'll move you in to your room, and I can tell you all of the rules that you'll need to follow for the first few weeks. After your Deputy Juvenile Officer has met with you, we can decide together whether you will have the same rules after that, or we can change them.*

Leading Questions   The way in which a question is asked can shape the response. **Leading questions** can manipulate clients into choosing a particular answer. Leading questions can mask the preferred approach of the social worker. Clients who have a need to be liked and/or those who are compliant are especially vulnerable to leading questions (Shebib, 2015).

Example of leading questions:

Social Worker: *Given all that you have tried in the past, don't you think it is time to call the police to get the drug dealers out of the neighborhood?*

Client: *Well, I guess so.*

Social Worker: *Do you want to call now to report what you just saw?*

Excessive Questioning   While questions are an essential part of the helping dialogue, the asking of questions also puts the social worker in control of that dialogue, which may lead to client resentment. When dialoging with clients, mixing different types of questions with empathic communication, summarizing, silence, and other approaches may help prevent client defensiveness, frustration, avoidance, and other responses that interfere with relationship building. When the social worker must ask many questions, it may be helpful to take periodic breaks to convey respect and recognition that the questioning may be taxing (Shebib, 2015).

Example of check-in:

Social Worker: *I have asked a lot of questions of you today. How are you doing so far?*

Multiple Questions   Asking two or more questions at the same time, or **multiple questions**, (also called "double-barreled" questions) can be problematic, because the client can become confused. The client may answer the last questions, while you think he or she is answering the first question, thus creating potential miscommunication.

Irrelevant Questions   To avoid asking **irrelevant questions**, which are questions that do not relate to the topic at hand, it is important to have a clear idea of the purpose of the dialogue. While you might be curious about details of situations or perceptions, consider whether the information is relevant before asking a question.

> **Examples of irrelevant questions:**
>
> Client: *My boyfriend broke up with me for the second time this week. He already asked my friend out!*
>
> Social Worker: *How did he tell you that he wanted to break up?*
>
> Client: *My mother wants me to wear clothes that are so out of style and boring. I don't want to wear her stupid clothes!*
>
> Social Worker: *Exactly what type of clothes does she want you to wear?*

Working with Interpreters or Translators   In an effort to communicate respectfully and effectively with clients from all ethnic, cultural, and linguistic backgrounds, social workers have a responsibility to provide services in the client's chosen language. Fulfilling this obligation may require the use of qualified language interpreters (for example, certified or registered sign language interpreters). Interpreters generally must be proficient in both English and the client's chosen language and must have undergone orientation and training. It is the social worker's responsibility to ensure that, at a minimum, interpreters maintain confidentiality, are properly trained in the ethics of interpreting in a helping situation, and understand terms and concepts specific to agency programs. Therefore, the use of children or neighbors as translators is problematic and should be avoided. Social workers may need to prepare for work with specific populations by learning at least the basics of other languages and cultural customs and by completing training about how to work with linguistically and culturally competent professional interpreters (NASW, 2015d).

Integrating the Core Qualities and Skills in Building Relationships

In social work practice, social workers use the core qualities and skills of warmth, empathy, genuineness, and unconditional positive regard in dialogue and interviews. These skills are vitally important; in fact, relationship factors may be more important to positive client change than specific practice models used. Social workers spend more time in dialogue and interviewing client systems than in any other professional activity, including with individuals, couples, families, small groups, and in direct practice, supervision, and in organizational task groups.

ARTICULATING PURPOSE: THE SOCIAL WORKER'S ROLE

In addition to demonstrating core qualities and basic skills, in the early part of the client dialogue, social workers must be able to articulate the purpose of their involvement with the client. **Transparency** refers to social workers' open communication about their intentions for their involvement with a client and ensures the client that the social worker has no preconceived idea of what the client should do (Miller, 2012). A social worker can demonstrate transparency by openly discussing their reasons for pursuing a particular line of questioning. This kind of openness can help the client understand the social worker's thought process and avoid possible obstacles in the working relationship. Transparency helps remove the mystery from the process for clients and lessens the distance and power difference that may exist between the worker and client. Social workers who are transparent with their clients will, if asked, acknowledge that they are students who will leave at the end of the year, are young and have no children, or are not persons of color.

The beginning of the professional relationship is often the most appropriate time to articulate your purpose through a clear, concrete description of what your roles or job responsibilities are—and what they are not. For example, a court advocate for a family violence shelter would want to clearly explain his role to clients and make sure that they understand that he could not provide counseling, medication, or other types of services for the clients and their children.

On a more subtle level, the overall purpose of the work should also be transparent and explicit for both the social worker and the client. To maintain a genuine and honest relationship with clients requires that you be open about the jointly agreed-upon direction of the work, the methods you will employ, and the goal of your intervention. It is sometimes tempting to engage the client in work on one issue and attempt, somewhat surreptitiously, to work on other issues you may think are more worthy. For example, if you and your client agree to work on the client's relationship with school authorities regarding her child, focus on this task without trying to covertly intervene in her parenting style, her negative relationships with men, or any other issue. If you believe that another approach to the issue is more relevant or that the goals should be different, you should raise this issue early and take your cue from the client's response. To remain genuine, it is important to avoid any hidden agendas. Doing so helps the client feel valued and accepted in the relationship.

This respectful stance regarding the client is one way to demonstrate a strengths-based approach. The following section elaborates on the use of the strengths approach in the engagement process.

MOVING FROM SPOTTING DEFICIENCY TO RECOGNIZING STRENGTHS

The **strengths perspective**, an orientation that emphasizes the client's resources, capabilities, support systems, and motivations to meet challenges and overcome adversity in order to achieve well-being, is a central hallmark of the profession (Barker, 2014). The strengths approach to engagement can be challenging due to the need to identify, focus, and intervene challenges or issues. Social work as a profession developed during the late 1800s, a time during which conversion about client morality was a focal point. The view of poverty as a reflection of moral deficiency or laziness rather than as a structural failing was fairly common, and efforts focused on trying to "improve" the morals of people in poverty. As professional fields of helping, such as psychology, developed more sophisticated and complicated assessment schemes (including the *Diagnostic and Statistical Manual of Mental Disorders DSM V Fifth Edition,* first published in 1958), the focus on pathology became more pervasive. Social workers have a long history of recognizing clients' strengths, but an emphasis on pathology, problems, or dysfunction is deeply embedded in the culture and traditions of the helping professions in general, and that emphasis on pathology persists in the current social service delivery system. Agencies frequently offer services tailored to specific types of problems (for example, substance abuse or major mental illnesses), and these problems define the agency's focus. Given an agency's purpose and milieu, developing the ability to focus on strengths when meeting a client may seem like an enormous challenge.

An increasingly visible body of literature reflects a different perspective from the various models of deficit, damage, or blame. Much of this literature focuses on **resiliency**, or "the human capacity to deal with crises, stressors, and normal experiences in an emotionally and physically healthy way" (Barker, 2014, p. 365). Most people raised or living in dire circumstances survive and sometimes even thrive. Communities demonstrate resiliency after a traumatic event or natural disaster when they process grief and shock using community resources to hold events and rituals, help victims, and function normally. Resilient clients can display strengths and coping capacities even in the most oppressive and compromising scenarios.

In the first encounter with a social worker, clients often wonder whether the social worker will be trustworthy, understanding, or judgmental and whether the social worker will be able to help. Clients are also often unsure whether they really need or want assistance (Shulman, 2015). Using the strengths-based approach and the engagement skills and methods discussed in the following section will serve to build effective professional relationships that can overcome these challenges. For example, sending clear verbal and nonverbal messages that you will not make negative judgments or try to change the client as a person, but rather that you will affirm their aspirations and work to help them achieve their goals, can build client trust. Engaging in enjoyable activities together, when possible, such as playing a game, and seeking to incorporate humor, joy, and laughter into the helping process is another strengths-based approach. Being sensitive to cultural factors, honoring diversity, and seeking to assist people in activities that hold meaning for them will serve you well in a great variety of practice settings (Kisthardt, 2013).

Engagement Skills and Methods

Rapp and Goscha (2012) identify a series of methods for building a strengths-based relationship. In addition to the core conditions described earlier, they suggest using mirroring, contextualizing, self-disclosure, accompaniment, reinforcement, and achievement.

Mirroring   When a social worker reflects the client's talents and capabilities, emphasizing their presence in the client's daily life and stressing their importance so that the client can see his or her strengths, that is called **mirroring**. The image the social worker reflects counters the negative reflections many clients have of their own value and worth. A client's self-image may be distorted, and the social worker can reflect a more positive view of the client. For example, if family members identify specific problems they are having in their relationships with one another, the social worker might reflect the care they are demonstrating for one another in their efforts to improve their family's functioning.

Contextualizing   When social workers **contextualize**, they view client issues from the community, society, and/or global perspective to discourage clients from blaming themselves and to encourage them to acknowledge the environmental and structural roots of their problems. For example, when landlords discriminate against a client receiving mental health services, the client might blame herself for somehow being "undesirable." In such a situation, the social worker can explore with the client the effects of stigma in an intolerant society or provide evidence that she is acceptable to other landlords. In another example, a social worker might point out to a group that funding cuts to city services may be contributing to the drug and violence problems in their community. In this way, the social worker shows them that they are not solely responsible for their problems and that insufficient city-sponsored security resources and job opportunities are partially to blame for their security challenges. The goal of contextualizing is to point out the environmental roots, causes, and contributions of the client's challenges, while working with clients to maximize their strengths and take advantage of opportunities and resources to address their specific challenges.

Self-Disclosure   The extent to which social workers should **self-disclose**—that is, share their feelings, values, and personal information with clients—remains a controversial issue in social work practice (Barker, 2014). Rapp and Goscha (2012) point to the inequities of expecting clients to disclose the most personal and profound aspects of their inner lives while professionals sit back and reveal little about themselves. A strengths-based approach aims to genuinely normalize the relationship and calls for some degree of worker self-disclosure to establish trust, validate the quality of the relationship, and model effective ways of managing emotions. There are no accepted standards governing the appropriate amount and nature of social worker self-disclosure. Social workers should carefully consider the purpose of self-disclosure and should avoid disclosures that meet their personal needs and goals, such as for expressing strong feelings about something, but that do not contribute to the achievement of client goals. For example, if a client's goal is to learn a certain skill, a social worker might share a story from her or his life to demonstrate that skill, but the social worker should never brag about how well they handled a certain situation.

While caution should be exercised about self-disclosure, in their efforts to foster open communication and a caring relationship, social workers may share relatively unimportant aspects of their lives with clients, while still maintaining a focus on the client. They might converse with clients about hobbies and interests or share information about their families if asked. Social workers are warm and genuine with clients and avoid strict formality by sharing information about themselves to further the relationship, yet avoid self-disclosure of significant information unless it serves a therapeutic purpose or is designed to achieve a client goal.

Accompaniment   Rapp and Goscha (2012) advocate for accompanying a client in the performance of a task. A social worker can literally accompany a client to court and/or metaphorically accompany a client, joining the client in her or his journey of change. When literal accompaniment is not appropriate, metaphorical accompaniment can be vital to the working relationship and can resonate with the client long after the work is over. Rapp and Goscha (2012) acknowledge the danger of a client becoming dependent on an accompanying social worker. Social workers may wonder if helping a client through a task serves the client's best interests in the long-term or whether they should encourage clients to complete tasks on their own. The need or desirability for accompaniment should be assessed critically according to the specific situation. When making accompaniment decisions, social workers should take into account the client's emotional, physical, and intellectual capabilities and the working relationship with the client. Cultural norms also play an important role in accompaniment decisions; the client's cultural and personal sense of the optimal level of independence, and not the social worker's, should be taken into consideration.

Reinforcement and Achievement   Praising a client's progress and accomplishments can be a powerful tool in a strengths-based social work intervention. **Reinforcement**, an action that encourages the tendency for a response to recur, can help build a solid working relationship (Barker, 2014). Some expressions of support, however, can affirm one person and embarrass another. A client may find indiscriminate praise insulting but may value purposeful, immediate, and specific positive feedback. Social workers using a strengths-based approach need to understand the meanings clients attach to being praised or recognized for their accomplishments in order to anticipate client responses in particular contexts.

Logistics and Activities

To establish a collaborative relationship with the client, strengths-based social workers give clients the choice of the location, day, and time to meet and, if possible, offer the option of meeting in a community location, rather than an office setting. Some clients may request a meeting at their home, either because they have small children, they lack transportation, or they are simply more comfortable in this setting. As is true of much of social work, the client's choice of location will likely be affected by the nature and context of the interaction, concerns regarding confidentiality, and the agency's purpose.

Incorporating recreational or fun activities can also help clients to engage and feel comfortable. Some clients may struggle with sharing aspects of themselves in an office, face-to-face setting and may be more comfortable in another setting or talking while engaged in another activity. For this reason, playing basketball with an adolescent, playing a board game with a group of children, or walking in the woods with a client struggling with mental health issues, for example, can create an environment that is much less intense (and therefore more tolerable for some clients) than a meeting in an office.

Some clients use metaphors (i.e., a figure of speech where they relate something to an object or action to which it is not literally applicable) as a way to communicate without exposing the specific details of their own lives until they are ready to do so. A skilled social worker can use these metaphors as a tool for working with these clients (Tay & Jordan, 2015). For example:

Client (Her small business has recently failed): *Have you ever thought about how trying new activities is kind of like wearing a new pair of shoes?*

Social Worker: *With new shoes, you are never really sure whether they are going to fit or be comfortable.*

(Client looks at the social worker, bites her lip, and nods.)

Social Worker: *Wearing new shoes can make you feel maybe a little vulnerable.*

Client: *I just want to wear my old slippers! I know they fit me.*

(Social Worker nods in agreement, giving the client a chance to be more direct if she is ready to be.)

Client: *It does not always feel good to feel vulnerable.*

(Sims, 2003)

The social worker responds using the same metaphors that the client suggests and is sensitive to the degree to which the client is or is not ready to be more direct. Using metaphors respects the client's communications using metaphors, rather than seeing the metaphors as a way to be less clear and avoid working on the issue. The social worker can use the information a client offers to support the client's efforts to communicate the depth of her or his experience. This strategy honors the client's meaning and validates her or his approach to engagement in the work. However, if at some point, the metaphors are confusing, it may be necessary to bring the metaphor into reality to confirm that both the client and social worker agree.

RECOGNIZING AND ARTICULATING POWER

Power is a component of social work relationships, from political advocacy to one-to-one counseling. The presence of **power**, or the possession of resources that enable a client to accomplish a task or to exercise influence and control over others (Barker, 2014), may not be readily apparent to you in your relationship with the client. In most instances, the obstacles clients face involve power, and the effective management of power can benefit the client.

Sources of Power

Four sources of power can affect the social worker–client relationship: agency resources, expert knowledge, interpersonal power, and legitimate power (Hartman, 1994).

Agency Resources   Social service agencies have access to and control over a number of resources. These include **tangible resources**, such as clothing for clients or money for emergency housing, and **intangible resources**, such as individual counseling and education groups. Traditionally, social workers and administrators have considered their agency's purpose and any guidelines or constraints that sources of funding may have imposed to determine how to allocate resources to client groups or individuals. However, some contemporary organizations, and even some federal programs, have experimented with arrangements that empower clients to determine and control what resources they receive. For example, an agency that serves children with disabilities might encourage the child's family members to identify the services they need, both within and outside the agency, rather than requiring them to undergo an agency-driven assessment in which a professional tells them what they need. By the same token, some Medicaid provisions include a waiver that permits a family member (usually a parent) to act as case manager, thereby coordinating services for the child and eliminating the costs of professional case management. Services that the family chooses and obtains with assistance are called **client-directed resources**. The concepts of power sharing and client-consumer advocacy threaten the notion that social workers and administrators should continue to control the disposition of agency resources. Given the professional background and experience of staff members, many agencies struggle with the idea of giving up their authority in this arena, and facilitating clients' self-determination without judgment.

Expert Knowledge   Some clients believe that social workers, due to their credentials and experience, possess **expert knowledge**, knowledge that the clients lack. However, expert knowledge does not make a social worker an expert about a particular person. For example, consider a client, a single mother who is trying to get off drugs and secure custody of her children. This client may believe that her social worker knows better than she does what she should do and how she should go about doing it. Using the strengths perspective, social workers can counter these kinds of assumptions by clearly articulating that clients are the experts on their own lives and by developing partnerships in which clients define their own goals.

Interpersonal Power The ability to build strong relationships, develop rapport, and persuade people is known as **interpersonal power**. Both social workers and clients may have this type of personal power, which is closely related to charisma. A social worker's interpersonal power can benefit clients, as when she uses it to attain resources or services, but it can also perpetuate a power imbalance between the social worker and clients if it diminishes the clients' efforts to claim power for themselves. Social workers must strive to reduce the interpersonal power exercised in relationships by establishing more egalitarian relations and genuine collaboration with clients (Hartman, 1994).

Legitimate Power The term **legitimate power** refers to the legal power to perform actions to control the behavior of others. Social workers need to be very careful about exercising this type of power. Social workers have a legal responsibility to protect clients and others (as in cases of child or elder abuse), and legitimate power should be exercised only as absolutely necessary to fulfill that purpose. Although social workers may retain their various powers for individual, family, group, or community client benefit, they may alternatively try to work to change structures that impact clients at the policy and organizational levels to empower clients. For example, social workers may facilitate group work according to the structure of the agency, while simultaneously working to institute a client advisory board to provide clients with a systematic way to provide input into the structure that governs group work.

Power in Client Lives: Jasmine Johnson

There are many ways to think about how power relationships affect clients. One approach focuses on power struggles outside the social worker–client relationship, either in interpersonal, community, policy, or larger cultural terms. For example, a community may be striving to convince their local government to allocate city funds for trash pickup in their area. Another approach involves power issues between the social worker and an individual client. This vignette about Jasmine Johnson provides examples of the types of power discussed earlier.

In your work at a family support agency, your client, Jasmine Johnson, is an African American mother who comes to you with a concern about parenting. Her teenage son is behaving poorly both at home and, increasingly, at school, and Jasmine is unsure how to deal with him. He often does not seem to respect her authority, and he ignores her attempts to discipline him. He is "sassy," talks back, and is occasionally quite rude to her. He ignores the limits she sets, and he does not obey school-night curfews or help with any household chores. Jasmine struggles to support him financially and receives only sporadic help from his father. Her job pays poorly, carries little status, and she unable to afford any recreational activities with him. Overall, Jasmine struggles with low self-esteem.

At first glance, Jasmine's challenges may appear to be strictly personal. Jasmine knows that she does not feel good about herself or her situation, and she assumes she needs to improve in some way. You might assume that she needs to address her self-esteem issues, or you might even conclude that she is depressed and needs medical attention. It is likely, though, that power, or lack of it, plays an important role in her experience. Jasmine experiences many interpersonal roles (i.e., ex-wife, single mother, daughter, worker, friend, and neighbor) and is part of a cultural group that has experienced pervasive and persistent oppression in our culture for more than three hundred years.

These external conditions and stressors can be examined toward the goal of empowering Jasmine (East & Roll, 2015; Scheuler, Diouf, Nevels, & Hughes, 2014). Although she may have interpreted her experiences as signs of her own deficiencies, she has also exhibited remarkable resilience in dealing with disadvantages and oppression. She has managed to survive in trying circumstances that have had far-reaching repercussions in her life. Recognizing the conditions and circumstances in which her life is embedded can be empowering. A skilled social worker can help empower Jasmine by purposefully articulating these circumstances.

This does not mean that Jasmine's own sense of her problem is erroneous. Rather, one of the social worker's goals is to validate client experience and to recognize the meaning she makes of it. Jasmine may not recognize how her experience on the negative side of the power differential has fed her feelings of inadequacy. That realization can open many doors. For example, Jasmine may begin to separate her feelings of inadequacy from her sense of identity and start to view her experiences as a function of her social location. This new perspective might inspire her to some action, such as establishing an informal support group for single, African American mothers. This group could share stories and experiences, provide day care arrangements, or coordinate grocery shopping. Adopting a different outlook and receiving encouragement from a social worker also might inspire Jasmine to eventually become a spokesperson for more stringent requirements regarding child support payments or increased benefits for working women with children. The possibilities for Jasmine's roles and activities are endless, and these types of activities may affirm Jasmine's experience even as they are instrumental in changing the quality of life for her and for others.

It may seem to Jasmine that there are few areas in which her social worker's life bears any resemblance to her own. As long as the profession sustains the concept of the social worker as expert, there will be a felt power differential between social workers and clients based on their distinct roles in the social worker–client relationship. There is also likely to be additional differences between client and social worker related to gender, age, race, socioeconomic status, and other dimensions of diversity. These differences, if perceived as problems, can complicate the engagement process, as clients may not think that they can relate to the social worker.

Suppose Jasmine's case is assigned to a social work student. Jasmine may find it challenging to think of social work students or younger workers in general as a genuine source of help to her. Students may come from a different cultural or ethnic background, and they may not have partners or children. They may also seem to her to be so privileged by their race and education that she thinks that they cannot relate to her experiences. Yet, social workers are supposed to be knowledgeable, and as such, they have some level of power that she may not really recognize or, conversely, notice and resent or admire. In most cases, these differences in social worker and client roles or attributes are, at the core, about power and power differences. It is necessary, then, to discuss these issues openly if they impede the work. Simply raising them can open up the relationship and facilitate client engagement. For example, in the early stages of the relationship, a social worker might ask Jasmine if she has any hesitation about working together. The social worker might acknowledge that their past and present life experiences differ and might ask that Jasmine tell her about her background and current life situation so that the social worker can better understand and help her. Asking the client to share this type of information, and giving the client the opportunity to talk about any qualms she may have about working together, gives the client the opportunity to talk about differences and the impact they may have on the relationship.

Situations that involve power differentials are sometimes awkward or even embarrassing. You may understand that the client sees you as having power simply because of your role as a helping person, an employee, or a student. At the same time, you may wonder about the extent to which you can help someone like Jasmine, an exasperated parent who might be of a different race and remote social class, when you might not even be a parent yourself. You may feel some hesitation at working with an oppressed client when you have enjoyed considerable privilege. Thus, power in social worker–client relationships can be quite complex.

When concerns about power in the social work relationship arise, you might hope that they will pass or that clients will just trust that you know what you're doing in spite of these differences. Once you or your client identify a difference as problematic, however, the issue will not simply go away. You and your client should confront it directly through open acknowledgment and exploration. Exhibit 3.3 provides an additional case example. In this excerpt, consider the ways in which the worker addresses the issue at hand. What impact do you think this approach will have on the future of the relationship?

EXHIBIT 3.3 *Recognizing and Articulating Power*	"Look, Mr. Cook, I know you think I'm a nice kid and that you like me," I said. "I do like you," he confirmed. "But, you know, I'm too young to have experienced what you go through every day!" I said. Silence. "And you may even figure that a kid like me can't help you." Silence. "Right?" I continued. A nod. "But you want to get out of this depression real bad, don't you." I said. "I sure do," he said. Then he sighed and added, "I'm probably being foolish. You

youngsters are right out of school with the latest techniques. I guess I'd just be more comfortable talking to someone closer to my own age. But here I am already talking to you, aren't I? So I guess I already decided to try it out with you."

I nodded. "How about if anytime you feel uncomfortable, you say so and every time I think you may be a little uncomfortable I'll say so?" I suggested.

"It's a deal," he said.

Source: Middleman & Wood, p. 163

The vignette in Exhibit 3.3 conveys an extended message. First, the social worker addresses the immediate obstacle, namely, that the social worker is much younger than the client and has comparatively less life experience. The social worker also paves the way for ongoing honesty in the relationship by addressing the obstacle openly and directly. The scenario is a relatively complex one in which both participants seem to feel an initial lack of power that is subsequently alleviated by open acknowledgment. Ultimately, the case suggests that there is a broader context for the work than the one-on-one issues that emerge between the social worker and client.

VIEWING THE CLIENT SITUATION AND VIEWPOINT FROM SOCIAL JUSTICE AND HUMAN RIGHTS PERSPECTIVES [EPAS 3]

When a client describes a situation that involves hardship or oppression, or that is otherwise emotionally challenging, social workers use their professional skills and methods to respond to the client. Social workers are human and are often personally moved by the situation a client describes. The experience of talking directly to an individual who is sharing a powerful story with you typically creates a bond. Larger perspectives of social justice and human rights may seem like remote, intellectual concepts in the face of your client's immediate pain. Nevertheless, social justice and human rights perspectives can provide the rationale for your practice, and they help to connect multiple client experiences together. They provide an organizing frame for your work so that your practice transcends individual emotional responses or simple empathy. A larger perspective can inform your practice so that it consists of carefully planned and cohesive activities that respond to clear, principled commitments to engage in efforts at the systemic level focused on prevented future client problems.

Full Participation in Culture

A number of "isms"—racism, elitism, sexism, heterosexism, ageism, and others—that you have probably already studied reflect the degree of social injustice that is prevalent in our culture. These society-generated prejudicial attitudes toward the "other" carry concrete repercussions for individuals, families, groups, and communities that take many forms, including exclusion from resources and limited class mobility. The term "exclusion from society" refers to the process through which people are barred from sharing in the benefits of public and cultural resources. This exclusion can be direct (for example, when there is no access ramp to a public library for people with disabilities) or more indirect (for example, when policies and poverty limit public investment in public schools). Exclusions like these represent the arbitrary and unjust allocation of access to public benefits and are social injustices. Quick Guide 5 examines these three levels of social and cultural exclusion. To impact larger systems, such as policies, communities, organizations, and societies, a practitioner must consider client situations relative to all three levels of exclusion. Although many practitioners see their labors in terms of individual achievements, collective achievements make a difference in the larger environment because they can affect a large number of people and potentially prevent future problems.

Strategies, Tactics, and Skills for Promoting Social Justice and Human Rights

When engaging with clients, it is helpful to remember that your contact with the client is framed by a larger context for the profession. Your beginning work with clients is focused on connecting with them for the purposes that they bring to the professional relationship. At the same time, social work deals with social justice and human rights issues. This broader mission calls for well-organized strategies and requires skill sets that usually fall within the realm of policy

QUICK GUIDE 5 THE THREE LEVELS OF SOCIAL AND CULTURAL EXCLUSION

Individual Exclusion

During your dialogue, clients may make an explicit reference to the way exclusion has influenced their situation. Individual exclusion refers to a person's perception of being left out of or barred from participation in interpersonal situations. For example, your client might feel that peers have harassed him on the basis of his race or that his teacher has dismissed him as having no future because of his ethnicity or ability status. Other clients may not give voice to any strong or concrete sense of their own exclusion or the violation of their human rights but may describe their exclusion as "fate" or the "way things are."

Organizational Exclusion

Like individual exclusion, organizational exclusion, wherein an organization prevents an individual or group from participating in its activities, can be obvious or obscure. For example, even hiring practices that appear to be fair on the surface may actually favor some groups over others through their written or unwritten rules, regulations regarding promotions, or subtle differences in work assignments. In fact, many battles over efforts like Affirmative Action arise from a concern for the organizational structures in which unjust practices and advantages have taken hold. For example, given that there is no income or racial equality in student access to this country's top-rated educational institutions, the organization that automatically hires the candidate with the most prestigious degree— even when the requirements of the job do not mandate it—is engaging in preferential practices rooted in injustice.

Just as Jasmine Johnson interpreted her difficulties as individual failings, your clients may not be sensitized to the role discrimination plays in their workplaces. Working with clients to recognize the manifestations of organizational exclusion and to help them examine the meanings they attach to those manifestations can be a liberating activity.

Structural Exclusion

Institutionalized conditions such as poverty tend to maintain and perpetuate themselves. Structural exclusion refers to the interconnected roles of institutions and societal forces in preventing participation or limiting access for certain groups or individuals. Structural exclusion can result in poverty, poor schools, limited achievement, limited employment options, restricted housing, poor health care, and shortened life expectancy. Recognizing poverty as a structural problem directly conflicts with presumptions about equal opportunity and the myth that anyone can get ahead. Social workers may need to work with clients over a period of time before clients and others can begin to see the roots of their personal challenges as stemming from structural exclusion.

practice. The following strategies, tactics, and skills are particularly applicable in such situations:

- Understanding and helping clients understand the repercussions of social injustices

- Helping clients gain access to legal entitlements through social advocacy

- Convincing legislative bodies to adopt, amend, or repeal laws when such changes would benefit clients

- Educating the community regarding certain populations, for example, giving a talk on the needs of refugee children or families with disabilities

- Developing resources—identifying and procuring resources that are needed but do not currently exist

- Facilitating the redistribution of resources

- Testifying in court regarding issues that affect clients

This list is by no means exhaustive, but it suggests the flavor of work focused on systems larger than the individual. These strategies do not negate the importance of connecting on a personal level, but they enrich the engagement and the worker's understanding in a way that is consistent with the complexities of people's lives in the contemporary world.

GRAND CHALLENGE

Close the Health Gap

Health inequalities in the U.S. is another of the most pressing challenges for today's society according to the American Academy of Social Work, who identified it as a Social Welfare Grand Challenges for Social Work. Walters et al. (2016) discuss health equity as a key social work concern.

Vast health disparities exist by race, ethnicity, gender, age, disability status, geography, sexual and gender identity, and socioeconomic status. In recent decades, the general population in the U.S. has been dying at younger ages than those of populations in peer nations. Yet, population health also has a social dimension; populations that experience high rates of social, racial, and economic exclusion also experience higher rates of poor health and premature mortality. Addressing the social, political, and economic dimensions of health is needed to secure sustainable, population-based health advances. Also needed is research and practice collaboration between disciplines to examine the social, political, and economic determinants of good health.

Social work's role in providing leadership on health equity is rooted in its historical social justice mission and commitment to serve disenfranchised populations. Social work has been involved in public health and the health care field for most of its history as a profession, including advocacy for conditions that promote good health, decreasing mortality, and increasing access to services.

To familiarize yourself with the issues related to health equity and social work's role, visit the Grand Challenges website and read Working Paper No. 19, *Health Equity: Eradicating Health Inequalities for Future Generations* (Walters et al., 2016) at: http://aaswsw.org/wp-content/uploads/2016/01/WP19-with-cover2.pdf. (See Exercise #a1 for additional exploration of this Grand Challenge.)

STRAIGHT TALK ABOUT THE RELATIONSHIP: INTERPERSONAL PERSPECTIVES

While engaging with the client, being transparent, or explicit about your work, means being clear about the restrictions you encounter as a practitioner. The social worker may not particularly relish discussing constraints or inviting critical evaluation. Nevertheless, a goal of the work is to establish a meaningful and trusting relationship with the client. Attending to the boundaries of your role early in the development of the professional relationship, along with maintaining confidentiality and client privacy as discussed next, is important to developing that trust.

Confidentiality

Confidentiality is important to the client engagement, as it is important to address boundaries and rules at the beginning of the professional relationship. However, there are at least three areas in which social workers may be required to break confidentiality. First, as mandated reporters, social workers, among many human service professionals, are legally required to report cases of child abuse, neglect, or exploitation. Second, most states also mandate that social workers report the abuse, neglect, or exploitation of older adults and persons with disabilities. Third, as mentioned in Chapter 2, social workers in many states have a duty to report if a client threatens to harm him- or herself or another person as a result of the *Tarasoff II* court ruling. Legal ramifications regarding these reporting requirements may vary somewhat by state or locality; however, social workers must report incidents of abuse, neglect, or exploitation that they witnessed or of which they become aware, and they must take steps to ensure the safety of a person whom a client has threatened.

Depending on the setting of the work, the mandate to break confidentiality may appear to be a significant obstacle to establishing a trusting relationship. For example, you may be concerned that clients will not share any information with you if they know that in certain situations you are obligated to inform the authorities. Although this concern is legitimate, to represent yourself fairly, you must communicate your responsibilities early in the work. Informing clients of the limits of your confidentiality may affect the relationship in unexpected ways. Clients may understand that they need help from authorities. For example, consider Kim, a social worker whose client struggled with substance abuse and had a difficult time keeping track of her five children, for whom she was the single caretaking parent. During their sixth meeting, she confided in Kim that she felt sure she was grossly neglecting her younger children and that she often struck the oldest child "hard" when he "mouthed off" to her. She told Kim that she finally revealed this information *because* Kim was a mandated reporter and she knew Kim would be able to get help.

Social workers must be honest with clients about their roles and not assume that an adversarial relationship will evolve simply because of the mandated reporter obligations. Most clients have good intentions. Even if the client is guarded about what she or he tells you (which you might expect), you still have significant opportunities to build a relationship. You can address the obstacles to, for example, a client's successful parenting (or caretaking for an older adult), model a genuine relationship in which you support the client's parenting competence rather than searching for deficits, and build the foundation for further work. The imminent safety of a child or adult should never be compromised, but this strategy is useful for work in those countless scenarios in which there is concern but no clear mandate for legal intervention.

Privacy

Client privacy can be a challenging issue for many reasons. Actions that some people interpret as caring may seem invasive to others. The initial negotiation regarding the nature and parameters of the work should include an open discussion of privacy issues. For example, a client may interpret your care and enthusiasm for the work to mean that you want both to know everything about her or his life and to become an active participant in it. If this is not your intention, you should let the client know. Similarly, in a group setting, it is a good idea to discuss what personal information individuals may choose to keep private and which pertinent information they will choose to share with the group. Straightforward discussions of social worker involvement and agreed-upon privacy parameters help prevent situations in which clients feel disappointed or even betrayed. For instance, if you have suggested that the client call you when she wants to meet again, but you then drop in unannounced "just to see how she's doing" (or to see how the children seem or if they have eaten that day), she may rightly perceive your visit as an invasion of privacy.

As a practitioner in your particular role and setting, you might consider the extent of privacy to which clients are entitled. For example, in a residential or correctional setting, what personal information does a social worker need to know about a client? If your work involves a social control function, how do you balance your client's privacy with the need to closely monitor? How does your agency's purpose affect the degree of privacy provided? Ensuring that clients are afforded as much privacy as possible involves several aspects: knowing yourself and the values, skills, and roles that you bring to the setting; noticing how you (and/or your agency) may or may not be influenced by predominant social norms about the rights (or lack thereof) of clients; and examining policy and procedures for opportunities to provide more client privacy, when possible.

Ongoing Evaluation

All through the engagement process, you invest your energy and skills to establish a solid initial connection with your client that will grow as your work together progresses. Throughout your work with a client, you must continually evaluate the effectiveness of your efforts. Relationships are easily misunderstood. You may be concerned that your client is hesitant to be as open as you would like, or that she or he seems uneasy in some way, or you may feel wonderful about the state of your professional relationship. Whatever your impression of how things are going, it is important to find out how your client feels about your relationship and to make any needed changes in response to that feedback. Although after services are finished the agency may provide a formal tool for client feedback, it is helpful during service delivery to ask the client how he or she feels about the work so far. For example, you might ask an individual client whether he or she is comfortable talking about the issues you have discussed. For example, how comfortable is he with the fact that you are of different racial or ethnic backgrounds? Is the process of meeting with you similar to, or different from, what he thought it would be? If it is different, how does he feel about it? What can you do to be more supportive, clearer, or more helpful? For group work, you might ask for feedback about your role as facilitator or teacher. At the community level, seeking feedback from individuals and colleagues in the community as well as from committees can elicit important suggestions.

At the individual level, the process of continuously monitoring your work also applies to your engagement with significant people in your client's life. As the work progresses, confirm your understanding of their role in helping to achieve your client's goals. This strategy is particularly important in contentious situations, such as the case of the reluctant landlord considered earlier in this chapter. While potential adversaries such as the landlord might assume that you will take your client's side, avoid alienating them from your client's goals.

Resolution of Case

Cynthia sat down, continued to attempt to make eye contact with the client, and began to speak softly to her. She stated how happy she was to see her, then she hoped that they could work together. She asked a few questions, to which the client did not reply. She next said, "I see that you do not wish to talk to me right now. If you are comfortable talking about it, I hope you can share what you are thinking about or feeling." She assured her that she did not have to talk if she did not want to, but if she changed her mind, that would be OK. After a few minutes, the client uncrossed her arms and began to talk.

CONCLUSION

Now that you have explored the importance of various aspects of engagement and relationship building in social work practice, you are ready to engage with clients. Although you are not likely to address all the issues presented here in the first interactions with a client, you now have the framework to go beyond initial connections to engage in an ongoing, dynamic association. If you have taken care to anticipate the meaning your client assigns to your work together, and ask for her or his feedback along the way, you will find that a positive working relationship is established and is shaped by the nature of your shared activities and experiences.

At first, you may feel that thinking about and trying to use these skills interferes with your spontaneity and/or responsiveness. However, as you use these skills, they will feel much more natural to you, and you will cultivate your own style. Engagement is a process that occurs throughout your work with clients—not only in the beginning. As the work progresses, you will continue to notice engagement dynamics; your own developing skills; and how engagement assists your client through the assessment, planning, and implementation of the work. In particular, the next step, assessment, builds on the relationship foundation that you create during the engagement phase.

MAIN POINTS

- The social worker's first and probably most important activity in the engagement process is carefully listening to the client's situation and perspective. This requires the worker to skillfully initiate a purposeful dialogue that nurtures the relationship.

- Social workers use the core relationship qualities of warmth, empathy, genuineness, and unconditional positive regard, along with strong interviewing skills, to establish a strong professional working relationship with the client.

- Negotiating the purpose and direction of the work enhances the trust between practitioner and client. For this process to be successful, the agenda must be made explicit.

- Respecting the strengths and resilience of the client is critical in establishing the relationship and must be pervasive throughout the work.

- The various sources of social worker power, the power in clients' lives, and the power between the worker and the client all play roles in social worker–client relationship. The social worker should recognize and articulate them as explicitly as possible.

- Although client stories may appear to be individual and are certainly unique, they can always be seen from the perspective of social justice and human rights. These perspectives lend meaning to the work and can help frame your commitments to address both individual situations and the systematic challenges.

- Social worker and client should discuss issues of confidentiality and privacy openly and directly, even when these topics make them uncomfortable. The client may not welcome direct conversation on some topics, but the worker owes it to her or him to be respectful and clear about them from the beginning.

- The social worker should evaluate her or his work, including the relationship, at all stages, beginning with engagement.

EXERCISES

a. Case Exercises

1. To apply learning about health equity discussed in Grand Challenges paper No. 19, *Health Equality, Eradicating Health Inequalities for Future Generations*, review the Riverton case at www.routledgesw.com/caseStudies and respond to the following items:

    a. Pretend that you are a social worker engaging a client in a health setting. The client is experiencing health problems related to asthma made worse by pollution created by the nearby heavy industry located in her low-income community. How might health inequity considerations emerge during in the engagement process?

    b. What are the environmental factors that could cause health inequity for Riverton residents as compared to residents of other communities?

    c. The director of the local health clinic would like to reduce health inequity in Riverton by increasing health services. Formulate a response that describes the limits of health services toward decreasing health equity.

    d. You are charged with creating community partnerships with a broad spectrum of local programs to attempt to tackle health inequities. Which Riverton community institutions and agencies would you approach to create a partnership? Provide a rationale for your choices.

2. Go to www.routledgesw.com/cases. Select the Sanchez case and review the Engagement phase and its tasks. With classmates, discuss the needs of the Sanchez family.

3. Review the Client History, Client Concerns, and Goals for the Client for Alejandro Sanchez. Next, click on "Explore the Town" (under "Case Study Tools") to review the neighborhood, Alejandro's Critical Thinking Questions, and his Interactional Matrix. Consider the following scenario:

    Alejandro is one of your clients. He presents as pleasant and respectful but melancholy. He says he is "unhappy" and seems to carry an existential sadness related to his family. He notes in the first interview that his father Hector was also 19 when he came to this country as an undocumented worker.

    Pair with a classmate and role-play for 10–15 minutes the first meeting between Alejandro and a social worker. In the session, the social worker should attempt to engage Alejandro and begin an assessment. The classmate who is playing the role of Alejandro should prepare by reviewing Alejandro's concerns and goals, as well as his strengths. Have other classmates observe and consult during the role-play. Afterwards, the entire class can debrief by considering the following questions:

a. Which attending skills did the social worker use? Which did she or he not use?

b. Did the social worker employ empathic responses? What were they? In what ways was the use of empathy challenging?

c. Was the social worker able to validate Alejandro's feelings of unhappiness, identify his strengths, and verbally share those strengths with Alejandro? Can the class think of other strengths the social worker did not mention? How can a social worker emphasize a client's strengths when the client is not receptive to hearing them?

d. What was the experience of the student who played the role of Alejandro? Did the student, in character, feel that the social worker demonstrated specific listening skills? Which skills?

e. What elements of Alejandro's experiences reflect social justice and human rights concerns?

4. Go to www.routledgesw.com/cases and, under the Sanchez family case, watch the videotaped interview with Emilia and the social worker. While watching the interview, note where in the interview each of the following skills is demonstrated:

a. Open-ended question

b. Closed-ended question

c. Reframing

d. Paraphrasing

e. Attending

f. Nonverbal communication

g. Clarifying

h. Summarizing

i. Empathic communication

What are the strengths of the interview and what could the social worker do differently?

5. Go to www.routledgesw.com/cases and become familiar with the Riverton case file (under the "Assess" tab). Using the questions in Quick Guide 4, consider the following scenario: A client arrives for her first appointment with you at the Alvadora Community Mental Health Center and she is clearly drunk. In a 1- to 2-page paper, state which of the questions might be most significant and your rationale. Would you use some of the questions to guide your interaction? Why or why not?

b. Other Exercises

6. You are a social worker in a neighborhood community mental health center. You are awaiting the arrival of a new client, Jasmine Johnson (discussed in this

chapter), who lives near the center. After you introduce yourself and she relaxes somewhat, she states, "My life is a mess; nothing I ever do is right; sometimes I think I can't go on."

Indicate how you would respond to her statement using each of the following relationship building and interviewing skills. Give a very brief verbal (one sentence or less, if possible) or behavioral example (if appropriate).

a. Attending
b. Responding nonverbally
c. Responding with minimal verbalization
d. Paraphrasing
e. Clarifying
f. Summarizing (make any needed assumptions about information provided in the dialogue prior to Jasmine's statement)

What other skills do you think would be helpful in this situation?

7. For the following role-playing exercises, create groups of three students so that one is the client, one is the social worker, and one is an observer.

a. Set a stopwatch for 3 minutes. The social worker may not speak during the 3 minutes. During this time, the client tells the social worker a peculiar story. The social worker conveys nonverbally that he or she hears the client. At the end of the three minutes, the observer provides feedback to the social worker, and the social worker and client share their perspective on the process. Each student should have the opportunity to play each role.

b. Set a stopwatch for 3 minutes. The client tells the social worker about a serious concern in their life. The social worker reacts in each of the following ways:
1. Disinterested
2. Inappropriate affect (forced smile, blank stare)
3. Distracting behaviors (e.g., foot tapping, excessive gesturing, fidgeting, head nodding)

After 3 minutes, the client provides feedback regarding the process. At the end of the 3 minutes, the observer provides feedback to the social worker, and the social worker and client share their perspective on the process. Each student should have the opportunity to play each role.

8. Review the following case to prepare for a role-play: Gina is your 16-year-old female client at a local teen drop-in center. Gina is usually talkative and outgoing with staff and other participants. Today, you notice that Gina is sitting in the corner alone, and she looks as though she has been crying. When you approach Gina and inquire about her day, she wipes her eyes and says in a quiet voice, "I can't do this anymore. My parents are always fighting and I just can't take it. I am not going back there."

For the role-play, create groups of three students so that one is the client, one is the social worker, and one is an observer. Using the case described here, the client begins the interview. The observer will tell the social worker whenever he or she becomes aware of the social worker using the following:

a. Excessive questions

b. Closed-ended questions

c. Jargon

d. Leading questions

e. Multiple questions

f. Irrelevant questions

Each student should have the opportunity to play each role.

9. For this exercise, the class instructor takes the role of Gina from the case in Exercise #7. Various students take the role of social worker. Each social worker demonstrates appropriate skills for the interview. When one individual social worker has a point where she or he feels stuck, he or she may return to the class, and the next student begins as the social worker where the previous student left off.

10. For this exercise, the instructor provides flashcards with various interviewing skills. For the role-play, create groups of three students so that one is the client, one is the social worker, and one is an observer. Use the case of Gina provided in Exercise #7. During the interaction between Gina and the social worker, the observer randomly presents a card with a skill listed on it to the social worker, who must demonstrate the skill in the interaction. Each student has the opportunity to play each role. After a 10–15 minute role-play, discuss the degree to which the social workers used the skills appropriately.

11. For this exercise, the instructor provides flashcards with various interviewing skills. For the role-play, create groups of three students so that one is the client, one is the social worker, and one is an observer. Use the case of Gina provided in Exercise #7. During the interaction between Gina and the social worker, the observer selects the card that corresponds with each skill the social worker is using and creates a pile. At the end of the role-play (10–15 minutes), a pile of cards that state the skills that were used is compared to the pile of cards that state the skills that were not used. The client, social worker, and observer engage in discussion about how the skills were used and whether any other skills may have been used appropriately during the interaction. Each student has the opportunity to play each role.

*Social Work Practice with
Individuals: Assessment
and Planning*

© Ron Chapple studios/Thinkstock

Barbara, a sixteen-year-old mother of a baby, is on public assistance, and lives alone in one room. She dropped out of school when she became pregnant, her family and the father of the baby have abandoned her, and her only social contact is a neighbor who works during the day. One afternoon, the young mother, lonesome and depressed, went out for an hour and left the baby alone. The baby fell off the bed and cut his head on an object, seriously injuring himself. When Barbara returned home she took him to the hospital, where the doctor in the emergency room, suspecting child abuse (maybe neglect?), referred her to the child welfare agency.

Carol Meyer (1993, p. 22)

Key Questions for Chapter 4

1. How can I prepare for assessment with individual clients? [EPAS 7]
2. What evidence-based theoretical perspectives will I use to guide my assessment and planning with individual clients? [EPAS 4]
3. What skills do I need to work with an individual? [EPAS 6–9]
4. How can I ensure that I engage in appropriate professional and personal self-care activities? [EPAS 1]

IN HER CLASSIC 1993 WORK *ASSESSMENT IN SOCIAL WORK PRACTICE,* Carol Meyer notes that there are many dimensions to the ways social workers think about situations like Barbara's and to the perspectives and boundaries they apply to them. Consider your own conceptual boundaries; as you read about Barbara, what first comes to mind? Do you see her as an unfit mother? As a lonely young woman? What are the major issues you see? What do you want to know more about? Where would an assessment begin? Are you concerned about child abuse, child neglect, a single teen mother without social support?

This chapter builds on the previous chapter on engagement and considers two facets of the planned change process: assessment and planning. Following the first phase of the intervention in which the social worker engages the client through rapport building, the phases of assessment and planning occur that serve to guide the implementation of the intervention, termination, evaluation, and follow-up phases of work. **Assessment** is the meaning-making process that helps social workers prioritize relevant factors in a client case and determine appropriate action. Assessment is a key social work practice skill that involves collecting information about the client to determine his or her strengths and his or her challenges (Jordan & Franklin, 2013). This chapter also discusses the history of assessment and the importance of client goals and considers approaches and skills through the lenses of theory and diversity. We will discuss the assessment of resources and explore approaches to pursue when resources are inadequate. This chapter concludes with a focus on two areas of challenges for assessment and planning.

Acknowledging the complexity of the situation and at the same time focusing with enough specificity to intervene in a helpful way can be challenging. The social worker's assessment process, therefore, attempts to identify and gain insight into the situation within the client's context to strive for accommodation of the client's desired goals.

The assessment and planning process begins right at the start of the social worker–client relationship when the social worker listens to the client's story and considers its meaning. Putting a client's story into the context of the values of social justice and human rights frames the social worker's understanding. By carefully listening, the social worker gains insight into how Barbara views her life and her goals and into the ways in which she feels the social worker might help her achieve those goals. The social worker may have reservations about the obstacles that seem to block Barbara from achieving her goals, about her or his agency's policies and restrictions, or even about the legal system. Thinking through these issues, including Barbara's strengths, is the heart of the assessment process.

ASSESSMENT AND PLANNING IN CONTEMPORARY PRACTICE [EPAS 7]

Since Mary Richmond published her pioneering work, *Social Diagnosis,* in 1917, assessment has been a critical component of social work practice. Contemporary social workers still consider assessment to be absolutely central to practice as it guides the focus of the social work intervention. However, some criticize the standard professional language social workers use in assessment and the implications regarding the social worker's expertise. The concept of assessment seems to suggest that the social worker has the power to define the client's situation and to impose that definition which may occur only in situations in which the client has been mandated to receive services. In Barbara's situation, she has been reported for possible child abuse and/or neglect and does not seek your services voluntarily. Initially, the social worker may impose her or his definition of the situation but, as they begin to work together, Barbara and the social worker can collaboratively frame the issues and determine the course of the planning and intervention processes. The assessment of the client's current situation should be framed by the client's perception of events, attitudes, and potential outcomes. The social worker's role is to gather and organize information and collaboratively interpret its meaning and implications with the client. A look at how the profession arrived at the word *assessment* may provide some perspective on this debate.

Since Mary Richmond introduced the term *diagnosis* into social work practice, the concept has been a part of the profession's history. However, **diagnosis** now firmly connotes a medicalized understanding of disease, dysfunction, symptoms, and the authority associated with the person who has the power to make a diagnosis and the declaration of an illness. As the concept of diagnosis is not rooted in a strengths-based perspective, social workers may find it challenging to use the diagnostic term.

Instead, contemporary social workers have adopted the term assessment to represent a more complete understanding of the client's context, one that focuses on strengths and resources as well as areas of challenge. Today, assessment is also considered a collaborative process by which clients can partner with a professional to make informed decisions about the work they can do together. Client resources include the environment in which the client lives as well as the history, culture, and traditions embedded in the life experience of the client. Treating assessment as an act of client-focused discovery stresses client definitions of the situation, including the parameters of the work, over professional definitions. This process can be a source of empowerment for clients.

A strengths-based systemic perspective invites social workers to examine the whole person, whose many dimensions can never be fully recognized in psychiatric diagnosis. Social workers stress the importance of dialogue as a way of getting a more complete perspective on client situations, considering their significance, hearing clients' goals, and understanding the ways in which clients believe they can achieve these goals. This larger view of assessment assumes that the client, rather than the social worker, directs the decisions about the substance of the work. In essence, assessment has evolved into an integrative collaboration between the social worker and the client from which the intervention flows (Jordan & Franklin, 2013). Consider the complexities of assessment in a situation like Barbara's. Her involvement with child protection services may mandate that she participate in services. Working with a client who may be reluctant or resistant requires sensitivity, and it may take more time to establish rapport and build trust.

When you and your client develop a shared vision and specify the goals, means, and end points for the work, you have the components of a solid, detailed plan. **Planning** is an interactive process between the social worker and the client that uses rational, incremental decision-making to choose and develop future objectives, alternatives, action steps, and evaluative strategies (Barker, 2014).

The key components that influence the concrete plan for work include:

- setting and prioritizing goals,
- identifying methods of reaching goals,
- developing a clear understanding of responsibilities,
- setting time frames,
- recognizing when an alternative plan is necessary,

- identifying resources, and

- identifying an end point for the work.

Incorporating these elements into a plan can enhance the client's understanding of the actions that will occur as a result of the assessment process. The issues that have been illuminated by both the client and the social worker during the assessment process provide a framework for the development of the intervention plan using the identified concerns, priorities, and available and needed resources. The client and social worker negotiate these components as an ongoing feature of the work, and this constitutes the mutually developed plan that can change over time. In sum, while assessment and planning may appear to occur simultaneously, they are, in fact, two distinct functions within the social work intervention. Assessment emphasizes the construction of the client's "story" (i.e., her or his history, current concerns, goals, and existing and needed resources) while planning is a collaboration between the social worker and the client to translate the information gathered during the assessment into a viable plan for implementation during the intervention.

WHERE DOES THE CLIENT WANT TO GO?

Many assessment processes begin with long, detailed social histories; these detailed histories have advantages and disadvantages. On the positive side, asking clients to talk about their life events can reveal important information, such as their great resilience in the face of childhood abuse, that might not otherwise be apparent but that is important to fully understand the client's situation. On the negative side, a social history that includes lengthy and detailed questioning can seem intrusive, irrelevant, or even judgmental to a client who, for example, only came to talk about a child care allowance so she can attend a class. Such histories may also seem to emphasize previous difficulties or situations that the client would prefer to leave in the past. Finally, the histories may seem disconnected and remote from whatever sense of urgency the client brings to the first interaction.

For example, Barbara may find an extensive history-taking process invasive and beside the point when she is being investigated by child protection services and may be interested only in getting her baby back. At the same time, such a process could reveal aspects of Barbara's life that might assist the social worker in helping her to achieve her goals using more or better-placed supports. The major requirement in this assessment process is that the social worker uses effective communication and relationship-building skills (as discussed in Chapter 3) to make the client feel comfortable and respected. By providing Barbara with information regarding why certain questions are important and by maintaining a flexible and patient approach, the social worker may be able to make Barbara feel more comfortable giving information. Whether the history is lengthy or brief, it is critical that the work start with you inquiring about the client's goals for the receiving service. The most detailed, painstaking social history is of little use if it—and not the goals of the client—becomes the driving force of the work.

IMPLICATIONS OF THEORETICAL PERSPECTIVES

Despite efforts to minimize prejudices and personal biases about the client's situation, assessments are not neutral gatherings of the facts. The questions you ask and the information you gather suggest, at the least, your theoretical preferences and biases. For every area on which you choose to focus, there are others you exclude. For example, if you focus on Barbara's relationship with her baby because you see her case as one of "mother and child," rather than considering her experience as a child herself, you are choosing to explore one area over another that could influence the work you and Barbara will do together. Likewise, if you stress one factor of her history (for example, teen pregnancy) but not another factor (for example, sexual abuse) those choices will affect the nature of the work.

In both scenarios, you take a specific approach based on your judgment about what is both relevant and important. This judgment is usually influenced by many of your personal attributes, such as who you are, what you believe about the nature of people, and where you work, and by the type of information you believe helps make a story understandable. The theoretical perspectives to which you and/or your agency most closely adhere and its assumptions will also influence what you consider useful here, as will the context and function of the agency. All of these components shape the kinds of questions you ask and, therefore, the information you receive. Framed as it is by your perspectives, the client's assumptions, and your own interpretation of a situation, the assessment process is never unbiased.

Classic Theories

The theoretical perspectives you adopt strongly influence the assessment and planning processes, the client–social worker relationship, and the subsequent work that the client and you do together. Throughout the history of social work, three classic theories have influenced assessments: psychoanalytic theory, attachment theory, and cognitive theory.

Psychoanalytic Theory Based primarily on the writings of the Austrian physician Sigmund Freud, **psychoanalytic theory** maintains that the unconscious is at the root of human behavior. Freud identified three structures that interact to determine human behavior: the *id, ego, and superego*. Each structure has a distinct function. The id is the repository of unconscious drives such as sex and aggression. In contrast, the ego is the managerial, rational part of the personality, which mediates between drives and perceived obligations. Finally, the superego serves as judge and conscience.

A social worker who believes that inner, unconscious motives and explanations determine the client's choices would orient an assessment toward interpreting the client's unconscious wishes or desire for rewards and gratification. For example, if Barbara repeatedly describes herself as a "loser," the social worker's assessment would likely be directed toward discovering the rewards and gratification Barbara receives from presenting herself as a perpetual failure. In actuality, Barbara may not be perpetually failing at all, but she may be receiving gratification by allowing others to see her as a failure. Perhaps she needs people to tell her that she is, in fact, successful and to be reassured that she has competence and self-worth. These rewards might include more attention from previously disinterested parents or protection from the high expectations of others. If Barbara labels herself a failure then perhaps people will not ask too much of her. If she does succeed, people will be pleasantly surprised, thus eliminating the pressure she feels. The first models of assessment were rooted in psychoanalytic theory, but as psychoanalytic theory gave way during the 20th century to evidence-based models, assessment approaches followed suit (Jordan & Franklin, 2013).

Attachment Theory   The social worker might first want to address Barbara as both a person who was parented and one who is now parenting. **Attachment theory**, originally proposed by U.S. psychologist John Bowlby (1982), holds that very early bonding occurs between a mother and an infant and subsequently plays a critical role in the child's future capacity to provide and sustain attachment opportunities for her or his own children. Most of this bonding activity occurs within the first two years of life, and it creates the foundation for the health of all of the child's future relationships.

A social worker who uses attachment theory focuses on Barbara's relationships with her early caregivers and the way in which these relationships may have contributed to her current struggles. To assess the attachment between Barbara and her child, a social worker might observe to identify behavior patterns that both the child and the mother demonstrate when a stranger enters the scene. In stressing these relationships of parental bonding during the assessment, the social worker would de-emphasize Barbara's other relationships in the environment.

Cognitive Theory   In contrast to psychoanalytic and attachment theories, if the theory guiding the work emphasizes the importance of **cognitions**, or thoughts, then the social worker may be using **cognitive theory**, which asserts that thoughts largely shape moods and behaviors. An assessment informed by the cognitive approach is likely to focus on what Barbara thinks about herself, the way in which she would like to think and act differently to achieve her goals, and the ways in which her thoughts and feelings influence her behavior (Beck, 2011). The cognitive approach assumes that people are thinking beings and that, if they change their thinking, their emotions will also change. It further posits that one's feelings influence both specific behaviors and general approaches to life. For example, because Barbara felt depressed, lonely, abandoned, or hopeless, she used poor judgment in leaving her baby. A social work intervention based on cognitive theory might involve helping Barbara appreciate her assets more fully, which in turn would help her feel better about herself and lead her to make safer caretaking choices for her baby.

All theories are predicated on assumptions that impact the way that the social worker perceives, relates to, and works with the client. Each social worker will have personal tendencies toward certain theories in certain situations. We are all guided by theories, formal or not. No one theory is "truth." You may use a combination of theories to frame the approach you will select for working with each client.

Contemporary Theoretical Perspectives

Like the classic theories, the worldview inherent in each contemporary theoretical approach influences assessment practice behaviors. We now turn our attention to two major contemporary theoretical perspectives, the strengths-based perspective and narrative theory, and to their implications for assessment approaches and skills.

The Strengths Perspective A strengths-based assessment does not focus on a history of client failures but instead concentrates on successes, resources, and goals for the future and examines the potential for the environment to nurture and support client strengths. Saleebey (2009, pp. 109–111) identifies two elements for strengths-based assessments that are useful with all client populations:

1. *The social worker meets the client in the struggle:* The line between supporting the positive dimensions of a client's personality, skills, or accomplishments and framing client experiences in terms of their negative dimensions (e.g., grief, terror, sorrow, or discouragement) may be a fine one. It is critical to the social worker–client relationship that the social worker validate the pain a client feels. Starting where the client is and listening to the client relate her or his concerns, painful though they may be, may help the client relate evidence of potential strengths on which you can work together to develop a strengths-based intervention.

2. *The social worker stimulates the discourse and narratives of resilience and strength:* A narrative approach can be helpful in reframing the work around the client's strengths. This reframing is dependent on the social worker supplying the words to help articulate the client's strengths, affirming those strengths, and emphasizing possibilities. Supportive questioning (i.e., questions that emphasize a positive aspect of the situation or a recollection of past successes) can focus the discussion on client strengths. Even in the face of repeated, entrenched

QUICK GUIDE 6   EXAMPLES OF STRENGTHS-BASED SUPPORTIVE QUESTIONS

Client Situation	Possible Supportive Questions
Middle-aged man who was recently laid off from his job and fears he will not be able to find new employment	"How did you approach your last job search?" "Who might be a good person or group with whom to network about employment opportunities?"
Single mother with four young children who is feeling overwhelmed with her life	"What strategies have you used to manage the demands of caring for your kids?"
Fifteen-year-old teenager who is stressed by daily arguments with her mother	"Can you recall times when you and your mother had fun together?" "What are those times?"
75-year-old male who is experiencing depression	"How have you handled other challenges in your life?"
33-year-old combat veteran who is experiencing post-traumatic stress disorder and is having difficulty adjusting to civilian life	"What were your best assets as a soldier?" "How might those transfer to this new chapter of your life?"
Middle-aged woman struggling with the decision to seek long term residential care for her mother, who is suffering from dementia. She feels that placing her mother would be a betrayal of the deathbed promise she made to her father to always keep her mother with her.	"How has your family traditionally handled difficult decisions?" "If your father were here to help you make this decision today, what might his response be?"

stories of trouble and pain, you can help clients recognize their capacities for survival and learn the language of strengths in order to uncover a seed of hope. Quick Guide 6 provides examples of supportive questions in various situations.

Exhibit 4.1 provides strengths-based assessment guidelines that focus on understanding client perceptions of the situation (Anderson, 2013). This set of guidelines is intended to empower clients to share their life stories, acknowledge their strengths and wisdom, and develop greater insight into the complexities of their lives and current circumstances (Anderson, 2013, p. 187).

This type of assessment includes two components (see Exhibit 4.2). First, the social worker explores a series of questions with the client to define the problem situation (Component 1). These questions help identify the client's strengths, life experiences (both positive and challenging), and strategies for coping with adversity. The social worker and client then work together to identify obstacles and relevant client strengths. These strengths and obstacles can be charted on a grid (Component 2), a visual representation of the assessment results.

Guidelines for a strengths-based assessment include:

- Document the client's story.
- Support and validate the story.
- Honor the client's self-determination.
- Give pre-eminence to the client's understanding of the facts.
- Discover what the client needs.
- Discover uniqueness.
- Reach a mutual agreement on the assessment.
- Avoid blame and blaming.
- Assess; but do not get caught up in labels (i.e., diagnoses).

Source: Anderson et al., 2009, pp. 186–188

EXHIBIT 4.1

The Strengths-Based Perspective in Assessment

A strengths-based assessment process helps clients identify their own strengths, use the resources in their environment, and tell their story about the current challenge. The approach is also explicitly political in that it recognizes and articulates the power relationships in clients' lives.

Narrative Theory   Recall from Chapter 1 that narrative theory, drawing on postmodern thought, focuses on the client's story as the central component in the work. Social workers using this approach are primarily interested in discovering client stories and in helping them to "re-author" those stories if they wish. In this context, a **story** is defined as events linked in sequence across time according to a plot (Morgan, 2000, p. 5). Narrative theory is consistent with the mission and values of the social work profession's commitment to "individualizing each client as unique, respecting each client's story, respecting cultural differences, and separating one's own beliefs and values from those of clients through self-understanding, and conscious use of self" (Kelley & Smith, 2015, p. 290). Narrative practitioners also subscribe to a person-centered approach that embraces the essentials of respectful listening, avoidance of labels, fostering empowerment, and emphasizing social justice (Kelley & Smith, 2015).

Narrative practitioners are interested in helping the client to broaden or "thicken" her or his story. For example, Georgia developed a negative self-story response to her experience of intimate partner violence. Before, her self-story was that of a strong and competent young woman, but with the experience, it slowly began to erode, reflecting her increasing doubt and finally wholesale dejection as she adopted the persona of an unworthy human being. It became a "thin" story in that it lacked complexity; it reflected only her self-rejection. Georgia's perception of herself as unworthy focuses on one dimension of her person (i.e., self-rejection) while ignoring her strengths, life lessons, and capabilities.

EXHIBIT 4.2

Two-Component Model for Assessing Client Strengths

In Anderson, Cowger, and Snively's (2009) two-component model for assessing client strengths, Component 1 is a process by which the worker and client define the problem situation and clarify how the client wants the worker to help. Component 2 is a graphic representation of the analysis of the problem defined in Component 1 (i.e., the assessment). It invites the worker and client together to chart strengths and obstacles in each of four quadrants. Quadrant 2 is highlighted and may contain subcategories relating to cognition, emotion, motivation, coping, and interpersonal relationships.

COMPONENT 1

Defining the Problem Situation: Getting at Why the Client Seeks Assistance

- *Brief summary of the identified problem situation:* The worker and client agree to a straightforward account of the circumstance, stated in plain language.
- *Who* (persons, groups, organization) is involved, including the client(s) seeking assistance?
- *How* or in what way are participants involved?
- *What* happens between the participants before, during, and immediately following activity related to the problem situation?
- *What* meaning does the client ascribe to the problem situation?
- *What* does the client want with regard to the problem situation?
- *What* does the client want/expect by seeking assistance?
- *What* would the client's life be like if the problem was resolved?

COMPONENT 2

	Strengths	
Quadrant 3		**Quadrant 4**
Social and Political Strengths		Personal and Interpersonal Strengths
• Civic engagement		• Cognition
• Social networks		• Emotion
		• Motivation
		• Coping
		• Interpersonal skills
		• Physical and physiological
Quadrant 1		**Quadrant 2**
Social and Political Obstacles		Personal and Interpersonal Obstacles
• Systemic oppression		• Powerlessness
• Legitimization of domination and violence		• Violation
		• Intense suffering
		• Isolation
		• Secrecy/silence
	Obstacles	

(left axis) Environmental Factors *(right axis)* (Client) Help Seeker Factors

Source: Adapted from Anderson et al., 2009, p. 192; Anderson, 2013, p. 194

In addition to trying to build a more in-depth story, the social worker recognizes the importance of the broader social context of the client's life. In one sense, Georgia's story is about her and her partner. In a broader sense, however, it is also about a pervasive social phenomenon that results in the deaths of thousands of women every year. The social work intervention aims to help Georgia rewrite her thin story of worthlessness into one that more accurately reflects her talents, competence, and attractiveness as a human being. This is the goal of assessment: to discover the alternative story the client wishes to author and to guide the development of a person-centered intervention to identify specific tasks and activities that will enable Georgia to tap into her talents, attractiveness, and competencies.

In Barbara's situation, the social worker using a narrative approach would first want to hear Barbara's story. How does she fill the day? What is it like to be mother to this baby? When are the best times? When did her loneliness first interfere with her life? When is she able to conquer it? Who would say she is a good mother?

These are a few of the most basic ideas of narrative theory and ways social workers use this approach to assess client needs. Though narrative theory differs from many more classic theoretical perspectives, it is similar in that the story is the emphasis of the assessment process. In a narrative approach, the person seeking assistance is the primary driver of the assessment, although you, as the social worker, contribute your ideas as well. A narrative approach aligns with the strengths perspective as it assumes that people are the experts on their lives and that they have multiple talents, values, beliefs, and skills for improving their lives. We will look more closely at the applicability of narrative approaches in interventions with families and groups in Chapters 6–9.

Solution-Focused Approach   Similar to a narrative approach, a solution-focused intervention builds on a strengths perspective and uses solution-related language to empower clients toward self-initiated change (Lee, 2015). Three primary assumptions and principles guide practitioners using this approach: (1) language is the mechanism by which clients and social workers understand the meanings of the client's life and actions; (2) because clients are the experts on their own lives, they have both the resources and the answers that will guide their solutions; and (3) clients, not professionals, function as the "knowers" within the intervention process and are therefore in the best position to create their solutions.

Clients work with the social worker in stages, using a series of questions, to develop solutions to issues. While the social worker poses these questions, their content is rooted in the story the client shared during the assessment phase. The social worker asks questions to fill in historical gaps, identify previous successes and solutions, and explore the client's perceptions for outcomes. Stages of solution-building include: (1) description of the problem; (2) development of well-formed goals; (3) exploring with the client exceptions to their experiences questions (i.e., questions aimed at identifying instances in which the problem did not exist); (4) provision of end-of-session feedback; and (5) evaluation of client progress

(De Jong & Berg, 2013, pp. 17–18). The social worker asks questions aimed at eliciting the client's self-evaluation of the meaning of her or his life events and an exploration of future possibilities that can be pursued by the client.

While similar in their strengths-based orientation, client-centered empowerment approach, and commitment to collaboration, narrative and solution-focused approaches are not the same. Proponents of the narrative approach emphasize the importance of "not knowing" (i.e., not being the expert on the client's life) and listening for unique outcomes to the client's presenting concerns, while solution-focused adherents delve into the possibility of "exception" questions (Kelley & Smith, 2015). In pursuing information regarding "exceptions," the social worker can ask the client to describe her or his life before the crisis or situation that brought her or him in contact with the social worker. Information regarding coping skills the client has used successfully in the past can provide insight into possibilities for a successful intervention for the client's current difficulty. Having some similarities, narrative, strengths-based, and solution-focused approaches all emphasize client empowerment and the mobilization of client strengths and resources, yet they also each have their own unique methods and strategies (Kelley & Smith, 2015). Some practitioners elect to combine these approaches with one another and with other approaches (e.g., cognitive behavioral interventions), but to combine approaches, a practitioner needs skills, knowledge, and competence in the areas being combined.

Evidence Matters [EPAS 4]

While theory guides and informs the development of social work practice knowledge, values, and competence, evidence can also help social work practitioners determine the appropriate skills, competencies, and behaviors to apply to the social work intervention. In fact, the Council on Social Work Education (CSWE) Educational Policy and Accreditation Standards (2015) calls for social workers to engage in practice-informed research and research-informed practice. **Evidence-based practice** (EBP) aids practitioners to "systematically integrate evidence about the efficacy of interventions in clinical decision-making" (Jenson & Howard, 2013). In evidence-based practice, social workers systematically determine, use, and assess interventions based on the consideration and integration of research findings; clinical expertise; client preferences, values, and presenting issues; and the values and circumstances that will best serve the client (Thyer, 2015). Evidence-based practice follows a five-step process: (1) converting need for information on needs for practice issues and potential interventions into answerable questions; (2) locating evidence to answer the questions; (3) critically appraising the evidence to determine validity, impact, and applicability; (4) integrating evidence into practice knowledge and the client's unique values and circumstances; and (5) evaluating the effectiveness and efficiency of using evidence to guide and improve the practice intervention (Thyer, 2015, p. 1194).

While the assumed focus of utilizing an EBP approach in social work practice is on informing the choice of and strategies for the intervention, using EBP as part of the assessment and planning process is equally important (Grady & Drisko, 2014). In order to collaborate with the client, a viable and effective intervention plan, with an evidence-based foundation for gathering and processing information from and about the client, helps to ensure a successful outcome. Drawing from available evidence on assessment and planning, a number of factors influence and shape the way in which assessment is conceptualized, including (Grady & Drisko, 2014):

1. *Social worker role*—If the social worker's task is to gather information but not develop a plan or implement an intervention with the client, the assessment will differ from one that involves an ongoing relationship as time and comprehensiveness of the assessment is critical.

2. *Agency/organizational factors:* While agencies rely on thorough assessments to guide and support service delivery, social workers need to have insight into the factors that influence the assessment/planning process, to include agency mission and purpose, services provided, the social worker's role, client needs, and agency culture about assessment (i.e., does agency policy mandate a structured assessment with little room for including the social worker's perspective; is the assessment a more open, narrative process, or a combination of the two?).

3. *Client availability and capacity*: A variety of issues may impact the client's willingness and ability to fully engage in the assessment/data gathering process, including cognitive capacity, mental illness, involuntary status as a client, cultural norms, language/speech ability, and values related to the helping process.

4. *Assessment format and structure:* The inclusion of well-accepted social work frameworks such as strengths and person-in-environment perspectives, the format (e.g., one session versus multiple sessions), and structure (individual versus couple or family) all serve to shape the approach and outcome of the assessment.

Utilizing the EBP process and the influencing factors described here, how would you apply this process to work with Barbara? Consider the following (Carter & Matthieu, 2010; Jensen & Howard, 2015):

1. Convert practice information into questions about background information, effectiveness of intervention, or policy:

   - *Information*: Barbara jeopardized her child's safety by leaving him alone.

   - *Question*: What are the risk factors most associated with teenage parent neglect?

   - *Information*: Barbara wants to be a good parent.

- *Question*: How can social workers provide assistance to teenage parents at risk of child neglect?

- *Information*: Barbara appears to be experiencing depressive symptoms.

- *Questions*: What assessment tools are most appropriate to assess for depression among teenage parents? What are the most effective intervention strategies to lower depressive symptoms in teenage parents?

2. Locate evidence to answer the questions.

    - Conduct a search of research and literature on child development, parenting, and assessment of and intervention with depression.

    - Consult with social work practitioner(s) who possess(es) knowledge and expertise in the areas of interest and ask for their opinions of best practices in the areas.

3. Appraise evidence.

    - Assess the quality of the best available evidence, including the appropriateness of the research design for the question, sponsorship of the research, the similarity of the research subjects to your client, and other factors.

    - Using the evidence compiled from your literature review, your judgment, and practitioners' discussion and experience, and the client's goals and social context, develop a plan for assessment and intervention.

4. Apply evidence to practice decisions.

    - Implement assessment and intervention plan.

    - Determine the appropriateness of the research methods for the client's situation while maintaining a client-centered approach; **cultural humility** (a commitment to self-evaluation and self-critique for the purpose of reducing the imbalances of power [Tervalon & Murray-Garcia, 1998, p. 117]); and applicability to the practice approach, setting, and client system.

5. Evaluate the process of using evidence to guide practice intervention.

    - At each step in the change process, conduct an evaluation of the efficacy of the assessment and intervention process. Questions to consider:

        - Was the assessment accurate?

        - Was the intervention effective?

        - Was the information compiled from the literature and practitioner helpful?

- Did ethical questions emerge in the process? How were those resolved?

- What would you have done differently? Why?

Evidence-based practice approaches are an evolving area for practitioners that can be used to guide practitioners to information regarding assessment, intervention, and evaluative strategies and other key resources needed for effective work with a client. An increasing number of social workers are accessing evidence to inform and guide their practice, however, social work students must continue to focus on gaining knowledge and skills to competently evaluate the array of evidence that is available from a variety of sources (Pope, Rollins, Chaumba, & Risler, 2011). The clinical judgment and skills required for competent and ethical social work practice also play an important role in effective interventions. When asked in a recent survey, most social workers reported that they do not use evidence "instrumentally"—applying it directly to practice, but rather they use it in a "conceptual" way—that is, to help them better understand information (Wharton & Bolland, 2012, p. 162). In other words, both the social worker and the client must view the evidence-based information and strategies to be viable, appropriate, and useful (Wharton & Bolland, 2012). Each client circumstance is unique and each situation must be assessed individually. Such an approach allows the practitioner to account for the complexities of client situations when implementing interventions.

IMPLICATIONS OF DIVERSITY AND CULTURE IN ASSESSMENT

Diversity and culture have a significant impact on assessment. To be a culturally competent practitioner, you must develop a set of "congruent behaviors, attitudes, and policies that come together in a system or agency or amongst professionals and enable the system, agency, or those professions to work effectively in a cross-cultural situation" (National Center for Cultural Competence (NCCC), n.d., p. 1). The NCCC (n.d.) further outlines five elements that contribute to one's ability to demonstrate cultural competence, including: (1) valuing diversity, (2) capacity for cultural self-assessment, (3) consciousness of the dynamics inherent in cultural interactions, (4) institutionalized cultural knowledge, and (5) service delivery adaptations that reflect understanding of cultural diversity (p. 1).

The social work profession is a cultural institution and is therefore affected by the same pressures and forces that influence other aspects of our society's culture. Shifting patterns of diverse populations in U.S. society require social workers to develop appropriate competencies and behaviors for different cultures. Consider these diversity-related questions as they may impact your work with Barbara:

1. What is Barbara's background, including race, ethnicity, family background, religious/spiritual beliefs, and education?
2. How might Barbara's experiences related to aspects of diversity impact her knowledge of parenting?

3. How does your background impact your knowledge of Barbara's ethnic, racial, and cultural background?
4. What information do you need to work with Barbara in a culturally competent way?
5. What culturally competent practice behaviors will be appropriate for working with Barbara?

The social worker who uses a strengths-based and/or narrative or solution-focused approach must be committed to affirming individuals' strengths and respecting their culture. Of critical importance to the assessment and planning processes is ensuring that every client encounter is viewed through the perspective of the client's **biopsychosocial-spiritual** and cultural lenses. Gathering and analyzing the information provided by the client through such a multifaceted lens can ensure that you are viewing the client as a "whole" person within the context of the physical, psychological, social, and spiritual environment in which she or he lives. The social worker must also acknowledge the implications of such a commitment for the assessment and planning processes, particularly in the areas of: (1) cultural competence, (2) connecting with the spiritual dimensions of a client's culture, and (3) making global connections.

Cultural Competence, Humility, and Intersectionality

A social worker who embraces a systemic, strengths-based perspective includes meaningful components of the client's culture in the assessment process (NASW, 2015a). Known as **cultural competence**, this behavior is defined as "the process by which individuals and systems respond respectfully and effectively to people of all cultures, languages, classes, races, ethnic backgrounds, religions, and other diversity factors in a manner that recognizes, affirms, and values the worth of individuals, families, and communities and practices and preserves the dignity of each" (NASW, 2015a, p. 13). Cultural competence requires that social workers be aware of their limitations and respect the unique, culturally defined needs of others. As you have learned, assessment involves discovering what is important to the client, and that includes those cultural influences that shape the client's values, how those influences have affected the client's experience, and how the client's perspectives differ from the social worker's.

Clearly, the social worker's ability to demonstrate cultural competence requires an ongoing exploration of her or his self-assessment and knowledge of her or his own culture (NASW, 2015b). That is, workers must understand their personal cultural influences, including power and privilege, and examine how those influences affect their work and understand the role culture plays in all of our lives.

Cultural humility, a concept that has recently been embraced by the social work profession that inherently exists within the professional–client relationship along with mutually beneficial and nonpaternalistic clinical and advocacy partnerships on behalf of those persons and groups being served (Tervalon & Murray-Garcia, 1998, p. 117). From a practice perspective, having cultural humility within the context of being culturally competent enables the social worker to function in the role as a learner and allows the client to serve as the expert on her or his life. As a culturally humble professional, the social worker acknowledges that she or he cannot know everything about all cultures. A social worker demonstrating cultural humility acknowledges that she or he cannot know everything about the client's cultural heritage and traditions, so might say to the client: "Forgive me, but I have not had much experience with your culture. I hope you will tell me more about it." Such a statement signifies your commitment to forging an open and collaborative relationship with the client.

Approaching clients with a perspective on **intersectionality** recognizes the multiple aspects of diversity that influence the client's life including, but not limited to, race, ethnicity, religion and spirituality, social and economic class, sexual orientation and identification, and abilities (NASW, 2015a). Intersectionality is an important diversity-related concept to incorporate into working at all levels of social work practice but is especially critical when engaged in the assessment and planning process with individuals. Taking such an inclusive approach enables the social worker and the client to holistically consider the many and varied aspects and identities associated with the client's life, thus embracing the person-in-environment perspective with a commitment to social justice.

An effective assessment and planning process depends on the social worker's level of cultural competence and cultural humility and commitment to intersectionality. You cannot simply assess the degree to which your client's intersectionality is different or similar from your own, but you must recognize the way in which your own cultural beliefs and experiences impact the client relationship and accept that you cannot be an expert on the client's cultural experience. Your understanding of the issues the client brings and the role the client's culture plays in those issues impacts how you perceive the presenting "problem." For example, when your client describes communicating with the spirit of his deceased father, you might wonder if he is demonstrating psychosis or hearing voices, unless you are willing to ask the client about his beliefs so you can develop a clear understanding that this kind of spiritual communication is part of his Latino cultural celebration of the Day of the Dead, which encourages reaching out and encouraging the spirit of the deceased to be present for a moment to hear the prayers and love of the family for them.

Culturally Competent Practice Behaviors

Developing the skills necessary to conduct a culturally competent assessment and plan, including the ability to ascertain, through talking to the client, the meaning of their culture, language, cultural norms, and behaviors, takes time and effort. It requires the social worker to see these attributes as strengths on which to build a culturally meaningful intervention (NASW, 2015a).

A social worker who adopts a strengths-based, culturally competent model of assessment and planning begins the relationship by initiating friendly yet purposeful conversations. Rather than focusing on long social histories, the social worker may consider some aspect of the client's cultural frame that she or he finds puzzling or particularly interesting and ask about it using a "global question." For example, consider the situation you encounter as you are working with your client, Emilia Sanchez (refer to www.routledgesw.com/caseStudies for information), a 24-year-old Mexican American woman with a history of substance abuse and the mother of a 4-year-old, Joey, who lives with her parents, Hector and Celia Sanchez. Joey has lived with his grandparents for most of his four years and, while he knows that Emilia is his mother, he sees Hector and Celia as his parents. Emilia has just learned that Hector and Celia are going to take legal action to officially adopt Joey. She is furious and has come to you for your help to prevent the adoption from going forward. As a culturally competent practitioner, you inquire about Emilia's cultural background and work to understand the impact it has on her beliefs and current situation. As the client (as a cultural guide) answers your questions, you remain highly attuned to the language she uses and you inquire about **cover terms**, which are expressions and phrases that seem to carry more meaning than the literal meaning the words would suggest. For instance, your client might respond to the question about what her family thinks with a comment like, "I don't care what those hypocrites think about me; I will never be the person they want me to be!" In this case, the cover terms are "hypocrites" and "person they want me to be," because they seem to have an ethnic or even familial cultural relevance to how she understands her social location.

Were you to exclude clients from the assessment and planning process, two negative consequences are likely to occur. First, important information that only the person experiencing the context can provide may be dismissed or ignored. Second, for many of these clients, exclusion contributes to the internalization of this kind of oppression; clients come to believe that they have no right or capacity to participate. The **internalization of oppression**—the process by which individuals come to believe and accept external judgments that devalue their sense of self—is one of the most sinister aspects of the oppression and domination dynamic (Van Soest, 2013), and one that clearly undermines the spirit of human rights.

Although extensive cultural interviewing could seem removed from the main issue, understanding the impact of the client's culture can contribute to the overall success of the work. It is particularly important to identify early on those cultural areas that have the potential to become barriers later in the working relationship. For example, given what you have discovered about Emilia, you know not to begin by suggesting a family conference with her parents.

Connecting with the Spiritual Aspects of the Client

In recent years, the social work profession has placed greater emphasis on the value of helping people define what gives their lives purpose and meaning (see, for example, Hodge, 2005a). Insofar as this effort might be seen as a spiritual quest, it can encourage people to find the most sustaining areas of their lives. People find such areas of meaning in many places, including religious practices, outdoor activities, and in social connections like volunteering in a hospice. The social worker and client can incorporate these areas of meaning into both the assessment and action stages of the work. For example, after inquiring about the client's religion and spirituality practices, you may encourage your client to identify her volunteer efforts as evidence of her value to the community, which in turn might reduce her sense of isolation. Facilitating a client's connection with her or his spiritual side is likely to be a lasting and significant contribution of the social work intervention.

Global Connections

In the United States, foreign-born migrants make up over 13 percent of the population, and these numbers are growing (Pew Research Center, 2015). Social workers may work with individuals who have come to live in the U.S. as nonimmigrants (e.g., visitors, students, and temporary workers); legal or undocumented immigrants; or refugees who fled political or religious persecution. It is therefore essential that social workers develop competence in internationally focused practice. At the individual practice level, social workers can work with international migrants in a number of different areas, especially health, including assessment of health beliefs and treatment expectation, case management, and health education; mental health, including case management, crisis intervention; individual, marital, and family therapy; and economic well-being, including job search and training-retraining assistance, coaching, and mentoring, interethnic relations, and conflict resolution (Potocky, 2013). Social workers may also work with individuals in foreign countries in such areas as relief and disaster interventions, international adoptions and cross-country adoptions, and working with immigrants and refugees (Healy, 2013).

Whether you are working with clients in your own country or abroad, you can build on your cultural competence and humility to individualize your approach for each client. When working with immigrants, a strengths-based approach is particularly appropriate. Because permanently leaving one's home country takes courage and coping skills, these clients can draw on considerable strengths.

Working in an international area can be a learning experience for you and for your client. To begin your journey toward becoming a culturally competent and humble practitioner, you must first become aware of your own cultural heritage, values (personal and differences), and belief systems and conflicts related to cultural assimilation and pluralism (Lum, 2013). Quick Guide 7 offers suggestions for beginning your cultural heritage journey. After exploring your own cultural make-up, you can begin to gain knowledge and develop skills to work with an international client. Learn as much as possible about your client's heritage and avoid making assumptions about the client's culture, particularly in terms of beliefs, knowledge of you and your professional value system, language proficiency, familiarity with their new home (as appropriate), or openness to working with a helping professional.

QUICK GUIDE 7   MY CULTURAL HERITAGE JOURNEY

The cultural heritage journeys of both clients and social workers impact their perspectives on life and work. Consider the following:

- Where do my family's roots begin?
- If my family emigrated to the United States, how long has each of my parents been living here?
- If I am in an adoptive family, what do I know about my biological family's cultural heritage?
- What traditions has my family passed down through the generations?
- Do my family's traditions relate to religion or spirituality, holidays, rituals, and/or significant events for the family?
- What values surrounding ethics, wealth, religion and spirituality, race, ethnicity, health, education, sexual orientation, and image have I learned from my family?
- Have I challenged any of my family traditions or values?
- Has my family had experiences that challenge their traditions and values? If so, how have I responded?
- What significant life experiences have shaped my view of the world and specifically of people who are different from me?
- How will my cultural heritage impact my social work practice?
- Would I like to change or add to my traditions? How might I start?

Not presuming to understand the individual client's life experience or goals is important in work with any client, and it is critical with a client who has relocated to a new country. Some clients may have fled their country of origin to escape trauma or torture, and some may have experienced trauma during relocation or challenges adjusting to the new culture and environment. Some clients may have concerns regarding their legal status in their new country. A client who is unfamiliar with customs, language, legal issues, or the role of helping professionals in the United States may have difficulty building the rapport and trust that are crucial to a successful social work relationship. In these situations, some strategies for developing a trusting working relationship may include: outlining your role, boundaries, and limitations as a social worker; asking questions about the client's culture, country of origin, traditions, and beliefs (being mindful not to be overly intrusive); sharing information about the culture of the agency and community, particularly as it relates to the provision of social and or health services; and creating an environment in which the client feels comfortable asking for clarifications on any issue. You will likely communicate with this client through an interpreter, which places a third person into the relationship. Working with an interpreter requires you to clarify your respective roles, the style of interpretation, and main-taining confidentiality.

SKILLS FOR ASSESSMENT AND PLANNING [EPAS 7]

During the assessment and planning phase of the social work intervention, the social worker and client can work together to form a shared vision for what the client hopes to achieve and how they will work together to reach that goal. In developing this vision, social workers help clients articulate the kinds of changes they want to make. Social workers ask questions that affirm the client's ability to make changes to improve her or his life. Building on the foundations of strengths, narrative, and solution-focused perspectives, skills for assessing and planning with individual clients emphasize a collaborative, client-focused approach.

An essential first step in the assessment and planning process is to create an environment in which the client feels comfortable and can develop a sense of trust that will enable the relationship to move forward with openness and honesty. Building trust varies depending on the setting and format of the service being

© fatihhoca

provided. For example, if you are staffing a crisis hot line, the entire intervention may occur in less than one hour so you must establish trust with the client in the first few minutes of the encounter. In this instance, you can state at the beginning how you can be helpful, that you are there to listen and offer options and resources, then allow the client to share her or his story without interruptions. Setting the parameters of the service and following through are helpful in building trust. In face-to-face settings with multiple opportunities to meet, the same guidelines can be followed but you have the benefit of seeing nonverbal communications and time.

Strengths Perspective

During the engagement, assessment, and planning phases, a social worker committed to the strengths-based approach fosters a climate in which both the social worker and the client recognize the strengths the client brings to the intervention and identify those resources that can be mobilized and those that can evolve.

Saleebey (2013) provides a group of questions designed to elicit information that focuses on identifying client strengths that may be factored into intervention planning. Quick Guide 8 contains eight such questions.

Narrative Theory

The ways in which social workers elicit and interpret client perceptions differentiate narrative approaches from solution-focused, strengths-based, and other empowerment approaches. Narrative practitioners first help clients "deconstruct" their stories. In other words, the social worker helps the client examine the way in which they have organized their life stories, which is then reviewed with the purpose of looking for new "truths" (i.e., new stories) (Kelley & Smith, 2015). Then, practitioners and clients work together to expand upon and externalize perceptions and meanings of the client's words by re-envisioning the way the client's life is organized and lived. This expansion can help the client to "reconstruct" those stories to develop a broader, more effective approach to functioning (Kelley & Smith, 2015).

Narrative social work practice may be viewed as a three-stage approach encompassing client engagement; exploring and deconstructing preconceived client stories and assumptions; and authoring new, more empowering stories (Roscoe, Carson, & Madoc-Jones, 2011; Roscoe & Madoc-Jones, 2009). When using a narrative framework in the assessment and planning stages, the social worker collaborates with the client to reconstruct the client's reality. Using a series of strategies and questions, the social worker and client together cast new meaning on the client's life in a way that empowers the client. Client and social worker views are of equal importance, which empowers each partner (Roscoe et al., 2011).

QUICK GUIDE 8   ASSESSMENT QUESTIONS FOR DISCOVERING STRENGTHS

Survival Questions:
How have you managed to survive thus far, given all the challenges you have faced? What have you learned about yourself and your world during your struggles?

Support Questions:
Who are the special people on whom you can depend? What do they respond to in you?

Exception Questions:
When things were going well in your life, what was different?
What parts of your world and your being would you like to recapture?

Possibility Questions:
What are your hopes, visions, and aspirations? How can I help you achieve those goals?

Esteem Questions:
When people say good things about you, what are they likely to say? When was it that you began to believe that you might achieve some of the things you wanted in life?

Perspective Questions:
What is your perspective on your current situation?
How would you describe your current situation to others?

Change Questions:
What thoughts do you have about ways your situation could change?
What strategies have worked well for you in the past? How can I help?

Meaning Questions:
What beliefs do you hold above all others? What gives you a sense of purpose? What are the origins of your beliefs?

Source: Adapted from Saleebey, 2013, pp. 107–108

After listening to the client's perceptions of her or his current realities, the social worker helps the client through the following process:

1. "Externalize" the problem by refocusing on the outcome rather than on the root cause and by de-emphasizing *problem-saturated stories* (self-perceptions in which problems dominate the client's life).
2. Discover "exceptions" (i.e., those instances in which the problem or concern did not exist for the client).
3. "Re-author" or reconstruct a new reality through mapping of the domain of the issue or problem (i.e., reviewing an issue or problem from a past, present, and possible future perspective to enable client to prepare for a desired change).

4. "Reinforce" the change by involving others who have been or are currently in the client's life who have an understanding or insights about the change situation and/or sharing/complementing the client's planned or actual change experience to identify unique outcomes and encourage a continuation of the same behaviors (Kelley & Smith, 2015; Nichols, 2014).

Throughout the assessment and planning process, the social worker poses different types of questions that aid the client in reaching her or his desired new reality. Using the case of your client who is struggling in her relationship with her wife, Alexa, to whom she has been married for one year, the following question types build on one another. Your client, Camille, feels that she and her spouse have different life goals, particularly in terms of having children, pursuing their careers, purchasing a home, and saving money. While these are her goals, she is coming to realize that her spouse does not share them at least at this point in their lives. Let us review questions a narrative-focused social worker may pose to Camille:

- *Deconstruction questions* re-focus on an outcome.
  Social Worker: *Camille, you have shared your concerns about you and your wife, Alexa, having different priorities for your lives. What goals and priorities did you have in common when you got married? Which of those do you continue to share?*

- *Opening space questions* create the possibility for unique outcomes the client may not have considered.
  Social Worker: *Camille, is there a possibility that you and your wife do want the same things in life but are not on the same schedule for achieving those goals? Is there a possibility that she appears to be resistive to your goals for other reasons? If that were the case, what could those reasons be?*

- *Preference questions* translate unique outcomes into preferred experiences.
  Social Worker: *If you learned that Alexa did share some or all of your life goals but does not feel capable of making plans now, how would your perspective change?*

- *Story development questions* create a new reality (or story) based on a client's preferred experiences.
  Social Worker: *Camille, if you and Alexa could create a new life plan/set of goals, what would that new reality look like? What are the strengths of your relationship that you can build on? Where are the possibilities for negotiation and compromise?*

- *Meaning questions* provide an opportunity for the client to replace negative perceptions with positive interpretations based on the strengths identified in story development.

Social Worker: *In thinking about a new reality with Alexa, how could the negative perceptions that you had at the beginning of our discussion be replaced with more positive perceptions of your life together?*

- *Extending the story into the future* empowers the client to see her- or himself in future situations. This phase may involve bringing others into the process to support the client as she or he embarks on a new reality.

Social Worker: *You have envisioned a new reality for your life with Alexa— what does that life look like in one year? Five years? Who else needs to be a part of this conversation?*

With an emphasis on deconstructing and re-envisioning one's life, a narrative approach can be an empowering experience for the client because negatives can be reframed as new and preferred outcomes can be built on her or his strengths and supports.

Solution-Focused Approach

Using overall strategies similar to those in a narrative-focused assessment and planning process, solution-focused assessment focuses on possible solutions as opposed to problems (De Jong & Berg, 2013). Compatible with a strengths-based approach, clients are viewed as the experts on their lives, their challenges, and their needs, further accentuating the collaborative nature of the client–social worker relationship (Nichols, 2014).

De Jong and Cronkright (2011) provide this overview of the benefits of the approach:

- Clients who are able to define what they want to be different in their lives make more progress than those who cannot.

- Clients make greater progress (and do so more quickly) when practitioners spend more time questioning them about what they want to be different than about the details of the problems.

- Clients make more progress, build solutions, and show less resistance when practitioners ask them about exceptions (i.e., their past successes) related to what they want to be different than when practitioners offer advice or confront resistance.

- Clients make more progress when held accountable for solutions instead of problems (pp. 22–23).

Like other empowerment approaches, a solution-focused approach incorporates a series of questions to elicit client perception, strengths, resources, and, ultimately, the solution. To facilitate the development of a trusting, collaborative relationship with the client, a social worker might first ask, "How are you hoping I could help you?" (Nichols, 2014, p. 230). This question invites the client to share her or his story and in doing so to provide insight into the reasons for seeking help. Utilizing the social work skill of starting where the client is, the social worker continues the assessment process, asking the client to share her or his concerns, and then working with the client to set goals. Let us return to the case of Camille and Alexa from the earlier discussion on narrative approaches in the context of a solution-focused approach. Solution-focused question types include the following (Lee, 2015, p. 595; Nichols, 2014):

- *Evaluative questions* engage the client in an evaluation of the "doing, thinking, and feeling" as these areas relate to the issue that brought her or him to you. Such questions enable the client to assess the current situation, associated feelings and actions, and potential solutions.

  Social Worker: Camille, you have shared your concerns about you and your wife, Alexa, having different priorities for your lives. What have you done about your feelings? What are your thoughts about your situation? What emotions are you experiencing when you think about your marriage?

- *Miracle questions* ask the client to "Describe a vision of the future in which the problem or concern no longer exists." Miracle questions promote creativity and hopefulness as well as client self-determination and participation in planning for concrete and achievable change.

  Social Worker: Imagine for a moment your future if the concerns about shared life goals is no longer a problem for you. What does that future life look like?

- *Exception questions* ask the client to "Consider a time when the problem or concern was not present. What was happening at that time?" These questions allow the client and social worker to identify existing assets and resources that may point to strategies client and social worker can use in the present situation.

  Social Worker: In describing your relationship history with Alexa, you indicated that you once shared the goals of marriage, children, buying a house, and saving for your future together. What convinced you at that time that you could build a life together based on these shared goals? What was happening at that time in your life? Her life?

- *Scaling questions* ask the client to "Consider your situation on a continuum from worst (1) to best (10). How would you scale it?" Quantifying issues enables client and social worker to frame goals, provide feedback, monitor progress, change course, and evaluate outcomes.

  Social Worker: Using a scale where 1 is your relationship with Alexa at its worst and 10 is your relationship with Alexa at its very best, what numeric score would you assign? In order for your relationship to be where you would like it to be, what number would you need to be at? Based on the value that you have given your current relationship, what change do you believe must take place in order for you to be happy with your marriage?

As described in this section, solution-focused approaches can help clients to evaluate their current situations and envision a time from the past and in the future in which the present concerns did not exist. Being able to quantify their evaluations of the situation can serve as a springboard for creating an action plan for change.

Developing a Shared Vision of Assessment and Planning

Preferred reality refers to the client's goal for a changed, improved circumstance. It reflects a postmodern (i.e., clients are the experts about their lives and situations) and narrative assumption that different realities can exist.

Our discussion of the assessment and planning process has emphasized the way in which the social worker engages in a dialogue with the client about the client's history, goals, and dreams. In that process, the social worker collaborates with the client to develop a picture of what could be. It is sometimes difficult for clients to see beyond the obstacles they face. Clients living at society's margins may be accustomed to seeing their dreams defeated. It is the social worker's job to help clients see that their lives can be different, that there are other realities, and that the client can work toward the reality that she or he desires.

For a social worker, maintaining and expressing a hopeful perspective can be a challenge. When you hear very painful stories, it can be natural to feel disheartened. For example, hearing about generations of violence or oppression can be discouraging. The concept of preferred realities benefits both the social worker and the client because the idea that the client's reality can be different helps both develop a hopeful view of the client's situation.

Remember that working toward a preferred reality does not necessarily require replacing poverty with riches or vicious violence with complete harmony. These are attractive long-range dreams, but they will appear elusive and unrealistic in many contexts if the client does not share them. However, such goals should not be ruled out—if the client seeks a goal that may initially seem unrealistic, the social worker can encourage the client to identify small, achievable steps that will move the client toward the ultimate goal. The starting point in any work should be the client's vision for change—not the social worker's vision. The client's vision may involve only small changes in her or his situation. In some cases, clients may frame their visions in clear, small-scale terms, while workers may be drawn to more ambitious transformations. While such perspectives are admirable, social workers should use caution not to overwhelm the client.

© Lisa F. Young

Support for the Client's Goals and Dreams

Consider once again the case of Jasmine Johnson, the single mother you met in Chapter 3. Recall that Jasmine is concerned because she sometimes hits her son when he speaks disrespectfully to her. Jasmine may ask you to help her find another way to respond to him. This request might seem like a relatively concrete goal for behavior change, but it also represents a vision of a preferred reality. Realizing this goal would result in a different mother–son relationship, which could have many positive consequences. Right now Jasmine is asking for help modifying her behavioral response. Her goal might be simply to avoid child protection charges or to reduce the likelihood that her son will respond violently. Therefore, you might work with her to explore her long-term goals. For example, Jasmine might want to establish a more satisfying emotional connection with the most important person in her life. She may not have allowed herself to emphasize feelings in her interpersonal experiences, or she may never have had the time to think that way. Maybe she is simply disinclined to view relationships in terms of personal feelings, or perhaps she has never known anyone who articulated such a goal. It is important to explore Jasmine's view of the situation without imposing your own meanings.

Based on the goals Jasmine articulates, and because you both agree that it is appropriate that you contribute to her work toward those goals, you develop a shared vision of a future in which Jasmine has learned other ways to respond to her son. As you work together toward achieving this vision, other, more encompassing dreams about her relationship with her son might evolve. Your role in this strengths-based assessment and planning strategy is to support Jasmine's dreams, always affirming her potential to achieve them. In order to help Jasmine turn her dreams into reality, you both need to specify her goals and articulate a plan for your collaboration.

Planning and Setting Goals   A thorough assessment is key to effective and, ultimately, successful goal setting and planning process. **Setting goals** gives the work a clear purpose and helps clients recognize the difference between current behavioral concerns and the long view of the dream. Depending on the client's goals and needs, the goals may take on multiple forms. Consider the following varieties of goals in the context of your work with Jasmine:

1. Goals that are *discrete* (a single outcome) or *continuous* (part of an ongoing plan). In Jasmine's case, a discrete goal might be for her to respond differently when her son speaks to her in a disrespectful way, while a continuous goal might be to improve her relationship with her son.
2. Goals that are *framed within different aspects of the client system* (individual, family, group, or community). In Jasmine's case, earning greater respect from others (e.g., family and co-workers) would be this sort of goal.
3. Goals that are related to *various behaviors and behavior changes*. In Jasmine's case, getting a new job or getting her son to speak to her more respectfully would be behavioral goals.
4. Goals that are *dependent on the individual client or that require the involvement of others* (e.g., couple or family). In Jasmine's case, as an incremental goal, invite her son to participate in family meetings with the social worker. (Garvin, 2015, p. 561–562)

There are a variety of ways to measure Jasmine's progress toward her goal of responding differently when her son is disrespectful to her. For example, does Jasmine want to "feel better" about their conversations? Does she want to halve the number of times she is tempted to respond to him physically? Does she want to eliminate those episodes altogether? Does she want him to report that their relationship has improved as evidenced by fewer conflicts? An appropriate measure reflects Jasmine's priorities. By setting priorities, Jasmine and the social worker determine the outcomes that are most critical within a particular time frame. For example, what if Jasmine's son is well behaved two times and then rude once, which provokes Jasmine to hit him? Do his two instances of positive behavior matter in terms of the goal? Is the goal to change Jasmine's behavior or to change her son's behavior?

Establishing goals and measuring progress toward achieving them can be complicated. Nevertheless, it is worth the effort to clarify how each party defines the goal of the work and how each one will know when the goal is achieved. Unless you are in clear agreement on an end point, Jasmine may believe you will work with her on her particular situation until some undefined time when she feels it is "fixed." To avoid misunderstandings, make sure you have a mutual agreement regarding this issue. Setting goals helps both client and social worker evaluate the degree to which their communication is clear, their expectations match, and they are making progress. Agencies and organizations also need to understand the purpose and goals of the work, often in concrete, measurable terms. Chapter 5 will discuss this topic as a function of formal evaluation.

Contracting In **contracting**, the client and social worker reach an agreement about priorities and determine who will do what and when. Developing a clear, measurable, and achievable contract with the client emphasizes the client's role in the planning and intervention and recognizes her or his right to self-determination (Rothman, 2015). Contracts vary greatly depending on practice setting, and they can be formal or informal. The planning document can serve as a formal contract, which is generally a written document signed by both parties. In contrast, an informal contract may be simply a verbal agreement. In crafting a contract, the social worker and client should be in clear agreement on details, including goals, individual roles, ways to change the plan, how progress will be monitored, meeting frequency, and the degree to which each goal needs to be met. Whether formally or informally executed, a contract should include: (1) goals; (2) objectives that emphasize action, timeframe, and strategies for determining success (or failure); and (3) proposed intervention specifying "who" is responsible for "what" aspects of the plan (Rothman, 2015). Whatever the nature of the contract, it is critically important that both social worker and client have a clear understanding of desired outcomes for the intervention. While the assessment and planning components of the intervention are dynamic, ongoing, and can change, social worker and client need clearly stated goals and a clear path to achieving those goals to avoid frustration or even putting the success of the intervention at risk. Quick Guide 9 provides an example of a contract you might find helpful in your work with Jasmine Johnson.

Even the most careful approaches cannot account for every potential obstacle that might arise. Many clients face real disabilities, which may include emotional, cognitive, or physical challenges that make it almost impossible for them to participate in assessment, planning, goal setting, and contracting. Although social workers

QUICK GUIDE 9   SAMPLE CONTRACT WITH JASMINE JOHNSON

Client Name: ____ *Jasmine Johnson* _____

Client Description of Issues to be Addressed:

__ *Relationship with my son* _____

__ *Deal with my anger toward my son when he is disrespectful to me* _____

Goals and Tasks:

Goal	Client Tasks/Timeline	Social Worker Tasks/Timeline	Three-Month Follow-Up
1. *Improve my relationship with my son*	*Begin attending weekly family therapy with my son as soon as an appointment can be made.*	*Within one week, refer Jasmine and her son to a family therapist and communicate regularly with the therapist regarding progress (with Jasmine's informed consent).*	*Social worker made referral and has had three contacts with the therapist. Jasmine and her son are attending therapy regularly.*
2. *Learn better strategies for disciplining my son, particularly when I am angry*	*Participate in weekly parents of teens class and support group (next group begins the first of next month).*	*Within one week, refer Jasmine to parenting class and support group and communicate regularly with the group facilitator regarding progress (with Jasmine's informed consent).*	*Social worker made referral and has had one contact with the therapist. Jasmine is attending class/support group regularly and finding it very helpful.*
3. *Get Devon's father to pay child support more consistently*	*As soon as possible, contact Legal Services Child Support Enforcement office to inquire if they can help.*	*Within one week, provide Jasmine with Legal Services contact information and eligibility requirements.*	*With information provided by social worker, Jasmine has made an appointment at Legal Services.*

Date Contract will be reviewed: __ *We will review the contract on a monthly basis for the next three months*

_____

I agree with the above stated goals, to complete the contracted tasks, and to participate in a review and evaluation of the contract on the specified date.

___ *Jasmine* _____   ___ *Julie* _____
Client   Social Worker

_____   _____
Date   Date

Source: Adapted from Berg-Weger, 2016

should never minimize these obstacles, they need to work directly with the client to the greatest extent possible, bearing in mind that many clients who have experienced lifelong challenges have never before been considered adequate participants in service provision planning. While these clients can make substantial contributions, they may be hesitant or even afraid to participate. Those who have experienced racial or ethnic oppression may have difficulty trusting the mutual assessment and planning process.

In their zeal to develop a plan, address issues, mobilize resources, and establish a contract, social workers may sometimes forget that certain elements of the work (e.g., client's emotional responses to loss and grief) are not as visible or as easy to categorize as others. By the time social workers have listened to clients' stories and collaborated to identify clients' preferred realities, they will probably have heard and felt a lot of emotional content related to clients' experiences. However, they may not recognize the power a client's complicated feelings about change can generate.

For example, whole family systems can be organized around one member's addiction to alcohol. In some families, everyone knows how to respond if Dad is drunk and has passed out on the couch. John, the eldest son, may be the one to carry him to bed; everyone else might ignore Dad, step around him, and pretend his drinking does not happen. Mom takes this opportunity to make decisions about the family finances that Dad once made. These specific patterns may not be as important as the idea of changing them. The social worker must be aware that, although Mom has come to an agency to get help with Dad's addiction because it is destroying his health, their marriage, and their family life, there is a cost to change. Mom may feel uniquely competent when she is put in the position to make major decisions she never made before, or John may take great pride in being able to endure the chaos and even feeling, at times, like the "man of the house." Again, the patterns that contribute to the overall problem are not as important as the disruption of the patterns. If Dad successfully withdraws from alcohol, Mom may have some regrets because she may feel she will have to give up the larger role that she felt forced to assume when Dad was drinking (and began to enjoy) to now return to her earlier role when her husband is more present. Similarly, John may lose his place as competent caretaker, and all members of the family will need to learn to relate to Dad and to each other differently. Renegotiating family roles can have disturbing emotional consequences.

A change in one part of the client system has the potential to change the entire system. Any change a client seeks is embedded in a social context and therefore can generate a powerful emotional response. This response may take the form of reluctance to engage in ongoing collaboration or hesitation when making progress on specific goals. In such cases, consider engaging in a dialogue with the client that goes beyond the specifics of goal setting and contracting to explore the meaning of the change itself in terms of emotional and logistical outcomes as well as the impact of the change on roles, functioning, and patterns.

Honest Responding

Up to this point, you have learned how social workers and clients can identify and work toward a preferred reality. This discussion has emphasized the importance of establishing a shared vision that reflects the client's goals and dreams. However, you might find yourself in a situation in which, after hearing a client's story, you are inclined to challenge her or his priorities. For example, if your client's overall goal is to avoid being arrested again for selling illegal drugs, you might want to contest that goal as a purpose for the social work intervention. You might instead encourage the client to abstain from using and selling drugs or to separate from a drug-using peer group. Conflicts over goals raise difficult questions for social workers. For example, do you have the right to disagree with a client's priorities? Are you inappropriately pushing your values? At the same time, how can you engage enthusiastically to achieve a goal you cannot support?

In these situations, the following questions may be helpful:

- Are you able to maintain objectivity about client goals?

- Do client goals reflect your priorities, values, or cultural practices?

- What are your legal, ethical, and professional commitments in this situation?

- Does not addressing an issue violate an ethical principle, even if the client would rather not deal with it?

- Do you think the client's goals are either unrealistic or not extensive enough?

- What is the value of working toward the client's ill-advised goal?

Although there are no easy solutions when client and social worker do not agree on appropriate goals, you can respond honestly if you "own" your own biases (e.g., you do not agree with the client's prioritization of her or his goals), one of which may be a greater belief in the client's potential than the client seems to possess.

When Confrontation is Necessary   In some situations of acute goal conflict, the worker has to directly confront the client. Consider the Jasmine Johnson case. Jasmine has requested your help to change the way she responds when her son, Devon, talks to her. You learn from Jasmine that she may be physically abusing him. How does this revelation ethically and/or legally affect the assessment and planning process? You may be convinced that you must call the child protection agency to investigate the serious allegations, and those authorities may in turn temporarily separate Jasmine from her son. If this occurs before you can begin to work with her on a different way of relating to him, you may decide that you must postpone that work until after you have established and achieved a new, short-term goal to carry out your professional and legal commitments. The assessment then moves to an intermediate plateau in which you address a dangerous, or potentially

EXHIBIT 4.3

Responding with Honesty

In an early meeting with Jasmine Johnson, the social worker learns that Jasmine routinely punishes her son physically when he treats her in a way that she considers disrespectful. The following is an example of the conversation the social worker is legally and ethically obligated to have with the client. In the conversation, the social worker balances honesty about her legal obligation with an expressed desire to keep working together:

Social Worker:	*Jasmine, it is my understanding from another source that when you feel Devon is being disrespectful to you, you hit him. Is that correct?"*
Jasmine:	*Yes, I just get so mad and he won't listen to me when I tell him he can't talk to me like that. I would never really hurt him, though. I just slap him, just to get him to stop mouthing off to me. I haven't even left any bruises or anything."*
Social Worker:	*I want to thank you for your honesty in confirming the report that I heard. Having a complete picture of the relationship you have with him and the way in which you use discipline can help me to help you find alternative strategies for responding to his behaviors.*

Before we can talk about other ways to handle your situation, I would like to talk about the issue of using physical punishment. We have to be certain that the form of punishment you are using does not constitute physical abuse. I want to make sure that you know that if I have reason to believe that you are physically abusing him, state law and my social work ethical code require that I report that concern to Child Protection Services.

Once a report is made, the agency will send a social worker to investigate. If the report is substantiated or found to be true, the agency will decide if they want to recommend that the court remove Devon from your care and place him in foster care. They could also decide, because you and I are already working together, not to pursue removal but to instead monitor the situation and get regular reports from me. If they find no support for the allegations, no case will be opened. I want to be very certain that you and I are both clear and comfortable with all this information and the possible outcomes. I will want to talk with Devon about those times when the two of you are having trouble. Using the information I have from the both of you, I will make a decision about making a report.

I understand that you may be angry with me for even raising these issues and angrier still if I do feel I have to make a report, but I want you to know that I am legally and ethically obligated to ensure the safety of children. I hope that we can continue to work together, but I understand if you don't feel you will be able to continue working with me.

Jasmine:	*I know you just got to do what you got to do. I don't think you will find that I have been abusing him, so go ahead and talk with him. If he says I have been, then we'll just deal with that.*

dangerous, situation that requires a more immediate (and ethical) response. You will need to be honest with Jasmine about your understanding of the situation and what you see as your ethical obligations; that is, you will need to confront her with the immediacy of reaching your short-term goal and the necessity of temporarily delaying her long-range goals. Exhibit 4.3 provides examples of practice skills that may be helpful when you must face a similar dilemma.

In this scenario, any decision that might lead to a separation between Jasmine and her son does not necessarily disregard her preferred reality of getting along with him better. Ideally, this temporary separation will improve her chances of working on her original goal after the crisis is past. It will be critical in your work with Jasmine to show that you support her dream, even though you must initiate another intervention first. Your honest dialogue with her will reassure her that you share her vision, that you want to help her work toward it, and that you can be trusted to tell the truth.

When Alternatives are Necessary   Occasionally clients need assistance clarifying and articulating their goals and their understanding of the situation. Their goals might seem unrealistic or even grandiose to you. This presents a complex challenge, particularly for strengths-based social workers. One strategy for responding in this type of situation is to help clients develop more realistic goals. To endorse goals that clients cannot achieve is to set them up for failure, which is to do them a major disservice.

At the same time, you are not in the position to determine for the client whether goals are realistic or to define the upper limits of the individual's capacity for growth and change. If social workers are to "hold high our expectations of clients and make allegiance with their hopes, vision, and values" (Saleebey, 2013, p. 19), you should not simply disregard a person's dream as unrealistic. Moreover, many strengths-based social workers insist that clients, like everyone else, have the right to fail in the pursuit of their dreams and important lessons can be learned from failure.

One useful approach in such a situation is to help clients determine the steps involved in achieving their goals. For example, if you are a high school social worker and your client states that she wants to be a physician, together you can consider what level of education she will need, what it might cost, and how long it might take. You should not use this kind of step-by-step discussion to discourage her but rather to provide information. You may then help her consider smaller, alternative goals that could serve as stepping-stones to her larger aspiration. Breaking down goals into workable and achievable subgoals, or procedural goals, can help clients clarify the practical side of their dreams and how far they want to take them. In the high school example, you might consider telling your client,

Let's put together a plan for you to achieve your goal of becoming a physician. The plan might include gathering information on the educational and training require-ments for medical school and completing a residency program. Once we know the

requirements, we can create a plan that includes strategies for each step you will need to take to reach each phase of the goal—what you can do while you are still in high school, the major and experiences you may want to consider for college, and what you can do to make yourself a strong candidate for medical school. What do you think about this idea for a plan?

Using Mapping Skills to Enhance the Dialogue

Your interpretation of the client's story influences the assessment and planning process. Human stories often have many layers and can be difficult to grasp. Frequently, a visual can make the information more accessible and organized. For instance, creating an ecomap or genogram during the first session can be an effective strategy in helping the client present her or his story in an organized way, which aids in your ability to grasp a great deal of information in an efficient manner. In **mapping**, complex phenomena are represented visually so that they can be absorbed perceptually rather than linguistically. Three fundamental types of mapping—genograms, culture genogram, and ecomaps—are discussed next.

Genograms Technically a family tree, the **genogram** usually represents at least three generations and indicates various aspects of the relationships of the individuals included. Exhibit 4.4 presents a sampling of the conventions for indicating these relationships, and Exhibit 4.5 is a genogram for the Sanchez family interactive case (see www.routledgesw.com/caseStudies). When used flexibly, a genogram can portray a broad range of issues and family patterns, such as strained relationships as well as stable marital relationships that can affect individual and family functioning. Using a genogram to review a family's history can add important information to the individual assessment, which may inform your work with a client on a contract. Your client can label the genogram to indicate such attributes as life accomplishments, substance uses/abuses and addictions, financial situations, and health issues, if you want to focus on a single issue. For example, identifying an intergenerational pattern of addictions that exists within her or his family may provide insight to a client struggling with a gambling addiction. Patterns can indicate family strengths as well (e.g., educational achievements or career choices and longevity).

With clients that are vulnerable, genograms should be introduced carefully and with sensitivity. For some people, the visual nature of a genogram may evoke more intense emotions (e.g., a sense of loss or regret) than mere words would. For example, a couple reviewing a genogram may become so distraught at the memory of a relative's suicide that they may abruptly leave a meeting with their social worker.

Like other assessment tools, genograms should be used with care. Genograms are frozen in time; that is, they represent relationships at the moment of the map's creation. They represent one person's perception, and they may seem deterministic,

People in a genogram are represented by the following symbols:

- Males = □ (occasionally represented by the medical symbol of ♂)
- Females = ○ (occasionally represented by the medical symbol of ♀)
- Unborn or aborted children are triangles (Δ)
- X through a person symbol indicates death (usually accompanied by age or year of death)

Relationships are represented by the following symbols:

- Jagged line = hostile relationship ─⋀─
- Strong, solid black line = strong, positive relationship _____
- Slanting vertical lines = separation or divorce (on line that depicts marriage or partnership) //
- Circle enclosing people indicates household
- Perforated line indicates a conflicted relationship with possible estrangement - - - - -

EXHIBIT 4.4

Genogram Symbols

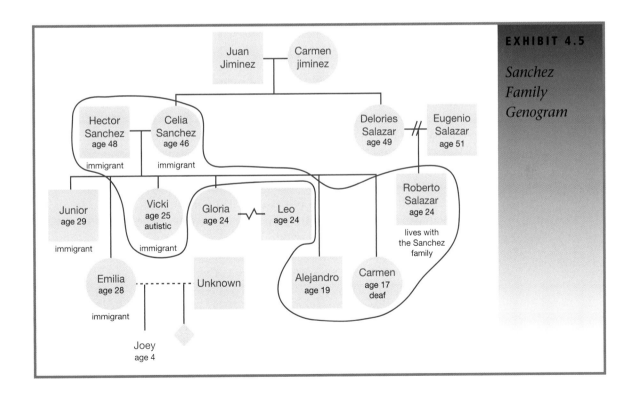

EXHIBIT 4.5

Sanchez Family Genogram

especially when they exhibit family patterns. For example, if a multigenerational exploration reveals that all or nearly all young male members on one side of a family have had major substance use problems, a client may be tempted to see such a pattern as inevitable. When discussing the genogram, the social worker can provide assurance that a family pattern does not doom the client to repeat family members' past behaviors and decisions. Rather, a family history provides context and can help you and your client locate the most effective intervention points.

Ecomaps   A diagrammatic representation of the client's world that illustrates the client's levels of connection to such institutions as schools, religious centers or spiritual practices, the workplace, extended family, friends, and recreation is known as an **ecomap**. An ecomap helps clients make sense of their experience by showing them how their day-to-day world looks and the resources and strengths that exist within that world. Ecomaps can also focus on a particular aspect of the client's life. For example, a social worker involved with children with special health needs can use an ecomap of medical and social supports relating to the child's health status to help shape the intervention. Some ecomaps include a miniature genogram.

Like all mapping techniques, the ecomap may enable your clients to explore patterns of everyday living not initially accessible to them in verbal form. For example, your client may complain about feeling lonely and estranged from the community. An ecomap could reveal that he has very few supports in the community—no satisfying work life, only one friend, no spiritual connections, and no outlet for recreation. Such a diagram would suggest that you expand your dialogue with him into these areas. Here, as always, it is important not to interpret and draw conclusions directly from the map without exploring the meaning of the indicators with the client. Consider the Sanchez family ecomap depicted in Exhibit 4.6 (refer to the Sanchez family case at www.routledgesw.com/caseStudies for more information). Can you identify strengths, resources, and areas for potential intervention in this ecomap? Note the stressful relationship described in the case between Celia and Emilia and that Celia perceives that the relationship is not a reciprocal one (i.e., Celia feels she is devoting more energy to the relationship than she is receiving from it). You can invite Celia to share with you the reasons behind her perception, her emotional response to the relationship, and the implications of her feelings for her relationships with Emilia and with others in the family.

Social workers occasionally use a sequence of ecomaps to evaluate the effectiveness and progress, or lack thereof, of the work. For example, if the client experiencing loneliness wants to expand his social world but fears that prospect, you might work with him to develop safe connections that the two of you could indicate on subsequent ecomaps.

Cultural Genogram   A mapping and assessment tool that facilitates the client's exploration of her or his cultural heritage and deepens your understanding of the

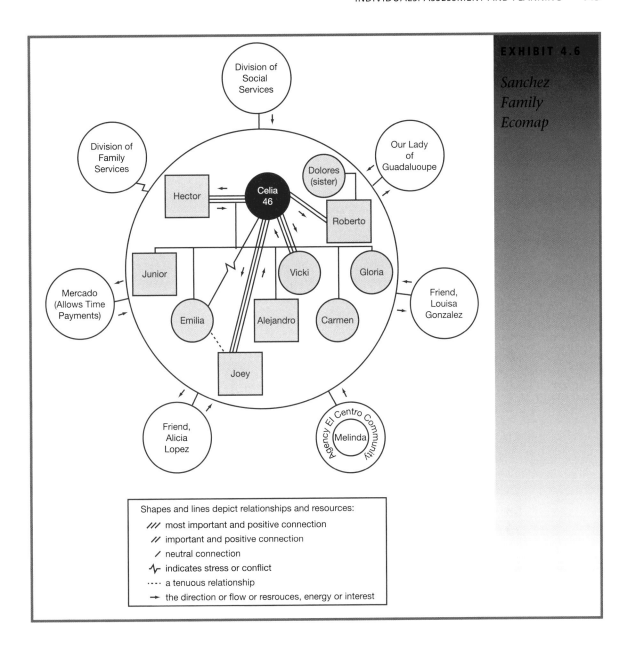

EXHIBIT 4.6

Sanchez Family Ecomap

Shapes and lines depict relationships and resources:

/// most important and positive connection

// important and positive connection

/ neutral connection

∿ indicates stress or conflict

···· a tenuous relationship

→ the direction or flow or resrouces, energy or interest

client's experiences and perceptions is the **cultural genogram**. Similar in some respects to the genogram described earlier, the cultural genogram, originally developed by Hardy and Laszloffy (1995) as a strategy for the training of helping professionals, is completed in three steps: (1) preparation includes identification of and mapping on a genogram culture of origin (the ethnic, racial, and cultural group(s) from which person is descended), the cultural group's organizing principles, and areas of pride/shame; (2) presentation to others; and (3) synthesis by reflecting on one's learning and viewing oneself as a cultural being (Warde, 2012, p. 572–573).

The importance of mapping as a part of the assessment and planning phases of work cannot be underestimated; therefore, the value of developing skills for collecting and organizing client-related information through mapping is a crucial skill for all social workers. There are numerous strategies for mapping client information and selecting the format and strategy that is the best fit with your setting, client population, and services should be your guide.

SKILLS FOR ASSESSING RESOURCES

Even the most skilled workers can rarely provide all the assistance a client needs. Social workers should familiarize themselves with resources available in the larger environment. There are qualities to consider when assessing resources that may be useful in reaching client goals, from their type and source to their availability.

Formal and Informal Resources

Structured opportunities for assistance, which usually take the form of services, are **formal resources**. Training in parent education, financial assistance, caregiver respite, and support groups for children in schools are all examples of the hundreds of services you might be able to name that are helpful to clients. These resources may be available within your organization (internal) or are offered by another organization (external).

Not all resources are formal, however. **Informal resources** may be people, your own creativity, or naturally occurring social networks, like church groups, neighbors, friends, or families. Informal, internal, or community-based assets can be mobilized to better serve clients. Within the practice context, natural helping networks, such as individuals, groups, families, and communities, can be the most important. These resources may endure long after formal resources are no longer involved with a client. For example, many children benefit from regular contact with an older child who befriends them, understands their troubles, or simply supports their abilities. An older adult may benefit from creating peer networks at a senior center or through volunteer work. It is not always necessary to hire someone or obtain a service. Some of the most meaningful relationships emerge from informal contexts of community life.

Assessment When Resources are Available or Unavailable

Your familiarity with both formal/informal and internal/external resources is an enormous benefit to your clients. Simply locating resources is not adequate. You also need to know enough about the client and the resources available from the client, the community, and/or other organizations to estimate the likelihood of a successful interaction between them. For instance, consider the case of a family support worker whose client asks for help managing a child with a chronic health condition. The social worker agrees that some supports would help her client become the effective parent she wants to be. The social worker might recommend some regular breaks from the demands of the child and also some assistance managing the child's challenging conditions. The social worker might then explore the availability of both formal and informal resources. For example, she could investigate informal parent support resources such as childcare cooperatives, family, and friends as well as formal parent support programs, focusing on the collaborative capacity of the trainers. The social worker would also consider concrete issues such as cost and schedule.

Unfortunately, even more careful social workers cannot always locate necessary resources. At some point in your social work, you will probably look for a particular way to help a client and find that it does not exist. Even in these situations, you are not powerless. You have at least two options when adequate resources are not available: You can advocate for improved formal resources, policies, or programs (e.g., updated adult day centers), or you can create resources where none have been developed. For example, you might assist single parents in a housing complex to organize a network of child care where none exists, or help a community write a grant proposal to fund summer youth employment for neighborhood teens.

Social workers need not simply accept, for example, that an uncooperative agency does not respond appropriately to their clients or that a housing project has no child care facilities. Social workers should remain hopeful and energetic in identifying and developing resources but must also be realistic and careful not to promise more than they can reasonably deliver. With clients who may be accustomed to broken promises, social workers foster trust when they are honest about possibilities.

Despite the possible risks, few experiences are more positive or powerful than a successful social action based in client–worker advocacy. Even if the results are somewhat less than hoped for, the process itself can be remarkably empowering for both social worker and client.

Although the scenario describing the tenants' story expands into the phase of intervention, it points to the importance of assessment and planning throughout the client relationship. Assessment and planning drive the intervention stage of the work and, therefore, must also address the action inherent in it.

STRAIGHT TALK ABOUT ASSESSMENT AND PLANNING: THE AGENCY, THE CLIENT, AND THE SOCIAL WORKER

The following discussion addresses a range of issues you will likely encounter as a social worker from agency, client, and professional perspectives. These insights can arm you with the knowledge and skills to respond competently and ethically in your social work practice.

The Agency Perspective

From the agency perspective, during the assessment and planning phase, the social worker needs to openly discuss work methods, schedules, the length of the work, documentation, and agency resources with the client. For example, you need to provide the client with information regarding your schedule, appropriate ways to contact you, the information and format in which you will be documenting your interactions, and which agency resources are available to her or him. Social workers should inform clients about their work processes from the beginning to avoid confusion or frustration as the relationship evolves.

Administrative Tasks With the increasing emphasis on brief, effective, and accountable (i.e., measurable, evaluated, and documented) treatment for individuals, families, and groups, managed care organizations (MCOs) and the Affordable Care Act (ACA) have influenced the assessment and planning process in significant ways (Corcoran, 2015). You may have limited time to complete the assessment, planning, intervention, termination, evaluation, and follow-up processes. Standardized, rapid assessment tools help practitioners complete assessments quickly while maintaining optimal accuracy. In the current service delivery environment, your agency may opt to use a rapid assessment process. There are numerous rapid assessment tools (RATs) to choose from; the key is to ensure the instrument relates to the client's issues and that empirical evidence validates its use with that population (Corcoran, 2015). Exhibit 4.7 provides an example of a rapid assessment for memory function, the Rapid Cognitive Screen (RCS) (Malmstrom & Morley, 2013). The RCS is a shortened version of the Saint Louis University Mental Status Exam (Tariq, Tumosa, Chibnall, Perry, & Morley, 2006). Both tools are psychometrically validated measures of cognitive function. While not a diagnostic instrument, the RCS may be administered in less than five minutes and identifies potential impairment in memory and cognitive function.

To have confidence in the efficacy of a standardized assessment tool, the social worker needs to see psychometric and clinical evidence that it is valid for use with the target population. Utilizing any assessment tool on a population for which it has not been shown to be effective can produce misleading outcomes in terms of age, gender, race, ethnicity, and culture. Evidence-based practice enhances the potential effectiveness of the intervention. Assessment tools can also be used as a strategy for monitoring progress toward goal attainment throughout the intervention and making changes to the intervention as needed (Corcoran, 2015). A note of caution regarding the use of standardized tools in the assessment process: while standardized measures provide helpful data on which to build a plan, they are not designed to "start where the client is," which is the

EXHIBIT 4.7

*Rapid
Assessment
Tool*

Rapid Cognitive Screen (RCS)

Name _____Age_____

Is the patient alert? _____Level of education_____

Please remember these five objects. I will ask you what they are later.

[Read each object to patient using approximately 1 second intervals.]

Apple Pen Tie House Car

Please repeat the objects for me. [If patient does not repeat all 5 objects correctly, repeat until all objects are recalled correctly or up to a maximum of 2 times.]

2. [Give patient pencil and the blank sheet with clock face.]

This is a clock face. Please put in the hour markers and the time at ten minutes to eleven o'clock.

   /2 (points) Hour markers okay

   /2 (points) Time correct

[When scoring, give full credit for all 12 numbers. If the patient puts only ticks on the circle, prompt them once to put numbers next to those ticks for full credit. Do not repeat the time. When scoring the correct time, make sure that the minute hand points at the 10 and the hour hand points at the 11.]

3. **What were the five objects I asked you to remember?**

   /1 (point) Apple

   /1 (point) Pen

   /1 (point) Tie

   /1 (point) House

   /1 (point) Car

4. **I'm going to tell you a story. Please listen carefully because afterwards, I'm going to ask you about it.**

Jill was a very successful stockbroker. She made a lot of money on the stock market. She then met Jack, a devastatingly handsome man. She married him and had three children. They lived in Chicago. She then stopped work and stayed at home to bring up her children. When they were teenagers, she went back to work. She and Jack lived happily ever after.

What state did she live in?

   /1 (point) Illinois

EXHIBIT 4.7

Continued

[Do not repeat the story but do make sure the patient is paying attention the first time you read it to them. Do not prompt or give hints. The answer of "Chicago" as the state she lives in gets no credit by you may prompt them once by repeating the question when "Chicago" is given as the answer.]

SCORING

8–10. . . . . Normal

6–7. . . . . Mild Cognitive Impairment

0–5. . . . . Dementia

_____ **Total Score [0-10 points]**

CLINICIAN'S SIGNATURE   DATE   TIME

Source: Malmstrom & Morley, 2013

cornerstone of the social work intervention, but standardized measures together with information from the client can provide a full picture of the client situation (Grady & Drisko, 2014).

It is also important to inform the client about other formalities related to administrative tasks and financial coverage. For example, if you are required to submit monthly reports to a judicial court, you should discuss this stipulation with your client. Even when clients are not happy about the requirement, they are likely to respect you for discussing it from the outset of the relationship. For another example, if your client must file a Medicaid or third-party reimbursement (i.e., insurance carrier) application in order to continue working with you, explain the need for action as early as possible. For many clients, filing for financial assistance may be a challenge because they may see it as admitting defeat, disability, or help-lessness. It is important to be sensitive to how your client views these aspects of your work together.

Increasingly, community agencies are mandating diagnosis as part of the assessment and planning process. Many institutions now demand a *DSM* diagnosis (from the American Psychological Association's *Diagnostic and Statistical Manual of Mental Disorders)* in order to bill for third-party payment (payment from an insurer). Complying with this mandate can be uncomfortable for social workers who believe strongly in helping clients to identify and use their own strengths. Formulating a psychiatric diagnosis requires a focus on deficiencies and can create a stigma. For example, a school social worker providing support to a 5-year-old whose parents are addicted to heroin may struggle with diagnosing the child with an "adjustment disorder," a label that will appear in school and other institutional records and follow the child for years to come.

If you are uncomfortable making or using diagnoses, you may decide not to accept a position with an agency that requires their use. Students are not likely to formulate diagnoses, but diagnoses inevitably categorize clients, and that categorization can impact the working environment. Others may find the process tolerable as long as it facilitates service provision. Still others may find the use of diagnoses helpful because they enable social workers to use evidence-based practice to provide the best possible service to clients for their challenges, and to collaborate easily with non-social work colleagues who also use the *DSM*. All social workers are ethically obliged to inform their clients when a diagnosis is required to access services. The client can then decide if she or he wants to participate in that exchange. For some clients and social workers, the diagnostic process may seem a small price to pay for receiving appropriate services and possibly medication, whereas for others, the benefits do not outweigh the costs involved in using the *DSM*.

Documentation   Social workers record encounters in virtually every setting, but the requirements and formats for each encounter are typically setting-specific. Social workers need to be able to create a variety of documents aimed at diverse audiences to serve a range of purposes. In work with individuals, social workers complete intake/psychosocial assessments, treatment plans, case notes, case studies, reports to external organizations (e.g., schools and court systems) and communicate in a variety of formats (e.g., memos, letters, and recommendations). Social work documentation begins with the first encounter and continues through each phase of the planned change experience. While documentation processes differ based on the setting and services provided, the purposes for record-keeping can generally be categorized into four categories: (1) opening a case, (2) monitoring progress toward goals, (3) reporting significant events, and (4) closing the case (Weisman & Zornado, 2013, p. 11). Recording information during engagement, assessment, intervention, and termination, evaluation, and follow-up encounters serves a number of key functions, including accountability (need for services, decision-making, evaluation, outcomes, and compliance), supervisory, and administrative purposes; practice enhancements; reimbursement; and planning (Kagle, 2013) as well as legal liability, continuity of care (specifically for case transferal), and coordination of multimember teams (Weisman & Zornado, 2013). Kagle and Kopels (2008) developed fifteen principles of recordkeeping that should be in the forefront of every social worker's practice (see Quick Guide 10).

While agencies' preferred documentation methods vary, some basic components are common. Kagle and Kopels (2008, pp. 38–40) suggest the following structure for creating a written record of the social work intervention:

1. Opening summary
2. Data gathering and social history
3. Assessment

QUICK GUIDE 10   PRINCIPLES OF GOOD RECORDS

- *Client goals* demonstrate balance in competing goals (e.g., accountability, improving practice, efficiency, and client privacy)
- *Agency mission* guides the documentation
- *Management of risk* for the agency, social worker, and client
- *Accountability* for service decisions, compliance, and legal issues is evident
- *Abridgement* (only information that is needed is included in the record)
- *Objectivity* includes observation, sources of information, criteria used in judgment, and appraisal
- *Client involvement* is evident
- *Sources* of information are cited in the record
- *Cultural context* factors are noted as each relates to the client's situation, service delivery, and outcomes
- *Usability* of the record includes organization, cross-referencing, and accessibility
- *Current information* is included in the record and summaries
- *Rationale* for service decisions and actions is evident
- *Urgent* situations are well documented
- Information that is unsupported or not relevant to the client's service status is *excluded* from the record.

Source: Adapted from Kagle & Kopels, 2008, pp. 10–11

4. Decisions and actions resulting from initial assessment
5. Service planning, including service options and purpose, goals, and plans of service
6. Interim notes
7. Special materials (e.g., forms, consents, emergency response, and service reviews)
8. Closing summary

The opening summary portion of the documentation covers the engagement phase of your intervention. Information typically included in an opening summary relates to the client's demographic characteristics (i.e., name, gender, address, contact information, birth/age, family and living composition, education, financial, and/or employment situations, insurance coverage, etc.); reason for requesting or receiving services; and eligibility status. The assessment and planning portion of the client record should include the social worker's observations (e.g., client's appearance and affect), descriptions, and impressions; sources of the information being recorded; criteria the social worker used to make judgments (e.g., formalized measures and information from past history with the agency or referring entity); history of service/treatment received; client perceptions; and social worker inferences and appraisals (Kagle & Kopels, 2008; Weisman & Zornado, 2013). This may be an appropriate place to record perceptions of strengths, resources, needs, cultural factors, and risks related to services that may be delivered.

While formats are agency- or program-dependent, there are elements of social work recording that are common across the profession. Most agencies have structured formats for documenting the assessment and planning process to include client encounters or meetings, intake or eligibility interview, social history, and treatment/intervention plan. Exhibit 4.8 lists the types of information to include in a client assessment; Exhibit 4.9 gives examples of information to include in a suicide risk and harm to others assessment; and Exhibit 4.10 provides an example of information associated with the planning phase to include in a treatment/intervention plan (adapted from St. Anthony's Medical Center, 2010). A typical treatment plan will include (Sormanti, 2012):

- a brief description of the issues to address, including client strengths, resources, and challenges;

- the theoretical orientation in which the intervention is grounded (may be optional);

- goals for intervention;

- specific and measurable objectives;

- an estimated timeline for the intervention;

- the planned intervention; and

- plans for evaluation and review of progress (p. 117).

A second form of documenting practice that social workers find helpful is referred to as **narrative recording**. Narrative recording can allow the practitioner to document client-specific, process-related information (Kagel & Kopels, 2008). Typically written out in complete sentences, a narrative report might include the nature of the client situation, the purpose of the service, service-related decisions and actions, the process of the service delivery, and the service impact (Kagel & Kopels, 2008, p. 125).

As the official record of the social work intervention, social workers must pay particular attention to the accuracy and professionalism of their documentation. Specifically, any documentation should first and foremost be grammatically correct and professionally presented. The document should be clear, concise, specific, factual, and written in an active (versus passive) voice and include no unnecessary or biased information, acronyms, or slang/jargon. Social workers should write their documentation with the assumption that every record could ultimately be subpoenaed for inclusion in a court case; therefore, you should view each word as important and meaningful.

EXHIBIT 4.8	**Demographic Data:**
Information to Include in a Client Assessment	

Demographic Data:

- Name
- Contact information
- Legal status
- All persons participating in assessment
- Presenting need
- Living situation (level of stability and safety)
- Social environment (level of activity, satisfaction, and relationships with others)
- Cultural environment (client satisfaction regarding services and view on help-seeking, and cultural view of help-seeking)
- Religion/spirituality (statement of beliefs and levels of activity and satisfaction)
- Military experience (branch, time in service, discharge status, coping with experience, and view of experience)
- Childhood (supportiveness of family, strengths, and significant events, including trauma)
- Family (composition—parents, siblings, spouse/significant other(s), children, and others; level of support; and family history of mental illness)
- Sexual history (activity level, orientation, satisfaction, and concerns)
- Trauma history (physical, sexual, and/or emotional abuse or neglect and experience with perpetrator(s))
- Financial/employment circumstances (employment status, satisfaction, financial stability, areas of concern or change)
- Educational history (highest level achieved, performance, goals, and challenges)
- Legal needs (arrest/conviction history and current legal status)
- Substance use/abuse (history of addictive behaviors—alcohol, drugs, gambling, sexual, or other). Addiction screen questions include: (1) Have you ever felt you should cut down on your drinking/drug use? (2) Have people annoyed you by criticizing your drinking/drug use? (3) Have you ever felt bad or guilty about your drinking/drug abuse? (4) Have you ever had a drink/used first thing in the morning or to steady your nerves or to get rid of a hangover (eye-opener)?

History of Emotional/Behavioral Functioning:

For each of the following areas, gather information regarding: current status (current, previous, or denies history); description of behavior; onset and duration; and frequency:

- Self-mutilation
- Hallucinations
- Delusions or paranoia
- Mood swings
- Recurrent or intrusive recollections of past events
- Lack of interest or pleasure
- Feelings of sadness, hopelessness, isolation, or withdrawal
- Decreased concentration, energy, or motivation
- Anxiety

EXHIBIT 4.8

Continued

- Crying spells
- Appetite changes
- Sleep changes
- Inability to function at school or work
- Inability to control thoughts or behaviors (impulses)
- Irritability or agitation
- Reckless behavior, fighting, or fire setting
- Stealing, shoplifting, or lying
- Cruelty to animals
- Aggression

Behavioral Health Treatment History:
- Date
- Program or facility
- Provider
- Response to treatment

Mental Status Exam:
- Attention (rate on scale of: good, fair, easily distracted, or highly distractible; and describe behavior)
- Affect (rate on scale of: appropriate, labile (fluctuating emotional status), expansive, constrictive, or blunted; and describe behavior)
- Mood (rate on scale of: normal, depressed, anxious, or euphoric; and describe behavior)
- Appearance (rate on scale of: well groomed, disheveled, bizarre/unusual, or inappropriate; and describe behavior)
- Motor activity (rate on scale of: calm, hyperactive, agitated, tremors, tics, or muscle spasms; and describe behavior)
- Thought process (rate on scale of: intact, circumstantial, tangential, flight of ideas, or loose associations; and describe behavior)
- Thought content (note: normal, grandiose, phobic, reality, organization, worthless, obsessive, compulsion, guilt, delusional, paranoid, ideas of reference, and hallucinations; and describe behavior)
- Memory (note: normal, recent (good or impaired), past (good or impaired); and describe behavior)
- Intellect (note: normal, above, below, or poor abstraction; and describe behavior)
- Orientation (note: person, place, situation, and time; and describe behavior)
- Judgment and Insight (rate on scale of: good, fair, or poor; and describe behavior)
- Current providers (including psychiatrist, primary care physician, therapist, caseworker, etc.)
- Community resources being used (including support groups, religious, spiritual, other)
- Client goal(s) for treatment
- Summary of social worker's observations and impressions

Source: Adapted from St. Anthony's Medical Center, 2010

EXHIBIT 4.9	**Suicide Risk Assessment:**
Information to Include in Assessment of Suicide Risk and Harm to Others	• Name, date, and time of assessment • Clinical assessment (include current suicidal thoughts, obsessions with death or indications of putting one's affairs in order, even with no specific plan). If yes to any items, follow-up questions include: is there a plan, is the plan lethal, is there potential access to plan? • Frequency of thoughts • Intensity of thought (rate on scale of: (1) no pressure to (5) high pressure) • Risk level (rate on scale of: negligible, mild, moderate, or severe) **Harm To Others Assessment:** • Name, date, and time of assessment • Clinical assessment (current thoughts of harming another person). If yes, follow-up questions include: is there a plan, is there a target/victim, and is there potential access to plan? • Frequency of thoughts • Intensity of thought (rate on scale of: (1) no pressure to (5) high pressure; and describe plan and victim) • Risk level (rate on scale of: negligible, mild, moderate, or severe) • Notify referring and/or primary care physician • Complete duty to warn protocol

Source: Adapted from St. Anthony's Medical Center, 2010

EXHIBIT 4.10	**Intervention/Treatment Plan:**
Information to Include in a Treatment/ Intervention Plan	• Preliminary assessment/diagnosis • Preliminary plan for intervention/treatment (to be developed at first visit) • Interventions for emergency/safety need • Other interventions needed • Needs (include identified need, status (active, inactive, deferred, or referred), and reason for deferral or referral) • Strengths • Facilitating factors for intervention/treatment • Limitations • Barriers to intervention/treatment • Other care providers/referrals and purpose (including plan for service coordination) • Plan for family involvement (note if client opts for no family involvement) • Termination criteria/plan • Planned frequency and duration of intervention/treatment

Source: Adapted from St. Anthony's Medical Center, 2010

The Client Perspective

Just as agency issues can present challenges for the social worker, some client situations can be difficult to address in the assessment phase of work. Involuntary, mandated, and nonvoluntary clients; violent situations, including suicidal clients; and crisis interventions all require specialized practice skills.

Involuntary, Mandated, and Nonvoluntary Clients When you first considered social work practice, you may have assumed that clients would come to you because they wanted your services and believed in the possibility, at least, that you would be able to help. The principles of self-determination and working toward a preferred reality seem the opposite of coercion, and some social workers question the appropriateness of working with clients who are required to participate in services. Yet, because of the constant tension between social work's dual roles as agent of social control and agent of change, a significant proportion of clients (in some settings, *all clients)* are involuntary.

Involuntary has several different meanings. In some sense, all clients are involuntary in that few are happy about the crisis (e.g., loss, illness, life change) that led them to need services. Certainly, those who seek public sector welfare services are likely to be involuntarily in their current situation. The distinction between voluntary and involuntary is not always clear-cut, but the profession generally accepts three ways of characterizing public sector welfare clients.

Clients, including mandated and nonvoluntary clients, are **involuntary** if they have been compelled to receive services (Barker, 2014). Typically, some authority (e.g., legal system, employer, etc.) requires **mandated clients** to receive services in order, for example, to reclaim children, escape criminal charges, or avoid institutionalization. Such mandates occur most often in systems of care that are heavily shaped and sanctioned by the law, such as child protection, mental health, and criminal justice. **Nonvoluntary** clients are not formally or legally obliged to participate in services but are pressured into receiving them. For example, an employer may "strongly encourage" an employee with substance abuse issues to seek help for her addiction, or a parent may "take" an adolescent to family counseling. In these situations, the client is in some way persuaded that she or he needs to get services in order, for example, to keep the peace, remain married, or stay employed.

Patterns of engagement with involuntary clients vary and may be unpredictable. Some angry mandated clients may become convinced that they can benefit from genuine involvement and will work for real change. Others will simply go through the motions, sometimes just to satisfy someone else. The whole notion of involuntary clients presents both challenges and opportunities.

Challenges in Working with Involuntary Clients For many social workers, whether they are students or more seasoned practitioners, the idea of working with a client who does not want to be there is uncomfortable, if not daunting. In some cases, this discomfort relates to the social worker's responsibility to interface with the mandating agency, which may seem restrictive or overly authoritarian. In others, social workers might dislike the involuntary client's behavior (for example, the client's engagement in child abuse, criminal activity, or substance abuse). In still others, social workers may be unsure how to build a relationship with an involuntary client. These are understandable concerns, but social workers should not assume that the involuntary client will not engage in or benefit from services.

For a first visit with an involuntary client, prepare yourself to interact with a client who may be angry, hostile, or fearful. If the client assaults you with spiteful or even hateful remarks at the beginning of a meeting, you may feel surprised and hurt; it is helpful to be aware of how you may react and to consider ahead of time how best to respond. In a hostile encounter, strive to remain calm and nonreactive. Clients who are emotionally agitated or distressed may seek to shock or outrage the social worker. A professional response to a client's outbursts can defuse a potentially volatile situation.

Involuntary clients often believe that they do not need anything you have to offer, and they may feel they have valid reasons for this belief (De Jong & Berg, 2013). As a result, they may not truly engage with you. While this may seem to be an overwhelming challenge, it can actually help you refrain from taking angry remarks personally, because the client has no expectations of you and/or makes few demands on you. Another way to prepare for resentment and negativity is to place yourself in the client's position by remembering times you have felt coerced, invisible, unrecognized, or ignored. This memory will help you to empathize and better understand the client's disinclination to trust anyone, including you.

Of course, not all clients will present this level of antagonism. Some may maintain a complacent or controlled demeanor, attempting to prevent you from touching them in any significant emotional way. Some may see meeting with you as an opportunity to think about making changes. Resist the temptation to assume the client is resistant before you start the work. As in any client situation, the most helpful approach is to listen. Find out how the client sees the situation. Ask the client how things could be different, respect the client's view of reality without challenging it, and assume the client has both strengths and competence despite the current predicament. Find out what is important to the client and how she or he wants things to change. This is often an excellent time to ask questions that probe for the client's perspective, because the client's answers can reveal parts of his or her identity beyond the involuntary situation—she or he is not, for example, merely "a B & E" (breaking and entering) or a "shoplifter." If an adolescent who is using substances feels like a "loser" and worthless, you might ask, "What would your best friend say is your greatest strength?" or "What would your favorite teacher say you're good at?" (De Jong & Berg, 2013). For more on approaches that may be useful with involuntary clients, see Quick Guide 11.

In most cases, you will have some externally structured pattern for delivering mandated services. This may be a set number of sessions (such as twelve) or a

QUICK GUIDE 11   INVOLUNTARY CLIENTS

Guidelines for Interviewing Involuntary Clients

- Assume you will be interviewing someone who probably will start out not wanting anything you might have to offer.
- Assume the client has good reason to think and act as he or she does.
- Suspend your judgment and agree with the client perceptions that are at the root of his or her cautious, protective posture.
- Listen for who and what are important to the client, including when the client is angry and critical.
- When clients are openly angry or critical, ask what the person or agency who offended them could have done differently to be more useful to them.
- Be sure to ask for the client's perception of what is in his or her best interest; that is, ask what the client might want.
- Listen for and reflect the client's use of language.
- Ask questions about the client's relationships with others to bring in the client's context.
- Respectfully provide information about any nonnegotiable requirements and immediately ask for the client's perceptions regarding these.
- Always stay "not knowing" (i.e., social worker's focus is on the client's frame of reference, not her or his own).

Source: De Jong & Berg, 2013, p. 184

curriculum to follow. Explaining this structure to your client can help encourage the engagement process. One of the major ways you can assist your client is to give her or him as much control as possible by emphasizing any choices (for example, you may be able to meet once or twice a week, on Tuesdays or Fridays) and by being as clear as possible regarding requirements. Let your client know if the court requires you to notify authorities if she or he misses a single session. Be sensitive to the fact that mandated clients often feel as if control and choice have been taken away from them. Provide all the information you can about contingencies as a gesture of respectful recognition and acknowledge that you are aware that the client does have choices (e.g., to work with you or not work with you), even if the client does not recognize those choices.

In spite of your best efforts to engage your client, mandated or not, you may find yourself having to take a position that is contrary to the client's wishes but may be in the best interests of the client's health, legal status, or safety, including children and older adults. This position can become difficult when you have been trying to respect the client's situation and work with their goals and wishes. For example, do not decide prematurely that the single parent in a child protection scenario is not ready to have her children back or that your older adult client cannot live safely in the community. You want to keep working toward the goals of the client to arrive at a point at which her or his preferred reality can be realized.

There will be times when you may have to take a conscience-driven stand that may seem to work against the client's wishes. For example, if, because of advancing dementia, an older adult is no longer able to maintain the activities of daily living, including cooking, shopping, and bathing, she may not be able to continue living alone in her home. You may recommend that the court seek care for your client in a residential setting. The client may be upset about your recommendation and feel you are not supporting her. In this type of case, make the client(s) aware of your intentions before any court hearing or other meeting. Avoid any surprises that would further violate your client's trust. For example, initiating an honest dialogue (e.g., "This is the way I see it") conveys respect even if the client does not agree with your assessment. Another way to help the client understand the perspective of others is to ask perspectival questions, such as "What do you think the judge might think about the times when you left the baby alone?" (De Jong & Berg, 2013).

Opportunities in Working with Involuntary Clients   Although involuntary situations are not ideal, they are seldom disastrous. Such interactions present the opportunity to engage people who might never undertake change without being forced to seek services. Work with involuntary clients gives social workers the opportunity to practice their most cherished social work skills. Listening to and respecting clients' perceptions, assuming clients can grow, and believing that their situation is workable enables you to engage them in ways that can potentially transform their lives.

Consider the following situation. The court judges a man to be a perpetrator of domestic violence, but because he has a substantial history as a client of mental health services and has just been discharged from a psychiatric facility, your supervisor asks you to meet with him individually. Normally your agency works with men in groups, but your supervisor has determined that this client would not respond well to the potential confrontation of a group. He is painfully embarrassed at being singled out as inappropriate for a group process, angry that he feels he is being treated like a "common criminal," and exceedingly hostile about meeting with you.

Using a basic approach of respect, a willingness to hear him out, and a position of wanting to understand his life, you are able to connect with him after several sessions. He then confides that he has never had the opportunity to talk about the challenging issues in his family and that before your work together, he felt humiliated and stigmatized about receiving mental health services. By the end of the twelve mandated sessions, he wants to engage in further work, and he has come to believe that he can change his violent behaviors by responding differently to stress. This is an example of the way clients may respond to an affirming approach that recognizes their strengths even when they are not initially involved in making treatment decisions.

Any kind of involuntary and especially mandated service involves coercive power. Regardless of the relationship or work that transpires, you may have considerable influence in determining events and actions that will occur in your client's life (e.g., probation, parole, or mandated treatment). In these situations, recognize the power you have, be as comfortable with it as possible, articulate your understanding of the power to your client, and elicit the client's understanding. Transparency about power creates a rich opportunity to demonstrate your genuineness and trustworthiness to clients and to discuss power and what it means to your client. It allows you to balance your roles as agent of social control and advocate for your client.

Focusing on power, especially with involuntary clients, provides a context for discussing client goals and strategies. A client's goal might be as simple as getting authorities "off my back," or it may involve much more complex efforts to change a system that she or he experiences as oppressive. For example, a woman trying to regain custody of her children who has to see you, get clean, get a job, and find a home, all without support from others, might want to join with others in an empowerment-focused approach to influence the system to help her meet her mandates.

Violence While violence looms in our culture, social workers cannot ignore the potential violence that may occur in their lives. From the wars waged overseas to violence in school settings, violence is manifest in ideological as well as interpersonal terms. Social workers frequently work with the effects of a violent culture and are not immune from direct exposure to violent threats in the workplace. The escalation of violence in our lives has become an insidious component of contemporary experience and should be addressed on personal, agency, and policy levels. The following discussion focuses on raising your awareness about your personal safety.

Workplace Violence in Social Work Practice Although it can be comforting to think of violent acts as discrete, chance occurrences, there is often a difficult-to-deny connection between violence and many historical, political, and cultural processes that reflect a cycle of escalation. In addition to being aware of strategies that can be implemented to eliminate the root causes of the violence, social workers must be prepared to respond to violence should it occur. Violence in any setting breeds negative, destructive attitudes and relationships, and periodic eruptions in social contexts reinforce those attitudes and relationships. Social workers must be knowledgeable about and prepared for violence within any practice setting. School bullying, interracial taunting, and sexual harassment are just a few pervasive examples of interpersonal persecution that may affect social work clients. Occasionally these situations escalate into physical violence on an interpersonal or social level in the form of isolated attacks, school murders, or race-related altercations. Some people rationalize violence because they believe it will allow them to meet their basic needs, and our society struggles to eliminate the barriers that prevent people from meeting those needs.

The NASW-issued policy statement calling for the development of organizational policies to address employee safety reflects the social work profession's commitment to minimizing the violence that occurs in the workplace (NASW, 2015c). When social workers observe the growing disparities between rich and poor in the United States and consider the political components that seem to spur people to hate one another, it often prompts them to renew their efforts to work for a just society. Building on the profession's systemic perspective, social workers can examine and advocate for less racist economic policies and welfare reform that does not punish people of color or maintain poverty and can analyze, for example, legal approaches to limiting the availability of weapons, their commitment to antiviolence principles, and their positions on war. These issues affect people at every level of society—from local to global—and as such are in the realm of social justice–oriented social work practice because of the social work profession's commitment to socially just policies and practices.

Considering that practitioners are very likely to work with people who are the most affected by the inequality and oppression that exists within society, it is not surprising that social workers are increasingly the objects of violence themselves (NASW, 2013a). As early as 1995, Newhill documented that "physical and emotional violence by clients toward social workers is increasing in all settings" (1995, p. 631). A recent survey of social service organizations in Massachusetts (Zelnick, et al., 2013) point to five significant findings related to workplace violence: (1) social service providers experience high rates of verbal and physical workplace violence, (2) direct care staff are at higher risk for violence than clinical staff, (3) the underreporting of incidents is likely due to workers' concerns that agency views them as incapable and have an unwelcoming environment for reporting, (4) workers in inpatient settings experience more violent incidents, and (5) the way in which workplace violence is reported is inconsistent (p. 81).

Unfortunately, the trend toward violence against human services workers is not abating as workers continue to report being subjected to verbal and physical assault such as outbursts of anger, profanity, or intimidation. Moving forward in an environment of decreased funding and increased client needs, social workers can and should work with researchers, agencies, and regulatory groups to gain a deeper understanding of the issues that fuel workplace violence and strategies (e.g., orientation, education, client risk assessment, and agency policies and practices to promote a supportive climate) for prevention to ensure preparedness (Kim & Hopkins, 2015; Zelnick, et al., 2013).

Skills for Working with Clients Who are Angry As a social worker in a context of potential violence, you can take reasonable precautions based on common sense and effective communication. Consider the strategies in Exhibit 4.11. Empathy may be the single most useful tool for working with a client who is angry or hostile. Empathic responses (e.g., actively listening while maintaining emotional and physical objectivity and distance) to clients demonstrate that you recognize they are

EXHIBIT 4.11

What Social Workers Can Do in the Context of Violence

- Always inform your client of the time you expect to make a home visit. Keep to that schedule as closely as possible. This is respectful, and you are more likely to be safe if your appearance does not take anyone by surprise.
- Consult with others (especially a supervisor) before entering a situation you think may be dangerous. If your client has a history of violence and is highly stressed or is known to have firearms or other weapons, do not make a home visit or an office visit after hours without talking it over with others who may have more experience and can consult with you about your decision.
- When you leave the office to make home visits, always inform someone about your schedule. Check by phone in worrisome (or all) situations.
- Pay attention to your surroundings. If you are on a home visit and you hear fighting or crying from outside the residence, reassess the timing of your visit and plan to return at another time. If there is activity that seems suspicious and/or is not what you expected, avoid confrontation.
- Do not put yourself in a position to be physically trapped in a potentially violent client's home. Keep a clear path to the door, so you can leave quickly if necessary.
- Connect with the local law enforcement if you work in a dangerous neighborhood or a rural area. Alert them of your plans when circumstances warrant and to the extent that confidentiality permits. Know when police should accompany you, and do not hesitate to ask them when appropriate.
- Do not challenge an angry client with rebuttals or consequences. A calm, kind, and reflective presentation can encourage de-escalation.
- If you sense that something is wrong and you are at risk, even if you cannot tell exactly what it is, leave. There is time for analysis later, and if you overreacted, you can explore that in a known safe environment.
- Report incidents of any kind to your supervisor, or use an agency-designated process if there is one. This both helps you work through your own reactions and skills and facilitates the agency's effective response to its workers.
- Recognize your own tension. Be alert for feelings of defensiveness and prepare yourself to avoid returning angry or hostile comments.
- Acknowledge the client's strengths as you listen and include them in your responses when they can be heard as genuine (rather than patronizing).
- Focus on positive and current alternatives that are realistic and available to the client.
- Avoid moralizing or lecturing, no matter how destructive you think the client's conduct has been.
- When necessary, focus on keeping your own control rather than on the client's anger.

upset, would like to understand the reasons for their distress, and want to assist them.

What Agencies Can Do In situations of potential violence, agencies need to assume some of the responsibility to avert danger. Employers can recognize and validate the hazards to which workers are exposed so that workers will feel supported and will report their experiences openly. Policies for preventing and handling incidents should be clear and worker-focused. Opportunities for reflecting on incidents and safety concerns and group consultation should be frequent and responsive. Preparation for workers entering possibly dangerous situations and debriefing for those who have experienced aggressive or violent clients should be standard practice and should not require that the worker initiate a formal request. Larger agencies should have established policies and practices, including a management team to address violence and should offer training on physical safety and verbal de-escalation procedures that meet worker needs and interests. The social work profession is committed to ensuring the safety of its members in their places of employment and has developed guidelines for social worker safety in the workplace (NASW, 2013a).

Crisis Intervention All social workers must develop competencies for responding to the range of crises they will encounter in their practice. While a life crisis may be the trigger that brings the client to the social worker, each client experiences a crisis in its own unique way. Crises occur when an intense, stressful event disrupts a person's life in a way that she or he cannot resolve using everyday coping mechanisms; when a client perceives a precipitating event to be emotionally meaningful or threatening; or when a client experiences fear, tension, confusion, and/or subjective discomfort following a period of disequilibrium (Yeager & Roberts, 2015, p. 12).

Regardless of the origins of the crisis (e.g., forces over which the client has no control or the result of a poor life choice), the trauma a client feels can be devastating. The social worker's ability to quickly and accurately conduct an assessment and develop an achievable plan can support and empower the client in her or his response to the crisis situation. Crisis situations provide the opportunity for the client to grow and change. It is incumbent on the social worker to have a repertoire of practice skills that can help the client view the crisis experience as an opportunity to strengthen her or his coping skills and even quality of life.

Social workers can benefit from having an evidence-based model, couched in theory, for responding to crises. Two models that lend themselves particularly well to assessing and intervening in crisis situations are Roberts' seven-stage model of crisis (originally developed in 1991) (Roberts, 2013; Yeager & Roberts, 2015) and the solution-focused approach. Roberts' (2013; Yeager & Roberts, 2015) model emphasizes the importance of assessment in an effective intervention plan. Specifically, initiating a rapid and timely assessment of and plan for responding to the client's crisis is a critical first step. In reviewing the seven stages of crisis intervention presented here, note the prominent roles assessment and planning play in the professional's response, both in the initial steps and throughout the intervention (Eaton-Shull, 2015, pp. 217–219; Yeager & Roberts, 2015):

1. Plan and conduct a crisis assessment including lethality, danger to self or others, and immediate psychosocial needs.
2. Rapidly establish rapport and the therapeutic relationship by genuine, empathetic expression of concern.
3. Identify issues pertinent to the client and any precipitants to the client's crisis contact.
4. Use active listening skills to deal with feelings and emotions.
5. During the planning process, generate and explore alternatives by identifying the strengths of the client as well as coping mechanisms the client has used successfully in the past.
6. Develop and formulate the action plan.
7. Establish a follow-up plan and agreement.

Through its emphasis on strengths, solutions, the present and the future (as opposed to the past), and short-term intervention, the solution-focused approach is effective in crisis intervention.

Suicide All situations related to suicide—whether a client is threatening or has attempted to intentionally take her or his life, a family is coping with the suicide of a loved one, or a client experiencing depression is at risk for suicide—present the social worker with an individual or a group in crisis. As with any client crisis, social workers are ethically bound to identify and assess clients who may be at risk for suicide and develop and implement plans to take appropriate actions to prevent suicide attempts. While advocating for the client's right to self-determination is a social work value, preserving life takes priority in the case of threatened or attempted suicide (Freedenthal, 2013). In the practice context, this means that the social worker intervenes when a client has threatened suicide to prevent the client from acting on the threat by contacting authorities or negotiating a no-suicide contract.

The key to effectiveness is rapid and timely assessment and planning. An important first step in preventing a suicide attempt is to conduct a suicide risk assessment (Freedenthal, 2013). In a suicide risk assessment, the social worker asks the client questions focused on any thoughts she or he may be having about death and suicide. The social worker then inquires if the client has developed a plan, a time frame, and/or a means for carrying out the suicide. The social worker then assesses the lethality of the client's plan. For example, does the client have access to the means of suicide that she/he has stated will be used, is the plan well formulated, or does the client talk about giving away personal possessions? These are indicators that the client is serious about ending her or his life. Also, has the client attempted suicide before or does the client have a family history of suicide attempts? Exhibit 4.12 provides an example of one agency's suicide risk assessment that you may find helpful in assessing a client's risk for suicide.

When assessing the potential for suicidal ideation in individuals in vulnerable populations (e.g., veterans, persons subjected to bullying, and LGBTQ youth), the social worker needs a specialized set of skills to competently and sensitively intervene. Considerations for assessing vulnerable populations and planning for action include the following:

- In assessing suicide risk, recognize that your client is likely to have experienced short-term (veterans) or long-term (LGBTQ youth) trauma or victimization and ensure that you do not revictimize or traumatize the client in your encounter.

- Allow the client to determine the pace of the assessment—she or he may or may not want to talk during the first meeting.

- In beginning to engage in the planning process, ask about and reinforce coping strategies that the client feels have helped her or him in the past.

- Use applicable general information and whatever the client shares to come to an overall understanding of your client's experience but do not make assumptions or presume to know her or his individual experience, even if you have gone through something similar.

- Acknowledge that you may have limited time to intervene.

- Do not be overly directive as your client may connect receiving instructions with her or his traumatic experience.

- Encourage the client to be in control as the crisis that brought on suicidal thoughts has likely robbed her or him of the sense of control.

- Do not minimize the crisis or offer positive prediction—you cannot know the client's experience or its outcomes.

- While some clients may find it helpful to share with others who have similar experiences or similar family situations, other clients may not feel comfortable in a group environment, so do not force the issue.

- For effective planning, be knowledgeable about services and resources available to clients by familiarizing yourself with evidence-based intervention practices and best practices for intervening with vulnerable groups.

- Above all else, maintain a nonjudgmental status.

EXHIBIT 4.12

Suicide Risk Assessment

CRISIS WORKER _____   DATE_____   TIME_____

Life Crisis Services, St. Louis   *Suicide Risk Assessment*
Caller Name _____   Phone# _____

1. Are you thinking of suicide? (If yes go immediately to assessment)	2. Have you thought about suicide in the last two months?	3. Have you ever attempted suicide?
Y N	Y N	Y N

RISK FACTORS	RISK LEVELS	LOW	MEDIUM	HIGH	IMMED HIGH

INTENT: *expressed intent to die; availability of means to and opportunity for attempt; specificity of plan; and preparations for attempt.*

Attempt in Progress	no	no	no	yes
Plan to hurt self/other	unclear	some plan	well thought out	
– time frame	in the future	>24hrs.	<24hrs	0–12hrs
– method	unclear	some plan	well thought out	
– location	unplanned	unsure	known	
Preparatory steps taken	none	some	many	
(giving items away, goodbyes, etc.)				
Expressed Intent to die	1	2	3	4

(on a scale of 1–4, with 1 being low and 4 high, when you think about killing yourself, **Details of method:** _____
how much do you really want to die?)   _____

DESIRE: *no reason for living, wish to die, wish not to carry on, desire for a suicide attempt*

Wants to hurt self/others	no	sometimes	most of the time	now
Hopelessness	none	sometimes	most of the time	always
Helplessness	none	sometimes	most of the time	always
Perceived burden	none	sometimes	most of the time	always
Feeling intolerably alone	not at all	sometimes	most of the time	always
Feeling trapped, no escape	not at all	sometimes	most of the time	always
Psychological pain	1	2	3	4

(on a scale of 1–4, how much hurt, anguish or misery are you feeling right now?)

CAPABILITY: *a sense of fearlessness to make an attempt; a sense of competence to make an attempt*

Means available	have to get	close access	have with	used
History of attempts	none	one	2–3 times	>3
Exposure to suicide	no	know someone	close relative/friend	
Hx of violence to others	none	occasionally	frequently	
Alcohol/drug use/abuse	none	average use	excessive use/abuse yes	
Currently intoxicated/impaired				
Recent dramatic mood swings	none	within last month	within last week	daily

EXHIBIT 4.12

Continued

Increased anxiety	none	monthly	weekly	daily
Decreased sleep	none	monthly	weekly	daily
Out of touch with reality	not at all	occasionally	frequently	now
Recent acts/threats of aggression	none	some	many	daily

BUFFERS/CONNECTEDNESS: *how many connectors to meaningful components of life are present?*

Immediate support present	available now	possibly available quickly	not possible
Other social supports	available now	available occasionally	no support
Future plans goals	concrete plans	some plans	no plans
Purpose in life	strong purpose	some purpose	no purpose
Ambivalence about death	much	a little	none
Beliefs about suicide	against belief system	belief system ambiguous	no belief system
Rapport with Crisis Worker	very engaged	somewhat engaged	not at all engaged

We've been talking for a while now . . . can I ask you about how you're feeling now? On a scale from 1–4, how likely are you to kill yourself?

	1	**2**	**3**	**4**
ENDING RISK	low	medium	high	Imm-high

____follow-up

scheduled   ____Pager called   ____traced call   ____Police called

Source: Life Crisis Services, n.d.

Exhibit 4.13 provides a sample dialogue between a social worker and a youth who expresses suicidal thoughts.

EXHIBIT 4.13

Suicide Risk Assessment with Vulnerable Populations: A Dialogue with Christopher

You are a social worker working in a multiservice not-for-profit agency that serves youth who are at risk. Your organization provides crisis intervention, emergency shelter, transitional and independent living, mobile street outreach, educational and employment programs, and individual and family treatment. You are conducting an initial intake interview and assessment the morning after Christopher arrived at the emergency shelter. Follow along with the interview below to learn more about assessing a client who is particularly vulnerable:

Social Worker: *Christopher, it's good to meet you. What brings you to our shelter?*

Christopher: *My parents kicked me out a couple of weeks ago. I've been staying with different people, just sleeping on their couches.*

Social Worker: *How are you feeling today?*

EXHIBIT 4.13

Continued

Christopher: *Okay.*

Social Worker: *Do you want to talk about your parents kicking you out of the house?*

Christopher: *They don't like my lifestyle, so they wanted me out of their house.*

Social Worker: *What is it about your lifestyle that you think they don't like?*

Christopher: *They found something and flipped out.*

Social Worker: *What did they find?*

Christopher: *Well, actually, they saw an email between me and my boyfriend.*

Social Worker: *What was it about the email they had a problem with?*

Christopher:`   *It's that I have a boyfriend. Turns out they didn't know I was gay.*

Social Worker: *Sounds like they didn't take it well?*

Christopher: *You could say that. . . .*

Social Worker: *How are you coping?*

Christopher: *So, my boyfriend breaks up with me because my parents called his parents, and now his parents won't let him see me anymore. They say I'm a bad influence. I'm just done. If my parents don't want me and my boyfriend doesn't want me and I don't have anywhere to go, then I'm just outta here.*

Social Worker: *When you say you're done, what do you mean?*

Christopher: *I mean . . . what's the point?*

Social Worker: *Again, let me ask what you mean.*

Christopher: *What's the point of living if I don't have a place to stay and nobody cares what happens to me?*

Social Worker: *It's your mention of "point of living" that concerns me. Are you saying you would think of ending your life?*

Christopher: *Yeah, I guess that's what I'm saying. I don't have anything to live for, do I?*

Social Worker: *Have you thought how you would do that?*

Christopher: *Yeah, I guess I have. There's a lot of times lately that I've sat at the Metro stop and thought how easy it would be to just step in front of that train. It would just end all the pain, you know, for everybody.*

Social Worker: *Do you have a time frame for when you thought you might do that?*

Christopher: *No, just been thinking about it sometimes.*

Social Worker: *What's keeping you from doing it?*

Christopher: *My friend, he saw this flyer at the Metro stop about you guys, and he said I should call. So, I did. I don't know what you can do to help though.*

Social Worker: *That was a good idea. That took courage for you to call. I'm glad that you came in. Let's talk about how we can help you to deal with some of these feelings you have without you hurting yourself.*

EXHIBIT 4.13

Continued

Christopher:	*{Silence. . . . he begins to cry}.*
Social Worker:	*I see this is emotional for you. Can you share what's going on?*
Christopher:	*I don't really want to die. It just seems like it's the easiest choice.*
Social Worker:	*Let's talk about something that would help you to be able to not follow through with this plan. Would that be okay?*
Christopher:	*Maybe.*
Social Worker:	*Let's talk about an agreement that includes some alternatives for when you are feeling bad.*
Christopher:	*Like what?*
Social Worker:	*We can both come up with ideas, write them down, and even sign them . . . just like a contract.*
Christopher:	*What kind of things?*
Social Worker:	*For instance, what makes you feel good?*
Christopher:	*Listening to my music.*
Social Worker:	*What is it about the music that makes you feel better?*
Christopher:	*I just connect with it.*
Social Worker:	*How about if you agree that when you are feeling bad, you will listen to your favorite band?*
Christopher:	*I guess maybe I could agree to that.*
Social Worker:	*What else do you do that makes you feel good?*
Christopher:	*Getting high.*

At this point, the social worker and the client go on to discuss healthy and unhealthy coping strategies and the long-term consequences of each. Eventually, they agree on a list of alternatives to suicide, which they write down. Each signs the contract, they make copies, and they agree to revisit the contract within the week. The social worker offers Christopher shelter and makes an appointment to meet in the new few days. Christopher agrees to talk with a shelter staff member if he begins to have feelings of harming himself.

It is critically important that the social worker have knowledge of agency and legal procedures to immediately and appropriately respond to suicidal ideations, threats, or attempts. Mobilizing an emergency response is imperative. Responses may include negotiating a contract in which the client agrees not to attempt suicide, involving members of the client's support network or community, facilitating the prescription of antidepressant medication, and/or seeking hospitalization for the client. Regardless of your response, a thorough and immediate assessment is critically important for your client.

The Social Worker Perspective: The Social Worker as a Whole Person

Just as it is necessary to be attuned to safety issues, social workers must be sensitized to their own physical and emotional health. As you have seen, challenges in social work practice may result in the social worker experiencing negative emotional and physical responses to their work situations. Working with clients who experience oppression and trying to help with inadequate resources, engaging involuntary clients who may challenge your capacities, confronting a violent culture and avoiding its direct expression against you, coping with the bureaucratic tensions of managed care—all of these may seem to confound and certainly challenge your best intentions in the practice of social work. Social workers' negative reactions to their practice experiences can result from work-related stress, secondary trauma from working with clients who are themselves experiencing trauma, and real or perceived lack of resources and support (Wagaman, Geiger, Shockley & Segal, 2015). When added to the pressures of adhering to organizational policies and practices (discussed in Chapters 10 and 11), social workers can experience frustration and alienation if they do not develop effective self-care strategies.

Social workers encounter phenomena in their work with clients that are particularly difficult to manage: learning about clients' painful events and the occurrence of events that trigger negative personal responses. Social workers need to develop self-care strategies to deal with the stresses that can lead to **secondary trauma**, **burnout**, and/or **compassion fatigue**. [EPAS 1] Secondary trauma can occur when helping professions react to the pain clients are experiencing, while burnout is a stressful response to the work. When both secondary trauma and burnout occur, the social worker may experience compassion fatigue, which is characterized by feelings of apathy, anxiety, depression, and hopelessness (Barker, 2014, p. 83). Given the intensity of social worker–client relationships and demanding work responsibilities, social workers, particularly in the early stages of their careers, are at risk for negative outcomes, including physical health problems, and should commit to a proactive approach to self-care (Kim, Ji, & Kao, 2011).

Painful Events Although most of social work practice deals with struggles clients experience, many (probably most) practitioners at one time or another encounter a particularly jolting event that shakes their confidence and makes them question their capacity or commitment. This event is often a crisis—for example, a client suicide, a murder, an unspeakable case of child abuse or neglect, or an annihilating fire. Such events can take a generally well-balanced human being off guard. Social workers who are usually able to cope without considerable difficulty may be reluctant to recognize or acknowledge when they have an unusual reaction. Ignoring the signs of secondary trauma can be dangerous for a social worker's own stability and ability to bounce back. Social workers need to allow themselves to be human in this profession, and the experience of overload, rather than showing that a social worker is somehow deficient, can reflect the traits of a caring, human person.

When isolated situations such as these occur, the social worker should seek and receive as much support as possible. Time away from work, debriefing sessions, or a shift in responsibility may be indicated. Supervisors should always assure social workers that these responses are appropriate to the situation; that is, the responses should be **normalized**. With appropriate supports and adequate time, most workers will come to terms with such situations and return to their practice as committed as they were before.

Personal Triggers In a related scenario, the social worker may have some unresolved or not-quite-resolved personal issues that affect her or his capacity to carry out the work of the agency. For example, a social worker who experienced abuse as a child may harbor a great deal of rage. While anger may be understandable and normal, it can be a serious problem if, for example, the social worker verbally or physically attacks a client who may be suspected of child abuse. In such cases, the agency is likely to address the issue administratively or with corrective action. Here, the social worker can engage in a process (i.e., therapy or education) to effectively change her or his behavior. An extreme reaction can be a difficult experience for someone who is committed to the profession and has the capacity to make a solid contribution. The intensity of the trigger situation can lead a social worker to self-assess as inadequate and not suited to the profession. However, appropriate consultation with a qualified professional (e.g., supervisor, mentor, or mental health practitioner) can help many social workers who experience an intense reaction to work through the emotional aspects of that reaction in order to reconcile the personal and the professional. All helping professionals can be triggered, so this phenomenon can be somewhat normalized. While no professional can claim perfect balance, social workers are obligated to identify and respond to those triggers that may impact their own personal and professional well-being.

A concern that arises for social workers, particularly in the early stages of their careers, is overempathizing with a client and developing feelings of sympathy, which they fear can take an emotional toll and ultimately become compassion fatigue. While some believe in this causal possibility, Nilsson (2014) contends that being overly compassionate about a client's situation does not result in compassion fatigue but can potentially create feelings of distress. Having the ability to regulate one's emotions, a supportive work environment, and a well-established self-care plan can aid the social worker in finding a balance when relating to clients.

While all social workers are at risk for compassion fatigue, most social workers actually experience **compassion satisfaction**, which, simply stated, is the positive aspect of helping others and driving pleasure from the work you do and those with whom you work (Stamm, 2010). Not surprisingly, social work students who experience lower levels of compassion fatigue report higher levels of compassion satisfaction, suggesting that finding balance and gratification from one's work mediates the negative effects of the stressors (Harr, Brice, Riley, & Moore, 2014). With increased awareness about the potentially negative outcomes associated with the practice of social work, students and practitioners are well served by committing themselves over their careers to self-care.

Self-Care   Even as they care for clients, social workers need to care for themselves. As in the case of safety, the profession has issued a policy statement deeming self-care a priority for all social workers, from students to individuals to administrators (NASW, 2015c). Although this process takes on different dimensions in different people, strategies that may prove useful include:

- *Learn to use yourself as a resource:* Knowing your own responses, biases, and limits in various processes of your work is a first step in self-care. Appreciating your strengths and accepting your vulnerabilities will help you make good practice connections with clients and avoid expecting too much of yourself, which frequently leads to feeling disheartened. In the face of extensive client need, you may expect to save the world and inspire clients to love you while you do it. When you know that about yourself, you can laugh at your own grandiosity, let go of the need for all clients to like you, and continue to strive for competent practice.

- *Understand shared power:* Within a model of planned change that includes engagement, assessment, intervention, termination, and evaluation, the strengths perspective assumes that clients have the ability to control their lives and do not need you to do it for them. Such an approach carries the benefit of reducing the pressure to be all-knowing and all-delivering, expectations that can be burdensome and harmful to clients and professionals. In essence, you do not have to assume responsibility for clients' behaviors; you cannot be responsible for any behavior other than your own.

- *Focus on practical goals:* If you strive to rid the world of all evil, you will always be disappointed and will continue to fail. When you concentrate on client strengths and their capacity to achieve their own goals, and when you stress social justice and human rights in ways the client can relate to, you are more likely to see joint successes. This in turn can bolster your commitment.

- *Find your own support systems:* Social workers understand how important support is for clients but may underestimate its value in their own lives. Support, inside and outside the workplace, is critical. Developing a group of peers at work can be helpful and enjoyable. Such a collective can function as a peer supervisory/support network, or it can be a strictly social group. Friends outside of work and family are also critical. Spiritual support, whether a formal religious affiliation or a more informal spiritual connection, can help put the occasional but inevitable disappointments and frustrations of the work into a perspective that helps keep you from feeling overwhelmed.

- *Prevention education and awareness:* Through education focused on self-care, increase your awareness of the risk and consequences associated with social work practice, particularly related to your own triggers (Harr et al., 2014). With increased awareness, you can identify effective coping strategies such as time management, problem solving, self–other awareness (i.e., separating yourself from others through maintenance of appropriate boundaries), recognizing and sharing your feelings with clients while regulating your emotions through mindfulness and controlling physical and verbal reactions (Harr et al., 2014; Wagaman et al., 2015).

- *Live healthy:* Balance compassion with humor, nonwork interests, and regular, healthy leisure activities (Harr et al., 2014).

Although social work will never be an easy job, it need not be overwhelming. Recalling the joys and connections of working with people can fill out the compensation side of the balance sheet. Taking control of your own reactions and caring for yourself will enhance your capacity to stay committed.

Just as social workers emphasize the whole client in context, they need to think of themselves as whole people, too. This means that they are not just social workers. Like clients, they are children, partners, bicycle racers, amateur politicians, musicians, parents, belly dancers, and artists. They are successful in some roles and need to improve in others. They may connect well with involuntary clients and yet steer away from children or older adults. They may be stimulated by institutional settings or find them hopelessly oppressive. They may be passionate about working to change urban agency policies, or they may thrive in rural locations where the sole agency has no walls and policy is an on-the-go venture.

Social workers may be subject to restrictions related to social justice themselves. Their identities are privileged in some contexts and devalued in others. When you see yourself as a whole human, belonging in a context, you will be more likely to engage in your work with enthusiasm and vigor.

Sustaining Ethical Practice in the Face of Challenges The *Code of Ethics* (NASW, 2008) requires social workers to care for themselves and to practice ethically in spite of setbacks; to keep growing in response to new ideas, perceptions, and client-informed experience; and to maintain a vision of what ethical social work practice can be and how they can contribute. The struggles social workers face can sometimes obscure ethical aspects of practice. Just as practitioners need to guard against rationalizing funding cuts or avoiding client contact, they need to keep the ethical considerations of omission as much in mind as those of commission. For example, not working for active reform of harmful systems (omission) is as neglectful as committing an outright violation of the *Code of Ethics* (NASW, 2008). If workers increasingly withdraw, defending themselves against the challenges of dehumanizing contexts, they can slowly lose the spirit of ethical practice without even realizing it.

One of the most effective ways for social workers to enhance practice experiences and reduce the risk for work-related stress and turnover in their positions is to have the benefit of a positive and supportive supervisory relationship (Kim & Barak, 2015) in which both the supervisor and the social worker can grow. As the social worker, you can contribute to that relationship by bringing something to the process; supervision is not a passive relationship but, rather, an interactive relationship. The term *supervision* may evoke a hierarchy. Literally interpreted as "watching from above," it suggests an authoritarian relationship in which one member judges and corrects the other. Fortunately, social work supervision is not limited to that configuration, in spite of the inevitable evaluative nature of the term.

Supervision in all its forms—individual, group, ad hoc, formal case, and peer— has the potential to contribute a great deal to sustaining ethical practice in challenging contexts. Hearing others' beliefs about the issues involved in a challenging practice situation, for example, can expand your thinking and help you work through the values and ethics of situations in which you feel immobilized or perplexed. Effective, collaborative supervision can provide technical support in that it has the potential to increase and improve your practice responses. It can also provide emotional support, reducing isolation and increasing hopefulness. See Exhibit 4.14 for tips on effectively engaging in supervision.

- Be prepared for each session by reviewing your work and identifying the issues you want to discuss.
- Demonstrate a genuine eagerness about learning more and expanding your knowledge and experience base in practice.
- Take responsibility for your work, your thinking, and your reactions.
- As much as possible, trust in the supervisory relationship so that you do not need to cover up mistakes or deny any struggles you have with the work.
- Be willing to take thoughtful risks.
- Understand the parameters of your work and the expectations your agency/supervisor has of you.
- Respect the difference between the focus of supervision (how an issue affects your work) and the focus of psychotherapy (how an issue affects your emotional life).
- Remain open and nondefensive if/when your supervisor suggests you do things differently.
- Demonstrate a respectful and professional approach to relationships with all colleagues, including your supervisor.

EXHIBIT 4.14

Tips for Using Supervision Effectively

<table>
<tr><td>

GRAND CHALLENGE

Eradicate Social Isolation

</td><td>

Identified by the American Academy of Social Work and Social Welfare Grand Challenges for Social Work Initiative as one of the most challenging social problems facing our society, social isolation is an issue that affects the physical and mental health of persons of all ages. As noted by Lubben and colleagues, authors of Grand Challenge Working Paper No. 7, *Social Isolation Presents a Grand Challenge for Social Work* (2015):

> Solid epidemiological evidence links social isolation to health. Both the World Health Organization and the U.S. National Institutes of Health have affirmed the importance of addressing social isolation. The American Association of Retired Persons (AARP) also has recently adopted social isolation as one of its top five new initiatives. Working in tandem with other key professions, social work possesses the unique expertise to greatly reduce the risk and consequences of social isolation by strengthening social ties among all populations (p. 1).

Created in response to an urgent need for change, the challenge to eradicate social isolation in our society calls upon the social work profession to collaborate within and outside the profession to conduct research and work with individuals, professionals, and organizations. The goal of this call to action is to develop and test interventions for individuals at risk for or experiencing social isolation in their communities (Lubben et al., 2015). In a comment in *NASW News* (Laurio, 2010), one of the authors of this Grand Challenge, Johnson, states that social workers are "uniquely positioned because our training has us looking at patients holistically. . . . Our training has taught us to look deeper, more broadly, at a person's situation. Social workers look at social health, mental health, and physical health as a complete picture" (p. 9).

The issue of social isolation has particular relevance in this chapter, which focused on assessment and planning with individuals as many clients who seek services from social workers are at risk for or may be experiencing marginalization as a result of physical or functional impairment, limited financial resources, mental illness, and lack of social connections and support. To familiarize yourself with the issues related to social isolation in children, youth, and older adults, visit the Grand Challenges website and read Working Paper No. 7, *Social Isolation Presents a Grand Challenge for Social Work* (Lubben et al., 2015) at: http://aaswsw.org/grand-challenges-initiative/12-challenges/eradicate-social-isolation/. (See Exercise #a1 for additional exploration of this Grand Challenge.)

</td></tr>
</table>

CONCLUSION

In an effort to help you experience the contemporary climate, this chapter has addressed a range of practice issues and skills related to assessment (including the very idea of assessment) and planning along with a variety of difficult and challenging issues that exist in social work practice today. Clearly, the assessment and planning processes involve a broad combination of efforts and tools. There are literally hundreds of instruments social workers can use depending on the practice setting, type of client served, and range of issues. Your agency will use a few selected instruments consistent with the mission and focus of the agency's services.

Social work assessment and planning are integrated activities that arise out of an effective engagement with the client and progresses into the action-oriented intervention phase of the work. The tone and focus of the assessment and planning processes should be consistent with the practice process as a whole. Assessment and planning continue throughout the practice process, sometimes shifting the work depending on changes that occur within the client's life situation.

MAIN POINTS

- Assessment involves dialogue to discover the goals and aspirations of the client while planning emphasizes the collaborative development of action steps aimed at achieving the client's goals and aspirations.

- The theoretical perspective the social worker uses has significant implications for the assessment, planning, and intervention processes. This chapter discussed six theoretical frameworks: psychoanalytic, attachment, cognitive, strengths-based, narrative, and solution-focused.

- The social worker develops a shared vision with the client by respecting and honestly responding to the client's preferred reality.

- Mapping is a useful addition to verbal assessment and planning. Two types of maps many social workers use are genograms and ecomaps.

- Assessment and planning evaluate the types of resources, both formal and informal, that the client and the client's environment can bring to bear.

- When resources are not present, adequate, or available to clients, social workers need to respond creatively and appropriately. In some cases, social action is needed.

- Assessment and planning move from a shared vision to the specific details of the intervention. Internalized oppression and the emotional impact of change can influence the entire assessment process and the client's capacity to participate in planning.

- Social workers are ethically bound to be clear and honest with clients about specific agency constraints and requirements that will influence the client's experience of the work.

- Social workers can meet the challenges of working with involuntary/mandated/nonvoluntary clients if they adequately frame these challenges and approach these clients with basic respect and a willingness to listen.

- Violence is a pervasive quality of U.S. culture that influences the work of the social work practitioner and that can affect her or his personal safety. Social workers can engage in social justice–oriented practice to try to minimize societal violence, and they and their agencies can develop skills and policies to deal with situations of potential violence associated with clients.

- Secondary trauma, burnout, and compassion fatigue reflect physical and emotional exhaustion in a complex practice context; these may arise out of painful events and personal triggers and can be mitigated through appropriate agency and social worker response.

- Holistic self-care is consistent with ethical practice, and it can carry you through difficult moments. As in your work with clients, think of yourself as a whole person, with strengths, vulnerabilities, and a need for your own support systems.

- Effective supervision is a useful interactive relationship for negotiating difficult practice contexts.

EXERCISES

a. Case Exercises

1. To integrate the issues of social isolation into social work practice, review the case of Carla Washburn at www.routledgesw.com/caseStudies and respond to the following items:
   a. Which of the social isolation risk factors identified in Working Paper No. 7 are present in the information on Carla Washburn?
   b. What is your assessment of Carla's level of emotional and physical well-being, social supports, needs, and risk for social isolation?
   c. To help you develop an assessment and plan for working with Carla, view the two videos located at www.bc.edu/centers/ioa/videos/social-isolation.html. Incorporating the information provided in the videos into your assessment of Carla, create a plan for intervening with her.
2. Go to www.routledgesw.com/caseStudies and review the case file for Emilia Sanchez, including the genogram and ecomap of the family for both its content and form. Click on the Assess tab and view the tasks you will need to complete. To prepare for this exercise, also review "Focus on Strengths" in the Values Inventory.

   Using Emilia as the anchor family member, develop two genograms. The first should reflect her relationships prior to age 14 and the second should be an "update" to her current age of 24. Include as much information as possible while ensuring that the drawing is informative and clear. After completing the first genogram and before completing the second, develop an ecomap that represents your interpretation of the systems and networks supporting Emilia's "change" (her involvement in drugs) that might have led to her estrangement from her family.

In class, partner with another student and exchange the three drawings. Are they similar? In what respects do they differ? What information is particularly helpful? What facets of Emilia's life are most effectively represented in a social mapping format? Which ones are the most challenging?

3. Go to www.routledgesw.com/cases and review Emilia's video vignette. After viewing the vignette, complete the following exercise.

Emilia Sanchez has come to you for help because she has decided she must conquer her substance addiction. Emilia's long history of substance abuse, her family's outrage regarding the out-of-wedlock birth of her son Joey, and the following abortion of another child resulted in her feeling discouraged. Specifically, she doubts her ability to make a place for herself in the family again and to make the changes she wants to make. Using the strengths perspective, the social worker can identify and assess Emilia's strengths. Respond to the following:

a. What was the most challenging aspect of identifying the strengths of someone who has had the number of challenges Emilia has experienced?

b. How do you as the social worker encourage Emilia to recognize her strengths?

c. Identify the strengths the social worker in the vignette points out.

4. Go to www.routledgesw.com/caseStudies and review the case of Carla Washburn. Click on Phase 2: Assess the Client System. Review the goals for this phase and complete Tasks #1, #2, and #3.

5. Go to www.routledgesw.com/caseStudies and review the case of Hudson City. Address each of the following areas:

a. Click on Engage and Discover. Select Case Files and review Your History, Your Concerns, and Your Goals. Respond to the questions posed under Your Goals.

b. Continuing with the engagement phase, click on Critical Thinking Questions. View Your Questions and respond to each question.

c. Moving to the assessment and planning phase, click on Assess the Situation. Select Biopsychosocial Perspectives. Review the biological, psychological, social, and spiritual lenses and respond to the questions related to each area.

6. Go to www.routledgesw.com/caseStudies and review the Brickville case. Address each of the following areas:

a. Click on Engage and Discover and complete the Tasks for this section with specific emphasis on strategies for engaging Virginia and other key persons in her life.

b. Review the ecomap centered on Virginia Stone and her family. Identify all relevant linkages Virginia has within her family and community, the character of those relationships, and strengths and areas for changes.

c. Review the Town Map and develop a list of Virginia's needs on the individual, family, group, and community levels.

7. Go to www.routledgesw.com/caseStudies and review the case of Hudson City. Two professional issues are relevant to the social worker in this case: dual relationship and self-care (compassion fatigue). After reviewing the case materials, conduct a literature search regarding one or both of these issues and develop practice strategies that are appropriate for your future as a social worker.

b. Other exercises

8. To begin the process of developing engagement, assessment, and planning practice skills, complete the following role-playing exercise. Begin by partnering with two other students.

Using Confrontation: Engage in brief re-enactments of the following scenarios with each student assuming the role of the social worker, the client, or the observer. Use the engagement and assessment behaviors highlighted in this chapter to role-play the beginning phases of work with clients in these situations. Upon completion of the role-play, each member of the triad will provide balanced feedback regarding the others' performance of skills. Select from the following list of potential client scenarios:

a. Client sporadically attends scheduled sessions.

b. Client reports that when she was angry with her 10-year-old son at the mall she spanked him in public.

c. Client is having difficulty obtaining employment. You recognize that the client's style of dress and hygiene may be a concern for employers.

d. Client continues to use language that you find offensive.

e. Your colleague is not completing tasks and you are experiencing negative consequences.

Upon completion of the role-play activity, reflect with your group (or in writing) on situations in which you have been involved that resulted in a confrontation between you and another person. If you cannot recall such a situation, remember a situation in which a confrontation may have been appropriate but did not occur. Imagine in that situation that you were confronted by a caring individual in your life. What was your reaction to being confronted? How did you receive feedback? How do you give feedback? How comfortable are you confronting others? What were the benefits to being confronted?

9. Review and discuss with other students the following situations. Evaluate your level of comfort in them. What makes you comfortable or uncomfortable? Be specific. Upon completion of the discussion, brainstorm with other students strategies for maintaining your safety.

a. Conducting a home visit

b. Working after dark at your agency

    c. Driving a client to an appointment

    d. Working with young males (if you are female) or females (if you are male)

    e. Working with individuals with mental illness

    f. Working with individuals with substance abuse issues

    g. Having an initial meeting with a client who is unknown to you

    h. Working with a client with a criminal record

10. Returning to the scenario at the beginning of this chapter that involved Barbara and her baby, develop a plan for conducting the assessment and planning phases of the social work intervention using one of the theoretical frameworks discussed in this chapter with attention paid to the biopsychosocial-spiritual, cultural, and mapping information that would enhance the assessment and planning process. This activity may be completed as an in-class role-play or discussion with other students or as a written exercise.

11. Exploring your own cultural heritage is an important part of becoming a culturally competent professional. Select one of the following options to gain insights into your journey:

    a. Quick Guide 7 provides questions to consider regarding the cultural heritage journey each of us takes the cultural heritage journeys of both clients and social workers impact their perspectives on life and work. Consider the following:

- Where do my family's roots begin?
- If my family immigrated to the United States, how long has each of my parents been living here?
- If I am in an adoptive family, what do I know about my biological family's cultural heritage?
- What traditions has my family passed down through the generations?
- Do my family's traditions relate to religion or spirituality, holidays, rituals, and/or significant events for the family?
- What values surrounding ethics, wealth, religion and spirituality, race, ethnicity, health, education, sexual orientation, and image have I learned from my family?
- Have I challenged any of my family traditions or values?
- Has my family had experiences that challenge their traditions and values? If so, how have I responded?
- What significant life experiences have shaped my view of the world and specifically of people who are different from me?
- How will my cultural heritage impact my social work practice?
- Would I like to change or add to my traditions? How might I start?

    Upon completion of your examination of your cultural heritage, turn your focus toward assessing your own cultural lens from a practice perspective. Specific attention can be devoted to the influence of your cultural heritage on your knowledge, awareness, and interactions with persons and groups different from yourself.

b. To create your own cultural genogram, go to the National Center for Cultural Competence at http://nccccurricula.info/awareness/D9.html. Using the guide provided, develop your own cultural genogram. Upon completion of your cultural genogram, reflect in writing about new or confirmed insights, yourself as a cultural being, and the connections between your insights and the influences of your cultural heritage (Warde, 2012).

CHAPTER 5

Social Work Practice with Individuals: Intervention, Termination, and Evaluation

Where after all, do human rights begin? In small places, close to home—so close and so small that they cannot be seen on any map of the world. Yet, they're the world of individual persons: the neighborhood he lives in; the school or college he attends; the factory, farm, or office where he works.

Eleanor Roosevelt (1958)

Key Questions for Chapter 5

1. How can I prepare to intervene with and empower individual clients? [EPAS 8]
2. How can I use the strengths-based perspective to guide the development of intervention, termination, evaluation, and follow-up strategies with individuals? [EPAS 8–9]
3. What social work roles enable me to effectively intervene, terminate, evaluate, and follow-up with individuals? [EPAS 8–9]
4. How do I determine which evaluation tool(s) are appropriate for interventions with individual clients? [EPAS 9]

INTERVENTION IS ONE COMPONENT of the planned change process, which includes engagement, assessment, planning, intervention, termination, evaluation, and follow-up. There are an infinite number of ways to intervene in practice with individuals; therefore, social workers must use theory and practice models to guide their interventions. For example, a critical constructionist lens, which posits that knowledge is created, acquired, processed, and relative, rather than transmitted (Barker, 2014, p. 90), suggests that what is a useful, direct intervention for one

One of the Grand Challenges for Social Work identified by the American Academy of Social Work and Social Welfare is the goal of helping older adults live long and productive lives and remain socially engaged. The authors of Grand Challenge Working Paper No. 8, *Increasing Productive Engagement in Later Life* (Morrow-Howell, Gonzales, Matz-Costa, & Greenfield, 2015) frame the challenge as follows:

> Economic security and health care, especially long-term care of older adults, are two challenges that have received the most attention. These two issues are clearly grand challenges, and most discussions about population aging have focused on these issues because of their complexity and importance. Another grand challenge comes as a response to these demands of population aging: increasing the productive engagement of older adults. This social development response seeks to shape social policies and programs to optimally engage the growing human capital of the aging population; to facilitate paid and unpaid work longer into the life course to offset the demands of population aging; and to ensure the inclusion of all segments of the older adult population, especially among those who are more likely to be excluded (e.g., by race, ethnicity, disability) (p. 1).

With advances in health care, environmental safety, and lifestyle, longevity is increasing around the world, particularly in the developed countries like the United States. For the first time in our history, older adults are routinely living decades after they have retired from paid employment. This Grand Challenge draws attention to the issue of productive aging and engagement for older adults and calls for society, in general, and social workers, in particular, to facilitate changes that will provide support and opportunities for older adults to continue making contributions to society. Changes are needed to change ageist attitudes, societal structures, and policies that will facilitate such shifts as: (1) employment policies that will enable an individual's work life to be extended should they choose; (2) educational institutions that offer learning and training opportunities for older adults; (3) increased volunteer opportunities; and (4) increased support for older adults who served as caregivers and strategies to reduce caregiver burden (Morrow-Howell et al., 2015).

The social work role in advancing long and productive lives relates to this chapter with its focus on intervention, termination, evaluation, and follow-up as social workers have the opportunity to identify and develop and mobilize resources to support older adults who want to be productively engaged. This Grand Challenge relates specifically to the case of Carla Washburn (www.routledgesw.com/caseStudies) as Carla is an older adult who has experienced multiple losses and is struggling to engage with others in her life. Guided by the principles of choice, opportunity, and inclusion, Morrow-Howell and colleagues (2015) suggest that social workers are well positioned to promote such solutions as:

- creating ample opportunities for engaging those who choose participation,
- eliminating barriers to engagement,
- supporting transitions between caregiving and other forms of productive engagement to prevent caregivers being negatively impacted, and

- restructuring social arrangements that exclude older adults from employment and social activities (p. 4).

To familiarize yourself with the issues related to advancing long and productive lives, visit the Grand Challenges website and read Working Paper No. 8, *Increasing Productive Engagement in Later Life* (Morrow-Howell et al., 2015) at: http://aaswsw.org/grand-challenges-initiative/12-challenges/advance-long-and-productive-lives/. (See Exercise #a1 for additional exploration of this Grand Challenge.)

GRAND CHALLENGE

Continued

person will not necessarily meet the needs of another person, even if he or she is in a similar situation. For example, a single woman with a 6-month-old baby may identify job training and finding suitable child care as the primary goals of the intervention. In contrast, another woman in seemingly the same circumstances may request assistance locating housing, handling roller-coaster emotions, and keeping a safe environment for her infant. Yet another single mother may require intensive advocacy efforts in order to deal with discriminatory practices in her place of employment. Social workers must expect differences and advocate against convenient, but not necessarily appropriate, one-size-fits-all interventions that health and social service organizations and public policies sometimes promote. To be effective and meaningful for the client, the assessment, intervention plan, the intervention itself, and the evaluation and follow-up must all connect to one another and actually address the problems/issues presented by the client and the desired outcomes. For example, your client seeks services at your agency for her eating disorder but refuses to address issues related to her family and her childhood (both areas known to serve as antecedents to eating disorders). If you were to work with the client only on the eating concerns and not integrate exploration of her relationships with her family, the intervention is likely not to be a successful one, whereas, if you and your client agree to combine strategies to address her eating patterns with an examination of family interactions, the intervention has the potential to be more impactful.

The context of the social work intervention plays a crucial role in shaping the meaning clients and social workers attach to the intervention experience. This chapter explores the impact of context on all aspects of practice with individuals. The choices and capacities of individuals, the systems in which they are embedded, and the accessibility of existing and potential resources make up the social work practice **context**. Whether you work with someone recently diagnosed with a chronic illness, an adult child experiencing the stress of caring for an aging parent, or an immigrant seeking U.S. citizenship, your actions will affect and be affected by the context of the work.

Each individual client's unique circumstances and what she or he defines as the most pressing issue will determine the starting point of your work. The decision regarding the intervention to be implemented should reflect the priorities for action the social worker and client agreed upon in the assessment and planning phases of work. Because each client is the chief negotiator of her or his change process, the work will first assume and then reflect the client's strengths and capacities to be successful in that journey.

This chapter examines generalist practice competencies and behaviors that support client strengths within their environments, as well as the variety of social work roles and methods that support client–worker relationships, including strengths-, narrative-, and solution-focused approaches. The chapter also includes case examples to help you bridge the gaps between strengths-based, environmental, social justice, human rights, and social construction perspectives. The chapter ends with a discussion of the termination and evaluation and follow-up of the planned change intervention, focusing on strengths-based strategies to help the client maintain accomplished goals.

INTERVENTIONS THAT SUPPORT CLIENT STRENGTHS [EPAS 7]

The goal of all social work interventions is to empower clients to make changes to enhance the quality of their lives and ability to function within their environments. There are obviously multiple approaches and frameworks that can be used to inform and guide the interventions. While not all evidence-based frameworks can be highlighted here, four intervention frameworks that are commonly used within the social work profession to guide and inform interventions will be discussed here, including strengths-based, narrative, solution-focused, and cognitive behavioral approaches.

The strengths perspective focuses on identifying, expanding, and sustaining the client's resilience and assets. A worker using a strengths-based method will not only seek out and identify client strengths in the assessment (see Chapter 4) but will also support and maximize those strengths throughout the working relationship. For many practitioners, this effort is the major focus of the work. The following discussion considers intervention from strengths-, narrative-, solution-focused, and behavioral perspectives.

Strengths-Based Perspectives and Intervention

Social work scholar Dennis Saleebey (2013, pp. 109–111) identifies four elements of the strengths-based approach that apply to the practice context and the action of intervention:

- *The social worker identifies hints and suggestions of strengths even in the struggle:* As the client relates her or his current situation, which often focuses on challenges and stresses, the social worker can "listen" for the client's inherent strengths.

- *The social worker stimulates the discourse and narratives of resilience and strength:* Most of us have difficulty recognizing our positive attributes. In addition to recognizing strengths, the role of the strengths-based social worker is to affirm any positives the client identifies, suggest the possibilities that exist for the client, and facilitate assessments and interventions that are grounded in the client's strengths and resilience.

- *The social worker and client develop goals grounded in strengths:* The strengths the client and social worker collaborate to identify are part of the context for the work. These competencies can be the focus of the assessment and intervention process and can guide the development of goals.

- *The social worker can work with the client to move toward normalizing (i.e., validating) and capitalizing on strengths:* A strengths-based assessment results in an intervention that brings together articulated strengths and resources, normalizes them, and puts them into action.

Acting in Context   Regardless of the theoretical approach that is guiding the social work intervention, the social worker's activity centers on helping the client use the strengths and resources that the client already knows and those she or he is beginning to recognize and to link them with her or his goals and dreams. That kind of effort might lead, for example, to the social worker supporting the client who desires more independence or to become more assertive. Inherent within the strengths-based perspective is the belief that social justice is the "ultimate goal," which requires a commitment to viewing the client–social worker relationship as one of equality (Gray, 2011, p. 8).

Consider Maria, who is having difficulty interacting with her landlord and feels she cannot successfully negotiate a lease arrangement. The client's capacities are identified within the context of the systems in which they are embedded and the client's ability to access/mobilize existing and potential resources. For example, in working with Maria, the social worker can help her identify her strengths and resources related to the goal of negotiating a lease that may include her rental/credit history, previous successes with negotiations, and existing resources (e.g., employment, letters of reference, etc.) and consider the advantages of establishing a positive rental history. The social worker can encourage Maria to recognize her capacity to understand the business-focused details of renting and to negotiate for those specific items or conditions she feels are important and fair. For example, if she is willing to paint the living room walls, in return, she can ask the landlord to provide the paint and reduce her rent for one month. This endeavor may require Maria to stretch beyond her usual comfort zone to initiate change, but it also gives her the opportunity to act on her own behalf. If the venture is successful—the landlord agrees to provide paint and a rental rebate if she will paint the living room walls—the client adds another competency to her growing list. If the effort is unsuccessful, she can use the experience to reflect on the specific areas in which she wants to direct her energies to make changes. She may decide to try to work to become a better negotiator or decide to seek out someone in her social network who has this competency to be her advocate in the next situation.

Capitalizing on Strengths Focusing on strengths allows the social worker and client to work together to recognize the client's success in establishing and stabilizing the client's competencies. In Maria's case, a strength on which Maria can build is her willingness to invest her energy toward a fair rental agreement. Following your strategizing with Maria, she found a new apartment she likes and works with the landlord to arrive at an arrangement where she paints the apartment for a reduction in rent. She has built on her strength of willingness to invest the energy needed to negotiate and gained competency in the area of negotiation. The social worker would then affirm the skills Maria demonstrated in her negotiation with her current landlord, encourage her to generalize those particular skills into other arenas (i.e., employment and personal and professional relationships), and support her ability to generate new skills. The social worker can also help Maria recognize that she is building useful relationships in the community. For example, when she has established a positive rental history, her landlord could become a resource if she needs a reference for a job or wants to find a larger apartment across town. Thus, a social worker's education, advocacy, and support efforts can enable the client to develop a network that links her accomplishments to her broader life goals. By framing the

© Alexander Raths

task as a normative life event, in this case, of securing housing, the social worker not only demonstrates the client's capacities, but also reinforces the availability of community resources (i.e., the social worker) and establishes that disengagement, or ending the work, is appropriate once the goal has been achieved. The ultimate normalization is the client's continued development and the recognition that she or he can successfully manage the everyday tasks of living.

Narrative Intervention

Building on the deconstruction of client perceptions that the social worker and client completed together during the assessment process (discussed in Chapter 4), a **narrative intervention** remains focused on the client, her or his strengths, and the meaning assigned by the client and social worker to current and future realities. In a narrative intervention, the social worker's questions are key. As opposed to eliciting information and interpretation, questioning that occurs during the intervention stage is aimed at helping the client move toward implementing changes in order to reach her or his goals. Return to Chapter 4 for a review of narrative-focused questioning strategies.

Once the client and social worker have deconstructed the original concern or issue in the assessment phase and conceived a plan, the social worker continues to question the client in a way that helps the client shift from the view that she or he *is* the problem to the view that she or he has a relationship *with* the problem (Nichols, 2014, p. 252). During the intervention, the social worker continues to help the client view her- or himself from a position of strength and to work toward a different understanding of the situation that separates the person from her or his situation. Upon achieving success with the intervention, using this strategy, the client can celebrate and share her or his new perceptions of her or his relationship with the problem with people who are important to her or him.

As with most interventions, the path from beginning to end may not be linear but feel more circular in nature. Helping the client to separate the person from the problem can aid the client in maintaining focus on solutions as opposed to her- or himself as the problem. In order to maintain a client-centered focus on the intervention when using a narrative approach, both the client and the social worker can periodically return to the problem as identified by the client and reconstruct it in light of new insights. Consider the earlier example of the client who seeks help with her eating disorder; it is important to not only expand the client's perception of issues for work (i.e., family relationships) and connect her goals (i.e., changing her eating patterns) to the intervention, but also to help the client to develop strengths-based measurable goals that are client-centered. In this scenario, measurable goals are those that are clearly stated, incremental, tangible, and focused on the client herself and the strengths that she possesses. For example, a goal for this client might be to build on her desire to become healthy by starting with a daily food journal in which she documents her food intake and graduating to the introduction of new foods, adding one at a time.

Solution-Focused Intervention

Solution-focused interventions are designed to achieve client goals in a relatively brief, time-limited manner. As you recall from Chapter 4, in solution-focused assessment and planning, the client engages in a self-evaluative process (evaluative questions) to learn how she or he views the situation. The client also envisions times when the problem did not (exception questions) and will not (miracle questions) exist; this provides insight into possible strategies for resolving the problem using the client's existing and created strengths and resources. In the intervention phase, the answers to these questions continue to be important reminders of the goal and connections to the client's past and future life.

Prompting the client to regularly assign a numeric value to a particular issue, experience, or behavior—that is, asking scaling questions—is a client-centered strategy that can empower her or him to continue to engage in self-evaluation and mutual feedback (i.e., activity in which both client and social worker provide feedback to each other) (Lee, 2015). This exercise is one you return to throughout the intervention as it serves to check and monitor progress toward goals. For example, if the client rated the situation as a "4" in July, what rating might the client assign in September? Is that second rating an indication that the intervention is moving in the desired direction or does it suggest that a shift in the plan is needed? Acknowledging small, concrete gains can be an effective motivator for both the client and the social worker. Developing measurable goals with regular client check-ins to monitor progress and connection to the goals (or lack of progress and disconnect with the goals) helps empower the client and inspires confidence that change can, in fact, be achieved or needs to be modified. Exhibit 5.1 provides

---

EXHIBIT 5.1

Integrating Scaling Questions into a Social Work Intervention: Virginia Stone

Virginia Stone of the Brickville neighborhood (www.routledgesw.com/cases) has identified a number of stressors in her life. Scaling questions can help Virginia identify and prioritize areas of concern and strength. They can be infused into the intervention process to frame goals and to track and empower Virginia's progress toward achieving those goals.

During engagement and assessment work, Virginia felt particularly stressed about the potential loss of her family's home. The following dialogue provides examples of how a social worker could use scaling over the course of several sessions:

Session #1: Engagement/Assessment phase:

Social Worker: *Virginia, on a scale of 1 to 10, with 1 being the worst and 10 being the best, how would you rate your stress today regarding your housing situation?*

Virginia: *I would say my stress level is a 1. I am so worried that we're not going to be able to prove the house belongs to my Grandma Stella. Then we won't even be able to sell it to that developer if he does move in here and take over.*

EXHIBIT 5.1

Continued

The social worker and Virginia worked together to develop a goal to reduce her stress. To achieve this goal, they determined that they would take action to obtain proof of Virginia's family ownership of the house. They mapped out strategies, which the social worker documented both in Virginia's case file and in the client contract.

Session #3: Intervention phase:

Social Worker: *Virginia, since we last reviewed your progress toward your goal, you visited Legal Services to ask for help locating a deed to determine ownership of the house. They told you that they believe you have a strong case. Using the same 1–10 scale, how would you rate your stress today related to this issue?*

Virginia: *I am feeling better about things today. I would have to say I'm at a 5 right now. It seems there is a chance we will be able to prove Grandma Stella was the rightful owner and that ownership passed to my mom when Grandma died. I'm still worried, though, that something will go wrong.*

The social worker asked Virginia to consider other actions that she could take while she waited on the outcome of the legal investigation. Virginia acknowledged that there was little she could actually do but wait. Once she realized that much was out of her control, she acknowledged that she was feeling better about not being able to take action and change the situation. The social worker documented the events and Virginia's perception of her current stress level.

Session #8: Intervention phase (three weeks later):

Virginia: *I heard from Legal Services, and they were able to find proof that Grandma Stella is the rightful owner of the house! I can't tell you how much better I feel about this thing.*

Social Worker: *Using that 1 to 10 scale we have used before, where would you rate your stress level on the housing issue today?*

Virginia: *On this one issue, I would say I'm at 3 today. I'm still worried about losing the house to that developer fellow, but at least now I know that if we do have to sell out, we will get paid a fair price for it so hopefully we can find another place for all of us to live.*

Once Virginia and her social worker were able to diffuse the effects of this particular stressor, they were able to turn their full attention to addressing other goals. While the client can certainly pose scaling questions to themselves, when a social worker instigates this exercise with the client, it may help the client to engage in self-assessment and to realize improvements even before the social worker has the opportunity to acknowledge the change, which can foster a sense of client empowerment. Though Virginia was working toward other goals, this particular stressor dampened her motivation to fully engage in working on her less tangible issues of caregiver stress and unresolved grief.

examples of scaling questions and strategies for monitoring scaling questions over the course of the social work intervention.

With its emphasis on concrete results, a solution-focused intervention can be impactful and empowering for the client. A social worker using this approach, by itself or in concert with another intervention model, attends to maintaining the client's motivation and focus on solutions and change while reinforcing respect for and confidence in the client's capacity to reach the desired outcome (Lee, 2015).

Greene and Lee (2011) offer the following suggestions for using a solution-oriented approach:

- Use questions to identify solution-focused patterns that guide the development of client-focused goals (e.g., "When you have encountered this issue in the past; what strategies have you used to resolve the situation?").

- Use solution-oriented tasks between meetings to amplify patterns and promote stability and change.

- For clients who are motivated, develop direct behavioral tasks for completion between meetings (e.g., engaging in a specific activity with client's family members). For clients who acknowledge a problem, but see an external cause or causes, use observational tasks for between-meeting activities (e.g., attending a presentation on parenting).

- At the end of each meeting, provide an end-of-meeting message to affirm the client's work.

- Use client's beliefs, language, metaphors, and figures of speech to guide tasks.

- Remember that clients have strengths, competencies, and resources to make change (pp. 126–127).

Returning to the earlier example of your client who is experiencing an eating disorder, how might you approach her intervention from a solution-focused perspective while also maintaining connections between her desired outcomes to improve her health and an intervention that includes measurable goals? Solutions-focused strategies that may prove particularly helpful in this scenario include the use of miracle and scaling questions. You can query the client to envision both a time in which her eating patterns were not unhealthy and how her life might be if she returned to healthy eating patterns. In establishing measurable and achievable goals, scaling questions can help to establish both a baseline and incremental goals that can be monitored and regularly linked back to her goals.

For both clients who are motivated and those that see external causes, work can be completed during the in-person encounter with the social work as well as between meetings in the form of "experiments" or homework assignments. Linking the between-meeting activities back to the client's goals, the client can be invited to develop an assignment that relates to a behavior she or he is already doing, thoughts, or feelings that will be a continuation of forward movement (Bavelas et al., 2015). Activities designed by the client her- or himself have a greater potential for success because the assignment is likely to be something that is familiar and desired and one in which the client can invest (Bavelas et al., 2015). An activity may involve observing actions and behaviors they want to see continue. To encourage the client in identifying an activity, the social worker might say, "What activity might you try this week that would be new for you and bring you one step closer to your goal?" For example, a teen whose goal is for her parents to treat her like an adult instead of a child is frustrated because she feels her parents are punitive and too restrictive and are not allowing her to grow up. She may be asked to note behaviors her parents do that she views as positive and would like to see continue. The social worker could encourage the client not to attempt wholesale change, which might be too difficult, but rather to think about an incremental step.

A solution-focused approach can be used in concert with other intervention strategies. Building on the basic solution-focused tenet of "if something is working, do more of it," clients and social workers can be incorporating aspects of solution-focused work with other interventions, including pharmacologic (medication), self-help, couple and family therapy (Bavelas et al., 2013, p. 22).

Cognitive Behavioral-Focused Interventions

Considered to be an effective modality for intervening with clients experiencing a range of mental health challenges, cognitive behavioral therapy (CBT) is another approach used by many social workers working in clinical arenas. CBT is based on the premise that thoughts drive one's feelings and actions and that changing one's thoughts can lead to changes in one's behaviors (National Association of Cognitive-Behavioral Therapists (NACBT), n.d.). CBT has been well studied, and the evidence suggests that this approach is particularly effective with such disorders as mood disorders, depression, anxiety, personality, eating, sleep, psychosis, and substance abuse (National Alliance on Mental Illness (NAMI), 2013). Using CBT-related research, NAMI (2013) also endorses CBT as an evidence-based approach for addressing relapse of depression, phobias, posttraumatic stress disorders, obsessive-compulsive disorders that serves as a complement to psychopharmacological treatment.

The primary components of CBT include the following (NABCT, n.d.):

- *Brief and time-limited format:* Meetings with the client can be limited to a specific number, with the client continuing to work on behavioral change following the formal relationship.

- *Collaborative relationship:* The social worker and client work together to identify and implement goals. The social worker's role is to listen, teach, and support, while the client focuses on expression and learning.

- *Structure, direction, and education:* The social worker facilitates change by teaching the client specific techniques during the session and in the form of homework the client completes between sessions that emphasizes learning as well as unlearning behaviors.

When identifying frameworks and strategies to incorporate into your practice, it is important to consider the congruency of your selections with the social work profession. CBT approaches are consistent with social work values through the emphasis on client self-respect and the strengths-based perspective, development of collaborative relationships that are client-centered, recognition of the intersections between the client's beliefs and the social context, and a social justice perspective (Gonzáles-Prendes & Brisebois, 2012). While the delivery of CBT requires advanced training and experience, generalist social workers can incorporate aspects of behavioral-oriented strategies into their interventions and can identify those clients who may benefit from working with a CBT-trained clinician. As the focus of change is directly related to client behaviors, CBT is a logical choice for working with the previously described scenario involving the client experiencing an eating disorder. Collaborative strategies can be explored, planned, and rehearsed during the client–social worker meeting, homework assigned that relates to eating behaviors and food-related interactions with others, and reflections on progress (or lack of progress) can be facilitated at future meetings.

Principles for Taking Environments into Account

In a classic application of a systemic intervention that embraces the client's environment, Wood and Tully (2006) identify six major principles that are relevant in contemporary social work practice. Consistent with the basic tenets of the social work profession, these principles strongly emphasize a client-centered social justice orientation that links the client's perspective and goals with the intervention planned and implemented. The following discussion provides an overview of these six principles:

The Social Worker Should Be Accountable to the Client   In being accountable to the client, the social worker responds to the client's perception of the problem or situation regardless of her or his estimation of its accuracy or clarity. The client's perception is the reality that she or he is working with and responding to that perception is consistent with the basic tenet of the social work profession to "start where the client is." If, for example, an individual client is experiencing substantial difficulty accessing certain public assistance benefits because he does not speak English fluently, but the client is focused on obtaining citizenship, the social worker can acknowledge the client's goal and develop a multistep plan for gaining citizenship while prioritizing the need to first obtain public assistance. To that end, but without losing sight of the client's ultimate goal, the social worker can direct their energies to addressing the need to access services. The social worker might employ a variety of strategies, such as arranging for an interpreter, requesting an agency worker who is fluent in the client's native language, or simply accompanying the client to the appointment to advocate for appropriate and equitable treatment.

The Social Worker Should Follow the Demands of the Client Task   One strategy for conceptualizing the demands of the client task is to create a frame of reference (Wood & Tully, 2006). See Quick Guide 12 for a quadrant diagram covering the parameters of the social worker's tasks that illustrates the frame of reference. This concept suggests that practitioners may work with client systems on behalf of an individual client (Quadrant A), client systems on behalf of the clients and others like them (Quadrant B), others (nonclients) on behalf of clients (Quadrant C), and others (nonclients) on behalf of categories of persons at risk (Quadrant D). In order to follow the demands of the client, the social worker must look beyond the individual client to see if there are others in the same situation. If so, the worker needs to move from one quadrant (as described in Quick Guide 12) to another or function in multiple quadrants simultaneously.

To learn how to apply the frame of reference to your work, consider the case of a social work practitioner working with Annalise, a mother whose child has severe disabilities and no viable transportation to school. The social worker, with the mother's agreement, can locate a driver or a person to accompany the child on the regular school bus or can request extended school hours so that the mother can pick up the child after work (working with a client on behalf of the client, Quadrant A). However, if the social worker discovers that there are four other children with disabilities in the school who also lack adequate transportation, she or he, still working with Annalise, might organize and coordinate a team of drivers for all five children (working with the client on behalf of the client and others like her,

QUICK GUIDE 12	FRAME OF REFERENCE FOR APPROACHING SOCIAL WORK TASKS	

INTENDED BENEFICIARY		
FOCUS OF INTERVENTION	SINGLE	MULTIPLE
Clients	Work with clients on their own behalf	Work with clients on behalf of themselves and others like them
Others	**Quadrant A** Work with others (nonclients) on behalf of clients	**Quadrant B** Work with others, such as (nonclients), on behalf of a category of persons at risk
	Quadrant C	**Quadrant D**

Source: Adapted from Wood & Tully, 2006

Quadrant B). If the social worker tries to enlist the aid of a community group to help locate and fund a small van that could hold six children, the work would fall in a different quadrant (working with others out of concern for specific clients, Quadrant C). Finally, if the worker contacts the state legislature on behalf of a category of clients—in this case, children with disabilities—to propose statewide transportation funding for children with disabilities, the work falls into Quadrant D, working with others on behalf of a category of clients. Although the social worker's efforts may vary, move from one quadrant to another, and/or operate simultaneously, the work is always client-centered, that is, performed on the behalf of clients and reflective of the client's needs and goals.

The Social Worker Should Maximize the Potential Supports in the Client's Environment This generic principle requires the social worker to identify, access, and, where necessary, modify or even create the supports that a client needs. These supports might include temporary housing for a family who is homeless, hospice services for a family dealing with an older member's imminent death, or child care services for a young mother who is employed outside her home. Chapter 3 discussed this aspect of resource development; attending to the client's environment remains a central focus for the intervention phase as well. On a cautionary note, it is important to have as much information as possible about existing resources before referring the client to the resource and to have realistic expectations when considering a plan to create new resources. It is also helpful to follow up after a referral to learn whether the referral was appropriate and helpful.

The Social Worker Should Proceed from the Assumption of "Least Contest" This tenet holds that the social worker should use the minimal amount of pressure required to meet a client's need. For example, if a client needs affordable child care, a social worker can explore the existing availability of such care before pressuring the mayor to initiate a city-sponsored child care system. If these attempts fail, and there is no adequate, affordable child care, the social worker can shift her or his focus to mobilize an effort to facilitate change at the community (i.e., neighborhood) level.

In a different situation, the "least contest" approach might encourage the social work practitioner to contact another service before engaging in advocacy. For example, a practitioner working with a young woman who was not accepted into a local parent support group might refer her to a different group. If a series of appropriate referrals does not yield the desired results, the social worker could consider other approaches of greater contest, such as advocating with the person who organized the original group.

The Social Worker Must Help the Client Deconstruct Oppressive Cultural Discourse and Reinterpret Experience from Alternative Perspectives This principle guides the social worker and client to discuss larger cultural and societal issues that impact the ways in which the client experiences the world. Exploring the oppression, discrimination, and/or violence that may be a part of the client's life experience can help the client understand the origins of these forces and the way in which they may have negatively impacted her or his life and view of the current circumstance and to construct alternative perspectives on possible change options. By gaining insight into the external forces that affect her or his experience, the client may realize that the current situation may not be the result of a personal failing. Creating a different view of oneself can free the individual to develop a new, healthier perspective by envisioning what her or his life *could* be. Consider the older adult who recently entered the country as a refugee with her large extended family after living for several years in a refugee camp. This client has endured a lifetime of oppression and discrimination, and she and her family are survivors of violence in their home country. As a social worker, you can help her create a new perspective on the United States, the culture in which she now lives, and ways in which she can preserve and respect her own cultural beliefs and practices. By examining her previous life experiences within the context of her new life, you can work with her to foster a new, more positive experience in the new, more supportive setting.

The **"Minimax" Principle** suggests the social worker should identify, reinforce, and/or increase the client's repertoire of strategic behavior for minimizing pain and maximizing positive outcomes and satisfaction. The principle cautions the social worker against holding the client responsible for the community's failure to develop resources or provide support. The principle recognizes that the client may need assistance developing behaviors likely to elicit community cooperation. For example, clients who have been excluded from the community on various levels might present as eager to the point of aggressiveness and might demonstrate a lack of interest in using an organization's grievance process to file a complaint when they have been treated unfairly. Such clients will likely improve their chances of being accepted by the community if they curb their enthusiasm somewhat, by speaking in a softer voice, and initially using an established grievance process, for example.

Because societal culture has led many people to blame themselves for the violence or oppression they experience, social workers and their clients must be careful not to attribute complete responsibility for difficulties accessing resources to our/their own failures, in essence "blaming the victim." Social workers whose clients blame themselves completely for their challenges can employ consciousness-raising techniques to challenge these client beliefs and to transform their views of such issues as child abuse and violence against women from being a personal issue into seeing them as political issues over which society has responsibility for addressing. Returning to the earlier example of the older adult woman who has recently arrived in the U.S., one focus of your work with her could be to examine the violence she experienced in her home country. Within the social work intervention, you can help her to recognize that the responsibility for the violence lies with the perpetrators of that violence and that, despite the pain and guilt she suffers, she and her family are not responsible. She may have made choices within that context that she regrets; however, it is helpful to discuss the idea that she was not responsible for the context and may have made the best decisions that she could at the time. Freeing the client from guilt can help her maximize her opportunity to create a new life with her family in the U.S.

Environment-Sensitive Processes and Skills

Regardless of the strategy used, when used effectively, many social work practice skills and behaviors can affirm client strengths and support clients' important role in the work. Social workers can also apply the groups of skills and behaviors previously discussed when relevant to supporting clients' effective use of environmental supports. What follows is a discussion of behaviors that social workers can use with individuals.

Cultural Humility   As discussed in Chapters 3 and 4, a client's cultural background is a potential source of strength, not an obstacle or a deficit. As you strive to become a culturally humble and competent social work practitioner, you can build your skills on four main assumptions (Kohli, Huber, & Faul, 2010):

1. Reality is socially constructed.
2. Diverse worldviews are valuable.
3. Multiple realities affect individual personalities.
4. Diversity education has a positive impact on the journey to cultural competence (p. 266).

Within the social, cultural, political, and historical context, these assumptions can inform the way you view both your client and yourself. These assumptions can also serve as reminders that a client-centered assessment and intervention are more accurately viewed within the context of the client's biopsychosocial-spiritual-sexual lens and should be connected to the client's perception of her or his situation, strengths, and goals.

Make use of those traditions or aspects of your client's culture that nourish and give meaning to life. For example, many cultures demonstrate great respect for authority and the wisdom of age. When you work with clients from such cultures and backgrounds, support those values; they are assets you and your client can incorporate into the intervention phase of your work. Although you should always confer with your clients regarding your actions, when conducting a client-centered intervention that includes clear and measurable goals, remain especially sensitized to how your approach "fits" your client's culturally influenced sense of propriety. Would it be appropriate, for instance, to encourage a client from a culture that has high respect for authority and older adults to participate in a rent strike aimed at a prominent elder statesman who owns a property if such an action would likely become highly adversarial? While such an intervention strategy may be client-centered and measurable, the option may be so incongruent with the client's cultural beliefs and practices that the strategy may be unsuccessful and result in the client feeling inadequate and disillusioned with the prospect of change.

Having confirmed the importance of recognizing and supporting client strengths and cultural influences in the intervention process, we focus now on identifying and intensifying the strengths of clients' environments. This dual emphasis on person and environment is consistent with the social justice traditions of the social work profession, and social workers often direct their efforts toward making clients' environments more responsive to client needs. This approach looks to institutions and policies outside of the client, rather than viewing the client's difficulties as a symptom of inner pathology. The process assumes that clients possess the capacity both to identify their difficulties and to participate in the work necessary to alleviate them.

Providing Information Clients often want, need, and ask for information about their environment, which may be their most valuable resource. You may worry that you will unintentionally overinfluence decisions, be too directive, or create dependency. While such concerns are legitimate, they also can be managed. Information in our society is clearly linked to power, and when we provide information to clients we empower those clients. The challenge arises when clients confuse information with advice or when the information provided is strongly biased. You can never have all the information related to a particular situation or circumstance, but you can offer what you know as a simple proposition, always framed by the limits of your knowledge. Consider again the situation of the older adult refugee. She is concerned about the impact previous experiences of violence may have on her younger female family members and does not want this information shared within their social networks. You have been working with her daughter and granddaughters, and she has asked you to share with her the information you have learned about them and to direct them not to discuss their experiences with anyone. While you are sensitive to her concerns, you are ethically bound not to share information about other clients without their consent. Moreover, your commitment to practicing social work in an ethical manner would not allow you to direct any client's beliefs or behaviors.

Let clients know that you have no expectations about what they will do with the information. It is not your prerogative to place restrictions on what clients do with the information you provide. For example, suppose you are a social worker working in child welfare helping a young couple learn more effective methods to care for their 3-year-old son who has received a diagnosis of being on the autism spectrum. You want to compile resources you think would be helpful to the parents. You believe that respite services would help the mother to develop some trust in a caregiver outside of the family. Therefore, you provide her with the names of several agencies that provide these services. When she does not follow up on this information, you may become frustrated or even irritated. In this case, the client used your "information" as "advice." The mother is either unable to or disagrees that she should act on the information in the way you hoped she would. This simple example illustrates the problematic nature of attaching expectations to the information you provide. When you provide information, make your suggestions transparent and let the client know that she is free to accept or reject that agenda without ramifications on your professional relationship.

Refocusing and Confronting   When you draw the client back to the heart of the work, you **refocus.** Refocusing can take several possible forms, including two discussed here: referring back to the original purpose of the work and recognizing clients' beliefs, plans, and/or behavior. Social workers frequently refocus to help clients take advantage of the potential in their environments.

When clients begin to move away from the agreed-upon focus of the work as outlined in the mutually developed contract, a simple reference to that agreement as laid out in the contract is sometimes all that is necessary. Occasionally the client (or the social worker) will become distracted by other compelling issues. Although such diversion is understandable and can, sometimes, be helpful, you are responsible for using your time with the client productively. If you are working with a client who seems to have lost focus on your agreed-upon goals, you might suggest that the two of you revisit those goals to determine whether you are both still focused on the plan. If together you feel your original goals are no longer realistic, propose revising the original plans. For example, if the agreed-upon goal was for the client to return to school to obtain a degree but the client was offered a promotion at her job that will require travel, the two of you may need to re-evaluate if returning to school at this time is feasible or if this goal can be revisited in the future.

In other situations, the client may not carry out the agreed-upon plan or contract because he or she does not embrace it as a priority, finds it uncomfortable, or for some reason is unable to implement it. For example, suppose your client, Jane, established a plan to seek counseling because she had been sexually abused and was experiencing painful memories. Initiating that contact required Jane to break family and cultural rules forbidding the discussion of such personal subjects with an outsider. Jane found the effort to initiate this counseling more difficult than she had imagined. In this situation, rather than refocusing Jane, you might instead confront her gently, saying, for example, "Help me to understand your concerns about discussing your painful memories with an outsider." Jane may simply need more informal support and acknowledgment from you to manage the unanticipated struggle. This development might also signal that the plan is not working for Jane and that it is not likely to lead to the desired outcome. In situations like these, return to the goals of the work to confirm that they continue to flow from the presenting issues (or do not), review the client's experience, and make changes as necessary. It is better to approach the speed of change at the pace comfortable to the client, however slowly, rather than try to move more quickly than the client is able to manage.

Significantly, clients often perceive gentle recognition of their behavior as not only helpful but supportive. A client may perceive a social worker's attempt to carefully contrast client actions with what the client agreed to do as a sign of respect because the social worker's effort affirms the client's capacity to meet agreed-upon commitments. For example, you may say to a client: "Your goal was to obtain employment, but you did not apply for any jobs this week. Please help me understand how your actions will help you reach your goal." Preventing the client from experiencing this type of confrontation as hostile or argumentative requires that you handle the interaction with sensitivity. In most cases, social workers try refocusing before confrontation. Instead, you might say, "Your goal was to obtain employment, but you were unable to apply for jobs this week. Are you able to identify any barriers that prevented you from applying that we could address today?" When a social worker uses confrontation selectively and sensitively, however, he or she can convey hope and respect to a client.

In some situations, a digression from the intended focus of the work is warranted. You will be called upon to exercise your professional judgment to recognize when a digression warrants a new focus. For example, if Jane came to your office with an eviction notice in her hand, you would place the original focus of your work on hold until she could resolve her housing crisis.

Interpreting Client Behavior   When the social worker makes sense of the client's behavior in ways the client may not perceive or acknowledge in the hopes of inspiring the client to consider her or his situation in a new or different way, the social worker is interpreting that behavior. From a social constructionist view, accurately interpreting can be one of the most challenging practice skills to master.

The meanings you and your client ascribe to a client's behavior may differ. Still, there may be a place for offering your interpretation, but you should be careful to test it out with clients and acknowledge that your interpretation of the situation is only one possibility. For example, consider the following conversation with Jane.

> Social Worker: *It seems to me that you do not feel ready to take on the kind of work likely to be involved in this type of counseling. Is that correct?*
>
> Jane: *I don't know what you're talking about.*
>
> Social Worker: *Each time we try to discuss your painful memories, you seem uncomfortable and change the subject. I think we might best use our time right now talking about other aspects of your life. When you feel more comfortable with me, we can revisit your memories. How does this sound to you?*

Although many of us have benefited from learning how others construe our behaviors, having others interpret our experience can also be frustrating and alienating. This is particularly true when their interpretation seems judgmental or "expert," that is, as if someone else possesses the secret to understanding our behavior. Interpreting is a widely applicable process, but one that should be used only in an established trusting relationship with the client, while participating in supervision, and you should always ask the client to evaluate the accuracy of your interpretations.

Mapping as an Intervention Strategy   Recall from the discussion in Chapter 4 that incorporating the client's family and community system is an important aspect of the assessment phase of the intervention. Just as mapping the client's family constellation and current living and relationships profile can be a useful assessment strategy, visual depictions of the client's environment can be helpful in the intervention itself. As you know, the genogram gives the client insights into her or his family history, behavior patterns, and a wide array of issues, including physical and mental health, substance use and abuse, relationship patterns, and estrangements. Ecomaps, on the other hand, visually depict the client's current life situation, including relationships, resources, assets, and challenges.

During assessment, plan development, and intervention implementation, you can incorporate the information you gathered using genograms and ecomaps into the client's goals and action steps for facilitating behavior and life changes. For example, consider the client who has experienced violence in her relationships and who, in the course of completing her genogram, identifies a multigenerational pattern of intimate partner violence directed toward the women in her family. Identifying this pattern of abuse can help her understand the nature of her previous relationships and select strategies she can use to seek out healthier relationships. Later you can use the genogram to help the client determine if she has successfully broken the pattern.

In the assessment phase, the ecomap helps the client identify strengths, the directionality of energy and benefits (i.e., where and how much energy the client is devoting to the areas of her or his life and what and how does this energy compare to the benefits received), and areas for change. Later, during plan development and implementation, the ecomap can enable the client to envision her or his life after the intervention is implemented. This new perspective on the client's current life can help her or him devise specific behavior and life changes. Previously unrecognized resources are mobilized, unhealthy behaviors are addressed, and dysfunctional relationships are targeted for change. The ecomap thus becomes a "work in progress" and serves as a mechanism for monitoring progress, determining a time frame for the work and termination, evaluating outcomes, and following up.

TRADITIONAL SOCIAL WORK ROLES IN CONTEMPORARY SOCIAL WORK PRACTICE [EPAS 8]

In thinking about the preceding descriptions of selected social work skills and behaviors, consider the specific roles workers assume in support of client strengths and environments. These roles include the following:

- Case manager

- Counselor

- Broker

- Mediator
- Educator
- Client advocate
- Collaborator

The following discussion focuses on the assumptions that underlie these roles and the ways the roles are actualized in social work practice.

Case Manager

Case management is "a procedure to plan, seek, and monitor services, resources, and supports from different social agencies to enhance client strengths and well-being in helping them achieve their goals" (Barker, 2014, p. 56). Clients with multiple challenges and needs particularly benefit from case management. For example, a client with a serious mental health issue, a back injury, and a housing issue may need medication, a referral to vocational rehabilitation, and a referral to a housing resource. Because of this client's multiple needs, he may be an appropriate candidate for case management. **Case managers** coordinate services and are responsible for monitoring how well services are meeting client needs by holding providers accountable, ensuring client participation, and collaborating with others to raise awareness of unmet needs. A case manager may also collaborate with others to advocate for and build needed resources in a community. Case managers work in a variety of settings including aging services; behavioral health; substance abuse and addictions treatment; child, youth, and family services; corrections; disabilities programs; educational settings; employee assistance; health care; housing; immigrant and refugee services; income support programs; military and veterans services; and tribal programs (NASW, 2013b). **Clinical case managers** provide specialized services that combine clinical and case management strategies and work with persons with serious mental illnesses (schizophrenia, depression, bipolar disorder, personality disorders, and substance abuse) around issues of social relationships, housing, income support, medical care, job training, recreation, counseling, and medications (Walsh & Manuel, 2015).

Common Components of Case Management   A planned case management process that incorporates the twelve challenges includes these steps (Roberts-DeGennaro, 2013):

1. Ensuring eligible clients are informed of available services at your organization
2. Assessing a client's needs and strengths
3. Developing a plan for intervention
4. Identifying and designing an appropriate network of services

5. Creating a written contract that includes achievable and measurable goals, time limits, agreed-upon actions, and consequences of failure to fulfill the contract (if any consequences exist)
6. Implementing the plan
7. Monitoring the plan to determine progress or a need to re-evaluate the contract
8. Evaluating the outcomes of the intervention
9. Terminating the case management relationship
10. Following up on the client after termination to determine if the client has maintained the desired change

The case manager may also serve as an informal, personal support/contact person or even therapist. Because therapy is an advanced-level intervention, the social worker is bound by the *Code of Ethics* (NASW, 2008) to possess an appropriate degree and training to deliver this service. In contrast to brokers, who may match a client to a single service, case managers take responsibility for assessing, monitoring, and evaluating the coordination of all services a client requires and providing follow-up services, as needed. This role may also involve client advocacy to ensure clients receive services from other agencies.

Purposes and Practice of Contemporary Case Management   For more than three decades, the profession has used the term case management to describe this overall coordinating function. Contemporary case management has two primary—and often conflicting—purposes: by coordinating services, to improve the quality of care while at the same time controlling its costs. While case management was originally conceived to address the integration of system-level services, it has become a functional and cost-effective practice approach for use with many types of work including family preservation, school social work, and substance abuse treatment as well as in different fields of practice, such as corrections and health care delivery systems and levels of practice (e.g., operationalization of services and policy). While social workers often work in settings where both are stressed (coordination and cost), the profession advocates that quality of service and client outcomes must be given priority over cost-effectiveness (Rothman, 2009).

NASW has developed a set of standards for the practice of social work case management. The NASW Standards (2013) are intended to support the case manager in competently and efficiently serving her or his clients by:

- strengthening the developmental, problem-solving, and coping capacities of clients;

- enhancing clients' ability to interact with and participate in their communities, with respect for each client's values and goals;

- linking people with systems that provide them with resources, services, and opportunities;

- increasing the scope and capacity of service delivery systems;
- creating and promoting the effective and humane operation of service systems; and
- contributing to the development and improvement of social policy (p. 17).

Counselor

The helping professions use the term **counselor** in a variety of ways. Within the social work profession, counseling is typically a specialized clinical social work skill that graduate-level social workers who have advanced training in working in health, mental health, and family service settings perform. In this context, a counselor serves individuals, families, groups, and communities providing suggestions, alternatives, and information and helping to articulate client goals (Barker, 2014). In the helping professions, a counselor also describes volunteers and professionals or paraprofessionals who work in group settings (e.g., camps and residential settings).

While the counseling role can include an array of different activities, the social worker functioning as a counselor typically works with the client on a specific issue or concern. The counselor uses different approaches and strategies based on her or his expertise and training and on the needs of the client but should always maintain a client-centered perspective that is viewed through a biopsychosocial-spiritual-sexual lens. Regardless of the theoretical or philosophical approach utilized by the practitioner working in a counseling setting, viewing the client and her or his environment from a holistic, comprehensive frame will guide the development and implementation of an effective intervention.

Broker

Social workers often act as **brokers**, linking clients to a needed service or resource. Needs may range from instrumental assistance (e.g., food, clothing, and children's toys) to services such as counseling, support groups, and advocacy. Consider the functions and context of brokering as the processes of building the necessary networks and of matching clients to services.

Brokering Functions and Context   Five social work functions of brokering are:

- assessing client need,
- assessing available resources,
- matching the client with appropriate services and initiate referrals,
- linking or networking services, and
- sharing information with the client and/or with the referring agency.

The brokering role can also entail modifying resources and creating new resources where none exist. For example, a social worker may work with a local church to start an after-school tutoring program when he notices that students at his elementary school are struggling academically and not completing homework assignments. All of these activities can strengthen the client's environment, or context, while supporting her or his strengths.

An early and esteemed role associated with the social work profession, brokering may have less status today because of the profession's increased interest in psychological and therapeutic roles and the availability of information through online sources. Brokering may also seem fairly simple at times. For example, if your client requests assistance locating used children's furniture, you simply "refer" her or him to the appropriate agency. It is somewhat misleading, though, to think of the brokering role as simple, because it requires that the social worker be familiar with resources and able to nurture and maintain a network of relationships with those resources. In the complex world of contemporary, urban social services, the ability to know one service or resource from the next can itself be a feat. In rural areas, where the service system may be much less comprehensive, with fewer choices, knowing and maintaining effective relationships with the available resources is even more important. Regarding the role in which the social worker is employed, brokering can be a necessary skill—even the therapist can find her/himself helping clients to access resources and services.

Building and Maintaining Networks for Brokering   In order to develop a brokering network, you must make initial and subsequent contacts with appropriate providers in other agencies and organizations, discover who will help your clients most effectively, and become familiar with program eligibility criteria and service elements. To broker effectively, you will also need to establish stable working relationships with people, organizations, and systems that will help your clients. In order to provide referrals that best fit the intended service, you may develop relationships with network resources in which you each utilize the other's services. Building and maintaining a network requires reciprocity and open, regular two-way communication.

To successfully build a network, you will need knowledge of both the formal and informal aspects of a resource. For example, it is helpful to understand the formal aspects of a resource, such as the mission statement of a particular community hospice program—the program's goals and methods of service delivery—as it will provide you with information on such important items as the population and geographic areas served, eligibility requirements, payment information, and philosophical approaches. It is also helpful to be aware of informal aspects of resources, such as news and happenings related to a particular resource. For example, it could be helpful to know that a program has received a large grant for an additional building, that the local university is about to install a field unit for student training, or that the board of an affiliated organization has approved funding to hire a development director. Your attention to, and continuous connections with, both the formal and informal aspects of the networks you maintain will enrich your understanding of and the ability of your clients to access and utilize your community's resource environment.

Making the Match in Brokering   Developing and maintaining a resource network (or "service system linkage") nearly always requires you to use the skills you first learned about in Chapter 3 in connecting with clients—that is, building rapport and trust to enable you to better assess the client's needs.

Following up on your referrals is important, both to determine if a client is participating in and benefiting from the service and to determine if the provider perceives your referral and the client to be appropriate for the organization. How well a client matches a service is important, not just from the perspective of the client, but also from the perspective of the service provider. When you take the time and care to learn about an effective and successful referral, you establish trust with these providers who will respect your competence and skills. Further, when you develop a genuine understanding of, and appreciation for, the work that others do, you are likely to develop an appreciation for how well "the system" is responsive to your client.

Mediator

Mediation has both a formal and informal function in the delivery of human services. Mediation as a professional practice has its own identity and is often associated more with the legal system and public policy than it is with social work practice. Some social workers complete specialized training to become mediators in such areas as divorce and child custody. Most social workers, whether or not they have specialized training, engage in some informal aspects of mediation fairly frequently. **Mediators**, as outsiders to a dispute, try to: (1) establish common ground between disputing parties, (2) help them understand each other's point of view, and (3) demonstrate that each party has an interest in the relationship's stability beyond the current differences.

Finding Common Ground   Locating points of agreement in the midst of a dispute is a common social work practice skill. Suppose you are working in a youth agency and have just seen Josh, a 15-year-old who has recently run away from home for the first time. From your conversation, you understand that he is troubled by the relationship between his mother and her new live-in boyfriend. He is upset and scared and is not certain about the ramifications of being on his own. He dislikes his mother's boyfriend and objects to the curfew and other house rules the boyfriend imposes. Josh misses his mother's companionship the way it was before "he" entered the scene. When you are satisfied that Josh will be safe at home (that he is not being abused in any way), you ask for his permission to schedule a meeting with his mother, her boyfriend, and Josh to explore the issues among them. He somewhat reluctantly agrees.

When his mother enters the youth center, she seems exasperated with her son, but she is also relieved to see him. She begins to cry and hugs him. Her boyfriend remains quiet, but when he catches Josh's eye, he smiles at the boy just slightly.

Walking Through It One mediation process you might try with Josh's family could involve the following:

- Represent yourself warmly and genuinely as someone who wants to help resolve the issue without taking sides. Convey to the family that you trust the process and will walk that journey with them. You might let the members of the family know that you are there to listen, explore options, facilitate, and possibly mediate but not to direct or advise.

- Attempt to establish common ground. In this case, Josh's present well-being is the immediate point of common interest. Josh is not prepared to support himself physically, financially, or emotionally (or legally in most places). He is scared and concerned about his future. At the same time, he is vocal about his freedom and does not want to be bound by all the rules his mother's new boyfriend has imposed. His mother cares for him and wants him to be safe. Her boyfriend wants a peaceful household and likes Josh well enough, although he has no strong connection with him. He cares deeply for Josh's mother.

- Help Josh, his mother, and her boyfriend understand and appreciate one another's points of view. Assume that Josh's mother and her boyfriend may have different perspectives and opinions, and acknowledge all points of view. Facilitate their direct dialogue with one another. The skills of planned emptiness and looking from diverse angles will be beneficial to this interaction. You might open a dialogue aimed at establishing a process in which each person is willing to listen to the others' points of view in the following way:

  "I would like each of you to be able to share your perspective on this situation. In order for each of you to be able to hear what the others are saying, it is important that we establish some ground rules for the discussion. For instance, I would like to ask that we each remain silent until the other person is finished speaking. If we have questions or thoughts to share, those should wait until the person has completed her or his statements. I will try to summarize what I am hearing each of you say so that you can confirm or modify our understanding."

- Establish with Josh, his mother, and her boyfriend that it is in all of their interests to work together during this interaction so that they can come to a resolution regarding Josh's living arrangements and his general safety.

- Help all parties recognize that each will benefit from an ongoing positive relationship in which they can settle differences that go beyond the current dispute. The quality of Josh's future, as well as the quality of the relationship between Josh's mother and her boyfriend, may depend on their ability to work together. These are the abiding points of common interest.

This scenario represents just one way in which this situation might play out. You might try other avenues to find common ground and identify solutions. You will notice that this process does not imply any *particular* solution. Josh, his mother, and her boyfriend might agree that Josh should return home, live with another family member, try to survive on his own on a trial basis, or any number of other possibilities. The major point is that the relationship between Josh and his mother (and her boyfriend) is collaborative and that each has a stake in working out a solution that affirms their mutual benefit.

Educator

In many ways, social workers function as educators. While the mission and scope of individual practice settings will determine the nature and level of such activity, some form of education is commonplace in most social work settings. On an interpersonal and concrete level, social workers serve as **educators** who provide information to an individual. You may teach clients about a range of topics; for example, you might teach clients how to complete an application, inform them of services and new programs, or show them the correct bus to take to travel uptown before noon. You may assure an adolescent client that she is indeed normal when she worries that her moodiness indicates she is not normal, or you might educate clients about the maximum allowable percentage of income they may have to pay to rent in public housing. Much of the direct service aspect of acting as educator relates to helping clients to access resources and to make the behavioral changes they want to make.

Developing Client Skills   On a direct practice level, you, as the social worker, can help clients develop the skills they need to participate in the intervention and reach their goals. The client's motivation for this kind of change needs to generate from her or his vision of change, rather than from your opinions about needed improvements. You can help clients understand the steps they need to take to accomplish that change through providing them with information they can use to develop change or through teaching them new skills by providing information, modeling, and practicing with the client. For example, if your client, Ramon, finds his co-workers or his supervisor intimidating and wants to be more assertive in the workplace, you might demonstrate for him a more assertive (but respectful) stance in a relevant interchange, and/or role-play or otherwise help him practice the new behavior. You can help older adult clients learn to organize their medications to increase their compliance with the health provider's medication directives. You can teach parents strategies for using positive feedback to support their children. You can model clear communication and gradually help your client participate more effectively in problem resolution situations. For example, if you are working with an adolescent who is frequently suspended from school because of her angry outbursts, you can work with her on appropriate ways to express herself effectively without alienating adults. You might accompany her to her first meeting with the school principal on her return to classes. You can support a more focused, direct, and respectful level of discussion based on her goals and help her describe her situation. You can help her process the session, evaluating what went well and areas for change, and support her ability to negotiate these relationships with further practice. To support her goal of self-sufficiency in these situations, you may then role-play the next meeting so that she will be ready to attend on her own. When you use skills with clients, you are engaged in **modeling** (e.g., demonstrating) behaviors that they may use on their own in their relationships. In all of these situations, the ultimate goal is to foster in the client a sense of strength—a change in clients' thinking about themselves and a greater integration of self and skills into the environment.

Working with the Public   Social workers frequently work with the public using the roles of educator, advocate (explained next), and mediator. For example, social workers educate large groups about issues that affect clients. In some instances,

© Adam Gregor

social workers engage in these efforts to prevent the development of a problem. For example, you may teach a parenting class or present a session on ways to support racial tolerance in the classroom to a group of preschool teachers. You may advocate for a population by providing testimony in a legislative hearing regarding the cultural needs of a group of refugee children, or you may respond to a community group's concerns about a new group home in their neighborhood that will house discharged clients with histories of psychiatric problems by mediation.

Client Advocate

Taking on an advocacy role in social work practice means to seek to secure the rights, well-being, and access to resources for clients who are at risk for a negative outcome. Advocacy typically represents a struggle for power. An **advocate** may strive to obtain resources, work to modify existing policies or practices, and promote new policies that will benefit clients. This role of defending, championing, or otherwise speaking out for clients is one of the profession's original commitments (Haynes & Mickelson, 2010). Social workers often advocate formally on behalf of the political or civil rights of clients or access to services for a group of clients. They also frequently advocate in informal, everyday situations when a client is treated disrespectfully or inefficiently or when a client is denied needed services.

Many social workers distinguish between **case (or client) advocacy**, that is, advocacy on behalf of an individual client or a single group of clients, and **cause (or class) advocacy**, which the social worker initiates on behalf of a category of clients. **Legislative advocacy** is a specialized version of cause advocacy that addresses some aspect of the law or regulations. We will take a brief look at each of these types of advocacy.

Case Advocacy   Social workers usually practice case advocacy at an agency or organizational level. For example, if your client is denied Supplemental Nutrition Assistance Program (SNAP) benefits (a.k.a. food stamps) to which she or he is entitled, you can advocate with the state public welfare income support organization that oversees the SNAP services. To be an effective advocate for your client, you will need to know SNAP eligibility requirements; agency appeal policies, regulations, and power structures; and contextual variables such as how SNAP fits into the overall welfare organization. You will also want to enter at the point of least contest so that you do not encounter unnecessary resistance. Therefore, you can address the situation with the worker who originally denied the SNAP application and use the agency grievance process before taking any other measures like involving powerful outside parties, calling the media, or organizing a protest.

Cause Advocacy   More political than case advocacy, cause advocacy involves both larger numbers of people and, by definition, a cause that affects them all, either because it imposes obstacles to attaining resources or because it directly deprives people of these resources. Cause advocacy involves speaking for a large number of people who are not necessarily your clients and who are not likely to be empowered to directly participate in forming the goals or the preferred methods of the advocacy effort. Cause advocacy is particularly effective when you partner with other concerned organizations in a coalition, and it can spur change that positively affects many people. It is also helpful when an issue is very clear and when the proposed solution is not imposed on people who do not choose it. For example, if your community has no adequate facilities for after-school child care, concerned agencies, churches, businesses, or other institutions may join together to advocate for the development of such a facility. Assuming that you require funding from local public sources, your coalition of interested partners (who are well organized and well rehearsed) will be in a position to advocate for adequate child care facilities. As in case advocacy, your coalition will need complete information on the proposed change; for instance, to understand how many children the facility will serve, what those children need, how much the service is likely to cost, how likely children and their families are to participate, how you will go about getting the issue on the city's agenda, and how the proposed facility will benefit all stakeholders. They will also need advocacy skills.

Legislative Advocacy   This form of cause advocacy is devoted to adding, amending, changing, or eliminating legislation in order to benefit a large group of clients. For example, when a social worker advocates to lower the legal alcohol limit for driving a motorized vehicle from .08 blood alcohol content (BAC) to .06, she or he is engaging in legislative advocacy designed to benefit a large cross section of people—drivers and passengers.

There are many scenarios in which a large group of people would benefit from a change in legislation because nearly all entitlement policies have limitations that may present obstacles to your clients. Access to controversial resources such as family planning and abortion clinics is likely to be more constrained (for example, by age limits or pregnancy duration) than less disputed services like food pantries.

Legislative advocacy usually requires intensive, cooperative work with one or several organizations. Initiating or collaborating in legislative advocacy is well within the purview of social work practice. It requires considerable knowledge, insight, and organization, but with careful preparation and diligence, it can produce desired results.

Thoughts about Power and Advocacy   Social work advocacy frequently involves trying to make changes so resources are allocated consistent with social justice; therefore, it is helpful to recall the assumptions about power that guide social work. In general, advocates recognize that those who have power do not readily relinquish that power. Power is not equally distributed, involves conflict, and is helpful to bring about substantial change. These points may seem harsh if you have not considered power and advocacy within such a context before. Familiarity with these

- When clients are directly involved, ensure that they genuinely support your advocacy efforts and understand the possible repercussions.
- Be prepared with relevant knowledge (e.g., eligibility requirements, entitlement limitations, number of people in a given category, history of advocacy on this topic).
- Be clear and specific about your goals; a complaint about a policy means little if you do not present a solution.
- Begin with simple persuasion efforts; first assume that there has been a mistake or an oversight.
- Understand when persuasion is not working with the targeted audience and you must progress to a more intense effort.
- Assess that more intense effort prior to action: Can you be successful? Are your clients still supportive? Do collaborative partners agree on the next step?
- Use carefully cultivated social work skills, including listening, empathy, clarifying, and firmness.
- Use the discourse of collaboration and common ground.
- Seek supervision and consultation. You are as vulnerable to "not seeing" in cause advocacy as you might be in the most intense interpersonal work.
- When entering into formal processes (e.g., legislative advocacy), learn about the technicalities of the legislative process.

EXHIBIT 5.2

Strategies Regarding Advocacy

concepts can prepare you to enter a political arena and can help you understand the social locations of those in our culture who are oppressed.

Case and cause advocacy are important to social work practice and strategizing about advocacy can be helpful. Exhibit 5.2 provides cautions and strategies for advocacy.

Collaborator

Collaboration is an inherent part of the daily fulfillment of the social work mission for most social work practitioners. In addition to using collaboration skills with clients to develop plans for change, social workers engage in collaborative relationships with other professions in many different ways. For example, social workers work with health, social service, and legal professionals to deliver client services, develop programs and policies, advocate, and research. While social workers sometimes interchangeably use terms to describe cooperative practices, these terms do have distinct connotations. **Multidisciplinary practice**, for instance, refers to groups of professionals working together toward a similar goal while maintaining their individual interventions and not necessarily coordinating and communicating their efforts with one another (Moxley, 2013). **Interdisciplinary practice** (also referred to as **interprofessional practice or collaboration**, collaborative practice, and partnered practice), on the other hand, involves professionals from different disciplines integrating their professional knowledge to work together, in a single intervention, toward a common goal. For example, professionals engaged in multi-disciplinary practice may each provide services to an individual but not discuss the client as a group or share information in the client record. An interprofessional practice approach involves regular communication and coordination of services.

Social workers often work in **host settings** in which the primary mission is not the provision of social work services. These include health care facilities and programs, educational institutions, law enforcement or legal systems, military programs, and even financial institutions. Social workers collaborate interprofessionally in virtually every setting in which they are employed, and it is essential that social workers working in host settings understand the philosophies, professional cultures, and language of those settings and other professions. Interprofessional collaborations, while often effective, can be complex and, sometimes, frustrating working relationships (for more on interprofessional collaborations, see Chapter 10). Social workers may encounter difficulty communicating with other professionals who have their own professional "jargon"; perceived hierarchy of professional influence; and conflicting opinions on approach, roles, implementation, and outcomes related to the work.

Social workers can use their training in collaboration and negotiation with clients to prepare for becoming effective professional collaborators and to initiate partnerships that emphasize that others are committed to positive outcomes for the client. Abramson (2009) suggests that learning about those professions with which they will collaborate can enable social workers to become competent collaborators. Specific strategies for enhancing your interprofessional practice competence include: (1) familiarizing yourself with the duties of other professionals with whom you work; (2) recognizing and respecting the philosophy and orientation of other professions and frame your activities and documentation accordingly, thus avoiding social work–specific language and excessive detail; (3) maintaining a focus on being flexible, accommodating, supportive, and empowering versus an emphasis on problem solving; and (4) appreciating and celebrating the progress and successes (no matter how small) achieved by the client and the team (Bathgate, 2016). Upon gaining familiarity with your collaborators' professional socialization experience, language, and culture, you can then seek out common ground on which to begin building a professional collaboration.

There is considerable overlap among these roles. For example, in your role as a social worker in the foster care unit of your agency, you have identified that your clients and their foster families have a number of unmet needs. You then determine that educating the legislature regarding the needs of foster children may pave the way for a future advocacy effort. Because this blending and overlapping of roles is common, it is important for your and the client's benefit in undertaking the roles that is clear. If roles are not realistically or clearly communicated, the client, social worker, and even other interested parties can become frustrated and unable to participate fully in the intervention process. For example, if you educate policy makers about adults who have experienced psychiatric hospitalization, you should indicate any intention you might have of advocating for a particular treatment for a client. While education and advocacy are often interlinked, it is important to be clear about when you are advocating for a client and when you are educating about the client system.

PUTTING IT ALL TOGETHER [EPAS 8]

Thus far, this chapter has explored various aspects of social work practice in action, including interventions that support clients' strengths and their environments and the practice activities associated with contemporary social work roles. The chapter now turns to empowerment practice as a model for examining the possible points of integration for social work roles within the context of a client-centered, strengths-based practice approach.

Empowerment Practice

The social work profession has long been committed to empowering clients. One of the early scholars of empowerment practice, Simon (1990) has asserted that, in its purest sense, empowerment cannot be given to someone else because empowerment is not one person's to give to another. Empowerment resides within the individual, and the social worker can only encourage or perhaps release empowerment. Ultimately, change comes from the client her- or himself. Best practices in the application of empowerment theory suggest that (Parsons & East, 2013, p. 124):

- Social workers should use a sociopolitical lens to frame client experiences (e.g., exploring the impact of societal and cultural influences and realities on the client's life).

- In the helping relationship, social workers should frame power within the context of client strengths, self-efficacy, and education, as opposed to pathology, to enable the client and you to build on each of these areas when planning and implementing an intervention.

- Informal social networks are integral to client system empowerment (e.g., family, friends, faith, employment, and education communities).

- Collectivity (seeking and receiving help from others) is key to the intervention, with a specific emphasis on support, mutual aid, validation, and social justice for the client.

Empowerment-focused social work connects a client's strengths, environment, and capacity for action that empowers her or himself. This connection supports intervention in multiple interconnected settings and recognizes the importance of the client's sense of self. As a departure from the traditional problem-solving approach

© monkeybusinessimages/Thinkstock

that emphasizes identifying the problem and its causes, an empowerment-focused model of social work practice can enable the client to focus on future-oriented solutions, rather than becoming discouraged and feeling victimized by her or his situation (De Jong & Berg, 2013). Exhibit 5.3 provides an illustrative case example of an appropriate and sensitive empowerment approach.

Empowerment and Roles

The concept of empowerment is applicable to each role a social worker assumes when intervening with a client. The social worker can use empowerment concepts

EXHIBIT 5.3

Thomas's Story

This story takes place in a small New England city in the 1970s. Thomas was born with cerebral palsy, a neurological disorder. His parents had little idea how to deal with his severe physical limitations and had three other children to rear as well. His parents cared about him and did what they could to learn ways to support him and his abilities and to learn strategies for them all to cope with his disability. He received the standard medical care of the time and was sent to school with his age group, being integrated into class with his age-peers.

Early on, it was evident that Thomas's physical challenges did not reflect his aptitude for schoolwork. He was, in fact, intellectually capable and did exceedingly well in the subjects in which teachers supported him. His family did not understand, however, the ways in which Thomas's physical impairments affected his socialization or how he experienced his life. Although Thomas had only a few friends, he attempted for several years to maintain a positive outlook, even developing an excellent sense of humor. Nevertheless, he continued to feel excluded by peers and adults alike.

COLLIDING WITH THE WORLD

Over time, Thomas became hostile with teachers because he had to prove himself over and over again every time he entered a new grade or school. Each teacher and school administrator he encountered initially assumed he was unable to do grade-level work. One teacher questioned his very presence in the regular classroom. His pastor advised that he seek supported employment through a public vocational program. Everyone seemed to think he was unable to do, know, or even feel anything. His medical treatment included the excruciating requirement, promoted in those days, that he walk in physical therapy. No one noted or responded to Thomas's pain.

When Thomas was an adolescent, his parents sent him to a psychotherapist to learn the reasons for his intense anger. To Thomas, this was yet another insult. His therapist told him he needed to "get the chip off his shoulder" and tend to his schoolwork as his parents did not have funds to pay for him to attend college—he would have to earn scholarships if he wanted to do more than sit in the living room until he got matched to a job he did not want.

MEETING MAURA

When Thomas was in need of a new wheelchair, his parents could not pay the required deductible, so he was directed by his physician to a social worker for assistance. That social worker, Maura, who worked in the primary care office of Thomas's physician, first spent some time getting to know him and hearing what he had to say about the wheelchair. She helped him get funding for his new chair and continued to ask about his overall experience. He began to talk about his options regarding school, his family, his anger, and his growing sense of estrangement from the world.

Maura listened with an openness and reflexivity that showed Thomas she believed he was the expert on his experience. She heard his story, took him seriously, and helped him look at what his disability meant to him by asking him to talk, not only about his physical pain, but also about the exclusion he experienced. She helped him appreciate his resilience

EXHIBIT 5.3

Continued

in the face of all he had been through. She respected his perception of his experience and did not challenge it. She asked him to articulate how he wanted his life to be different in view of his strong capacities. She encouraged him to reflect on his own position and how he might address his goals. As time passed, Maura helped Thomas secure vocational rehabilitation funding for college and validated his by-then strong commitment to working in human services on disability issues. She also met with Thomas's family to help them understand his choices and the impact these choices would have on the family.

CHANGING DIRECTION

Thomas earned a master's degree in disabilities, and is preparing for a career in which he can advocate for people with disabilities. He is a full participant in his community and in the surrounding context of his family, friends, and culture. He is still angry sometimes, but he is not fearful or alone.

Reading this (almost all) true story, you can see how Maura implemented the empowerment focus: She helps liberate Thomas's "potent self" and encourages his interpersonal connections. She supports his understanding of his environment and helps connect him to a direction in which he can address the more political aspects of his experience. Consider now the connections between Thomas's experiences with other social work perspectives.

Social justice: Maura works diligently to expand Thomas's access to the benefits, helping him find funding for education. She does not accept the status quo in which those with private resources are privileged and those without are not. To complete this role as advocate for social justice, Maura would work toward reallocating educational funding for all people, not just for Thomas.

Human rights: The fact that Thomas is a person with a disability cannot be considered as a rationale for discrimination in education. Further, Article 26 of the United Nations Universal Declaration of Human Rights states that his disability must not preclude the "full development of [his] personality" through education. Recognizing Thomas' human rights, Maura recognizes Thomas as a person who has needs, abilities, and the right to fulfill his life as he chooses.

Strengths perspective: Maura recognizes Thomas's considerable strengths, validates them, and encourages linking the full expression of his strengths to his goals. She sees him as a whole human being with many talents to offer, not as a "victim of cerebral palsy."

Critical social construction: Maura sees Thomas's disability as a social construction resulting from the prevailing collective meaning our culture ascribes to it. She questions the limitations that construction imposes, and she believes Thomas can do what he sets out to do. Maura accepts that there are multiple realities and honors his experience of exclusion and oppression. Because his experience has developed within the context of his social location, on which he is the expert, she makes no attempt to "correct" his understanding. Her effort focuses on changing his future experience so that it is more consistent with how he wants to arrange his life.

to carry out the tasks associated with being a case manager, counselor, broker, mediator, educator, client advocate, and collaborator. Even in crises or tragedies that impact entire communities, regions, or the country as a whole, the social worker, working at any level of practice and any of the strategies discussed in this chapter, can approach interventions with an empowerment perspective in mind. If you are working with individuals who have experienced violence, a natural disaster, or community-wide crisis, your role can be not only to meet their immediate needs by establishing measurable and attainable goals, but also to help empower them to survive, advocate for themselves or others, or change the system. As Kohli and colleagues (2010) write: "We should appreciate the strengths of individuals that help them to survive in the worst of situations and use their strengths to empower them" (p. 266). Consider the resilience and fortitude of a client who has survived a significant life event and begin the intervention at that point of strength.

A social worker can play a strong role in empowering the client to engage in self-advocacy by building on the strengths of the client and the client's self-efficacy and life experience. Activities that promote self-advocacy and empowerment include helping clients prepare, providing education and support, and accompanying them during the advocacy process. Consider the situation in Brickville in which Virginia Stone fears losing her family's home to a real estate developer. What strengths and experiences do Virginia or her family members possess that she and her family might use to advocate on her behalf?

Empowerment Practice and Different Strategies

Social workers need different strategies to fit different situations to initiate and facilitate a strengths-based intervention that empowers clients. For example, while the narrative approach does not provide specific therapeutic skills, a social worker using the narrative approach can help empower clients to construct, deconstruct, and finally reconstruct the conceptualizations (i.e., stories) that have defined their lives. The social worker's role is to help clients determine if they wish to change their perceptions by challenging and broadening their thinking about their lives. Because the narrative approach is consistent with the social work values of strengths, collaboration, and viewing the client as the expert on her or his life, social workers can use it with other clinical (solution-focused) and cognitive behavioral approaches (Parsons & East, 2013).

One such empowerment-focused strategy that social workers can use to help clients reconceive how they view their lives is **motivational interviewing (MI)**. Initially developed for practice with clients mandated for services, motivational interviewing builds on the client's strengths and right to self-determination to implement a client-directed plan for change (Miller & Rollnick, 2013). Aimed at helping clients who are ambivalent or reticent about change, MI is a collaborative process in which the practitioner helps the client become more aware of the implications of her or his decision to engage (or not) in the change process (Lundahl,

Kunz, Brownell, Tollefson, & Burke, 2010). Psychologists Miller and Rollnick provide a more technical definition of MI: "a collaborative, goal-oriented style of communication with particular attention to the language of change. It is designed to strengthen personal motivation for and commitment to a specific goal by eliciting and exploring the person's own reasons for change within an atmosphere of acceptance and compassion" (2013, p. 29).

In a 2010 meta-analysis of 119 research studies using MI, Lundahl and colleagues concluded that MI can help clients with a variety of issues including addictions (e.g., substance abuse and gambling), high and low levels of distress, increasing healthy behaviors, and decreasing unhealthy behaviors, and it can enhance client participation in the intervention process. As with life circumstances and behaviors, the evidence further supports the use of MI with different cultures, populations, and settings, making it an attractive option for the social worker who receives specialized training in MI (Johnson, von Sternberg, & Velasquez, 2015).

Motivational interviewing is an evidence-based communication strategy in which the social worker uses empathy and reflective listening to help clients address their ambivalence regarding change (Hohman, Pierce, & Barnett, 2015; Wahab, 2005). Currently, social workers use MI in a variety of settings with a range of client situations (e.g., child welfare, treatment of substance abuse and other additions, intimate partner violence, and family and group work). As the expert on her or his life, the client is responsible for articulating her or his story and developing motivation to initiate life changes. While MI can be an effective strategy for working with behavioral change, MI can also be applied in situations in which clients are struggling to identify and accept a life event, adjust to a new life situation, and clarify feelings about an experience. As preparation for embarking on a change process, MI can also serve as a strategy to empower clients to enter into a treatment environment. For instance, MI can help individuals experiencing eating and anxiety-related disorders who often have considerable fear about even seeking help by reducing ambivalence about the process and increasing trust in the practitioner (Romano & Peters, 2015).

Four interrelated components underlie the perspective or "spirit" of MI: partnership, acceptance, compassion, and evocation (Miller & Rollnick, 2013, p. 15). Quick Guides 13 and 14 detail these components, the principles of MI, and skills and strategies for integrating motivational interviewing into practice. They review change talk, evoking change, and the four processes of MI, known as OARS—Open questions, Affirmation, Reflection, and Summary. Chapter 7 will discuss how social workers can use MI with families.

Motivational interviewing builds on a strengths-based, person-centered framework. To determine if MI is an appropriate intervention strategy for a particular client, consider the following (Miller & Rollnick, 2013, p. 25):

1. Are you and your client discussing change? MI is an appropriate strategy for virtually any type of change effort but particularly helpful in working with clients who are reluctant to engage in a change effort (e.g., addiction).

QUICK GUIDE 13   THE SPIRIT AND PRINCIPLES OF MOTIVATIONAL INTERVIEWING

Motivational Interviewing embraces the following concepts:

Partnership: The client is the expert on her or his life, and behavior change is most likely when the social worker and the client work together to determine areas of and strategies for change.

Acceptance: The social worker believes in the client's absolute worth, genuinely attempts to understand the client's perspective, respects the client's autonomy, and affirms those strengths and efforts the client demonstrates.

Compassion: The social worker conveys compassion by actively promoting and prioritizing the client's needs.

Evocation: Clients possess strengths and self-wisdom. They have reasons for their actions and have the motivation and resources to make desired change.

The principles upon which Motivational Interviewing is built stem from this spirit. They emphasize the social worker's ability to:

1. *Express empathy* to enhance client rapport and comfort and to decrease client resistance.
2. *Develop discrepancy* to help client see any gaps between her or his value system and current behaviors.
3. *Avoid arguing with client.*
4. *Roll with client resistance* to convey to the client that the social worker respects her or his apparent resistance to change and views it as normal.
5. *Support client self-efficacy* to promote the client's confidence in her or his ability to change behavior.

Source: Lundahl, Kunz, Brownell, Tollefson, & Burke, 2010 pp. 137; Miller & Rollnick, 2013, pp. 14–21

2. Should you initiate a conversation about change? The client may initially present to you not asking for help with change (does not see the need and/or thinks others are forcing the change) and MI techniques can help the client to view the change issues from a broader perspective.
3. Will client changes influence client outcomes? MI strategies can be used to help the client connect her or his own behaviors with desired outcomes.
4. Is the client ambivalent about change? MI techniques have long been used in working with clients who are uncertain or resistant to making changes in their lives.

The process of implementing an intervention using motivational interviewing encompasses four components (Miller & Rollnick, 2013, pp. 26–29):

- *Engaging:* establishing a connection with the client that promotes a positive working relationship;

- *Focusing:* developing a specific agenda for change;

- *Evoking:* drawing out the client's motivation for and articulating arguments that support making a change; and

- *Planning:* helping the client transition from being motivated for change to being ready for change. A client might exhibit this readiness if her or his conversation shifts from the "ifs and whys" of change to the "where and how" of change.

QUICK GUIDE 14   SKILLS AND STRATEGIES FOR MOTIVATIONAL INTERVIEWING

Three skill areas related to motivational interviewing include (Miller & Rollnick, 2013):

- *Change Talk* occurs when the client makes statements that encourage her or him to make a change in her or his life. Change talk contrasts with *Sustain Talk,* statements that favor maintaining the status quo (p. 7).
- *Evoking Change Talk* is a type of talk in which a social worker, using a person-centered approach aimed at initiating a desired change, elicits clients' wisdom and experience, including their ambivalence about change.
- *OARS* is a mnemonic that embraces the four core skills social workers use to facilitate the four processes of MI (pp. 32–34):

  ○ *Open Questions* involves questions such as "How are you feeling about your goal to lose weight?" to engage the client in expanded, reflective discussion about potential change.
  ○ *Affirmation* is when the social worker makes positive statements regarding the client's intentions, strengths, efforts, resources, and courage related to the proposed change. For example, the social worker may say to the client striving to lose weight: "I admire your commitment to living a healthier life. You are a good role model for your children."
  ○ *Reflective Listening* explores the client's previous statements, clarifying and deepening their meaning. The social worker might say, "It seems you are able to maintain your weight loss plan well, but you struggle with compliance in times of stress, like when you lost your mother."
  ○ *Summarizing* briefly recaps previous reflections, preparing the social worker and client to transition to the next phase of work. Summaries bring together the most important aspects of the conversation and aid in both the planning of the change process and the evaluation of change that has occurred. The social worker might summarize discussions with the client working on weight loss as follows: "We have talked about your past efforts to lose weight, the strategies you feel worked and did not work, and your commitment to being successful this time. We have also explored the triggers that make it more challenging for you to stay on your diet and exercise plan. We have brainstormed some strategies you can put to use when you are feeling particularly stressed and want to revert to your old eating patterns."

The role of the social worker is to focus on the client and her or his desire to make a change. Specifically, the social worker engages in MI when she or he listens and reflects, affirming those behaviors/activities that the client is doing well; identifying change talk, drawing out the client's motivation, wisdom, and strengths; and resisting the "righting reflex" (i.e., advice-giving, confronting, or arguing) (Miller & Rollnick, 2013, p. 324).

STRAIGHT TALK ABOUT INTERVENTIONS: UNEXPECTED EVENTS AND ONGOING EVALUATION

If you practice sensitive engagement, carefully assess both the client and the environment, and plan consistent methods for taking action on behalf of your clients, you might be seduced into thinking that the work will always go smoothly. This is a mistake.

In the practice world, not everything goes as planned. Because social work is so immersed in the lives of our clients, social workers have limited control over their work with clients and must accept (or at least tolerate) the up-and-down nature of the work. In the world of practice, people get sick, have accidents, change their minds, get fired and laid off, become disheartened, and move. Their kids get into trouble, and they experience violence. On the positive side, people also get promoted, find their strengths, find their voices, fall in love, get jobs, read inspiring books, discover new friends, and develop insights. All of these factors and many more have the potential to interrupt, postpone, redirect, or even terminate your work together.

In some cases—for example, if a client becomes discouraged or simply loses interest—you will want to inquire about how your words or actions might have contributed to these developments. In many cases, your responsibility will be to honor, acknowledge, and explore the meaning the client ascribes to the new situation and to reconfigure your work when indicated. It will be helpful for you to *expect the unexpected*. Flexibility is one of the most critical of all social work attributes. Consider the volatile couple with whom you have been helping to work toward as amicable a divorce as possible. The divorce is granted, and they come to you for help in reconciling—most likely a development you did not anticipate!

Just as you have consistently evaluated the progress of your work with your client and others involved throughout the engagement and assessment processes, you will want to periodically evaluate the direction of the intervention as well, particularly if the client has experienced substantial changes or unexpected events. Due to inertia and a tendency to continue going in one direction, it can be difficult to divert from the plan you so carefully crafted, even when it no longer fits the client's situation and/or needs very well. It is a good idea to check in with the client frequently during the intervention process. In that way, you can ensure that you are always providing relevant service that can become particularly important should the client encounter a crisis in her or his life.

The social worker's ability to intervene effectively in crises is contingent upon a timely response and accurate assessment. After ensuring, during the engagement and assessment phase, that the client is safe the social worker needs to focus during the intervention phase on empowering the client to resolve the crisis by reconstructing the client's self-perceptions of strengths, assets, and resources (Eaton & Roberts, 2009). The social worker and the client should collaborate to devise a viable plan to address the root causes of the crisis. The plan should emphasize concrete action strategies and include clear, agreed-upon steps for follow-up and maintenance.

SUPPORTING CLIENTS' STRENGTHS IN TERMINATION, EVALUATION, AND FOLLOW-UP [EPAS 9]

"Important things are almost never easy." Clients may demonstrate both positive and negative feelings about their termination process. They may view termination with a sense of accomplishment, ambivalence, sadness, or as a loss (possibly one of many) in their lives (Fortune, 2015). Even when all participants in a relationship agree that it is time to move on, the termination phase can be a wrenching process, often punctuated with doubts about whether the social worker has given or done enough, or wishing, in some vague way, to start over. This is a common experience that you have probably had yourself, perhaps when you left home or ended a significant relationship. Endings tend to raise ambivalence: On the one hand, they may be sad, while on the other hand, they represent a kind of freedom to be on your own, make a fresh start, gain new experiences, and be who you want to be.

The ends of relationships between social workers and clients often reflect these tensions. Some clients and social workers are tempted to minimize the significance of these endings; they may simply choose to "slip out the back." Others tend to take scrupulous notes with contact information and schedules and agree to call, text, connect on social networking sites, or email each other (which raises ethical questions that must be addressed within the policies of the agency). Many people develop patterns about how they deal with endings; these usually serve to mitigate the loss one inevitably experiences at the end of any significant relationship. Just as with the earlier phases of the social work intervention, supporting client strengths is important during the final stages of your work together.

The remainder of this chapter addresses the process of ending a professional relationship with your clients and the ways in which the social worker and client can continue to build on the strengths that the client brought to the relationship and developed during the intervention. It explores strategies for evaluating the practice intervention on multiple levels. Terminations that occur at the family, group, organization, or community level are unique; we will explore them in the following chapters. Our discussion in this chapter emphasizes general termination and evaluation issues relevant to social work relationships with individual clients.

ENDINGS AND TERMINATION [EPAS 9]

Endings can represent a metaphorical death, and it is important to recognize your responses to that, and to respect your clients' responses to it, in order to say goodbye to clients in an effective, positive, and professional way.

Endings occur in social work practice in numerous ways depending on the age, gender, ethnicity, socioeconomic status, cultural experience, working style, and personality of both the client and the social worker. The social location of the work, its purpose, the agency, the perspective used, and the organizational pressures surrounding the work also have an impact on the way in which the social worker–client relationship ends. Whatever the nature of the social worker, the client, and the intervention, general planning is important to bring closure to the professional social work relationship.

Planning the Process: Overview of the Termination

The following termination tasks are common to a range of relationships and are consistent with ethical social work practice. These tasks will not apply to all social work relationships, and their order need not be rigid. Your theoretical orientation and the specifics of the practice situation (e.g., your knowledge of the client and agency policy and practice) will guide when and in what order you complete these termination tasks.

- Negotiate the timing of the termination

- Review the agreement for the work

- Process successes and shortcomings

- Develop and clarify plans for termination and maintenance of change

- Share responses to ending

- Practice cultural humility

Negotiating the Timing   Because termination is a goal that social worker and client establish at the beginning of the relationship, it should not only guide the intervention but remain a focus for discussion as you progress through the intervention. In some circumstances, you and your client can specify the number of sessions at the start of the relationship and determine the closing date during your first meeting. The same is often true of mandated arrangements or managed care situations in which the agency must adhere to prearranged stipulations regarding the length of the service provided. The prearranged guidelines are, of course, artificial proclamations that the work is done, and they are all externally imposed. Predetermined boundaries do not always coincide with the ideal timing for termination, which is when the social worker and client have achieved the mutually formulated goals. In some cases, clients may request additional sessions (as in task-centered models), and social workers may petition for an extended number of sessions (as in managed care).

Determining if goals have been reached may not be apparent. Consider your client who has recently shared with his family that he is gay but is struggling with sharing the information with his teachers and classmates. Even when you and your client state goals in precise behavioral terms (for example, "The client will contact the school social worker to ask for help and guidance"), there is no guarantee that the intervention will realize those established goals and plans. For example, your client may have unsuccessfully attempted to contact the school social worker, or he may have made contact but was unable to clearly articulate his message; in this case, achieving the stated goal did not address the real issue. If the goal(s) have not been met, it is your responsibility as a social worker to make a reasoned judgment that the client no longer needs your services. You and your client may not agree on the exact moment when that occurs, and in many cases, the two of you will need to negotiate the timing of and criteria for ending the professional relationship, remembering that you are each subject to your own interpretations of the situation.

There are at least three areas to consider when you negotiate the termination of a social work relationship. First, as a social worker, you are obligated to provide the client with full information about the possible nature and timing of termination. In many circumstances, you will not have control over the timing, but in others, you can at least anticipate, if not change, the conditions. For example, a state contract or managed care restrictions may determine an end date that you think is inappropriate. In such a situation, you can prepare the client for the possibility that your appeal for more time/sessions may be denied. You may encounter similar complications if your agency is about to eliminate services or programs, your position is threatened, or you know you are leaving your job or internship on a particular date.

Second, just as you have ongoing discussions with your client about goals, contracts, and progress, you should also discuss termination throughout your relationship. It is important to maintain dialogue with your client to determine whether or not your work together is helping and to consider what else might need to happen for the client to know she or he has met the goals. Even when the agency or your intervention plan determines the end point, ongoing discussion about termination can and should be integral to the work.

The final issue involves predetermined endings. When you and your client both know from the outset how many times you will meet, you can regularly check in with the client to reinforce your shared understanding of the point at which the work will be completed. Some clients may assume that you can or will extend the number of sessions at your discretion, and others might expect that, if they behave/perform well (especially in mandated sessions), you will "dismiss" them early. Always be as clear as possible about any limits that are imposed on you for the work and be as open as possible to discussing what those limits mean for your client.

Even when both sides clearly understand the end date, either may still experience difficult relationship ending dynamics.

Reviewing the Agreement for Work   In the process of finishing your work together, you and your client should review your prearranged formal or informal agreement for the work. You may want to renegotiate the understanding each of you has about the agreement, as it may have changed in view of your completed work, circumstances in your lives, or changes in the agency's ability to offer services.

Processing Successes and Shortcomings   You and your client should discuss and process those aspects of the work that are going well, those that miss the mark, and any approaches that are clearly heading in the wrong direction throughout the work; this type of assessment should not be reserved for your last meeting. Nevertheless, a culminating summary of successes provides valuable perspective on the experience as a whole and insight into the client's view of the work. In fact, you may consider framing a termination as a "graduation" as the term imparts a sense of achievement for which the client may feel pride and satisfaction. Sometimes, for example, you or your client may find that, in retrospect, you now associate with personal growth an experience that seemed difficult at the time. Recall the example from earlier in the chapter of the client with mental illness who struggled to locate housing. Perhaps at the time she found challenging your suggestion that she was ready to meet with the landlord on her own. As your work together progressed, however, she may have come to see your suggestion as a useful push that helped her recognize her strengths. From an empowerment perspective, your client's success suggests her ability to act on her own needs. She no longer views herself as a victim but instead sees herself as someone who has defied the power imbalance that people impose on others when they use negative labels to describe them. Power and human rights definitions are one useful tool clients and social workers can use to process successes.

At this point in the social work relationship, it is not uncommon for some clients to indicate that they have not made as much progress as they want to make or you believe they have. A client may point to various criteria to demonstrate her or his shortcomings. The client may feel that ending the work at this point represents a sort of abandonment and may raise the possibility that it would be premature and possibly harmful to end the working relationship. On the other hand, some clients may express these doubts to convey a lack of confidence in their ability or readiness to make their way independently. One effective way to address such dynamics is to be transparent about the process and to engage the client in a detailed discussion of the issues throughout the relationship. Whether or not you offer to continue to work with a client is a matter of your professional judgment, your supervisor's judgment, and other agency or funding constraints.

Some clients, anticipating the end of the working relationship, will threaten to leave the relationship early. This "I'll fire you before you fire me" response, sometimes called **flight**, may minimize a client's sense of abandonment. In a case like this, make every effort to engage the client in the process for at least one more session/meeting in which you can address the end of the relationship and strive for closure. A positive ending process sometimes results in the most personal growth for clients who pointedly (and physically) avoid the ending steps in the work.

Some clients may identify shortcomings in your own work. When you ask for ideas about those aspects of the intervention that did not unfold as you or the client had hoped or expected, you must be truly open to receiving a critical answer. An account of your shortcomings or those of the process itself may surprise you, especially if the client has not expressed any dissatisfaction along the way. Although it can be difficult to hear critical comments, you can choose to learn from them and remain open to the message your client is attempting to impart to you.

Making and Clarifying Plans   Sometimes the work is clearly finished and the client is ready to move ahead without further assistance. Other times, though, you may determine that your best course of action is to refer a client to a different type of service or to transfer a client to another social worker, either in your agency or in a different agency. Suppose that, throughout your practicum, you have worked with a client named "Sam." As the month of May and your graduation nears, you realize that Sam is not likely to complete the work he had hoped to do before you leave your position. In negotiation with him, you will need to reassess his progress, where he wants to go from here, and through what arrangement he is mostly likely to continue his work effectively. You can help him to clarify his options and to assess his own needs at termination. After you terminate your working relationship with your client, it is possible that he will receive no further services. He may experience this independence as a setback, or it may promote his continued growth.

When you decide to refer a client to another agency, you assume the role of broker. Fulfill this responsibility with great care; regardless of your experience, your skill level, or the level of success of your work with the client, your inappropriate or ill-conceived referral can undo any client gains.

A client who is ready to end professional services needs a plan to maintain gains and/or continue further growth without your ongoing support. Some clients may find it difficult outside the client–worker relationship to maintain changes without some clear way to reinforce them. You can help the client to identify and explore potential situations and to consider strategies for addressing future stresses or events. You can also encourage the client to identify a support network within her or his community before ending the work or direct the client to other available community resources. Suppose that you and Sam identify formal (e.g., agencies, services, organizations) and informal (e.g., individuals) resources that will be available to him following the termination of his relationship with you. At termination, most clients will return to (e.g., following residential treatment) or continue to live in the environment in which their struggles arose, so having a strategy to cope with those environments can be critical to their ability to maintain gains. You might suggest that, once your work together is terminated, Sam can "rehearse" his response to potential situations that may arise on his own.

Sharing Responses to Endings   Identifying and articulating feelings about termination may be the most sensitive dimension of ending the work. You will need to anticipate, to the extent that you can, the way in which your client will respond to termination and those issues that will require attention. Many clients have endured a series of difficult endings in their lives. For example, clients may have endured difficult breakups, or they may have been removed from abusive homes, been abandoned by others, or witnessed violence that resulted in death or separation. Clients living in poverty and with social exclusion may have experienced turbulence in their living situation and abrupt disconnection from others, such as with the experience of eviction. If ending well turns out to be the most positive aspect of your work together, that, in and of itself, will be work well done and could provide your client with a model of a healthy ending to a relationship. Clients will often thank you for helping them through a difficult time in their lives. Should a client express gratitude for your helping her or him, you can remind the client that she or he is the one who did the actual work—your role was to serve as the "coach" or "facilitator."

Social workers, too, may have experienced chaotic, sometimes traumatic, disruptions. In termination, many social workers struggle as much as or more than clients. Many new social workers are surprised to realize how attached they have become to a client and find themselves unprepared to respond appropriately with objective emotional distance. This understandable reaction is an issue to discuss in supervision. To facilitate a professional approach, the social worker should keep in mind that the purpose of the relationship is to promote the client's—and not the social worker's—well-being.

When you discuss feelings about termination, let your clients know about your own ambivalence: express your own sadness about ending the relationship, that you have enjoyed knowing them, and that you are confident they will meet their own needs effectively in the future. It is generally inappropriate to express acute feelings of loss so that clients feel they must help you cope, just as it is inappropriate to continue the relationship beyond whatever follow-up arrangements you might make without initiating a new process. Utilizing colleagues and/or supervisors, processing your feelings about terminations can be an important part of your own professional development and self-care. For example, after working with Mrs. Jones in which she attempted suicide, the new social worker debriefed her strong emotions with an experienced colleague to process and manage her emotions about the client, their work together, and the termination process.

Exhibit 5.4 depicts two opposing termination-related exchanges between Virginia and her social worker as they move toward ending their working relationship.

Over the course of a career, many client situations challenge these guidelines for termination. Some situations, particularly in rural social work practice, may have the potential to become dual relationships when both a professional and

EXHIBIT 5.4 *The Dialogue of Termination*	These two examples of an exchange between Virginia Stone (www.routledgesw.com/cases) and her social worker demonstrate the power of an effective termination process. As you recall, Virginia and her social worker have been working on a number of challenging issues, including housing, caregiving, grief, and loss. Due to the number and intensity of the issues they have worked on together, their relationship has spanned more than a year. There are many ways to handle terminations. Which of these two examples would you choose?

Termination Option #1	**Termination Option #2**
Social Worker: *Virginia, as we discussed the last time we met, today will be our final meeting. I want to take this opportunity to review our progress.*	Social Worker: *Virginia, I think today should be our final meeting. You will recall that we discussed at our first meeting that we would end our work at some point. I feel we are at that point now. What do you think of this idea?*
Virginia: *I've been thinking a lot about this since last time and I feel good about things.*	
Social Worker: *Let's take a look at each of the items in the contract we developed early in our time together.*	Virginia: *What do you mean? I didn't know we had to stop. Did I do something wrong?*
Before we get started looking over the list, I want to let you know that I have enjoyed working with you and seeing you make such positive changes in your life. I will miss our meetings. I want you to know that you can feel free to contact me if any further needs arise in the future.	Social Worker: *No, you haven't done anything wrong. I just decided that we have accomplished as much as we are probably going to. Let's do a quick re-cap. I think that will help you see what I mean.*

personal relationship exist. For example, a social worker would be in a dual relationship if she or he works with the client in a social work capacity and also purchases real estate from the client. The boundaries in such situations are less than clear. In situations like these in which no simple rule is adequate, the social worker can seek dialogue with supervisors and peers to resolve issues. When dual relationships are unavoidable, it is always the social worker's responsibility to avoid exploitation in the personal relationship.

Respecting Cultural Consistency   Due to cultural differences, clients may differ from the social worker in their approach and reaction to endings, which gives the social worker the opportunity to practice cultural humility. As in all aspects of the work, the social worker must incorporate cultural diversity into the termination process, ensuring that it is culturally appropriate for the client (Fortune, 2015). For example, if a client lives in a culture with tightly woven informal ties, the client may view the formal aspects of ending the work and cutting off the relationship as a reflection of your annoyance or rejection. The social worker may need to address this situation to ensure that the client understands the nature of the termination.

Some clients may have difficulty speaking about their emotions because their cultural orientation encourages a restrained and private approach to sentiment. In cases such as these, it may be productive to emphasize how the client's return to a supportive and nurturing ethnic community will help to consolidate her or his gains. This rejoining with the community is often especially critical in communities of color (Lum, 2004). In some situations, a client may bring you a gift, a gesture that may represent a more comfortable way to express feelings, reflect celebration, and offer a suitable token of closure. In others, you may prefer to maintain a more formal, businesslike relationship. Note that your ability to accept gifts, no matter how small, is dependent on the policy of your organization.

STRAIGHT TALK ABOUT TERMINATION AND ENDINGS [EPAS 9]

The termination processes discussed thus far assume conditions in which ending is planned. When, as often happens, endings are unplanned and not under your control, your role is to negotiate the unexpected. Earlier we explored scenarios in which the client leaves the relationship before you expect. Clients may terminate a relationship early because of a life-changing event, or they may terminate early because they do not feel the relationship has been fully established or productive. For example, if the client is not clear about expectations or does not share the social worker's understanding of the purpose of the work, she or he may feel that the meetings lack focus and direction. Social workers may identify outcome goals that the client may not find relevant (even when clients "agree" to them). If a client is unclear about the end point of the work, she or he may not remain engaged in the process. In such cases, the work may continue, but the client may grow discouraged.

There are multiple reasons the client might prematurely end the work, all of which present the social worker with dilemmas regarding the appropriate response and its meaning to the client. If the reason for the premature ending is a result of the client withdrawing, the most useful strategy is to make low-pressure contact, if possible, and to encourage the client to return to the work, if only to end it in a more purposeful way. This approach conveys respect for the integrity of the work while leaving the client able to determine if the work will resume. You can use this contact to explore the dynamics of the relationship, which may provide important information to inform your future work.

In institutional settings, your work with clients may be prematurely terminated when the client is transferred to another unit or service. In this case, you may want to petition your supervisor for a single meeting to reconnect with your client, if only briefly, to review the work and acknowledge the shift in care. Although institutions tend to organize themselves in terms that meet the staff's, rather than clients', needs, make an effort to prioritize the latter whenever you can. When you have made every effort and your client does not respond, respect the manner of ending she or he has chosen. At that point, it is the client's choice, and by humbly understanding the limits of your influence on the client, you respect his or her self-determination.

At least once in your career, it is likely that you will terminate one or more client relationships before the work is completed when you leave an organization. When the social work relationship ending is worker-initiated, the client may feel a loss of control, disappointment, and/or anger, both over the ending and over the future of her or his intervention (Siebold, 2007).

Following up with clients can be an important part of the termination process for clients and social workers as it provides information regarding client status, progress, and sustainability of change but may or may not be an option for social workers. Agency policy and the client's situation will determine if having contact with the client after termination is appropriate; therefore, you should clearly communicate your ability and intentions regarding follow-up to the client during the termination process.

FORMAL EVALUATIONS

While many practitioners feel anxious at the mention of evaluation, most social workers appreciate the importance of evaluating practice. Evaluation can provide feedback regarding goal achievement, the utility of a particular method, and the client's experience of the work. It can be globally focused, behaviorally directed, and process-oriented. The evaluation process can also reflect on individual progress, group development, and changes in power structures. In short, evaluation is a useful tool for practitioner development, rather than a threat.

Evaluation Priorities

The profession has long debated which evaluative strategies are relevant to and most appropriate for social work practice. As we discussed in Chapter 4, many scholars maintain that social work practice should be informed by empirical, evidenced-based practice to function in our contemporary society. Practice evaluation data has multiple uses; it can inform and improve your practice assessment and interventions, provide data for use in funding proposals, and aid in program planning. Scholars Bloom, Fischer, and Orme (2009, p. 15) suggest that, in order to be an evaluation-informed practitioner, one must strive to be a **scientific practitioner**. A scientific practitioner uses evidence and evaluation without compromising the "art and creativity of practice." Thus, scientific practice includes: (1) using research and evaluation to identify interventions that are proven to be effective; (2) systematically monitoring and evaluating one's practice using single-system designs (described next); (3) engaging in ongoing learning to improve practice competencies; (4) approaching social work practice with problem-solving, investigation, and discovery goals; and (5) remaining committed to the values and ethics of social work practice (p. 15).

Though social work ethics mandates that the provision of service obligations take precedence over data collection and evaluation efforts, evaluative strategies are an important component of effective practice. Evaluation of one's practice can provide information that is consistent with social work practice requirements, values, commitment to informed practice, and serve to empower both the client and the social worker. Imagine how empowering it can be for a client to realize she or he now has experience of successfully overcoming a year-long challenge. Evaluation of practice has become an important component of agencies' ability to secure and maintain funding for services. Virtually all public and private funding entities require service providers to evaluate practice interventions and outcomes using standardized and multiple forms of data collection.

The following sections present two major methods of evaluation: empirical design processes and reflective assessment. These two methods serve complementary purposes. Together, they contribute to evidence-based practice while validating the contemplative, postmodern social worker's inclination to critique traditional practice and evaluation processes through focused critical reflection.

Quantitative and Empirical Processes: Evidence-Based Practice

Quantitative and empirical evaluation processes have two tools in common: single-subject design (SSD) and goal attainment scaling (GAS).

Single-Subject Design   Applicable to any theoretically guided intervention, **single-subject design** (SSD) is a group of evaluative procedures based on an intuitive framework for examining behavioral changes in one client over time (Fischer & Orme, 2013). Single-subject design evaluation plans assess and monitor interventions, adapt to changes in the intervention plan, and compare the effectiveness of different interventions (Bloom et al., 2009, pp. 264–265).

The single-subject design is highly flexible and generally easy to use. Usually, the social worker and client measure an action, feeling, or behavior multiple times over the course of their work together. Consider Virginia's return to her walking program. The two of you could use a single-system design approach to chart and monitor her progress. The visual depiction of her activity would provide an accounting that could serve as the basis for discussion, revising the intervention plan, and evaluating Virginia's progress. Conversely, a social worker could use one intervention with a series of clients. Consider that you are working with a client who wants to stop smoking cigarettes. Utilizing a single-system design approach in which you track the clients individually and compile the results may help you to identify those strategies that are more effective than others, possible time frames for interventions, and events that trigger relapses.

To administer this design effectively, the client and social worker meet over a period of time to allow for repeated measurements. The social worker and client first agree on the behavior, attitude, or belief they will measure and how they will measure it. As in developing any intervention plans, the behavior or behaviors selected should be client-centered and reflect the client's goals of the work. Single-subject design evaluations do not typically focus on peripheral concerns, such as how often the client arrives on time. There is no maximum number of attributes that the social worker and client can select, but in general, you will want to select no more than a few after considering a wider range to promote a more focused, measurable, and achievable intervention (Bloom et al., 2009).

You can measure the frequency (the number) of occurrences, or you can use a standardized measurement tool that yields a numerical result. The social worker and the client should establish a relatively consistent schedule for taking measurements throughout the course of the evaluation. For example, if you want to monitor the number of new social contacts your client initiates, consider the accumulated frequency of contacts over a standard period (e.g., every two weeks).

In most cases, the phases of your evaluation will include a **baseline**, which is the rate at which or number of times the behavior occurred before the client came to you (for example, the number/pack of cigarettes a client smokes/day); intervention (strategies to promote smoking cessation, including behavioral and/or pharmaceutical); **maintenance** or the period of stabilizing client gains (tallying smoke-free days or instances of relapse); and follow-up (checking-in period). All of these measures, once completed, can be charted to depict a visual pattern. If you and your client cannot establish a baseline because your client needs immediate intervention, you can still plot improvements as they occur during the intervention (for example, at one-week or one-month intervals).

If you are able to establish a baseline prior to the intervention, your measurements can show the differences before and after the intervention. This suggests that the improvement is a result of your work together as it assumes that, without your intervention, the baseline measurement would remain unchanged (this is, of course, a big assumption). In the example of smoking cessation, it is possible that the client could end her or his smoking without your intervention, but conducting and reflecting on a single-subject design evaluation can aid the client in gaining insight into the process of behavior change. If the intervention is interrupted (e.g., one of you goes on vacation), reducing the frequency of your client's social initiations, you can see if improvement resumes when your work starts up again. If it does, that strengthens the connection between your work and your client's improvement. However, such interruptions may not be in the client's best interests, and you should never disrupt the course of the work simply to demonstrate its success. Exhibit 5.5 provides an example of an SSD graph.

Goal Attainment Scaling   Suitable for use in a variety of settings, **goal attainment scaling** (GAS) is a standardized framework that social workers can customize to fit

This graph is an example of the single-subject design model. From the graph you can see that, in the baseline period before the work began, the client initiated three, then two, and then no new social contacts at two-week intervals. During the weeks of service, those numbers increased from two to seven, with a setback at week eight. After the work ended, the client initiated seven, then five, then six, and then seven new contacts. This shows improvement from the baseline period.

EXHIBIT 5.5

Simple Single-Subject Design

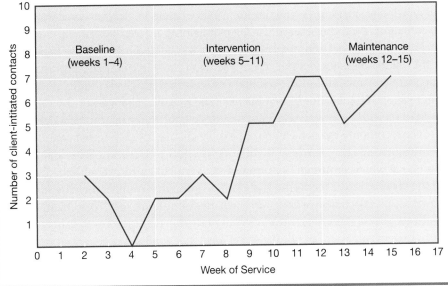

individual client-initiated goals. The first step of the multiphase GAS process is to identify two to five client goals and develop a scale for each based on the quality of the outcome on a continuum from most desired to least desired potential results. The following is one useful scale (Bloom et al., 2009):

0   Most unfavorable outcome thought likely.
1   Less than expected success.
2   Expected level of success.
3   More than expected success.
4   Most favorable outcome thought likely.

Using this model, the social worker and client describe in a few words the client's condition or status for each goal before the intervention (the baseline). This baseline condition or status represents position 1 on the scale. Next they indicate what a deteriorated condition or status might look like at the lowest point (0).

Finally, the social worker and client describe the best possible scenario (4), a very good scenario (3), and an expected scenario (2). For example, if one of your client's goals is to attend parenting classes as part of a plan to regain custody of her children, you may agree to use the status descriptions in the chart in Quick Guide 15. The chart also provides status descriptions for two additional goals: attending GED classes and maintaining a clean apartment.

Following this process, you and your client can measure goal achievement more precisely by assigning a relative weight to each goal, reflecting its importance in the individual case situation. As you can see in Quick Guide 15, the individual weight is 75 for attending parenting classes, 15 for maintaining a clean apartment, and 10 for attending GED classes, for a total of 100. To track a client's progress, place a check mark in the cell that best describes the client's status at the start of the social work relationship (baseline) and an X in the cell that best describes the client's status at the end of that relationship (outcome). Then calculate the weighted change score by subtracting the start score from the end score and multiplying the difference by the weight.

Next, compute the percentage of possible change for each scaled goal. To calculate this percentage, determine the highest possible mark on the scale and divide it into the actual weighted change score. Finally, calculate an overall score by adding all the possible scores for all the goals and dividing that number into the sum of the actual weighted change scores. Although this procedure may seem daunting and overly empirical, it becomes intuitive with practice. You may want to gain familiarity with this evaluative strategy by using a change that you have experienced personally.

Originally developed for use with individual clients, goal attainment scaling is well suited to a range of social work interventions, including child and adult mental health and work with families and organizations. GAS is also a proven effective strategy for evaluating crisis interventions (Roberts, 2013). Crisis interventions and GAS both emphasize short-term, structured, and specific characteristics, and the social worker engaged in crisis intervention work can easily and quickly use GAS to evaluate for both the client and her- or himself the process and outcomes of their work together.

Other Forms of Evaluation   There are other quantitative measurement scales and other methods of attaining evaluative data that are not always quantitative (empirically based) but may be qualitative (narratively based). The latter include instruments like client satisfaction scales or client evaluations of the agency, the social worker, or both. Although these tools are often considered highly subjective and not particularly rigorous, they frequently provide both the social worker and the agency with valuable information about the client's experience, but they may or may not yield specific outcome-based information about the client's experience with change.

Postmodern Views of Evaluation   In this world of managed care and increasing calls for evidence-based accountability, effective social workers must understand

QUICK GUIDE 15   GOAL ATTAINMENT SCALING

Client: Clarissa			
	Key:✓ = Beginning level		× = Ending level
Attainment Grade	Task 1: Attend parenting classes	Task 2: Attend GED classes	Task 3: Keep apartment clean
0 Most unfavorable outcome likely	✓ No attendance at parenting classes	No attendance at GED classes	✓ No satisfactory ratings for cleanliness
1 Less than expected success	Attend less than 50% of the time	✓ Attend less than 40% of the time	Receive satisfactory ratings less than 60% of the time
2 Expected level of success	Attend 50%–75% of the time	Attend 40%–60% of the time	Receive satisfactory ratings 60%–80% of the time
3 More than expected success	× Attend 76%–95% of the time	Attend 61%–85% of the time	Receive satisfactory ratings 81%–95% of the time
4 Best anticipated success	Attend 96%–100% of the time	× Attend 86%–100% of the time	× Receive satisfactory ratings 96%–100% of the time

Summary	Task 1	Task 2	Task 3	Total
Percent of goal	75	10	15	100
Change in score	3	3	4	
Total score	225	30	60	315
Possible total score	300	40	60	400
Percent of goal attained	75%	75%	100%	79%

how to document, evaluate, and account for the usefulness of their efforts. To make an informed choice from among many evaluative methods, you should know the shortcomings and criticisms of each. Critics charge that many evaluative models exclude the richer, nuanced contributions of the less quantifiable aspects of client situations (e.g., those aspects related to the social worker–client relationship), as well as qualitative research, and that they overshadow ethnographic forms of evaluation that explore cultural phenomena and ultimately question the assumptions of the everyday world.

Practitioners who use quantitative evaluation methods recognize they are based on expectation, researcher bias, and a political agenda that some social workers find unhelpful. Even when workers find themselves in a situation in which they must demonstrate the value of their work through empirical evaluations in order to accommodate their organizations and/or funders, they cannot afford to de-emphasize the possible vulnerabilities and opportunities for error in the evaluations themselves. In this case, it is helpful for social workers to possess a form of bilingualism—that is, you will need to speak the language of contemporary demands while remaining alert to and keeping up with critiques of those demands. For example, it is important to separate the outcomes of the client intervention from the client's feelings about the agency. In this case, the client may have achieved the goals that were established but have negative feedback about the agency or even you. The opposite can also occur—the client does not accomplish the desired goals but feels she or he had a positive experience with the agency and/or you.

Social workers who find these empirical methods mechanical or lacking in substance may want to examine their work on other levels. Although support for quantitative evidence-based practice is strong and gaining momentum in the profession, social workers are not restricted to these evaluative strategies but can use other acceptable replacements. Social workers can also reflect on their practice, as discussed next.

Qualitative and Reflective Processes

We now turn our attention to other ways to evaluate social work practice, including case studies, explorations of compatibility with theoretical perspectives, and quality of relationship. These methods can expand your thinking about social work practice. They are not meant to compete with empirical processes but, rather, can be combined with them to create a well-rounded evaluation process.

With any of these methods, many questions about the client's experience and outcomes could be asked; we suggest some here. Whichever method you choose, you should purposefully focus your inquiry on a specific set of outcomes. If you want to gain an additional perspective on a case, consider engaging your supervisor as a second reader in a case study (discussed next) or your peers in a group conversation to explore particular issues. With this additional information, you can reflect on and expand your options for intervention and evaluation. Examining specific issues can also help focus ongoing staff meetings and professional development activities. Available technology can also enrich the data that you are able to gather about your practice. Meetings can be audio or videotaped, which allows you to review and reflect on the content at a later time.

Case Studies   Like single-system designs, **case studies** involve intensive analysis of one individual, group, or family and depend on accurate, careful, and detailed record keeping. A case study typically spans the course of the work. Case studies do not generate empirical data from planned comparisons but are instead an accounting of the client's situation while working with you and, as such are often lengthy and fairly detailed. Case studies have long been used in social work practice as the basis for the evolution of the formal evaluation process (Bloom et al., 2009). While space prohibits the presentation of a complete case study here, we encourage you to review the interactive cases for the Sanchez and Stone families or for Carla Washburn, which are available on the book's companion website at www.routledgesw.com/cases. As you review the cases and complete the interactive assignments, you can document your thoughts, reactions, and plans in the online notebook. These notes can provide the foundation for a **case study**, a method of evaluation that systematically examines the characteristics of one individual, group, family, or community over an extended period of time (Barker, 2014, p. 57). The case study is compiled only after the full planned change effort has been completed and you have ample information to evaluate progress and outcomes.

You can use a case study for postmodern reflection. For example, in reviewing the initial contact, you might ask if your sensitivity matched the client's need for validation, consider other ways you could have articulated your purpose, or reflect on how your work might have progressed had you taken another tack. Perhaps you thought you expressed agency requirements clearly, but looking back on the records, you can see where your language may have been confusing. How might the work have gone differently if those requirements had been clear to the client? There are hundreds of potentially helpful ways you can reflect on the work, both in supervision and on your own. A record of your observations, what you thought about the work, and what the client said—all of these can provide material for later analysis. When you review your experiences and those of your client using case studies, you often come to appreciate how you have grown as a professional.

In order to compile a case study, a social worker must have excellent communication and documentation skills. The documentation guidelines we discussed in Chapter 4 are essential throughout the intervention, termination, and evaluation phases to ensure both client and social worker have well-organized, articulate social work records. Quick Guide 16 provides guiding principles for clinically focused practice writing, and Quick Guide 17 presents a sample case summary. With the integration of standardized forms and electronic records, case summaries may be created using a "fillable" online form, but the data gathered and compiled continues to include key items of information related to the client's situation, including the identified need for services, assessment and planning, actions taken, and termination and evaluation notes.

Explorations of Compatibility with Theoretical Perspectives   Another way to evaluate your work is to explore how well the intervention strategies adhere to the theoretical perspectives you embrace. This approach is especially helpful when those perspectives challenge you and stretch your thinking.

In this text, social work practice has been placed with four frameworks thus far: social justice, human rights, the strengths perspective, and critical social construction. These theoretical frameworks represent multiple perspectives, each of which suggests a set of broad criteria for evaluating the work you have completed. For example, are you consistently recognizing your clients' strengths, or do you tend to be pulled into a pathology orientation? Are you alert to social justice concerns when you meet with

QUICK GUIDE 16   GUIDING PRINCIPLES FOR CLINICAL WRITING

- Social work values and ethics should guide your writing. Your commitment to client's self-determination, strengths, empowerment, and cultural competence must be ever present as you write about clients in any form of documentation, including case records, case studies, letters, emails, and court reports.
- In keeping with your commitment to ethical practice, use words that do not label, denigrate, depersonalize, or marginalize clients (e.g., do not use words like "abusive parent," "handicapped boy," or "welfare mother").
- Extend the strengths perspective into your documentation, using strengths-focused language to give "voice" to the client's narrative story (e.g., "In sharing her experiences of surviving a sexual assault, Mary focused on the coping strategies she used to regain her sense of safety and security.").
- Maintain person-centered practice standards to emphasize the client's rights to confidentiality and self-determination. Operationally, respectful writing only includes information that is relevant to the current situation. If you believe collateral sources can benefit from additional information, consider an alternative form of communication (e.g., case conference, telephone contact, etc.) and secure a signed release from the client.
- Understand and follow agency and state requirements regarding what client information you may communicate, including health or disability status and compliance with the Health Insurance Portability and Accountability Act (HIPAA).
- Keep in mind those individuals and groups who may have access to the documents you create, including clients and their families, co-workers, court systems, or even media outlets, and ensure that your writing is fact-based and that any opinion-based content is clearly labeled as such.

Source: Sormanti, 2012, pp. 129–131

Resources to Support Practice-Related Writing:

American Psychological Association. (2010). *Publication Manual of the American Psychological Association* (6th ed). Washington, DC: American Psychological Association.

Green, W., & Simon, B.L. (2012). *The Columbia Guide to Social Work Writing.* New York: Columbia University Press.

Kagle, J. D., & Kopels, S. (2008). *Social Work Records* (3rd ed). Long Grove, IL: Waveland Press, Inc.

Purdue Online Writing Lab (OWL). https://owl.english.purdue.edu/owl/section/2/10/.

Szuchman, L.T., & Thomlison, B. (2011). *Writing with Style: APA Style for Social Work* (4th ed.). Belmont, CA: Cengage Learning.

Weisman, D., & Zornado, J.L. (2013). *Professional Writing for Social Work Practice.* New York: Spring Publishing Company.

QUICK GUIDE 17   CREATING A CASE SUMMARY

Effective and accurate documentation is essential for social work practice. While formats and content are agency-specific, the following example provides an abbreviated presentation of a typical case summary. For this example, let us return to Jasmine Johnson, a client discussed in Chapters 3 and 4.

Opening summary

Jasmine is a 33-year-old African American woman and a single parent to a 14-year-old son, Devon. Jasmine requested services to help her improve her relationship with her son and to find better strategies for disciplining him. She admits to having hit him when she believed he was being disrespectful to her but denies any current or past abuse or neglect.

Assessment

Family history: Jasmine was married at age 18 and gave birth to Devon when she was 19 years old. She and Devon's father divorced two years ago when Devon, then 12, was starting middle school. Jasmine was awarded sole custody of her son and monthly child support, but the payments are sporadic. To save money, Jasmine and Devon moved out of the family home and live in a one-bedroom apartment across town where Devon sleeps on the fold-out couch in the living room. The move required Devon to attend a new school.

Employment and financial situation: Jasmine has worked in the housekeeping department of a large hospital for the past eleven years. The hospital provides comprehensive benefits (e.g., health insurance, retirement, and educational support), but her salary is low, and she often struggles to pay all her bills each month.

Social support and resources: Jasmine and her family did not have any family living in the community where she moved with her then-husband for his job. Her ex-husband remains in the area but has remarried and is expecting a new child. He seems to have little time for Devon but does see him occasionally, usually when Jasmine contacts him and asks him to see his son.

Jasmine's supports in the community now include a tight-knit group of co-workers, a neighbor, and members of her church. Her co-workers provide emotional support and often invite the Johnsons for holidays. The neighbor frequently "cooks too much food" and brings dishes over for Jasmine and Devon. Her church friends have provided spiritual support, which Jasmine finds comforting.

Jasmine and Devon have received support through the church's Christmas adopt-a-family program, the youth programs, and the food and clothing pantry. Devon is eligible for the breakfast and lunch program at his school.

Prioritized concerns: Jasmine's primary concern is her relationship with her son. While she wishes that he did not speak disrespectfully to her or violate the rules she has established, she recognizes that he is a teenage boy and that the divorce, the move to a smaller apartment and a new school, and the lack of support from and contact with his father have turned his life upside down. She wants to improve her relationship with Devon and find alternative ways to establish and maintain acceptable boundaries for his behavior.

Strengths and areas of challenge: Jasmine possesses a number of strengths, including: (1) the desire to be a good parent and not use physical discipline, (2) a history of consistent employment that provides benefits, (3) an active if not extensive support system, (4) a willingness to seek help for relationship challenges and to use community resources, and (5) the resilience to overcome adversity.

Areas of challenge for Jasmine include: (1) a history of physically striking Devon and a lack of knowledge about other parenting possibilities or strategies; (2) low self-esteem—Jasmine assumes her son's disrespect for her is her fault because she divorced his father and took Devon away from him, moved Devon to a new area and school, and never has never had enough money to provide Devon with anything beyond the necessities; and (3) stress related to her income, including sporadic child support payments from her ex-husband.

Intervention plan: With monthly reviews, Jasmine and her social worker jointly developed a three-month contract:

Goal	Client Tasks/Timeline	Social Worker Tasks/Timeline	Follow-Up	Termination
Improve my relationship with my son	*Begin attending weekly family therapy with my son as soon as I can make an appointment.*	*Refer Jasmine and her son to a family therapist and communicate regularly with the therapist regarding their progress (with Jasmine's informed consent).*	*At 3 months, Jasmine and Devon are attending family therapy.*	*At 6 months, the social worker recommends the case be closed as goals have been met.*
Learn better strategies for disciplining my son, particularly when I am angry	*Participate in weekly parents of teens class and support group (next group begins the first of next month).*	*Refer Jasmine to parenting class and support group and communicate regularly with the group facilitator regarding progress (with Jasmine's informed consent).*	*At 3 months, Jasmine is a regular member of the class/support group.*	*At 6 months, social worker recommends case be closed as goals have been met.*
Get Devon's father to pay child support more consistently	*As soon as possible, contact Legal Services Child Support Enforcement office to inquire if they can help.*	*Provide Jasmine with Legal Services contact information and eligibility requirements.*	*At 3 months, Jasmine has made an appointment with Legal Services.*	*At 6 months, social work recommends case be closed as goal is in process of being met.*

Intervention (including service options and purpose, goals, and plans of service)
Goal #1: Jasmine and Devon attended eight sessions with the family therapist. They continue to attend, although Devon sometimes refuses to go with his mother. He has attended six of the eight sessions and agrees to "keep trying it for a while." The therapist reports to the social worker that she believes the Johnsons are making small strides toward improving their relationship. As suspected, Devon is extremely angry with his mother and does not understand why things had to change. Jasmine refuses to disclose

to Devon that his father's drinking and infidelities are the reason for the divorce. Early on, there was an episode at home of physical contact in which Jasmine slapped Devon for calling her a name.

Goal #2: Jasmine has been regularly attending the Single Parents of Teens classes and support group. Not only has she found the information provided very helpful, she has found a new group of friends who share her experiences, empathize with her, and offer helpful suggestions.

Goal #3: Jasmine was slow in contacting Legal Services, but once she got an appointment and completed the application, she met with an attorney and social worker. The attorney sent a letter to her ex-husband regarding his delinquent payments. He has yet to respond. Should he not respond, she will have to return to court and request enforcement.

Closing summary
During the six months that Jasmine has been collaborating with the social worker, she has initiated work on each of the three goals outlined in the contract. Positive changes have been slowly occurring in her relationship. There have been no episodes of physical contact in five months. While Devon still sometimes violates curfew and speaks disrespectfully to his mother, he no longer does so frequently.

Shortly after the implementation of the intervention, the social worker learned that someone called a child abuse hotline to allege that Jasmine had abused Devon. Upon further investigation, the social worker learned that Devon himself made the call months earlier after a particularly emotional confrontation with Jasmine. The report was unsubstantiated.

The social worker is recommending closure of this case as substantial progress is being made on all goals. Jasmine and the social worker will discuss termination and evaluation. Should Jasmine feel she is in need of additional services, she will be invited to request that her case be reopened.

Sample case/progress/interim notes (brief excerpts from the case record):

October 1: Jasmine Johnson came to the agency seeking help with her 14-year-old son. She believes he is "out of control," and she is worried that she will become abusive. She has physically struck him on several occasions when he has violated her rules or spoken disrespectfully to her. She feels she is at her "wit's end." Intake assessment forms completed. Social worker asked Jasmine to bring Devon to the next meeting so his perspective could be included.

November 28: Jasmine and Devon have attended two family therapy sessions. Devon was a reluctant participant but did agree to attend with his mother. Jasmine reports that he said very little in the first meeting but opened up more in the second session. Her fears are confirmed—he is very angry with her. Jasmine has attended two Single Parents of Teens classes and support group meetings. She reports that she is getting a lot out of the sessions, particularly in terms of tips for ways to interact with Devon. She has not yet contacted the Legal Services office.

clients who seem unable to make their way in this culture? Can you truly remain open to the multiple realities that critical social construction emphasizes? Do you rationalize human rights violations because they are so common in our culture?

These considerations also apply to more specific practice perspectives, such as feminist or narrative lenses. If, for example, you adopt a feminist theory that stresses the importance of power analysis, is your work consistent with that type of analysis? Do you return to a more traditional perspective regarding the issues that your client brings, emphasizing her reluctance to leave an abusive relationship or her lack of self-esteem? Can you keep an analytical structure of gender relations at the forefront of the work rather than falling back into our society's tendency to blame women for occupying a power-down position? Which aspects of feminist theory do you carry out well, and which can you better integrate into your work?

If your framework is narrative, are you completely open to the complexity of the client's story? Do you wish you had responded to it in a more transparent way? Do you recognize your client as expert, or are you tempted to believe you know better? Which aspects of the perspective are you having trouble fulfilling? Which seem to come naturally? These considerations, of course, do not yield empirical data; rather, they can help you decide to what degree you can work within the constraints of particular perspectives, and they can help you identify ways in which you want to develop skills and grow intellectually. The process of posing such challenging questions for yourself can be evaluative in and of itself and is an important routine to establish early in your career. Reflection on these areas can be illuminating and help to shape and refine your theoretical practice stances.

Explorations of Quality of Relationship   The nature of the relationship you develop with your client offers another opportunity for exploration. Is the relationship consistent with your purpose of the work? Was the intervention client-centered and connected to the client's stated needs and goals? Was openness a characteristic of the connection early on? Did either you or your client have difficulty establishing openness? What can you learn from the client's struggle? What can you learn from your own? What cultural dimensions influenced the development of the relationship, and what did you do to work through those issues (see Maramaldi, Berkman, & Barusch, 2005)?

This investigation might highlight your own idiosyncrasies. For example, do you respond more easily to people who are most like you? Do you wonder if you encouraged the client's dependence on you? Do you struggle to maintain useful boundaries between you and your client? Are you comfortable with the amount of self-disclosure you engage in? Do you have trouble being positive about some kinds of clients?

Some questions that arise from this kind of self-examination may point to more general issues: What is the ideal relationship between client and worker? What does it look like? Is it different in different settings? Is it likely that all your client relationships will fall into this ideal range? How does the ideal relationship interface with the client's goal attainment?

STRAIGHT TALK ABOUT EVALUATION AND REFLECTING ON OUR PRACTICE KNOWLEDGE

As the discussion on intervention, termination, and evaluation comes to a close, consider the distinctiveness of the social work profession and its greater purposes. Social justice, human rights, strengths, and the value of multiple realities all inform social workers, who in their work combine a practical orientation and a strong sense of caring and compassion. Context and compassion are always difficult to measure, and as long as you are pressured to assign numerical indicators, you may miss some of your most important contributions. Recall the term "practice wisdom," which we introduced in Chapter 1. Practice wisdom is the social worker's application of her or his "accumulation of information, assumptions, ideologies, and judgments" (Barker, 2014, p. 331). Practice wisdom is a dynamic process that enables the social worker to apply insights, skills, and values while recognizing one's limitations and need for further knowledge (Thompson & West, 2013). Practice wisdom does not replace evidence-based practice but, instead, serves to enhance and promote its application. Social workers' distinctive knowledge, based on an individual or group practice wisdom of person-in-environment, strength and struggle, and heart and grit, is the "humble stuff of lived experience and values and flies in the face of most current views about how social workers know what they know" (Weick, 1999, p. 327).

As an empowering practice that involves real people and real misery as well as real joys, social workers will ask other questions about its effectiveness, including:

- Who benefits from this work? If the goals of social work relate to empowering clients, how can clients realize those goals? If a client demonstrates improved capacity to manage a household budget, for example, does that affect her experience of poverty? Is it identified and challenged? Will she quietly and skillfully manage on close to nothing (and is this progress?), or will the benefit go beyond, to others like her, and to challenge the structure that supports poverty?

- Whose values are most salient? Social work values are at the heart of the work. Do they dominate the client relationship? How do social workers negotiate differing values? This is one of social work's most challenging dilemmas.

- What changes have occurred in the societal power structure in a given time period? Have social workers helped to raise consciousness about oppression and the internalization of it? Have clients joined with others to respond to oppressive imbalances in our culture's structural arrangements?

These questions lead us back to the beginning of our exploration of social work practice. As a social worker, you will likely find satisfaction in connecting with clients. You may initially struggle to identify the theoretical framework that best guides your work and will find it challenging to meet the demands of the client's preferred realities and to document the demands. You will experience frustrations and successes in each of these areas, answer many questions, and come up with many more. You will figure out how to respond to it in ways that are consistent with your values, your social work ethics, your sense of social justice and human rights, and your respect for different views and experience.

Your own story as a social work practitioner will be embedded in the hundreds of stories of your individual clients, groups, and families; the organizations and communities you serve; and in the story of global change. Your choices are legion, and your opportunities, enormous. In the end, these will return to the story of the profession. You, as a member of the next generation of citizen/social workers, will author the next chapter of social work practice.

STRAIGHT TALK ABOUT PRACTICE ISSUES RELEVANT TO INTERVENTION

A critical component for social workers implementing the intervention phase of the planned change effort is to maintain a focus on professional behaviors and issues. In addition to gaining skills in selecting and applying theoretical frameworks and executing appropriate strategies and techniques, social workers must attend to an array of professional issues that can both positively or negatively influence their work with clients. Regardless of the theoretical approach that is utilized in the intervention, there are several areas that are critical to the well-being of both the client and yourself, including: therapeutic use of self, managing countertransference, professionalism, and self-care. While your attention to these areas of practice begins during your social work education, you will continue to grow and develop in each throughout your social work career.

Therapeutic Use of Self

Sharing personal information with a client has and will continue to be a controversial social work practice issue. "Use of self" in the worker–client relationship occurs when the practitioner shares information about her or his own life with the hope that the client can relate the professional's experience to her or his own. The practice is controversial as some consider that it is a violation of professional–client boundaries, suggesting that the two can relate on a social (versus professional) level. Others view the time spent on the professional's life experiences as potentially distracting the worker and the client from the intended work, which is to focus on the client. Despite the concerns noted here, social workers are generally in favor of sharing personal information with clients that is specifically related to building trust with the client to promote honesty and open communication and create a therapeutic alliance (Knight, 2012). Factors known to influence a social worker's position on self-disclosure include the social worker's own professional socialization and culture (i.e., is self-disclosure viewed as appropriate) and the length of time/number of meetings with the client (i.e., longer relationships increase comfort with self-disclosure) (Knight, 2012). In order to determine if self-disclosing personal information with a client is appropriate, Knight (2012, adapting from Peterson, 2002) suggests asking the following questions:

1. Is self-disclosure necessary to protect client's informed consent?
2. Who benefits, the client or me?

3. Will client be able to use the information I disclose and/or affective reaction I share in a way that is useful?
4. Will disclosing information and/or sharing a reaction interfere with our progress and with the working alliance? (p. 303)

Inserting your own experiences into the relationship you have built with your client can be a powerful and meaningful experience for both you and your client. In determining if you want to share personal information with your client, be intentional and not impulsive and determine if the client can truly benefit (Knight, 2012).

Managing Transference and Countertransference

When a client has a strong reaction to the social worker (typically negative in nature), the client may associate the worker's behavior with an experience from her or his past—this phenomenon is known as **transference** (Barker, 2014, pp. 434). Conversely, when a social worker consciously or unconsciously experiences an emotional reaction (i.e., feelings, wishes, or defensiveness) to a client, this response is defined as **countertransference** (Barker, 2014, p. 98). As a professional or a client, identifying with the other can help in establishing rapport and trust; however, over-identifying can be disruptive to the intervention and can be potentially damaging for the client, the workers, and/or their ability to engage in an effective intervention with each other. All client relationships should be monitored for the emergency of either of these reactions. Should you determine that either the client or you is experiencing transference or countertransference, you should consult with colleagues and/or your supervisor to identify an appropriate strategy for responding, which can include raising the issue with the client or referring the client to another practitioner if the situation has become unhealthy for one or both of you.

Professionalism

Maintaining professional standards and behaviors is paramount to being a competent, ethical, and effective practitioner and part of the lifelong learning and professional development process for social workers. As noted in the *2015 CSWE Educational Policy and Accreditation Standards*, social workers:

- make ethical decisions by applying the standards of the NASW *Code of Ethics*, relevant laws and regulations, models for ethical decision-making, ethical conduct of research, and additional codes of ethics as appropriate to context;

- use reflection and self-regulation to manage personal values and maintain professionalism in practice situations;

- demonstrate professional demeanor in behavior; appearance; and oral, written, and electronic communication;

- use technology ethically and appropriately to facilitate practice outcomes; and

- use supervision and consultation to guide professional judgment and behavior (p. 7).

Being a professional social worker means that you possess and demonstrate competence in applying the knowledge, skills, and values of the profession. Within these constructs, professionalism means ensuring that you identify yourself as a social worker, act in an ethical manner with and on behalf of your client, maintain at all times appropriate boundaries with the client, and commit to further your knowledge and skills through lifelong learning and professional development.

Self-Care

Related directly to your ability to demonstrate professionalism is your ability to engage in caring for yourself particularly during the phase of work in which the client and you are implementing the agreed-upon intervention as this can be a stressful and challenging time for you both. During this phase, goals and intervention plans may have to be re-negotiated, clients may question their ability to move forward, or your work may have to cease altogether due to an unforeseen crisis. As highlighted in Chapter 4, self-care is essential to your ability to function as a competent social work professional. While effective self-care routines are unique to the individual, there are aspects of professional/personal self-care that are common for social workers that can be particularly helpful during the more intense times of work with the client, including: regular and frequent monitoring of your own stress levels; ongoing use of supervision, consultation, and mentoring; diligence in adhering to your personal health and well-being regimens; and realistic expectations of your client and yourself. Social workers can benefit from practicing the same principles they promote to their work with clients.

CONCLUSION

In this chapter, we have explored social work intervention, termination, evaluation, and follow-up actions. The practice setting, theoretical perspectives, and social worker and client perception of roles influence your work to support clients' strengths and their environments. The overall fit of intervention activities with your beliefs about people create a sound backdrop for expanding your work into other client system levels as long as they fit well and the beliefs are serving clients' needs. The next chapters integrate and extend these same processes to groups, families, groups, organizations, and communities. They consolidate the principles and skills in this first part of the book and apply them across system levels.

In the paradoxical way that some things constantly change while they remain the same, so endings and evaluations continue and evolve. We will all experience new ways of executing social work practice in the future. Some of you will work in complex settings that integrate the public and private sectors through partnerships and alliances. Some of you will choose relatively radical forms of practice in which you will challenge what you see as unjust or obsolete historical and professional legacies. Others will continue to practice using largely the same models they learned in social work training. All of these dimensions of practice will have implications for beginning and ending the social work relationship, for executing and evaluating the work, and for grappling with the obstacles that get in the way of the vision. There are no magic formulas for anticipating all of the implications of change for social work. Your flexibility, integrity, and creativity, as well as your caring for people who struggle, will be your own best guides for your future practice.

MAIN POINTS

- The intervention starts with the issue(s) the client perceives to be most pressing. The context of the client's situation and the actions you mutually agreed upon in the assessment and planning phase define the issue.

- Evidence-based approaches are used to guide social work interventions with individuals; three are highlighted in this chapter, including strengths-based, narrative, solution-focused approaches.

- To support clients' strengths, social workers act in context to normalize and capitalize on those strengths. Social workers respond to feelings, determine their meaning, and support diversity.

- To support clients' environments, social workers are accountable to the client. They follow the demands of the client task; maximize the potential supports in the client's environments; identify, reinforce, and/or increase the client's repertoire of strategic behaviors; and apply these principles to themselves.

- Examining traditional social work roles and their assumptions within the context of contemporary practice provides another perspective on the roles of case manager, counselor, broker, mediator, educator, client advocate, and collaborator.

- Exploring a case situation through an empowerment lens puts the work in context and demonstrates its fit with the perspectives emphasized in this book.

- The planned ending process includes several components that can benefit and empower clients by consolidating the gains of the work and the relationship. Social worker and client must share a clear understanding of the timing of the ending, the original agreement, the successes and failures of the work, and their responses to termination.

- Unplanned endings pose a special challenge to both social workers and clients. Social workers can attempt to reconnect with clients to end the work on a different note, but they may have to acknowledge the limits of their influence and honor client self-determination.

- Social work practice increasingly requires quantitative and empirical evaluation processes. Single-subject design and goal attainment scaling are two evaluation options.

- Qualitative and reflective practices are another important method for evaluation and professional growth. They relate to philosophical commitments, theoretical perspectives, and relationship building.

EXERCISES

a. Case Exercises

1. To apply your learning of the Grand Challenge for Social Work—Advancing Long and Productive Lives—that was highlighted at the beginning of this chapter, visit the Grand Challenges website and read Working Paper No. 8, *Increasing Productive Engagement in Later Life* (Morrow-Howell et al., 2015) at: http://aaswsw.org/grand-challenges-initiative/12-challenges/advance-long-and-productive-lives/. To gain insight into strategies for empowering older adults to optimize their engagement and productivity in later life, we will consider the case of Carla Washburn at www.routledgesw.com/caseStudies. After reading Working Paper No. 8 and reviewing the Washburn case, respond to the following questions:
   a. Based on the definition of productive engagement and utilizing the information provided about Carla Washburn, assess her current level of productive engagement, specifically addressing those areas of her life you would deem provide her gratification.
   b. Building on the assessment you have developed, identify potential activities in which Mrs. Washburn might get involved. Resources that may be helpful include the community map and the sampling of innovations described in the Working Paper No. 8.
   c. Develop a plan for intervention, termination, and evaluation with Mrs. Washburn that is focused on optimizing her productive engagement and aging.

2. Go to www.routledgesw.com/cases, review the video vignette with Emilia Sanchez, and respond to the following questions:
   a. What strengths does Emilia possess?
   b. What thoughts and/or feelings do you have after watching the video that, if you were to verbalize them, would not reflect a strengths-based approach?
   c. As the social worker, what are your next steps with Emilia?
   d. With a group either in or outside of class, develop a strengths-based intervention plan for Emilia.

3. Go to www.routledgesw.com/cases and click on Carla Washburn. Review the engagement and assessment phases, and then click on Phase 3: Intervention. Complete each of the tasks identified in the five steps (introduction, goals and needs, client tasks, social worker tasks, timeline, and coalitions).

4. Go to www.routledgesw.com/cases and click on Brickville. Focus on Virginia Stone and her family. Review the engagement and assessment phases and then click on Phase 3: Intervention. Complete each of the tasks identified in the five steps (introduction, goals and needs, client tasks, social worker tasks, timeline, and coalitions).

5. Go to www.routledgesw.com/cases and click on Brickville. Focusing on Virginia Stone and her family, review the four components of the social work intervention, including engagement, assessment and planning, intervention, and termination and evaluation. Upon completing the tasks identified in each section, develop a case summary using the sample in Quick Guide 15.

6. Go to www.routledgesw.com/cases and click on RAINN. After reviewing the information, click on Engage, review the two client scenarios (Sarah and Alan), and respond to the three questions listed below the scenarios. In addition, develop a list of skills you would need to develop to work competently with a survivor of sexual assault.

b. Other exercises

7. The admissions unit of a psychiatric care facility where you work issues a one-page daily report summarizing all the patient admissions, discharges, visits, legal proceedings, and other activities for the preceding 24-hour period. This summary is meant to convey useful information for all staff, and social workers view the summary as helpful for monitoring client status. One of the categories on the form, "body count," is a tally of the number of patient/residents in the hospital at midnight. A social worker from a local community mental health agency visits her client in the hospital and hears reference to this sheet. She is horrified by the use of "body count," a phrase you have become accustomed to seeing in the reports.

   Answer the following questions based on this scenario and be prepared to discuss your answers in class or to submit your written response.

   a. What is the issue here? Why does it matter? Be as specific as you can.

   b. How would you address this issue? Would the way you address the issue be consistent with your view of a social worker's role?

   c. Develop a plan that includes at least three steps you might take. Compare your plan with those of other students.

8. Tammy is a 35-year-old Caucasian female seeking treatment after her release from a 21-day residential drug/alcohol treatment facility. The public child welfare agency refers her to your agency. Because Tammy was convicted of driving under the influence with her 8-year-old son, Jared, in the car, and

because of her continuing substance abuse, the court places Jared in Tammy's mother's physical custody.

Tammy has a 20-year history of drug and alcohol abuse, and she has been diagnosed with bipolar disorder. The staff psychiatrist at the residential treatment facility recently wrote her a prescription for the disorder. It is a new medication and is not covered by her insurance. She has been noncompliant with medication in the past due to the side effects and her drug/alcohol use. She has had brief periods of sobriety but often relapses after a few weeks. This is the longest she has been sober since the birth of her son eight years ago.

Tammy has never been married and has a difficult relationship with her family of origin. Because of Tammy's behavior, her mother placed her in foster care at the age of eight. Tammy reports that her mother was physically and emotionally abusive to her and often would leave her with various relatives to go out with boyfriends. Tammy's father is not involved. Tammy has few friends and little contact with her mother. She is angry that her mother has custody of her son. Tammy has been involved with her son's father sporadically for the past nine years. Currently, she names him as a source of support.

Tammy is not currently employed but receives public assistance in the form of Medicaid, disability assistance, and SNAP (food stamps). She lives with her boyfriend but would like to have her own apartment. She has her high school diploma and is interested in continuing her education.

Partner with other students and complete the following exercises:

a. Using narrative interventions, reconstruct this case from a strengths-based perspective.
b. What roles would you play to help Tammy?
c. Construct a strengths-based, solution-focused intervention plan.
d. Share your findings with the class and compare your plans.

9. Reflect on a time in your life when you contemplated making a change. What did you do? Were your actions successful? What factors led to the success? If your actions were not successful, what was missing?

10. Identify an area or behavior in your life that you would like to change (e.g., texting while driving, exercising, budgeting money, or time management). For 1 week, chart your journey in a journal, and note those factors that are helping you to change and those that are a negative influence on your change efforts. At the end of the week, reflect on your progress or lack thereof. Consider your feelings before the change, during the change, and about the results.

11. Write your own life story from a strengths-based perspective.

CHAPTER 6

Social Work Practice with Families: Engagement, Assessment, and Planning

The social work profession and the family have traveled a long distance together, sometimes in close companionship and sometimes on divergent paths, only to meet once again on the same road. Our profession began in the company of the family and has returned to it once again.

Ann Hartman and Joan Laird (1983, p. vii)

Key Questions for Chapter 6

1. What competencies do I need to engage with and assess families? [EPAS 6 and 7]
2. What are the social work behaviors that enable me to effectively engage with and assess families? [EPAS 6 and 7]
3. How can I use evidence to perform research-informed practice, and how can I use practice-informed research to guide engagement and assessment with families? [EPAS 4]
4. How do my perspectives on and experiences with my present family and/or family of origin impact my engagement with and assessment of client families? [EPAS 1]

The Patel family lives in Hudson City (www.routledgesw.com/cases) and is one of the many families displaced by Hurricane Diane, which swept through the community a few weeks earlier. The members of the Patel family include:

- *Hemant and Sheetal—both in their late 40s, they emigrated to the U.S. from India fifteen years earlier. They own and operate a family restaurant in their neighborhood.*

- *Rakesh, Kamal, and Aarti are the Patel's three children. The oldest son, Rakesh, is 18 and in his first semester at the University of the Northeast. He lives at home and commutes to school. The younger son, Kamal, is a 16-year-old high school junior. The Patels' daughter, Aarti, is age twelve and in the 7th grade.*
- *Bharat and Asha are Mr. Patels' parents who came to live with their son and his family when the restaurant opened ten years ago. They are both in their early 70s and help part-time in the restaurant. Bharat had cardiac bypass surgery last year; Asha suffers from hypertension. The family left behind their medications when they fled from the storm.*

All members of the Patel family work full- or part-time in the restaurant. The Patels' restaurant and home sustained major damage in the storm. While the restaurant and house can be rehabilitated, the damage is extensive, and repairs will likely take weeks to months to complete. The Patels are staying with friends in a nearby community, but they feel they must quickly make other arrangements and not impose on their friends' hospitality. As the entire family derives its income from the restaurant, money is a concern. While everyone in the family is devastated at their losses, Hemant and Sheetal are especially worried about the older couple's health and their children's education and stability being disrupted.

FAMILY IS THE EARLIEST, MOST BASIC, AND, SOME SAY, most challenging small group one can experience during a lifetime. Family is also probably the most powerful in shaping who we become. For some, family means home, safety, and acceptance, but even the most secure family environments can be shaken when crises or tragedy strike, as in the case of the Patel family. For others, family means violence, danger, or neglect. Some people may feel important and cherished with family, while others may feel never quite good enough or even useless. Some may feel swallowed up in their family's dysfunction, or they may long for or bask in unconditional support. Most of us experience a mix of these feelings. Family is a complicated enterprise, and many of us find it both joyful and troubled. Virtually all members of society have experienced some kind of family, and most have ideas or dreams of the qualities that an ideal family could or should possess.

In this chapter, we will explore the concept of family—its definition, meaning, and place within the contemporary social context—and the process of engagement and assessment with families from a biopsychosocial-spiritual perspective. We will also look at theoretical perspectives for working with traditional and contemporary family structures as well as the dynamics, skills, and tools for working with a range of families. This chapter will also guide you through strategies for understanding the impact family issues can have on you and your clients.

FAMILIAR PERSPECTIVES AND SOME ALTERNATIVES

Enormous and rapid changes in social rules in most Western countries have led many to contend that the "traditional" family is a thing of the past. A traditional vision of the ideal U.S. family is a nuclear group consisting of two heterosexual adults married to each other and two or perhaps three children. The father supports the family economically, and the mother supports it emotionally. There are clear rules, and each member is responsible for playing certain roles and doing certain jobs. If the mother also works outside the home, she is still free to, for example, participate in the children's car pools, do the laundry, entertain friends, and "be there" for her husband and children. In many families, a father is sensitive to the feelings and needs of his wife and children, though his work still takes priority. In contrast, a contemporary view of family is one in which the members "assume certain obligations for each other and generally (but not necessarily) share common residences" (Barker, 2014, p. 155). This inclusive perspective on the family embraces units in which parents are divorced, separated, or unmarried; grandparents rearing grandchildren; gay, lesbian, bisexual, transgender, or questioning families; and adoptive, multigenerational (e.g., three or even four generations co-residing, like the Patel family), and fostering families, along with couples who have no children, partnered couples, and families caring for older adult members. The purpose of the family, regardless of the form, structure, or composition, is to help the individual members grow and develop and to create and sustain a connected family unit over the life course (Paris & DeVoe, 2013).

To engage in effective service delivery, social workers must recognize the range of diverse contemporary family constellations (Rasheed & Rasheed, 2013). For example, to avoid assumptions and confusion, the social worker should ask the client to describe and define her or his family unit (Samudio, 2015). Given the changing nature of the family and the fluidity of membership in some families, it is important to ask each member of the family, "Who do you consider to be part of your family?" A follow-up question may then be, "Of these people, who is biologically and/or legally related to you?" For instance, a client's "aunt" may not be a legal or biological family member, but the client may consider her to be family.

Those with nostalgic visions of family may be appalled at what they see today as a lack of morality in many young families. They may be distressed about young adults who live together with no permanent commitment. Single women often choose to become parents and do not suffer the social stigma they would have experienced only a few generations earlier. Parents who are lesbian, gay, bisexual, transgender, and questioning (LGBTQ), who, in earlier generations would have had to conceal their sexual identities, are joyfully marrying, parenting biological, foster, and adopted children. In the past, LGBTQ individuals were not even given the option to foster or adopt children; now, state child protection agencies recruit them.

Although some may lament these developments in U.S. cultural norms, fear of change should not be allowed to overshadow research about new, more inclusive family and parenting and caregiving arrangements. While the widespread belief for several decades has been that at least half of all marriages in the U.S. end in divorce, a shift in that trend has occurred, resulting in a decreasing divorce rate that is well under 50% at this point (Miller, 2014). A variety of reasons are offered for this decline in divorce, including: later marriage, birth control, couples living together before marriage, changing gender roles (resulting from the feminist movement), level of education (fewer divorces among college-educated couples), and fewer marriages (Miller, 2014).

Despite a declining rate in divorce, there are issues surrounding the contemporary family that create concerns for social workers and that also impact service delivery. One particular area of concern is closely related to the ever-growing number of children who live in single parent-headed households with incomes below the poverty level. The percentage of families who live in poverty with a single mother remains over 30%, while the percent of all families and two-parent families experiencing poverty are currently at 11.5% and 5.7%, respectively (U.S. Census, 2014b). Social workers who work with single mothers must be aware of the higher poverty rate for these families. A second area of concern for social workers is the persistence of poverty for children born to teen mothers. While the number of births to teen mothers in all racial and ethnic groups continues to decline (24.2/1,000 teen females in 2014, down 9% from 2013) (Hamilton, Martin, Osterman, Curtin, & Mathews, 2015), teen births are associated with unplanned pregnancies, legacies of perpetuated poverty, increased family violence, and health and mental health issues, and with a sense that two generations—the child and the child's child—have sacrificed much of their potential. Thus, teen mothers often have a wide range of challenges to reaching their dreams for their adulthood.

There are many ways to look at the concept of family. In keeping with this book's consideration of multiple realities, we will explore the experiences of an array of family constellations to expose popular misconceptions about the family and to develop a balanced perspective. This chapter will discuss the experiences of both traditional and nontraditional families. Consider Exhibit 6.1, which describes the experience of family for countless people who have been marginalized.

HISTORICAL ANTECEDENTS FOR FAMILY SOCIAL WORK

The contexts of the times have shaped the long history of social work with families. In today's context, social work to strengthen families occurs in community mental health centers and youth agencies, hospitals and schools, and social welfare and child protection efforts. Collins, Jordan, and Coleman (2013) encourage social work students interested in working with families to seek answers to

EXHIBIT 6.1

Family: Views from the Margins

© Harry Hu, courtesy of Shutterstock® images

- What we may consider now to be the ideal family has never actually flourished in any culture for any length of time. Historically, families considered children commodities that enhanced the economic status of their fathers, who owned them and who often equated their value to the amount of work they did. Childhood as a time to be nourished and cherished is a relatively new and narrowly prescribed phenomenon of Western culture and some nations in the East. The United Nations instrument "The Rights of the Child" reflects the need to consider children as genuine people and not possessions. In contrast, in parts of the United States, children are prostitutes, drug dealers, and hired thieves. In much of the world, they are all of these things and also soldiers.

- Historically, ideal conceptions of the family have restricted and diminished women's role as categorical caretakers. Many women throughout history have been required to abandon their dreams, and like children, many have been viewed as property to be exploited. Men, too, have historically been pressured to fit into tightly proscribed roles that may not be compatible with their identities or goals.

- In the past, infant and childhood mortality was high, and some parents died by their early 40s. Such circumstances produced a crisis for remaining family members, who were sometimes placed with distant relatives, with community members, or in orphanage care. The idealistic notion of earlier times turns a blind eye to realities of disease, early death, and other forms of danger that surely shaped the overall experience of family.

- Even in contemporary U.S. society, the family and the support of the community are the primary forces for the socializing and nurturing of children. As an example,

EXHIBIT 6.1

Continued

families still provide most of the care and nurturing for adult children experiencing mental illness, in spite of federal and state programs designed to assist them. Family members are the primary providers of informal care for older adults who require care.

- Rigid definitions of family that focus on biological and legal ties and heterosexual partners or adoptions have always marginalized and scapegoated significant numbers of people. Many people have meaningful and productive relationships and make significant contributions to the community, the socialization of children, and the general economic and social order though their families do not fit such rigid definitions.

- More contemporary notions of family have liberated both men and women to develop and carry out child caretaking, economic provision, management, personal development, and health care roles in ways that do not deny their individual aspirations and talents. The same principles hold for gay, lesbian, bisexual, and transgender families with biological or adopted children.

- Contemporary families have greater biological control over the number and timing of pregnancies and can plan family composition in a way that is consistent with their financial capacities and other internal demands (for example, if one partner is in school or another is committed to the care of a parent). Women are now more able to exercise control over their reproduction and to make decisions about their futures.

the following questions during their studies, in order to prepare for practice in this area:

- What is the purpose of family social work?

- How does family social work differ from family therapy?

- How can I work effectively with families who are different from my own family?

- What is my role as a family social worker?

- How will I know what factors contribute to the family's difficulties?

- How should I work with an entire family and with all members in the same room at the same time?

- How will I know what questions to ask family members? What do I say to the family?

- How do I engage all the members of the family, particularly if some seem resistant or uncommunicative or seem to feel blamed or overpowered by another member?

- What should I do if family members become angry with me or another member of the family?

- What do I need to know to help families change? What new knowledge will help the families begin to change (e.g., parenting, financial capability, or physical and mental health care)?

- What skills will I need when there are young children in the interview? What about older children?

- What can I do to protect individual family members when the rest of the family is attacking or blaming?

- How do I help families that are paralyzed by a crisis to rise above it and solve their problems?

- What do I need to know about when working with families of different ethnic, racial, or sexual orientation backgrounds?

- What skills do I need in order to prioritize the family's problems? What skills do I need for each of the phases of work with families (pp. 1–2)?

Why is there such a concern for the maintenance of the family? What does our culture expect the family to do, and how do we think the family should work? Although there are many possible responses to these questions, we examine two particular perspectives that seem to have special relevance for social workers today—the family as a functioning unit and the family as a system.

Family as a Functioning Unit

A concrete way to think about the importance of the family is to explore what our society requires of families. Our society typically expects contemporary families to serve the following functions:

- Provide material and economic necessities for family members' sustenance and growth

- Offer members emotional security, respect, safety, and a place for appropriate sexual expression

- Provide a haven for privacy and rest

- Assist, protect, and advocate for members who are vulnerable or who have special needs

- Provide support for members' meaningful connection with and contribution to community life

- Facilitate the transmission of cultural and/or religious heritage

- Provide a socially and legally recognized identity

- Create an environment in which to nurture and socialize children

One strategy for conceptualizing needs that families may or may not meet is to classify family needs by levels, such as the following (Kilpatrick, 2009; Kilpatrick & Cleveland, 1993):

Level 1—Basic survival: Needs are in the areas of food, shelter, and medical care.

Level 2—Structure and organization: Needs center on setting limits and safety concerns.

Level 3—Space: Needs relate to issues of privacy, access, and boundaries.

Level 4—Richness and quality: Needs exist in areas of inner conflict, intimacy, and self-actualization (p. 4).

The responsibilities reflected here emphasize, not only the functional roles of individual family members and their needs and identities, but also family members' connection to their communities and to the overall societal environment. This compilation is not prescriptive; that is, it does not specify *how* children should be nurtured but allows for individual and cultural interpretation. Rather than seeking individual or family dysfunction, the exploration of these tasks in various areas of family life tends to highlight strengths as well as areas for improvement. In that respect, this set of functions serves as a useful guide for assessing the degree to which any particular family meets societal expectations. Returning to the Patel family's situation, the parents' worries as they are unable to fulfill their familial obligations of providing shelter, safety, economic security, and a sense of stability are consistent with the idea that families provide material and economic necessities for one another. While the Patels' situation is likely to be temporary, consider the level of anxiety one might have if the situation were chronic or even permanent.

Despite the society mandate to serve a critical function in society in meeting members' needs, some may have difficulty fulfilling the mandate, and thus they may require the involvement of a helping professional. Taking into consideration the type and level of need, you can focus the social work engagement, assessment, planning, intervention, termination, evaluation, and follow-up process within a conceptual framework that encompasses both the context of those persons with whom you work (i.e., family/community, couple/dyad, and individual) and the orientation (e.g., theoretical approach) of the intervention you choose with the family. For example, will the intervention focus on behavioral/interactional change (e.g., intimate partner violence); on experiential aspects of clients' thoughts and feelings (e.g., anger felt by one or more family members toward another member); or on client history, emphasizing family-of-origin issues (e.g., childhood abuse by a parent) (Kilpatrick, 2009, p. 10)? Incorporating the complexities of the family system into the intervention, you can gain insight into the way the family functions, their needs, and the most effective strategies for helping them reach their desired goals.

Family as a System

Because social work focuses on interactions among people and between people and the environment, the profession enthusiastically adopted systems theory in the 1970s. Whether you are working with an individual, a family, group, or community, systems theory (also referred to a perspective or framework) posits that a system involves a series of highly organized components that depend upon each other in an orderly way. The social work profession applies systems theory to each level of practice—individuals, families, groups, organization, and community. Though a growing number of critiques suggest that the systems theory is too rigid and that it tends to place the social worker outside the work, it remains a guiding influence on many views of structural arrangements, particularly the family. Three elements of systems theory are particularly important:

- Change in one component affects all other components

- Subsystems and boundaries

- Family norms

Change in One Component Affects All Other Components   Possibly the most powerful systems theory idea for social workers is that change in one part of the system will affect all other parts of the system. Social workers, therefore, seek to learn about every aspect of a client's environment, including family functioning. For example, when you are exploring why a child is having angry outbursts or sullen withdrawals in school, it is useful to know that the child's father has just been sent to prison. Similarly, a woman's fragile health is likely to suffer when she learns that her mother is experiencing intimate partner violence. Social workers often find such connections intuitive and useful but guard against assuming that a particular situation will automatically produce a certain response. In systems theory, one set of actions can predict multiple sets of reactions. For example, a child may become more attentive to her or his mother or work harder in school in response to her father's incarceration. Not all individuals within a family with react to an event in the same way. Consider, for example, a family in which the primary wage earner becomes unemployed. This could create a ripple effect within the family. While one adolescent child may seek employment to help the family, another may demonstrate anger.

Subsystems and Boundaries   Components of a system that also have interacting parts, known as **subsystems**, provide a mechanism for organizing relationships and planning ways to engage with them. In systems theory, the individual is a subsystem of the family, the family is a subsystem of the community, and the community is a subsystem of the culture. A family may be a subsystem of more than one larger system, or of differing systems, so you must avoid making unqualified judgments regarding the place an individual or group occupies within the system. For example, in a blended family, some members may consider themselves part of the family and community from the previous marriage in addition to being members of the new, blended family and community. Social workers can support and facilitate healthy transition relationships for this type of client system. Exhibit 6.2 illustrates the components of a family system.

In thinking about the concept of family, social workers often distinguish between the subsystem of the parents and the subsystem of the children. The types of **boundaries** or limits that separate the subsystems a family constructs reflect the relationship between these subsystems in that particular family. If the children are included in most family decisions, these boundaries are **permeable**, meaning that information and interchange goes easily across them. In families in which parents have little or no decision-making authority, the boundaries are so permeable as to be almost nonexistent. These are called **diffuse boundaries**.

Appropriate boundaries between the subsystems of parents and children may vary considerably depending on culture, the era, background, and/or the boundaries within which the parents themselves were reared. While you may consider a mother whose preteen daughter is her primary confidante as lacking appropriate boundaries, particularly related to her relationship with the child's father, other families may view this as acceptable. Can you cite examples of boundaries in your

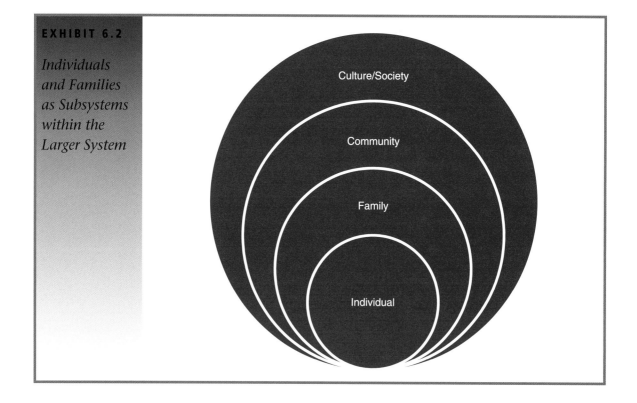

EXHIBIT 6.2

Individuals and Families as Subsystems within the Larger System

Culture/Society

Community

Family

Individual

own family that are similar to or different from those of your friends or other extended family members? Consider the way in which your experience with your own family might relate to families with whom you will work.

Some family boundaries may be so diffuse that they result in **enmeshment**, which suggests that family members are too close, have few distinctions in role or authority, and enjoy little autonomy or independence (Nichols, 2014). For example, consider the family in which the adult children share virtually every life experience with their mother, seldom make decisions without consulting one another and her, and are emotionally dependent on each another. In an enmeshed family, one member's routine life experience, such as a job change or change in relationship status, creates strong reactions in other family members.

On the other hand, in a **disengaged** family, boundaries between family members are too rigid. In this situation, subsystems are so unconnected that the family has little sense of identity, and parents are apt to relinquish much of their caretaking role as they and their children pursue their own separate interests. In a disengaged family, members may barely acknowledge significant life events, such as a significant job change or a divorce.

When you read about or work with youth/young adults who seem to have little or no effective family connections, and who have experienced school or legal problems, you may wonder about the boundaries (or lack of) their parents established and how their parents perceived their own roles. This theory can help you understand the misplacement or laxness of parental boundaries when children are experiencing life challenges. In such cases, professionals will work to restore clear and appropriate boundaries between children (including adult children) and parents that support parent caretaking, authority, or influence. When, for example, a judge requires the parents of an adolescent who has been arrested to undergo family management training or requires them to supervise a child's curfew restrictions, that judge is acting in a manner consistent with family systems theory.

Family Norms   Most families establish **family norms**, or rules of conduct, related to boundaries and subsystems. These can be similar to the group norms we will describe in Chapter 8, but in families, they have an additional complication as they are often held as sacrosanct and not negotiable. Family norms can be deeply ingrained, even if no one in the family has ever articulated those norms. This implicit aspect of norms can make them difficult to address and challenge, so much so that while everyone in the family understands what behavior is allowable, family members may not even realize that there are rules. For example, all the members of a family may understand that no one will enter into a dispute with Dad at the dinner table, that everyone will attend religious services, or that all of the children will go out of state to college. Some of these rules apply to everyday boundaries and may simplify everyday interactions (for example, if a door is closed, one is not to enter without knocking). Other rules may signal secrets that are taboo or too difficult to talk about or that perpetuate unjust or oppressive situations, such as all the female children knowing not to find themselves in the same room alone with Grandpa or the understanding that no one asks Mom how she got a bruise on her face.

When applying a systems analysis to family norms, a social worker may recognize that interrupting the family's patterns of behavior or relationship by breaking a rule is, in fact, both feasible and desirable. For example, a social worker may point out that one of the children spoke up one day about the bruises on Mom's face. This disclosure could lead the mother to talk about the violence she experiences, which might initiate the empowerment process and decrease family violence. On the other hand, this disclosure might render the child who raised the issue in the first place vulnerable to violence; therefore, the social worker would not likely encourage a child to take such an action without support and protection. Family norms in such cases are often very powerful and should be carefully evaluated to avoid putting any family member at risk.

Implications of Systems Theory for Generalist Practice with Families

Norms, subsystems, and boundaries create family structure and intergenerational patterns, which are two specific dimensions reflected in family systems theories, have influenced generalist social work practice with families. In many respects, these dimensions represent a classic approach to conceptualizing the family, and they have influenced how social service policies and agencies respond to families. You may discover that these ideas have shaped your thinking, too.

The following principles for social work assessment and intervention with families grew out of the systems theory (Rasheed & Rasheed, 2013) and provide a useful basis for considering family structure and intergenerational patterns:

1. Family is considered within a "context" that is comprised of multiple systems.
2. Rooted in the basic systemic foundation, the family "is more than the sum of its individual parts," which function together as a unique system.
3. A change within one part of the family system creates change in the entire system and affects the family's ability to find balance or instability.
4. A systemic-focused assessment and intervention provides a view of the family as a complex system.
5. A systems perspective views behaviors as a product of the multifaceted system and not as the result of one individual or action and should be viewed as circulator (versus linear) and having multiple causations.
6. A systems perspective that promotes a strengths-based approach frames the family assessment within the context of their environment and allows for building on family resilience and cohesiveness and incorporate the family's biological, psychological, life cycle, cultural, spiritual, and historical environments.
7. A systems perspective views family members, particularly those in diverse groups, within the context of their family system as well as within the larger societal system.

8.   The legal, social, and economic biases and discrimination that affect families with members considered to be cultural, racial, ethnic, religious, or sexual minorities may impact family function.
9.   Viewing the family as a unique system within the larger community (i.e., different from the broader community) allows the practitioner to more objectively focus the assessment on issues that present challenges to the entire system in order to guide prioritization and intervention planning.

Family Structure   The relationship among the generations of a family, especially between the subsystems of children and parents, is the **family structure**. One of the early scholars in defining models for family interventions, Salvador Minuchin (1974) posits that boundaries between children and parents should be clear and that, because they carry out appropriate caretaking functions, parents should be in charge of major decisions. Often, it is the blurring of the boundaries between these two subsystems that causes family difficulties.

Intergenerational Patterns   The identification of **intergenerational patterns**, the idea that families transmit their patterns of relationship from one generation to the next, has played an important role in social work practice with families (Papero, 2015). For example, if your adult client, Jeanae, is so closely connected to her mother that she experiences great anxiety when they are separated and therefore cannot work outside the home, Jeanae is likely to establish that same kind of relationship with her own daughter. The anxiety that any effort to be separate from her mother generates is contagious and makes it difficult for Jeanae to think clearly. In this way. she becomes dysfunctional, tending to be dominated by her feelings, and she passes that pattern on to the next generation. This overemphasis on feeling in a family sometimes results in frequent emotional uproar, violence, major feuds, difficulties with the law, and generalized struggle accomplishing the basic family functions considered earlier.

Phrases like "welfare families" and "incestuous families" reflect the use of intergenerational theory. These terms reflect the assumption that problematic, emotional patterns and the resulting behavioral consequences (such as violence, inability to focus on work, and substance abuse) appear to be transmitted from generation to generation. Social workers seek to eradicate such thinking and cycles, to bolster families' strengths, and to support an appropriate level of autonomy in individual family members. Many social and educational programs designed to break patterns of economic dependence, addictions, and lack of educational focus and to build up healthy bonds between family members reflect these principles.

Family systems theory, like any other theory, does not explain all situations. For example, professionals using a systems perspective when they relate crime, addiction, or school violence among youth to the families involved, regardless of evidence may not be accurate. Sometimes children engage in illegal or violent behavior even when they have caring, hardworking parents who are doing the best they can. It can be tempting to use familiar methods to find a rational cause for human behavior. People are often eager to blame a child's problems on the family's behavioral shortcomings or background while not viewing the behavior within an even wider systems theory lens of the broader aspects of poverty, disenfranchisement, challenging school situations (e.g., bullying), or racism. Placing blame on the parents/family is a simpler explanation and removes people from responsibility of addressing societal problems that may contribute to the problem behavior.

Systems perspectives can be helpful and can support logical approaches to assessment, especially of complex arrangements like the family. These perspectives have a general cultural appeal, but they do not constitute a "magic," one-stop answer for conceptualizing, assessing, or working with families. While systems views are highly valued in today's analyses of social issues, other ways of thinking about issues may be relevant. Be careful not to blame or scapegoat any particular person or the family simply because it seems logical or fits with a possible systemic interpretation of any situation. As you continue your social work education and develop your approach to practicing social work with families, you will be exposed to a wide array of philosophical and theoretical frameworks. You are professionally obligated to consider all available options and to determine the evidence-based approach(es) that is(are) most appropriate for the families you serve.

THE CONTEMPORARY CONTEXT FOR FAMILY SOCIAL WORK

As previously noted, today's real-world families rarely resemble the idealized outdated television (usually white) families with a stay-at-home mother, fully employed father, and two bright, talented children. Social workers often work with families who were once seen as "other"; that is, families that did not fit these prevalent fantasies of family life. The following sections briefly identify several types of family constellations that have not traditionally been considered mainstream but that are a vital part of the contemporary family landscape and suggest specific strategies for working with them. Family constellations include:

- grandparents rearing grandchildren;

- gay, lesbian, bisexual, transgender, and questioning parents;

- single-parent families;

- families of multiple racial and ethnic heritage;

- families that include persons with disabilities;

- blended families;

- international families; and

- families with multiple problems.

© Comstock Images/Thinkstock

Beyond these types of families, other current configurations include adoptive families, foster families, step families, multigenerational families, and, of course, many combinations of these types. In the coming generations, the social work profession will need to expect and remain open to ever-evolving forms of the family. This area of sociocultural change provides social workers with the opportunity to serve clients across all levels of society in a culturally competent and humble manner.

Grandparents Rearing Grandchildren

In many past cultures, grandparents played a significant and ongoing role in the nurturing and socialization of children. Some cultural groups today, typically those who are less mobile or those with strong ethnic identification(s), have maintained those patterns consistent with their cultural and instrumental needs (e.g., the Patel family). Mainstream societal changes in the industrialized and "informationalized" 21st century have obscured age-old extended family organization patterns. These changes reflect a break with the traditional cultural patterns of today's grandparents and their parents' parents.

In contemporary society, there has been a reemergence of grandparents assuming primary (rather than supportive) parenting roles (Ellis & Simmons, 2014), many as a result of family violence, addiction, and/or the incarceration of their adult children. In fact, of the over 7 million grandparents who co-reside with their grandchildren, 2.7 million have responsibility for the children's care, and only one-third of these households have one or both of the child's parents living in the home (Ellis & Simmons, 2014). Growing pressures on many child protection agencies have contributed to these increases because child protection workers often see biological relatives as preferable to, and more available than, unrelated foster parents. While many of the custodial grandparents are healthy, active, and potentially able to take on the responsibility of rearing their children's children, many experience increased poverty and physical disability because they assumed responsibility for their grandchildren (Ellis & Simmons, 2014).

Much more is involved in assuming primary caregiving responsibilities, however, than simply being physically and financially "able." The typical grandparent caring for grandchildren is a female who is between 50 and 59 years of age and has been caring for the grandchildren for five or more years (Ellis & Simmons, 2014). Many of these custodial grandparents have reached a point in their lives when they can pursue their own interests and the dreams they put on hold while they worked and reared families, or they may still be engaged in the workforce on a full- or part-time basis. Others may find it exhausting to keep up with young children, particularly those who have come from dysfunctional situations and have multiple needs, demands, activities such as health/mental health appointments and co-curricular activities. Some grandparents take on the unexpected role joyfully and fully, while others are enormously burdened and sometimes guilt-ridden because of their own children's inabilities to parent (which they may blame on themselves). In any event, many parenting grandparents, even if they are eager to care for grandchildren, are likely to want and need significant support from social, educational, and health care agencies.

Social workers working with grandparents need to use generalist practice skills and perspectives. Generalist practitioners are trained to recognize the need for and offer several types of support as they sensitize themselves to the complexities of the emotional and instrumental (e.g., meeting physical and financial care needs) stresses grandparents' experience. Grandparents who may or may not have been financially stable prior to assuming full-time care of their grandchildren may find their financial resources depleted and/or unable to cover all the children's needs and local resources unable to adequately fill the gap, particularly in rural communities (Bailey, Haynes, & Letiecq, 2013). Research has additionally shown that grandparents caring for a grandchild who has a disability have a more even challenging experience, resulting in increased demands, financial support, and difficulty accessing and navigating both formal and informal supports (Kresak, Gallagher, & Kelley, 2014).

Not surprisingly, grandparents raising grandchildren can find caring for their grandchildren to be stressful and, therefore, can be empowered by interventions that focus on cognitive behavioral (e.g., problem-solving and coping) and skill-based strategies that they can practice with support (McLaughlin, Ryder, & Taylor, 2016). Specifically, interventions should include content related to: (1) emotional support, parenting, and legal and financial issues and resources (Fruhauf & Hayslip, 2013) and (2) creating and strengthening parenting, legal and financial knowledge, skills, and natural support systems (Kresak et al., 2014).

In some situations, birth parents recovering from substance abuse or other challenges have visiting privileges or partial child caretaking responsibilities on a preliminary or trial basis. These arrangements can cause considerable tension between grandparents and parents. These and other conflicts may indicate the need for additional ongoing assistance from social workers. Despite the multiple challenges present in such situations, assessment and intervention should focus on the child(ren) (as opposed to the caregivers and birth parents) and can be enhanced through collaborations with the school system and other involved community resources (Bailey et al., 2013; Shakya, Usita, Eisenberg, Weston, & Liles, 2012).

Lesbian, Gay, Bisexual, Transgender, and Questioning Couples and Families [EPAS 1]

Social workers work with LGBTQ clients as both couples and larger families. Social workers can play an important role when working with families in which one or both parents is the same sex, transgender, or questioning and need knowledge and skills to practice with cultural humility and competence. The following discussion highlights current characteristics and issues related to social work practice with LGBTQ families.

According to the most recent U.S. Census, there were 783,100 same-sex couple households in the United States (U.S. Census Bureau, 2014a). Data is not collected regarding couples and families who have a member who is bisexual, transgender, or questioning.

With the 2015 landmark Supreme Court ruling making same-sex marriage legal in all states in the U.S. (Supreme Court of the United States, 2015), same-sex couples have achieved marital equality. Despite same-sex marriage being legalized in the U.S., LGBTQ couples, when compared to heterosexual couples, continue to face discrimination from some members and organizations within society. LGBTQ couples may be considered unique in that they struggle for recognition of their legal standing and commitment within societal culture. They may have to overtly psychologically support one another (more than a comparable heterosexual couple). They also have unique challenges regarding gender roles; that is, traditional gender roles they learned growing up in their families of origin may not be applicable, and they must negotiate them. The legalization of same-sex marriage does not equate with acceptance by all. A recent poll commissioned by the LGBT acceptance advocacy organization, GLAAD, revealed that even with progress made in acceptance of LGBTQ persons, many non-LGBT individuals remain unaccepting (GLAAD, 2014) in such areas as: same-sex couples and weddings, in particular; children displaying non-gender-conforming behaviors; and transgender persons.

In all couples and family interventions, social workers need culturally specific, competent, and humble knowledge, skills, and values, but attention to these areas is particularly important in working with LGBTQ families. Practitioners can convey support of and validation for the same-sex relationship by advancing clients' psychological health and wellness, promoting their self-determination, and encouraging them to meet their human intimacy needs (Rostoky & Riggle, 2011). In working with LGBTQ couples, social workers should prioritize cultural competence and humility in the area of gender roles. Research shows that these roles have a greater impact on the relationship than sexual orientation (Butler, 2009). As highlighted throughout this book, using a narrative approach, social workers can work with LGBTQ couples to deconstruct gender role expectations (Butler, 2009).

Social workers can also support same-sex couples by collaborating with them to implement strategies for coping with the stress that accompanies discrimination in the form of societal acceptance, treatment of their children, and accessing services. A strengths-based approach and intervention is also helpful to enable same-sex couples to identify and appreciate the stresses they have faced and overcome together (Rostoky & Riggle, 2011).

Social workers can also help LGBTQ families address the discrimination they face by providing psychoeducational support and consultation within the community (Rostoky & Riggle, 2011) and connect LGBTQ couples with wider systems, such as other families and community programs (Butler, 2009). Social workers can work with local community organizations, schools, faith groups, and other agencies to reduce the prejudice and discrimination directed toward LGBTQ couples and families (Rostoky & Riggle, 2011). Social workers can also engage in political advocacy efforts to support all sexes and genders as well as educate themselves about issues that affect their clients (Rostoky & Riggle, 2011).

Parenthood   While not all LGBTQ individuals and couples choose to have children, those that do can approach parenthood in ways that work for their relationship and situation. They may have children from previous relationships, or have a child by birth. There are options for parenting, including: adoption, foster care, kinship care, surrogacy, donor insemination, birth from a heterosexual union, sharing parenting from a custody agreement between lesbians and gay men, and shared parenting with gay men and a heterosexual mother (Mallon, 2014).

Recently, states have begun to support the adoption or foster care placement of children in state's custody with LGBTQ parents. The ever-increasing pool of children needing a home and the increasing number and type of adoptions being granted has led, just as with grandparents, to less traditional, more creative placement planning efforts (Barth, 2013). These arrangements have been highly controversial within the child welfare community because they are at odds with the idealized version of the family. Researchers have investigated concerns about identity issues and the overall mental health of the parents and children. Recent research continues to demonstrate that children reared by LGBTQ parents suffer no detrimental emotional, psychosocial, or behavioral effects (Bos, Knox, van Rijn-van Gelderen, & Gartrel, 2016). When comparing same-sex and different-sex families on issues as partner and parent–child relationships, parent stress, and child health and behaviors, Bos and colleagues (2016) report differences only in same-sex parents experiencing more stress than different-sex parents but no differences in any child-related outcomes.

As prospective parents, LGBTQ persons and couples can still face obstacles in their pursuit of foster care or adoption and still experience institutionalized stigma, even from social workers. In both policy and practice, social workers should support the efforts of all persons seeking parenthood who, through the assessment process, are deemed eligible (i.e., able to provide a loving, supportive, and stable environment for a child). Social workers can de-emphasize the search for dysfunction and pathology as they give expression to the strengths and resilience of the parents (see Goldberg & Allen, 2013). Social workers can also recognize the effects of lingering cultural discrimination directed against the LGBTQ community regarding the strengths and viability of such people as parents.

The strengths perspective may be particularly helpful in working with LGBTQ parents. Helping these parents identify not only their own strengths, but also the strengths of the system in which they live, can be an informative, and even transformative, strategy for your work together. Being committed to an LGBTQ-affirming approach that embraces the belief that the quality of care, not the family constellation, is key to a child and family's well-being and health (Mallon, 2014).

Competent practitioners must also reflect on their own attitudes, values, and feelings about working with LGBTQ families (McGeorge & Carlson, 2011). Social workers should acknowledge that LGBTQ families and parents face many of the same challenges all parents encounter (e.g., parental roles, discipline philosophy, and expectations of children) as well as some that are unique (e.g., lack of legal protections if not married, community supports, etc.). Consider the family in which one of the partners of a lesbian couple gave birth to a child conceived through a sperm donation. If the couple is not married and ends the relationship, the nonbiological mother may have no legal rights to share custody of the child. These family arrangements are strengthened by strong social worker emotional and logistical support.

Single-Parent Families

Being raised in a single-parent family is more common than ever; currently, over one-quarter of children in the United States live in a household headed by a single parent (DeNavas-Walt & Proctor, 2015). Society and, at times, some social service providers have historically viewed single parenthood as a blight that necessarily leads to insecure, delinquent, and otherwise unhappy and dysfunctional households. While the data suggest that families headed by a single parent do have unique challenges, such generalized assumptions are unwarranted. It is important to recognize the specific challenges when working with single-parent families. For example, when working with single-parent families, it is helpful to know that generally, if the household head is female, these families report lower levels of income than two-parent families (DeNavas-Walt & Proctor, 2015). Specifically, of the 20% of children living in poverty, 46.5% of those live in female-headed households compared to only 10% who live with parents who are a married couple (DeNavas-Walt & Proctor, 2015). Children who reside with single fathers do not experience poverty at the same rate as children living with single mothers as fathers tend to come to single parenting later than single mothers and often do not experience the financial disadvantages that single mothers do. A review of research indicates that these fathers may approach parenting differently than both their counterparts who are single female parents and married male parents, primarily due to established gender norms and available supports, but they are also shown to be engaged and effective parents to their children (Coles, 2015).

While research has shown that children reared in single-parent families can face more economic, educational, and well-being challenges than their counterparts in two-parent families, having two parents in the home does not ensure the absence of negative outcomes (Musick & Meier, 2009). Growing up in a family in which conflict is handled in a healthy manner also has a strong correlation to a child's later well-being (Musick & Meier, 2009). On the other hand, there is some support, both in the scholarly literature and in the practice community, for recognizing the unique challenges of single parenting and the way that such parenting impacts both the social work relationship and parenting functions. Four major issues that frequently arise from divorce or separation are: (1) a lack of resources to cope with stress, finances, or other responsibility; (2) unresolved family-of-origin (family in which you grew up) issues, often brought on by the single parent's need for assistance from her or his parents; (3) unresolved divorce or relationship issues, such as anger, grief, or loneliness; and (4) an overburdened older child.

An older child who is not yet an adult may be pressed into providing excessive household chores or care for another family member. Such a child is termed a **parentified child**. The experience of being parentified has been viewed as having both positive and negative outcomes for the child. On the negative side, parentification is seen as a developmentally inappropriate life experience that can may compromise the parentified child's own physical and emotional health and well-being, particularly in the areas of feelings of injustice about the situation (Jankowski, Hooper, Sandage, & Hannah, 2013). From a more positive perspective, parentified children develop "extraordinary ability in influencing their environments and contributing to their families" (Chee, Goh, & Kuczynski, 2014, p. 210). Social work with families in which a child has assumed parental responsibilities can commend the child for her or his capabilities, help the child express and regulate feelings of unfairness, and negotiate a healthier balance of roles and responsibilities (Jankowski et al., 2013).

Focusing engagement, assessment, planning, intervention, termination, and evaluation and follow-up on the family itself, social work practice with single-parent families can use the family's strengths to create and stabilize coping skills. Drawing from the work of several family scholars whose work has influenced social work practice with families, skills for social work practice with single-parent families include (Atwood & Genovese, 2006; Jung, 1996):

- *Joining*, similar to engagement, reflects the social worker's effort to show clients that they are cared about and that the social worker understands them and their struggles.

- *Empowering clients* supports their activities and capacity to address their own issues, and it values their uniqueness and skills. In particular, the social worker can help the parent clarify and reinforce the parental role, while the parent also strives to nurture and support the other family members.

- Maintaining a focus on the family, the social worker can *help individual members identify strengths and resources within the family unit* (e.g., the parent is fully employed with a flexible work schedule to allow for involvement at the children's school); the extended family (e.g., grandparents are committed to helping with childcare); and the community (e.g., the community has active, well-organized after-school programming).

- *Involving significant family members* emphasizes collaboration, reduces stress, and pools resources.

- *Allocating agency resources* focuses on agency planning, outreach, and networking.

- *Highlighting small changes* emphasizes making small shifts that ease overextended schedules and increase energy; such changes can also highlight success and autonomy.

- *Articulating self-efficacy* emphasizes competence, accomplishments, and empowerment to exert greater control over management of family issues, ideally for all family members.

This knowledge and these values are consistent with a strengths-based, empowering approach that recognizes both internal and external factors and supports single parents in their ongoing efforts to provide security and nurturance for their children. Further, this knowledge and these values can enhance the social worker's efforts to engage and assess the family system by conveying a sense of care and concern for the individual members, identifying and building on the strengths of each member and the unit as a whole, and emphasizing their self-efficacy.

Families of Multiple Racial and Ethnic Heritages

Interracial and interethnic marriages, civil unions, and partnerships have been gaining in acceptability since the 1960s and currently comprise over 6 percent of all marriages (U.S. Census Bureau, 2015a). Shifting immigration patterns in the United States, globalization, and the breakdown of ethnic barriers all appear to have an effect on the incidence of racially and ethnically mixed families being a well-accepted family structure.

Perhaps few other developments in the everyday life of our communities offer a greater opportunity to view people differently than the growing numbers of families with multiple racial and ethnic heritages. While many in our society value the contributions of other cultures and challenge the notions associated with racial privilege, there are gains yet to be made for people of color within society as a whole. It is important to recognize the negative power of the persistent oppression many ethnically diverse families experience in our culture. Becoming aware of U.S. cultural and ethnic heritage and values and of our history of oppression, some of which persists today, is a critical step toward becoming a culturally competent (and humble) practitioner (Kohli, Huber, & Faul, 2010). Flexibility, shared goals, and a commitment to explore and address challenges are critical in working across culturally and ethnically diverse communities. As with all other aspects of individual and family assessment and intervention, a family should not be defined solely in terms of its group characteristics (e.g., race, ethnicity, or culture) but should be assessed with a lens on the individuals who are members of the group (Van Hook, 2014). However, being able to recognize and explore the unique situation and needs that exist within a multiple heritage family can help to lessen the more negative aspects of their lives (Henriksen & Maxwell, 2016). On the other hand, social workers should not assume that being a family whose members are from different races, ethnicities, or cultures defines that family or their current challenges.

A number of models can guide your intervention with a multiracial or multiethnic family. We briefly highlight two here. The **posture of cultural reciprocity** is an approach for working with diverse families that requires social workers and families to recognize and respect the cultural aspects of their own personal values and to collaborate toward the agreed-upon goals that incorporate their values (Kalyanpur & Harry, 2012). As Exhibit 6.3 illustrates, this posture occurs in four steps. These steps imply a constructionist understanding of cultural difference, value the client's distinctions without the imposition of the social worker's orientation, and provide a useful framework for working with people of other cultures. Because they enhance inclusion and reflect a basic assumption of cultural strengths, they are consistent with a commitment to social justice and human rights.

Cultural attunement uses self-awareness to inform practice. Being culturally attuned to multiracial/multiethnic families requires social workers to go beyond raising their awareness of their own and others' cultural heritage to gain new information about "racial legacies" and the way in which those legacies influence racial/ethnic self-identity (Jackson & Samuels, 2011, p. 239). When you assess and plan

STEP	EXAMPLE	
"Step 1: Identify the cultural values that are embedded in the professional interpretation of a student's [or client's] difficulties or in the recommendation for service."	Ask why, for example, a culturally different client's behavior bothers you. Is she late for appointments? Does she interrupt you? Does she respond to you indirectly? How do you interpret her behavior?	**EXHIBIT 6.3** *Working with Diverse Families: Racial and Ethnic Diversity*
"Step 2: Find out whether the family being served recognizes and values these assumptions and, if not, how their view differs from that of the professional."	For example, you may discover that you and your client have differing senses of time and that punctuality has little meaning for her. Here you would want to explore how she approaches time, what it means to her, and whether she recognizes your approach to it.	
"Step 3: Acknowledge and give explicit respect to any cultural differences identified, and fully explain the cultural basis of the professional assumptions."	This requires you to enter into a dialogue regarding your assumptions and beliefs and how they differ from those of your client. For example, you might recognize and appreciate the client's less frantic approach to time and deadlines while you explain your agency's need to abide by a schedule.	
"Step 4: Through discussion and collaboration, set about determining the most effective way of adapting professional interpretations or recommendations to the value system of this family."	Work out a solution that respects the nature of the family's values. You might settle on a more flexible appointment time at the end of the day, agree on a time range, or make outreach visits if that is possible.	

Source: Kalyanpur & Harry, 2012, p. 17

using a culturally attuned framework, in addition to learning more about the racial legacies in the community in which you are delivering services, the following social work skills can be particularly useful (Jackson & Samuels, 2011):

- Ask open-ended questions regarding racial/ethnic identity.

- Connect multiracial families to appropriate resources.

- Be vigilant about racial/ethnic-focused issues that are raised by the client and reactions experienced by the client and you.

- Develop practice wisdom regarding the unique experiences of the multiracial family.

Families Including Persons with Disabilities

Social workers work with families in which one or more members have a physical, cognitive, and/or mental health disability. In fact, the number of children and young adults aged 6–21 years who are identified as having a learning disability is on the rise, with the greatest increase occurring in the area of autism (Samuels, 2016). Note that the increase may be an artifact of improved identification and reporting and not necessarily an increase in the number of persons with a disability.

Family-centered care is an empowerment-focused philosophy of care that creates a partnership between the individual/family and the professionals (Institute for Healthcare Improvement (IHI), 2016). Family-centered care emphasizes (IHI, 2016):

- developing care pathways (i.e., sequencing of plans to promote access) that are co-designed and co-produced with individuals and their families;

- ensuring that care preferences are understood and honored, including at the end of life;

- collaborating with partners on programs designed to improve engagement, shared decision making, and compassionate, empathic care; and

- working with partners to ensure that communities are supported to stay healthy and to provide care for their loved ones closer to home (para 4).

Family-centered care assumes that the family determines what it needs, and thus services are "family-driven" (Seligman & Darling, 2007, p. 14). This strengths-based approach is a promising method for working with families in many arenas, especially for working with those who have disabilities. When children have comprehensive and severe health challenges, such as neuro-developmental delays, **interprofessional teaming**, in which professionals from different disciplines work together toward the client's goals, is an appropriate response. Social workers can play an important role on such teams to help address the many needs of children with disabilities that go beyond medical and educational requirements across the life span. With our commitment to a strengths-based, person-in-environment perspective, we have the opportunity to empower families by recognizing that they are the experts on their lives (Tomasello, Manning, & Dulmus, 2010). Many agencies employ family-centered social workers to help adults with developmental disabilities learn job skills. Thus, it is very valuable for social workers to be able to work with adults who have developmental, mental or physical health, or cognitive disabilities and their families and support networks.

As another example, when a child with profound disabilities is born, family members usually have to reorganize both their everyday lives and their long-term plans. One parent may have to stop working to facilitate the services and treatments the child needs. The time requirements for involvement with school teams, health care teams, and interprofessional teams, as well as the individual services of a speech therapist, audiologist, occupational therapist, physical therapist, pediatrician, psychologist—the list is sometimes quite long—can turn a family upside down. Siblings are affected, family interactions are affected, and parents often struggle with the emotional ramifications and the physical consequences of exhaustion. Social workers can offer support, time management ideas, and help with expanding parents' ability to identify resources. In addition, many families struggle to access services to which they are entitled and therefore may need social work advocacy to negotiate a complex system.

Societal views of individuals and families that emphasize deficits may challenge social workers working with families that include individuals with disabilities. In response, social workers and disability scholars have proposed the following set of beliefs to serve as a foundation for working with such families (Mackelprang & Salsgiver, 2015):

- Persons with disabilities are capable, have potential, and are important members of society.

- Devaluation and a lack of resources, not individual pathology, are the primary obstacles facing persons with disabilities.

- Disability, like race and gender, is a social construct, and intervention with people with disabilities is political in nature.

- There is a disability culture and history that professionals should be aware of in order to facilitate the empowerment of persons with disabilities.

- There is a joy and vitality to be found in disability.

- Persons with disabilities have the right to self-determination and the right to guide professionals' involvement in their lives (pp. xvii).

Social workers have the opportunity and ethical responsibility to empower clients to embrace this belief system. When individuals and organizations within our society do not embrace a strengths-based perspective, the social worker may need to become an advocate for people with disabilities.

A diversity (or social) model that views societal attitudes, structures, policies, and institutions as responsible for imposing limitations on persons with disabilities is most appropriate for work with individuals with disabilities. Person-first language is currently in use in some segments of society, but "disability identity language" (e.g., man with a disability) may more appropriately frame the disability as a dimension of diversity, similar to race/ethnic group. Social workers may need to advocate for disability to be seen as a dimension of diversity in society, which implies that social workers need to engage in public dialogue about advocacy, structural principles, and the skills to work for social justice.

There is a growing need for social workers who want to work with families in which a member has a disability. Social workers can help empower the family and the person with a disability to engage in self-determination, self-advocacy, and independence negotiating life transitions with family members, organizations, and themselves (Beaulaurier & Taylor, 2007). It is important to ask the family members, including siblings, what roles they would like to have in the assessment and intervention process. While family-centered care is built on the notion of the professional partnering with the family members, not all family members may want to play high-level roles (Lotze, Bellin, & Oswald, 2010).

Within a framework of promoting client needs and self-determination, the person with a disability and their family members can be empowered to: (1) expand their range of options and choices; (2) be more effective in dealings with professionals, bureaucrats, and agencies that often do not understand nor appreciate their heightened need for self-determination; and (3) mobilize and help groups of people with disabilities to consider policy and program alternatives that can improve their situation (Beaulaurier & Taylor, 2007, p. 65). Lastly, consider that the family may be faced with multiple, and sometimes contradictory, demands for attention and resources. These can be viewed as a "pileup of demands" (Van Hook, 2014) and can result in a family feeling overwhelmed. For example, a family may have more than one member experiencing a disability, a member with a disability along with financial difficulties, or a child with a disability and another child with a substance abuse issue. Such situations can create a crisis for the family as well as the social worker in terms of prioritizing needs and goals and allocating limited resources. In each of these examples, the family is experiencing multiple stressors and feels incapable of making decisions. The social worker's role may be to focus a part of the intervention on prioritizing the needs of the all the members of the family.

Blended Families

Families become blended in different ways. A blended family is considered one in which separate families come together through marriage or other circumstances

© Rob Hainer

(Barker, 2014). Other blended families include kinship and nonkinship groups including domestic partner relationships, civil unions, and nonrelated families who co-reside in the same household who assume traditional family roles (Barker, 2014). Approximately 16 percent of children are part of a blended family (Manning, Brown, & Stykes, 2014).

While most blended families come together without specifically seeking the services of a helping professional, some families value a social worker's contribution as they blend into the new family constellation. An intervention with a blended family can provide education and support on such issues as: realities of stepfamilies, strengthening relationships through respectful communication and conflict resolution, incorporating the past, parenting strategies, and relating to the biological parents (Zeleznikow & Zeleznikow, 2015). Social workers working with a blended family should be aware of the families' histories and be sensitive to the dynamics that may occur when two families merge into one. Incorporating information about family blending is a critical component of the engagement, assessment, planning, and intervention processes. Family members may not be aware of or able to articulate the challenges they are experiencing regarding the "merger" of the two family units. Social workers who strive to stay attuned to the issues that can occur when families consolidate can identify the reason the family is struggling.

Work with a blended family begins with identification of individual and family strengths. Within the engagement and assessment process, the social worker can help the family identify and discuss the roles of individual members along with boundaries between members of the multiple families coming together. It is important to remember to view each member of the newly created family unit within the context of both of the systems (i.e., original family and new family) in which they exist. Competence in working with blended families requires knowledge of family development and transitions. You may need to involve noncustodial parents and extended families to help families negotiate new and different family roles, boundaries, relationships, and traditions. The social worker can also engage with and assess blended families by helping them identify their expectations for the forming of this new family. The following questions for clients from the work of Gibson (2013, p. 798–799), may be helpful to this process:

1. What does it mean to be family? Who influenced your beliefs? How have your beliefs of family influenced your stepfamily?
2. As each person responds, the other members may be asked: What was it about what he or she said that made you believe them? Is there anything that was said that does not fit with your individual values now?
3. Are your beliefs about stepfamilies influenced by any outside sources like friends, TV, media, or social media? In what way?
4. If a child has been open to new roles in the blended family, the family may be asked: What benefits have transpired from you being open to your stepparent or stepchildren's different view of family roles?
5. What positive influences do you think you have brought to your stepparent's life? How do you think your stepparent feels about the influence you have had on her/him?
6. Do you have friends at school or work who are part of a stepfamily? What do you think that family is doing well together? How do they do that?

International Families

Social work practice with families in contemporary society requires global competency. If you are practicing social work with families in the U.S., you will likely encounter families who have arrived in the U.S. as immigrants or refugees. If you are a social work practitioner outside the U.S., you will need extensive knowledge of international issues. While working with families abroad may require a different knowledge base regarding immigration, legal and governmental issues, cultures, and customs than working with families in the U.S., the same practice skill set is common to all family social work practice regardless of setting. You should be prepared for working with families who are new to their country, as well as those that are "stuck" in countries for many years and wish to be elsewhere (back in their home country or as an immigrant to their country of choice).

    To become competent in thinking and working internationally, learn as much as possible about the family or families with whom you will be working. Before you meet the client(s), expose yourself to information about their relocation history and experience and their home culture, heritage, language, customs and traditions, spiritual practices, and community. While reading about your client's country of origin and culture can be helpful, seek out others who can provide you with firsthand personal or professional experiences and guidance.

While some characteristics may be common to groups of people who share a country of origin, culture, or traditions, social workers should view each person within a family and the family itself as individuals. Remember also that the client family can ultimately be your best source of information and insight. You may find as many similarities between a family from the U.S. and a family from Ghana as between two families from Ghana. Learn from them and learn about them as a unique family. Learning about the lives of the families with whom you work is an ongoing process that can unfold as you build rapport and trust. As with all clients, it is especially important to explore these families' perceptions and beliefs about working with a helping professional.

While much of the social work practice knowledge and skills you learn is applicable to all families, certain competencies are unique to working with a family that has relocated from their country of origin. First, it is critical to understand the cultural norms of your client family related to the definition of family. As with any family, be reminded that you need to have a clear understanding of who is considered a member of the family, how family members relate to one another, the meaning of those relationships, and any hierarchical traditions that may exist within the family unit. For example, does the word "family" describe the nuclear unit or the larger, extended family? Are persons who are not biologically or legally linked considered part of the family? What rules and tasks guide family members in their daily lives and in making major life decisions such as marriage, parenting, residential arrangements, education, careers, religion/spirituality, and financial priorities?

Regardless of the family's origins, you can use a strengths-based approach to complete your assessment and intervention planning. Using the International Family Strengths Model, DeFrain and Asay (2007a, p. 452) suggest that family strengths can be assessed on the basis of: (1) appreciation and affection, (2) positive communication, (3) commitment to the family, (4) enjoyable time together, (5) a sense of spiritual well-being, and (6) the ability to manage stress and crisis effectively. While you can apply these attributes to families of any ethnic, cultural, or heritage background, they are particularly helpful when considered within the cultural context of the family with whom you are working, as these family dynamics can have different meanings when viewed within the cultural background of the client system.

Building on family strengths can be a particularly helpful strategy as families work to adjust to their new country and environment. Parents, for example, may struggle with their children to adopt the customs, language, and dress of their culture, or older adults may find it challenging to live in a world that is unfamiliar to them. When a family experiences a crisis or tragedy, as in the case of the Patel family going through a hurricane, they may find that usual coping and support systems are not available in their new country. Using the family's strengths can empower family members to find their place within their new home while maintaining their connections to their heritage. You can help to make global connections between the world from which the family has come and the one they have entered by pointing out and affirming the family's ability to rely on one another in times of need despite the challenges they face adjusting to life in their new country and home.

In summary, while the preceding discussion focused on family situations and circumstances, in the real world of social work practice, individuals and families may present multiple concerns and dilemmas that include a combination of challenges in financial, relationships, and physical and mental health. For example, a grandparent rearing her adolescent grandson may face a custody battle with the child's biological parent; a couple with a child born with a disability may, at the same time, grapple with a grandmother's cognitive impairment; a blended family may cope with employment layoffs and foreclosure proceedings on their home.

As with any family, the social worker's role with families facing multiple challenges is to approach each as a unique system with strengths and individualized needs. Listening to each member of a family unit enables the social worker to gain insight into each individual's perceptions, relationship dynamics, and possibilities within the collective family system. Social workers who are competent in working with families have developed a repertoire of behaviors that include family-focused knowledge, skills, and values. The social worker can focus on organizing problem solving into short- and longer-term goals and promoting a supportive and nurturing environment. She or he may discern the need to pay special attention to both internal and external challenges that confront the family (Janzen, Harris, Jordan, & Franklin, 2006). For example, a family may face an internal challenge—substance abuse by one of the members, or they may face an external challenge—the family's inability to qualify for subsidized housing or financial assistance. While the social worker may need to use different strategies to address internal versus external issues, she or he may serve a number of roles (e.g., broker, advocate, counselor, or educator). The remainder of this chapter will highlight a sampling of the behaviors within these roles that are needed to work effectively with families.

CONTEMPORARY TRENDS AND SKILLS FOR ENGAGEMENT AND ASSESSMENT WITH FAMILIES [EPAS 4]

As with social work practice with individuals, a wide array of theoretical approaches are available for assessing and intervening with families. The family social worker relies on multiple and interrelated theories to guide her or his engagement and assessment processes (Rasheed & Rasheed, 2013). We present three different theoretical perspectives here; throughout your career, you will develop the approach most consistent with your philosophical and practice perspectives and agency context. Each of the perspectives highlighted here has some components in common and each corresponds in some ways to traditional perspectives. Regardless of the theoretical approach(es) you use, your goals in social work practice with families should be situational-focused, structured, realistic, concrete, and achievable (Rasheed & Rasheed, 2013).

Narrative Theory in Family Engagement and Assessment

As discussed throughout this book, narrative theory is based on a postmodern, constructionist perspective that enables clients to make sense of their lives through "stories," that is, through the client's perception of an individual or a situation. Family interpretations of ongoing events may support the ongoing narrative that most people believe, refute the narrative, or include a combination of the two. Families use the stories to organize their subsequent experiences. When experiences do not fit their chosen narratives, families often dismiss those experiences as not representative of the real family. The language families use to interpret and describe various family stories is significant and shapes how they view the experience. For example, one family may frame one member's alcohol addiction as an "occasional problem."

Exhibit 6.4 outlines the tenets on which a narrative family assessment and intervention is based. The following examples explore the ideas central to a narrative approach.

As opposed to seeking a diagnosis, conducting an assessment from the narrative perspective involves helping family members tell their family and individual stories, which can then be used to inform the intervention. In essence, using a narrative

---

1. Language (i.e., word choice) helps determine how families assign meaning to life events and provides the context for change.
2. Stories, much like language, help families give meaning to their life events.
3. The stories each family member creates shape subsequent life events, and family members may recall life events differently. It is important to acknowledge all stories, as multiple realities can and do exist simultaneously.
4. Social context, specifically culture, influences values, social roles, gender relationships, and concepts of justice, which, in turn, serve to define the stories family members create.
5. Stories are not necessarily based in fact; they may instead be the result of family members' perceptions of life experiences, which may not include strengths and positive alternatives.
6. Stories can encompass possibilities for growth and healing.
7. Families are not the problem; families experience problems.

EXHIBIT 6.4

Tenets of a Narrative Family Intervention

Source: Adapted from Van Hook, 2014, p. 250–251

approach intertwines the assessment and intervention processes as the stories bring to light the family's strengths and provide direction for the deconstruction of old stories (Williams, 2009). The goal of a narrative approach is to help the family alter their interpretation of themselves and their current situation to one that is more liberating and the role of the professional is to serve as a co-editor and collaborator with the family in creating new meanings (Van Hook, 2014, p. 251).

In our first example, a family comes to the social worker out of concern for the daughter Liza, who is 6 years old, the youngest child, and the only girl in a single parent, male-headed household in an economically affluent neighborhood. The family casts Liza in the role of family "misfit." They describe her behavior as oppositional and say that she is clumsy, speaks disrespectfully, and is disruptive. The family uses any incident involving Liza (e.g., forgetting her pencil or knocking over her milk) as just another piece of evidence supporting her misfit status. When Liza's first-grade teacher reports to her father that Liza is exceptionally well liked, by both her peers and teachers, and that she is bright and fun, Liza's father is incredulous. He suspects the teacher has her confused with another student or that Liza must be faking at school. From his perspective, the *real* Liza, as everyone knows, is oppositional, clumsy, disrespectful, and disruptive, as misfits are inclined to be.

The story that Liza tells about herself is different from her family's story about her. Each individual story carries the power to perpetuate and expand the family story, which in turn will influence the way Liza, as the major character, plays her role. If her family persists in maintaining their original negatively focused perception of Liza and not be able to view her in a more positive, strengths-based light, she is likely to respond over time by becoming increasingly rude, failing, or developing truly disruptive conduct. On the other hand, if her family at any point re-authors their perceptions, recognizing the exceptions to their ideas about Liza, her story may unfold quite differently. Everyone has multiple stories, but some have more power, relevance, and a wider audience than others. Liza's alternative story (told by her teacher) has the potential to influence her future in positive and significant ways.

Thickening the Story The narrative framework has many components. This chapter focuses on the concepts most relevant to generalist social work practice with families. You may recall that **thickening the story** refers to the social worker's effort to expand "thin" (Morgan, 2000) or **problem-saturated stories**, one-dimensional perspectives on a truth that clients created about themselves that may or may not be based in fact (Kelley & Smith, 2015). This attempt to create a more complex story may achieve the larger goal of instilling hope that the client can make positive changes. Liza's first story is a good example of a thin account. In the account, she has no redeeming virtues and is simply oppositional, clumsy, disrespectful, and disruptive. A thickened version of Liza's story reveals her likable personality, talents, and ability to connect with people in spite of, or in addition to, any behaviors that are oppositional, clumsy, disrespectful, and disruptive. By assuming an unknowing position with the entire family, the social worker can allow the family to be the experts on their lives.

Our second example comes from the Smith family, who illustrate the value of reframing the story. The Smiths have experienced considerable child rearing challenges. One child has been taken into state custody for behavioral concerns, and now child protection workers are investigating to determine whether they should remove another child for safety reasons. The mother disparagingly claims, in defeat and sarcastic resignation, that the Smiths are "just one of those families." Child welfare workers may likewise view them as "just one of those families" because various Smith children have been in custody for three generations (as was Ms. Smith).

Rather than assessing the narrowly defined dysfunction of this family, the narrative social worker would search for exceptions to this story to enrich it and make it more complex. Rather than maintaining a focus on problem solving, the narrative social worker collaborates with her or his clients to "enhance their awareness of how cultural forces have lulled them into accepting problem-saturated ways of living" (Williams, 2009, p. 205). For example, the social worker can ask about Ms. Smith's ability to keep a family together for ten years in the face of poverty, to overcome a major childhood health challenge, or to survive homelessness. As part of the engagement and assessment process, the social worker can ask questions of the family that will help to identify the family's risk factors and negative beliefs systems (Van Hook, 2014). The social worker's aim is to expand the narrow failure story so that the family can see its potential, which in turn can support re-authoring the story to reflect the way the family would like it to be. The family then can shape its future to fit the new story. Such a narrative approach contrasts with the one in the section "Intergenerational Patterns" earlier in the chapter. Through a different lens, it offers the potential for hope through development of the family's resilience and positive attributes.

A narrative approach can provide an opportunity to highlight the fact that a family's resilience can be a powerful aspect of the social work intervention. In keeping with the practice approaches presented here, the social worker should perceive that resilience begins with the beliefs, socially constructed judgment, and evaluations that each family member creates (Benard & Truebridge, 2013, p. 205). Some families need help identifying their areas of resiliency. Social workers can help families by incorporating the family's stories into the assessment and planning phases of work by focusing on the following resiliency-oriented beliefs about families (Benard & Truebridge, 2013):

- All people have the capacity for resilience.

- Most individuals survive and even thrive despite exposure to severe risk.

- One person can make a difference in the life of another person.

- Coming from a risk environment does not determine individual or family outcomes.

- Challenging life experience and events can be opportunities for growth, development, and change.

- There is nothing wrong with you that what is right with you cannot fix.

- Bad behavior does not equate with being a bad person.

- As a practitioner, it is how you do what you do that counts.

- To help others, you need to help yourself.

- Resilience begins with what one believes (p. 207).

You can conceptualize resiliency as the family's ability to "absorb the shock of problems and discover strategies to solve them while finding ways to meet the needs of family members and the family unit" (Van Hook, 2014, p. 15). The social worker's role is to empower the family to operationalize their capacities for resilience specifically by:

- incorporating a sense of hopefulness and purpose into the meaning families assign to situations (e.g., pointing out ways in which the family can show support for the family member who has just completed a substance abuse treatment program, and the importance of that support);

- supporting organizational structures that provide effective leadership and a balance of flexibility and stability can help build family resilience by streamlining access and service delivery;

- promoting clear, empathic, and supportive communication patterns among family members;

- emphasizing existing positive family members' relationships;

- promoting family members' problem-solving abilities; and

- to the extent possible, improving and enhancing the social support system and community and economic resources accessible to the family (Van Hook, 2014, p. 30).

Externalizing Problems   Within the narrative approach, the notion that problems are considered outside of the family is known as **externalization**. The problem is not the client itself; the problem is the result of an issue separate from the client, and thus the focus of the intervention is also external to the client (Kelley & Smith, 2015). Narrative social workers try to identify and help the family to name the issue that is creating their difficulties. By objectifying or personifying it, family members can develop a relationship with the challenge, rather than be consumed by it, and ultimately they may control it.

For example, if a family feels overwhelmed by the demands of raising a child with disabilities, the social worker may externalize their resulting "worry." To do this, the social worker asks about the feelings of being overwhelmed, help family members label their feelings, and support all those times when the family takes control over "the worry." By separating the issue (or "worry") from the family's identity, the worker and the family can explore ways to defeat their concerns or at least to keep them at bay.

Unearthing the Broader Context   One of narrative theory's most relevant contributions to generalist social work practice is a consistent emphasis on the political context of the family. Social workers are highly sensitized to the danger of reinforcing the oppressive dimensions of a dominant pattern (such as racism) in society. For example, consider 6-year-old Damion, who appears to be having a fearful reaction about going to school. Damion's reaction seems extreme for the situation. The social worker will not want to externalize the reaction prematurely as "the school creeps" or "school scares" if in fact Damion is being taunted and bullied because of his ethnicity. Using narrative theory, the social worker seeks to identify any political factors that affect the situation with the client and family and, through a partnership with the client and family, to address those factors that negatively shape and impact the challenge at hand. In the case of Damion, it is important for the social worker to elicit the client's and his family's perception of the climate at his school that may promote an environment in which Damion does not feel safe. The social worker can work with Damion and his family to develop an externalized version of the story and to incorporate the school into the situation. Helping Damion, his parents, and school personnel to articulate a detailed description of the classroom environment and Damion's specific interactions with his peers begins the externalization of his reluctance to go to school. Externalizing the situation beyond Damion himself allows the group to identify strategies to address his fears.

Solution-Focused Family Work

Like many contemporary family models, **solution-focused practice** de-emphasizes history and underlying pathology by defining the family broadly rather than limiting its conception to traditional forms or even requiring all members to be present in the meeting with the social worker (Nichols, 2014). Solution-focused practice involves using brief interventions that narrowly define the arena of specific problems within the context of particular environmental variables. Therefore, solution-focused family work can be used with a range of life situations and groups. A solution-focused engagement, assessment, and planning process emphasizes the "presence of something positive, rather than the absence of something negative" (Van Hook, 2014, p. 228).

Solution-focused family social work is grounded in the following assumptions (Koop, 2009):

1. The family is the expert.
2. Problems and solutions are not connected.

3. Unsolvable problems can be solvable.
4. Change is constant and inevitable.
5. Only a small change is needed to make an impact.
6. Interventions can be brief.
7. Interventions should focus on the future.
8. The focus should be on the family members' perceptions (pp. 147–148).

Solution-focused social workers usually emphasize a cognitive approach, support a collaborative stance with clients, and reject notions that problems serve any unconscious or ulterior motive. Accordingly, solution-focused social workers believe that individuals want to change, and they believe that attributing resistant behavior to families says more about the social worker than it does about families. Early in his work, the founder of solution-focused therapy, Steve deShazer (1984), declared resistance "dead" and in turn redefined clients' balking at practitioner directives as their way of educating the social worker about the help they need. Exhibit 6.5 lists the seven tenets of solution-focused family interventions.

Solution-focused social workers emphasize the future and its possibilities, in which solutions can be implemented within the specification of clear, concrete, modest, and achievable goals. Solution-focused work has become an important contemporary model as it generally aspires to short-term, specific, and direct results, thus avoiding costly, protracted professional relationships. Long used in community-based programs, solution-focused interventions have shown promise in addressing family and relationship problems, particularly related to children, youth, and families and in school-based settings (Bond, Woods, Humphrey, Symes, & Green, 2013). Solution-focused practice is popular in school settings because of its client-focused strengths orientation and its portability, adaptability, brief time frame, and the

---

EXHIBIT 6.5

Tenets of Solution-Focused Family Interventions

1. Emphasize the future and ways in which it will differ from the past.
2. Solutions may be unrelated to the problem's history; therefore, understanding the past may not aid in developing future-focused solutions.
3. Negativity and pessimism can overshadow family members' abilities to see positive alternatives to their ways of relating to one another.
4. People want to change. Resistance can be a trigger for the social worker to identify different strategies for intervening.
5. Because the social worker can influence family members, the practitioner should focus on empowering the family to understand their problems and possible solutions.
6. Social workers can encourage family members to switch from using problem-oriented language to using solution-oriented language to discuss their issues.
7. Family members determine those areas of focus that are important to them and, as a result, that are most appropriate to formulate goals for the intervention.

Source: Adapted from Van Hook, 2014, p. 226–227.

opportunity for small changes to matter and applicability for cultural competence (Kelly, Kim, & Franklin, 2008, p. 8).

Solution-focused work with more than one person focuses on the relationship, not the individual, and concentrates on finding and maintaining a common goal (De Jong & Berg, 2013). Solution-oriented social workers need specific skills to work with families, as families often have one or more of the following preconceived notions about their needs (Sebold, 2011):

- Families see problems stemming from the relationships among family members.

- Families often perceive that one person needs to change.

- Families often view problems as relating only to the child(ren) (p. 211).

With a focus on developing solutions and de-emphasizing ongoing descriptions of the problem, the solution-oriented social worker enables the family to "know" their problems *and* the possible solutions to those problems and to work together to build on one another's ideas and competencies to develop preferred solutions (Sebold, 2011).

Assessment Process   The assessment process begins with a series of questions to elicit the perceptions of each member. The social worker then uses the family's perceptions to co-construct an intervention plan (De Jong, 2015). With families, questions can focus on relationships among members, even those who are not present. Next, the phases of an assessment process for the solution-focused approach are described. Included are questions that relate to the solution-focused assessments:

- *Joining:* This phase is characterized by initially chatting informally with family members and asking them general questions about themselves and their lives to build rapport (Koop, 2009).

- *Normalizing:* When possible, ask the family questions to help them view the current situation as normal. This can enable them to envision a future in which they do not feel in crisis (Koop, 2009). For example, "What would your lives be like if you allowed your daughter to have more freedoms?"

- *Goal-formulating:* Questions aimed at goal-formulation prompt the client to consider how their situation will be different when their problem is solved (e.g., "What will be different if the problem is resolved?"). "Miracle" questions can help the client envision what life would be like if a miracle eliminated the presenting problem. In the engagement and assessment phases of work, goal-formulation can serve several purposes. It can enable family members to communicate their individual goals to one another, focus family members on a common direction for the work, and enable family members to identify and build on individual strengths in pursuit of agreed-upon goals.

- *Exception-finding:* Questions developed to identify exceptions are critical to the assessment process. They help family systems recall experiences in which they were successful (and the problem either did not exist or existed but was not identified as a problem). These questions provide opportunities to identify available strengths and resources to incorporate into the intervention.

- *Scaling:* Scaling questions invite the family system to quantify the past and the future within the context of the problem or crisis they are experiencing. These questions ask clients to rate on a scale of 1 to 10 their belief that they will find a solution for the issue that brought them to see you. During the engagement and assessment phases of the intervention process, scaling questions help establish a starting point for the work and identify current and past successes and areas for future growth.

- *Coping:* Coping questions strive to connect family members to coping strategies that they have used successfully in the past or that they could use now and in the future. Such questions can engage and invest the client in the helping process as well as assess past successes and failures, which you and the client can then use to develop the plan of work for the current intervention.

- *Circular questions:* Family members' perceptions of what other people (including other family members) think of them can influence their actions; therefore, asking family members what they believe others think of them can help you better understand clients' concerns (e.g., "What do you believe your wife thinks about you when she feels you are not listening to her?") (Koop, 2009).

In applying the strategies listed here, specific solution-focused questions that may be asked in a family assessment include (Nichols, 2014):

- What do you think the problem is now?

- How will you know when the problem is solved?

- How will you know when you don't have to come here any more?

- What will the signs be? (p. 228)

Like narrative proponents, solution-focused social workers concentrate on identifying and bolstering family's successes. As early as the assessment and planning process, the conversation begins to shift from problem-talk to solutions-talk (Van Hook, 2014). When solution-focused social workers ask families to remember when their efforts worked, even when it may seem their successes have been small and infrequent, they are directing their attention to those exceptions and explore the contextual factors that made the exception possible. A solution-focused social worker shows families that they have the strengths to cope, that they have in fact done it successfully before, and that they can do it again (De Jong & Berg, 2013). In this way, the family's vision is translated into them determining their goals and using their own skills, even if the skills have to be recovered or expanded (Van Hook, 2014).

When solution-focused practitioners use "exception" questions, they emphasize strengths, encouraging families to identify and focus on those strengths that are relevant to the current situation (Weick, Kreider, & Chamberlain, 2009). "Exception" questions allow clients to place strengths within the context of times and situations in which they were successful.

Environmental Focus   Using an ecological orientation, solution-based social work looks to the community as a resource and seeks to understand problems in terms of their relationship to the surrounding context.

For example, a social worker who views the client within the context of the environment in which the client has grown up and currently lives may view a client who abandoned her children in the context of the culture in which the client is embedded, a culture in which she experiences gender discrimination, poverty, unmet mental health challenges, or perhaps racism. This context can help explain the client's current inability to care for her children. The intervention may then focus on education, mobilizing resources, and developing a support system for the client.

Constructionist and Social Justice Approaches to Family Social Work

The contemporary approaches described in this chapter are complementary. They share some constructionist notions as reflected in the client-defined meanings of family, the lack of rigid ideas of so-called normal family development, and the collaborative partnerships built with clients. Critical social construction (also referred to as constructivism) suggests the development of a perspective that focuses directly on constructionist ideas and social justice principles. Specifically, constructivist approaches embrace the belief that "knowledge is created, acquired, and processed" and unique to each individual's perception, thus resulting in all knowledge being relative (Barker, 2014, p. 90). Both narrative and solution-focused approaches are grounded within a constructivist foundation based on the importance of individuals being able to voice their perceptions of their lives and relationships and give them meaning that is relevant in their lives. Additionally, the approaches presented in this book also relate to social justice issues in their concern for the daily contexts of client's experiences. In that respect, the approaches are more alike than they are different, and each makes a positive contribution to contemporary social work practice.

Whether one is utilizing a strengths-based, narrative, solution-focused, or other approach, social work interventions with families that are rooted in a constructionist perspective enables the social worker to help families to tell their stories and to acknowledge the meaning of those stories for them. During the assessment and planning phase of the intervention, the social worker using a constructivist approach to elicit the family's stories to identify individual and family strengths, to pinpoint times when the family was able to respond in a beneficial way (i.e., exceptions), and to explore the implications of those stories on family functioning and opportunities for change (Holland & Kilpatrick, 2009). The following principles of constructionist thought are helpful in working with families (Holland & Kilpatrick, 2009):

- Family stories transmit meaning, create sequences that are coherent within the context of the family's assigned meaning, shape identity, organize values and explain choices, and involve alternative interpretations.

- To function as a family, family members must have shared meanings.

- Outside individuals cannot change the meanings of stories ascribed by the family (p. 26).

Critical Constructionist Emphasis When viewing the family from a critical constructionist lens, social workers explore the meaning of family within a broad contextual framework. Constructionist descriptions of the family provide the social worker with multiple critical perspectives, each with its own implications for social work practice. For example, if you assume a theoretical model that considers the family basic for human survival and absolutely sacrosanct, you might view the family, as many did for centuries, as immune from external interference in its internal dynamics, including family violence. If, however, you assume that the meanings (or realities) clients make of their lives occur within a larger community, you and the client can view their situation within the context of the groups to which they belong (e.g., racial, ethnic, socioeconomic, religious, etc.) (De Jong & Berg, 2013). Using a critical constructionist emphasis, the solution-focused intervention becomes a collaboration between the social worker and the family in which family members explore their realities (i.e., problems, miracles, successes, strengths, and solutions) while incorporating the influence of the multiple groups within which they live their lives (e.g., neighborhood, extended family, schools, job settings, and church) (p. 369).

Social Justice Emphasis Constructionist theorists call for consideration of both external and internal dimensions of social justice. From an external perspective, social workers direct their attention to ensuring that all families—not just the idealized families of dominant groups—are granted the rights and privileges of society. Diverse families, whether they differ from the majority because of their ethnicity, sexual orientation, socioeconomic class, or any other difference, should be guaranteed equal access to the benefits of the culture. When they are not, the social worker is called upon to intervene in whatever ways are applicable, including legal advocacy, legislative advocacy, public education, or other forms of social action.

From an internal perspective, the social worker looks within the family itself to ensure justice for all family members. The social worker challenges overt and specific oppressive behaviors, such as intimate partner violence and child abuse, but also looks at family structure, gender dynamics, and roles. Critical constructionist social workers address external influences that have clear internal ramifications by educating and advocating for more just family practices and policies. This perspective reflects the continuous and energetic efforts of the social work profession to develop practice models that confront unjust and support just dimensions of contemporary society.

Generalist Practice Skills Guidelines for Family Engagement and Assessment [EPAS 6 and 7]

While models may differ somewhat, the following list includes the family-oriented engagement and assessment behaviors common to most models:

- Ensure the family is as physically comfortable as possible.

- Work to facilitate a respectful tone throughout the meeting.

- Use verbal and nonverbal behaviors that transmit positive regard or warmth, support, and respect.

- Engage with and hear from each member of the family, inviting each to share her or his perception of the family's purpose, strengths, areas for concern, and reason for seeking services/goals.

- Agree upon the expectations and focus of the work.

- Recognize your own biases around family forms and norms and seek to avoid demonstrating your biases.

- Observe the family's communication and interrelationship patterns.

- Inquire about, observe, and discuss the role and emotional function each family member serves within the family, particularly within the context of intergenerational relationships.

With all the models discussed here, the engagement and assessment process should be focused and thorough. In the engagement process, it is key that the social worker "join" with the client. In joining, the social worker greets each family member, attempts to place each person at ease, and starts to develop an alliance with the family members in order to build trust and rapport (Van Hook, 2014). An established, trusting relationship is critical for moving forward into the assessment and planning phases of the social work intervention. Because family systems are complex and encompass multiple perspectives, the assessment process cannot be rushed and must account for the perspective of each family member (Rasheed & Rasheed, 2013). While the engagement phase of work provides the basis for ongoing work with the family, it is important to recognize that not all family members may be positive about working with a social worker or may be ambivalent about change altogether (Van Hook, 2014). You can take this opportunity to acknowledge these feelings and review your collaborative approach, issues of confidentiality, and the timeframe for your work together.

The agency typically determines family assessment processes. Your agency may or may not use a standardized assessment process. If you are in a setting where you use a formalized assessment protocol with standardized measures, your role is to clarify for the family the purpose and logistics of the measures to allay any potential anxiety and frustration. Specifically, you can clarify the timing, place, persons present during assessment administration, purpose, format of the standardized assessment measure(s), the meaning of the score(s) or outcome(s), and the way in which the information will be shared and used (Corcoran, 2015). While agency protocol may provide a structure for completing the assessment, content areas a social worker can address include the following (Van Hook, 2014, p. 67):

- *Risk factors:* What are the sources of distress in the lives of family members? What aspects within the family and their extended world contribute to these sources of distress?

- *Appraisal:* How do family members view these issues?

- *Additive factors:* Are there additional factors, if any, that contribute to this distress?

- *Protective factors:* What resources for coping and support do family members, the family as a whole, and their external world, possess?

- *Access to resources:* How can family members use these resources?

- *Strengthening of resources:* How can these resources be enhanced?

- *Barriers to resources:* What barriers prevent family members from using these resources?

Family assessment encompasses an array of assessment tools and strategies. Regardless of the process or protocol you use for conducting an assessment of the family, consider the possibility of incorporating a pre- and postintervention measurement. If a formalized assessment format is used, pre- and postintervention scores can be compared and used to determine progress toward goals. If the assessment process is more informal, a pre- and postintervention comparison can allow the family and you to reflect on the work that can be completed. The following discussion highlights the use of mapping with families.

Mapping: A Family Assessment and Planning Tool   Competent family-focused assessment and planning requires mapping skills. Chapter 4 discussed the use of genograms and ecomaps in work with individuals. Genograms and ecomaps also are compatible with most models of social work practice with families. For example, you might ask everyone in the family to participate in the genogram, or you might have each member make her or his own map of the family's relational patterns (see Exhibit 6.6). Whether you use a genogram or another mapping activity, the process of collecting the information can provide you with insights into the way family members define family membership, perceive the current situation, and interact with one another within the interview and on paper (Minuchin, Colapinto, & Minuchin, 2007).

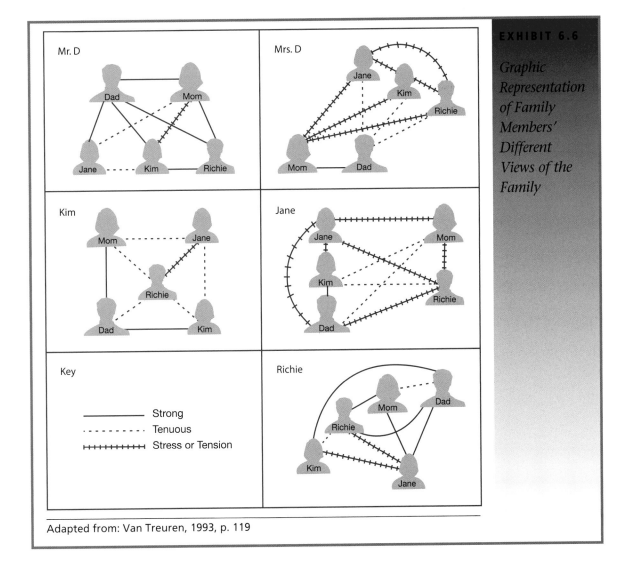

EXHIBIT 6.6

Graphic Representation of Family Members' Different Views of the Family

Adapted from: Van Treuren, 1993, p. 119

Genograms are particularly illuminating assessment tools for family social work because, in visually depicting family structure and patterns, they can serve as an "information net" in which data and insights are captured within the larger, intergenerational context. For example, a genogram may enable you to view the presenting problem within the larger context of the family's issues, or it may facilitate an understanding of the immediate household within the context of the extended family and community. It might show you how the current family situation matches a family's history of similar patterns, how family members perceive nonthreatening questions in light of painful inquiries, and how family members compare factual information to judgments regarding family patterns and function (McGoldrick, 2015, p. 415).

One type of genogram, the cultural genogram, has multiple purposes—developing rapport, family assessment, and supporting culturally competent practice (McCullough-Chavis & Waites, 2008). Building on the foundation of the genogram, a cultural genogram incorporates the perspective of the client on areas of culture that impact the family's experience. Culture can encompass, but is not limited to, race, ethnicity, sexual orientation, social and political influences and oppression, socioeconomic status, and religious and spiritual influences. According to McCullough-Chavis and Waites (2008), the role of the social worker in completing a cultural genogram is to identify intergenerational patterns and to focus on strengths within the context of the larger socio-cultural-political world in which the family lives.

First developed by Hardy and Laszloffy (1995) for use with family therapy students, the cultural genogram has been adapted for use with social work practice (Warde, 2012). In learning how to administer the cultural genogram, students are encouraged to complete their own cultural genogram to gain insight into how the family might experience this aspect of assessment. Warde (2012) presents a modified list of eleven questions social workers should consider when completing a cultural genogram with clients (see Quick Guide 18).

Ecomaps and other variations that demonstrate relationship patterns can liberate some families from what seems like endless talking, and they usually enjoy developing them and examining the final product. You can use ecomaps in a visual service evaluation when the goal is to expand community connections in general or specifically (for example, engaging in more recreational pursuits) or to alter them (such as improving the relationship between the school and the family of a child with disabilities).

Other mapping techniques can prove helpful in social work practice with families. The use of maps is limited only by the imagination. Maps can represent relationship complexities, the passing of time, interacting components, interpersonal interactions and patterns, levels of intimacy, specific types of connection (such as material or emotional support), and spirituality (Hodge, 2005b; 2013). One such map is the **culturagram**, which represents a family's experiences relocating to a new culture (Congress, 2004; 2015). Targeted specifically for use in engaging and

QUICK GUIDE 18   QUESTIONS TO CONSIDER WHEN COMPLETING A CULTURAL GENOGRAM

1. If you are not Native American, under what conditions did your family come to the United States?
2. What were/are your family's experience with oppression?
3. What significance do race, skin color, and hair play in your family?
4. What role does religion play in your family?
5. How does your family define gender roles?
6. How does your family view people who are lesbian, gay, bisexual, transgender, or questioning?
7. What prejudice or stereotypes does your family have about your own racial group and about other racial groups?
8. What principles have shaped your family's values about education, work, and interactions with people outside the family?
9. What are the pride/shame issues of your family?
10. What impact do you think these pride/shame issues will have on your work with clients who are culturally similar and dissimilar?
11. As you reflect on your answers to the previous questions, how do you think the values you got from your family of origin will influence your ability to work with clients whose values and beliefs are discernibly different from yours?

Source: Warde, 2012, pp. 574–575

assessing families who have immigrated to this country, the culturagram can empower clients from their own cultural perspective. The resulting map illustrates content from inquiries relating to the specifics of the family's experience, from immigration to their celebration of values in a new land. Exhibit 6.7 is an example of a culturagram and the areas for discussion that generated it. This visual and interactive tool helps social workers and families understand the family's internal experiences, recognize differences between and within families, see ways in which the family has been successful, and, importantly, pinpoint areas for planning for potential intervention (Congress, 2015).

More literal maps of physical arrangements, such as floor plans in housing situations, illustrate challenges in daily living or disparities in economic circumstances. For example, a map that shows five children's cots in a tiny bedroom, a stepchild sleeping on a couch, or an older adult sharing a room with an infant demonstrates a person-in-environment reality that may be difficult to comprehend fully through verbal means. A legend on the map that describes the meaning of all symbols and a general heading to orient the reader can be especially helpful in any creative or unconventional mapping.

The Family Interview is the core of the assessment and planning process. The goal-setting, intervention, and evaluation and follow-up processes are all guided by

EXHIBIT 6.7

Culturagram

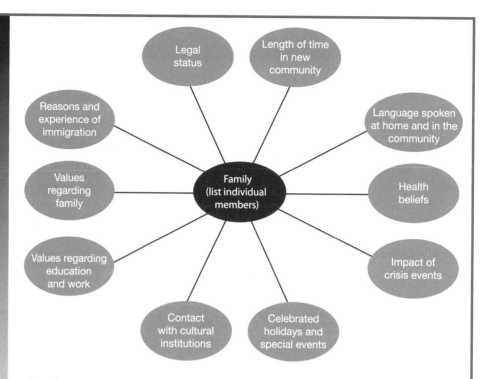

The culturagram addresses the following culturally-focused issues with an immigrant or refugee family:

- Reasons for and experience of immigration
- Legal status
- Length of time in new community
- Language spoken at home and in the community
- Health beliefs
- Impact of trauma and crisis events
- Contact with cultural and religious institutions, holidays, food, and clothing
- Oppression, discrimination, bias, and racism
- Values about education and work
- Values about family (structure, power, myths, and rules)

Source: Congress, 2015

the information that is gathered from the family members. It is essential to the process to ensure that each family member who is present for the assessment is given ample (and safe) opportunity to have voice and to be able to provide her or his perspective on the issues. While the social worker facilitates the family assessment interview, she or he should also be actively listening to the statements made by the individual members, observing the verbal and nonverbal interactions and messages being communicated by the family members. A typical interview guide for a family assessment can include the following items/observations (Van Hook, 2014):

- Verbal and nonverbal messages

- Thematic dimensions: verbal and nonverbal communication and content

- Observed patterns and alliances

- Practitioner use of self and response to family members

- Current stressors: onset, context, impact on family, and additive factors that have made the situation more stressful

- Family appraisal of the situation: attributions of responsibility, view of impact, appropriate ways to address situation

- Potential resources available to family: coping strategies; belief systems (self-efficacy, mastery, and hope); family trust and loyalty; and spirituality/ faith

- Family organizational patterns: cohesion, leadership, communication, flexibility of family roles, and humor

- Community context: resources and definitions of the situation and coping

- Levels of family functioning: basic needs, family structure and organization, boundaries, and intimacy and its meaning (p. 75)

Planning Depending on the approach you are using, you may be asking other types of questions as well. After assessment information has been gathered from the family, the planning phase of work can begin. As with individuals, intervention planning with families is a collaborative process, albeit a potentially more complex one as all members must have the opportunity to have input and to contribute to the final plan. While the family's goals will guide the planning of the intervention, the social worker can help the family to identify the goals by identifying those areas or issues that are creating the most concern for the family, the family's protective factors, and those areas most amenable to change at that point in time (Van Hook, 2014, p. 381).

To serve as a guide for the intervention, a family-focused plan should be a mutually agreed-upon contract between the members of the family and between the family and you. Items essential to the development of a clearly articulated and documented plan include: measurable goals, objectives, outcomes, evidence-based intervention strategies, time frame information, termination, and evaluation and follow-up plans (Jordan, Franklin, & Johnson, 2015).

STRAIGHT TALK ABOUT FAMILY SOCIAL WORK PRACTICE

Families are a powerful ingredient in our lives. They have inspired fierce loyalties, lethal conflicts, abject miseries, and quiet pleasures throughout all of history and continue to do so today. Whether you view your own family as supportive, toxic, or something in between, coming to peace with your own feelings can enhance your work with other families. It is difficult to assess and intervene with the family situations of others if they trigger feelings because of their similarity to (or difference from) your own. Your family concerns need not be clearly understood or even fully resolved, but your feelings and concerns about your own family situation should not intrude on or influence your work in ways you do not recognize. If they do, your supervisor may need to become involved. You will benefit from sharing with your supervisor any current struggles in which you are engaged with your own family, especially if you are seeing families in your practice.

Self-Care

At some point in your work with families, you will likely experience situations in which your feelings are difficult to manage. Egregious abuse exists in some families, and although contemporary theoretical perspectives can help you temper your responses and recognize that individuals and families do the best they can, the litany of injuries or aggressions emerging in court reports, police accounts, or living room conversations can bring on powerful emotions in the most seasoned and balanced social worker. Fortunately, you can use supervision, agency supports, peer connections, and personal strategies to cope with such feelings and reactions. Many social workers see professional therapists to process their family challenges in order to avoid the influence of their family challenges on their professional practice. The most encouraging dimension for social workers is that the majority of families with whom we work inspire the greatest admiration for their resiliency, spirit, resourcefulness, and agency in the midst of potentially demoralizing circumstances.

Documentation

Another important "straight talk" item for social work practice with families is the need for accurate and comprehensive documentation. Family-related interventions requiring documentation can include child welfare situations (i.e., child protective services and foster care), adoptions, and early interventions. Such cases may require the creation of intake assessments, progress/case notes, reports, case referrals or transfers, treatment planning, and evaluations (McGowan & Walsh, 2012). Social workers working with adult families may have to initiate documentation for family members with addictions, disabilities, health concerns, relationship challenges, or residential placements. In all situations, the social worker should include only relevant information, consistent with a strengths-based framework that represents the perspectives of all members of the family.

As in social work practice with individuals, documentation is a critical, although more complex, behavior when working with families. Chapters 4 and 5 covered the

---

QUICK GUIDE 19   DOCUMENTING A FAMILY ASSESSMENT

Demographic Data (include all members participating in the assessment and intervention):
- Names, birthdates, and relationship to others
- Contact information

Family Information:
- Presenting need(s) or concern(s)
- *Living situation:* e.g., members of household and level of stability
- *Family composition:* parents, siblings, spouse/significant other(s), children, and others (extended family and friends); level of support; and family history of mental illness, as applicable. A genogram and/or ecomap may be a good way to gather and depict this information.
- *Timeline:* significant life events the family has experienced
- *Cultural environment:* traditions and cultural view of help-seeking
- *Religion/spirituality:* statement of beliefs and levels of activity and satisfaction
- *Family strengths and significant events*: including trauma (e.g., physical, sexual, and/or emotional abuse or neglect and experience with perpetrator(s))

Individual Family Member Information:
- Individual family member information, including:
  - Educational history of each member (highest level achieved, performance, goals, and challenges)
  - Substance use/abuse (history of addictive behaviors, alcohol, drugs, gambling, sexual, or other)
  - Emotional/behavioral functioning and treatment history
  - Risk factors
  - Physical health
  - Legal status or concerns
  - Financial/employment circumstances (employment status, satisfaction, financial stability, areas of concern or change)

Social and Environmental Information:
- Strengths and concerns regarding physical environment, as applicable (e.g., structure, neighborhood, and community)
- Safety issues (e.g., risks of and/or concerns for individual members and social worker)

Summary:
- Current providers, including psychiatrist, primary care physician, therapist, caseworker, etc.
- Community resources being used including support groups, religious, spiritual, other
- Family goal(s) for intervention
- Summary of social worker's observations and impressions

Source: Adapted from St. Anthony's Medical Center, 2010

QUICK GUIDE 20   DOCUMENTING A FAMILY INTERVENTION PLAN

Intervention Plan:

- Preliminary assessment
- Preliminary plan for intervention and plan for change (to be developed at first visit), including:

  - What will each family member do differently?
  - How does each family member view themselves accomplishing changes?
  - What support and services does the family need to accomplish the plan for change?
  - Who will provide support and services?
  - Who will arrange for support and services?

- Interventions and plans for emergency/safety needs
- Other interventions needed
- Needs, including date, identified need, status (active, inactive, deferred, or referred), and reason for deferral or referral
- Strengths
- Facilitating factors for intervention
- Limitations
- Barriers to intervention
- Other care providers/referrals and purpose, including plan for service coordination
- Plan for involvement of individual family members, extended family members, significant others and friends
- Review and termination criteria/plan
- Planned frequency and duration of intervention

Source: Adapted from St. Anthony's Medical Center, 2010; Missouri Department of Social Services, n.d.

---

components of basic documentation and provided documentation guidelines. While these same guidelines apply to documenting family interventions, it is important to consider the "group" aspect of family work. Recording the assessment and intervention phases of social work practice with families requires the social worker to include all participating family members and to give voice to and provide perspective on individual contributions. Quick Guides 19 and 20 provide guidelines specific to documenting a family assessment.

CONCLUSION

Social workers can both support and challenge the contemporary family. Social workers engage with the family and its struggles in our culture, thus a goal for the

The American Academy of Social Work and Social Welfare Grand Challenges for Social Work Initiative identifies one of the areas the profession should address is to ensure healthy development for all youth. The authors of Grand Challenge Working Paper No. 10, *Unleashing the Power of Prevention* (Hawkins et al., 2015) provide the following basis for considering the prevention aspects of this challenge:

> Every day, across America, behavioral health problems in childhood and adolescence from anxiety to violence take a heavy toll on millions of lives. For decades, the approach to these problems has been to treat them only after they have been identified—at a high and ongoing cost to young people, families, entire communities, and our nation. . . . The challenge now is to mobilize across disciplines and communities to unleash the power of prevention on a nationwide scale. We propose a grand challenge that will advance the policies, programs, funding, and workforce preparation needed to promote behavioral health and prevent behavioral health problems among all young people—including those at greatest disadvantage of risk, from birth through age 24 (p. 3).

Decades of research have provided evidence of the significant and negative impact of behavioral health problems on the individuals, children and adolescents and their families, in particular. The social work profession is being challenged to focus on the development and mobilization of services and programs to identify and prevent such behavioral health concerns as: anxiety; depression; autism; alcohol, tobacco, and other drug use; risky driving; aggressive behavior and conduct problems in childhood; delinquent behavior; adolescent violence; self-inflicted injury; risky sexual behavior; and dropping out of school. Using evidence to guide interprofessional intervention planning, actionable goals include (Hawkins et al., 2015) the following:

- Increasing public awareness of preventive interventions to promote healthy behaviors for all
- Spend 10% of all public funds spent on youth to support effective prevention programs
- Implement community-assessment and capacity-building tool to assess and prioritize risk and protective factors
- Establish and implement criteria for preventive interventions
- Increase infrastructure to supply preventive interventions
- Monitor and increase access of children, youth, and young adults to effective preventive interventions
- Prepare practitioners in health and human service professions for new roles in promotion and preventive interventions (pp. 14–15)

To familiarize yourself with the issues related to ensure healthy development of all youth, visit the Grand Challenges website and read Working Paper No. 10, *Unleashing the Power of Prevention* (Hawkins et al., 2015) at: http://aaswsw.org/grand-challenges-initiative/12-challenges/ensure-healthy-development-for-all-youth/. (See Exercise #a1 for additional exploration of this Grand Challenge.)

GRAND CHALLENGE

Ensure Healthy Development for All Youth

profession is to develop additional and relevant models for working with families that recognize their strengths, agency, and resilience. Further, social workers need to educate and advocate for shifts in the structural and political arrangements that impede families in their efforts to provide support and nurturing for their members. Ideas about what makes a family evolve and differ, but as a culture we still value the family, and social workers can help create environments that validate and support families of all kinds.

As the structure and meaning of family itself continues to change, it is important to be aware of and to maintain your personal capacity to honor how others conceptualize the family. As a form of "group," the family has particular resonance for many social workers and serves as a grounding point for understanding human collectives. With that dimension in mind, the next chapter will explore the intervention, termination, and evaluation and follow-up phases of work with families.

MAIN POINTS

- Historical antecedents for involvement with families, including family function and systems theories, shape the way social workers engage with and assess families.

- An idealized, or fantasy, notion of the American family still exists today, but social workers recognize and work with many forms of family, including grandparents raising grandchildren; lesbian, gay, bisexual, transgender, and questioning families; single-parent families; families of multiple racial and ethnic heritages; families with members who have disabilities; blended families; and families who have immigrated from their home country.

- Several contemporary theoretical perspectives have emerged for working with families that are consistent with a critical social construction perspective, the strengths-based framework, and social justice orientations, including narrative and solution-focused approaches.

- Your practice setting will guide much of your work with families, but the skills and behaviors that you have learned for engaging and assessing individuals and groups from a biopsychosocial-spiritual perspective will apply to your work with families. Specific family-oriented skills and behaviors you will use include engaging the whole family, reframing, and recognizing your own biases around family forms.

- Mapping tools can be helpful in assessing and evaluating work with families; they can also help empower families to change.

EXERCISES

a. Case Exercises

1. To apply your learning of the Grand Challenge for Social Work—Ensuring healthy development for all youth—that was highlighted in this chapter, visit the Grand Challenges website and read Working Paper No. 10, *Unleashing the Power of Prevention* (Hawkins et al., 2015) at: http://aaswsw.org/grand-challenges-initiative/12-challenges/ensure-healthy-development-for-all-youth/. To examine issues within a prevention context, consider the Sanchez family at www.routledgesw.com/caseStudies. After reading Working Paper No. 10 and reviewing the Sanchez case, respond to the following questions:

   a. Identify the children of Celia and Hector who are at risk for or are experiencing one or more of the behavioral health issues discussed in the Working Paper. Create an assessment of each of the children and the issue(s) that she or he is experiencing.

   b. Building on the assessment you have developed, discuss ways in which each of these areas may be approached from a prevention perspective.

   c. Consider resources in your community that could be mobilized (or developed if none currently exist) to serve as prevention strategies for each of the areas identified in this exercise.

2. Go to www.routledgesw.com/cases and review the case file for Roberto Salazar. As the undocumented nephew of Hector and Celia Sanchez, Roberto has consistently earned an income but has also experienced several health challenges. He is currently living with the Sanchez family due to an injury that prevents him from working. He has a number of skills, but his current injury and inability to work has him feeling defeated.

   You are the social worker charged with monitoring the status of Hector and Celia's Section 8 housing voucher. While Hector and Celia generally manage their rent payments, they are having difficulty meeting the payment schedule due to extra expenditures they incur supporting Roberto. Your agency is responsible for controlling Section 8-related expenses and complying with federal regulations. Your supervisor is especially concerned with this aspect of the program.

   On your visit to the Sanchez home, Hector assures you that—even though he knows the landlord can evict him and his family for violating regulations regarding occupancy—Roberto is family, and of course, he and Celia will house and feed him. He remembers his own loneliness when he came to the U.S. and how his uncle helped him. He has no doubt that he can assist Roberto by providing temporary housing and support. Hector explains to you that it is important for immigrants to stick together and support one another, especially family. You are feeling some pressure from the agency to report and help resolve the issue of Roberto's unacceptable presence in the Sanchez home. You are concerned that your supervisor will look unfavorably on you if you allow Roberto to continue to live in the house.

Respond to the following questions:

a. How might a family focus differ from an individual focus in this situation?

b. How will you respond to Hector? Your supervisor?

c. How might diversity be a factor in this situation? Compare your responses to those of your peers. Identify and team up with another student whose response seems similar to yours and develop a unified approach. Brainstorm in class regarding different or creative ways to approach this situation.

3. Go to www.routledgesw.com/cases and review the case for Carla Washburn. Create a genogram of her family. Explore connections between Carla and her family members and ways in which those connections impact her relationships within the family. Address the following:

a. What are the strengths of the family?

b. What issues have impacted the family?

c. How have those issues impacted the various family relationships?

d. Who has the most/least "power" in the family?

e. If you were a social worker working with this family, what issues do you think should take precedent?

4. Go to www.routledgesw.com/cases and review the case for Brickville, focusing on Virginia Stone and her family. Review the genogram for the Stone family and analyze the information provided by responding to the following questions:

• What additional information do you believe would be helpful to include in the genogram?

• What patterns emerge as you review the Stone's genogram? In addition to general patterns, comment on potential themes in the areas of:

  ○ boundaries between family members

  ○ intergenerational family relationships and patterns

  ○ single parenting

  ○ grandparents rearing grandchildren

• What strengths and areas of challenge are evident?

• What information does the genogram yield that suggests priorities for planning a social work intervention?

5. Go to www.routledgesw.com/cases and review the case for Hudson City. You are working as a volunteer mental health disaster responder when the Patel family (described at the beginning of this chapter) comes to the Emergency Center. Complete the following:

• Develop a list of culturally competent and humble engagement strategies that will be helpful as you begin your work with the Patel family, including additional information and resources you will need.

• Select one of the theoretical frameworks presented in this chapter and develop a plan for conducting an assessment of the Patel family.

6. Go to www.routledgesw.com/cases and click on the case for Hudson City. Returning to the information provided regarding the Patel family, click on Assess the Situation and respond to My Assess Tasks. Using the Patel family information provided here, complete Tasks #1 and #2 as they relate to the Patels. Once you have assessed the issues and needs facing the Patels, develop a preliminary plan for your social work intervention.

b. Other exercises

7. You are a social worker on an interprofessional team that works with children who are on the autism spectrum and their families. Three-year-old Jenny is referred to your team. She is the light of her father's life—she is lively, energetic, and bright-eyed. In the last year, she has become quiet, preferring to play by herself, and she is less interested in the special outings her father loves to share with her.

   After a series of anxious appointments with the pediatrician, Jenny was referred to a specialist in developmental pediatrics. Many observations and checklists later, Jenny was diagnosed on the autism spectrum. Her parents, Catherine and Jason, were devastated. Her 2-year-old brother, Sammy, was oblivious.

   Over a period of a month, Catherine began to adjust to the diagnosis. She connected with a supportive group of parents coping with children on the autism spectrum and read all she could about autism. She also spent considerable time with Jenny, playing and coaxing her to interact with her. Jason, however, was notably uninterested in Catherine's activities. He began to refuse to go to Jenny's doctor's appointments. During one argumentative dinner with Catherine, he stated that he did not believe the diagnosis; he thought Jenny was fine, that she was just going through a stage, and he accused Catherine of "selling out" her own daughter. Jenny's pediatrician referred her to the interprofessional team. Catherine engaged in the process enthusiastically, if painfully. Jason attended the assessment and seemed sullen, participating very little. The team concurs that the family would benefit from your "support work" around the diagnosis. Catherine and Jason agree to meet with you, and you speculate this might be your only chance to engage Jason.

   Respond to the following questions and then compare your responses with those of your peers.

   a. What is your assessment of this family? Identify a theoretical perspective that is most applicable to working with this family. How does your choice of perspective influence your approach to this family? Be specific.

   b. Generate a list of three questions or issues you think are important to address in your first meeting.

   c. How might you attempt to engage the family, especially Jason? As you compare responses with your peers, what perspective (different from your own) was most useful to you?

8. Develop a solution-focused plan for the assessment and planning phase of the social work intervention with the family in Exercise #6.

9. Use a narrative approach to develop a plan for assessment and planning in your work with the family in Exercise #6.

10. This chapter mentions a range of contemporary family structures about which social workers must have knowledge and skills for competent practice. Select one of the families discussed in this chapter and conduct a search of the evidence-based practice approaches social workers currently use with the family you have selected. Prepare a brief summary of the knowledge and skills needed for effective practice with this family.

11. Create a genogram of your family. Explore the connections within the family and the ways in which those connections impact the relationships within the family, particularly your relationships. Address the following:

    • What are the strengths of your family?
    • What are the issues your family has faced?
    • How have those issues impacted the various relationships?
    • Who has the most/least "power" in the family?
    • If you were the social worker working with your family, what issues would take precedence?
    • What have you learned about your family from this exercise?

12. Family Assessment Movie Review: to integrate an understanding of family systems dynamics by analyzing a fictional family:

    a. Select one movie to review that portrays family members in relationship with each other and in transaction with their environments (your instructor may provide a list or approve your choice).

    b. Select a *research* article (published within the past ten years) that studies an aspect of family.

    c. View the movie and write a description of your analysis of the family relationship dynamics viewed in the movie. Include discussion of the following: family rules (spoken and unspoken), boundaries, rituals, power, communication patterns and problem-solving skills, family secrets, roles, family strengths, the family's transactions with the environment, and the manner in which these transactions seemingly influenced the family and the environment. Use quotes and scenes from the movie to support your analysis.

    d. Briefly discuss the research article (including information on the research question, sample, methods of data collection, and findings) and compare and contrast the findings to your assessment of the family (i.e., is the experience your family exhibits similar to what research says you should expect to find?). Support your assertions.

    e. Include in your critique the manner in which the family dynamics were presented in the movie, including movie's realism, bias, and family strengths and areas for growth.

Source: Ruth T. Weinzettle, Ph.D., LCSW-BACS, Professor of Social Work, Northwestern State University of Louisiana. Personal communication, April 15, 2016

CHAPTER 7

Social Work Practice with Families: Intervention, Termination, and Evaluation

[T]o think larger than one to think larger than two or three or four this is me this is my partner these are my children if we say, these are my people who do we mean? How to declare our bond how to keep each of us warm we are in danger how to face it and not crack.

Melanie Kaye/Kantrowitz (Kaye 1980)

Key Questions for Chapter 7

1. What competencies do I need to intervene with families? [EPAS 8]
2. What are the social work skills and behaviors that enable me to effectively intervene with families? [EPAS 8]
3. How can I engage in research-informed practice and practice-informed research to guide the processes of intervention, termination, and evaluation with families? [EPAS 4, 8, and 9]
4. What potential ethical dilemmas might I expect to encounter in intervening with families? [EPAS 1]

The Williamson family reside in the Riverton community (www.routledgesw.com/ cases).

While the Riverton case initially appears to focus on a neighborhood and a community, each community is comprised of individuals and families. In your role as the social worker who has just moved into the Riverton community, consider your new neighbors, the Williamson family (not described in the case file). Jocelyn is a 48-year-old single mother who lives with her two children, 18-year-old Tori and 17-year-old Jamal, and her mother, 77-year-old Nina. Jocelyn divorced her husband because of his chronic alcoholism and unwillingness to seek treatment. She is worried about Jamal because she knows he regularly drinks and uses marijuana, and she fears he is on the verge of graduating to harsher substances. She has come to your agency to ask for your help with Jamal. In light of the alcohol and drug issues in the neighborhood, she feels powerless to handle the situation alone. Her mother owns the house, and she cannot afford to move out of the neighborhood because she is unable to work full-time due to her responsibility to care for her mother and her desire to be with her children as much as possible.

SOCIAL WORKERS HAVE A LONGSTANDING HISTORY OF intervening in family situations and crises. Dating to the era of Mary Richmond and the Charity Organization Society and Jane Addams and the Settlement House movements, social workers have focused on intervening with families (Rasheed & Rasheed, 2013). Just as social work practitioners respond to societal changes, social workers also adapt their practice knowledge, skills, and values to the developmental stages of families or changing structure of families. While families are generally self-sufficient in meeting their ongoing financial, emotional, and caregiving needs, when they seek help outside the family, they require a response that has been developed to meet their family's specific structure, race, ethnicity, sexual or gender orientation, socioeconomic status, and (biopsychosocial-spiritual) needs (Briar-Lawson & Naccarato, 2013). Family social workers intervening with families must develop specific competencies to address the complexities of contemporary families, which may include culture, racial, and ethnic diversity; financial and legal challenges; and intergenerational relationships and dynamics. Unlike family therapy, family social work is based on generalist social work skills for intervening with families who are at-risk for negative outcomes. Family social work practice interventions may focus on: (1) reinforcing family strengths to prepare families for long-term change, such as a member arriving, leaving, needing care, or dying; (2) creating concrete changes in family functioning to sustain effective and satisfying daily routines independent of formal helpers; (3) providing additional support to family therapy so families maintain effective family functioning; and/or (4) addressing crises in a timely way to enable the family to focus on longer-term concerns (Collins, Jordan, & Coleman, 2013, p. 3).

Building on the previously conducted assessment that focused on the family's strengths and self-determined needs, the intervention process is an opportunity to collaborate with the family to facilitate growth and change. Contemporary family social work is influenced by a variety of factors, one of the primary ones being managed behavioral care. With its emphasis on brief, efficacious, and evidence-based interventions, managed behavioral care has influenced social work practice with families by focusing the social worker clearly, systematically, and succinctly on identifying and assessing the problem or concerns; developing and implementing an intervention plan; terminating; and evaluating the working relationship (Jordan,

Franklin, & Johnson, 2015, p. 433). This chapter will highlight theoretical frameworks and skills and behaviors for social work practice interventions with families that include the processes of termination, evaluation, and follow-up.

THEORETICAL APPROACHES TO INTERVENING WITH FAMILIES

Like interventions with individuals, interventions with families are planned change processes in which the social worker and client work together to implement steps to reach goals they establish together in the assessment and planning process. An array of theories underpin approaches to social work practice with families, including systems, ecosystems, family life cycle, cultural and social diversity, strengths-based, and empowerment theories (Rasheed & Rasheed, 2013). When you are well grounded in theoretical approaches for working with families, you can select the approach or approaches and techniques best suited to your practice philosophy and to the needs of the client family. In an effort to best serve the families with whom they work, practitioners "frequently use a combination of couple and family techniques from different models rather than adhering to one particular approach" (Franklin, Jordan, & Hopson, 2015, p. 439). **Integrationism** (i.e., blending models and techniques), **technical eclecticism** (i.e., using different techniques), and the use of common characteristics or core components can be effective ways to address the needs of specific populations (Franklin et al., 2015, p. 439). As a practitioner, you will recognize that there is no one ideal theoretical approach or technique that is appropriate or effective for all families; rather, you must incorporate such characteristics as the family's culture, race, ethnicity, and lifestyle into the social work intervention (Rasheed & Rasheed, 2013). However, the family intervention models that are most effective typically share certain elements, including education, opportunities to practice and model new behaviors and skills, and multifaceted intervention plans (Franklin et al., 2015). As an ethical and culturally competent social work practitioner, you are responsible for undergoing the training necessary to use the evidence on available family models and to select the approach or combination of approaches that you believe will be most effective for your client.

Exhibit 7.1 depicts a framework for approaching family intervention from a multidimensional perspective. As the exhibit shows, the process of developing a family intervention involves first viewing the family within their environment; then selecting a relevant theoretical approach; and finally creating an intervention, termination, evaluation, and follow-up plan that uses appropriate techniques.

The following discussion explores theoretical approaches that use the strengths and empowerment, narrative, and solution-focused perspectives. In keeping with the overall approach of this book, the theoretical perspectives presented here align with postmodern frameworks. While postmodern approaches may seem counter to traditional systemic approaches, Rasheed and Rasheed (2013) posit that, in fact, the two complement one another. Systems theories help the practitioner view and

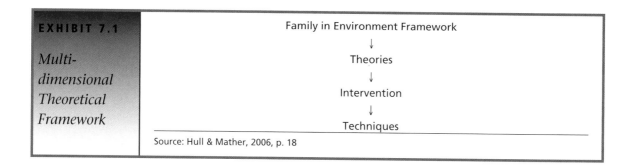

Source: Hull & Mather, 2006, p. 18

frame the family within the context of their environment, while postmodern constructs help the social worker view the family within the context of the family's interpretation of the meaning of the presenting issues as provided by the family themselves. We will also explore how to help families grow and change by aiding them in identifying and building on strengths, reconstructing their life experiences, and developing new realities.

Strengths and Empowerment Perspectives and Family Interventions

An intervention in the strengths tradition strives, not only to enhance the family's assets, but also to empower the family to develop new coping and resiliency strategies. A strengths perspective views challenges as opportunities and possibilities (Saleebey, 2013). An intervention grounded in a strengths perspective builds capacity and assets and focuses on solutions (Briar-Lawson & Naccarato, 2013). For example, an intervention that emanates from the traditional deficit-based perspective views the family as the source of its own problems (e.g., poor parenting, dysfunctional relationships, or irreparable problems). A strengths-based intervention identifies the family's assets (e.g., the parents are committed to placing value on being together as a family, and the family has remained together in the face of adversity) and capacities and focuses on solutions (e.g., the family is willing to work on the challenges that brought them to a social worker).

In the face of the complexities families face in contemporary society, practitioners may be tempted, when developing an intervention plan with a family, to focus on the problems that exist within the family rather than on the family's strengths. Instead, taking a strengths-based approach, a social worker might ask family members to describe the characteristics of a healthy, strong family, and this might lead to a discussion about which of those characteristics the client family shares with that idealized family. This discussion could lead to insights around which the planning and intervention are incorporated (Jordan et al., 2015). Exploring those actions family members can take that build from their individual and collective strengths can alter the family's perspective of themselves and also, possibly, of the social worker. Gaining insight into interacting in a new way with one another and with the environment can be an empowering experience for the family. For example, consider the case of Virginia Stone, one of the residents of Brickville (www.routledgesw.com/cases). Recall from previous chapters that Virginia is struggling with an array of challenges. In your initial intervention, you might lean toward focusing on the most compelling issues (e.g., her caregiving stressors or home ownership dilemma). It may be most helpful to Virginia in the longer term to help her to identify the strengths and resiliency (from previous experiences of coping with challenges) that she and her family possess so that she may use those strengths-based experiences to help resolve her current challenges. For example, Virginia's family's strengths may include their dedication to caring for older members and remaining connected to one another even through times of adversity.

Grounded in a commitment to build on family strengths, empowerment-oriented practice has applicability for intervening with families. Having evolved over the past several decades from a conceptual, philosophical perspective to a set of practice-based principles and methods, empowerment-oriented interventions encompasses the personal, interpersonal, and sociopolitical aspects of the family's life (Parsons & East, 2013) and is applied to work with families with various presenting challenges. For example, Dunst and Trivette (2009) have continued to develop their family-focused model for early childhood and family support interventions. This model embraces empowerment and strengths- and resource-based family-centered models that emphasize a capacity-building paradigm (p. 128). This paradigm shift is intended to aid professionals in developing helping practices that align with a capacity-oriented approach to identifying and mobilizing family concerns and priorities, abilities and interests, and supports and resources. In a capacity-building approach, the role of the social worker in providing services is relational and participatory. In addition to demonstrating traditional social work practice skills of active listening, compassion, empathy, and respect, the capacity-focused family social worker emphasizes possibilities for change in an individualized, flexible, and responsive manner (Dunst & Trivette, 2009, p. 131).

Empowerment-driven interventions are helpful for families in crisis—especially those who have experienced a history of crises—and can aid the social worker in helping the family create solutions. An empowerment perspective is grounded in a belief that a repertoire of protective factors are available in the family's environment (i.e., family provides caring relationships, maintains high expectations, and affords opportunities for meaningful participation and contributions) can buffer the stressors and trauma that a family experiences (Benard & Truebridge, 2013, p. 208). In essence, the family has the skills and resources they need to be resilient and adaptive in the face of adversity but may need help in identifying and mobilizing those skills and resources. For example, consider a family who in 2012 survived Hurricane Sandy but lost their home. They are a large family and could not find temporary housing together in one place. Instead, they were forced to stay in different locations with family, with friends, and in shelters. They came together once each week to work on rehabilitating their home so they could return there as a family. This family might be viewed as unconnected and "falling apart" when, in fact, they could be seen from a strength-based perspective as being a family who is working to stay together.

An empowerment approach uses seven principles of practice (Wise, 2005):

1. *Build on strengths and resources and diminish oppressive factors:* As noted, the family must first identify the strengths they can use to address their challenges. The family can then review existing and potential resources and begin mobilizing those resources. Oppressive factors or barriers to growth and change may lessen as family members perceive options and possibilities. Strategizing with the family about ways in which they may confront, ameliorate, or minimize oppressive factors can also empower them. A first step, however, may be for family members to confront the oppressive factors that they may perceive to exist *within* the family. For example, family members may be stifling anger at one member for having a disability or an addiction. Until all family members acknowledge and address this anger, the family is unlikely to be able to collaboratively work toward resolving the presenting concern.

2. *Exhibit multicultural respect:* Multicultural respect requires attention to a wide and growing array of phenomena, including race, ethnicity, gender, age, socioeconomic status, religious/spiritual beliefs, sexual and gender orientation, differing ability, language, and developmental phases. The family may be impacted in multiple areas. The role of the social worker in helping the family create an intervention is to ensure that all family members are aware of their perceptions and experiences in these areas, to help them understand the meaning and impact of those perceptions and experiences, and to work with them to confront stereotypes and barriers.

3. *Recognize personal, interpersonal, and community empowerment needs:* While family members may well know their needs, they may have difficulty, particularly during a crisis, articulating those needs to one another or the social worker. A successful empowerment-focused intervention relies on the social worker to help the family create solutions that are directly linked to their biopsychosocialspiritual needs. Regular individual and family check-ins ensure that the needs have been accurately and thoroughly voiced and that the intervention plan is addressing those needs. The social worker can help the family to recognize that needs can and do change and to maintain a realistic approach to success.

4. *Help connect the family with sufficient resources so that they can empower themselves:* In implementing the intervention, resources are identified and mobilized. The social worker does not have the ability to complete the work for the family but can monitor and interpret the family's use (or lack) of resources. For example, consider the value of helping the family mobilize resources from their religious or spiritual community. The religious community can not only provide tangible and emotional resources but can also serve as a recognized authority that may help engage and intervene with family members (Nakhaima & Dicks, 2012).

5. *Connect families to the support they need from each other, from other families, and from the community:* Receiving support both within and outside the family can be the impetus the family needs to reach their agreed-upon goals and solutions. The role of the social worker may be to normalize experiences, provide information, and connect the family to each other and to individuals outside the family. For example, helping the family to access services from a hospice organization can help to support the member who is terminally ill along with the members of the immediate and extended family.

6. *Establish and maintain a "power WITH" relationship:* Power can be an asset and a barrier in a family intervention. To use power for growth and change, you can convey to the family that each member has power, the family as a group has power, and the social worker has power. Most importantly, the social worker and the family can share power for the purposes of achieving the goals of the intervention. Interventions should not rely on the "power" of any one group or subgroup of the family–social worker partnership. Rather, it should be shared in a collaboration using the strengths, assets, and resources that each person or subgroup brings to the intervention.

7. *Use cooperative roles that support and assist family members:* Implementing the intervention requires that each member assume a variety of roles over the course of the relationship. Such roles may include co-consultant, co-collaborator, guide, co-teacher/learner, co-investigator, and co-creator (pp. 86–88). The social worker is in a position to point out ways in which family members can use their knowledge and skills to implement these roles.

To bring these principles to life, consider the current situation of the Murray family, a three-generation family living together in the same house. William, a 55-year-old high school teacher, and Genevieve, a 50-year-old occupational therapist, have been married 27 years and have three children. Their daughter Elle, a 25-year-old, unemployed, licensed practical nurse (LPN), recently returned to her parents' home with her two children ages 4 and 2 years following a divorce. Their son Stephen, 21, lives at home, works part-time, and attends a local university. Their youngest daughter, Samantha, is 16 and a high school junior. Not long ago, William's mother Edna, who is 76, moved into the house after she had a car accident where she was at fault. Edna suffers from Alzheimer's disease, which is progressively getting worse. When Edna and Elle and her children arrived, Stephen and Samantha had to give up their bedrooms. The family created a makeshift bedroom for Samantha in the basement, and Stephen is sleeping on the fold-out couch in the den. The Murray family comes to your agency when Samantha is arrested for driving under the influence of alcohol and is subsequently suspended from school. It is immediately evident that this is a family in crisis in several additional areas: Edna's illness and increasing need for care, Elle's adjustment to divorce and single parenting, displacement and lack of privacy for Stephen and Samantha, and the stress William and Genevieve experience supporting the family.

Using strengths- and empowerment-based perspectives, how can this family be supported through this challenging period in their lives? First, consider the family's strengths and the resources to which they have access. William and Genevieve have a longstanding marriage and are both employed. They have opened their home to their daughter, her children, and William's mother, and they are willing to provide care for these family members. The family can be a resource for itself, but it is important for the social worker to ascertain from each member his or her perception of the issues and any factors they consider barriers to resolving the issues. Samantha, for example, may view her grandmother as the problem, as Edna has taken her room and her parents' time and resources. This has led Samantha to argue constantly with her parents and to spend as much time away from home as possible. Helping the family articulate their needs in a multiculturally respectful way is the next step in creating alternatives with the family. For example, providing the family with information about Alzheimer's disease and its course may help them better understand and accept Edna's behavior and needs. The social worker can enlist ideas from each family member about ways in which they each can help and can offer suggestions for accessing resources outside the family.

Collaborating with the family to access and mobilize resources can provide a model for them and at the same time engage them in an alternative to their present incapacitation. Examples of collaborating with the family include:

1. Capitalizing on Elle's professional expertise as an LPN, the family can apply for a family caregiver program in which one member can be paid to care for an older adult. Elle can contribute to the family financially, care for her grandmother and her children, and work toward rebuilding her life.
2. Co-investigating with Stephen ways he can use his experience as a camp counselor to apply for a live-in resident assistant position on campus can provide him with space and privacy.
3. Samantha's substance use and arrest has effectively gotten her parents' attention. Guiding the family to consider the various responses and treatment options can enable them to make choices together and learn from one another to co-create a new way of being a family. While the social worker may guide the family members toward resources, the members would be encouraged to handle as many of the logistics of accessing resources as possible.

Narrative Theory and Family Interventions [EPAS 4]

Like strengths and empowerment approaches, a narrative approach to intervening with families also incorporates strengths, views the family as experts on the family unit, and emphasizes collaboration between the social worker and the family. Using a narrative approach, in hearing each family member's perceptions of the family and the problems that brought them to a social worker, family members are able to give meaning to the problem and to discover alternatives to that meaning that will aid in helping to improve the family's interactions (Kelley & Smith, 2015). Like the narrative approach to working with individuals, the narrative approach to working with families uses respectful listening to assess the problems confronting the family and the planning and interventions processes. The social worker and the family reflect upon and deconstruct the family's perceptions and then challenge perceived truths to reconstruct those perceptions. The reconstruction process facilitates collaboration between family members and the social worker in which they create an intervention plan that enables the family to arrive at unique and meaningful outcomes that have viability within their family unit. For example, you are working with the Taylor-Crofts, a same-sex couple who are divorcing, and their 11- and 13-year-old children who are struggling to adapt to the change. You begin by encouraging each member of the family to voice their perceptions and concerns then move to helping them, as a family, deconstruct the story, and, finally, move into a reconstruction in which each member offers a potential outcome that the family evaluates for its meaning and viability. Through a collaborative process, the family agree on a new story in which the children 1) have more input into the visitation arrangement and 2) spend more equal time with each of their mothers.

Implementation of a narrative-based intervention represents the culmination of the family–social worker partnership. The family members' story with its history, identified meanings, and potential reconstructions becomes the intervention, and the social worker's role is to empower clients by supporting their strengths (Williams, 2009). A narrative approach provides the social worker with a variety of strategies to optimize the family's strengths in order to expand their perceptions of themselves and of their problems and to create a new vision. Within the discovery process, the family has the opportunity to envision a future in which the current problem persists or one in which they take action to alter or resolve the problem. Clients who collaborate with a social worker who hears their stories become empowered to construct new stories (and realities) (Williams, 2009).

To empower clients for change using the narrative approach requires a variety of strategies and questioning formats. Interventive techniques can include (Van Hook, 2014, pp. 253–260; Williams, 2009):

- *Listening to the family tell their problem:* Ask each member of the family to share their concerns.

- *Normalizing:* Listening and empathizing can serve to build rapport and trust between the family and the social worker.

- *Externalizing the problem:* The social worker can collaborate with the family to help them separate the problem from the person(s). The social worker and the family can then form a team to tackle the problem, rather than targeting one or more of the individuals who make up the family.

- *Mapping the problem:* Through the use of relative influence questions (e.g., "How does the problem affect you/your family?"), looking for patterns from the past can help the family understand ways in which the problems were sustained and the impact the problems had on the individual members and the family. Mapping strategies can include:

o Searching for a unique outcome, identifying a time when the family successfully overcame a problem.

o Asking spectator questions to help the family consider how others outside the family view them and their current situation and functional capacity.

o Re-authoring the family's story to emphasize a perception in which the members have been able to overcome adversity (also known as asking significance questions).

o Identifying cultural messages that support problem-saturated stories, that is, examining how previously received cultural messages have influenced the family's ability to interact with one another and to handle life's responsibilities.

- *Finding news of a difference:* Identifying evidence of change, no matter how small, can move the family beyond problem behaviors and into a new, alternative reality.

- *Asking therapeutic questions:* Ongoing questioning can help the family to continue to tell their stories and to author new stories that create a healthier environment. Therapeutically-focused questions can concentrate on opening space for possibilities, effecting change to amplify news of differences (e.g., "Would it be possible that you could ask your siblings to help with the care of your parents?"); preference questions (i.e., comparing past and present and identifying which is preferred); developing stories that highlight differences; meaning questions (e.g., uncovering how the family perceives the meaning of their actions); and future-oriented questions.

- **Scaffolding:** Once the social worker and the family begin to deconstruct the old story (e.g., "Since your mother had a stroke, have you asked your siblings to help with her care?"), a new story (one of competence like "Do you feel you can ask your siblings to help you?") can be constructed to replace it. Scaffold questions are defined as using a series of questions to shift client focus from the known to the potentially known (White, 2007). They can help to shift the story's focus from exceptions (e.g., a time when the family was happy) to significance questions (e.g., acknowledging the importance of an action/event) to spectator questions (e.g., understanding ways in which family members experience one another).

- *Collapsing time and raising dilemmas:* The past and present are both important aspects of evolving the way in which the family views the problem to a newly constructed story (e.g., "Can you describe a time from the past when your siblings and you worked together to support your parents?" and "If your siblings were to help you in the future to care for your parents, what would that look like to you?").

- *Enhancing change:* The social worker may challenge the client's problem-saturated story to motivate clients to examine and abandon their reliance on that version of the story.

- *Predicting setbacks:* The social worker can help the family recognize and accept that they may find it difficult to give up on problem-saturated stories and that they are likely to experience setbacks. Anticipating such an eventuality may lessen the potential impact of the setback.

- *Creating ways to reinforce the new narrative:* Encourage family members to identify strategies and individuals who can help them maintain the changes they have made. For example, the social worker can provide a written communication to the family to encourage progress.

A social worker using a narrative approach to frame the Murray family crisis would listen to each member share her or his views on the family situation. As you can imagine, each member of the family is likely to perceive the situation in a different way. William and Genevieve may share that they are doing their best to provide for all the members of the family and that they feel betrayed by Samantha's arrest and suspension. Samantha (as noted earlier) may believe her parents have given more to other members, particularly to her grandmother, than they have to her. Edna may feel that, because she is struggling with cognitive impairment, she is a burden to her family and feels powerless to change the situation. Elle may express guilt for being unable to support her children and herself. Stephen may feel pressured to hold down a job and to maintain his grades and scholarship so that he not further upset his parents and continue with his plans to move out of the house. At this point, identify the strengths that each person brings to the current situation. After reaching a consensus with the family regarding their desired outcomes, the social worker can work with the family to deconstruct and reconstruct their perceptions by externalizing the problems (i.e., focusing the family on the issue, not a person). Should the family, for example, choose to focus on stabilizing the situation regarding Edna's care, the social worker can externalize Edna's behaviors as, because of her cognitive impairment, outside her control. The social worker can then help the family envision their lives if they take no steps to improve their perceptions of Edna's situation and then to envision their lives when they understand the disease, coping strategies, care and respite options, and ways to enjoy their remaining time with Edna. While reconstructing a story of Alzheimer's disease will not alter the course of the disease, challenging the family's problem-saturated perceptions can enhance the quality of life for Edna and her family. The family can view Edna as an honored member of the family, not as a burden, while also acknowledging the changes needed to care for her.

Solution-Focused Family Interventions [EPAS 4]

Like other postmodern family-focused interventions, solution-focused family interventions emphasize strengths and empowerment, client self-determination, and client–social worker collaboration to mobilize assets and resources in order to construct new realities. Solution-focused interventions differ from other similar approaches in the use of a series of specific and focused questions that move the family from the crisis that brought them to seek services to a solution through the co-construction of solutions (De Jong, 2015).

Family solution-focused interventions emphasize relationships and explore client skills, strengths, and competence in a way that is consistent with many postmodern approaches. This orientation solidifies the social worker–client relationship as a collaboration focused on building on past successes (De Jong & Berg, 2013). As a foundational premise in social work assessment, planning, and intervention is to consider the client within the context of their environment, the social worker is encouraged to look for solutions in environmental, structural supports rather than for pathology in internal dynamics. Social workers do not disregard individual responsibility for behaviors such as those that occur in the family (e.g., abuse of a family member or substance abuse/addiction). Instead, the focus is on two areas: (1) recalling times when the issue did not exist and (2) identifying resources that exist in the individual, family, and beyond (Van Hook, 2014). For instance, family violence may occur when a family experiences stress and does not make use of internal resources (e.g., internal coping strategies) or external resources outside the family (e.g., social, health, mental health, or financial aid services) to deal with that stress.

Employing a solution-focused intervention encourages the family to adopt a hopeful, strengths-based, and future-oriented view of their lives. The social worker's role in facilitating interventions is to encourage and mobilize the family to think and talk about solutions (versus problems). Families must focus on establishing and achieving a series of modest solutions using existing and expanded coping strategies in a concrete behavioral way, which often means that the solutions already exist within the family's skills and experiences (but have to be re-mobilized) (Van Hook, 2014).

You will recall from Chapter 6 that social workers use a series of questions in the assessment and planning of solution-focused interventions that are used to guide the plan for change and intervention. While the family's identified needs, goals, strengths, and resources should drive the intervention process, the social worker can be most helpful by developing a repertoire of skills and strategies to aid the family in achieving their mutually determined goals. Exhibit 7.2 lists six tasks for implementing a solution-focused approach. Once the plan is underway, the social worker uses "what's better?" questions to monitor members' progress. A review of the solutions and exceptions that surfaced in response to the scaling questions the social worker asked in the assessment phase can highlight changes as they are made

EXHIBIT 7.2

*Solution-
Focused Social
Worker Tasks*

- Create interactional balance and balance between talking about the problem and talking about the solution. Maintaining balance among the persons who speak ensures that each voice is heard. Maintaining a balance of content ensures that the emphasis is not primarily focused on the problem but includes a focus on solutions.
- Use effective listening and summarizing skills. Staying tuned in to the contributions of each member of the family and regularly summarizing their input can re-energize the clients and the social worker to remain focused on the goal and to ensure that each person's voice is heard.
- Introduce transitions that will move the conversation from problem-focused to solution-focused. To maintain the focus on solutions, the social worker can regularly affirm the family's strengths with statements that convey support for the family's efforts.
- To sustain the emphasis on solutions, the social worker must focus on the family's current realities, that is, key in on those issues family members raise. When the intervention does not address specific and timely issues, there is a tendency for the family and the social worker to generalize and not attend to the identified problem areas. The social worker can help to redefine issues from problem-focused to solution-focused and can promote that process by staying focused.
- Facilitate a "family reflecting pool." In discussing issues and initiating solutions, each family member must have the opportunity to reflect on the issue or change from her or his vantage point, as each is likely to view the item or issue in a unique way.
- Establish goals and negotiate tasks. "Homework" is typical in any social work intervention, and solution-focused tasks should emphasize desired goals and solutions rather than problems. For example, suppose one stated goal is for the family to spend more time together. Before the next session, the family agrees to have dinner together three times in the upcoming week.

Source: Sebold, 2011, p. 217–228

and to addressing potential resistance and setbacks (Nichols, 2014). For example, the social worker might ask family members to rate on a scale from 1–10 how they felt about an issue when they first came to see the social worker and to compare those ratings with how they currently rate their feelings on the same issue. The social worker can also use scaling questions to anticipate future feelings and behaviors (e.g., "On a scale from 1–10, how confident are you that you will be able to sustain this change?").

The case of the Williamson family described at the beginning of this chapter provides examples of additional techniques for completing solution-focused interventions, which include the following (Koop, 2009, pp. 158–160; Nichols, 2014, pp. 233–236; Van Hook, 2014, p. 155):

1. Provide compliments as often as possible to emphasize strategies that have been successful. Compliments may be:
    a. *Direct:* "Jocelyn, you are to be commended for the concern that you show for your mother and your children."
    b. *Indirect*: "Jocelyn, what kind of things have you tried to address your son's alcohol and drug use?"
    c. *Self-compliments:* "Jocelyn, I'd like you to identify something in your life that you feel good about."
2. Focus attention on family members' relationships with one another. Questions such as "Jocelyn, how is your relationship different when you actively listen to Jamal when he speaks?" can help the family concentrate on changing their relationships.
3. Throughout the intervention phase, maintain a positive, future-oriented emphasis on "who, what, when, where, and how" questions. For example, "Jamal, what do you think your mother could do differently?"
4. Once the family has identified goals, shift the focus to a range of behavioral tasks in which the family can engage, including:

    • *Doing more of what works*: Encourage the family to continue to use any effective interactions and strategies they have identified. For instance, "Jocelyn, Tori, Jamal, and Nina, it is clear that you all care about one another but have difficulty expressing your feelings. What things have the other three done that send the message that she or he cares about you?"

    • *Doing something different*: introduce the idea of trying new strategies for relating to one another. Consider a question such as "What do you each think it would be like if you were to commit to having a meal together several times a week?"

    • *Going slowly*: Promote a slow, incremental approach to change. Building on the previous question, "Would it be possible to start with having three meals together each week?"

    • *Doing the opposite*: Encourage family members to engage in behaviors and interactions that are the opposite of what they are currently doing. As an example, "Jamal, what would happen if you did not leave the room/house when you feel like your mother is giving you a hard time about your friends?"

    • *Predicting tasks*: Help the family to predict outcomes and to identify patterns that occur when they experience change. For instance, consider saying to the Williamson family:

        We have talked about making some big changes in the way you interact with one another. I think we have established some achievable goals, including a commitment from each of you that you will agree to share a meal together three times a week. It is possible that you will not always be able to achieve that goal. If that happens, you should not feel you have failed. We can talk about ways to address the challenges that come up.

5. Find, amplify, and measure progress in order to monitor signs of positive movement toward desired goals. The social worker might say, "You have all done a good job of keeping to your commitment to have dinner together three times a week. What has that been like?"

6. Take a break within an interaction for the social worker and family to provide feedback to one another. For example, "Let's take a brief break, during which time we will reflect on the work we have done here today."

7. At the end of the meeting, recap the work the family and social worker have accomplished and provide suggestions for future work (i.e., "homework" that focuses on observing successes, engaging in new tasks, and predicting desired changes). Tasks can be divided into three separate categories:

    a. *Formula*: General tasks in which the family considers what they might do differently. With the Williamson family, you might compliment them on the work they have done thus far and suggest they increase the number of meals they share together from three to five.

    b. *Perception*: Observational tasks in which the family notes the differences in one another's behaviors. As an example, "Next time we meet, I'd like to have each of you share your thoughts on any differences you observe in yourself or your family."

    c. *Behavioral*: Tasks in which family members take action and interact differently with one another. Suggestions may include: "Jocelyn, I would like to encourage you to identify something you believe that Jamal is doing well that you would like him to continue doing."

Continuing to explore additional strategies for the implementation of the solutions-focused intervention, let us consider miracle questions. During the assessment and planning phase of your work with the Murray family, you asked each of the members regarding their perceptions of life in their household. Imagine how William and Genevieve might respond to goal-formulation or miracle questions. Perhaps they will talk about having imagined a near "empty-nest" household with their two older children living on their own and Samantha about to head off to college. In response to the "miracle" question, Samantha might express the desire that that she not face legal issues related to her arrest for driving under the influence and her school suspension and that her grandmother no longer live with the family. Elle's "miracle" might include employment, a supportive partner, and a home of her own. Stephen's miracle may involve a room of his own. Edna may wish desperately to have her memories back and to return to independent living.

Given the diverse array of goals family members may express, helping the Murray family to connect with a realistic set of goals may be a complicated process. Highlighting the fact that the family members care for one another can foster good-will and establish common ground on which the members can agree (De Jong & Berg, 2013). Reminding the Murray family of their commitment to and concern for one another can be a regular part of the intervention. Imagine that the agreed-upon goal is to find a solution to their overcrowded housing situation. Your role can be to work with the family to develop concrete and achievable short- and long-term solutions, to check in regularly with "what's better?" questions, and to terminate the professional relationship when you and the family agree the goals have been achieved.

Your social work values and ethical standards provide the foundation on which you develop interventions in your work with families, regardless of the theoretical approach that guides your work. For example, the client's right to self-determination, their strengths, and their diversity should be honored as top priorities. To help you to engage in social work practice with families, the following discussion emphasizes the behaviors that will enable you to become a practitioner who is competent and ethical in social work practice with families.

CONTEMPORARY TRENDS AND SKILLS FOR INTERVENING WITH FAMILIES [EPAS 8]

Families are groups of individuals, and, as such, they benefit from the careful use of the same practice approaches and skills that assist individuals and groups that are consistent with contemporary societal and family trends and challenges. Interventions with families are likely to vary according to practice setting and agency mission and programs and trends. Because the social work profession has always functioned within the context of the larger and ever-changing society, social work practice with families must use evidence to respond to the evolving structure of families and service delivery systems. For example, if you are a member of the intake unit of a public agency child protection team, your intervention with the family will probably differ from that of your colleague who works in a nonprofit mental health agency or family preservation program. The theoretical lens through which you work will also influence the way you intervene with family members. You may develop an intervention plan from a systems focus in which you work with family members to build an intervention plan based on their perceptions of ways in which you might help them, as in solution-focused work. In any situation, your intervention begins with an invitation to the family to tell their story, but your agency mission and purpose and your own theoretical preferences influence the intervention approaches you take.

Social work practice interventions with families share many similarities with individually focused interventions. Recall the Chapter 5 discussion on social worker roles in work with individuals (e.g., case manager, counselor, broker, mediator, educator, client advocate, and collaborator). Each of these roles applies to work with families, particularly in light of the setting in which the intervention may occur For example, the social worker working with a family in a child welfare setting may engage in all these roles but may also emphasize case management and brokering activities in particular in order to reunify the family. In a health care setting, the social worker may emphasize education and self-advocacy, for instance. As with social work interventions with individuals, it is important to use a biopsychosocial-spiritual lens in viewing the family, to recognize relationship dynamics, and to consider all family members' perspectives and the strengths-based intervention goals that will optimize family functioning.

As in your work with individuals, the setting in which you practice and your philosophical and theoretical approach will frame your intervention activities. In addition to the model-specific behaviors already discussed, general skills and behaviors transcend the continuum of theoretical approaches discussed here. The following strengths-based skills for intervening with families build on the behaviors social workers use in family engagement, assessment, and planning (Benard & Truebridge, 2013, p. 207; Hull & Mather, 2006):

- Identify the issues and concerns, use active listening to enable family members to share their perspectives on the challenges, and reflect on the information family members share.

- Acknowledge family members' pain.

- Look for and point out individual and family strengths.

- Ask questions about survival, support, periods of time that were positive for the family, interests, dreams, goals, and pride.

- Encourage the family to recognize that resilience begins with the belief that all people have the capacity for resilience.

- Link strengths to the goals and dreams of family members (both as a group and as individuals).

- Find opportunities for family as individuals and as a whole to help educate one another and to serve as helping agents in achieving the family's agreed-upon goals.

- Brainstorm for solutions to help the family view the situation and themselves differently.

Strategies like written homework assignments, task designation, and teaching can be helpful if they are appropriate to the family's situation, their investment in the process, and the framework you are using in the intervention. Return for a moment to the Murray family scenario and consider the previous list of practice skills. To mobilize the family toward crisis resolution, you can begin by asking each member her or his priorities for change. From those verbalizations, you will likely glean the pain, strengths, goals, and dreams each of the family members feels. You may choose to engage the family in brainstorming strategies they can use to address each of the areas of concern, or you might assign the family homework in which they develop ideas to address their concerns. An alternative may be to ask the family to have a **family conference** (a meeting of all members of the family in which they use a predetermined agenda to have a focused discussion on a matter relevant to the family) and to bring the resulting ideas to the next meeting with you. Once the family has developed a range of ways to address their prioritized concerns, consider asking them to identify and assign specific tasks. Be sure to explore the possibility that the expertise for problem solving resides within the family and that individual members can function as teachers and guides.

In addition to individual and family skills, practice strategies with evidence-based efficacy, when used carefully in many family situations, include reframing, perspectival (or circular) questions, family group conferencing, motivational interviewing, and reenactments (i.e., role-playing or rehearsals) (all described next), among others.

Reframing

Reframing is a practice skill in which the social worker conceives of and describes a situation in different terms. Social workers use reframing to focus on strengths and positive alternatives in work with families, individuals, groups, communities, and organizations. Reframing can be particularly helpful in family conversations in which one member makes an incendiary statement to or about another family member. Careful reframing can help defuse a situation so that both recipient and "sender" can begin to listen to each other. In order to have a meaningful impact, reframing must be appropriately timed. To have a significant effect, the social worker must be carefully attuned to family members' dialogues to identify opportunities for reframing as they occur (Minuchin, Colapinto, & Minuchin, 2007).

Suppose a 15-year-old boy, who sees his mother as an autocratic barrier to his freedom because she will not allow him to go out with his friends who drive, tells you, "There is no person on the face of this earth who is more controlling and overprotective than my mother. She is just like Hitler! She keeps me locked up in the prisoners' camp." After acknowledging his strong feelings and yearning to be free, you may suggest that the teen's mother cares for him so much that she fears he will be hurt in an automobile accident because his friends are driving him around, and they just recently obtained their driving licenses.

When reframing, offer a plausible alternative that does not resonate as a "gimmick" type of effort to diffuse strong feelings and that, accordingly, will be heard by the parties involved. Avoid interpreting the thoughts or feelings of another person without that person's direct input. In the example of the 15-year-old teen and his mother, it is quite unlikely that the mother is intentionally attempting to torture her son (and quite likely that she truly worries about his going out with friends who drive), but he may or may not be able to "hear" this reframed interpretation as being her being genuinely concerned. Another reframing effort may be more effective depending on the nature of the relationship between the family members (and possibly the social worker and family) and the people involved. Effective reframing requires judgment and skill; reframe with caution and only when conditions are relatively straightforward. How can a social worker reframe the Murray family's situation? Instead of focusing on the upheaval that Edna, Elle, and Elle's children moving into the house has created, consider emphasizing strong family commitments, caring environment, and flexibility.

Perspectival Questions

Perspectival questions can be effective in family social work. Seeking the perspective of another family member can help you clarify the feelings and meanings of one member's view of another. If the family is experiencing stress because the eldest son is leaving home, you may ask the teenage daughter, "What do you think your mother will do to prepare for Johnny's leaving for college?" Or you may ask the mother, "What do you think your daughter will miss most about Johnny?"

Responses to these questions can communicate ideas and feelings that no one in the family previously recognized. Such communication assistance is vital when family members assume they know all they need to know about the ideas and feelings of other family members as a result of long-term, "stuck" patterns of argument, difference, or "saving face." Use perspectival questioning carefully and only when you are confident that you can respond appropriately to any statement. The daughter in the example just provided might respond with, "Mother will sew name tags in Johnny's underwear so he won't lose it in the dorm laundry room at college," or she might say, "Mother will no doubt start to drink again." The same element of the unexpected that can create new ways of thinking for families can also catch the unwary or unprepared social worker off guard. Perspectival questions can elicit illuminating responses. Suppose, for example, that when asked about the support her son and daughter-in-law have provided to Elle and her children, Edna responds that they should not have invited Elle and the children to move into their house. By expecting the unexpected answers and maintaining flexibility, a social worker can effectively incorporate perspectival questions.

Family Group Conferencing

Family group conferencing (FGC) is an empowerment-focused intervention strategy that aims to create or strengthen a network of support for families who are experiencing a crisis or transition. The strategy was originally developed in New Zealand (Child, Youth, & Family, n.d.) for work with families in which children

© Lisa F. Young

were at risk of abuse or neglect, and social workers have adopted it for use in other family situations, including families with older adults experiencing life changes. The family conference is an intervention and is a collaborative effort that includes the social worker, the family (including extended family members), and members of the family's community who are or may be resources for the family (Wise, 2005).

The goal of the conference is to gather family members and people who are connected to them to decide how to respond to the presenting challenge. The social worker confers with each potential participant individually prior to the conference to ensure that each agrees to be actively involved in decision-making and action steps. During the conference itself, the participants are encouraged to identify their strengths and strive for openness, trust, and respect to enable them to become partners in achieving their goals (Chandler, 2013). Once a plan is established, the group adjourns; they may reconvene after implementing the plan to discuss progress or renegotiate the plan.

Return for a moment to the Murray family. If you were to convene a family group conference with the Murrays, consider whom you would invite to participate and a rationale for that choice. What goals could provide an opportunity for the Murrays to mobilize their support network and strengthen their coping skills? What are the family's strengths? How might they benefit individually and collectively from participation in a family group conference? What is your role? While answers to these questions can only be speculative, you can use this exercise to begin to see yourself in the role of a family social work practitioner.

Motivational Interviewing

Recall from Chapter 5 that motivational interviewing (MI) can be used with a variety of clients, including those who are nonvoluntary or who are experiencing substance abuse or intimate partner violence (IPV)(Wagner, 2013). Motivational interviewing provides another opportunity for you, as a social worker, to engage the client family in a collaborative partnership aimed at providing the opportunity for change. The four processes of MI—engaging, focusing, evoking, and planning—promote behavior change and make MI well suited to situations in which a client is uncertain about making a change and/or has limited time in which to make it (Miller & Rollnick, 2013; Wagner, 2013).

Motivational interviewing is also useful in social work with families. Miller and Rollnick (2013) offer strategies for engaging in motivational interviewing with families with adolescents. Using the FRAMES strategy, the social worker can conduct a family check-up that provides the social worker with the opportunity to perform the following actions (Miller & Rollnick, 2013, p. 375):

1. Provide **F**eedback regarding family members' personal status relative to family norms
2. Designate **R**esponsibility for personal change to the family as individuals and a group
3. **A**dvise family members regarding their situation and the benefits of change
4. Provide the family with a **M**enu of change options to choose from
5. Use an **E**mpathetic counseling style to validate family members' concerns
6. Reinforce family members' **S**elf-efficacy

Note the strategies described here are do not necessarily occur in a linear sequence but are concepts that guide MI. For example, using the FRAMES strategy with the Murray family, the social worker may opt to check in with the family in this way:

1. Provide *Feedback* to each family member on strengths and areas for consideration related to their proposed solutions for the identified stressors currently affecting the family based on the perceptions they have shared with you regarding the various crises they are experiencing. Encourage the family to also provide feedback to one another.
2. Designate *Responsibility* for change, clarifying roles and tasks for each member of the family.
3. *Advise* the family on change by providing information on the impact of ongoing stress for the family, Alzheimer's disease, and the potential positive outcomes of collaborative change.

4. Provide family members with a *Menu* of options for behavior change, healthier interactions, services, and resources that may be mobilized within and outside the family.

5. *Empathetically* validate the concerns each family member expresses and acknowledge the pain they are experiencing. Reiterate that the family members are the experts about themselves and that it is within their power and responsibility to implement change. Try to create an environment in which the family is empowered to view themselves as having the capacity to respond to their crises with resilience and efficacy.

6. Regularly reinforce each family member's *Self-efficacy*, identifying their strengths, their commitment to change, and their progress toward goals.

While motivational interviewing into social work practice with families can be an effective strategy for change, it can present challenges that do not exist in working with individuals. Given that families often come to social workers as the result of their inability to resolve relationship challenges on their own, it is critical that you ensure that each member of the family is given adequate opportunity to speak (Miller & Rollnick, 2013). Moreover, the social worker should balance the interactions to maintain a focus on positive change as opposed to continuing arguments and negative discussions.

Re-enactments

Re-enacting a particularly challenging interaction and then role-playing or rehearsing the scenario with alternative behaviors can be a powerful mechanism that allows the family to "try on" new ways of relating to one another. Role-plays are a safe way to share feelings and to rehearse, and they can be carried out in a variety of settings for a range of situations. You can revisit a role-play as the work progresses. Considerations for developing role-play activities include (Hull & Mather, 2006, pp. 163–164) the following:

1. The social worker and the family should collaborate to determine the purpose and parameters of the role-play.

2. The social worker and the family should collaborate to determine whether members will play themselves or other members of the family.

3. Members should play the roles as accurately as they can and should consider their feelings as they move through the rehearsal.

4. The role-play can be stopped so members can discuss, reflect, and change interactions.

5. The social worker and the family should debrief after the role-play to explore alternatives to the interaction they have just enacted.

A re-enactment may be an ideal approach for the Murray family with a role-play or rehearsal to follow once the family has identified the issues that are their highest priority. You can use the re-enactment of a previous experience to guide the development of an experiential exercise to "rehearse" the change strategies they have brainstormed. Given the multiple generations, issues, and priorities that exist within the Murray family, role-playing can be a valuable way for the family to work on individual issues and relationships. Imagine a role-play in which William and Genevieve share with Samantha their feelings and concerns regarding her life choices and decision-making. The family may be encouraged to envision a dialogue between Samantha and her parents that any one of the three may stop so they may regroup, change course, or ask for input. Such a rehearsal may enable the family to change a negative pattern of interactions.

Mapping as an Intervention

Mapping strategies are often discussed in the context of assessment. They do, however, have a place within the intervention process itself. During the intervention, mapping—in particular genograms—can be used to clarify family patterns, frame and detoxify family issues, and develop intervention plans (McGoldrick, Gerson, & Petry, 2008). Using the identified patterns and unhealthy family issues to develop and facilitate change plans can be a liberating experience for family members. McGoldrick and colleagues (2008) promote the use of genograms as an intervention strategy that empowers clients to change existing relationships. Being able to see historical patterns of loss, relationships (healthy and unhealthy), physical and mental health issues, substance use/addictions, responses to stress and crisis, and cultural traditions can make family members aware of the options they have for change. Creating and discussing genograms can also provide family members with an opportunity to engage in intergenerational dialogue. Consider the Murray family. If the family members engage in dialogue with Edna, they might discover family history they have never heard before and have a meaningful experience with Edna before her memory fades away. The social worker can incorporate the genogram into the development of the intervention by asking members to identify strengths as seen in the genogram on which they can rebuild relationships and continue cultural traditions (McGoldrick, 2015). They may also be able to identify patterns of substance abuse/addictions, involvement with the criminal justice system, or other distressing patterns that can inform their collective and individual work.

Similarly, ecomaps and culturagrams are also assessment tools that social workers can use in interventions, terminations, evaluations, and follow-up. Using a baseline ecomap or culturagram to monitor change throughout the intervention provides the family and the social worker with a visual depiction of the work. The ecomap or culturagram can be updated to track and evaluate progress and to note any barriers preventing success. Social workers can work with families to construct new maps as a means of ritualizing a successful outcome and also reflect during the termination process on changes achieved or not achieved.

Documentation for Family Interventions

As with social work practice with individuals, documentation is a critical component of family interventions. The client portfolio includes copies of the assessment tools mentioned here as well as a record of the intervention plans. Exhibit 7.3 offers a sample family intervention plan template, and Exhibit 7.4 provides an example of intervention plan documentation a social worker might develop with the Murray family.

As with your work with individuals, interventions with families require social workers to complete comprehensive, ongoing assessments from which they can collaborate with families to create flexible, individualized interventions. The outcome of a successful intervention is, of course, the termination. We now direct our focus to the termination, evaluation, and follow-up phases of family interventions.

EXHIBIT 7.3

Family Intervention Plan Documentation

Intervention Plan:

- Preliminary assessment
- Preliminary plan for intervention and change (to be developed at first visit), including:
  - What will each family member do differently?
  - How does each family member think they will accomplish changes?
  - What support and services do family members need to accomplish change?
  - Who will provide support and services?
  - Who will arrange for support and services?
- Interventions and plans for emergency/safety needs
- Other interventions needed
- Needs (include date, identified need, status (active, inactive, deferred, or referred), and reason for deferral or referral)
- Strengths
- Facilitating factors for intervention
- Limitations
- Barriers to intervention
- Other care providers/referrals and purpose (including plan for service coordination)
- Plan for involvement of individual family members, extended family members, significant others, and friends
- Review and termination criteria/plan
- Planned frequency and duration of intervention

Source: Adapted from St. Anthony's Medical Center, 2010; Missouri Department of Social Services, n.d.

EXHIBIT 7.4

Documenting the Intervention Plan: The Murray Family

Preliminary assessment

The Murray family has requested services from this agency to address a number of crises and concerns within the family. The family is comprised of William, a 55-year-old high school teacher, Genevieve, a 50-year-old occupational therapist, and their three children Elle, Stephen, and Samantha. Elle is a 25-year-old divorced single mother of two young children, Stephen is a 21-year-old college student, and Samantha is a 16-year-old high school junior. Along with William's mother, 76-year-old Edna, all members of the family reside in the couple's now overcrowded home. Stephen and Samantha were displaced when William and Genevieve gave their bedrooms to Edna and Elle and her children. Edna is experiencing cognitive impairment (Alzheimer's Disease) and can no longer live alone as she presents safety concerns at her assisted living facility.

When Samantha was arrested for driving under the influence and suspended from school, the Murrays sought help. During the assessment, the family shared information that suggests that the family has been in crisis for some time and that Samantha's arrest and suspension brought that crisis to a climax.

Preliminary plan for intervention and plan for change

During the first meeting of the entire family, each member shared their concerns, needs, and potential solutions. Then, the social worker shared a summary of that information and collaborated with the family to create a list of priorities. Through this collaboration, the social worker and the family developed the following preliminary plan:

1. Genevieve agreed to contact the local chapter of the Alzheimer's Association to obtain information on services available for families experiencing dementia. She will specifically inquire about programs that provide information on Alzheimer's disease and offer financial support for care needs (e.g., Family Caregiver Support Program).
2. All family members agreed they would attend a presentation for families about the disease provided by the Alzheimer's Association.
3. Stephen will contact the campus housing department at his university to learn about applying for a resident advisor position, which would provide him with tuition support and free housing in exchange for living in one of the student residential facilities. While he waits to find out if his application will be accepted, William and Genevieve have agreed to work with Stephen to fix up the basement so he may have a private bedroom and workspace.
4. Genevieve, William, and Samantha all agreed to attend the court-mandated program for teens arrested for driving under the influence.
5. Samantha agreed to attend the alternative school program for the duration of her school suspension.

Interventions and plans for emergency/safety needs

The first meeting yielded two areas of immediate concern regarding the family's safety needs. All family members agreed upon the following plan:

EXHIBIT 7.4

Continued

1. Elle agreed to provide care for Edna during the day when Genevieve and William are at work. This will reassure Genevieve and William that Edna is safe and that her supervision and transportation needs will be met. Elle will be able to remain home with her children and will not have to bear the expense of child care.
2. Samantha agreed not to drink and to be subjected to periodic alcohol tests if her parents are uncertain about her sobriety.

Other interventions needed

Longer-term interventions may include:

1. Exploration of all family members' feelings regarding their overcrowded living conditions and stressful relationships,
2. Discussion regarding Stephen's living arrangement if he is not accepted for a resident advisor position,
3. Decision-making regarding Edna's ongoing care needs as her disease progresses,
4. Discussions regarding Elle's permanent employment and living situations, and
5. Re-establishing a trusting and healthy relationship between Samantha and her parents.

Needs

At this preliminary phase, the family's primary needs are to:

1. Establish a safe environment for Edna;
2. Address Samantha's legal, school, and alcohol issues;
3. Provide adequate space for Stephen and Samantha; and
4. Address family stressors.

Strengths

The Murray family has several important strengths on which to build, including:

1. Genevieve and William's longstanding marital and employment history and commitment to each other and their family members as evidenced by their willingness to open their home to Edna and to Elle and her children.
2. The families' commitment to care for one another.

Facilitating factors for intervention

The family members' willingness to care for one another is the primary facilitating factor in this intervention. Additionally, the family's resources, both internal (e.g., Elle's availability to care for Edna and her expertise in nursing care) and external (e.g., Alzheimer's Association, alternative school, etc.) enable them to access needed services.

Limitations and barriers to intervention

1. While plans are underway to address the family's overcrowding situation, change may take time. Coping with the stress of the cramped living quarters in the interim presents a particular challenge.

2. While she agreed to attend the alternative school and to participate in family therapy, Samantha appears angry and may be reluctant to actively engage, particularly if the home continues to be a stressful environment and she feels she gets no attention or privacy.

3. The multitude of issues and tasks they are working to address may overwhelm the family, and this may render them less able to mobilize for change.

Other care providers/referrals

1. School personnel at the alternative school and Samantha's regular school
2. Alzheimer's Association
3. Family Caregiver Support Program
4. Substance Abuse Treatment Program

Plan for involvement of individual family members, extended family members, significant others, and friends

At this time, there is no plan to include other family members. However, the family mentioned that William has two sisters who live out of town and who may be willing to help with Edna's care at some point.

Review and termination criteria/plan

All agreed that the goals will be achieved when the family members feel they are in better control of their lives, specifically when:

1. The overcrowded housing issue is resolved,
2. Plans for Edna's long-term care needs are determined,
3. Elle's employment and housing plans are clarified,
4. Samantha has successfully completed the court-mandated program and is once again a student in good standing at her school (one-year minimum of no school violations), and
5. Stephen has a permanent housing solution.

Planned frequency and duration of intervention

The initial plan is for the social worker and family members to meet weekly. The social worker will be available by telephone in the interim. After the first four meetings, social worker and family will discuss plans for ongoing contact. As issues resolve, meeting frequency will decrease. Termination is scheduled to occur within three months of the intake.

Source: St. Anthony's Medical Center, 2010

ENDING WORK WITH FAMILY CONSTELLATIONS [EPAS 9]

General principles for termination and evaluation apply to all levels of practice. The need for culturally sensitive practice is paramount with individuals, families, groups, communities, and organizations. As in all terminations and evaluations, it is important to explore the meanings of endings for families. This discussion builds on prior discussions of terminations, evaluations, and follow-up and applies those ideas as appropriate for interventions with families.

In social work with families who have sought services voluntarily, endings tend to occur when the family is satisfied that they have achieved their goals. In some circumstances, the restrictions of third-party insurers or managed care companies may mandate an end point that occurs before the goals are achieved. Family work often focuses on the ways the family wants the dynamics of their relationships with each other or with outside entities to change and on the extent to which the family successfully achieves that change. The work also often focuses on preparing for future situations so that the family can anticipate how best to respond. For example, if a family is struggling with the decision to allow an adolescent son the freedom to develop a unique identity when he has a history of legal altercations, it may help them to consider how they will manage that issue when he leaves for college. These positions are all consistent with the principles of review and exploration highlighted in Chapter 5.

The following discussion will consider ending work with families from a strengths and empowerment perspective and through narrative-focused and solution-focused perspectives. These approaches strive to minimize the difficulty of endings. In general, they propose a comfortable, flexible process that gives clients control whenever possible.

Endings with Strength and Empowerment

Viewing each family unit both as individuals and as a whole requires the social worker to help each member articulate her or his feelings about the ending and the work that was completed (Wise, 2005). Family members can benefit from openly discussing feelings and insights about the strengths each individual and the family brought to the intervention. In an evaluative spirit, these insights can reinforce what the family has accomplished in the intervention and enable members to acknowledge the ending. Keeping in mind the original goal, the social worker and the family can focus on the future and on how the family can sustain change. If the relationship is terminating even though the family did not achieve their desired goals, the termination and evaluation phases can focus on lessons learned that the family can use in the future. In terminating with the Williamson family, for example, they acknowledge they were not able to fulfill their goal of having dinner together three times each week. While they did not achieve their goal, the family and you can use this time to reflect on changes made, insights gained, reasons the goal was unmet, and strategies for the future if they want to continue to work on a goal.

© Lisa F. Young

A strengths- and empowerment-oriented social worker can focus the termination and evaluation around the strengths identified in the assessment process and those identified or created during the intervention phase. Existing and new strengths can become the basis for the family to sustain the changes they have made. Together, the social worker and the family can review the family's strengths. The social worker can then ask the family to consider how they can apply these strengths to future situations. The family can also use these strengths as coping skills when and if they encounter new challenges. For example, the social worker may ask family members, "How can ending our work together help you achieve your goals?" (Wise, 2005, p. 215). Further, you can ask family members to speculate on their motivation and ability to continue working on their goals even after the formal intervention has ended.

Endings in Narrative-Focused Work

Narrative social workers often punctuate endings by working with families to develop rituals or ceremonies in which the family invites an audience to witness the changes the family has made and to celebrate their achievements. When siblings, other professionals who have worked with the family, and/or extended family attend a meeting, the experience can be validating for all involved. Using such strategies as certificates, celebratory activities, and definitional ceremonies in which family's successes are highlighted can affirm change and inspire continuation of change (Van Hook, 2014). This focus, like solution-focused work, represents a departure from traditional views of endings while acknowledging the same concerns about maintaining gains. In revisiting the termination with the Williamson family, consider that they not only achieved the goal of dining together three times a week but were able to increase that to five times a week. A celebratory termination activity to commemorate their progress may be to bring food that is special to the family (e.g., dessert) and share as a group.

Endings in Solution-Focused Work

Solution-focused work emphasizes endings almost from the beginning. As a short-term intervention approach, a solution-focused approach stresses that clients have abilities to competently manage their lives. Because this approach is built on the premise that change can occur within a brief, time-limited period, a social worker can use scaling early in the process, perhaps asking, "What [number] do you need to be in order not to come and talk to me anymore?" (De Jong, 2015). This question refers to the number from 1 to 10 that reflects the degree of well-being that the client reports. This approach honors a family's concerns about needing further work, and the family determines the number and content of further sessions. The approach places very little emphasis on the relationship between the social worker and the family; it views "not coming to talk to me anymore" as the preferred reality and a natural and comfortable conclusion to a problem for which the family likely already has a solution (which the social worker may help bring to light). In this approach the ending is, by definition, a success. Termination; evaluation; and, when possible, follow-up (e.g., checking in with the family, inviting the family for a return of follow-up session, or making referrals) are as important to the planned change process as any other stage of the relationship. Bringing the intervention to a close can serve as an opportunity for the social worker and family to: (1) review the work through a summary or a demonstration; (2) create an awareness of the changes made; (3) consolidate gains (i.e., celebrate changes and successes); (4) provide feedback to the social worker; and (5) prepare the family to handle challenges that may arise in the future (Collins et al., 2013, p. 447).

Not only should the termination of the social worker–family relationship be a time of mutual reflection, it can also serve as an opportunity for final declarations of hope for the future. Specifically, the social worker can remind the family that they should recognize that they fully own their strengthened and enhanced ability to cope with the challenges in their lives (Van Hook, 2014, p. 380). Moreover, this can be a final time in which the social worker and the family can review those new or remobilized resources within (e.g., beliefs and relationships) and outside (e.g., extended family, friends, and community) the family; abilities; and strategies that have been integrated into their interactional patterns so that they can readily access them when the inevitable challenges arise in the future (Van Hook, 2014). Engaging in these reflective activities during the ending phase of family work leads naturally into the process of formally and informally evaluating the work you have done together. We will now focus attention on this phase of work.

Evaluation of Social Work Practice with Families

Evaluating family interventions helps you as a practitioner and helps your organization determine if the intervention has been complete and effective. Evaluation can be critical in determining the selection of strategies in future work, maintaining funding, and continuing programs and services. During the evaluative process, the social worker and the family collaborate to reflect back on their work together, note progress, and determine if the intervention has achieved the agreed upon goals (Rasheed & Rasheed, 2013). If you have used evidence-based practice approaches, your evaluation can provide insights and contributions to your practice or your agency's practice. While evaluating your interventions with individuals can yield similar information about your practice, the same evaluative strategies are not always applicable to family interventions. Just as families are unique, so, too, are evaluations of family interventions.

The context and goals of the original contact often determine how a social worker conducts ongoing evaluation of work with a particular family. For example, if you are working with a family in child or adult protective services, the first priority may be the continued safety of the child(ren) or of an adult. There may be other goals, such as improving the parents' family management skills, meeting the health needs of a particular child or adult, or providing appropriate care for an older adult. In most cases, you will document these goals in writing and refer to them throughout the work.

When evaluating interventions with families, social workers focus on the family unit itself and not on the individuals within the family. An examination of the family's ability to exhibit new behaviors and coping skills, realistic attitudes, and new information and learning promotes enhanced well-being for the entire family (Wise, 2005). For example, if you and the family are able to determine that power has shifted among and between family members, this could indicate that the intervention has been effective. Alternatively, family members might deem the intervention successful because they agree that the stress level within the family has decreased or the quality of their interactions has improved. Family evaluations may focus, not only on the outcomes of the goals established during the assessment and planning phases, but also on the relationship with the social worker and the agency.

Strengths-Based Measures for Families

While family-focused intervention evaluations differ from evaluations of individual and group practice, the same evaluative strategies described in Chapter 5 provide a basis for developing plans for evaluation of family interventions. To promote a family (versus the individual) focus for the evaluation, strategies such as single-system design, goal attainment scaling, and case studies can be effective evaluation tools. An array of evaluation measurements has been developed specifically for use with families. While the scope of this book cannot address all of them, the following discussion will briefly explore the selection of measures that are grounded in a strengths-based perspective.

Several instruments that are designed for use in strengths-based practice with families allow social workers to document their service effectiveness (see Corcoran & Fischer [2013] and Early & Newsome [2005] for detailed reviews of family assessment tools). Standardized evaluative tools are increasingly important as funders, boards of directors, client advocacy organizations, and the social work profession itself hold agencies and practitioners accountable for measuring outcomes. Additionally, practice evaluation instruments can be helpful in maintaining the social worker's focus. Some of the instruments that have emerged as strengths-based emphases were introduced in the 1980s and remain useful tools today because they measure family perceptions and assets. The advent of evidence-based practice brought an increase in the number of standardized family assessment measures. Early and Newsome (2005, pp. 390–391) offer the following guidelines to consider when incorporating standardized assessment measures in family-focused social work practice:

1. Select a measure that emphasizes consistency and that is appropriate to the client situation.
2. Explain to the family the reasons for using the measure (e.g., method for efficiently collecting information to guide the helping process) and provide specific details about the contents of the measure and its expected outcomes.
3. Provide adequate and appropriate time, space, and materials to complete the measures.
4. Ensure that family members understand the items and feel comfortable asking questions about the assessment tool.
5. Whenever possible, score the measure in the family's presence.
6. Share the scores and interpretations with the family.
7. Maintain the evaluation tool in agency records for future review and comparison.
8. Repeat the measure over time to assess progress toward goals.

You or your agency will select the evaluative strategy that is most appropriate to your setting and to the families you serve. The following is a small representative list of reliable strengths and empowerment-focused evaluation measures that may be of help to you as you consider evaluating your practice:

- *The Caregiver Well-Being Scale* (Berg-Weger, Rubio, & Tebb, 2000; Tebb, 1995; Tebb, Berg-Weger, & Rubio, 2013): A strengths-based clinical measure to help family caregivers of adults and/or children identify the strengths and areas for change in their caregiving experience. See Quick Guide 21 for an example.

- *The Parent Empowerment Survey* (see Dunst, Trivette, & Deal, 2003): Designed to measure parental perceptions of control over a life event (see Herbert, Gagnon, Rennick, & O'Loughlin [2009] for review of empowerment measures).

- *The Family Support Scale* (see Dunst et al., 2003): Measures what is helpful to families. See Quick Guide 22 for an example.

- *The Family Strengths Profile* (see Dunst et al., 2003): Designed to chronicle family functioning, this profile provides a qualitative format for identifying and assessing family strengths and type of resources needed. Quick Guide 23 provides an example of this measure.

- *The Family Resource Scale* (see Dunst et al., 2003): Measures the adequacy of resources in households with young children, identifies needs, and emphasizes success in meeting those needs.

- *The Family Functioning Style Scale* (see Dunst et al., 2003): Measures family values, coping strategies, family commitments, and resource mobilization. Families indicate to what degree various statements are "like my family."

- *The Family Empowerment Scale* (Koren, DeChillo, & Friesen, 1992): Measures family empowerment on three levels: family, service system, and community/political.

- *The Behavioral and Emotional Rating Scale: A Strengths-Based Approach to Assessment* (Epstein, 2004) and *The Behavioral and Emotional Rating Scale (2nd edition): Youth Rating Scale* (Epstein, Mooney, Ryser, & Pierce, 2004): These scales focus on children and youth to determine the presence of behavioral or emotional conditions.

Self-Reporting   In strengths- and empowerment-oriented measurements, self-reporting is an asset. Self-reporting can complement traditional, scientific measurements in which the goal of objectivity conflicts with the biases in self-reporting. Bias is inherent in self-reported information because it is difficult to be objective about yourself. However, the strengths perspective supports the expertise of individuals and families about their own lives, experience, and aspirations, thereby making self-report a natural and theoretically consistent method of data collection.

The evaluation tools and procedures mentioned here are just a few among many. Some are flexible and, with creativity, you can apply them to a variety of situations. Using both quantitative and qualitative evaluative strategies (i.e., narrative comments) can provide the social worker and the profession with a comprehensive picture of the social work intervention, including the engagement, assessment, planning, implementation, and termination process and plans for follow-up. Remember that

QUICK GUIDE 21   CAREGIVER WELL-BEING SCALE

I. ACTIVITIES

The list below includes activities that each of us do or that someone does for us. Thinking over the past three months, indicate by circling the appropriate number on the scale provided to what extent you think each activity has been accomplished in a timely way. You do not have to be the one who did the activity.

1=Rarely   2=Occasionally   3=Sometimes   4=Frequently   5=Almost Always

	1	2	3	4	5
1. Buying food	1	2	3	4	5
2. Taking care of personal daily activities (meals, hygiene, laundry)	1	2	3	4	5
3. Attending to medical needs	1	2	3	4	5
4. Keeping up with home maintenance activities (lawn, cleaning, house repairs, etc.)	1	2	3	4	5
5. Participating in events at church and/or in the community	1	2	3	4	5
6. Taking time to have fun with friends and/or family	1	2	3	4	5
7. Treating or rewarding yourself	1	2	3	4	5
8. Making plans for your financial future	1	2	3	4	5

II. NEEDS

The list below includes a number of needs we all have. For each need listed, think about your life over the past three months. During this period of time, indicate to what extent you think each need has been met by circling the appropriate number on the scale provided below.

1=Rarely   2=Occasionally   3=Sometimes   4=Frequently   5=Almost Always

	1	2	3	4	5
1. Eating a well-balanced diet	1	2	3	4	5
2. Getting enough sleep	1	2	3	4	5
3. Receiving appropriate health care	1	2	3	4	5
4. Having adequate shelter	1	2	3	4	5
5. Expressing love	1	2	3	4	5
6. Expressing anger	1	2	3	4	5
7. Feeling good about yourself	1	2	3	4	5
8. Feeling secure about your financial future	1	2	3	4	5

Source: Berg-Weger, Rubio, & Tebb, 2000; Tebb, Berg-Weger, & Rubio, 2013.

QUICK GUIDE 22   FAMILY SUPPORT SCALE

Name _____   Date _____

The list below includes people and groups who are often helpful to members of a family raising a young child. This questionnaire asks you to indicate how helpful each source is to your family.
   Please circle the response that best describes how helpful the sources have been to your family during the past three to six months. If a source of help has not been available to your family during this period of time, circle N/A (Not Available)

How helpful has each of the following been to you in terms of raising your child(ren):	Not Available	Not at All Helpful	Sometimes Helpful	Generally Helpful	Very Helpful	Extremely Helpful
1. My parents	N/A	1	2	3	4	5
2. My spouse or partner's parents	N/A	1	2	3	4	5
3. My relatives/kin	N/A	1	2	3	4	5
4. My spouse or partner's relatives/kin	N/A	1	2	3	4	5
5. Spouse or partner	N/A	1	2	3	4	5
6. My friends	N/A	1	2	3	4	5
7. My spouse or partner's friends	N/A	1	2	3	4	5
8. My own children	N/A	1	2	3	4	5
9. Other parents	N/A	1	2	3	4	5
10. Co-workers	N/A	1	2	3	4	5
11. Parent groups	N/A	1	2	3	4	5
12. Social groups/clubs	N/A	1	2	3	4	5
13. Church members/minister	N/A	1	2	3	4	5
14. My family or child's physician	N/A	1	2	3	4	5
15. Early childhood intervention program	N/A	1	2	3	4	5
16. School/day-care center	N/A	1	2	3	4	5
17. Professional helpers (social workers, therapists, teachers, etc.)	N/A	1	2	3	4	5
18. Professional agencies (public health, social services, mental health, etc.)	N/A	1	2	3	4	5
19. _____	N/A	1	2	3	4	5
20. _____	N/A	1	2	3	4	5

Source: Dunst, Trivette, & Deal, 2003, pp. 155–157

QUICK GUIDE 23 FAMILY STRENGTHS PROFILE

Recording Form

Family Name ____________________________ Interviewer ____________________________

INSTRUCTIONS
The Family Strengths Profile records family behaviors and notes the particular strengths and resources those behaviors reflect. Space is provided to list behavior exemplars down the left-hand column of the recording form. For each behavior listed, the interviewer simply checks which particular qualities the family exhibits in their behavior. (Space is also provided to record qualities not listed.) The interviewer also notes whether the behavior is viewed as a way of mobilizing intrafamily or extrafamily resources, or both. A completed matrix graphically displays a family's unique functioning style.

FAMILY MEMBER	DATE OF BIRTH	AGE	RELATIONSHIP

FAMILY BEHAVIOR	Commitment	Appreciation	Time	Sense of Purpose	Congruence	Communication	Role Expectations	Coping Strategies	Problem Solving	Positivism	Flexibility	Balance			TYPE OF RESOURCE	
															Intrafamily	Extrafamily

NOTES

Source: Dunst, Trivette, & Deal, 2003

all evaluative measures have their limitations. It may not be possible to draw conclusions regarding the impact of a change because the change may have occurred separately from the intervention (Hull & Mather, 2006). Further, positive or meaningful change may occur even if the family is unable to achieve the goals of the intervention. In those situations in which the family does not reach identified goals by the time the intervention must end (i.e., as in the case of managed care, court- or school-mandated treatment, etc.) or when the family terminates the relationship prior to the agreed upon ending point, the social worker must process this experience. Talking with a supervisor or colleagues regarding the possible reasons for this unanticipated outcome can be a valuable professional development opportunity. While practice evaluations can be immensely helpful tools, they must be viewed within a context for family, yourself as a practitioner, and your agency.

Practitioner Reflection   The evaluation phase also provides you with the opportunity to engage in evaluating your own practice, including selection of theoretical approaches and strategies. In order to broaden the family-focused intervention beyond a set of techniques that you use, you can reflect on several areas of your practice, including (Nichols, 2014):

- the goodness of fit between the approach that you employed and the family's response and ultimate outcomes and

- the presence of conceptual themes and balance to ensure your intervention maintained a focus and forward movement on the family's prioritized issues with appropriate depth and breadth (pp. 279–280).

Consider your role with the family and reflect on the quality or competency of your work. Reflection with families is typically an introspective and interactive process. Some questions you can ask include:

- Does each family member feel that his or her contribution to the work is valued?

- Are there issues regarding the family's culture?

- Does the family still agree with the direction of the work?

- How is the work changing their experience?

At all levels of practice, it is important to check in with clients, through a dialogic process, to make sure they feel heard, understood, and are invested in the work you are doing with them. Remain attuned to nonarticulated feedback from family members. Lack of follow through on assignments or commitments and nonverbal gestures can be indicators of the family members' feelings about the intervention (Hull & Mather, 2006).

© monkeybusinessimages/Thinkstock

STRAIGHT TALK ABOUT FAMILY INTERVENTION, TERMINATION, EVALUATION, AND FOLLOW-UP

Practice with families is a complex enterprise, and the intervention, termination, evaluation, and follow-up processes can include the unexpected. Family members have individual relationships, networks, and influences outside the family, and those external persons or groups can positively or negatively affect the work the family accomplishes within the intervention. Family members may establish internal alliances that strengthen or, in some cases, undermine the work. Staying attuned to family members' descriptions of their activities, relationships, and pressures may help you accept that the unexpected is inevitable.

Like terminations with individuals, ending work with families can be emotional, particularly if family members have developed a positive relationship with the social worker. The family may even view the social worker as a member of the family; therefore, termination can elicit powerful reactions from the family. It is always important for the social worker to be sensitive to the family's cultural norms and feelings (Rasheed & Rasheed, 2013). The process of terminating and evaluating the social work intervention can elicit negative responses from some family members, some of whom may refuse to participate or may display anger, denial, anxiety, or even regression as the termination approaches (Fortune, 2015). As a social worker, you may find yourself juggling a variety of different responses from family members to the ending of the family intervention. Addressing individual and collective reactions to termination and evaluation, while building on the strengths and gains of the intervention, can serve as an intervention in and of itself. Empowering the family to handle a change (one they may perceive to be another loss) can be a meaningful new experience for the family; they can support each other, model new behaviors, and mobilize the strengths and resources they developed during the intervention.

Evaluations of family interventions may also yield unexpected results. If you opted (as described in Chapter 6) to complete a preintervention assessment, you can compare that data with a postintervention evaluation. You may be surprised at the family members' perceptions. You can explore these unexpected responses with the family in order to gain insight into their differing interpretations.

Due to agency policy or family preference or availability, having contact with the family after the formal termination and evaluation processes are completed may not always be possible or advisable. In those situations in which you are able to communicate with the family, you can utilize this contact to receive an update on the family's status and continued progress on maintaining the goals and outcomes from the intervention. If you learn that the family has been unable to sustain the change, you can take the opportunity to reflect with them on the barriers that prevented the change from being maintained, and you can (with their consent) brainstorm with them about ways in which they can return to their planned strategies.

The American Academy of Social Work and Social Welfare Grand Challenges for Social Work Initiative identifies one of the areas the profession should address for you is to end gender-based violence, both within and outside of families. The authors of Grand Challenge Working Paper No. 15, *Ending Gender-Based Violence: A Grand Challenge for Social Work* (Edleson, Lindhorst, & Kanuha, 2015) provide the following basis for this challenge:

GRAND CHALLENGE

Ending Gender-Based Violence

> Efforts to protect and support survivors of violence while also holding perpetrators accountable and working to rehabilitate them abound at the international, national, and local levels. Existing initiatives to prevent GBV (gender-based violence) and promote violence-free intimate relationships including building healthy teen and parenting relationships, emergency shelter programs, screening to identify those at highest risk of lethal violence, and coordinated community responses to address system-level barriers. Culturally responsive interventions for survivors and perpetrators are less prominent but are emergency worldwide (p. 4).

Decades of research have provided evidence for the prevalence and long lasting effects of an individual's experience of gender-based violence (GBV), including intimate partner violence (IPV), sexual violence, and exposure to violence as a child. While there is no one

<table>
<tr>
<td>

GRAND CHALLENGE

Continued

</td>
<td>

intervention or best practice that can be used to end GBV, the social work profession is being challenged to focus on the development and mobilization of interventions at the research, practice, and policy levels within the criminal justice and social service systems. Within the coming decade, the social work profession has the opportunity to address GBV through initiatives that: measure progress toward ending GBV, produce practice innovations, and transform perceptions and changing norms related to GBV (p. 8).

To familiarize yourself with the issues related to ending gender-based violence, visit the Grand Challenges website and read Working Paper No. 15, *Ending Gender-Based Violence: A Grand Challenge for Social Work* (Edleson et al., 2015) at: http://aaswsw.org/grand-challenges-initiative/12-challenges/stop-family-violence/. (See Exercise #a1 for additional exploration of this Grand Challenge.)

</td>
</tr>
</table>

CONCLUSION

Facilitating an intervention with a family from engagement through termination, evaluation, and follow-up can be an immensely rewarding professional accomplishment for you and transformative for the family. Working with families requires the social worker to develop a repertoire of theory- and evidence-based behaviors and skills to optimize family strengths and to create and mobilize needed resources. This chapter explored the integration of several theoretical approaches into social work practice with families and provided examples of ways the approaches can be applied to family situations. While refining your theoretically driven social work practice is a lifelong process, identifying the theoretical approaches that are most consistent with your professional and personal values is an important early commitment toward your development as a social worker. Clarifying your own views on families and your role as a family social worker can be helpful along your journey. This chapter highlighted strategies for working with families that you can use in a range of settings and with diverse types of families.

MAIN POINTS

- Social workers can choose from an array of theoretical perspectives to guide interventions with families. Social workers' training, philosophical and value system, available empirically supported evidence, and agency orientation influence which perspectives they select.

- This chapter highlights several approaches for developing intervention plans with families including strengths, empowerment, solution-focused, and narrative perspectives. While each perspective shares some similarities with the others, each has characteristics that make it unique.

- While different models of family intervention require certain specific skills and behaviors, the following basic skills for working with families are common to most models: collaborating, using strengths, and supporting the voice of each member of the family.

- Your experience with your own family can influence your work with client families. Ongoing evaluation includes, not only documenting the achievement of externally imposed goals (e.g., school or court system), but also determining if your role and relationship with the family are working.

- Each family social work intervention is multifaceted, and the termination and evaluation process should include candid discussion of potential inside and outside influences. When ending work with families, the social worker must consider how the professional–client relationships that formed may have affected the work; the effectiveness of chosen theoretical perspectives; and the practical, contextual dimensions of the work.

- The evaluation of the social work intervention with families may emphasize an empirical process and/or a qualitative one. Standardized tools may be helpful in the process of evaluating family social work. Some models emphasize the family's qualitative satisfaction with the outcome of the work.

- Some situations allow for following up with the family. In such situations, the social work can focus on the degree to which the changes have been maintained and support the family in making appropriate adjustments.

EXERCISES

a. Case Exercises

1. To apply your learning of the Grand Challenge for Social Work, "End Gender-Based Violence," which was highlighted in this chapter, visit the Grand Challenges website and read Working Paper No. 15, *Ending Gender-Based Violence: A Grand Challenge for Social Work* (Edleson, Lindhorst, & Kanuha, 2015) at: http://aaswsw.org/grand-challenges-initiative/12-challenges/stop-family-violence/. To examine GBV-related issues, review the information about Hector and Celia's daughter, Gloria, and her spouse, Leo, at www.routledgesw. com/caseStudies. After reading Working Paper No. 15 and reviewing the information on Gloria and Leo, complete the following:

   a. Select one of the family intervention approaches discussed in this chapter. Using assessment strategies identified in Chapter 6 (including mapping), complete an assessment for Gloria and Leo.

    b. Building on the assessment that you completed for Gloria and Leo, develop an intervention plan that includes existing and needed resources and services.

    c. Develop a plan for the way in which you would complete the termination and evaluation processes.

2. Go to www.routledgesw.com/cases and review the case files for each member of the Sanchez family. A number of potential ethical issues may emerge as you work with this family. Using the NASW *Code of Ethics* (available at naswdc.org), identify the ethical issues or dilemmas that could arise, citing the core social work and ethical principle relevant to each issue you identify. Upon completing this task, write a brief reflection on your findings. [EPAS **1**]

3. Go to www.routledgesw.com/cases and review the case file for Carmen Sanchez. Address Critical Thinking Questions #1, #2, and #3. For Critical Thinking Question #2, identify at least one article in each of the two areas that concern Carmen: the impact on families of children with special health needs and outcomes of children in different types of families.

    Gather into groups with 4–5 of your classmates and develop a potential work plan for the family based on your answers to the Critical Thinking Questions. In your plan, focus on the following:

    a. Identify areas of potential challenge.

    b. Develop strategies for working with the entire Sanchez family around these challenges.

    c. Develop a plan to insure Carmen's maximum participation in the process.

4. Go to www.routledgesw.com/cases and review the case file for Carla Washburn. While Carla does not have a traditional family network, she is connected to a support system. Strategize about ways in which you might integrate each of the members of her support network into your intervention with Carla, identifying the strengths and potential contributions each can make. You may wish to review the case files and ecomap to develop your plan.

5. Go to www.routledgesw.com/cases and review the case for Brickville, focusing on Virginia Stone and her family. Based on the initial assessment and planning process you conducted in collaboration with Virginia (you may want to review Exercise #3 in Chapter 6), you and she have determined that a family conference will help address the multiple concerns related to her mother's care, home ownership, and response to the proposed plans for neighborhood development. Using the information available to you (including the ecomap and genogram), develop two separate written plans for a family conference from two perspectives (narrative and solution-focused), including your responses to the following questions:

- Whom should you invite to participate in the family conference?
- What location is optimal for the conference?
- Based on discussions with Virginia, develop a list of:

- ○ potential agenda items,
- ○ individual and family strengths and areas of concern, and
- ○ available and needed resources (within the family and community).
- What is your anticipated role?
- How might the family genogram and/or ecomap be incorporated into the family conference to develop a collaborative intervention, particularly as it relates to providing care for family members?

Upon completing your plans for a family conference, reflect in writing on three areas:

- Differences and similarities of a narrative or solution-focused approach
- Ways in which you can integrate a strengths-based perspective into the conference
- Possible motivational interviewing strategies you can employ during the family conference

6. Go to www.routledgesw.com/cases and review the case for Hudson City and the information provided in Exercise #4 in Chapter 6 regarding the Patel family. Using a strengths-based, solution-focused approach, develop a summary of the planned change model intervention (engagement, assessment/planning, intervention, termination/evaluation) you would facilitate with the family. Be sure to include your theoretical approach(es) and to incorporate the available resources in Hudson City.

7. Go to www.routledgesw.com/cases and review the case for Riverton. Returning to the Williamson family (described at the beginning of this chapter), utilize your knowledge of the Riverton community, its resources, and its current culture to develop a strategy for engaging, assessing, planning, intervening, terminating, evaluating, and following up with the Williamson family. Include all members of the family in the intervention plan.

b. Other exercises

8. As a social work practitioner at a community mental health center, you serve primarily individuals and families. Later today, you will conduct an intake appointment with the James family, who recently called you. You have the following information about the family:

- The father, who self-identifies as African American, made the appointment.
- The family includes the mother, father, their two adolescent sons, and the father's parents who live with the family.
- The eldest son, age 18, is of most concern to the family. He has expressed suicidal thoughts and has recently been increasingly withdrawing from school, family, and community life. Last year, this son was a well-known school athlete, and this year he is not active in any school or athletic activities.

- The parents suspect that their sons are using alcohol or other drugs.
- Both sons are reluctant to attend the appointment, but they will do so because their father has indicated they will.
- The mother will "go along" because she wants to avoid conflict.

In your preparation for this appointment, you consider several dimensions of the work. In small groups, discuss these dimensions and explore the questions. Report back to the entire class.

a. You are not African American but are of Jewish heritage, which is relatively rare in the town. You know there are differences between your culture and this family's culture, but you believe you can bridge those to some extent because you consider yourself different culturally as well. What might you need to consider about your own assumptions? Identify the differences that may occur between the two cultures and strategies for addressing such differences.

b. What model of family social work (among those discussed in this chapter) do you believe will provide the most useful base for work with this family? Discuss the reasons for this selection.

c. What specific information will you want to clarify from the start?

d. What specific approaches will be most important with this particular family?

e. How will you begin your intervention with this family? What skills and behaviors will you use? What might you actually say? (Give an example.)

9. Using the strengths-based strategies highlighted in this chapter, review the following list and describe in detail the way in which you would incorporate each item into an intervention with the James family (from Exercise #6):

- Identify the issues and concerns, use active listening to enable family members to tell their stories, and reflect on the information they share.
- Acknowledge their pain.
- Look for and point out strengths.
- Ask questions about survival, support, periods of time that were positive for the family, interests, dreams, goals, and pride.
- Encourage the family to recognize that resilience begins with what one believes, and all people have the capacity for resilience.
- Link strengths to the goals and dreams of family members (both as a group and as individuals).
- Find opportunities for family members to contribute to the intervention by helping to educate other members and to serve as helping agents in achieving the family's agreed-upon goals.
- Brainstorm solutions to help the family view the situation and themselves differently.

10. Using a solution-focused approach, identify the techniques reviewed in this chapter that you believe will be appropriate for use with the James family described in Exercise #6. Describe the specific way you would implement the strategies.

11. Termination and evaluation are critical aspects of the social work intervention. Conduct a review of the research to identify evidence-based practice skills and practices that are applicable to facilitating an effective termination and evaluation with a family. Share your findings in class and compare the results of your review.

CHAPTER 8

Social Work Practice with Groups: Engagement, Assessment, and Planning

© SerrNovik/Thinkstock

Alone we can do so little. Together we can do so much.

Helen Keller (1880–1968)

Key Questions for Chapter 8

1. What competencies do I need to engage with and assess clients in social work group practice? [EPAS 6 and 7]
2. How can I use evidence in research-informed practice and practice-informed research to guide engagement and assessment with groups? [EPAS 4]
3. What potential ethical issues may arise in social work practice with groups, particularly in the early phases of the group's development? [EPAS 1]
4. What knowledge and skills do I need for culturally competent group-level engagement and assessment practice? [EPAS 2]

The residents of the Riverton community (see case at www.routledgesw.com/cases) are becoming increasingly concerned about alcohol consumption and its negative impact on the residents and businesses, particularly on the children and youth who live in the neighborhoods. As this chapter will highlight, there are multiple strategies and formats for intervening in this problem at the group level. The Riverton community members have proposed three potential group interventions to address their concerns about alcohol use in their neighborhoods: (1) Riverton Against Youth Drinking (RAYD)—a voluntary group of residents and professionals who receive in-kind support (meeting space, office supplies, etc.) from the Riverton Association of Neighborhoods whose goal is to prevent problems by creating alternative activities and options for the community's youth as an alternative to substance use; (2) Riverton Children's Grief Support Group—a group facilitated by the Community Service Agency for children who have lost a family member to drug- or alcohol-related death; and (3) Riverton Mental Health Center Groups for Persons with Co-occurring Diagnoses—a therapeutic treatment group for persons who are experiencing substance abuse and mental health challenges.

NONE OF US LIVES WITHOUT SOCIAL CONNECTIONS. Many of us spend much of our lives negotiating our closeness to family, neighbors, friends, associates, and colleagues. Regardless of the ways in which we experience connections and whether we perceive them as positive or negative, virtually everyone has relationships to small collectives of other people or groups. In this context, **group** refers to the natural or planned associations that evolve through common interest (e.g., supporting the local Little League Association), state of being (e.g., having a child with a disability), or task (e.g., working together at a place of employment to improve workflow). Connectedness to groups depends not only on an individual's needs for affiliation but also on cultural norms; social arrangements (e.g., marital/relationship status, family status (parent or child), and personal affiliations); and social location (e.g., faith traditions, children's school, or neighborhood of residence). Within social work, **group work** is a "goal-directed activity that brings together people for a common purpose or goal" (Toseland & Horton, 2013, para. 1).

This chapter addresses the nature of groups, briefly reviews the history of group work in social work practice, and explores the dimensions of group work that relate to types and purposes of groups. In this chapter, you will explore the purpose of groups and the relationship of groups to other areas of social work practice along with engagement and assessment skills. Chapter 9 will build on the engagement and assessment of group practice addressed in this chapter by presenting skills and behaviors for approaching the various aspects of the process of group work through intervention, termination, evaluation, and follow-up.

GROUPS: THE SOURCE OF COMMUNITY

The social dimension of social work implies that people need and want to relate to others within the context of a "community." Yet the ways to meet this need are not always clear to social work professionals or to the clients they serve. In contemporary U.S. culture, there is a pervasive emphasis on independence, mobility, and the pursuit of success. Employment opportunities for many that are far away from home; socioeconomic achievements; and/or pressures to advance professionally, socially, and economically influence people and have spurred new definitions of and parameters for community. Such influences are not necessarily negative, but they can take a heavy toll on one's sense of connection and linkages (i.e., community) to stable, consistent groups on which they can depend over time.

A brief online search using the term "support groups" or a review of the advertisement section of any major newspaper provides evidence of our need to connect with others. The number of announcements for therapy groups, support groups, community groups, and educational groups suggests that, as a western culture, people are looking for a way to relate to others that is outside of themselves. In other words, people seek out groups in order to form community. Such groups provide a safe environment in which to share goals, information, give and receive mutual aid, and make connections with others (Steinberg, 2014). By implication, social work practice with groups affords people the opportunity to participate in meaningful experiences that the contexts of their personal and/or professional lives do not provide. Family, friends, and co-workers may be empathetic to and supportive of our challenges and form one type of group that provides community, but it might not be enough. We may find a stronger connection with nonfriends or family who share lived experiences, issues, or perspectives than our natural groups.

Group Orientation as a Cultural Dimension

Culture has an important impact on the amount and type of connections people seek. "People relations" (Diller, 2015, p. 99) is one of the cultural paradigms that distinguish one cultural group from another. For example, European Americans are more inclined to be individual in their social relationships; this contrasts with the collective focus of many other cultures—Latino/a Americans, in particular. The social worker facilitating the group must be culturally astute, aware of group participants' cultural backgrounds, and attuned to the cultural influences that affect group dynamics. Brown (2013) offers the following strategies for culturally competent group facilitation:

- Ask questions of group members to draw out cultural differences and attempt to integrate learning into the group process.

- Do not overwhelm group members with too much information at one time.

- Regularly check in with group members to ensure clarity of understanding by all members of the group regarding goals, purposes, membership, and processes.

- Attend to your communication skills; use open-ended questions and avoid technical words and jargon.

- Ask group members to share their own traditions related to respectful interactions, culturally sensitive issues, and taboos (p. 52).

Exhibit 8.1 provides additional suggestions for developing culturally competent group practice skills.

Social workers practicing with groups can benefit from incorporating culture-specific strategies, like those listed here, that build on culturally competent practice with individuals and families. These practice guidelines do not apply to all members of these populations, and they should be used in conjunction with, and not in place of person-centered skills that focus on the individual members of a group.

EXHIBIT 8.1

Cultural Competence in Group Work

Latino/a Americans: With a commitment to collectivism, family traditions, harmonious interpersonal relationships, and respect, consider the following as you develop a group:

- Attend to issues of language, both written and oral, including ensuring that written materials are available in Spanish, pronouncing names correctly, and asking if group members prefer English or Spanish and, if the latter, clarifying the word/phrase meanings if group members speak different variations of Spanish.
- Assess level of group member acculturation within various contexts, including physical and mental health, school, family, and work and consider potential conflicts if members are newly arrived in the country or if they are longtime residents.
- Make no assumptions about group members, and be open to learning about individual group members' language, origins, and history.
- Be flexible and fluid with the timing and flow of the group meeting.

EXHIBIT 8.1

Continued

- Allow adequate time for engagement and for trust and relationship building. Encourage facilitators to share personal information about themselves and their families.
- Use story circles/storytelling to enhance relationship building, collaborations, and social action.
- Integrate activities that encourage artistic expression (e.g., painting, acting, theater).
- For curriculum-oriented groups, ensure content and materials are culturally specific and appropriate.

Source: López and Vargas, 2011, pp. 144–145; Paniagua, 2014, pp. 104–105.

African Americans: To consider the use of an Afrocentric approach that brings together Western and African cultures:

- Emphasize the interconnections among the individual, family, and community to enable the individual to see her or himself within those contexts.
- Maintain a focus on African American culture and its strengths.
- Present yourself as respectful and genuine.
- Upon gaining the group's acceptance, maintain a consistent and active role in the group process.
- Be aware of and attend to group members' expectations regarding the group experience (e.g., will the group be multi-racial/ethnic and or have a communalistic focus?).

Sources: Greif & Morris-Compton, 2011; Harvey, 2011, p. 268; Paniagua, 2014.

Asian Americans—Understanding Asian American cultures can help you to:

- Recognize that the importance many Asian Americans place on what Westerners might sometimes see as conflicting values (such as family (versus the individual), harmony, independence, privacy, expression of feelings, and respect for authority) can complicate a group intervention.
- Consider your own assumptions, biases, and lack of information with regard to the diverse groups within Asian cultures. Take heed of the implications of each of these for the intervention.
- Understand that potential differences in communication styles (i.e., emphasis on nonverbal communication) can, for example, enable you to be comfortable with silence.
- Acknowledge group members' strengths, particularly in terms of bicultural skills.
- Consider the impact of similarities and differences in terms of: length of time in the U.S., cultural origins, migration and loss issues, acculturation to Western culture, intergenerational and gender roles/conflicts, and experiences in the U.S. (particularly related to discrimination and oppression).

EXHIBIT 8.1

Continued

- Consider normalizing feelings and experiences, psychoeducational activities, nonconfrontational approaches, and self-disclosure.
- Assess member's level of comfort with sharing feelings and avoid invasive questions until trust and communication norms are established.

Source: Paniagua, 2014; Ringel, 2005.

Native Americans: While few group work approaches have been developed with specific emphasis on Native American culture, consider the following strategies:

- Strive to ensure that each member's voice is heard, specifically in terms of sharing individual stories and making decisions for the group.
- Acknowledge and gather information on tribal-specific traditions, ceremonies, spiritual implications, and context.
- Incorporate positive and honest humor.
- Be consistently "present" and genuine with group members.

Source: McWhirter et al., 2011, pp. 79–80; Paniagua, 2014

Undocumented Immigrants: With their diverse array of personal and family histories and potentially high level of anxiety regarding legal status and possible deportation, group work with undocumented immigrants can benefit from the social worker's use of the following specialized skills:

- Acknowledge and celebrate group members' resilience in the face of challenges and the strengths they have developed as a result of their lived experiences.
- Be knowledgeable about the legal issues associated with undocumented status.
- Ensure that agency administration supports the provision of services to this population.
- Consider active outreach to enable this population to feel comfortable joining a group.
- Clarify for yourself what you do and do not need to know—group members may be reluctant to share specific information regarding their living situations.
- Promote relationship building and trust by inviting members to share their stories and later addressing such issues as marginalization, isolation, and discrimination.

Source: Chen, Budianto, & Wong, 2011, pp. 90–93

Implications of Global and Cultural Connections for Social Work Group Practice [EPAS 2]

An increasingly global perspective on social work practice underscores the need for sensitivity to global awareness in social work group practice. In 1996, NASW amended its *Code of Ethics* (2008) to include the following statement: "social workers should promote conditions that encourage respect for cultural and social diversity within the United States and globally" (Standard 6.04). This addition to the *Code of Ethics* called on the social work profession to embrace a more global consciousness, a perspective that has become well integrated into social work practice, in general, and with groups, in particular. Due to the increased globalization of our society, social workers engaged in group work will need heightened awareness of the expectations and needs of group members of diverse cultures.

As a practicing helping professional, you will benefit from exploring the degree to which your own orientation to achievement, independence, and competition as cultural variants might be incompatible with the cooperation and collaboration that clients from other cultures may value more highly. Regardless of your own cultural heritage, be careful to avoid valuing your orientation to the ideals in your culture or privileging your cultural values as normal just because they are familiar. Suppose, for example, that you encounter a child, Jared, in a school setting who appears to lack an eager, competitive spirit; who seldom raises his hand when a teacher asks a question; and who always defers to others, and you attribute these behaviors to a personal deficit. You may find him slow, shy, or lethargic, and you may see him as dependent, or even as depressed or developmentally delayed. Rather than correlating with some deficit, however, Jared's behaviors may simply reflect a cultural orientation to cooperate, to prioritize the communications of others, and to maintain modesty in the company of people who are older and who have authority.

The nature of "groupness" is complex and variable according to social location. While all people need and seek social connections, their cultural expectations related to family and community, customs, propriety, loyalty, authority, individualism, and the way in which these factors fit together can temper and shape this phenomenon. Although Western values of competitiveness and individualism have been responsible for much of the accomplishments and power of U.S. culture, these values have the potential to create disconnection, isolation, and detachment. While individual self-determination is an important hallmark of social work practice, a group social worker must also understand that it could be perceived as oppressive to clients whose cultural orientation is more collective in nature. Group social workers should be able to adjust group work processes and expectations to account for the range of cultural orientations about collective versus individualistic orientations of group members.

Historical and Contemporary Contexts for Group Work

Like other legacies in social work, social work group practice has roots in the settlement houses in England in the 19th century. The political and economic context of this time period disrupted lives and broke down social connections within and among families. Such a sense of isolation led people to come together in groups around common interests and needs. With a sense of mission, volunteers, often through charity organization, of this era brought groups together for socialization, recreation, advocacy, and social action. The time was ripe for the development of group social work, although there were disagreements among professionals regarding the question of whether social or individual change should be the focus of group work (Alissi, 2009; Furman, Bender, & Rowan, 2014 requested; Toseland & Horton, 2013).

Group work developed in the United States in the late 19th and early 20th centuries at a time when many in our society perceived a need for public, religious, or philanthropic organizations to involve themselves in the lives of U.S. citizens. Inspired by the work of religious and philanthropic organizations in the U.S. with individuals and families, the concept of bringing people together in small groups became a popular strategy for helping clients within community-based settings (e.g., YMCA/YWCA, Boy/Girl Scouts, and faith-based community centers). One approach focused on individuals and their need for change. In contrast, another group of helping professionals of the time focused group efforts on social reform with a humanitarian impulse and believed that social change was the critical ingredient in making a positive difference in people's lives. These reformers were more likely to see the group (rather than the individual) as the medium for that form of intervention. The differences between these groups of professionals echo the social control/social change tension discussed in Chapter 1. By the end of the 19th century, the Progressive Era promoted continued growth of group work. In response to the influx of immigrants and needs of the teeming urban environments, group work (particularly groups with a self-help focus) were being offered within settlement houses and community organizations, and self-help groups. These organizations stressed group methods (e.g., language classes, cooking groups, recreation, the arts, and youth services) and aimed to address the social justice issues of inclusion and acculturation. They sought to increase access to society's assets for newly arrived residents in order to maximize their ability to achieve their desired quality of life. Still, group work was not clearly identified with social work during this period.

Throughout the 1930s, many social work professionals tended to assign lesser status to group work than to social casework. This perception was due in part to the fact that recently developed curricula in schools of social work, reflecting Freud's pervasive influence, focused on individual casework. With the pervasive Freudian focus, existing group work was strongly associated with recreational activities (e.g., sponsoring dances or creating arts and crafts with children) as well as inclusion and acculturation. Such activities were not held in as great esteem as more clinically focused casework. That slowly changed, and as the profession began to accept group work as equal status with casework, practitioners declared it a part of social work, but as a discrete unit with distinctive methods.

In the 1950s, group work expanded from the community into hospitals and psychiatric facilities and social workers introduced **therapeutic group work** or **treatment groups**. These therapeutically focused groups were designed to heal or help people change. This shift took a more professional stance than the former community-based model. Through the process, the distinctions between group work and casework began to blur.

Three classic models for group practice—the **social goals model**, the **reciprocal model**, and the **remedial model**—emerged between the late 1950s and the 1970s. Social workers still use these perspectives in contemporary social work practice with groups, and we will discuss them in detail later in this chapter and in Chapter 9. See Exhibit 8.2 for a brief description of the origins and aims of these three classic models.

By the 1970s, the Council on Social Work Education (CSWE), the accrediting body for social work education in the United States, required all schools of social work to adopt a generalist focus throughout undergraduate programs and for the first half of master's programs. With an aim toward integrating all practice methods across levels, the generalist focus requirement served to de-emphasize the distinctive role of group work as a method and, many believe, to lessen its importance. Most school curricula already emphasized casework, and with the CSWE mandate, there was little incentive to develop more group work courses. As a result, many social work students did not complete coursework that focused on social work practice with groups. Nevertheless, a strong core of social workers committed to the

EXHIBIT 8.2 *Classic Models for Social Group Work, 1950s to 1970s*	MODEL TYPE	MAJOR FOCUS	SOCIAL WORKER ROLE	EXAMPLE	ORIGINAL AUTHORS
	Social Goals	Democratic values, social conscience, responsibility, and action; uses strengths of members.	Fosters social consciousness and serves as a model for democratic values.	School groups that promote student affiliation and contributions to student governance.	Pappell and Rothman, 1962
	Reciprocal	Interaction in an attempt to fulfill mutual affiliation goals; mutual aid.	Serves as mediator between each member and the group as a whole; finds common ground.	Adolescent children of incarcerated parents developing coping skills.	Schwartz, 1961
	Remedial	Prevention and rehabilitation aimed at behavior change and reinforcing individual behaviors.	Works both inside and outside the group to ameliorate conditions in environments; acts as motivator.	Discharge group in mental health settings to increase patient capacity to negotiate community.	Vinter, 1974

power of social work with groups remained, and they founded the Association for the Advancement of Social Work with Groups, Inc. (AASWG) in 1979 (later renamed as **International Association for Social Work with Groups (IASWG)**). The IASWG first issued *Standards for Social Work Practice with Groups,* a guide for effective practice with groups that is widely used in contemporary social work practice, in 1999. The second edition of the *Standards,* issued in 2006 and updated in 2015, provides practitioners with guidelines and practice perspectives for gaining the knowledge, tasks, and skills needed in group work. These guidelines include core values and knowledge, phases of the group process (i.e., pregroup planning, beginning, middle, and ending), and ethical considerations. The Standards are derived from practice wisdom, theories of group work practice, and empirical evidence (AASWG, 2013, p. 270).

The climate of social work practice today offers practitioners a unique opportunity to work with groups to help individuals meet their needs for genuine connection and social action. A group-focused orientation is one of the characteristics that distinguish social work group practice from psychology or mental health counseling groups. In group work, the social worker's effort focuses on the development of the group as a whole through which individual well-being is promoted through interactions and group structures.

DIMENSIONS OF SOCIAL WORK PRACTICE WITH GROUPS

For this discussion of the dimensions of type, form, and function and the logistics of social work group practice, we define a social work group intervention as a small, face-to-face gathering of people who come together for a particular purpose which can be focused on the individual or community. The major feature of a group experience is the interdependence among person, group, and social environment for such purposes as individual or community growth and social advocacy/policy change.

Types, Forms, and Functions of Groups [EPAS 4]

At the most basic level, social work groups are either formed (or constructed) groups or unconstituted, **natural groups**. Natural groups occur in the context of socialization and are not organized from the outside. These may be based on spontaneous friendships, common interests, or common social location, such as living in the sophomore wing of a college dormitory. Families are the original natural group. Natural groups usually do not have formal sponsorship or agency affiliation, but social workers may have occasion to work with them (particularly families). Social workers and their agencies can also provide support to these naturally formed groups in a variety of ways (e.g., offer meeting space, access to office equipment, or staff consultation).

© Blaj Gabriel

Social workers are more likely to engage with or facilitate **formed groups**, which are organized by an institution or organization, such as a school or hospital, an agency, or a community center. There are three primary models of formed groups that accomplish different functions: **task groups**, which are designed to accomplish a specific purpose; **social action** or **goals groups**, a type of task group that focuses on advocating for social justice; and **client groups**, which are geared toward personal change. More specifically:

1. Task groups include task forces, committees and commissions, legislative bodies, staff meetings, interprofessional teams, and case conferences and staffing. A task group aims to facilitate a change that is external to the group with a focus on a specified purpose, such as developing policy, completing a product or a plan, or creating a mechanism for collaborative decision-making (Strand et al., 2009, p. 42). The social worker can function as a convener, member, chair/leader, facilitator, or a combination of these roles. The social worker in the leadership role is responsible for initiating and monitoring the meeting and the group's progress toward stated goals and objectives, managing group interactions, and maintaining focus (Furman et al., 2014, p. 18). We explore task groups in more detail in Chapter 10. You may also visit http:// routledgesw.com//riverton/engage/video to learn about a task group, the

Alvadora Neighborhood Association that oversees the activities and growth of the community of Riverton. The video provides an example of a social worker-led task group in action as the members use Roberts Rules of Order to discuss purchasing streetlights and issuing a liquor license.

2. Social action or goals groups are a form of a task group that addresses a social issue to empower individuals or a community (Toseland & Horton, 2013). A social action group inevitably incorporates a political focus that may address issues of social justice, equity, and human rights, all of which require the social worker to have knowledge of the political and social challenges faced by those being served (Dudziak & Profitt, 2012). The social action approach has a number of strengths: (1) the collective effort of a group of people can be more powerful than that of an individual; (2) the social worker is not the expert leader, but rather a facilitator or supporter of the group; (3) groups can help harness the individual's capacity to create social change; (4) professionals and group members work in partnership; (5) group members determine the agenda; and (6) groups can create a safe environment for the individual and collective exploration of issues of oppression, discrimination, and disadvantage (Fleming, 2009, pp. 275–276). As with task groups overall, the social worker can function in a variety of roles. For example, as described at the beginning of this chapter, a group of residents of the Riverton community came together with professionals who work in the community to address their growing concerns about alcohol abuse among the youth in their neighborhoods by forming a social action group, Riverton Against Youth Drinking (RAYD). With in-kind support of the Riverton Association of Neighborhoods, RAYD has established the goal of developing organized activities and programs to deter the youth from engaging in drinking behaviors and worse. To reach their goals, the group plans to apply for grants, hold fundraising events in the community, and partner with family service organizations.

3. Client treatment groups may be aimed at support, education, growth, therapy, socialization, empowerment, and remediation. Client groups can be formed for two purposes:

   a. **Reciprocal groups**, also referred to as support, self-help, and mutual sharing groups, form to enable members who share a common experience to provide mutual aid to one another. With an emphasis on self-help and not specifically on therapeutic intervention, reciprocal groups can range from informal to highly structured to **psychoeducational** (blending mutual support and educational focus). Reciprocal groups provide members with an opportunity to experience "shared empathy," which is the experience that brings members together and provides the potential for cohesion and mutual problem solving (Furman et al., 2014, p. 69). Finding others who share similar life experiences can be validating and affirming for group members and can provide them with opportunities to share valuable insights and coping strategies.

This model for group work intervention has wide applicability, particularly among adults who face a new or unanticipated struggle and can benefit from education and group support. Psychoeducational groups focus on educating group members regarding a psychological condition. One approach in particular has been especially helpful to parents of young adult children experiencing mental illness. These individuals frequently develop new symptoms in their early 20s, and their parents may not have been touched by mental illness before. Local community mental health agencies often offer group sessions to these families to help them learn more about mental illnesses, what to expect in terms of their children's behavior and symptoms, how they can best provide support, and how they can cope with their own grief. The **National Alliance for the Mentally Ill (NAMI)** first established these groups, and they have been particularly effective. Psychoeducational groups usually incorporate considerable factual information, but they also rely on the supportive and accepting attitudes of worker/facilitators and other group members. Groups can be structured, with a curriculum and lessons in sequence, or they can be freer in form. In some locations, parents who originally attended these groups have become group facilitators themselves, generally with training and technical support from the local agency.

Social work involvement in reciprocal groups can range from initiator to facilitator to "silent" support person. The social worker role will be related primarily to the origins of the group (i.e., a larger role if social worker-initiated and a lesser role if member-initiated). In the case of a psychoeducationally focused group, the social worker may play a more formal role based on possession of particular knowledge or skill expertise. A grief support group for children living in the Riverton community who have lost a family member to alcohol or drug abuse is one example of a psychoeducational group. As described at the beginning of this chapter, the Riverton Children's Grief Support Group is offered by the Community Service Agency and facilitated by a social worker. The group relies primarily on community professionals from the school, Community Service Agency, and Alvadora Community Mental Health for referrals.

Groups for persons who are in the early stages of dementia are one example of contemporary support groups. Social workers frequently work with persons who either have dementia or live with or love someone who has dementia. The stigma and isolation some of the men and women living with dementia experience can be as devastating as the disease itself. This makes support a critical component of work with these individuals, and the support group can offer a chance to share feelings, combat loneliness, gain information, exchange resources, and normalize the overall experience. Similar issues arise for families and other loved ones of someone with dementia, and social workers may facilitate groups for them as well. Social workers need to understand the effects, symptoms, and issues that people with or effected by dementia's experience. Alzheimer's disease and other dementia can invoke volatile emotions; therefore, it is particularly important for facilitators to acknowledge and understand their own reactions to and biases regarding the disease and those living with it.

b. **Remedial groups** aim to change behaviors, restore functioning, or promote coping strategies of the individual members who either voluntarily or involuntarily join the group (Toseland & Horton, 2013). The social worker's role in these groups is typically that of facilitator or leader because they bring the clinical knowledge and skills needed to direct the group. Returning to the Riverton community as an example, a remedial group may be formed at a mental health center or hospital to provide therapy for persons struggling with **co-occurring illnesses** (i.e., substance abuse/addiction and mental illness). The Alvadora Mental Health Center Groups for Persons with Co-Occurring Diagnoses is co-facilitated by two clinical social workers with training in addictions and mental health treatment.

Groups may also be distinguished by the role the social worker plays. In treatment or therapy groups, the social worker may use methods consistent with counseling and interpretation, while educational groups may focus on teaching and processing. Task groups are likely to direct the social worker's focus on facilitation, as she or he assists the group in taking action to address an undertaking. See Exhibits 8.3–8.5, which depict phases of group interventions, including social worker and member roles. Using the descriptions of the four groups in the Riverton case, these exhibits give examples of the beginning phases of group processes—pregroup planning, engagement, and assessment—that illustrate the social goals/action, reciprocal, and remedial models.

During the group planning process, a decision you must make is to determine if a group experience will meet the needs you have identified. Group interventions can be powerful and have the potential to address a number of individual, community, and societal needs. A group approach is more suited to some situations than it is to others. In addition to bringing together people who have a common life experience, concern, or need, a group effort can promote creativity and problem solving, influence individual thoughts and behaviors, and provide a convenient strategy for delivery of services to a large group of clients with similar issues (Garvin & Galinsky, 2013). While all of these can be valid reasons for launching a group intervention, consider whether the potential gains for the group, both as individuals and as a collective, are optimally efficacious and efficient or if another type of intervention will be better given a particular situation or need. For example, having a number of male and female clients of all ages who share a life experience (e.g., childhood sexual assault) does not ensure that developing a group intervention is the most appropriate intervention as practice wisdom has shown that mixing ages and genders around an issue as sensitive and personal as childhood sexual assault is not

<table>
<tr><td>

EXHIBIT 8.3

*Riverton
Against Youth
Drinking
("RAYD"): An
Example of
Social Goals/
Action Group*

</td><td colspan="2">

PHASE I: BEGINNING

Background: Concerned about the use and abuse of alcohol among their adolescent children, a group of parents, residents, and professionals in the Riverton community approaches a local community service agency to ask for help addressing this problem. Chapter 9 will highlight later phases of the group's work.

Note: While the stages of group interventions are not linear and may, in fact, overlap, the following depicts a possible approach to responding to the identified need.

</td></tr>
<tr><td></td><td>

PREGROUP PLANNING AND ENGAGEMENT

</td><td>

ASSESSMENT

</td></tr>
<tr><td></td><td>

Meet with parent groups to gather information

</td><td>

Determine individual and group members' "agendas"

</td></tr>
<tr><td></td><td>

Identify current and potential stakeholders who are/may be invested in the issue

</td><td>

Conduct community assessment, including needs, assets, and resources (see Chapter 10 for further information on community assessment)

</td></tr>
<tr><td></td><td>

Identify interests of group members

</td><td></td></tr>
<tr><td></td><td>

Research evidence on approaches for facilitating social goals groups on this topic

</td><td>

Gather and analyze data from assessment; identify and prioritize options for intervention

</td></tr>
<tr><td></td><td>

Determine general focus/goal of launching an intervention

</td><td>

Re-determine/confirm focus of intervention

</td></tr>
<tr><td></td><td>

Identify roles for agency and social worker

</td><td>

Finalize plan for intervention, including objectives, tasks, activities, persons/groups responsible, time frame, and plans for evaluation and sustainability

</td></tr>
<tr><td></td><td>

Arrange first meeting and logistics, including time, location, refreshments, etc.

</td><td>

Re-clarify agency and social worker roles and responsibilities

</td></tr>
<tr><td></td><td>

Develop agenda for first meeting

</td><td>

Revisit needs

Make plans for continued assessment

</td></tr>
</table>

the most effective approach. Individual and same-gender/age interventions may be more helpful to the clients.

Recognizing that the individual's work is completed within the context of the group's fluid, interactive, and sometimes conflictual dynamic, ask yourself if your desire to establish a group meets the client's needs or your needs to efficiently serve a larger group of clients. Would group work primarily meet your agency's revenue goals, or would it mount an advocacy effort, or some combination of the two?

PHASE I: BEGINNING

Background: A social worker in a local community service agency has become aware of a number of children in Riverton who have lost a parent to alcohol and substance-related deaths. The social worker takes steps toward offering an educational support group in the community. Chapter 9 will highlight later phases of the group's work.

Note: While the stages of group interventions are not linear and may, in fact, overlap, the following depicts a possible approach to responding to the identified need.

PREGROUP PLANNING AND ENGAGEMENT

Gather information to support the need for and appropriateness of this group intervention

Analyze data and confirm plans to move forward with forming a group

Research evidence supporting approaches to facilitating reciprocal groups with children

Determine group components:

- Composition of group (number, age range, and gender)
- Recruitment strategies
- Format (open or closed)
- Time frame (time-limited or ongoing)

Determine and implement appropriate recruitment strategies

Conduct screening interviews with potential members (see note in Assessment regarding group membership)

Invite group members (for minors, obtain written permission from legal guardians)

Determine roles of agency, social work facilitator, children, and legal guardians

ENGAGEMENT AND ASSESSMENT

Pregroup

Prior to first meeting, meet individually with parents/guardians and separately with children to assess interest in and appropriateness (i.e., "fit") for a psychoeducational support group

First Session

Lead introductions

Orient members to the group; review purpose, goals, rules, norms, format, time frame, intervention plan, termination, evaluation, and confidentiality

Assess individual member goals, functions, and interactions with other members

Assess group cohesiveness

Continue to assess individual and group needs (for support and education), interests, strengths, and "agendas"

Monitor and assess social worker role

Administer pregroup measurements to be used in the evaluation process

EXHIBIT 8.5

Riverton Mental Health Center Group for Persons with Co-Occurring Diagnoses: An Example of a Remedial Group

PHASE I: BEGINNING

Background: A new social worker at the Riverton Mental Health Center has recently assumed co-leadership with another social worker for a clinical intervention group for persons with co-occurring diagnoses (i.e., substance abuse and mental illness) who receive outpatient services at the agency. The group is diverse; members represent a mix of gender orientation, racial/ethnic group, and age and both mandated and voluntary participants. Membership turnover depends on members' "graduation" from the treatment program; therefore, group membership is fluid. Two new members have been referred to the group. This will be the first time new members have been referred since the social worker took over co-responsibility for the group. Chapter 9 will highlight later phases of the group's work.

Note: While the stages of group interventions are not linear and may, in fact, overlap, the following depicts a possible approach to responding to the identified need.

PREGROUP PLANNING AND ENGAGEMENT	ENGAGEMENT AND ASSESSMENT
Obtain information on potential new members from referral sources and agency records, as appropriate	*First Session*
	Facilitate introduction of new members to group and review group expectations, norms, and rules
Research evidence on incorporating new members into an existing group	
Determine structure for admission, including criteria and process	Assess individual member goals, interests, and "fit" with group
Meet with potential new members to screen for potential "fit" with group purpose, goals, and other members	Assess member reactions to new group members
	Assess group cohesion
Invite new members to first session, introduce self, and provide orientation (e.g., composition, goals, expectations, norms, and rules)	Monitor/assess progress of other members

Quick Guide 24 provides a set of questions to consider as you weigh the pros and cons of forming a group.

Group Work Logistics

Social work groups may form and meet in community agencies, schools, community mental health centers, medical practices, public assistance offices, job training centers, residential care settings, church or faith organizations, or any other setting in which participants come together. The physical location may be a setting that

QUICK GUIDE 24   THE PROS AND CONS OF CREATING A GROUP: QUESTIONS TO CONSIDER

As you weigh options for intervening with client, organization, and community systems, first determine if a group intervention is the most effective approach. To clarify your goals, consider the following:

- What are my reasons for choosing a group intervention over an individual or family intervention? Specifically, what needs have I identified within my clients, my agency, or the community?
- What type of group intervention am I considering—social action, task, reciprocal, or remedial? What are my reasons for selecting this format?
- What would the goal(s) of the group be? For the group? For me? For the agency or community?
- Will the group be an open or closed group (i.e., continuous group of members or open to members entering and leaving as needed)?
- Will the needs of members best be met in a time-limited or open-ended group?
- Who and what will determine the eligibility criteria for group membership?
- Do I have the requisite competence to facilitate a group intervention?
- Should I be the sole facilitator, or would having a co-facilitator better serve the group?
- Do I have the support of my supervisor and agency administration? If not, am I aware of the process for gaining approval?
- What resources do I need to offer the group? Possibilities include meeting space, supplies, and funds for recruitment, refreshments, transportation, and child or adult care.
- What options exist for gaining the resources needed for the group?
- If this is a client group, will there be a charge for participation?
- What is the optimal group size?
- Is there an adequate pool of potential group members within those my agency serves or the larger community?
- If I am uncertain about the pool of candidates for the group, how would I recruit members? What marketing strategies would be appropriate?
- What are the appropriate meeting dates, times, frequency, and longevity for the group?
- When will group meetings begin?
- How much time do I need to prepare to lead the group?
- How will group activities be recorded and evaluated?

group members already use (such as a school), or it may be a local community facility that makes itself available to group activities (a community hospital that houses a grief and loss group, for example). Many residential settings that host social work groups, like law enforcement centers or mental health facilities, restrict their use to residents and their significant others.

Social work groups may differ in other ways, such as the number of group meetings or the way in which they are organized. A group may meet for a fixed number of sessions, or it may be ongoing, with changing membership over time. Some groups are structured as **closed groups** in which group membership and the number of sessions are fixed. Many others are **open groups**, which allow new members to join at any time (or occasionally only at fixed times, such as after the third and sixth sessions). Group interventions are often intentionally time-limited because of the nature of the work (e.g., mandated groups or psycho-educationally focused groups), financial or agency resources, or characteristics of the group members (e.g., children or adolescents). In developing plans for a group intervention, consider which of these formats will best meet the needs of the target population. Open groups may offer flexibility for the facilitator and group members and economic advantages for the organization, but this format may lack the cohesiveness and continuity of a closed group format. Consider also the similarities and differences in the skill sets required to facilitate each type of group. For example, to effectively lead an open group, the social worker must be able to quickly develop an empathetic connection to group members, promote cohesion in each meeting, and know when it is appropriate to use more active or less active facilitative skills (Turner, 2011).

Whether group participation is voluntary or mandated is another important distinction. In mandated situations, the social worker may have lower expectations (not always realized) of member investment, and the influence of the mandating institution (such as the court) is likely to be greater than it is in voluntary groups. Many involuntary treatment scenarios employ groups. For example, recall the innovative family group decision-making model in Chapter 7, which used a large group of community and extended family members in a case of a child protection violation. More traditional models also use involuntary groups for work with clients who experience intimate partner violence, parenting issues, and substance abuse/addictions. Group work focuses particularly on interrelatedness and extension to the "outside" world, thus creating opportunities to engage involuntary clients in a process from which they can benefit long after completing treatment. During the engagement, assessment, and planning phases of group work with members who are mandated to participate, the social worker's role is to take an empathetic stand toward the goal of finding a mutual purpose, including acknowledging to her- or himself and the clients the presence of anger and hostility while creating options for decision-making (Doel & Kelly, 2014). For example, consider your approach if you are facilitating a group for adolescents who have been convicted of nonviolent criminal offenses in which the members are mandated by the court system to participate and are, not surprisingly, unhappy to be there. Rather than attempting to create an illusion of willingness or complacency about their situations, you may opt to address the involuntary aspect at the outset of the group with a statement such as,

I know that you are each required to participate in this group as a condition of your legal situation and that you may prefer not to be here. I also know that you have a choice in how you want to handle your time in this group and I want to let you know that I will respect your right to participate at the level you feel comfortable.

THEORETICAL APPROACHES TO ENGAGEMENT AND ASSESSMENT WITH GROUPS [EPAS 6 AND 7]

As with social work practice with individuals and families, developing competencies for engaging, assessing, and planning in group practice begins with identifying a theoretical stance from which you will work. Just as in social work practice with individuals, families, and communities, social workers are obligated to utilize a theoretically evidence-based intervention that incorporates empirically supported group interventions and process, evidence-supported guidelines, and practice evaluation (Macgowan & Hanbidge, 2015).

Regardless of the theoretical perspective selected for group work, you should maintain a commitment to the strengths-based perspective. The following discussion is grounded in the premise that all members in a social work group have strengths on which the goals and objectives can be built. As Kurland (2007) notes, "the very act of forming a group is a statement of our belief that every member of the group has something to offer the others, something to give to others, not just to get from them" (p. 12).

Since all groups are created and function as a system, most theoretical frameworks for group practice derive from the systemic perspective (Garvin & Galinsky, 2013). You can apply your knowledge of systems theory as it relates to work with individuals and families to your work with groups. You may begin by viewing groups as fluid, dynamic interactions between a set of individuals who become interdependent. Any change in group composition (e.g., a member joins or exits) changes group dynamics and interpersonal interactions. A systemic perspective suggests that, through group members' exchanges and feedback, the work of each phase of the group process "coalesces into a meaningful whole" (Manor, 2009, p. 101). Group work can be highly effective when approached from a strengths-based perspective. When a group focuses on members' strengths and abilities as opposed to their limitations, it can have a powerful impact on those individuals (Ephross, 2011). Building on the conceptualization that systemic and strengths-based frameworks guide social work group practice, the following discussion looks at narrative and solution-focused perspectives within group work.

Narrative Approach in Group Engagement and Assessment

Social workers have integrated narrative theory with other theoretical and practice approaches to group work just as they have in their practice with individuals and families. Incorporating a narrative approach with groups begins with viewing the clients as collaborators with one another and the social worker. With a group, the number of potential collaborations is significantly increased as compared to individual work. Having a group of individuals who share common experiences can further aid in the process of engaging the individual group member to elicit her or his story, then challenging the client's perspective and partnering to reconstruct a new story/reality. Members can benefit, not only from sharing and reconstructing their own narrative, but also from listening to other group members and contributing as they reconstruct their own individual stories.

The narrative framework emphasizes the client's expertise on her or his life (Kelley, 2013). Within the context of assessment in group practice, group members can work with one another and with the social worker to identify members' strengths. The assessment process can also help members externalize or separate themselves from their problems for the purpose of planning for change. Next, we explore using a narrative approach blended with a solution-focused approach.

Solution-Focused Approach in Group Engagement and Assessment

Recall from earlier discussions of social workers using a solution-focused approach with individuals and families that this approach emphasizes brief, targeted interventions. A solution-focused approach "encourages more purposeful interaction among group members" (De Jong & Berg, 2013, p. 286). With its grounding in a strengths-based perspective and its emphasis on solutions, this approach can quickly focus group members on the issues that brought them to the group, aid them in collaborating with one another on the development of a plan for change, and activate the planned change—all with the input and support of other group members and of the social work facilitator.

In engaging potential group members, the social worker can emphasize the time-limited, targeted, future-oriented nature of a solution-focused group. This orientation clearly sets the stage from the engagement phase that the work together will be purposeful, will occur within a specified time period (ideally 6–12 meetings), and will emphasize concrete, achievable outcomes. Such an approach is likely to appeal to potential group members who may be reticent about joining a group. De Jong and Berg (2013) report that the relatively brief, time-limited nature of the solution-focused group intervention can serve as motivating and purposeful for group members. Solution-focused strategies have been shown to be particularly helpful when addressing bullying behaviors with children and youth (Young, 2013), with clients mandated for intervention (e.g., prison inmates and offenders of intimate partner violence) (Uken, Lee, & Sebold, 2013; Walker, 2013), and substance abuse (SAMHSA National Registry of Evidence-based Programs and Practices (NREPP), 2012).

Because of the pragmatic, outcomes-oriented nature of the solution-focused approach, the assessment phase of solution-focused group work can promote a range of helpful techniques. For example, creating individualized therapeutic goals and using scaling questions to gauge members' concerns enables group members to monitor their own progress throughout the intervention. Using a standard series of solution-focused questions to introduce assessment highlights previous successes, strengths, and resources while focusing the individual client (and the group) on viable solutions. For example, as a social worker working with the group of Riverton residents who have lost someone to substance abuse/ addiction, you could begin the assessment phase by asking individual members the "miracle" question: "How would your life be if you were no longer acutely grieving the loss of your loved one?" You could then ask the group member to recall a time when he or she successfully coped with a challenge or crisis. Recognizing that grief is not easily resolved, you can guide group members to consider alternative strategies for coping with their loss. The benefit of such a pragmatic, time-limited nature of the group process is that group members can share ideas and strategies, help identify strengths in themselves and others, and support and nurture one another.

Social workers can effectively integrate solution-focused approaches with other intervention approaches. For example, incorporating strategies from the strengths- and narrative-based schools of thought can enhance the impact of the intervention (Kelley, 2013). All three approaches emphasize engagement, assessments, and planning focused on the resources of each person with the goal to empower and change. Narrative-focused techniques can elicit the stories of the group members and help develop alternative and unique change outcomes for the individual and the group. Specifically, the interactional nature of the group experience can promote the group members' comfort and motivation to articulate their stories as well as enable them to support one another as they explore and strategize potential solutions that will work for them.

Regardless of the orientation(s) to which you subscribe, remember that your client in group work is, in fact, the group itself, and the group experience can be powerful for both you and for group members.

CONTEMPORARY TRENDS AND SKILLS FOR THE BEGINNING PHASES OF GROUP WORK: ENGAGEMENT AND ASSESSMENT [EPAS 6 AND 7]

As with practice with individuals and families, pre-planning, engagement and assessment, and planning are critical to an effective social work intervention with a group. These areas coincide with the phases of the group intervention: (1) engagement including preplanning and planning for the group experience; (2) assessment and planning for the group process planning; (3) intervention focused primarily on the middle phase of group work; and (4) termination, evaluation, and follow-up encompassing the ending phase. Group practice skills build on the skills and knowledge needed in work with individuals and families; here we will discuss new skills for pregroup formation planning (i.e., screening, engaging and assessment, group logistics, and process (Macgowan & Hanbidge, 2015).

Pregroup Planning

A successful social work group intervention requires careful planning prior to the first meeting. As the practitioner, there are nine areas you need to consider before organizing a group (adapted from Kurland & Salmon, 1998, p. 24):

- Client need

- Purpose

- Composition, eligibility, and appropriateness

- Structure

- Content

- Agency context

- Social context

- Pregroup contact

- Contacting prospective group members

You should think about each of these areas within the context of the agency, your supervisor's input or direction, and the larger social environment. These areas are interrelated; decisions in one area may influence decisions in another. The considerations here do not presuppose certain answers. They are simply areas to keep in mind in order to avoid unexpected obstructions later. See Exhibit 8.6 for schematic drawings related to preplanning models and Exhibit. 8.7 for an example of the operationalization of the preplanning process.

Let us return to Jasmine Johnson's situation in which she asks for your help to learn alternative strategies for interacting with her teen son. A component of her contract with you was to participate in a Parents of Teens Support Group. Look at Exhibit 8.7 from the perspective of the social worker who will create and lead that group.

Client Need   To determine if a group approach would be most appropriate for clients, you may begin by identifying the major relevant issues that confront the client population. You want to know your clients well and to be aware of their needs as they perceive them. In order to establish a vital, functioning group, you must understand members' lives and struggles and be able to focus on some aspect of their lives that is important to them. In-depth knowledge of your target group can influence your recruitment and retention strategies, meeting location, group agendas and activities, and the impetus for potential members to participate (Finlayson & Cho, 2011, p. 491). For example, in working with the parents of teens group in which Jasmine Johnson is a member, consider the decisions you will make

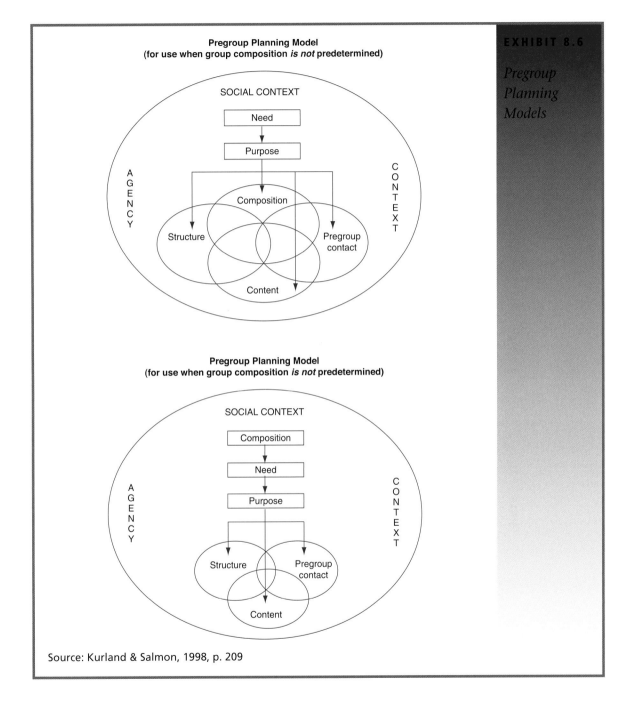

Pregroup Planning Model
(for use when group composition *is not* predetermined)

SOCIAL CONTEXT

AGENCY

CONTEXT

Need

Purpose

Composition

Structure

Pregroup contact

Content

Pregroup Planning Model
(for use when group composition *is not* predetermined)

SOCIAL CONTEXT

AGENCY

CONTEXT

Composition

Need

Purpose

Structure

Pregroup contact

Content

Source: Kurland & Salmon, 1998, p. 209

EXHIBIT 8.6

*Pregroup
Planning
Models*

EXHIBIT 8.7

Preplanning for a Group Intervention: Parents of Teens Support Group

Your agency has experienced an increase in the number of parents of teens seeking services out of concern for their relationships with their adolescent children. Together with your supervisor and colleagues you reach a decision to form a support group for this population. You have been asked to lead this effort. Building on Kurland & Salmon's (1998) classic list of preplanning tasks, you consider the following:

Preplanning Issue/Task	Consideration for Parents of Teens Support Group
Need	62% increase in the past six months of parents of teens seeking services out of concern for their relationships with their teenage children.
Purpose	After discussion at a staff meeting, family service staff agree that parents can benefit from a reciprocal, psychoeducationally focused group intervention.
Composition, eligibility, and appropriateness	*Composition:* The group will target parents of adolescents aged 12–19 years and will not have a minimum or maximum number of participants.
	Eligibility: Based on the changing needs of the target population, the group will be open to any interested parents of teens. Participants need not currently receive services from the agency.
	Appropriateness: Due to the psychoeducational/support orientation of the group, any parents who feel they need support will be appropriate for the group. This type of group is consistent with other services your agency offers.
Structure	The group will meet monthly for 90 minutes in the agency's multipurpose room. You will serve as primary facilitator while the social work student completing practicum with you this year will serve as co-facilitator. The agency will provide refreshments and will offer child care for any parents with young children. Service learning students from a nearby university will oversee the childcare area.
Content	As the group intervention focuses on the provision of mutual aid and education, each session will begin with a brief presentation by one of the facilitators or another professional. The parents will collaborate with the co-facilitators to determine topics of interest.
	Following the presentation and discussion, members will be given the opportunity to "check-in" with one another, raise issues, and ask for input from the group regarding their concerns.

EXHIBIT 8.7

Continued

Agency context	With support from your supervisor, agency administration, and your co-workers, this group intervention helps promote the agency mission to provide services to families and children.
Social context	A psychoeducational, reciprocal support group meets a need within the community that no other agency or institution is currently meeting. Should members need additional support, your agency provides individual and family services.
Pregroup contact	Together with your social work student, you will develop a program flyer to circulate among agency staff and post on the agency's website and bulletin boards. You will also promote the program to other social service agencies that serve this population, school social workers, a community service website, and in the organization section of the local newspaper.
Contacting prospective group members	Social service professionals may refer prospective group members or prospective members may contact the agency directly. You and your social work practicum student will conduct a brief intake interview with each potential member to determine her or his appropriateness for the group. If you determine that the individual is a good fit, you will invite her or him to the first meeting.

regarding the scheduling and location of meetings and the parents' schedules, transportation, and child care needs. Keep in mind the challenges these parents face in balancing challenging parenting situations with work, the needs of other family members, and their own well-being and focus on an issue relevant to their lives rather than on something they may deem irrelevant (e.g., retirement planning). On the other hand, self-care strategies (e.g., exercise, social activities, or creative arts) may be very appealing to parents who are feeling stressed and concerned for their teenage children. The point is to know your clients' needs and respond to them in a way that is consistent with your agency's purpose. Community needs assessments, agency service statistics, and interviews with staff and clients can all provide data that can help you make these decisions.

Purpose   Consider both collective and individual objectives: What hopes will the group as a whole have? What expectations will individuals have? Ask yourself, what is the function of the group and what will your role be? The group may focus on, for example, counseling, teaching, or facilitating social action. Consider ways in which member interaction will contribute to the purpose of the group. A structured group intervention should always focus on meeting participants' goals for growth and to gain knowledge that they can apply to their own lives (Ephross, 2011). Returning to the parents of teens group in which Jasmine is a member, the group as a whole may hope to normalize the experience of living with and parenting their children during the often turbulent years of adolescents. Individual goals may be to gain strategies and wisdom for responding to the challenges of parenting an adolescent that can be gained through group member sharing and psychoeducational content.

Composition, Eligibility, and Appropriateness   Group composition refers to the number of group members and their characteristics, such as gender orientation, age, experience, skill, beliefs, and values. The major concern in determining the composition of a group is the degree of homogeneity or heterogeneity that is most condu- cive to achieving desired outcomes. In general, scholars agree that some common characteristic or situation optimally provides a unifying focus, but there should also be enough difference to sustain members' interest and the potential for growth through exposure to different ideas. Frequently, a particular condition, such as living with cancer or caregiving for a family member with a chronic illness, can bridge many differences on other dimensions, such as age or ethnic background, but these aspects should be evaluated carefully in each situation. In the case of the parents of teens group, Jasmine and the other parents share the experience of finding challenges in trying to help their children through adolescence, which can be a shared similarity, but each will bring a different lived experience, attitudes, and beliefs about their situations which can show diversity of perspectives.

In addition to individual descriptive variables, behavioral characteristics are also important. The group has the potential to be more successful if members have compatible interpersonal styles, levels of verbal development, and understandings of the potential for groups. Different types of groups will vary on the balance of these components—for example, similar ages in children's groups would probably be more important than in most adult groups. In thinking about the parents of teens group, the parents will likely be a range of ages and varying degrees of parenting experience, both of which can be an asset in the group's ability to support and guide one another.

The need and purpose of the group intervention helps determine the eligibility criteria and type of members that are appropriate for the group. As you explore the possibility of forming a group, take into consideration the focus of the group and members' ability to connect to one another. For example, consider these questions. Will caregivers of spouses with Alzheimer's disease have issues that are similar to or different from caregivers of adult children with a developmental disability? Will people in recovery from an addiction be eligible to remain in the group if they are found to have relapsed? Focusing on the goals of the group intervention will help you answer these questions and create a group who will be able to help each other.

Structure Determine if a group will be open or closed and if there will be any "trade-offs" for your particular group. What is the agency's position on this question? What challenges might you face in an open-ended group? What about challenges in a closed-ended group? What type of group will best address the short- and long-term needs of group members?

Group leadership is another area to address as you begin developing a group intervention. Will the group have a sole facilitator, or will co-facilitators better meet the needs of the group? While a single facilitator may be more economical in terms of time and financial resources, there may be compelling reasons for co-facilitation, including physical safety for members and facilitators, opportunity for a student to gain group experience, and the benefits of facilitators as role models (Ephross, 2011).

Structure also refers to the logistical arrangements of the group—location, frequency of sessions, time of meetings, and duration. Other practical questions include: What type or size of room will work best? Will group members require transportation or child care? Will there be a fee for participation in the group? How will members maintain confidentiality? What level of agency coordination will be required? Using the parents of teens group as an example, taking into consideration the parents' work and family obligations and schedules will be critical to the parents' ability to join the group. Similarly, knowing that the information that each one shares will be maintained inside the group will enable the group to share more openly and without fear of their family issues becoming public knowledge.

Content You should determine the content the group will cover by analyzing the purpose of the group, its members' needs, and agency and personnel resources. The activities or other means used to accomplish the group's purpose may require special equipment or educational or art materials. Consider the agenda and content of the meetings. Who will be responsible for making arrangements for the group, establishing timelines, creating an agenda, and developing a group purpose? If the group will use discussion, will the content facilitate interaction among members? For the parents of teens group, providing the members with an opportunity to establish their own rules, agendas, and areas to be discussed can serve to more accurately meet the parents' needs and to empower them as individuals and parents.

Agency Context Consider how the agency will affect the group and how the group will affect the agency. Specifically, do agency administration and personnel endorse group work for the population served, and is group work consistent with the agency's mission and emphasis? Do not assume you have the agency's support without confirming it. Your group is likely to have repercussions for others. For example, a children's group that meets at the agency is often noisy and may be disruptive to other staff and clients. The addition of group work to the agency's repertoire of service may increase the support staff's administrative responsibilities. Individual social workers may feel possessive of their clients and may be reticent to refer current clients to a group experience. It is to your advantage to address these and other concerns as directly as possible prior to creating the group.

Social Context   Consider social and cultural influences that may influence the group's bonding and functioning. Will the group complement other community services? Are there appropriate supports and resources for members after the group to help them maintain changes? Do members' cultural contexts support group participation? For example, if you want to facilitate a group for adolescent girls, consider whether their families will approve of and provide support for the group and their daughters' participation.

Pregroup Contact   Prior to a first meeting, consider the following questions: How will members be recruited or referred to the group? Will you conduct individual pregroup screening interviews to determine whether individuals are appropriate for the group? How will members prepare themselves for the group experience? How will you facilitate members' orientation to the group process so they can experience maximum participation and benefit? While each group and each potential member is unique, developing a plan to address these questions can enable you to assemble a group with whom you are familiar and who are already oriented to the purpose, structure, and format of the group they may be joining. While raising each of these questions is important, in general, meeting with each potential group member is an appropriate strategy for providing relevant group information to the person, for determining if she or he can benefit from a group experience, and for determining if there is a fit between the individual and the other members of the group.

Pregroup contact can also be an opportunity for the social worker and the client to discuss the client's participation in and balance with other services. The client may be receiving individual and/or family services so strategizing about ways to maximize benefits from both types of services can be helpful for the potential group member. The social worker can also let the potential group member know that, during the group experience, it is not unusual for the social worker to suggest individual or family services be initiated. The social worker can help the client who receives multiple services process and make use of the information gleaned from each of these intervention approaches.

Contacting Prospective Group Members   There are many ways to build up the membership of a prospective group and to connect with potential group work clients, including outreach and on-site service referral. **Outreach** is a method for contacting people in their homes and communities to inform them of services and information about which they may not have been aware (Barker, 2014). You may reach out to potential group members through connections with other professionals in the community (e.g., school social workers). Other times, outreach may require a more concerted coordination campaign (e.g., advertising, posting to agency website or social media, and individual contacts), particularly if potential clients fear discrimination or barriers to eligibility. It may be helpful for current group members to recruit prospective group members. Having firsthand knowledge of the group's purpose and focus can be an effective strategy for recruitment of new members.

On-site service referral is often a useful way to connect with potential members. You may, for example, recruit members from your caseload of individual clients, or you might ask your colleagues for referrals after they give you their support. Postings and announcements are helpful, but they must be paired with personal contact, such as another staff member's enthusiastic recommendation, to be effective.

In nearly all scenarios, a pregroup interview is ideal. First, it allows you to get an in-depth sense of the potential member to determine her or his "fit" with the goals and purpose of the group and whether she or he is an appropriate member. A pregroup meeting also provides an opportunity to assess any potential concerns about the person's interaction with other members of the group. It also provides the opportunity for the prospective group member to air any anxieties, to develop a sense of this new experience, to ask questions, and to make a more empowered choice about joining the group. A pregroup meeting is a time to raise questions or concerns regarding fees or costs associated with joining the group. Finally, this contact with group members is a form of engagement, assessment, and planning. As such, it requires the same level of knowledge and skills as individual engagement and assessment and planning.

You can ease a potential or new group member's entry into the group by providing online or printed information regarding the group experience. Such a document may contain information on (Brown, 2013):

- group purpose and goals;
- the format of the group and techniques, activities, and procedures that will be a part of the group experience;
- the individual's right to refuse participation;
- limitations of the group intervention;
- potential risks and benefits;
- the leader's credentials and group experience;
- the leadership of the group if the leader is not available;
- implications of any diagnoses that may have been made and the role of testing, if it occurred;
- documentation, including recordkeeping, reports, and client access to records; and
- payment process, if applicable (pp. 19–20).

Engagement

Overlapping with the important pregroup planning phase, engagement is the beginning phase of the group intervention. The *Standards for Social Work Practice with Groups* (IASWG, 2015, pp. 6–9) provides behavior guidelines for the practitioner working in the engagement or beginning phases of the group work intervention, including such pregroup activities as:

- identifying member aspirations and needs as perceived by the member, agency, and yourself;
- confirming organizational support for offering a group;
- determining the group type, structure, processes, and size that will complement group purpose and goals;
- developing strategy for and recruit potential group members;
- completing organizational requirements for admission to group;
- clarifying member goals and expectations along with the person's feelings about joining the group;
- establishing meeting time and location to ensure comfort, safety, and access;
- developing a group purpose (will be finalized during first group meeting); and
- planning group content, activities, and documentation format and obtaining needed resources.

Following the pregroup phase of work, skills and behaviors needed for continuing the engagement and assessment of group members include:

- developing contracts for explication of individual and group goals, tasks, and activities for the duration of the group and beyond;
- following your own introduction and clarification of your role in the group, inviting members to introduce themselves and to share their reasons for joining and their hopes for the group;
- in collaboration with group members, developing a clear statement of purpose, rules and norms, and roles that incorporates the individual and group member and agency goals, needs, and perceptions;
- developing, as appropriate, content, activities, and resources relevant to the group's purpose;
- highlighting common interests and goals, direct interactions, and potential linkages in order to promote group cohesion among members, and between the members and you;

- in cooperation with group members, establishing the work plan for the group for the rest of the beginning phase and for the remainder of the group's planned time together (or for the individual's time in the group if the group is open-ended and not time-limited); and

- building awareness and overt recognition of the unique characteristics of each group member, including but not limited to cultural and ethnic heritage, age, gender, sexual orientation, presenting concerns, and note that each person brings strengths to the group process.

The first session ideally begins with you and group members sharing your expectations for the group. Be transparent about what you (you alone or with a co-facilitator) hope to accomplish. Likewise, encourage members to talk about their perceptions of their roles. Confidentiality is often one of the first dimensions you will discuss, and, as you can imagine, unless all members feel safe in revealing their struggles and feelings, it is not likely that many will participate fully.

Establishing **norms**, or expected rules of conduct, creates a productive group climate and requires members to actively participate so the social worker is not in the position of dictating group regulations. The actual norms will depend on the type of group. For example, the major expectation for a socialization group for 7-year-old boys in residential treatment may be "no hitting." "No shouting" might be applicable to an anger management group, or "celebrating holidays and accomplishments" to a single-parents' group. Some groups also discourage members from contacting each other outside the group because it may dilute the group process, and others encourage it because it fosters translation of group benefits into the "real world." The primary purpose of norms should be to facilitate group members' involvement through a relatively clear set of behavioral expectations that in turn will increase their comfort in the group and encourage their maximum participation. If, for example, group members have differing cultural heritages, and some members interpret lateness as disrespectful while others view it as culturally appropriate or simply flexible, the social worker may opt to explore timeliness as an area for negotiation. Knowing the membership can help you anticipate particular issues that may affect group process. Like the interview, all of these early negotiations with group members serve as important opportunities for both engagement and ongoing assessment.

The engagement phase can be challenging for both the social worker and for group members. The social worker is trying to engage with each individual member and the group as a whole, to promote cohesion among the members themselves, to establish the group structure and format, *and* to keep the group on task and on target for the previously stated goals. Creating an environment that is safe, comfortable, and supportive is essential to group members' ability to establish rapport and engagement with the process and with you as the facilitator (Furman et al., 2014). When a group is engaged, group members become empowered to begin sharing with and supporting one another, alleviating the need for the social worker to take full responsibility for leading the group. Engaging new members or facilitators who join an established group can be challenging. The social work facilitator is responsible for engaging the new member and for encouraging the group to do the same, or, if the social worker is new to a group, he or she is responsible for reaching out to members. If members do not feel engaged in the first meeting, attrition may occur. Members who join a group voluntarily but who do not feel connected to the group or to the facilitator may feel reticent about returning to the group.

The beginning phases of group work can present challenges for group members as well. Whether the group member is voluntarily or involuntarily participating in the group, she or he may be reticent to engage with the group facilitator, fearing possibly that the facilitator does not understand the member's situation or is judging the member for life choices or circumstances. Regardless of the reasons for the member's hesitancy, the social worker can use "**tuning in**," with each of the individual members. In "tuning in" to the individual members, the social worker conveys empathy, acknowledges the reasons that the member may be reluctant to engage with the social worker or other group members, and invites feedback (Shulman, 2015). Being attentive to individual reactions and responses will ensure that individuals are not "lost" or deterred from investing in the group experience. "Tuning in" to the group members can also help to create a **therapeutic alliance** (i.e., development of a trusting working relationship) with the members of the group as individuals which can then allow the individual members to create alliances with the other members of the group (Shulman, 2015).

Assessment and Planning [EPAS 1]

As with social work practice with individuals and families, the transition from one phase of work to another is rarely linear or clearly defined and must relate both to the group and the individual members. Just as engagement can be an ongoing process, you can revisit assessment and planning throughout the duration of the group experience. Both assessment and planning logically and naturally occur as you recruit and screen potential members and again as the group forms and collaborates on the development of individual and group contracts. You may find that you need to assess and plan at different points throughout the life of the group as individual and group goals change and evolve, as members arrive and depart, and as unanticipated events influence group interactions (e.g., conflict, change of facilitator, or termination). Ongoing assessments must be conducted to establish the individual member's goals and desired outcomes, the group's outcomes, and the group processes (e.g., group cohesion and productivity) (Macgowan & Hanbidge, 2015).

Regardless of the timing and frequency assessment occurs, bringing a biopsychosocial-spiritual lens to the information is essential for the group intervention. Within the context of group practice, the biopsychosocial-spiritual assessment is a strategy both for determining the context of the client's situation, if the issues and characteristics a group member presents are consistent with those of other members, and for monitoring individual and group progress toward goals. Recall the earlier example of the group for Riverton children who had lost a family member to substance abuse or addiction. As the facilitator of this group, you may initiate a group discussion about the biopsychosocial- spiritual aspects of addictions and grief.

You can also conduct assessments to measure group-related issues such as cohesiveness (Macgowan, 2009b). Upon determining what you want to assess, you can opt to use standardized measures, observation, group member self-reports, or feedback from an external source (e.g., in person, through videos, through audio recordings).

As with any area of social work practice, group leaders must be cognizant of the ethical obligations associated with engaging and assessing members of a new group. Social work ethical guidelines dictate the following (Brown, 2013):

- All assessment techniques and instruments must have sufficient and appropriate validity and reliability.

- Group facilitators must have formal training and supervised practice assessing group members.

- Group leaders must always practice within their areas of competence.

- Group members must provide informed consent for participation in the group experience and the group leader must inform them of any information resulting from the assessment that will be shared with others (p. 23).

Planning within the assessment phase of group work often requires vigilant attentiveness and flexibility. While most group facilitators spend considerable time and effort on pregroup planning and developing an agenda or plan for each group session, the experienced group practitioner can attest to the need to be willing and able to quickly and creatively shift plans. Regardless of the type of group you are facilitating, it is likely that at any meeting a member or members will have an issue, crisis, request, or behavior that will take precedence over your plans for that session. While you will want to be responsive to each individual's needs, you must try to balance the needs of the entire group. You may be able to set aside your plans for that session to devote time to one or more specific individuals, but use caution to ensure you do not sacrifice the needs of other members or agenda items in the process.

Shulman (2011) offers the following suggestions for helping group members manage their feelings during these early phases of a group intervention:

- Reach inside the silences by asking the members of the group to share the reasons for their silences.

- Help the group member to put their feelings into words.

- Convey to the group members that you understand their feelings.

- Share your own feelings with the group members (p. 18).

STRAIGHT TALK ABOUT GROUP ENGAGEMENT AND ASSESSMENT

Acting as a facilitator or co-facilitator can help you develop important practice skills as you learn to share the helping role and some control of relationship(s) with group members and to allow the group to forge its own path. For many students and new social workers, however, learning to trust the group process and to maintain a stance of facilitator (not necessarily "leader" and certainly not "runner of") can be challenging. A tolerance for relinquishing control will serve you well. That said, despite your best efforts to refrain from controlling the group and to strive for empowering the group to assume increasing levels of power, it is important to recognize that there may be a hierarchy with you being perceived as having more power than the group members. Addressing these issues to both the group and yourself can directly diffuse any potential conflicts (Doel & Kelly, 2014). Fortunately, early anxieties regarding control and its management usually abate with experience.

When embarking on an experience in which you will serve as a group leader or facilitator, it is particularly important to think about the experience in the context of the members' participation. With that in mind, consider the following assumptions one can make about group members and their roles (Brown, 2013):

- Each group member has a unique personality and history and can make a unique contribution to the group.

- Group members are not always aware of the fantasies and fears that may influence their lives.

- Some group members may be at a crossroads in their lives that prompts fears and anxieties about group participation. Such dilemmas may present in the form of defensiveness within the group.

- Group members use different strategies to make sense of their experiences (p. 59).

Preparation

Surprisingly, many social workers fail to adequately attend to the logistics of group preparation and implementation. While it is important to consider the philosophical dimensions of launching a group intervention, equally important is logistics, such as making sure there are enough chairs, the meeting is not scheduled on a religious holiday, that all members have transportation, and that child/adult care is provided as needed. Ensure, for example, that a group for male perpetrators of violence does not meet at the same time and place as a group for their survivors. Consider competition with other known schedules, so that a parenting group does not conflict with a mothers' and children's group. While it is not possible to avoid all conflicts or awkwardness, giving thought to as many of these aspects as you can is worth the effort.

Engagement

Actively listening to the messages group members convey to you is particularly important to the engagement and assessment phases of group work (Shulman, 2009). This requires you to be aware of your own thoughts, feelings, and reactions and to have empathy for those of group members and others (e.g., family, staff, or referral sources). For example, if you are facilitating a group for Riverton residents concerned about local teens' use of alcohol and drugs, it is crucial that you "tune in" to your own experiences and feelings related to substance use and abuse and to the origins and meanings of what the Riverton residents have to say about the problem in their community. Tuning in can enable you to understand the influence your own attitudes, feelings, and experiences may have on a client situation. For example, if you grew up with a parent who is an alcoholic, you may not be completely objective when a group member in a substance abuse treatment group talks about her or his inadequacies as a parent. Listening is important to your work with any population, as it enables you to determine if you have biases, unresolved personal concerns, or conflicted values that may prevent you from objectively and empathetically serving a client.

In keeping with being in tune with the needs of group members, be mindful to use the following additional facilitative strategies (Ephross, 2011):

- Say less (as opposed to more) to avoid interfering with the group's process. You may need to play a more active role in the beginning, but your role should decrease as the group process unfolds (i.e., eventually group members should be doing approximately 80 percent of the talking).

- Recognize that the power of the intervention comes from the group interaction, not from the social worker.

- Summarize group members' discussions and provide a bridge to the next topic or area of work.

- Set limits. Use clear and transparent expectations and policies, negotiate individual and group contracts for work, and transition the group through the various phases of the group process.

Assessment and Planning

The early phases of a group experience can present unique and possibly unexpected challenges for the social worker, particularly related to the ongoing assessment and planning activities. To your surprise, you may find that group members have conflicting agendas and roles from what emerged during your assessment and not all members will be committed to supporting other members (Zandee-Amas, 2013). You may encounter situations in which your goals for the group differ from those of group members or your role as a provider of individual and family services conflicts with your role as a group facilitator. Or you may find that some members of the group are not able to or interested in productively engaging with other group members. Challenges that can occur within any group experience include: norms and patterns of nonproductivity being established by group members and conflict between group members and one or more members and the social worker (Macgowan & Hanbidge, 2015). Each of these situations relates to group member expectations and dynamics. Group members who struggle to see how the group process benefits them, particularly when compared to an individual helping relationship or in an immediate time frame, may leave the group. Group members often find that their common experiences extend beyond the group; this can lead to alliances within the group session and/or socializing outside the group. While not necessarily a problem, such relationships can be disruptive to the group process.

© Yuri Arcurs

As assessment and planning are activities that continue throughout the entirety of the group social work intervention, it is critical to have skills that will enable you to engage in evaluating the individual members' concerns and issues. Shulman (2011) offers these recommendations for helping the group members manage the issues they are facing: (1) to decrease the possibility of the members having unrealistic expectations of the social worker, regularly clarify your purpose and role in the group; (2) utilize the group members to provide feedback to one another and to you regarding the issues being raised; (3) identify and partialize the concerns being introduced; and (4) when the members bring up sensitive or "taboo" topics, provide support so the issues may be discussed openly (p. 18).

Documentation

Another logistical detail that social workers sometimes fail to adequately address is that of documenting the group experience. While documenting the process of the group experience presents a unique set of challenges, it need not be an overwhelming or complex task. Documenting any group experience serves a range of purposes. It records (1) the group process, including interactions and dynamics; (2) assessments and evaluation of individual and group change and outcomes; (3) group leadership skills; (4) referrals; and (5) accountability for payment and the sponsoring organization (Doel & Kelly, 2014; IASWG, 2015). Typically, the facilitator maintains two separate records of the group experiences. The group's record includes information on attendance, general themes, cohesion, interactions, and plans, while documentation in the individual group members' record includes only information regarding that client and her or his goals, needs, etc. In order to protect individual client confidentiality, the names of other group members should not be included in an individual client's documentation. Typically, these two records are never co-mingled in the same paper or electronic record; the only exception to this would be if the records are subpoenaed by the court. At that point, the social worker would need to clarify for the court record that the information contained in the group document on any members not related to the court action should be redacted to protect their confidentiality.

Documentation should reflect the tenor and flow of the session itself. For example, if you are using a solution-focused approach, your assessment documentation should focus on solutions rather than problems (De Jong & Berg, 2013). Exhibit 8.8 provides samples of documentation that you might include for assessing potential members of a client-oriented group, while Exhibit 8.9 provides a list of questions a social worker can ask an individual client to assess and document whether she or he is appropriate for membership in the group.

EXHIBIT 8.8

Intervention Plan Information to Include in a Group Assessment

AGENCY/ORGANIZATION NAME

GROUP NAME

Demographic Data:

- Name
- Contact information
- Legal status and needs
- Group participation needs (e.g., child or adult care needs, transportation, etc.)
- Presenting concerns as they relate to the group purpose or focus
- Current living situation (level of stability, support, safety)
- Social environment (level of activity, satisfaction, relationships with others)
- Cultural environment (client satisfaction with and views on help-seeking and cultural views of help-seeking, particularly in the group environment)
- Religion/spirituality (statement of beliefs and levels of activity and satisfaction)
- Military experience (branch, time in service, discharge status, coping with experience, view of experience)
- Childhood (supportive of the client, strengths, and significant events—including trauma)
- Family (composition—parents, siblings, spouse/significant other(s), children, and others; level of support; family history of mental illness)
- Sexual history (activity level, orientation, satisfaction, concerns)
- Trauma history (physical, sexual, and/or emotional abuse or neglect and experience with perpetrator(s))
- Financial/employment circumstances (employment status, satisfaction, financial stability, areas of concern or change)
- Educational history (highest level achieved, performance, goals, challenges)
- Substance use/abuse (history of addictive behaviors, alcohol, drugs, gambling, sexual, other)

History of Emotional/Behavioral Functioning:

For each of the following areas, gather information regarding current status (current, previous, or denies history), description of behavior, onset and duration, and frequency.

- Self-mutilation
- Hallucinations
- Delusions or paranoia
- Mood swings
- Recurrent or intrusive recollections of past events
- Lack of interest or pleasure
- Feelings of sadness, hopelessness, isolation, or withdrawal
- Decreased concentration, energy, or motivation
- Anxiety
- Crying spells
- Appetite changes
- Sleep changes

EXHIBIT 8.8

Continued

- Inability to function at school or work
- Inability to control thoughts or behaviors (impulses)
- Irritability or agitation
- Reckless behavior, fighting, or fire setting
- Stealing, shoplifting, or lying
- Cruelty to animals
- Aggression

Past and Current Behavioral Health Treatment History (i.e., individual, family, and/or other group experiences):

- Date(s)
- Program or facility
- Provider
- Response to treatment

Mental Status Exam:

- Attention (rate on scale of good, fair, easily distracted, or highly distractible, and describe behavior)
- Affect (rate on scale of appropriate, changeable, expansive, constrictive, or blunted, and describe behavior)
- Mood (rate on scale of normal, depressed, anxious, or euphoric, and describe behavior)
- Appearance (rate on scale of well groomed, disheveled, or inappropriate, and describe behavior)
- Motor activity (rate on scale of calm, hyperactive, agitated, tremors, tics, or muscle spasms, and describe behavior)
- Thought process (rate on scale of intact, circumstantial, tangential, flight of ideas, or loose associations, and describe behavior)
- Thought content (note normal, grandiose, phobic, reality, organization, worthless, obsessive, compulsion, guilt, delusional, paranoid, ideas of reference, and hallucinations, and describe behavior)
- Memory (note normal, recent (good or impaired), past (good or impaired), and describe behavior)
- Intellect (note normal, above, below, or poor abstraction, and describe behavior)
- Orientation (note person, place, situation, and time, and describe behavior)
- Judgment and insight (rate on scale of good, fair, or poor, and describe behavior)
- Current providers (including psychiatrist, primary care physician, therapist, caseworker, etc.)
- Community resources being used (including support groups, religious, spiritual, other)
- Client goal(s) for treatment
- Summary, including social worker's assessment of client "fit" with the group (see Exhibit 8.9 for assessment questions).

Source: Adapted from St. Anthony's Medical Center, 2010; Safe Connections, n.d.

EXHIBIT 8.9

Screening Questions for Group Assessment

When you determine a client's appropriateness for membership in the group, you ensure the emotional and physical safety of all group members. The following list of general questions can help you evaluate clients for possible group membership.

- How does the client respond to opinions, thoughts, and insights that differ from her or his own?
- When the client becomes angry or upset, what is her or his reaction and thought process?
- Is the client able to express her or his emotions in an appropriate way? Does the client assume responsibility for the emotion?
- What triggers the client's emotional responses?
- What is the client's developmental age? Is the client able to cope with negative emotions and thoughts at a level appropriate to the developmental level of other group members?
- Does the client demonstrate:
  - Impulse control challenges?
  - Appropriate boundaries?
  - Self-awareness?
  - Self-destructive behaviors?
  - Potential to monopolize or disrupt the group?
  - Ability to respond to social cues?
  - Sensitivity toward others?
  - Potential for personal growth?
  - Appropriate group interaction behaviors?
  - Difficulty making decisions?
- Might the client's behavior limit group participation or benefit?
- If the client is currently experiencing a crisis, will the benefits of participating in the group outweigh risks for the client?

Source: Adapted from Safe Connections (n.d.)

While the documentation of the work of nonclient groups—social goals/action and task groups—may include some of the same basic information you would record with a client group (e.g., attendance, themes, and plans), the focus is more typically directed toward recording actions and decisions. Often compiled in the form of minutes or notes, the documentation of group process and outcomes for social action/goals or task groups emphasizes the work being completed as opposed to the interactions among group members. See Quick Guides 25 and 26 for templates you can use to record the work of nonclient groups. Quick Guide 25 provides a template for a matrix-style record, while Quick Guide 26 provides an outline for a narrative-style document.

QUICK GUIDE 25   TASK GROUP NOTES TEMPLATE

AGENCY / ORGANIZATION NAME
GROUP NAME

Date
Present:
Absent:
Minutes submitted by:

ISSUE	DISCUSSION	FOLLOW-UP/ RECOMMENDATIONS	PERSON(S) RESPONSIBLE
Call to Order			
Minutes			
Announcements			
Old Business			
New Business			
Adjournment			
Future Meetings			

QUICK GUIDE 26   TASK GROUP MINUTES TEMPLATE

Agency / Organization Name
Group Name
Date

In attendance:
Absent:

1. Call meeting to order
2. Review meeting agenda
3. Review minutes from previous meeting
4. Announcements
5. Old business
6. New business
7. Adjournment and next steps

Respectfully submitted,
[Note taker's name and title]

Regardless of the challenges you may encounter as a group facilitator or leader, maintaining a transparent, open, and equitable style will best serve you and the group. Remember, the "basic reason for doing group work is the power of the group, *not the worker*" (Ephross, 2011, p. 13). Gaining as much group experience as possible throughout your social work education, particularly as facilitator or leader, can prepare you for being a contributing member and capable leader throughout your social work career. As we continue to explore social work practice with groups in Chapter 9, consider the valuable lessons you can learn from experiencing different roles within a group, including member, facilitator, and observer.

GRAND CHALLENGE

End Homelessness

The American Academy of Social Work and Social Welfare Grand Challenges for Social Work Initiative identifies one of the areas the profession should address is to end homelessness. The authors of Grand Challenge Working Paper No. 9, *The Grand Challenge of Ending Homelessness* (Henwood et al., 2015) emphasize that philosophy regarding homelessness has shifted from management and reduction to elimination:

> To eradicate all forms of homelessness in 10 years, interdisciplinary and cross-sector collaboration will be necessary for accurately assessing the scope of the problem; improving data; establishing innovative and clear solution to family, youth, and other subpopulation homelessness; and disseminating existing effective solutions. Ending homelessness cannot be accomplished simply by focusing on how best to respond to individuals who experience homelessness; it will require ongoing effort to address the structural, macro-level factors of poverty and income inequality (p. 4).

With the profession's expertise in working across all levels of social work practice, social work can and should have a significant role in the effort to end homelessness. However, new strategies are needed to provide housing and access adequate health care and educational opportunities. The authors of the Grand Challenge charge the social work profession to engage in such innovative activities as: gather evidence to accurately measure the number of persons who are homeless, particularly those who are transient or hidden, and evaluate the efficacy of interventions; better utilize community resources and services; promote evidence-based intervention practices; and identify and leverage funding to support interventions (p. 14). These activities could involve the extensive use of task groups among a wide variety of professionals, including social workers, working in an array of settings, such as government agencies, nonprofit social service agencies, and for-profits (e.g., banks and other lenders).

To familiarize yourself with the issues related to ending homelessness, visit the Grand Challenges website and read Working Paper No. 9, *The Grand Challenge of Ending Homelessness* (Henwood et al., 2015) at: http://aaswsw.org/grand-challenges-initiative/12-challenges/end-homelessness/. (See Exercise #a1 for additional exploration of this Grand Challenge within the context of the Riverton community.)

CONCLUSION

This chapter advocates for social work practitioners to address the culturally imposed isolation of many individuals through groups. We have explored some of the exciting adventures into group work using contemporary theoretical perspectives in the pursuit of social justice. Group work can provide opportunities to address issues related to social justice, diversity, and human rights connections that give social work its meaning.

Chapter 9 will turn to the next phases of social work practice with groups. Building on preplanning, engagement, and assessment work, the social worker–facilitated group moves first into the intervention or middle phase of work and then to the termination, evaluation (or ending), and follow-up phases of the group experience.

MAIN POINTS

- All people are members of groups that provide meaning to their lives and interactions and critical human connections. Western culture tends to de-emphasize the gifts and powers of group connection.

- Group work in the social work profession remains a vital part of practice that lends itself especially to social justice, diversity, and human rights perspectives.

- Organizing a group requires careful planning and continuous consideration of the value the work to the group as a whole and its individual members.

- Traditional theoretical models for group work include the task group, social action or goals model, the reciprocal model, and the remedial model.

- Social work group practice employs a variety of theoretical frameworks. This chapter highlighted strengths and empowerment, narrative-focused, and solution-focused perspectives.

- Engaging and assessing group members individually and collectively from a biopsychosocial-spiritual perspective is the first step in group formation.

- While primarily completed during the beginning phases of group work, engagement and assessment can be ongoing aspects of the group experience. The fluid and evolving nature of group work can result in changing membership and leadership, new and unexpected issues, and interpersonal dynamics and conflicts that can influence the course of the group intervention.

EXERCISES

a. Case Exercises

1. To apply your learning of the Grand Challenge to end homelessness that was highlighted in this chapter, visit the Grand Challenges website and read Working Paper No. 9, *The Grand Challenge of Ending Homelessness* (Henwood et al., 2015) at: http://aaswsw.org/grand-challenges-initiative/12-challenges/end-homelessness/. To examine the issue of homelessness in the Riverton community, review the case information at www.routledgesw.com/caseStudies. After reading Working Paper No. 9 and reviewing the information on Riverton, complete the following items:

   a. Using the town map, sociogram and interaction matrix (matching the homeless community icon with each of the other community entities), prepare an analysis of the homelessness situation in Riverton.

   b. Develop a plan for engaging members and organizations in Riverton in group work using task groups and conducting an assessment of homelessness in Riverton, including but not limited to identifying potential partners, strengths, barriers, and resources needed.

2. Go to www.routledgesw.com/cases, review Carla Washburn's video vignette, and complete the following tasks:

   a. Summarize the group's activities as depicted in the vignettes.

   b. Document the group practice behaviors that the social worker, Shannon, uses.

   c. Identify any potential challenges that may occur in a group intervention with the members of this group.

   d. Brainstorm the next steps you would take as a social worker facilitating this group.

2. Review the Carla Washburn video vignette and explore options for facilitating this group using a range of different approaches, including the following:

   a. Psychoeducational group

   b. Reciprocal group

   c. Remedial group

   Now respond to the following questions:

   a. How does the focus of each group differ?

   b. How does the social worker's role differ in each group?

   c. What engagement skills did the social worker use?

   d. Using the case vignette as an example, role-play with classmates the group as one of each of the following:

      1. psychoeducational

      2. reciprocal

      3. remedial

3. Go to www.routledgesw.com/cases and review the case for Brickville, focusing on Virginia Stone and her family. In the Intervention section, review Vignette

#3, which describes the use of a social action group intervention focused on Virginia's efforts to save the park memorializing her family members who were lost in an apartment fire twenty years earlier. Using the information available to you, develop a written plan for:

a. Determining the need for this group

b. Identifying the purpose a task group would serve in this situation

c. Propose appropriate group composition and each member's potential contributions

d. Develop your thoughts regarding group structure (e.g., meeting time and place, documenting group activity, and leadership) and content

e. Reflect on the meaning of forming this group in the context of the agency and the community

f. Describe your plans for initiating pregroup contact, engaging group members, and assessing members' potential commitment and contributions

g. Assess available and needed resources and potential barriers to success

4. Go to www.routledgesw.com/cases and review the case for Hudson City. Recall from Chapters 6 and 7 that the Patel family experienced significant impact from Hurricane Diane. Several weeks after the hurricane, Sheetal (wife of Hemant and mother of Rakesh, Kamal, and Aarti) confides in you that she is concerned that her 12-year-old daughter, Aarti, is not coping well with life following the hurricane and the family's displacement from their home and restaurant. They have been able to return to their home and are working on re-opening the restaurant. Aarti has returned to her school, but she continues to have nightmares about the storm, is uncomfortable being away from her parents, and seems to have less of an appetite. Other parents whose families were affected by the storm are expressing similar concerns, both to you and to your co-workers. Describe in writing your plan for developing a group intervention to address the needs of children who survived the hurricane, including:

- Type of group approach (include format and structure)
- Plans for member eligibility, recruitment, and parent involvement
- Strategies for engaging group members in a culturally competent manner, keeping in mind the diversity of the community and its large immigrant population
- Strategies for assessing group members' appropriateness for the group

5. Go to www.routledgesw.com/cases and review the case for Riverton, then, referring back to the discussion of the Riverton community's concerns about alcohol consumption at the beginning of this chapter and Exhibits 8.3, 8.4, and 8.5 in this chapter, conduct a search of the literature on group-level practice in order to find evidence to support development of the following group interventions:

a. Riverton Against Youth Drinking (RAYD): evidence-based practices for facilitating social goals groups on teen drinking.

b. Riverton Children's Grief Support Group: evidence-based practices for facilitating reciprocal groups with children.

c. Riverton Mental Health Center Groups for Persons with Co-Occurring Diagnoses: evidence-based practices for facilitating a treatment group for this population and for incorporating new members into an existing group.

b. Other Exercises

6. As a skilled individual and group practice social worker at a local community health center, you have several young clients who have been diagnosed with attention deficit hyperactivity disorder (ADHD). The clients are Hispanic children between 6 and 8 years of age. When they come to pick up their children, you notice that some of their parents appear sad about their children, while others appear anxious, frustrated, or angry. The children themselves seem somewhat isolated and all are experiencing social, academic, and behavioral problems in school.

   Assume that you have the time, interest, and agency support to offer to form and lead a group. Choose one of the following interventions from this list that you think will be the most helpful:

   a. A play/social skills group for the children
   b. A support group for the parents
   c. A psychoeducational group for the parents
   d. An empowerment group for the children

   Be prepared to provide a rationale for your choice to your classmates. How might one choice intersect with another? Compare with peers.

7. You work for a child welfare organization and are facilitating a support group for adolescent females who have recently given birth and are preparing to return to their high schools. In some cases, the babies' grandparents are helping with their care, and some babies have been adopted through the agency. Some of the group members have concerns about returning to school while others are eager to get back into a "normal" social life. Most group members are participating well, although one member, Janine, has said almost nothing in the first three meetings. All members of the group are African American. You are a white, 23-year-old female social work practicum student.

   At the beginning of the fourth meeting, the mood of the entire group seems contentious. After you share in brief preliminary pleasantries and restate the agenda for this session, you realize that Janine is quietly crying in the corner. At the same time, two of the other members start calling your name angrily, competing for your attention. They tell you they are annoyed at the group, at the plan for today, at the agency, and at Janine who is sitting there acting like a "baby."

   Respond to the following:

   a. Identify two skills from the chapter that you would use in this situation and give an example of the way in which you would use these skills.

   b. Provide a rationale for your selection of these particular skills. What results do you expect from the use of these skills?

   c. Which of the models described in this chapter offers the best explanation for these group dynamics?

8. Attend a mutual aid group in the community and write a reflection about your experience.

   a. Describe the group type, purpose, and structure.

   b. Identify group leader and member roles.

   c. Reflect on your previous experiences as a group member. What role do you often play? Why? Do you want to do things differently?

9. In small groups of three or four, create your own social action group.

   a. Identify an issue of mutual interest to group members.

   b. Determine the roles for each member.

   c. Develop a plan of action for the group. Prepare a presentation for the class.

10. Your field instructor at your practicum has invited you to join her in co-facilitating a psychoeducational support group for persons who serve as caregivers for a family member experiencing Parkinson's disease. Most members of the group are wives and adult daughters. In addition to co-leading the group each session, your field instructor has suggested that you assume responsibility for leading one session on a topic of your choice that will be relevant for this group. This is your first group work experience, and you are unfamiliar with this medical condition. To accomplish your task:

   a. Review the literature to learn about Parkinson's disease.

   b. Develop a plan for the session that you will lead, including identifying a relevant topic and strategies for engaging the group members in the discussion.

Social Work Practice with Groups: Intervention, Termination, and Evaluation

I found myself slipping into that self-trashing thing, man, you know, putting myself down, thinking and saying I'm a dumb broad, ugly and worthless, just like J. used to tell me. But they got on me, those awesome women! They told me I was breaking the friggin' rules! Me! Breaking the rules, and then I remembered what they meant. We're not doing that stuff in this group. The end. Not okay. They are really the most awesome! What would I be without them?

Marcy (of the Debbie, Joan, Marcy,
and Kate Group for Survivors of Intimate Partner Violence)

Key Questions for Chapter 9

1. What competencies do I need to intervene, terminate, and evaluate with clients at the group level of social work practice? [EPAS 8 and 9]
2. How can I use evidence to practice research-informed practice and practice-informed research to guide the evaluation of a group I am facilitating? [EPAS 4]
3. What is the appropriate response for a social worker leading a group if one group member violates the confidentiality of another member of the group? [EPAS 1]
4. What is the distinction between the appropriate social worker role in facilitating an intervention with a self-help support group and a therapy group? [EPAS 8]

From the perspective of social work practice with groups, there are multiple opportunities to work with the Stone family of the Brickville neighborhood (www.routledgesw.com/cases), including: (1) Virginia Stone, who is a family caregiver of her mother who may benefit from participation in a support group for caregivers of older adults; (2) Virginia's son, David, a participant in the Brickville Community Development Corporation's Youth Leadership Program (YLP) who is developing his leadership skills by serving as the Chair of the youth-led Committee for Healthy Teens; (3) Virginia's two granddaughters, Tiffany and Suzanna, who are the children of an incarcerated parent and are both having behavior and academic challenges in school that might be addressed in group work; and (4) the trauma of the tragic fire twenty years ago and the family's sense of racial bias by the fire and police departments has been reignited by incidents that have occurred across the U.S. from which groups like Black Lives Matter have emerged.

THE EFFICACY OF SOCIAL WORK PRACTICE INTERVENTIONS, terminations, evaluations, and follow-up with groups stems from effective engagement and assessment. The middle and ending phases of work—the interventions, terminations, and evaluations—are the parts of the group experience in which the "majority of the work of the groups gets accomplished" and is "the time to consolidate the work of the group" (Toseland & Horton, 2013, para. 22, 23). Terminations and evaluations are complex because of the dual focus on both the individual and the group.

To complete our exploration of social work practice with groups, this chapter follows the group experience from the development of the intervention process through the termination, evaluation, and follow-up phases. We will focus on theoretical frameworks for group interventions and models of group intervention and look at the social work behaviors you will need to intervene with groups. The chapter then examines the final phase of the group intervention: termination, evaluation, and follow-up. To set the stage for delving into the middle and ending stages of group work practice, let us first consider social justice, diversity, and human rights.

INTERFACE: SOCIAL JUSTICE, DIVERSITY, AND HUMAN RIGHTS [EPAS 3]

Social work with groups is a natural setting for practitioners who are committed to social justice, diversity, and/or human rights concerns. As discussed elsewhere in this book, much of social injustice is rooted in exclusion—from resources, opportunities, respect, and supports. This kind of exclusion is especially evident in the experiences of those persons and groups who are considered by society as "other" or

© Glynnis Jones

different. Those may be persons with disabilities; persons of color; people living in poverty; people from other racial or ethnic backgrounds; older adults; persons who are gay, lesbian, bisexual, transgender, or questioning—unfortunately the list is long (see Greif & Ephross, 2011). The most appropriate and effective social work response to diversity within the group intervention is a subject of ongoing debate. For example, are group interventions more effective if the group is heterogeneous or homogenous? Most scholars agree that evidence-based practice is critical for group work; therefore, social workers must provide evidence to support the intervention(s) and to inform the decision to offer a heterogeneous or a homogenous group structure (Toseland & Horton, 2013). The need for supporting group work with evidence will be discussed within this chapter. Diverse groups reflect the world in which most people live, but not all individuals may feel comfortable or safe taking personal risks around others who are different from them in some way meaningful to them, or with others whose reasons for joining the group are different from their own. In addition to utilizing research on group diversity to inform and guide interventions, social workers can also benefit by examining their own views (including their own "isms") on the groups (e.g., population, ethnicity, and affiliations) they will be bringing together for a group intervention (Toseland & Horton, 2013). Social workers must also factor in their prior life and professional experience and the preferences of the members of the group.

Group work practice brings people together in meaningful ways that can serve as a forum for increasing understanding, appreciation, and respect for others. In short, group membership can reduce the effects of exclusion and the injustices associated with feelings of marginalization. When working with groups, you can identify, establish, articulate, and mediate the rights and the needs of group members. This can be an important and empowering experience for those who may have rarely (or never) understood their own social contexts in terms that affirmed their rights as human beings (Kurland et al., 2004), and model such behavior for other members of the group. Viewing group intervention as reinforcing human rights can further integrate human rights practice into the profession.

Approaching group work with a focus on social justice requires a commitment to learning about and embracing a number of conceptual foundations. Singh and Salazar (2011) suggest that social justice-oriented group work is based on the following foundations:

- *The centrality of multicultural competence:* Social workers must strive to become culturally competent with many different cultures (multicultural competence) throughout their entire social work career. The diversity of our contemporary society means that, as a social worker, you will routinely interact with and serve a wide range of individuals who are members of various groups; thus, the need for not just cultural competence, but *multi*-cultural competence and cultural humility becomes paramount to your practice.

- *The interplay between content and process:* A commitment to a social justice orientation enables the social worker conducting groups to address the substance and interactions related to social inequities and oppression that may occur in any group setting and among the group members.

- *The influence of privilege and oppression:* Delving into the impact of group leader and members' experiences with privilege and oppression is critical for social justice-oriented group work. Questions to consider may include: "What are group members' needs, perceptions, experiences, and wants with regard to the injustices they face? What are their efforts toward their own empowerment and freedom from self-blame? How are these injustices experienced by others in the community? How do community members, both individually and collectively, define and perceive empowerment?" (p. 218).

- *Effects on power dynamics within and outside groups:* Emphasizing issues of power within the group can and should have the added benefit of empowering group members to engage in advocacy and change in other areas of their lives.

THEORETICAL APPROACHES TO INTERVENING WITH GROUPS [EPAS 4]

Just as there are many theoretical models for social work intervention with individuals and families, there are well-developed theoretical approaches related to group interventions, processes, skills, and ending points. When the social worker subscribes to a specific theoretical perspective, she or he can use the theory to guide the formation of the group, define roles, and impact group dynamics to guide the content of the group experience (Macgowan, 2013).

In this section, we will continue our examination of theory-driven approaches to group practice. Following an overview of theoretical applications to group interventions, we will explore several classic, contemporary, and developmental models. Later, we will look at intervention skills, examples of current groups, and, finally, contemporary innovations in group work.

Strengths and Empowerment Perspectives on Group Intervention

As you recall from Chapter 8, this book is grounded in the premise that social workers should approach practice with groups from a strengths orientation. A strengths approach can affirm and motivate the individual's change process through a focus on "possibilities versus problems." The strengths perspective helps identify and integrate individual members' strengths into strengths for the whole group. For example, within the intervention itself, the social worker can use group members' strengths for a range of purposes, including developing individual and group goals and sharing resources. Individual strengths can serve as models when group members share ideas and resources. For example, the group member who has experienced multiple losses in her life (Virginia Stone from Brickville, for instance) and continues to remain strong can serve as a role model for other group members. Approaching the group intervention from a strengths-based perspective requires the social worker to help create an environment in which all group members accept the following three norms (Benard & Truebridge, 2013):

- *Participation:* Group members recognize one other as equal participants, each with the same rights and opportunities.

- *Communication:* Interactions among group members and the facilitator must be respectful (e.g., everyone should be allowed to speak without interruption or side conversations).

- *Interactions:* In order for all group members to contribute equally, members and the group leader should be committed to arriving on time and staying for the duration of the group (p. 215).

A strengths-based perspective integrates easily with other theoretically-driven intervention approaches, such as the empowerment perspective. Arising from an ecological perspective, empowerment-focused group interventions align with a strengths perspective in their emphasis on addressing social injustices and fostering reciprocal connections with members' environments (Hudson, 2009, p. 48). Within this context, empowerment is a process as well as an outcome that encompasses the personal (individual person), the interpersonal (interactions between persons), and the social (interactions within society) (Cattaneo & Goodman, 2015). In **empowerment groups**, committing to joining a group can itself support the personal and interpersonal dimensions as well as the empowerment felt from helping and receiving help from other members. Critical analysis of the political environment and individuals' participation in change efforts is also important to the empowerment process. This means that group members are empowered from the earliest planning for the group and participate in the identification of needs (Breton, 2006).

In helping to negotiate a change between group members and their environment, the social worker's role is to collaborate with members to mediate between them and the entities or issues within their environment that create oppression or injustice (Hudson, 2009). The social worker is a "co-activist," working with the group to achieve their goals. Such an approach works with many types of group interventions, including social goals/action and reciprocal mutual aid groups.

Recall Georgia's situation from Chapter 1: Georgia experienced intimate partner violence, and after working with a social worker individually, she joined an empowerment group with other women who had been in violent relationships. This group supported Georgia's needs for esteem and dignity; offered her the opportunity to identify her priorities (for example, have a viable safety plan, stable work situation, and protect her children); built new skills so she might competently access needed information, services, and help; and enhanced her self-efficacy through increased confidence, sense of community, and asking for and accepting help (Cattaneo & Goodman, 2015). The quote from Marcy, another survivor of intimate partner violence, that opens this chapter, shows us just how powerful the group process can be.

Narrative Theory and Group Interventions

Building on a strengths- and empowerment-focused engagement and assessment process, a narrative approach to intervening with groups emphasizes, not only the collaboration between the client and the social worker, but also the collaboration among group members. A narrative-oriented group intervention requires the social worker and group members to listen to each member's voice and to aid in the deconstruction and subsequent reconstruction of the individual or group "story" (i.e., their experience through their own perspective). In the case of a mutual aid or therapy group, stories are individual, but in a social goals/action group, the "story" may be the group's story. Reshaping individual or group perceptions can provide a basis for setting a plan in motion for members to achieve the unique outcome the individual group member(s) desire(s). Group members can then work together to brainstorm and process members' motivations, options, and behaviors.

One of the hallmarks of the narrative approach is the use of witness groups and community supports. The social worker calls people together into **witness groups** to "witness" discussions between the social worker and the client and/or among group members. In the case of a group intervention, group members are in place to serve as witnesses to their own discussions. Known as the outside-witness group (because they are outside the individual's personal situation), these group members both contribute to, and listen to, dialogues and provide feedback to the social worker and to individual group members (Morgan, 2000). Such feedback can include questions, observations, and interpretations. The individual receiving feedback may then ask questions and respond. This process can help the client develop an alternative approach to her or his current dilemma or concern.

Using "insider" knowledge (i.e., hearing from others with similar life experiences) is a staple of the narrative approach. Group interventions are good opportunities to use this practice strategy, particularly if group members share similar life experiences and are at different phases of those experiences. For example, Hall (2011) describes how a social worker used a narrative approach with a group of males who had battered their partners. Using narrative strategies, the group leader was able to work with group members to address issues of male power, privilege, and entitlement by externalizing the violence outside of the individual. This helped the males in the group to gain insight into the origins of their belief systems, which freed them to determine if they wished to continue their behavior or to change (Hall, 2011, p. 180). Understanding the beliefs that underpin your behavior promotes assuming responsibility for one's choices. As noted in Chapter 8, narrative approaches are also well suited to many other theoretical frameworks.

Solution-Focused Group Interventions

Solution-focused interventions with groups are similar to family interventions and require the same knowledge and skills. During the beginning phases of group work, you asked clients a series of questions to identify their desired new realities and the strengths and resources available to help achieve the clients' goals for change (De Jong, 2013b). When you develop a solution-focused intervention plan, you can ask clients to reconsider the "miracle," "exceptions," and "scaling" questions to solidify the plan for change. While you pose these questions to individual group members, the entire group can contribute to the development, implementation, and evaluation of individual change plans, and they can continue to be a resource throughout the change process, presenting their own questions, observations, and experiences. Once the plan is developed and underway, you can monitor members' progress by asking group members to describe the changes they are experiencing (i.e., "What's better?").

Solution-focused approaches at all levels can be used in conjunction with other approaches (e.g., solution-focused, empowerment, and narrative therapy approaches) to enhance the effectiveness and accountability of interventions. De Jong and Berg (2013b) suggest that social workers implement a solution-focused intervention with a group after becoming competent with solution-focused work with individuals and families.

The solution-focused group intervention is well suited for a variety of client populations and settings. With its emphasis on positive changes in the client's life and client-developed individualized treatment plans, this intervention has reaped promising outcomes with adults, adolescents, and children and with involuntary clients (Greene & Lee, 2011). When used with adults who are incarcerated, in mental health settings (in- and out-patient), and in substance abuse treatment programs, solution-focused interventions "can often be like doing individual therapy in front of a group" (Greene & Lee, 2011, p. 203) when individual clients are engaged in dialogue about their individual situation in front of the group.

The integration of solution-focused group interventions with adolescents and children is equally promising. Social workers and their adolescent and child clients can build solution-focused group interventions around a specific topic or theme. In addition, their brief time-limited format, flexibility, future-oriented focus, and de-emphasis on problem "talk" makes solution-focused group interventions particularly well-suited to work with adolescents and children (Greene & Lee, 2011).

Developmental Models

One of the classic theoretical perspectives on group work, the **developmental model**, is based on the assumption that group members (individually and collectively) grow and change as the group process unfolds. Developmental models assume that groups change and grow in semipredictable ways. This assumption does not mean groups go through rigid progressions but rather that group relationships ripen. Members are perhaps ambivalent about joining the group at the beginning. Then they jockey for position within the membership, grow closer together through the work of the group, establish differences from one another, and finally separate at the group's ending. This perspective reflects the idea of stages (also referred to as phases) and has been extremely influential in contemporary group work. Developmental models are still the norm in many practice contexts. They are frequently useful in alerting the social worker to possible dynamics, gauging what is happening, and thinking about how to intervene. We now examine two different developmental models—the Boston Model and the relational model.

Boston Model   First developed at Boston University's School of Social Work, the **Boston Model** outlines five stages of group development: preaffiliation, power and control, intimacy, differentiation, and separation (Garland, Jones, & Kolodny, 1965).

- During **preaffiliation**, members may feel some ambivalence or reservations about joining the group as well as excitement and eagerness. For example, someone joining a support group for people diagnosed with an illness may be eager to connect with others who have a similar experience but may at the same time wonder if she or he will find others in the group who share common experiences, fears, and needs.

- In the **power and control stage**, members vie for influence and status within the group. In a support group for individuals who share a diagnosis, members who are further along in their illness, treatment, or recovery may perceive themselves as having more status and influence than those who are recently diagnosed.

- **Intimacy** occurs when group members, having worked through their power issues, become closely connected; they may seem more homogeneous at this stage than at any other time in the group. Having processed the issues of power and control, they can begin to support each other around their common life experiences. Members will often share coping strategies and develop relationships outside of the group sessions to help each other through crises.

- During **differentiation**, members feel they are safe enough to express and value the differences among themselves and the worker; the homogeneity of the former phase matures into a respect for difference. In this phase, members of an illness support group may become comfortable enough to confront one another on differences of opinion, coping behaviors, or lack of compliance. Such confrontations can occur successfully only when members have reached a point of mutual respect for one another.

- In the final stage, **separation**, members begin to withdraw from the group in anticipation of its ending. Members of an illness support group may separate as they finish treatment, recover, or learn that their illness is terminal.

Although the creators of the Boston Model propose a general progression through these stages, they do not assume that progress will occur as a rigidly linear sequence. There are likely to be points in the life of a group at which one or more members seem to loop back to the behavior typical of a previous stage or tend to jump ahead to another one. See Quick Guide 27 for ways these developmental stages can be applied to three different group populations. As you can see in the Quick Guide, some of the groups exhibit these stages in slightly different orders than the Boston Model, or skip some stages. While these phases of group process are not typically associated with task groups, one could argue they are, in fact, relevant for work with tasks groups since task groups form, bond, and progress through similar relationship-building stages.

Other models of group development divide the stages slightly differently, and some include additional substages. The group population also influences the degree

QUICK GUIDE 27   APPLICATIONS OF THE BOSTON MODEL PROTOTYPE TO THREE POPULATIONS

	BOSTON PROTOTYPE	FEMINIST	FEMALE ADOLESCENT FOSTER CARE GROUP	OLDER INSTITUTIONALIZED PERSONS: FLOOR GROUP
	Garland, Jones & Kolodny, 1965	*Schiller, 1995, 1997*	*Lee & Berman-Rossi, 1999*	*Berman-Rossi & Kelly, 1997*
Stage 1	Preaffiliation	Preaffiliation	Preaffiliation: • Approach-Avoidance • Power and Control	Approach-Avoidance
Stage 2	Power and Control	Establishment of a Relational Base	Intimacy and Flight	Intimacy
Stage 3	Intimacy	Mutuality and Interpersonal Empathy	Differentiation	Power and Control 1: Challenging the Institution
Stage 4	Differentiation	Challenge and Change	Termination	Power and Control 2: Challenging the Worker
Stage 5	Termination	Termination		Differentiation & Empowerment

Source: Adapted from Berman-Rossi & Kelly, 2003

to which members progress through the phases and the ways in which they progress. For example, in an application with an online group of nurses developing best practices, Kelly, Lowndes, and Tolson (2005) found that separate stages emerged, including preaffiliation, work/intimacy, work/amalgamation, with a return to work/intimacy, and group development was influenced by member characteristics, structure, and group purpose.

With its emphasis on power and control, the Boston Model may be most appropriate for use with group members who are more comfortable with competition, power, and conflict (e.g., younger groups) and groups that can move through stages quickly and with independence from the facilitator (Schiller, 2007).

Relational Model   Feminist theorists and practitioners established the relational model in response to developmental theory building that excludes women. Many feminists challenge Erik Erikson's famous male-normed psychosocial sequence of life stages on the grounds that he stereotyped girls as being concerned with "inner space" and boys with "outer space." Some feminists believe the intimacy stage, a clearly relational dimension, actually precedes the identity stage in girls, which reverses Erikson's order. Over two decades ago, Carol Gilligan (1993) suggested that the identity and intimacy stages are intertwined in girls.

The feminist orientation to the importance of the relational aspects of development appears in group work models as well. The **relational model** proposes that women go through different stages than those in the Boston Model. The second and third stages of the relational model emphasize the relationships established before the conflict, or challenge, stage. The model is as follows (Schiller 1995; 1997; 2003):

- *Preaffiliation:* Members experience ambivalence about joining.

- *Establishment of a relational base:* Members build strong, affective connections with others.

- *Mutuality and interpersonal empathy:* The connections deepen into a commitment to mutual aid.

- *Challenge and change:* Members recognize differences, and the connections may change in nature.

- *Termination:* Members conclude their work and separate.

While useful in all groups, this model is particularly helpful in feminist groups or in groups composed mainly of women because it supports one of the more accepted

© Blaj Gabriel

gender constructions relating to women's development and theory (Lesser et al., 2004): that is, the importance of established relationship and relational patterns as a precursor to engagement in challenge, such as self-advocacy, or taking risks previously not attempted. Specifically, women benefit in a group environment when they are able to develop relationships with other women who share similar life experiences and/or are similar to one another in other ways. Creating connections can enable participants to feel secure and safe within the group, leading to a comfort in sharing with others (Lesser et al., 2004). A relational approach may also be applicable for other groups who may have experienced oppression or displacement and for whom confrontation is not motivating (e.g., immigrants and refugees) (Schiller, 2007).

Relationships and connections lie at the heart of this model of group intervention. Thus, a key role for the social worker leading a relational group is to help empower group members to feel safe so they may move into the phases of the group process in which they will take risks and address areas of concern (Schiller, 2007).

Many valid theories and perspectives can guide group interventions. Each social worker must determine the theoretical perspective that is most compatible with her or his philosophy and professional and personal value systems, given agency structures, guidelines, and funding sources. Once a practitioner identifies one or more perspectives with which she or he is comfortable, that practitioner must develop competency in the chosen approach(es). Regardless of which theory you choose, it is essential that you demonstrate competent behaviors.

© Design Pics/Don Hammond/Thinkstock

CONTEMPORARY TRENDS AND SKILLS FOR THE MIDDLE PHASE OF GROUP WORK: INTERVENTION [EPAS 8]

In the middle phase of the group experience, the social worker, the client, and the entire group implement the plan to work toward their goals. The social worker and the group move into a pattern of interaction that enhances cohesion, unity, integration, trust, and communication (Macgowan, 2013). The primary function of intervention phase of group work is to carry out goals that were established during the assessment phase of group work. The *Standards for Social Work Practice with Groups* (IASWG, 2015) provides guidelines for organizing this phase of work and identifying needed skills:

1. *Support progress toward individual and group goals:* Having established both individual and group goals in the assessment phase, members can develop and implement a plan to accomplish the goals. The social worker must be attentive to the potential need to re-negotiate goals during this phase of work.
2. *Attend to group dynamics and processes:* The social worker must be vigilant in her or his ongoing observations of group dynamics and processes. As group members become familiar with one another, they may feel more confident confronting one another, which can create conflict within the group. Moreover, the social worker must be mindful of alliances that form within the group and outside the group and of the impact of those relationships on individual and group functioning.
3. *Use evidence-based group practices (see discussion next) and utilize resources inside and outside the group:* As the work phase progresses, the social worker should be aware of and have access to resources that may be helpful to group members.

Examining the literature for evidence-based group interventions can help your group practice. Group work that is informed by both quantitative and qualitative evidence to support the "best available" practices is known as **evidence-based group work** (EBGW) (Macgowan, 2009a, pp. 132–133). Using rigor, impact, and applicability as the criteria for determining the strength of the evidence, EBGW enhances practice and policy accountability, enables social workers to improve practice competencies using empirically validated tools and research outcomes, and ultimately bolsters the efficacy of the group intervention. Exhibit 9.1 outlines the seven considerations of an evidence-based approach to implementing and evaluating a group intervention.

Examples of Different Types of Social Work Group Interventions

As we discussed in Chapter 8, there are four types of groups within which practitioners often work—task groups, social action/goals groups, reciprocal groups (including psychoeducational groups and support groups), and remedial groups.

When reviewing the research on approaches to group interventions, consider each approach with regard to the following:

1. The way in which the approach assesses client needs and strengths
2. How the approach identifies desired outcomes
3. Potential legal and physical risks involved
4. Group member compliance with the intervention plan developed by group members
5. Client responses to intervention
6. Assessment of outcomes
7. Distinction between individual and group outcomes

Source: Comer & Meier, 2011, pp. 464–470

EXHIBIT 9.1

Considerations for Evidence-Based Group Work

These groups often have overlapping outcomes. For example, the support group promotes mutual aid among members, the psychoeducational group supports and educates, the social goals group educates and advocates, and all deal with some aspect of social justice, diversity, or human rights. In each type of group work, the members are experiencing some dimension of exclusion or are concerned about others experiencing exclusion (such as intimate partner violence and groups concerned with those in correctional facilities), which in turn leads to unmet needs and violation of rights (see Goodman, 2004).

Each effort described here represents an attempt to counter the negative effects of a contemporary social issue, and each demonstrates creativity and courage. Note that, as works in progress, these efforts may not be proven effective. Although they are based on recognized social work perspectives and guided by research inquiries, they will no doubt evolve in response to evaluation procedures that gauge their effectiveness and pinpoint needed improvements. In forging new territory, they take risks and reflect group work's potential.

Constructionist Groups for Women Experiencing Intimate Partner Violence   A **constructionist group** is a group intervention facilitated from a social constructionist perspective. In this approach, the facilitator recognizes that group members create reality through shared meanings. The constructionist group process offers members the opportunity to develop new understandings of themselves. A constructionist group intervention embodies feminist and narrative theories as well as the postmodern approach of the way in which a person develops a new and preferred **representation of the self** (i.e., view of her or his own worth and identity). In a feminist group for women experiencing intimate partner violence, members accomplish new representations of the self in part by resisting and protesting male violence. The work of the group includes three processes: (1) revealing and undermining society's oppressive discourse relating to women experiencing violence, which has historically been manifested through *political* processes; (2) identifying and detailing the protest that women can and will use in response to violence, the recognition of which reflects *change*; and (3) reconstructing participants' identities based on the protest. These activities work together to encourage members to first seek resistance (i.e., to confront difficult issues) and to then anchor resistance (i.e., identify potential change), culminating in a new story that elaborates a new identity (Roche & Wood, 2005). Group members celebrate this last process in an empowering **"definitional ceremony"** (a concept developed by Myerhoff, 1982, and applied by Wood & Roche, 2001, p. 17), which allows the women to present to an audience of people important to them their new understandings of self. In the definitional ceremony, one group member tells her story, a witness responds with a retelling of the story, and finally the original speaker retells the story, incorporating the new insights the witness provided (Leahy, O'Dwyer, & Ryan, 2012).

In one example, the social worker points out the common themes that arise in the women's conversation relating to their reactions to violence. Some women adopt a socially imposed understanding that incorporates shame and guilt when male partners are violent toward them. They believe that their own shortcomings cause violence against them and that they are responsible for changing their behaviors in exchange for safety. After first expressing support for the women, a social worker can help to counter the woman's feelings of shame and guilt by asking perspectival questions that help to break the logic of self-deprecation (for example, "What would your sister say about the way Mike treats you?" or "What did the court say about this?"). Over time, such questioning encourages a focus on multiple realities by helping women see that others would not think they "deserved" violence, "had it coming," or should "just put up with it."

At this point, the social worker seeks descriptions from the women in the group regarding their actual responses, that is, the ways in which they have resisted and protested. Protest may take the form of simply not accepting the batterer's negative statements, or it may be considerably more confrontational, such as obtaining a restraining order. Some protests may be viewed by the client and the social worker as passive (giving older bread and milk to an abusive partner while saving fresher food for a child). Incidences of protest, however they are expressed, begin to form the basis for a new understanding of the self as a person of agency who can make real and meaningful life changes.

Group members ask where a woman got her ideas for the protest or the courage to carry it out, and they also consider what the protest says about her. These explorations lead to a new view that challenges the woman's identity as helpless and worthless. The social worker and other group members then reinforce, or anchor, this new more positive representation by seeking to enrich the story through the woman's further detailed description. Finally, they celebrate her new identity as she sees it through a collective definitional ceremony. By emphasizing process rather than group stages, the group commits to helping each woman discover the other side of their survivorship and become who they want to be.

Models like this one, based on narrative ideas of story and constructionist ideas of self, are especially useful in political contexts that highlight contemporary views of gender and power relationships. In particular, they are appropriate in any situation in which the goal is to strengthen an individual's self-esteem (e.g., community mental health centers and for groups addressing sexual assault, intimate partner violence, and relationship issues).

Restorative Justice Groups for Combating Crime   Seeing the criminal justice system as mired in practices that neither heal nor rehabilitate, scholars and practitioners have developed what they believe is a more relevant approach that better responds to the issues of offenders as well as survivors, particularly in cases involving gendered violence against women (see van Wormer, 2009). A loosely associated collection of strategies called **restorative justice groups** focuses on crime as an interpersonal conflict with repercussions on the victim, the offender, and the community at large. Well suited to the social work profession's grounding in the value of the biopsychosocial-spiritual perspective, the strategies of restorative justice emphasize healing, growth, and enhanced functioning for all those affected by crime (see, for example, the systematic review of social work involvement in restorative justice in Gumz & Grant, 2009). Communities suffer when their members are engaged in crime, and they benefit when healthy and productive climates are restored within the community; therefore, it is important to focus on securing community involvement when addressing crime.

In one example, a series of three groups of offenders conducted at the Washington State Reformatory focused on balancing (1) offender accountability, (2) the rights of victims, and (3) citizen involvement in the justice process. The three groups accomplished their work through participants' stories of their personal crime experiences. Each week, one victim, one offender, and one community member shared her or his personal accounts of experiencing crime. Such storytelling increases understanding, validates experience, reduces isolation, and increases the vision for change. Group participants then determined how offenders could respond to the needs of individual victims and what offenders and community members could do to repair the harm.

The progress and process variables of these groups were largely consistent with classic models of developmental group work theory (that is, initial anxiety and a stage of conflict, followed by greater connectedness) with individual members also influencing the meetings so that each reflected different stages of development. A number of additional obstacles to the development of group unity occurred, such as the emphasis on crime, the large number of participants, emotional fragility, at times problematic group dynamics, safety concerns, confidentiality issues, and the implications of diversity, among others. This emphasis on an alternative crime response strategy that heals and helps people reconnect with each other holds promise in a society struggling with the alienation of both victims and perpetrators. A recent addition to this concept is the enactment of Neighborhood Activity Boards. In many communities, groups of volunteers come together to meet with first-time, nonviolent offenders and those people victimized by the criminal activity to discuss the impact of the crime. Typically, the offender must complete community service along with participating in the impact panel.

Motivational Interviewing Groups   Chapters 5 and 7 discussed motivational interviewing (MI) in the context of working with individuals and families. MI is also useful in a group setting, where it is known as GMI (group motivational interviewing). GMI builds on the same premise of engagement, focus, evoking, and planning. GMI in particular requires the facilitator to emphasize collaboration, autonomy, support, and empathy through reflective listening and change talk (Hohman, 2012). MI scholars Miller and Rollnick (2013) support the use of MI with a range of group interventions, but they offer two cautionary notes: (1) the group leader should be competent in the facilitation of MI with individuals before attempting to incorporate it into a group experience, and (2) due to the larger number of participants, there will be fewer opportunities for change talk, which may result in less predictable outcomes.

The examples provided here present just a small sampling of the types of group interventions available to social workers. Identifying the intervention approach, format, and structure that best fits your goals for working with groups is the key issue to consider whether you are developing a task, remedial, reciprocal, or social action group.

Social Work Skills for Group Interventions

While social workers must possess certain skills to apply any theoretical model, and while group work interventions may seem different from one-to-one models in social work settings, many of the same generalist practice roles and skills that social workers use in individual and family interventions are both applicable to and vital for group work interventions. As you work to maintain a group-centered focus during an intervention, you will find that listening, supporting, and empathizing all play as important a role in group work as they do in work with individuals. Exhibit 9.2 provides a comprehensive list of general skills that are important for group interventions, and the section that follows discusses specific skill areas in greater depth.

The following additional skills critical to group practice are adapted from the authors' practice experience as well as from Brown (2013), IASWG (2015), and Middleman and Wood (1990, pp. 96–102).

Leadership Skills   Social work practice with groups requires the social worker to demonstrate leadership in initiating and facilitating the group, including:

- To maintain a "**thinking group**" posture, you, as the social worker, consider the group as a whole first and individual members second. This concentration

As a social worker, you will use a diverse array of skills when working with groups of any type, including the following:

1. Understanding your relationship to your agency and the way in which you and your agency fit within the context of the larger community.
2. Understanding the flow of group work from beginnings through endings, including the ongoing assessment of and attention to the group's level of cohesion.
3. Conducting group interactions with multicultural awareness and sensitivity.
4. Advocating for individual clients, the group, and your agency.
5. Practicing within the ethical guidelines of the profession.
6. Helping the group establish adaptive norms.
7. Ensuring that self-disclosure is consistent with agency policy and meets the needs of the group (as opposed to your personal needs). Use of self (incorporating your own experiences) can help reflection and role modeling for the group.
9. Collaborating with group members to identify individual and group short-and long-term goals.
10. Ensuring that the goals the group establishes are consistent with the purpose of the group.
11. Regularly seeking feedback from the group regarding members' feelings about the group and the process.
12. Clarifying members' perceptions of time needed to make change, since we often expect change to occur more quickly than is realistic.
13. Providing group members with information that is relevant to the purpose of the group (e.g., medical/health information or information about legal processes).
14. Admitting when you lack information or knowledge.
15. Incorporating a variety of strategies and techniques into group process (e.g., art or writing projects; role-playing; relaxation exercises; or videos, speakers, or exercises).
16. Promoting expression of feelings within the group.
17. Demonstrating your respect for the group when members share feelings by listening actively, reflecting, and tracking.
18. Normalizing group members' feelings.
19. Engaging members on a cognitive level (i.e., thoughts and feelings).
20. Incorporating past experiences and family history to help group members connect with emotions.
21. Partializing (i.e., separating and prioritizing) the presenting issues to help group members avoid feeling overwhelmed.
22. Confronting individuals and the group as needed regarding issues related to compliance or engagement, for example.
23. Maintaining a focus on the present, such as using current events to emphasize human nature and social justice.
24. Offering strategies for resolving interpersonal conflicts.
25. Modeling empathy and the use of "I" statements and contracts.
26. Promoting member self-esteem and competence.

Source: Adapted Greif & Ephross, 2011, pp. 489–493

EXHIBIT 9.2

Knowledge and Skills for Group-Level Interventions

on the whole can require a paradigm shift. For example, you may avoid a prolonged exchange with a single group member because that focus would hinder the group's communication.

- Exhibiting "**balanced leadership**," you encourage the group to have some control over the process and outcome. This leadership can challenge social workers who believe they must have complete control of the group and its agenda or it will explode or become chaotic. If the social worker allows the group to evolve without close attention to process, it *can* become chaotic, members' feelings may be hurt, or the group may fragment and lose its meaning for group members. The social worker's ability to effectively facilitate depends on many factors including group connection, group functioning, and the presence of internal or **indigenous leadership**, that is, leadership that evolves within the membership.

Generally, the social worker is more directive in the early stages of groups, in groups with lower-functioning members, in groups with little indigenous leadership, in open-ended groups, and in task-oriented groups. As the group progresses, the social worker's role is to gradually retreat and to encourage growth in the group's ownership of the activity. The key here for any social worker is to recognize group needs and to be flexible with the degree of direct leadership. Typically, the overall goal for social workers in groups is to reduce their activity to as little as possible while maintaining self-awareness and a safe environment and encouraging members to take charge of their own group.

- **Scanning**, engaging in ongoing observation and engagement with all members of the group, is a strategy for maintaining visual observation of all members—the group version of the attending skill.

- Maintaining **cohesiveness**, or connectedness, means sustaining a sense of "we" through the use of "we" language, the encouragement of rituals (for example, marking the beginning and end of each meeting in a specific way), and the recording of the group's progress. When groups have too much or too little cohesiveness, the leader can attempt to uncover the causes (e.g., group member anxiety) (Berg, Landreth, & Fall, 2013). The use of these skills can contribute to group members' spirit and can facilitate a sense of belonging to something significant. Development and recording (through a chart on the wall, for example) of the group's agreed-upon norms or customs contributes to a sense of connection as well.

- **Facilitating change**, which can occur by assisting group members in making progress toward goals through support, programmatic activities, addressing obstacles, assessing progress, and making new contracts for goal achievement, as needed.

- **Promoting the development of mutual aid**, which may involve a review of group norms, group values, and conflict resolution.

- **Facilitating and monitoring groups**, which is completed by reviewing and reiterating definitions and rules related to confidentiality, particularly those germane to sharing information about other group members outside of group meetings.

Leadership Communication Skills

- Carefully choose the patterns of communication you will use in your group. If you respond only to the members who speak up, you will likely marginalize or exclude a subset of members. On the other hand, if you always go around the group, member by member, some members may feel pressed to contribute, and all will feel a certain amount of routinization. Instead, endeavor to encourage a respectful balance so that all members have an opportunity to speak without any one member dominating. Alternatively, you may choose to invite all members (especially those members who remain quiet) to participate and ask if others in the group share the speaker's thoughts or feelings. Periodically remind members of the norms they agreed upon and emphasize the group's accomplishments and history when appropriate.

- Responding empathetically is a critical skill in the group intervention that requires the group leader to: focus on the person speaking, restrict questioning to only those areas that need clarification, allow the group member to finish speaking, and resist the temptation to provide answers to client situations.

- **Redirection**, or redirecting questions and concerns away from you back to the group or to individual members, can be challenging. Some members will continue to address you as the source of authority for the group. Given the power dynamic, many group members may have experienced as clients in other services, such behaviors are not unexpected. Some members may complain about other members through a third party (often you). In both of these situations, you can redirect the message. Your goal is to facilitate direct, constructive communication within the group and its supporting environment. Exhibit 9.3 provides an example of a redirection within a group using the two scenarios mentioned here.

- You establish both consensus and difference when you invite agreement and disagreement on issues. A group member who has not been especially vocal will likely find it challenging to register dissent when a group approves something heartily. Early feelings of connectedness and strong group bonds can make that dissent even harder. Later, as the group matures, expressions of difference should be less troublesome, but you should continue to support difference and encourage others' capacities to respond.

As the group facilitator, you can use the following example to redirect a group session in which one member of the group appears to be leading the group away from its goal.

A member asks if visitors can attend a group meeting. Because the group has not addressed the issue before, you submit the question to the full membership:

"How do others see this question?" or "How do you as a group want to handle this?"

You may invite quieter members to participate and attempt to soften the messages of louder voices.

A second scenario involves one member of the group complaining about another member. In this scenario, you may simply say:

"Why don't you tell Bernice that?" or "I don't think you need my help talking to Kate about that."

- If the facilitator is talking, members cannot, so it is important that you, as a facilitator, work on **exercising silence**. The social worker's well-placed silence encourages the group to engage in the bulk of the interchange, which allows members' communication patterns to develop.

Leadership Problem-Solving Skills

- *Connecting progress to goals* by summarizing progress, identifying options, prioritizing decisions, mediating conflicts, confronting lack of progress and group interactions, and weighing potential outcomes are skills and activities that a social worker employs in problem solving during the intervention phase of group work. On occasion, the social worker may have to negotiate an amended contract with individual members or the entire group. The social worker may also identify the next discussion areas for future group meetings.

- In problem solving with groups, it is important that the social worker participate in *locating resources to benefit group members*. This involves working with members to identify resources, to include natural assets (e.g., friends, family, or neighbors) into the helping network, and to emphasize the connections between the group and the community. Engaging in a joint discussion among members early in the process conveys the expectation that the group has both the ability and the responsibility to deal constructively with its own issues. Identifying resources outside the group expands the potential network for all members and supports the interdependence between members, groups, and the environment. Another potential resource for the members of a group can be to incorporate activities in which the members can engage, including outside speakers, videos, group exercises, or journaling.

- The social worker can *make use of the unique characteristics of the group in the act of problem solving.* A social worker's goal in work with groups is to negotiate the tension between individual member and whole group needs, coming to a genuine compromise that encourages creative enrichment that benefits both the individual and the group. The group must establish an acceptable expression and appreciation for difference. Consider the following example from a social worker's notes of the eighth meeting of a socialization group of 12-year-old girls.

The girls were bustling around preparing crepe paper streamers and searching for birthday candles, giggling and joking about how old Lila was really going to be. Some said she was probably going to be 60 or so, judging by how glum she had seemed last week about the party they were planning. Lila was late, and when she finally showed up, she looked more miserable than ever. Finally, she blurted out, "I HATE BIRTHDAYS!!" in a voice very unlike her usual somber tones. The other girls were horrified and silent for a moment—almost unheard of in this group. Lila started to cry. Finally, she choked out the story: Her mother had died the night before her birthday two years ago, and she didn't know how to tell anybody in the group that before. The very word "birthday" was a terrible reminder. She didn't want to celebrate.

The girls seemed to feel sorry, they liked Lila, but they also really wanted to celebrate birthdays in this group. It was an important ritual for them. I confess that, as their facilitator, I didn't have a clue what to do. After a moment, Betsy, whose grandmother came from France, cheerfully volunteered, "Well, let's be trés français in this group and say we're celebrating our anniversaries! That's what the French call them, the anniversary of birth!" The others responded loudly, hoping their ritual was rescued from certain demise. Lila was silent. She looked up. Finally she almost smiled and said, "I think that would work." And that was that. The group took on a "French theme" ever after and was the only group of 12-year-olds I ever knew that celebrated their anniversaries!

Management of Group Function and Process   All effective social work interventions make use of the social worker's ability to interact competently with clients with strengths-based and biopsychosocial-spiritual perspectives. Within those interactions, the social worker and group members may fulfill a broad spectrum of potential roles. While this and the previous chapter have highlighted social worker roles within groups, this chapter will focus on the role of the social worker during the intervention, termination, evaluation, and follow-up phases of group work. The summary of those roles is examined here, followed by an overview of the roles group members play.

Social Worker Roles

While the social worker's primary role is to provide leadership for the group intervention, the type, format, and goals of the group determine what specific role the social worker will play. The social work group practitioner may find her- or himself needing to function in one or more of the following roles (Berg et al., 2013; Furman, Bender, & Rowan, 2014; Collins & Lazzari, 2009, pp. 299–302; Reid, 2002, pp. 435–436):

- As a **facilitator**, the social worker must be a skilled listener who invites sharing and participation, reframes and links issues, and maintains group boundaries and rules to promote appropriate interactions. In a task group, the facilitator may set the agenda, maintain the group's focus on tasks, and document the meeting. Regardless of the group setting, the social worker should foster an ongoing awareness of the "unconscious group process" (i.e., understanding issues that permeate the group's functioning) (Levy, 2011, p. 155).

- As a **synthesizer**, the social worker summarizes group members' discussions, identifies themes and patterns, and connects content from one session to the next to promote continuity and substantive discussion.

- When a social worker models appropriate group behavior and directs feedback, she or he acts as a **setter of norms**. For example, the social worker establishes appropriate group interaction by encouraging the use of direct interactions, "I" statements, appropriate challenges, and concrete examples and by helping set the rules at the beginning of the group. Norm setting includes the challenging issue of self-disclosure. As the leader, you can appropriately share information about yourself and suggest group activities that focus on attitudes, values, and beliefs rather than more threatening exercises that emphasize sensitive content areas.

- Social workers functioning as **educators** or teachers within a group setting provide factual information specific to group goals.

- As group leaders, social workers can empower group members by promoting **self-advocacy** that can be applied both inside and outside of the group setting. The group can serve as a place for members to rehearse their newly learned self-advocacy skills.

- As with social work practice with individuals and families, social workers may **collaborate** with other professionals. Co-leadership is often an effective strategy in group interventions as it can involve equal commitment, motivation, and vision on the part of each of the co-leaders that can build on the strengths that each leader brings to the intervention.

Group Member Roles

Group members bring their unique characteristics and traits to the group experience regardless of the type of group or its purpose, often serving as both learner and teacher (of others in the group). The social worker may experience these qualities as both strengths and challenges. Ideally, group members will be open to new information, growth, and change and will be willing and able to actively participate in the group process to provide the same for others (Furman et al., 2014). These are obvious strengths, but even challenging behaviors can be reframed and used for positive individual and group outcomes. If a group member displays resistant behaviors (e.g., disruption or an unwillingness to engage) and cannot fulfill their roles as learner and teacher, she or he may lack trust or feel insecure (Berg et al., 2013). See Quick Guide 28 for a list of questions that may be helpful in managing resistance. The social worker can encourage appropriate group member interactions by setting expectations from the outset of the group intervention, but individual group member's idiosyncrasies may still lead to challenging interactions within the group process.

Some group member roles commonly emerge. Individual personalities influence and interact with group dynamics (much like the dynamics of a family interaction). The competent group practitioner can begin to anticipate these roles and behaviors and, having previously considered these possibilities, can be prepared with an appropriate response. You must exercise caution, however, to ensure that you do not generalize or stereotype group member behaviors but respond to each person as unique. Six potentially challenging group member roles you can expect and possible social worker responses include the following (adapted from Berg et al., 2013; Furman et al., 2014; Yalom & Leszcz, 2005, pp. 391–405):

- *The "silent" group member:* The "silent" group member is challenging because it is difficult to determine if the individual is not speaking because she or he

QUICK GUIDE 28   QUESTIONS THAT MAY BE HELPFUL IN MANAGING RESISTANCE

If you encounter a group member or members who seem resistant to engaging in the group process, consider the following questions:

1. What is the nature (e.g., behavior and attitudes) of the resistance?
2. Are the member's behaviors disrupting group function and process?
3. How does resistance impact other areas of the individual's life?
4. How do other group members respond to the group member who is displaying resistance?
5. How are you responding to the group member displaying resistance?

After reflecting on these questions, share your observations with the group and collectively brainstorm possible causes and responses.

Source: Berg, Landreth, & Fall, 2013, p. 125

is not engaged or because he or she is uncomfortable or intimidated and thus not able to benefit from the group experience. Silence does not necessarily mean that the person is not engaged. While it is possible to experience vicarious gains without active engagement, the social worker typically strives to turn the reticent group member into an active participant. Inviting the individual to participate, noting nonverbal gestures, and speaking with the member outside of the group about her or his silence are all strategies for promoting participation. Should these strategies fail, the social worker may either allow the individual to continue as a silent member of the group or develop an alternative intervention outside the group for the individual. As you consider the way in which you will address the silence, take into account the responses from the other group members.

- *The "monopolizer":* Equally as challenging for a group leader is the "monopolizer," who is perceived as talking too much. In this role, the group member may attempt to offer her or his opinion on virtually every statement made by others or may spend an inordinate amount of time describing her or his own situation or needs. Monopolizing can present itself in different forms, including the "compulsive talker," the "intellectualizer," the "special interest pleader," or the "manipulator," all of whom may be operating out of fear or a need to control the situation. While understanding the reasons for this person's behavior is important for changing the behavior, the impact on the group process and members can potentially be negative as members may perceive that the person is being singled out, the group is not safe, and/or they may be next to be confronted. As with the "silent" group member, the social worker may personally address a group member's monopolizing behavior or may encourage the group to address the behavior. The social worker might work with the monopolizer outside the group to address the reasons she or he feels compelled to speak so frequently, or the worker may develop an alternative intervention strategy.

Subgroups or cliques within the group can also monopolize the group's time and energy and can isolate some members or create internal divisions or conflicts. Allowing the group to manage any subgroups when they form is ideal; the social worker can ensure that the process is fair and respectful.

- *The "help-rejecting" or complaining group member:* A social worker may view a group member who appears to reject help or ideas as both a challenge and a resource. Avoidant behavior can signal a member's depression or lack of problem-solving skills. The "help-rejecting" or complaining group member is likely to have a negative influence on the group's dynamics and may be unable to experience change or to grow. On the other hand, other group members may use the avoidant member's negative perspective to see alternate possibilities (if only as a reaction to the negativity). The social worker can respond in a way that maintains a focus on concrete feedback and on the group process and that encourages the group to respond to this member as well. The leader may also seek to build trust with the member displaying avoidant behaviors.

- *The "caregiver":* A "caregiver" (also known as the coordinator or rescuer) is a group member who strives to take care of others, including the group facilitator. Not surprisingly, caregivers often use caring for others as a way to avoid addressing their own individual challenges. The social worker can respond to caregivers by acknowledging their history of altruistic caregiving, praising their willingness to now take care of their own needs, and gently confronting them when they attempt to care for others as a way to avoid dealing with their own issues

- *The "attacker":* An "attacker" may verbally assault another member or the facilitator, which may either stimulate or disrupt the group. Acknowledging an attacker's aggressive behavior is a first step toward exploring the underlying reasons for that behavior. Confrontation is required if attacks become personally targeted.

- *The "dependent" group member:* Certain "dependent" behaviors can be challenging in the group setting. For example, the "harmonizer" strives to maintain peace within the group, the "clown" uses humor (often to mask depression or fear), and the "poor me" member seeks constant affirmation.

© vm

QUICK GUIDE 29   SUMMARY OF INTERVENTION SKILLS FOR SOCIAL WORK GROUP PRACTICE

The social worker engaged in the intervention phase of social work practice with groups should:

- be knowledgeable and skilled in group leadership (e.g., logistics and time management);
- facilitate group communication and group dynamics;
- be competent with individual and group problem solving;
- focus on promoting progress toward group and individual goals; and
- manage group functions.

As a facilitator, you can initiate a discussion focused on the interactional and communication styles the members possess and the functions those styles serve in their lives. As the discussion of the intervention or the middle phase of the group work process comes to a close and the exploration shifts to the termination and evaluation phases of group work, a review of the skills needed to competently intervene with groups may be helpful. See Quick Guide 29 for a recap of these skills presented.

CONTEMPORARY TRENDS AND SKILLS FOR THE ENDING PHASES OF GROUP WORK: TERMINATION AND EVALUATION [EPAS 9]

While the concepts we explored in our discussions of terminating (i.e., ending), evaluating, and following-up with individuals and families can be applied to work with most clients, there are some additional considerations and dynamics to consider in social work practice with groups. As in social work terminations and evaluations with individuals and families, the intensity of the phases of ending a group and evaluating the work will depend on the type of group and its purpose.

Social Work Group Endings

The social worker's role in termination is to "help members examine their accomplishments, review their experience together, and prepare for the future . . . and express and integrate positive and negative emotion" (Garvin & Galinsky, 2013). Social work practice with groups can end in many ways. Terminations may occur when a member opts to leave the group, when the group reaches a predetermined time limit or meets its collective goals, or when the leader leaves the group (Furman et al., 2014). Regardless of the reason for the group's termination, endings may evoke a range of member responses and interactions. Group members may experience positive emotions, including feelings of success and elation, and/or negative emotions such as loss, threat, rejection, abandonment, or anger—all of which may relate both to their individual and group experiences (Furman et al., 2014). At termination, the group leader may notice that group members regress back to previous behaviors, withdraw from the group, panic, or begin to devalue the group experience (Brown, 2013). Response often depends on the group purpose and lengths. For example, members of an educational or task group are likely to experience fewer highly emotional responses than those of a treatment group. A group that has met only six times will probably not be as highly invested as a group that has met for three years.

Negotiating terminations with groups is an often-complex endeavor in which the social worker deals with endings on three different levels:

- The relationship between group members and the social worker

- Relationships among the group members

- The structure of the group itself

The theoretical framework a practitioner uses should guide the termination phase of group work. We will now consider endings from each of the theoretical perspectives discussed earlier in the chapter.

Using the Strengths and Empowerment Approach in Group Work Endings

Integrating strengths and empowerment concepts into the termination phase can enable both individual members and the whole group to review progress toward their goals and to develop strategies for sustaining change. The social worker can invite each member to review and reflect on her or his individual experience in the group, including: the strengths they brought to the group process; their status in the beginning, middle, and endings phases of the work; the changes they experienced; and their plans for using the group's strengths to maintain the change(s). Having individual members engaged in this review and reflection process provides an opportunity for the social worker and other group members to contribute to that individual's own experience of the group process. Group members can take advantage of fellow members' reflections for their own review and sustainability processes.

A strengths-based perspective can further enable the social worker and group members to reflect on how the group's strengths have evolved as the group moved through various phases. For example, a group strength may be the respectful and supportive way in which the members interact with one another. The social worker can provide feedback on the changes she or he has observed in the group's engagement, cohesion, and work, and group members can reflect on taking part in a strengths-focused group experience. Such reflection can empower group members and the social worker to integrate this enhanced sense of confidence and competence into the group process.

In situations in which individual or group goals are not realized, the formal ending of a task or social action group can still be oriented toward a strengths perspective. One strategy is to engage in an exercise in which members review the strengths the group had from the outset, those strengths they gained or mobilized during the group, and those strengths members can carry on after the group is terminated. While group members (and the social worker) may be dismayed at the group's failure to achieve its goals, planning ways in which members can continue to work toward achieving those goals can be empowering.

Narrative-Focused Group Work Endings   Ritual or ceremonial activities and public acknowledgement of growth and change work well in narrative-focused group terminations that emphasize strengths. Group members and the social worker can collaboratively plan a celebration to recognize the formal ending of the group's work together. This "definitional" ceremony can acknowledge the achievement of goals and the next phase of growth as well as help individuals reclaim or redefine themselves (Morgan, 2000, p. 121).

As with individual and family work endings, the group termination process involves public testimonials (Morgan, 2000). Group member feedback on individual testimonials can reinforce members' changes and solidify plans for maintaining change beyond the formal group experience. A social worker can use a process similar to one she or he might use with individuals, with group members serving as outsider-witnesses. The definitional ceremony begins with the social worker and group members listening as an individual group member re-authors her or his work in the group. The witnesses then reflect that re-authored story back to the individual, the individual member responds to the feedback, and the entire group engages in a discussion about the process. This activity can be helpful both as a tool for recognizing individual and group strengths and goal attainment and as a means of evaluating the change process.

Solution-Focused Group Work Endings   Termination of the solution-focused group intervention can be viewed by the social worker and the group members as the achievement of the initial and overall goals for the work of the group even if all of the members' individual goals were not realized. Solution-focused group interventions identify issues and plan and implement a change effort. In group interventions, group members provide opportunities for individual members to process their issues and potential solutions. Recall that solution-focused interventions are grounded in the ongoing use of a series of questions to elicit strengths, thoughts, and feelings regarding change and to develop plans for change. During the termination phase, you can ask members about the progress they've made via scaling progress questions (e.g., "On a scale of 1 to 10, where were you when you joined this group? Where are you now? Where do you need to be in order to maintain this change when you leave the group?" "How will you know when it is time to leave the group?" "What will be different?") (De Jong, 2015). Group members can provide their own observations of an individual member's change process. Shifting the emphasis from the present to the future can help the individual and group members to perceive themselves as separate from the group and from the social worker leading the group, thus enabling them to view themselves as empowered to implement and maintain the desired changes.

Regardless of the theoretical perspective you choose to guide a group intervention, you will need a number of competencies to effectively bring an intervention to an end. As with any social work intervention, groups are made of unique individuals and situations, and the social worker must be attuned to those aspects. In addition, a social worker needs to possess a set of termination-related skills specific to group practice.

Skills for Social Work Group Terminations

Even planned group endings can be complex and intense, and social workers need a skill set that reflects the unique features of the group intervention. During the termination phase, the social worker emphasizes bringing together the different phases of the work, beginning with the engagement, assessment, and intervention, to achieve closure for the individual group member, the group itself, and for her- or himself (IASWG, 2015; Toseland & Horton, 2013). The social worker should recognize and attend to all the feelings of the group members as well as her-/himself and frame the ending as a new beginning (Furman et al., 2014). Individual and group reflection during termination is particularly powerful. Group members and the facilitator can reflect on accomplishments as well as the way in which each person experienced the group process and ending (Furman et al., 2014). Let us take a closer look at each of the multiple skill sets social workers use in group endings.

Ending the Relationship between Group Members and the Social Worker   The end of the relationship between group members and the social worker places particular demands on the social worker. In this final phase of any type of group (i.e., task or client group), you, as the social worker, have several responsibilities with respect to the entire group, including the following (Brown, 2013; IASWG, 2015; Furman et al., 2014; Kurland & Salmon, 1998; Toseland & Horton, 2013):

- Preparing members for ending (from the mid-point of the group intervention)

- Assessing progress toward achievement of group goals

- Helping stabilize member and group gains

- Anticipating and eliciting individual and group responses to ending

- Planning timing and content to maximize remaining sessions/meetings

© Yuri Arcurs

- Helping group members express their ambivalence about the group's ending and addressing individual and group reactions and behaviors to individual or group accomplishments, including affirmations and confidence building regarding achievements

- Sharing observations of progress and confidence in members' abilities to function successfully without the group, or, in the case of a task group, continuing to work toward identified goals (it may be helpful to identify any obstacles to success and needed connections to resources outside the group)

- Supporting members' efforts to begin the process of separating from the group and identifying strategies for implementing change and applying new knowledge

- Developing awareness of ways in which individual and group change will impact systems external to the group

- Helping members connect their experiences in the group to life experiences in the future

- Developing awareness of your own feelings regarding ending and reflecting on and sharing feelings with the group

- Eliciting feedback from group members about the group process

The social worker's task is to help the group end positively and to help members translate their achievements into the "real world" outside the group. The social worker also has to monitor her or his own responses; after all, she or he has invested a great deal of effort in facilitating an effective experience, and groups in which significant personal and group changes have occurred can experience more difficult endings as groups may be reluctant to end as they have developed strong bonds with one another and the social worker. Recalling the overall purpose of the group and focusing on the specifics of the process can help the social worker to balance her or his response between task and emotion.

There are also a number of group behaviors typical to endings that may be directed either at the social worker or at the group as a whole. These include: (1) denial, or simply "forgetting" that the group is ending; (2) **clustering**, moving toward more connection rather than less; (3) **regression**, either claiming verbally or acting out in behavioral terms that the group is not ready to end; (4) withdrawal or passivity related to active participation; (5) rebellion; or (6) flight, leaving the group before it ends (Furman et al., 2014; Reid, 1997).

The responses to ending in groups are similar to those that occur in intervening with individuals and families. The fact that the number of people in the group may multiply those responses can make them feel quite momentous to you as the social worker. For example, when an entire collective of 13-year-old girls makes it clear, through sudden and orchestrated hostility toward you, that they do not want the experience to end, you can certainly feel the power of the group. In this case, just as in individual or family work, you can view the group's reaction as a function of the process (and perhaps of the success of the group), rather than as a focused personal assault.

Social work skills that are particularly useful in ending work with groups include the following (IASWG, 2015):

- *Preparing for termination:* The social worker has the responsibility to ease the transition and promote sustained change by ensuring that the end of the group experience (whether individual or entire group) is anticipated and planned.

- *Discussing impact of the group experience on the individual, the group, and the group facilitator and reflecting on gain:* Reflecting with the individuals and group-as-a-whole on the gains made and not made and strategies for sustaining changes is a useful strategy for ending group work because it allows the group to discuss their achievements and verbalize plans for maintenance.

- *Preserving group information:* This skill involves the facilitator verbally and in writing documenting the group goals, processes, achievements, and referrals/connections in individual and group records. In the process of ending, the social worker can help the members to focus on maintaining the changes they experience as a result of the group into their world outside of the group.

Ending Relationships among Group Members   In ending relationships with other group members, individuals may exhibit a range of responses, from denial or flight behaviors to gratification to actual celebration. Some members may not attend meetings specifically dedicated to ending activities. Others may attend but refuse to enter group interactivity about endings, or they may simply resign themselves to feeling they have been rejected by the other members or the social worker. Individuals may become increasingly short-tempered and impatient with other members, as if to negate the importance of their relationship and to render the ending insignificant or even a relief. This behavior may occur among those members who have worked the hardest to connect with one other.

In other situations, individual members may question their ability to maintain change without the assistance of the group and the social worker. These members will sometimes lobby for individual sessions with the worker or a reconstituted "mini group" in which only a few members of the original group would attend. Some individuals may initiate more intense relationships with other group members outside the confines of group meetings, as if to negate the need for the group. The most helpful thing you can do is to articulate your observations regarding group dynamics, reflecting on your perceptions of their individual and group starting places, work completed, changes made, and goals achieved with the group members. Such a reflection can help the members examine their own experiences through the lens of another person. Staying focused on the group, rather than on individuals, can be challenging, but it is part of negotiating a successful ending.

Ending the Group Itself   The ending of the group itself is at once philosophical and technical. On the philosophical level, it requires you to reflect on your feelings about ending this unit of work and this group of unique characters. How will the experience contribute to your professional growth? What could you have done differently? How will group members benefit from it? If the group has been difficult, you may struggle with feelings of inadequacy or a sense of work left undone. When there is an overall sense that the group went well, you may feel exhilarated by a sense of accomplishment, of having crossed a particular hurdle, or of entering into the realm of the skilled. What metaphor will you use to describe your experience? Death? Divorce? Disengagement? Completing a required course? Graduation?

On a much more practical side, when the group ends, you will need to close out records of participation, complete the evaluation process (discussed in the next section), and terminate logistical arrangements such as space and place. Finally, you will need to honor follow-up commitments and successfully make any referrals or transfers.

Consider the issues that arise in the following group termination scenario:

A community-based agency that serves new immigrants offers a group for high school-aged students focused on the students' transitions from their country of origin to their newly adopted country. The group also has a secondary purpose: it provides an opportunity for the students to practice their English skills in a safe environment. The group is composed of a mix of genders and ethnicities. The social worker charged with facilitating the group has developed her cultural competency through a commit-ment to learn as much as she can about the students' heritage and traditions, language, cultural rules and norms for gender interactions, and faith traditions. She personally interviews each student who is referred to the group and her or his parents/ family/guardians so she can be familiar with the individual student's needs and goals for joining the group.

The social worker has become aware of a potential dilemma. The current group of students has developed into a cohesive group, particularly around becoming "Americanized" as they enthusiastically adopt the customs of teens in their new country. The time-limited group is scheduled to come to an end, but a number of parents who are distressed that their children are abandoning their heritages have approached the social worker and have asked her to continue the group for the purpose of reconnecting the teens to their ethnic and cultural roots. While the teens enjoy the group, they have already planned their "graduation" celebration and appear ready to move on with life outside the group. The social worker is conflicted—she empathizes with the parents' concerns but believes the group should terminate as planned.

What options or alternatives might the social worker in this scenario consider in order to meet the needs of both groups?

Endings can and should be a time for reflection and celebration. It is important that all social workers in group practice, particularly those in the early stages of their career, review the group process as it has impacted their personal and professional growth.

Evaluating Social Work Practice with Groups

Evaluating practice with groups serves the same purpose as evaluating practice with individuals and families: to assess the work, the process, the progress, and the social worker's skills (Furman et al., 2014). Unlike family intervention evaluations that focus exclusively on the unit and individual intervention evaluations that focus solely on the individual, the evaluation of a group intervention encompasses both the individual and the group, thus elevating group evaluations to a higher level of complexity.

As noted previously, individuals arrive at the group with distinct goals, personalities, needs, and expectations. Oftentimes, the social worker must consider evaluative strategies within the context of a large, diverse group of individuals who perceive their experiences differently from one another. You must frame an evaluation of any group intervention within the context of the purpose, type, structure, and format of the group. Further complicating group evaluations, the social worker must work within the agency or organizational structure in which the group is conducted. Having to address multiple needs with a group of individuals requires the social work group practitioner to have a clear and thoughtful approach to evaluation of the group intervention *prior* to the first meeting of the group.

Regardless of the method(s) used to evaluate the group intervention, it is important for everyone involved in the intervention to participate in the evaluative process (Garvin & Galinsky, 2013). The many strategies for accomplishing the goals of this phase of the group intervention include the following (Bloom, Fischer, & Orme, 2009; Furman et al., 2014; Garvin & Galinsky, 2013):

- Related to individual and group goals, reviewing individual and group member accomplishments with an emphasis on preparing for the future, sustaining change, and ensuring the inclusion of support systems to reduce risk for failure.

- Gathering group members' impressions of the group experience and the activities/programming. You can collect data publically as part of the group process (orally within the group or in written evaluations which are discussed in the group) or anonymously (in writing), using caution to avoid "satisfaction-only" surveys in which members are asked if they enjoyed the experience, as they typically do not accurately reflect growth and change, but members' feelings about the facilitator, setting, etc.

- Administering pre- and postgroup measures of behaviors, attitudes, and group function. Consider the use of previously validated and standardized measures that have been used with comparable groups. Such measures will provide you with evidence-supported data from which to interpret your findings. While standardized measures of the individual are appropriate for use in group interventions, also consider the use of standardized measurements developed specifically for group interventions (e.g., see Group Engagement

Measure (originally developed by Macgowan, 1997; further psychometric testing and review of research: 2000, 2003 (with Levenson), 2005 (with Newman), and 2006).

- Through direct observation, documenting behaviors and changes in individual group members and in the group. You may gather data quantitatively and/or qualitatively.

- Completing a self-evaluation, including exploration into such areas as: meeting group member needs, developing appropriate structures and interventions, and assessing your own performance as a social work practitioner. As part of reflecting on your role within the group, you may want to conduct a self-evaluation so that you can grow and evolve as a group facilitator. Quick Guide 30 provides a strategy to help you engage in a self-evaluation.

- Soliciting direct observation and feedback from other professionals.

While each group develops its own personality and each group experience is unique, there are aspects of each phase of the group process that are often replicated. Recall from Chapter 8 the examination of the engagement and assessment phases of three group models (social goals/action, reciprocal, and remedial models) used within groups of parents from the Riverton community. Returning to the Riverton example, Exhibits 9.4, 9.5, and 9.6 depict the intervention, termination, and evaluation phases from the perspectives of the three models.

QUICK GUIDE 30   GROUP FACILITATOR SELF-EVALUATION

When reflecting on your experience leading a group, ask yourself the following questions:

1. How did the group experience me?
2. What feelings did I experience in this session? Did I express those feelings? Did I have some feelings with which I did not feel comfortable?
3. What were my reactions to various group members? Did I feel "turned off" by some members, or rejected? Do all members know I care about them? Do they feel that I accept them?
4. What general message did I communicate to each member? Did I say what I really wanted to say? Did I clearly state my message?
5. How much time did I spend focused on the content of the discussion rather than on the interaction taking place or the feelings and needs subtly expressed?
6. What do I wish I had said or done? What would I do differently next time?
7. Did I dominate? How willing was I to let someone else assume the leadership role?

You can complete this reflection following each session as well as when the group comes to a close. Upon finishing this reflection, consider ways in which you may strengthen your group skills.

Source: Berg, Landreth, & Fall, 2013, p. 138

EXHIBIT 9.4	PHASES II AND III: MIDDLE AND ENDING WORK
Riverton Against Youth Drinking ("RAYD"): An Example of a Social Goals/ Action Group	*Background:* A group of parents in the Riverton community, concerned about the use and abuse of alcohol among their adolescent children, approaches a local community service agency to ask for its help.

Work thus far: Stakeholders and their interests and goals have been identified. The social worker's role has been agreed upon. A community needs assessment has been conducted, including strengths, resources, needs, and priorities. A plan for intervention, termination, and evaluation has been established; it will focus on developing and mounting a public education campaign to raise awareness about the issue of teen drinking.

Note: While the stages of group interventions are not linear and may, in fact, overlap, the following depicts a possible approach to responding to the identified need.

INTERVENTION	TERMINATION	EVALUATION
Identify community partners who will support and help to disseminate the education campaign	Conclude campaign	Conduct evaluation
		Analyze data gathered from evaluation effort
Confirm the plan, time frame, and resources for intervention, termination, and evaluation continue to be viable		Implement plan for sustainability
		Document findings
Launch the intervention		
Monitor progress, particularly dissemination and relationships with community partners		
Adapt the intervention, as needed		
Revisit plan for evaluation and sustainability		

PHASES II AND III: MIDDLE AND ENDING WORK

EXHIBIT 9.5

Riverton Children's Grief Support Group: An Example of a Reciprocal Group

Background: A social worker in a local community service agency has become aware of a number of Riverton children who have lost a parent to alcohol and substance-related deaths. The social worker takes steps toward offering to the community an educationally-focused support group.

Work thus far: Based on the social worker's assessment of community need and interest, group members were recruited, screened, and invited to join the group. A first session was planned and has been held, at which time the social worker and group members collaborated to determine group rules and norms. Individual group goals and needs were shared. The social worker's role as a facilitator/educator was established.

Note: While the stages of group interventions are not linear and may, in fact, overlap, the following depicts a possible approach to responding to the identified need.

INTERVENTION	TERMINATION	EVALUATION
Social worker begins each session by reviewing group rules and norms and conducting member check-in	Begin termination as planned	*Individual*
	Check in with each group member regarding feelings about the termination of the group and the process	Determine if goals were met (informal or formal)
Social worker engages in ongoing assessment of individual member needs, group interactions, and group cohesiveness		Administer post-group collection of data
	Invite each member to talk about individual gains and continuing needs	*Group*
Social worker has developed a repertoire of available agency and community resources to suggest as needed	Discuss plans for sustaining change and any perceived obstacles to maintaining desired changes	Determine if group goals (informal or formal) were met
Revisit group needs and adapt intervention and educational programming plans as appropriate	Provide resources as needed to help members sustain change	Ask members to provide feedback regarding satisfaction with the group process
Share information, as agreed upon prior to group initiation, with legal guardians	Conduct termination ritual or celebration	
Monitor individual and group progress and adapt as needed		

EXHIBIT 9.5 *Continued*	INTERVENTION	TERMINATION	EVALUATION
	Regularly revisit time frame and plans for termination and evaluation		Document findings
	Invite suggestions from group members regarding plans for recognizing group termination		

EXHIBIT 9.6

Riverton Mental Health Center Group for Persons with Dual Diagnosis: An Example of a Remedial Group

PHASES II AND III: MIDDLE AND ENDING WORK

Background: A new social worker at the Riverton Mental Health Center recently assumed leadership for a clinical intervention group for persons with dual diagnoses (i.e., substance abuse and mental illness) who receive outpatient services at the agency. Group membership is diverse and includes a mix of genders, ages, and mandated and voluntary members. Membership turnover depends on members' "graduation" from the treatment program; therefore, members are often entering and exiting the group. Two new members have been referred to the group. This will be the first time new members have been referred since the new social worker took over responsibility for the group.

Work thus far: The social worker has gathered information on eligibility criteria for group membership and integrating new members into an ongoing group. The social worker has met with the two persons who have been referred and determined they would be appropriate for inclusion. The two members have been oriented and attended their first meeting. During this session, the social worker introduced the new members to the group, revisited group rules and norms, and assessed the individual goals and needs and group cohesion.

Note: While the stages of group interventions are not linear and may, in fact, overlap, the following depicts a possible approach to responding to the identified need.

INTERVENTION	TERMINATION	EVALUATION
At the beginning of each session, social worker reminds members of group rules and norms	Ongoing, as membership is open	Complete formal evaluation as required by agency

Social worker conducts check in by asking members to share with the group events/actions since the last session

Social worker assesses individual member needs and goals and monitors progress towards goals (critical as each person may be at a different point in their progress)

Social worker assesses group cohesion

Members with longer membership serve as guides/mentors for newer members

Determine termination ritual appropriate to an open-ended group

Prepare existing and remaining members for termination

Check in with members regarding their feelings about termination

Obtain information from existing members regarding achievement of goals and experiences with group format and process (e.g., open vs. closed and time-limited format) and social worker leadership

Document findings

EXHIBIT 9.6

Continued

In addition to the type(s) of evaluative strategies for examining group interventions that we have discussed, consider using the data that you gather and analyze to develop evaluation tools that you can use with future groups (Garvin & Galinsky, 2013). For example, you and other group facilitators may find it helpful to have a menu of strategies for monitoring group progress or a manual for conducting a group intervention. Exhibit 9.7 offers a sample of a facilitator evaluation that group members can complete.

STRAIGHT TALK ABOUT GROUP INTERVENTION, TERMINATION, AND EVALUATION

The social worker's overall role and purpose is to encourage and mobilize the group's strengths. The social worker's concern for individual well-being and growth is augmented by the individual relationships within the group, one member to another. Consistent with trusting the group process, the social worker should strive to avoid overinvestment in the centrality or power of her or his role. The goal, after all, is for the group to gain its voice and develop its strength, even as individual members continue to grow. You will not be able to take credit, even in your own mind, for all of the potential successes in your group. In exchange, you will have the

<table>
<tr><td>

EXHIBIT 9.7

*Group
Counselor
Rating Scale*

</td><td>

Instructions: Rate your group counselor as you see her/him functioning in your group.

Respect: Shows respect for group members by attentiveness, warmth, efforts to understand, and supports freedom of personal expression.

5.0	4.5	4.0	3.5	3.0	2.5	2.0	1.5	1.0
Very high		high		moderate		low		very low

Empathy: Communicates an accurate understanding of group members' feelings and experiences. Group members know the counselor understands how they feel.

5.0	4.5	4.0	3.5	3.0	2.5	2.0	1.5	1.0
Very high		high		moderate		low		very low

Genuineness: Realness. Everything she/he does seems to be sincere. That's the way she/he really is. This person doesn't put up a front.

5.0	4.5	4.0	3.5	3.0	2.5	2.0	1.5	1.0
Very high		high		moderate		low		very low

Concreteness: "Tunes in" and responds to specific feelings of experiences of group members. Avoids responding in generalities.

5.0	4.5	4.0	3.5	3.0	2.5	2.0	1.5	1.0
Very high		high		moderate		low		very low

Self-Disclosure: Lets group know about relevant immediate personal feelings. Open, rather than guarded.

5.0	4.5	4.0	3.5	3.0	2.5	2.0	1.5	1.0
Very high		high		moderate		low		very low

Spontaneity: Can respond without consistently having to "stop and think." Words and actions seem to flow easily.

5.0	4.5	4.0	3.5	3.0	2.5	2.0	1.5	1.0
Very high		high		moderate		low		very low

Flexibility: Adapts to a wide range of conditions without losing her/his composure. Can adapt to meet the needs of the moment.

5.0	4.5	4.0	3.5	3.0	2.5	2.0	1.5	1.0
Very high		high		moderate		low		very low

Confidence: Trusts her/his abilities. Acts with directness and self-assurance.

5.0	4.5	4.0	3.5	3.0	2.5	2.0	1.5	1.0
Very high		high		moderate		low		very low

Open-ended questions like the ones below may also yield insightful group perceptions about the facilitator:

</td></tr>
</table>

1. Of what changes have you become aware in your attitudes, feelings about yourself, and relationships with other people since your group experience began?
2. How did the group experience help these changes to come about?
3. What did the group leader do that was most helpful and least helpful to you?
4. Was the group experience hurtful to you in any way, or did it have any negative effect on you?
5. Briefly identify any group exercises you especially liked or disliked.
6. In what ways do you wish you had been different in the group?
7. How are you most different as a result of the group experience?

Source: Berg, Landreth, & Fall, 2013, p. 143–144.

EXHIBIT 9.7

Continued

privilege of experiencing the power of group connection and the autonomy the group ultimately can exercise as it liberates the power of its members. The emphasis on the group does not mean that your own role is any less important. You are responsible for the structure of the group, for the emotional and physical safety of each member in the group, and for ensuring the group processes its own activity. Accordingly, your role is to evaluate group process and functioning on an ongoing basis, just as you do in other forms of social work practice interventions. This evaluation will vary according to the nature of your group purpose, goals, and format. For example, if you are working in a task group, the intervention and evaluation processes will focus on monitoring progress in completing the group's project. If you facilitate a group for school-aged children, you must make sure to use an appropriate developmental level. Other forms of evaluation that are especially useful come from members: Is the group meeting their social and affiliation needs? Do members continue to feel safe in the group? Is it a helpful forum to address the issues they want to deal with? As always, consider the work of evaluation as an ongoing process.

The American Academy of Social Work and Social Welfare Grand Challenges for Social Work Initiative identifies one of the areas the profession should address is to use technological innovations in social work practice, including group practice. The authors of Grand Challenge Working Paper No. 12, *Practice Innovation through Technology in the Digital Age: A Grand Challenge for Social Work* (Berzin, Singer, & Chan, 2015) charge the social work profession with investing in resources to leverage information and communication technology (ICT) to enable the profession to better prepare students and practitioners and serve consumers:

GRAND CHALLENGE

Harness Technology for Social Good

Technology shifts at a rapid pace and social work is poised to be part of these advances. Social workers can begin to play a more active role in guiding the development side with their content knowledge and exploiting technology created for other purpose by ensuring . . . meaningful progress (p. 13).

While the profession must consider the ethical and practical implications of further integrating technological advances into individual, family, and group practice, there are a number of potential benefits, including: increasing accessibility and flexibility in service delivery; using social media to reach more people, using global positioning systems (GPS) and sensor systems to personalize treatment processes and gather evidence for practice innovations; and redefine social work roles and boundaries. The authors of the Grand Challenge advocate for the social work profession to promote evaluation of cutting-edge technologies to support practice interventions, develop training programs to encourage adoption of technologies, and advocate for regulations to support online service delivery (p. 13–14). This Grand Challenge is timely as Technology Standards in Social Work Practice are jointly launched by the National Association of Social Workers, Association of Social Work Boards, Council on Social Work Education, and the Clinical Social Work Association to provide the profession with guidelines related to the use of technology in social work practice (for more information, visit www.socialworkers.org). To familiarize yourself with the issues related to the use of technology, visit the Grand Challenges website and read Working Paper No. 12, *Practice Innovation through Technology in the Digital Age: A Grand Challenge for Social Work* (Berzin et al., 2015) at: http://aaswsw.org/grand-challenges-initiative/12-challenges/harness-technology-for-social-good/. (See Exercise #a1 for additional exploration of this Grand Challenge within the context of the Hudson City community.)

CONCLUSION

This chapter has presented social work practice with groups as functioning to mediate a range of social and emotional issues, including isolation, oppression, and life crises. Group work harnesses the relationship component of humanity toward individual and group goals. Currently, there are many exciting adventures in social work practice with groups that build upon contemporary theoretical perspectives, social justice, and diversity. The scenarios presented in this chapter that emphasize process over stages and story over problem all point to the empowering direction that social group work is taking. Social work practice with groups offers significant potential for the future and is particularly relevant for the social justice, diversity, and human rights connections that give social work its meaning.

MAIN POINTS

- Effective social work practice interventions with groups provide an interface for the promotion of social justice, diversity, and human rights.

- Strengths and empowerment, narrative, and solution-focused approaches are useful middle-phase (intervention) and ending-phase (termination) strategies.

- Developmental models, such as the Boston Model and others based on it, are widely used in group work. Many applications of and departures from these models can be found in the contemporary practice environment.

- Social workers working with groups add to the skills they've honed for intervening with individuals, developing additional skills for group intervention in the areas of group leadership, community, problem solving, and management of group functioning.

- Contemporary examples of innovative, evidence-based group practice models, such as constructionist groups and restorative justice groups, help to provide vision and possibility for responding to current cultural and social issues.

- Termination occurs in three distinct areas of group practice interventions: between group members and the social worker, among group members, and of the group itself.

- While evaluation of group practice shares some commonalities with evaluation of individual and family interventions, evaluating group interventions is more complex, as it requires both examinations of the individual members of the group and of the group itself.

EXERCISES

a. Case Exercises

1. To apply your learning of the Grand Challenge to use technology for social good that was highlighted in this chapter, visit the Grand Challenges website and read Working Paper No. 12, *Practice Innovation through Technology in the Digital Age: A Grand Challenge for Social Work* (Berzin et al., 2015) at: http://aaswsw.org/grand-challenges-initiative/12-challenges/harness-technology-for-social-good/. To examine the potential use of technology in the aftermath of Hurricane in the Hudson City area, review the case information at www.routledgesw.com/caseStudies. After reading Working Paper No. 12 and reviewing the information on Hudson City, complete the following items:
   a. Using the town map, sociogram, and interaction matrix, identify potential

group interventions in each of the four areas of social work group practice discussed in this chapter.

b. For each of the proposed group interventions, research existing technological models and resources that could be utilized to provide or enhance the social worker's ability to develop and conduct the group intervention.

c. Reflect on the potential strengths, weaknesses, and ethical dilemmas associated with each of the proposed technological strategies.

2. Go to www.routledgesw.com/cases, review Carla Washburn's video vignette and consider the roles each member plays in order to complete the following activities and answer the following questions:

a. *Gather into groups*: Start with the group session from the conclusion of the video vignette, and role-play the next session. What happens next? Process the group session with the class.

b. *Round robin*: Each student takes the opportunity to role-play the social worker. Change roles when the "social worker" is not sure how to proceed with the group. Debrief about the experiences and practice behaviors demonstrated for each role-play. What were strengths and areas for growth for each student as a facilitator?

c. Select a member of the group and discuss her or his role in the group process.

d. Identify the social worker's strengths as a group facilitator along with those practice behaviors that she or he may be able to improve.

3. Terminating a group intervention can be challenging. Returning to the grief support group depicted in the Carla Washburn video vignette, role-play the final session. Consider the following:

a. What is the most important role the social worker plays at this stage of the group process?

b. What practice behaviors are critical for the termination phase of a group intervention?

c. Brainstorm strategies for responding to the array of possible member reactions to the ending of the group experience.

4. At the conclusion of a group intervention, the evaluation of the effectiveness of your interventions is critical. Research various evaluation tools and complete the following for the grief support group in which Carla Washburn is a member:

a. Create a satisfaction survey.

b. Create a pre-test/post-test.

c. Create a six-month evaluation tool.

5. Go to www.routledgesw.com/cases and view the Riverton video vignette that depicts a group meeting of the Riverton Neighborhood Association. Upon viewing the video, respond to the following:

a. What model of group intervention is being conducted in this vignette?

b. Identify the practice behaviors and skills covered in this chapter that the group facilitator demonstrates in the meeting.

c. Compare and contrast group facilitation skills needed for a group such as the Riverton Neighborhood Association and for a client-focused group.

6. Go to www.routledgesw.com/cases and view the Riverton video vignette that depicts a group meeting of the Riverton Neighborhood Association or the Carla Washburn video vignette that depicts a grief support group. Using the Group Counselor Rating Scale (Exhibit 9.7), evaluate the group leader. Write a reflection identifying the group leader's strengths and areas for growth and change.

7. Go to www.routledgesw.com/cases and review the case for Brickville, particularly Virginia Stone and her family. In Chapter 8 (Vignette #3), Virginia was involved in the creation of a social action group targeted at saving the park that was built in memory of her family members who were lost in the apartment fire twenty years earlier. The exercise in Chapter 8 focused on determining the need, purpose, composition, structure, and content for such a group. Using the information available to you, develop a written plan that includes the following:

a. Development of the social action plan

b. Strategies for implementing the plan

c. Resources needed to implement the plan, including individuals, groups, organizations, and funding, as appropriate

d. Plan for determining the success or failure of the social action effort

e. Your reflection on the process of implementing a social action plan at the community level.

8. Go to www.routledgesw.com/cases and review the case for Hudson City. Recall from Chapters 6, 7, and 8 that the Patel family experienced significant impact from Hurricane Diane. As a result of her response to the experience, you refer the 12-year-old daughter, Aarti, to a group to help her develop her coping skills. While Aarti was a regular and active participant in the support group, there is mounting concern that she continues to struggle with the challenges that resulted in the referral to the group (e.g., nightmares, discomfort when required to be away from her parents for activities other than school and group, and decreased appetite). Describe in writing your thoughts about the concerns her parents and the leader of the support group express and a plan for addressing the ongoing challenges that Aarti and her family are experiencing, including:

- Continuation in the support group
- Alternative intervention strategies
- Resources needed for a revised intervention plan

9. Go to www.routledgesw.com/cases and review the case for Brickville, then, referring back to the discussion of the Stone family potential participation in group interventions at the beginning of this chapter, conduct a search of the literature on group-level interventions to find social work skills needed to conduct and evaluate the following group interventions:

a. Through a community needs assessment of services for older adults, the Bethany Catholic Church additionally identified a number of community members who are caring for older family members and determined that offering a group for family caregivers would be of service to the caregivers and their older family members.

b. The Brickville Community Development Corporation Youth Leadership Program (YLP) uses evidence-based practices for training and facilitating a task group focused on helping teens to make healthy life choices.

c. The Catholic Charities Community Center offers a group for children experiencing behavioral concerns.

d. A group of residents in the Brickville area have banded together to form a group to bring attention to issues of police and fire department lack of/slow responses to their community.

b. Other Exercises

10. To relate the information covered in this chapter to your own group experience, reflect on a specific experience you have had as a member of a group by responding to the following items:

a. Describe in detail a group to which you belonged (may be a current group). Include the following:
   - Type of group (may use one of the types described in Chapter 8)
   - Purpose of group
   - Structure of group (e.g., open or closed membership, time-limited or open-ended, number of members, eligibility for membership)
   - Your role within the group

b. Consider the quality of your involvement by reflecting on:
   - How did you feel about being a member of the group? How did you feel about your role? Your contributions?
   - Did the group fulfill stated expectations? Your expectations? If not, explain the reasons.
   - What were the strengths of the group?
   - What are areas for the group's growth or change?
   - Was group leadership formally determined or did it evolve naturally? What was the style of the leader(s)?

c. Based on your experience and your new knowledge of the group process, reflect on the following:
   - Would you engage with the group differently? If yes, how would your involvement change? Explain your reasons.
   - Was the group formally or informally evaluated? What were the outcomes?

11. Develop a plan for the way in which you, as a group leader, will respond to each of the following behaviors that may emerge during the course of your experience in group work:

a. "Silent" group member

b. "Monopolizer"

c. "Help-rejecter/avoider"

d. "Caregiver/coordinator"

e. "Attacker"

f. "Harmonizer"

g. "Clown"

h. "Poor me" group member

After developing your response plan for each behavior, reflect in writing on the challenges you anticipate facing and strategies for learning and growing as a group facilitator.

12. Recall from Chapter 8 that you, as a practicum student, were invited to serve as a co-facilitator for a psychoeducational support group for family caregivers of persons experiencing Parkinson's disease. In the previous exercise, you focused on familiarizing yourself with Parkinson's disease and developed a plan for the session that you would lead. In preparing for the intervention, terminations, and evaluation phases of group work, respond to the following items:

a. Identify potential needs for ongoing psychoeducational support that care-givers of persons with Parkinson's disease will likely experience.

b. Develop a plan for evaluating the support group with a specific emphasis on strategies you will use to gather feedback from group members.

CHAPTER 10

Social Work Practice with Communities: Engagement, Assessment, and Planning

Change will not come if we wait for some other person or some other time. We are the ones we've been waiting for. We are the change that we seek.

Barack Obama, Feb. 5, 2008

Key Questions for Chapter 10

1. What competencies do I need to engage and assess communities? [EPAS 6 and 7]
2. What are the social work practice behaviors that enable me to effectively engage and assess communities? [EPAS 6 and 7]
3. How can I utilize evidence in research-informed practice and practice-informed research to guide engagement and assessment with communities? [EPAS 4]
4. How can I apply social work values and ethics to community engagement and assessment? [EPAS 1]

Many issues that arise in individual, family, and group practice can also be addressed through community practice. Community practice includes social planning, which means planning human services for a geographic community based on resident needs. It also includes community organizing and development work. The Sanchez family members (see www.routledgesw.com/sanchez/engage/casefiles) have a range of challenges that could be the focus of community practice. For example, Celia struggles with low English proficiency, and the family has financial struggles and does not access health care often due to barriers. These struggles may be shared by other families in their community and may be addressed by community practice. Beyond

*just being referred to existing services for their challenges, the family may also ulti-
mately benefit from a community engagement and needs assessment process
(discussed in this chapter) to uncover how common these issues are in the community, and whether there are other issues that need to be addressed community-wide.*

IT IS IN COMMUNITIES THAT PEOPLE FIND identity and meaning for their lives in their various roles as individuals, parents, children, partners, friends, and professionals. **Community** is the structure, both tangible and metaphoric, that supports interaction and connectedness among people over time. The characteristics of the community in which people grow, live, and develop can have important implications for the resources and opportunities available to them. For example, growing up in some communities that offer a safe environment and strong schools helps children grow into secure and well-educated adults with strong prospects for the future. Communities are the central context of social work practice with all types of clients: therefore, community practice is an important aspect of generalist social work.

This chapter examines the concept of community and your relationship to it as a social work practitioner. It will explore the types of community and the functions that give community meaning. We will consider methods of inquiry into the study of community, including community analysis; community needs assessment; and community asset mapping. Finally, the chapter will consider the need for and avenues by which to have a global perspective on community practice.

FAMILIAR PERSPECTIVES AND SOME ALTERNATIVES ON COMMUNITY

Encouraging individuals, families, and groups to work to improve their communities is part of social work practice. Sectors such as education, housing, health, recreational opportunities, local businesses, religious/faith communities, and employment opportunities are important to the quality of life for the residents of a community. Local relationships, experiences, resources, and opportunities continue to play an important role in our daily lives, and local residents invest time, energy, and resources into creating community resources and opportunities that will positively impact their quality of life. For example, local residents and business owners work hard to maintain and increase property values and to decrease crime in their neighborhoods. Similarly, residents strive to keep materials that are hazardous to the environment (e.g., some chemicals and landfills) out of their neighborhoods and to garner resources to increase the quality of public education in their communities. Challenges and issues compel residents to take action on behalf of their communities. **Interdependence**—the idea that individuals depend upon on one another—resonates in practice models with individuals, families, and groups that emphasize health and recovery based on both professional and peer support.

Forces Working against Connections within Communities

Much of contemporary research and literature about community focuses on how the increasingly impersonal and complex nature of U.S. society works against some types of community work (Brueggemann, 2013a). As an example, the forces working against connections within local geographic communities include technology that allows people to share interests and build bonds with people outside of their immediate community and all over the globe and the individualistic character of U.S. culture, which provides less social reinforcement for community involvement than other cultures. Globalization provides another example; it may also work against the development of strong place-based community connections, as corporations and financial capital shift quickly from place to place to find the most profitable locations for business, and workers move to find optimal employment opportunities. Third, the human service system also reinforces society's focus on individualism in its emphasis on the individual and family and the perpetual pursuit of self-fulfillment. Many human service agencies focus on individual and family counseling. Encouraging individuals, families, and groups to work to improve their communities is part of social work practice.

Community Practice and Generalist Practice

Promoting community involvement is important for social workers working with clients at every level. Communities are critical because it is within communities that individuals live their lives, and communities are the formal conduits through which resources; formal and informal systems; and political, social, and economic forces shape individuals, families, and neighborhoods. Communities therefore influence our experiences and the ability of social workers to affect outcomes for their clients. Even when social workers never go outside of the traditional one-to-one social work relationship, the success of their efforts depends, in large part, on the nature and responsiveness of the clients' communities. For example, a community's overall capacity to provide decent, affordable housing for single persons who receive public assistance will impact a young, low-income client with two children who is seeking shelter. If this client asks for your help finding housing, you need to know about the resources for shelter, transitional housing, and low-income housing available in her community, as well as resources to combat discrimination if she suspects that she is denied housing illegally (if, for example, she is denied rental housing because the landlord will not rent to single mothers who receive public assistance). Other factors to consider surrounding her housing choices may include employment, schools, child care, the quality and quantity of afterschool programs, and the existence of a community center. She may be interested in information about the overall safety of the community, including the rate of crime, the proximity of a former partner who may pose safety concerns, and the presence of specific gangs in the area. To practice competently, social workers need knowledge of community resources and skills to address challenges related to those resources; the entities that make decisions about resources; and ways to secure resources for clients. A social worker also needs to know about the various dimensions of a community in order to be an effective catalyst for change in that community. Skills honed working with individuals, groups, families, and organizations are vital to community practice, and skills honed working with communities are important to every other type of client.

Working with communities requires mastery of many social work competencies and behaviors (CSWE, 2015). For example, social workers must be able to respond to the contexts that shape practice [EPAS 7] by being proactive and engaging in community work that will seek to prevent problems and unnecessary challenges from occurring. As in work with other types of clients (individuals, families, and groups), social workers in community practice must also employ ethical principles [EPAS 1] and cultural competence [EPAS 2]. Community practice uses research-informed and evidence-based practice [EPAS 4] to advance human rights and economic justice [EPAS 3]. Lastly, like practice with all other types of clients, community practice utilizes the change process (i.e., engagement, assessment, intervention, termination, and evaluation) [EPAS 7, 8, 9, and 10]. This chapter will explore many of these competencies and will discuss the practice behaviors associated with them. We will also consider the different types of communities, the nature of community functions, and ways to understand a community.

DEFINITIONS AND TYPES OF COMMUNITY

Several types of community are discussed in the social work literature. This section describes three of the most common—spatial, social, and political—as well as personal communities (Chaskin, 2013).

Spatial Community

One type of community is a geographic entity, such as a town, city, small neighborhood, or college dormitory. These **spatial communities** are structures of connectedness based on a physical location. In some cases, these communities have clear, physical boundaries, such as a river, mountain, gate, wall, or a legally defined boundary. In other cases, **stakeholders**—those who have an interest in community affairs, such as county or city officials, or neighborhood leaders—agree upon their boundaries. People also construct cognitive maps of their communities that inform their relationship to their physical space, movement within their spatial community, and their social interaction. These boundaries may provide safety and security for community members, but they may also be a means of excluding others. The degree to which community residents perceive themselves as community members depends on many dimensions, but access to the community's benefits is among the most influential. Those residents of a community who do not have access to community benefits such as community centers, public libraries, and other resources may not feel personally affiliated with the communities in which they live. In large spatial communities, such as New York City, there are likely to be many smaller communities within the larger community. Spatial communities of all sizes can be diverse. For example, Jackson Heights, New York, a community within the borough of Queens with 175,000 residents, is one of the most diverse communities in the U.S. and the world, with 167 spoken languages (New York Times, 2015).

Social Communities

Groups that share common interests, concerns, norms, identity, or interactions and share a similar sense of belonging are **social communities**. One type of social community, a community of identity, relates more to affiliations than to a location. Student communities, Asian communities, lesbian communities, veterans' communities, and skateboard communities are all examples of communities of identity. As in spatial communities, members attach different meanings to their communities and affiliate with those communities to varying extents over time. For example, the Jewish community may play a significant lifelong role for some but have less significance for others, or a community of skateboarders may play a very important role in members' lives for several years but fade in importance as they reach adulthood. Some social workers focus their careers on specific communities of identity, such as women who experience intimate partner violence or those who have lost a partner to Alzheimer's disease or related dementia. Social workers may develop interest in a particular community of identity based on their personal experiences or early professional experiences. While social communities have the potential to function as exclusionary associations, they can also offer members a powerful sense of connection and commitment.

People are often part of more than one type of community. For example, a person may be affiliated with a spatial community in which they live, a worship community, an online community of gamers, a community of yoga teachers, her/his dorm, and a community of undergraduate students. A social community consists of a collection of both spatial and social communities, where people can build a sense of belonging. They often serve to provide meaning to one's identity. These unique arrangements of place and nonplace communities are networks within which one interacts, and they serve to integrate one's personal and professional lives. Social workers may be interested in clients' social communities because social communities provide socialization and resources, such as helping networks (formal and informal), that may be helpful for clients facing a crisis or challenges. Social communities can also provide cross-cultural dimensions that aid in a wider world view.

© vm

Political Communities

Political communities serve as venues through which people participate in demo-cratic governance and promote social change through community organizing and political mobilization. The spatial community, as a formal political unit, and the social community, through which people interact, are both incorporated in a political community since they can both serve political functions. Efforts to promote democracy using political communities focus on increasing the capacities of both geographic and social communities to practice self-determination and be involved in governing. Social workers may utilize the political community of clients to encourage civic engagement through attending neighborhood meetings, supporting candidates for office, meeting with elected officials to share ideas about local needs, voting, and being involved in grassroots community organizing efforts.

COMMUNITY FUNCTIONS

A traditional view of community holds that communities perform certain necessary functions for their residents or members, including the following (Streeter, 2013):

- *The production, distribution, and consumption of goods and services:* This may include basic needs like food, clothing, shelter, health care, and employment. Communities provide adequate wages so people can access goods and services.

- *The transmission of knowledge, social values, customs, and behavior patterns:* This socialization process guides how residents view themselves, others, and their rights and responsibilities. Both formal institutions, such as schools and faith communities, and informal institutions, such as friends and peer groups, can be involved in this function.

- *The maintenance of conformity to community norms through social control:* Formal governmental entities, such as law enforcement and court systems, enforce laws, rules and regulations. Informal systems of enforcement, such as schools, families, peers, and organized neighborhood watches, reinforce community standards. Patterns of service provisions that regulate access to resources (e.g., eligibility guidelines for local food pantries) also serve as mechanisms of social control.

- *Social participation through formal and informal groups:* Interaction with others through groups, associations, and organizations provides social outlets and helps build natural helping and support networks. People engage in social participation when they join sports leagues, volunteer, vote, attend Parent Teacher Association (PTA) meetings, and attend local music festivals.

- *The provision of mutual support:* Families, friends, neighbors, and volunteers provide aid, support one another, and assist individuals and families to solve problems independent of professional help. Due to the complexities of modern society, the work of human service professionals, such as social workers, often supplements this function.

UNDERSTANDING A COMMUNITY

Given their complex nature, understanding the many ways that communities can be conceptualized is imperative before moving into the change process of engagement, assessment, intervention, and termination and evaluation. We will examine communities as social systems; as ecological systems; as centers for power and conflict; and from two contemporary perspectives: the strengths, empowerment, and resiliency perspectives and the postmodern perspective.

Community as a Social System

General systems theory offers a helpful framework with which to analyze and understand communities. General systems theory posits that a system, such as a community, is composed of multiple intersecting components that relate to one other and that are also part of larger systems, such as a larger community. Some communities are part of subsystems that perform specialized functions for the larger system—the community as a whole (for example, a community of business owners within a larger geographic community). Through community assessments (in the "Assessing Communities" section), social workers can critically assess the extent to which subsystems, such as the function of mutual support or the business subsystem within a community, meet the community's needs. If necessary, they can then advocate for higher functioning to improve the subsystem (Netting, Kettner, McMurtry, & Thomas, 2017; Streeter, 2013).

Community as an Ecological System

The ecosystems perspective focuses on the interdependence of people and their environment in our understanding of communities. It emphasizes the spatial organization of community resources, the relationship of these resources to one another and to groups of people, and the corresponding social and economic consequences. For example, a major road or highway bisecting a community can have implications for the social organization and economics of the community. It may bring in more customers for some businesses and shut down others. The social organization implications of the road include the possibilities that individuals and groups may interact more or less with one other. The ecosystems perspective is also concerned with competition for resources: one or more communities may compete with each other, or groups within a community may compete. For example, competition for land is common in many communities, as some groups want to develop land for residences and businesses, while others would like to keep land available for parks, community centers, and hiking trails, and still others may advocate to keep land devoted to family-based agriculture. The political or economic dominance of communities over one another or of one group over another group within a community often results in decreased access to resources for some groups that have less power and has consequences for the social interactions within a community. A group's dominance can ensure its access to better schools, employment, health care facilities, and public services such as police and fire protection. The ecological systems perspective can therefore help in understanding a hierarchical, uneven power structure in a community. Other related concepts including segregation (i.e., the isolation of groups within a community); centralization (i.e., concentration of resources in one part of a community); and succession (i.e., the movement of groups of people into and out of areas of a community) are also useful in analyzing communities (Netting et al., 2017; Streeter, 2013). These concepts help explain the ways in which populations move and settle in various areas of communities and why resources differ among particular areas of communities.

Communities as Centers of Power and Conflict

Political and social dynamics and conflicts are powerful forces in communities. Power significantly influences opportunities and constraints for community members. Often, the interests of one segment of a community clash with the interests of another segment, and a struggle can emerge. Applying conflict and power theories can create conditions that promote change (Weil & Ohmer, 2013). The following theories assist in our understanding of the community as a setting for power and conflict (Hardina, 2002). Individually or together, the theories can help explain power and conflict within communities.

Power dependency theory focuses on the dynamics associated with a community's dependent relationships with the external entities that supply needed resources. The effects of these dynamics can be dramatic. For example, a community's dependence on a funding source with close ties to a large retail chain may influence its decisions about promoting small, locally owned businesses. Therefore, the small businesses may go out of business due to the community's dependence on the interests of a funding source.

Conflict theory views the community as divided into influential ("haves") and noninfluential ("have-nots") groups that compete for limited resources. This theory further assumes that the influential group has power over the noninfluential group and that dimensions of diversity play a central role in oppression. For example, people with greater income and political connections may have more influence over decisions that affect the community than those who are of lower income and fewer connections. Therefore, community decisions may favor those with more income and political connections over those with less of both.

Resource mobilization theory focuses on the conditions needed to promote change through community practice. Large-scale community change occurs more easily when groups that feel excluded from a decision-making process come together and protest their exclusion as a group. These groups can use an appealing message and an inclusive structure to attract more members. For example, delegates to the 2016 Republican National Convention from all over the U.S. who did not endorse Donald Trump as the Republican Party candidate for President came together at the Convention around the message of "Never Trump" and staged a protest.

Taken together, the theories just discussed inform the social work profession's thinking about the community as a setting in which power and control play crucial roles. Groups within a community vie for power and control to implement change that will benefit their interests, even if the change may oppress others within the community. Communities can bring about change through rational planning and collaborative efforts, or through confrontation, efforts to build power, and negotiation. Dimensions of diversity, such as race, socioeconomic status, and ethnicity, as well as special interests, such as area of the community, can be driving factors in community conflicts, and underscore the need for cultural competence in community practice. Viewing the community as a center for power and conflict can help social workers assess the community power structure and understand the process of community decision-making, the reasons behind it and their roles in community processes. Social workers may also use this lens to learn more about ways in which marginalized groups are oppressed in communities and how powerful forces in communities maintain their power (Netting et al., 2017; Streeter, 2013).

Contemporary Perspectives for Community Practice

Now that we have a general understanding of communities, we turn to a discussion of the strengths, empowerment, and resiliency perspectives and the postmodern perspective. These perspectives move us toward a deeper understanding of community and toward assessing communities.

Strengths, Empowerment, and Resiliency Perspectives   As previously mentioned, the strengths perspective, originally presented by Saleebey (2013), focuses on identifying possibilities and assets of individuals, groups, and communities, rather than on their deficits and problems. It may be challenging to apply the strengths perspective in communities that have few resources. As in all communities, identifying strengths in these communities can help them empower themselves. Assisting them to recognize the resources they possess helps them develop the power to effect change. The recognition of resources can lead to resiliency and can increase the potential for successful problem solving. For example, the strengths perspective can encourage leaders in communities with large plots of vacant land and boarded-up homes to think about the land and homes as valuable assets, rather than as problems. Perhaps the vacant land could be used for community gardens or for greenhouses for small businesses. A community's strengths also include the skills and talents of its residents. Later in this chapter, we will discuss community asset mapping as a means to implement the strengths, empowerment, and resiliency perspectives (Kingsley, Coulton & Pettit, 2014; Netting et al., 2017; Hillier & Culhane, 2013).

Community in a Postmodern Perspective   The postmodern perspective assumes that knowledge is socially constructed and that multiple "truths" exist, depending on a person's perspective. Postmodern approaches, including social construction and critical social construction, invite the examination of the cultural assumptions that underlie many arrangements of power and politics. These approaches tend to be critical of assumptions or theories that claim absolute or authoritative truth. Social workers using postmodern approaches are interested in assumptions, explanations, and causes of perceived problems in the community and in examining situations from multiple perspectives. For example, social workers using the postmodern perspective would seek out different perspectives and assumptions surrounding the presence of undocumented immigrants in a community to learn about various community members' views and assume that there could be multiple "truths" about how welcome they have been and how they are viewed by other community members. They would also be interested in the cultural symbols and norms a community uses, such as the ways in which the social structures of specific populations are organized, and the cultural symbols used to signify those structures (Weil & Ohmer, 2013).

ENGAGING COMMUNITIES [EPAS 6]

This section will discuss traditional and contemporary perspectives on community work and the ways in which these perspectives can inform engagement and assessment with communities. Traditional and contemporary perspectives on community allow us to use different lenses to understand the dynamics and decision-making processes in communities. The perspectives also help explain the sources of and barriers to change in ways that inform the change process (i.e., engagement, assessment, intervention, and termination and evaluation with communities).

Engagement of Communities

In their work in communities, social workers can approach engagement, the first step in the change process, in many different ways. Engagement with communities involves working with clients and institutions on behalf of entire communities. Many of the engagement and assessment skills we discussed in previous chapters are helpful in work with communities. Active listening skills, for example, are as useful in working in community practice as they are in work with individuals, families, and groups and organizations.

Social work with communities begins with a focus on challenges and opportunities. For example, a social worker working for a community-based education program attached to a local public school may discover that community residents lack adequate employment opportunities. Alternatively, social workers employed by a local or state correctional system may learn about an opportunity to apply for funding to prevent juvenile crime and engage community members to plan and write a grant to benefit the local community. Social workers may also engage in community practice through their work with a particular population. A social worker in a health care setting may learn about a lack of respite services available for the family caregivers of older adults. The social worker may help the caregivers organize themselves to approach a potential funder—such as local, state, or federal legislators or a local foundation—to advocate for funding for respite care. Social workers also engage with communities based primarily on setting. For example, a social worker employed by an elementary school may learn that a local factory is dumping hazardous waste materials in a nearby neighborhood, endangering the health of the children of the community. The social worker may work to engage local community leaders to conduct community-wide meetings and/or communicate with appropriate decision-makers and work toward a resolution to protect the health of the children. Social workers become engaged with communities in many ways, either through formal employment or volunteering at the community level or through involvement with a challenge/opportunity, population, or setting they learned about through their primary professional roles with individual, family, group, or organizations (Netting et al., 2017).

Engagement with community members can take place in a wide variety of ways. Often different types of groups are used to learn more about community issues. For example, using the Sanchez family, a school-based group of parents may be formed to try to engage parents and families about improvements needed in the school for children with disabilities. As part of the group process, many issues may emerge, including the difficulty in accessing primary health care in the community. With skilled facilitation that encourages members to share their stories and build group solidarity, groupwork can also facilitate engagement in wider community issues (Hardina, 2013).

Interprofessional Engagement Community engagement often includes interacting with institutions and professionals that provide resources or potential resources, make decisions for, or have influence in a community. Engaging institutions and professionals that specialize in health, public health, mental health, counseling, psychology, urban planning, theology, education, business, and/or law is common in community practice. Professionals with these backgrounds work in a variety of roles, such as business leader, politician, community planner, program manager, faith leader, and others. Interprofessional collaboration skills, including such interpersonal skills as active listening and building trust, are needed to effectively engage these professionals and their institutions. Social workers also need a strong understanding of social work values and ethics to guide them in collaboration. Other professions often have different values and ethics, or codes of ethics; therefore, interprofessional collaboration requires a curiosity about the differences between and among the knowledge, skills, and values of various professions, as well as a strong social work identity. In the engagement process, the goal is to build relationships useful for working together on a shared vision within a climate that is trusting and capable of resolving conflicts productively and professionally (Hardina, 2013).

For example, a social worker who is facilitating the school-based group of parents that includes the Sanchez family may work with other professionals, such as those with legal and educational degrees, along with the parents, to pressure the school district to provide more resources for children with disabilities. Throughout the process, the social worker should be mindful of the National Association of Social Workers' (NASW) *Code of Ethics* (NASW, 2008) to guide her in the advocacy work and should be aware that those with legal and educational background may be guided by different professional values and ethics.

ASSESSING COMMUNITIES [EPAS 7]

The assessment process in community work often occurs in tandem with the engagement process, and it can involve several different techniques. The following discussion will explore two prominent techniques: comprehensive community-based analysis and a community needs assessment. Community asset mapping will also be discussed as a strengths-based community assessment technique.

Comprehensive Community-Based Analysis

Social workers in different settings and jobs need an understanding of the overall community in which they serve clients, as well as an understanding of the specific population they serve and the primary challenges that population faces. Understanding communities involves learning about their structures and how they function. Developing an accurate knowledge base about a community can lead to more effective assessments and interventions with individuals, families, groups, organizations, and communities.

When you learn about key aspects of a particular community, you discover its unique characteristics, including its strengths, challenges, and history and the concerns of its residents. You can use the answers to the questions suggested next to create a formal document for an organization or community or in an informal fashion.

One useful tool for understanding the connections among aspects of a community is the **sociogram**. A sociogram (similar to an ecomap) is a visual tool for assessing community connections and dynamics. It is important to note which subsystems interact and the nature of the interaction. It is also important to note which subsystems do not yet have any interactions so that you can consider potential linkages. The use of a sociogram can lead to understanding both isolated and well-connected aspects and the nature of those connections. The focal system is considered the "client," that is, the system that is the focus of intervention, as displayed in Exhibit 10.1.

To achieve an overall understanding of a community, the following major community domains must be explored during a community assessment (Netting et al., 2017) using assessment techniques discussed later in this chapter. The following provides a guide for domains for a spatial community:

- *Physical setting:* The physical setting of a community includes the geography (e.g., presence of water or flat or hilly land), main geographical boundaries and natural barriers, and the degree to which communities are integrated into or isolated from surrounding neighborhoods. For example, is the community near a downtown area, a vital entertainment or shopping district, or a medical complex? Do the streets dead-end or go through to other communities?

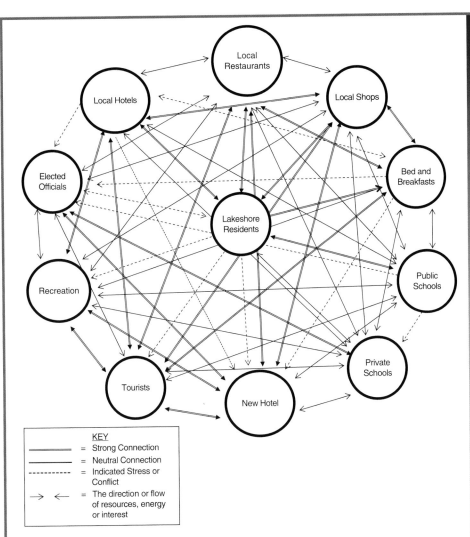

EXHIBIT 10.1

*Lakeshore
Sociogram*

Lakeshore is a town in the northern part of the United States. It is a popular tourist destination in the warmer months because of the beautiful lake and beaches that surround it. Its many restaurants and shopping districts prosper in those warm months. As evident from the sociogram, the relationships among the various entities in the town vary. A few are described in the following list:

1. The restaurant owners have a strong positive relationship with the local shops because the shops recommend the restaurants to tourists. The residents also are supportive of local shops, and they enjoy a strong positive relationship.

2. There are many thriving small bed and breakfasts and locally owned hotels, but this year a large, high-rise hotel is scheduled to be built in the town. This will be the first hotel of this kind in Lakeshore, and there are mixed feelings about what this hotel

EXHIBIT 10.1

Continued

will bring the town. Therefore, the relationship between the hotel, the bed and breakfasts, and smaller local hotels is stressed/conflicted.

3. Due to the tourism industry at the lake, there are many recreational opportunities in the town such as miniature golf courses and lake/water activities, but residents get upset in the tourist months when they are very crowded and increase their prices. Therefore, the relationship between the residents and the tourists, and between the residents and recreation, is stressed/conflicted.

4. There are both public and private schools in Lakeshore. The public school leadership feels that the private schools drain resources from the public schools, because the parents of the private school children are not as supportive of campaigns for additional public funds for schools, and fewer students in the public schools means fewer state funds for the schools. Therefore, the relationship between the two is stressed/conflicted, with a one-way energy flow.

5. Elected officials voted and passed plans for the addition of the new, high-rise hotel in town. The owners of the new hotel therefore have a positive relationship with elected officials, while the local hotels, bed and breakfasts, and residents have a conflicted relationship with the elected officials. While some residents believe the hotel will benefit the town's small businesses and overall economy, most prefer to support locally owned, smaller hotels and bed and breakfasts.

- *History:* The history of a community includes the identity of the population(s) that originally settled the community, when it was settled, and the major historical events that shaped the community. Additionally, you might also consider the ways in which the architecture and layout of the community reflect early inhabitants and whether the community history impacts the current dynamics of community functioning. Consider asking the following: What is the history of different populations settling in the community? Have transitions occurred? If so, have these transitions been marked with conflict?

- *Demographics of the population:* Knowledge of the current population of the community, as well as the well-defined and informal subpopulations with their own distinct cultures within the community, is very important. Questions to consider include: What are the largest population groups in the community? Can the community be characterized as homogeneous or heterogeneous, considering different variables?

- *Economic system:* The economic system includes employment for community residents; types, number, and industry of large businesses; the presence of small, locally owned businesses; the presence of stores that residents can utilize for their basic needs, such as grocery stores and co-ops, farmers' markets, clothing stores, and hardware stores; the rate of employment in the community; and the type of transportation available to community residents. You may ask: Who are the major employers? Where are the jobs located? Are the jobs conveniently located to the unemployed or underemployed? What is the employers' relationships to the community? What are the needs of the employers?

- *Political system:* An awareness of a community's political system provides helpful information about who makes key decisions affecting the community. To understand the community, it's important to learn about all types of elected officials who have the authority to make decisions for the community. It's also important to seek information about the level of political activity in the community (for example, by looking for bumper stickers and yard signs). Information about the degree to which the business community is organized into a business association and involved in politics is also helpful. You might inquire about the degree to which human service systems are involved in the local political system, the degree to which the political system is organized and connected to community residents, and the level of activity of local politicians.

- *Social characteristics:* Social characteristics include the demographics of the residents in terms of social class, race, ethnicity, age, and other dimensions of diversity, as well as places where people gather. Questions to consider regarding the social characteristics of a community include: Do new residents and visitors consider the community friendly or unfriendly? Are there many places of worship? What size are the congregations and which denominations are present? Are there formal or informal meeting places besides places of worship (i.e., coffee shops, meeting halls, clubs, associations, etc.?) What is the condition of the parks or recreational areas? What are housing conditions in terms of upkeep, quality, and the proportion of rental versus family owned? Does it vary by neighborhood? Is housing for sale? Is the for-sale housing dispersed or clustered? Is there evidence of construction and home repair? Are there strong institutions in the community related to social needs?

- *Human service system:* The human service system includes education, health, and social services of all types. Questions to consider include the following: What kinds of public and private schools are located in the community? Investigate their educational quality, physical condition, and funding sources. What kinds of voluntary agencies are located in the community? How available are services to residents? How well organized are the organizations within the community? Are professional networks in the community strong or weak?

- *Values, beliefs, and traditions:* While observing and building relationships to learn about values, beliefs, and traditions, consider what community residents value. Are differences based on race, ethnicity, and sections of the community, or on another dimension of diversity? Do members of the community celebrate specific traditions that may be unique to that community or to a sub-population of the community?

- *Evidence of oppression and discrimination:* A social justice perspective requires social workers to look for oppression and discrimination within the community, and/or from other communities. Questions to consider include: Is there a history of oppression and discrimination in the community (such as separate recreational facilities, housing patterns that suggest discrimination, and/or school enrollment and quality patterns that suggest discrimination)? Are there current patterns of discrimination and oppression?

Community Needs Assessment

A community **needs assessment** is a formal process for identifying unmet community needs, placing needs in order of priorities, and planning to target resources to solve problems. A needs assessment can be conducted to focus on the overall functioning of a community. Alternatively, many social workers begin to learn about a community through the focus of the predominant population they are serving, or because of a specific community challenge such as poor quality housing, gangs, or truancy. A focus on a particular community of identity or population and to assess the degree to which the social services system meets their particular needs is another way to do a needs assessment. The process concentrates on the gap between needs and resources. The findings inform the planning process for specific social work community interventions and are often more practical than comprehensive studies. Ideally, community analyses and needs assessments are integrated processes rather than an either/or choice.

The overall process of a community needs assessment can be compared to a research project. As with a research project, the goals of the sponsor of the study may shape the purpose of the assessment. For example, a social service organization may want more information about the needs of the older adult population in a community, but may not be as interested as you are, as a researcher, in examining the growing LGBTQ older adult population. This difference of interest may require a negotiation about the needs assessment process, tools, data sources, and reporting. Regardless of the sponsor, the social worker should use the following six recommended steps to conduct the needs assessment (Mulroy, 2013);

1. Reviewing the evidence
2. Assessing local knowledge
3. Selecting study methods
4. Conducting the study
5. Processing and studying the data
6. Reporting the findings

The principles of evidence-based practice, as discussed in the next section, should guide the research process.

Using Evidence-Based Practice in Community Practice [EPAS 4]   Following the steps of evidence-based practice, social workers begin community practice with a review of relevant research literature about similar communities and theories of change to guide the design of the needs assessment. The next step is to clarify the unit of analysis for the study, whether that is a specific population, a geographic area, a particular challenge—such as homelessness or a combination of units. Consultation with community members, the sponsor, and other interested parties about the current evidence; local knowledge; research design; study methods; analysis; and the structure of the report can help achieve the highest-quality needs assessment (Mulroy, 2013).

Social workers can use the same research methods they used for comprehensive community analyses when they perform comprehensive needs assessments or needs assessments focused on particular populations or challenges. An understanding of each approach can help determine the most appropriate evidence-based method(s) to use in a particular situation. In the following discussion, we consider several sources of data gathering, including observation, census and administrative data, interviews with key informants, focus groups, community forums, and survey data (Royse, Staton-Tindall, Badger, & Webster, 2009; Ohmer, Sobek, Teixeira, Wallace, & Shapiro, 2013). We go on to discuss the use of maps to visually display data and community asset mapping.

Community Needs Assessment Process   Social workers are involved in community needs assessments for many reasons, including seeking new resources and support for a program, targeting a program to best meet community needs, or simply getting to know the community in order to better serve individuals, families, and groups. Funders considering a request to back a program will often ask the agency or institution making the request to justify the proposed program or services by demonstrating community need. Policymakers can use the findings of a community assessment to modify policy. For example, if, due to increased demand, a food pantry must consider changing its eligibility policy, the program can use data from a community assessment to determine which population has the highest unmet need. Organizations that wish to improve services for a particular group of clients may undertake a needs assessment to learn about, for example, the unmet needs of single men in the community. Finally, social workers may become involved in a needs assessment to establish or strengthen partnerships. For instance, a homeless shelter may increasingly encounter children who are medically fragile. The staff of the organization may conduct a community needs assessment to collect data about the health needs of homeless and near-homeless children so that they can present that information when they approach local health providers to develop a service partnership.

Sources of Data for Community Needs Assessments

There are many potential sources of data, including primary and secondary sources of both quantitative and qualitative data, for a community needs assessment. Some of the most common and useful forms include observation, service statistics and previous studies, census data, administrative data, interviews, focus groups, community forums, and survey data. Several of these types, as well as guidelines for making decisions about methods, are discussed next (Mulroy, 2013; Netting et al., 2017; Iowa State University Extension and Outreach, 2016; Ohmer et al., 2013).

Observation   The purpose of observation is to collect information about community processes and events as they occur. Observers can attend popular community events such as free concerts, plays, and/or political rallies to notice aspects of community life including ethnic composition, geographical divisions, and apparent patterns. For example, an observer may detect the presence or absence of late-night street activity, the number of older adults visible in a community, the number of children playing outside during school hours, and the number of young adults hanging out on the streets during the day. Other aspects to notice include interpersonal relationships, patterns and styles of how residents relate to one another, and residents' relationships to the community space. An observer may simply witness events, or she or he may actually participate in the community activities being observed.

As a nonparticipant, an observer may walk around and/or attend events within the community in places like the city hall, coffee shops, community centers, busy parks, commercial strips, fairs and markets, and schools. Using this method, the observer can gather notes about observations, items in local newspapers, pamphlets that describe community resources, local maps, local directories, and historical markers.

Participant observation occurs when an observer joins in community events and interacts with local residents. For example, a participant observer could learn about a community by eating at local establishments and interacting with patrons and staff. During the interaction, a participant observer asks questions from the perspective of a respectful learner and avoids taking the stance of an expert or a change agent.

Service Statistics and Previous Studies   Data from local human service organizations may be helpful for the needs assessment. Such data can include rate of utilization of services, types of services provided, waiting list information, and caseload data. Data from other types of organizations, such as businesses, faith communities, neighborhood groups, and youth organizations, can also be helpful. This information may be available through a variety of sources including annual reports, public data available on the Internet, a contact person at an organization, or an elected or appointed community official. Similarly, previous studies about the origins of community problems, such as studies from the public health department or community organizations, may be helpful.

Use of Census Data   The U.S. Census Bureau conducts a national census every ten years, gathering extensive demographic information about people living in the United States. The Census Bureau also conducts the American Community Survey each year, collecting some data from a sample of residents. A variety of databases and websites, some of which are very user friendly, provide access to census data. These resources allow you to access data at small geographic levels within broader communities.

Administrative Data   School districts, public assistance offices, child welfare offices, public health agencies, and police departments make administrative data available to the public. Administrative data can help illuminate a wide variety of community issues including local academic performance, truancy, child abuse, rate and prevalence of sexually transmitted disease, teen pregnancy, crime, and other issues. These data are typically available at the zip code level. The data may provide information about the topic you are interested in directly or indirectly. For example, the drop-out rate and teen pregnancy rate together may serve as a proxy for the number of young people who drop out of high school because of the demands of parenting, which may be data not directly collected by any institution or organization. See Exhibit 10.2 for ideas for sources of census and administrative data.

Other Data   Many state, local, and human service organizations provide data about the clients they serve and/or community-level data on populations or issues. These data may be publically available, or organizations may be willing to make them available at the social worker's request. These organizations may collect data to ensure that their services are meeting the community needs that are the highest priority, or they may be required to collect data in order to retain funding. The data may be collected across the community, or it may be only a sample.

Mapped Data   Mapping can help to establish relationships among different sets of data. **Geographic information systems (GIS)** are enhancing the usefulness of data that is attached to a specific geographic location. GIS utilize the geocoding of spatially mapped data to allow researchers to identify spatial patterns among challenges and resources (Hillier & Culhane, 2013). Using GIS, census and other types of data may be visually combined onto one map. For example, as Exhibit 10.3 demonstrates, plotting both minority populations and home purchase loans on the same map can add to the depth and complexity of a needs analysis and provide even more useful data. This map can illustrate the possible relationship between subprime minority populations and home purchase loans in the St. Louis, Missouri region, informing a local task force's efforts to encourage minority homeownership. GIS also offer the possibility of adding more layers of data, such as income, to this map, so that

EXHIBIT 10.2	National Center for Health Statistics	This Center for Disease Control and Prevention site provides access to information regarding recent health surveys and data collections on vital statistics.
Sample of Sources for Census and Administrative Data	Bureau of Labor Statistics	The Bureau of Labor Statistics site, updated by the Department of Labor, provides FTP links to download raw data on Local Area Unemployment Statistics and Geographical Profiles.
	County and City Data Books	County and City Books, from the U.S. Census Bureau, provide information about individual cities and counties in the United States by year.
	FedStats	This site includes a listing of approximately 100 federal agencies (e.g., National Center for Health Statistics) with links to information on statistics and other resources.
	U.S. Census Bureau	This site provides the most up-to-date information from the U.S. Census Bureau. The "QuickFacts" feature allows you to search statistical information about a particular state.
	Bureau of Justice Statistics	This site contains information on crime, criminal offenders, victims of crime, and the operation of justice systems at all levels of U.S. government.
	Statistical Abstract	This U.S. Census site provides a summary of statistics on the social, political, and economic organization of the United States.
	National Neighborhood Indicators Partnership	This network of the Urban Institute and 36 cities supports the development and use of neighborhood indicators across many domains. Each partner city maintains neighborhood-level indicators across topic areas.
	DataPlace	DataPlace is a free resource for housing, economic, and demographic data. It includes guides and analysis to help users understand data sources and interpret indicators.
	The Census Bureau's Data Ferret	The Data Ferret allows users to map census data for specific geographic locations.
	The Centers for Disease Control and Prevention	The Centers for Disease Control and Prevention site provides available health-related data, such as mortality, births, and sexually transmitted morbidity, for specific locations.
	Annie E. Casey Foundation Data Center: Kids Count	The Kids Count website provides access to hundreds of measures of child well-being on a national and state level.

Sources: St. Louis University Pius XII Library (n.d.); Ohmer et al., 2013

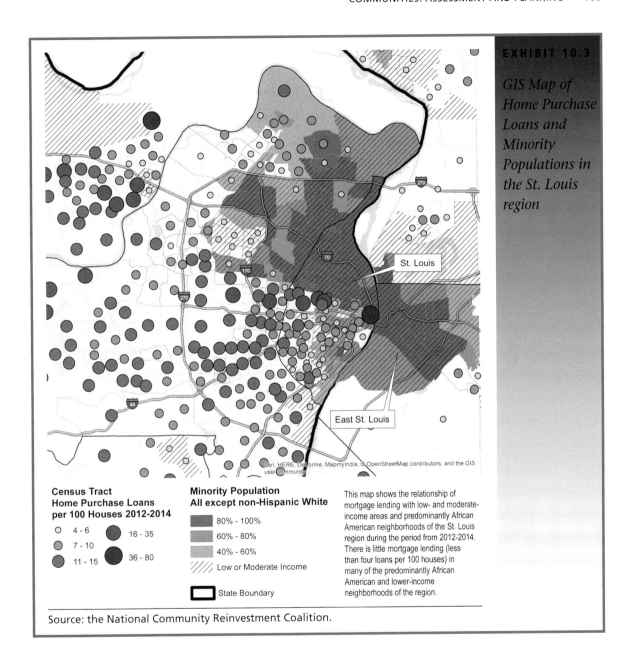

Census Tract Home Purchase Loans per 100 Houses 2012-2014

○ 4 - 6   ● 16 - 35

◔ 7 - 10   ● 36 - 80

● 11 - 15

Minority Population All except non-Hispanic White

■ 80% - 100%

■ 60% - 80%

■ 40% - 60%

///// Low or Moderate Income

☐ State Boundary

This map shows the relationship of mortgage lending with low- and moderate-income areas and predominantly African American neighborhoods of the St. Louis region during the period from 2012-2014. There is little mortgage lending (less than four loans per 100 houses) in many of the predominantly African American and lower-income neighborhoods of the region.

Source: the National Community Reinvestment Coalition.

the task force might study possible relationships among race, home purchase loans, and income.

Interviews with Key Informants   Although any person with some level of knowledge can be an informant, relationships with key informants who can act as guides to the inner workings of community life can be particularly useful. **Key informants**

are individuals who have expertise in a given area, such as the history of the business sector of a community, or who have formal or informal influence on an issue or with a population of interest. These may be formal leaders (e.g., mayors, business association chairs, executive directors of organizations, clergy members, or alderman/city council people), or informal leaders (e.g., longtime citizens' advocates, volunteers for the community association, or gang leaders).

If you are seeking information about systemic and political barriers to solving community problems, carefully select key informants who have extensive history with the community, population, or issue studied. Choosing a key informant who is well informed about the institutions involved in shaping the community, population and/or challenge, both past and present, is also helpful. This person can provide information about both the day-to-day dynamics and the past and present forces that impact those dynamics. If you are just seeking a key informant to learn the lived reality of community life, you may want to consider someone who does not necessarily have the qualities mentioned here, but who has a helpful perspective to provide to the data collection, such as a longtime resident or the matriarch of a family who has been in the community for several generations. This type of key informant may be able to provide information about residents' lived community experience, values and beliefs, oppression, and discrimination. To locate key informants, begin by approaching leaders of community meetings and organizations and those quoted in local news sources like websites and newspapers. Your first key informants may direct you to other people you might contact for an interview. Quick Guide 31 provides a structure for a key informant interview and examples of questions to ask key informants. The questions relate to informants' personal views and their sense of significant community facts, relationships, and dynamics.

Focus Groups   A moderated discussion among a group of people who share a common characteristic, or a **focus group**, is another method of collecting data about a community. The common characteristic among participants might be that they are enrolled in the same program, living in the same community, or caring for an older adult. In focus groups, you can ask questions about the issues that are most important to participants, the reasons they find something challenging, and how a challenge exists in a community. You can ask participants about their attitudes, beliefs, and opinions. Focus groups are an inexpensive, flexible, and efficient way to collect data. The open discussion allows participants to build their thoughts and ideas off of comments from others. Quick Guide 32 provides more detailed guidance for focus groups.

Community Forums   When people meet in a public space to exchange and debate information and to consider and critique strategies, they are engaging in a **community forum**. In these forums, community residents can learn about an issue, state their preferences, and/or present their demands. Forums can be organized to introduce an idea for solving a problem or debating an issue. Forums may be open to all community residents or to a select number of persons chosen based on specific criteria. Quick Guide 33 provides in-depth discussion of community forums.

QUICK GUIDE 31   GUIDE TO KEY INFORMANT INTERVIEWS

General Guidelines
Based on your previous research about the community, prepare a few general questions prior to conducting the interview.

The format should be flexible enough to allow for more depth on some questions, depending on the informant's answers.

Prepare for a 30–40 minute interview, with the option for a longer interview if the key informant is amenable.

Educate yourself ahead of time with available census and administrative data, prior needs assessments, observation, and/or other available data.

Interview Format
Practice the interview skills discussed in Chapter 3, such as empathy, genuineness, and warmth.

At the beginning of the interview, develop rapport by engaging the key informant, define the purpose of the interview and agree on the time allotted for the interview. Provide the key informant with the interview format (such as the topics and number of questions, the issue of confidentiality, etc.) and information about what you will do with the data you collect. If you want to tape the interview, obtain the informant's consent to do so.

At the end of the interview, consider asking the key informant to share any other pertinent information that may not have come up.

Questions
Consider funneling the questions (i.e., moving from general questions to specific).

Avoid using jargon. Avoid double-barreled, leading, long, and negative questions.

Ask about the strengths of and challenges to the community.

Ask about the internal structure of the community (i.e., organizations and decision-makers within the community) as well as the external structure (i.e., organizations and decision-makers outside of the community).

Sample Questions for Key Informants
- Tell me a little bit about your history with the community. Why have you chosen this community in which to live/work/volunteer?
- What are the advantages to living/working/volunteering in this community? What are the main challenges?
  What are the organized groups in this community? How do these groups relate to one another?
- Who is significantly involved in community affairs in this community? To which groups, if any, do they belong? Are they elected or appointed to any official positions? Who are key decision-makers in this community? Who influences them?
- Who has been involved in efforts to make changes to or advocate for the community?
- What were those efforts? What were the results of those efforts?
- What groups or types of individuals is the community not serving? In what ways?
- What groups or individuals are not involved in community affairs? What might explain their lack of engagement?

*Key Informant
Interview*

© CREATISTA

Survey Data   Surveys are a common method of collecting data for community practice. Survey data can help researchers gauge attitudes, beliefs, and opinions about an issue or a proposal. Researchers should disseminate surveys widely, and surveys should be clear and easy to complete. In order to quickly survey a large number of people door-to-door, via web, telephone, or other technology, or face-to-face in public spaces, researchers should focus on closed-ended survey questions. Surveys can deliver information about specific needs within a community or population that even census data and administrative data cannot provide. Surveys can provide information about the availability and accessibility of services, and they can identify unmet needs or gaps in services. Depending on the amount of resources available, you can create a survey or purchased one that has been tested in the past. Targeted surveys involve collecting data from a small group within a larger group or community without trying to generalize the finding to the larger population. Small surveys may be given to certain types or groups of residents, business owners, organizations, and service providers. For example, you might collect data on the impacts of the use of methamphetamine in a community by surveying treatment providers, physicians, social workers, clergy, health providers, lawyers and judges, and others directly involved. Quick Guide 34 provides sample needs assessment survey questions.

QUICK GUIDE 32   GUIDE TO FOCUS GROUPS

General Guidelines

Focus groups can get closer to what people are really thinking and feeling about problems or ideas and can assist to obtain public opinion in an interactive method. They have a specific, focused discussion topic, such as the improvements needed within a particular school or the features of a new planned playground. Like with Key Informant Interviews, preparation is needed to facilitate effective focus groups. Use prior research (census and administrative data, prior needs assessments, observation, and/or other available data) about the community to prepare a list of questions prior to conducting the group. However, focus groups are seeking more depth, nuance, and variety of responses than can be typically obtained with many other data collection methods. Facilitators encourage members to express their opinions and to comment on each others' thoughts and ideas. Nonverbal behavior and group interactions can also be observed.

Logistics

Focus groups' discussions should be recorded—either audio recorded (using, for example, a smartphone app or a digital recorder) or through note-taking. Either way, group permission should be given for recording the discussion. Generally, focus groups run for approximately 45–60 minutes, and consist of 8–10 people.

Group Composition

Group members should be a representative sample of those whose opinions you want. For example, if you are collecting information about the needs of older adults in a spatial community, you want to consider inviting older adults from various areas of the spatial community, as well as those with varying demographics, such as age, race, ethnicity, marital status, gender, ability status, and others. You might run several focus groups to ensure that you hear from a variety of the population of interest. To get people to the meeting, you might consider offering transportation, food, a small monetary incentive, child/elder care, public recognition, or other things that prospective members might need or want. Participants can be recruited through personal invitation to specific people, or publicity for willing volunteers.

Sample Questions

- What are some of your thoughts about what is going on now?
- Are you satisfied with the current situation? Why?
- What needs to be changed about the current situation?
- Some people have suggested [XXX] is needed. What do you think about this? Do you agree?

Facilitation

Facilitators should feel free to follow up participant answers by asking

- Can you say more about that?
- Can you say why you think that?
- Can you give us an example?

Facilitators should also work toward a balance of discussion by asking the quieter participants directly for their thoughts. If some members are dominating, the facilitator can ask people who have spoken already to wait until others have spoken before speaking again. It is helpful to occasionally summarize the group discussion to check for accuracy.

Source: University of Kansas Work Group for Community Health and Development, 2016.

QUICK GUIDE 33 GUIDE TO COMMUNITY FORUMS

General Guidelines
Like focus groups, community forums also collect public opinion but in a more public and open format than focus groups, and with potentially a wider group of people (such as a broad cross-section of the whole community). Additionally, forums can provide a link to people interested enough in the topic that they might later be involved in a community intervention.

Logistics
If possible, hold several forums in various locations comfortable to various populations and at various times to facilitate attendance by a broad cross-section of people. Publicity is key to getting people to attend, so all avenues should be utilized (print, media, word-of-mouth etc.). It is helpful to personally invite people as well and ask them to recruit others to attend. Providing food/drink, transportation, childcare, and other incentives can be helpful. Like with focus groups, community discussions should be recorded (audio and/or note-taking).

The Program
The format usually consists of a short formal presentation, and a general or breakout sessions to facilitate a higher level of interaction. There should be some sort of interactive portion, such as discussion, prioritizing issues or ideas, and/or voting. Next steps should be announced at the end.

Sample Discussion Questions
- Did the presentation include the most important challenges/ideas? What was missed?
- What are the barriers to solving these challenges? How can they be overcome?
- Are the challenges widespread? Who is most affected?

What resources are needed to address these challenges?

Facilitation
The facilitator should be someone who is neutral on the topic, and can keep the program and discussion moving. Careful facilitation is needed to ensure that everyone feels welcome to participate and that a small minority of participants do not dominate the discussion.

Source: University of Kansas Work Group for Community Health and Development, 2016

Determining Your Assessment Approach

There are several important considerations to take into account when designing a community needs assessment. Key principles include the following (Mulroy, 2013; Ohmer et al., 2013):

1. *Value participation from diverse constituencies:* Seek multiple perspectives on the community and experiences in the community, particularly those of disadvantaged and oppressed populations that may have been overlooked and undervalued in the past. While it may be difficult to gather data from diverse constituencies, carefully consider the way in which you can fairly report on dissenting opinions in your final report.

QUICK GUIDE 34   SAMPLE NEEDS ASSESSMENT SURVEY QUESTIONS

Circle any of the following that are needs for you or your family.

Medical Health Care	Job Transportation	Childcare
Dental Health Care	Medical Transportation	Elder Care
Vision Health Care	Housing	Legal Services
Prescriptions	Disability Assistance	Utilities
Mental Health Care	Housing Loans	Counseling
Hospice	Housing Repairs	Domestic Violence Services
Clothing	Employment	Income Tax Preparation
Food	Education	Senior Services

What are your barriers to childcare services, if any? (Circle all that apply)

None needed	Location of childcare providers	Not enough childcare providers
No barriers		
Cost	No transportation	Quality of childcare providers
Hours not sufficient	Children have special needs	

How many household members do NOT currently have health insurance? (Including insurance from Medicare, Medicaid, CHIP, Private Insurance) _____

Of those with NO health insurance, how many are: Under 18: _____ Over 65: _____

What are your barriers to health care? (Circle all that apply)

No barriers	No doctor in my area	No childcare during
Cost	No doctor will take my	appointment
No insurance	insurance	No transportation to doctor
Fear		

What are your barriers to employment? (Circle all that apply)

No barriers	Pay too low to support	Lack of training or
No jobs for my field	family	experience
No transportation	No childcare during work	Mental disability
	Physical disability	

What are your barriers to reliable transportation? (Circle all that apply)

No barriers	Price of gas	No routes near work
No car/Can't afford car	No private transportation	No public transportation
No routes near home		

What are your major housing concerns? (Circle all that apply)

Rent too high	Utility costs too high	Can't find house in price range
House needs major repairs	Can't afford house payments	No concerns

Circle if you HAVE a:

Phone	Computer	Internet access

QUICK GUIDE 34   CONTINUED

What do you feel is the primary cause of unemployment in this community? (Check only one)

☐ Lack of child care
☐ Not enough jobs
☐ Wages are too low
☐ Lack of encouragement to work

☐ Lack of education
☐ Not enough on-the-job training
☐ Lack of transportation

☐ Not enough help available to find a good paying job
☐ Other
_____

What do you feel is the primary cause of transportation barriers in this community (Check only one)

☐ Suspended driver's license
☐ Lack of reliable/ affordable vehicle
☐ Insurance prices

☐ Gasoline prices
☐ Bus service not available/ reliable

☐ Other
_____

What do you feel are the biggest problems facing youth (ages 5 to 17) **in the community? (Check up to three)**

☐ Not much to do away from school
☐ Lack of adult role models
☐ Adults not in touch with needs of youth
☐ Stress

☐ Depression
☐ Alcohol/drug abuse by youth
☐ Alcohol/drug abuse in family
☐ Other _____

☐ Lack of opportunities to develop skills needed as an adult
☐ Violence

What do you feel are the biggest problems facing adults in the community? (Check up to three)

☐ Inability to pay all bills and on time
☐ Stress
☐ Bad credit
☐ Lack of education

☐ Lack of assets
☐ High rent/mortgage costs
☐ Alcohol/drug abuse
☐ Low wages

☐ Nowhere to turn for help in crises
☐ Unemployment
☐ Other
_____

Do you have and use a bank account (checking or savings)? Yes No

Do you presently use a prepaid card, check cashing, or cash advance services instead of banking services? Yes No

Source: University of Kansas Work Group for Community Health and Development, 2016

2. *Use multiple methods:* Both quantitative and qualitative methods offer unique types of data for the project. Quantitative data, such as service statistics, census and administrative data, mapping, and survey data, offer reliability, repeatability, and transferability. Qualitative data, including participant and nonparticipant observations, interviews, focus groups, and community forums, offer a richer, holistic picture of communities and their inhabitants. The most informative community needs assessments use both types of data.

3. *Encourage civic participation in technical elements:* Encourage key stakeholders and/or community members to participate in the design and selection of technical elements. Seek their input when formulating research questions, and when selecting data collection methods, survey questions, focus group participants, and key stakeholders. Involve them in the collection and analysis of data and in formulating recommendations, if appropriate. Their full participation helps build capacity in the community while ensuring that the data gathered is relevant and that it may be useful for efforts to improve the community.

4. *Keep the assessment realistic:* Community stakeholders and agency staff want usable evidence for local community and agency decision-making and community improvement. Lengthy assessments and overly long documents may not be helpful.

5. *Value strengths and asset building:* Along with needs, note the strengths and assets of the community. Institutional resources, such as churches, locally owned businesses, nonprofit organizations, schools, financial institutions, networks of organizations, and individuals can all be considered strengths. Asset-building programs, such as those that encourage savings, employment, small businesses, local investment of resources, and other types of assets, are intended to increase the individual and collective assets of a community. Local control of resources empowers residents and strengthens the community.

When selecting your methods, the purpose, desired impact, and potential uses of the assessment and resources must be major considerations (University of Kansas Work Group for Community Health and Development, 2016; Ohmer et al., 2013). Questions to consider include:

- What do you/your sponsor hope to learn?
- How will you use the information?
- Can existing data provide the needed information?
- Can you combine existing data with newly gathered data?
- What resources do you have for the project?
- What might be some of the other potential benefits of choosing particular methods?

The purpose of the assessment will help to shape the specific data you collect. For example, if you are conducting a needs assessment about financial services for low-income residents in a community, you might ask a key stakeholder, "When you think about the residents using financial institutions in this community, what services do they need that currently do not exist locally?" or "What type of institutions, if any, would be more beneficial to local residents?"

If the public or decision-makers view your project as controversial, or if you anticipate a skeptical or even a hostile response to the findings, plan the most rigorous data collection your budget allows. Political issues surface in a needs assessment, because the data may be used to convince decision-makers to approve and/or fund a program or service, to modify or end a program or service, or to acknowledge a previously unrecognized challenge in the community. Assessments can challenge the status quo in communities, and therefore, they may be contentious. Including specific influential individuals and organizations in the assessment may lend credibility to the findings. Using data supplied by less credible individuals and organizations may cast doubt on your findings.

It's also important to consider the financial resources and time available for an assessment. For example, social workers interested in creating a new financial education program for local youth may have few resources to conduct a needs assessment and little time before a proposal is due. In contrast, a new city councilor may ask a social work staff member to provide a more comprehensive community assessment, and that councilor may be able to provide adequate resources and more time to carry out a longer, more involved assessment. If you are short on funds and time, consider using publically available data, including data available from government sources, the local chapters of the United Way, and nonprofit organizations. You might also consider including a focus group and/or a community forum. If you have more time and/or resources, you may add targeted surveys, key informant interviews, and/or larger surveys. Exhibit 10.4 shows the interrelationships among time frame, budget, expertise, and possible designs in developing a community needs assessment.

In sum, key considerations about needs assessments, the scope of the type of information you need, how you intend to use the data, political considerations, and available funding and time influence the methods you choose. For examples of community needs assessments and to see a sample assessment conclusion, see Exhibit 10.5.

Assessing Specific Population Needs and Social Problems

Social workers often work with community members who are vulnerable, at risk, or otherwise in need of particular services. These may include runaway youth, older adults, people with HIV/AIDS and their families, persons with disabilities, working families who are poor, and former psychiatric inpatients. Likewise, social workers often work to alleviate issues in the community. Creating or continually modifying services to effectively and efficiently meet the needs of specific populations or to target services at a specific issue is critically important. It can help ensure long-term program funding. Needs assessments often focus on a particular population or social problem. General needs assessments and those targeted to a specific population or community challenge use the same process and data collection methods.

The goal of a community needs assessment is to learn about a community from the perspective of a particular challenge or the needs of a particular population. In

TIME FRAME	FINANCES	RESEARCHER EXPERTISE	POSSIBLE DESIGN	EXHIBIT 10.4
6 months–1 year (or even longer) to complete	Grants or other significant funding in excess of $1500 *	Primarily research and/or evaluation staff with some experience in needs assessment*	• Probability surveys • Personal interviews	*Considerations for Needs Assessment Designs*
3–6 months to complete	Small grants or funding ($500–$1500)	Primarily staff with some experience in research	• Small targeted surveys	
Less than 3 months	Very small grants or funding ($500 or less)	Primarily agency staff or students who have other commitments and limited research or statistical expertise	• Focus group • Community forum • Unobtrusive measures including secondary data collection from agency files	

Resources (vertical axis label on left)

Scientific Rigor (vertical axis label on right)

* *Note:* In needs assessment projects that are funded by larger grants, a professional organization may be used.

Source: Royse, Staton-Tindall, Badger, & Webster, 2009

the process of conducting a community needs assessment, social workers strive to understand the history and characteristics of a population or challenge and to profile the specific dimensions associated with the population or challenge. When assessing the needs of a population, it is important to identify the following: (1) the population's perspective on the community and its patterns of resource availability; (2) the community's strengths, issues, and problems from the perspective of a specific population; and (3) the differences between groups in the community, such as the dominant values of each and the methods of oppression and discrimination the dominant group(s) in communities use to subjugate other populations. For needs assessments focused both on populations and community challenges, learning about the power structure of the community while learning about other aspects of the structure of the community is helpful. Questions about resource distribution and decision-making processes can help uncover these dynamics (Netting et al., 2017). For example, if a social worker is investigating the needs of a Filipino population within a city, asking key informants about the Filipino leaders'

EXHIBIT 10.5 *Examples of Needs Assessments*	• Community Action of the Franklin, Hampshire, and North Quabbin Regions in Massachusetts conducted a comprehensive community needs assessment for 2015–2017 that provides an overview of the community economic and social conditions. They will use this document to identify major issues and needs and design to strategies to address them within their service area. • The Fairfax County Department of Family Services–Office for Children published a community assessment for Head Start Programming in 2015. The document provides the latest information on trends in the service area, including data about health, dental, nutritional, and special education needs of the children eligible for Head Start in their service area. • The Princeton Department of Human Services in Princeton, New Jersey, published a community needs assessment in 2014. The assessment identifies community needs in the areas of housing, food, health care, employment, transportation, legal matters, and safety. They found that residents prioritized their need for a living wage, job training, and affordable medical care. • Spectrum Health Care System in Kent County, Michigan identified community health needs in their needs assessment for 2014. They will use the data for problem and asset identification, and policy and program development. *Summary: The need for affordable housing in the District of Columbia (Washington, DC)* The data gathered through the Needs Assessment demonstrate that: • the need for affordable housing is significant; • the majority of households in DC were nonfamily households (either single people or unrelated people); • housing construction has been booming, but the majority of housing was built over 50 years ago; • the majority of areas are majority renters; • the most common problem is housing costs exceed what residents can afford, especially for renters and those with household incomes that are half of the area median income or less; and • based on current projections, there will be 33,000 more households with extremely low incomes than affordable units available to these households. Source: Tatian et al., 2015

relationships with leaders of the wider community may help the social worker learn about power, dominance, and oppression. If the needs assessment focuses on a particular community challenge, such as homelessness, researchers may ask key informants about the history of the location of shelters in the community, the history behind the funding patterns for homeless services, and/or the relationship

EXHIBIT 10.6

Social Impact Assessment

A needs assessment can be used to determine how a potential change in a community will impact the human social fabric of the community. Researchers may conduct this type of assessment to analyze the potential social impacts of any policy, plan, program, project, or proposed facility—for example, a new development project or a change to an existing facility. This type of assessment discerns the potential ways in which a change—such as a new housing, commercial property, or transportation development—may affect how people live, work, recreate, relate to one another, and organize as a community, or change their norms, values, and beliefs. All types of impacts, including social, cultural, demographic, economic, social–psychological, and political, may be assessed (IOCPG, 2003).

Census data, surveys, key informant interviews, focus groups, public meetings, and historical documents are all useful data sources for conducting social impact assessments. Giving affected populations the opportunity to be heard through the assessment and to therefore have input into the decision-making process about a proposal is key to the social impact assessment process. The assessment can measure population characteristics, community structures, resources, and potential individual and family changes (IOCPG, 2003).

Social Work: Practice in Action–Social Impact Assessment

A semirural community near an urban area in New Mexico was under threat of significant disruption from a proposed 14-acre development. This proposed development could have significantly changed the social fabric and quality of life of neighborhood residents. The Rio Grande Educational Collaborative proposed a 35,000 square foot learning facility on land that had been planned for a storm water drainage pond. Students and faculty affiliated with The Resource Center for Raza Planning engaged in data collection through the use of census data, historical documents, previous studies about the site, survey interview data, key informant interviews, and focus group data. They collected data related to the programmatic and facility characteristics. At the conclusion of their assessment, they produced an 82-page report, and presented their findings to the public and to decision-makers. Their findings included community concerns about traffic and parking, property values, and the potential displacement of residents. They recommended criteria for site selection for the facility and offered alternative activities for the site that reflected community preferences. While the residents were supportive of the learning programming, the ultimate impact of the facility on the community would be a negative one. County officials rejected the proposed development; instead, a water retention pond with walking trails and a working community farm were built on the site.

Source: Cordova, 2011

of key providers to political decision-makers in the community. Exhibit 10.6 provides an example of a needs assessment that focuses on the human social impact of a proposed change, and Exhibit 10.7 provides an example of a needs assessment that focuses on a particular community challenge.

EXHIBIT 10.7

Community Practice and Child Welfare Assessment

A social worker working in child welfare services in a small community can engage in community practice in a variety of ways. One social worker in child welfare was working in a community within a county characterized by higher-than-average rates of poverty, substance abuse, and criminal violations. A substantial number of children in the county endure prolonged childhood sexual abuse. These children are initially placed in foster care, but many are removed shortly thereafter and placed in residential facilities because they express their acute emotional disruptions in dangerous or out-of-control behaviors. Residential care is more costly than foster care, and it has implications for both the current quality of life and for the future community integration of the children.

Due to the behaviors children who have been abused display, the social worker forms a group of caseworkers, supervisors, foster parents, former foster children, and allies in other organizations to complete a needs assessment. After reviewing previous needs assessments of foster children in that community, as well as U.S. Census data, public health data, juvenile court data, educational data, and other administrative data, the group decides to use a survey to complete the needs assessment. All foster parents and those providing any services to foster children, including teachers, complete the survey. The survey is designed to elicit strengths, resources, and stressors.

The plan is, as a group, to analyze the data, integrate the survey data with previous data and studies, and issue a report, which will include recommendations, to the child welfare supervisor for the county. The group will ask the supervisor to share the needs assessment with other local decision-makers, including politicians, in an effort to change policy and possibly raise funds for additional services, if needed.

Asset Mapping

Social workers using a strengths-based approach in community work seek to learn about and identify the people, institutions, and organizations in the community, as well as those who work on behalf of that community. In order to effectively address the challenges that face communities using a strengths-based approach, social workers must possess knowledge of the resources (or assets) available to work on local issues. The key to this approach is the idea that, collectively, the resources available within the community offer the capacity to address local issues. **Asset mapping** is a technique to systematically learn about a variety of different types of assets that could be helpful in an intervention. It prepares the way for an intervention that focuses on effectiveness and interdependencies within a community and that seeks to empower people by identifying ways that people can contribute to a community change effort (Hillier & Culhane, 2013). Like individual, family, and group assessments, asset mapping provides information that can be useful in planning a community intervention.

The community mapping process is the first stage of an asset-based community intervention, generally called the asset-based community development approach.

McKnight and Kretzmann (1996) first developed this approach, and today the Asset-Based Community Development Institute at Northwestern University spearheads its use. Using a strengths-based approach, the first activity of community practice is to inventory—to "map"—the assets of a community. These assets include members of the community, both those that currently participate in community affairs and those who do not, as well as institutions and formal and informal organizations. Conducting an inventory of the assets of individual people requires the identification of the abilities, talents, gifts, and capacities of community members. For example, community members may have underutilized home repair, child/older adult care, craft, music, and other types of skills. Exhibit 10.8 provides an example of the topics included in an individual capacity inventory. Researchers mapping assets would first ask people questions on these topics and then ask them to prioritize their skills and to comment on their involvement in community activities, their interests in starting a small business, and their current business activities. Researchers would also map formal and informal organizations and associations that exist within the community, including economic, education, political, religious, and kinship groups. Associations can include many types of formal and informal organizations and groups, such as self-help groups that assist with addictions, youth groups, environmental groups, and charitable groups. Institutions can include parks, libraries, schools of all types, law enforcement, hospitals, and other health care resources. Exhibits 10.9 and 10.10 provide examples of community asset mapping tools for associations/organizations and institutions. Several helpful asset

CATEGORY	EXAMPLE OF SKILLS	
Health	Caring for an older adult or person with a mental illness	**EXHIBIT 10.8**
Office	Typing, writing letters, telephone skills	
Construction and Repair	Painting, roof repair, tuckpointing, demolition	*Capacity Inventory for Individuals*
Maintenance	Washing windows, mowing lawns, gardening	
Food	Catering, bartending, baking, washing dishes	
Child Care	Caring for children, assisting with field trips	
Transportation	Driving a taxi, truck, or ambulance; hauling	
Operating Equipment and Repairing Machinery	Repairing electronics, using a forklift	
Supervision	Completing forms, planning work for others	
Sales	Operating a cash register, selling services	
Music	Singing, playing an instrument	
Security	Guarding property, installing security systems	
Other	Sewing, upholstering, managing property	

Source: Adapted from Kretzmann & McKnight, 1993

EXHIBIT 10.9	Types	Examples of Types
Capacity Inventory for Associations/ Organizations, Abbreviated List	Artistic	Artists coalition
	Business	Business association
	Charitable Groups and Drives	American Red Cross, United Way
	Church Groups	Service, prayer, youth, women's and men's, choir
	Civic	Lions and Rotary Clubs
	Collectors Groups	Stamps, antiques
	Community Centers	Senior centers
	Ethnic Associations	League of Americans of Ukrainian Descent
	Health and Fitness	Basketball league
	Interest	Antique car owners, book clubs
	Local Media	Local cable TV, local community radio
	Mutual Support	La Leche League, Alcoholics Anonymous
	Neighborhood	Block Group, Community Development Corporation
	Outdoor	Biking, hiking, rollerblading
	Political	Ward, Democratic Party
	School	Parent-Teacher Association
	Service/Nonprofits	Habitat for Humanity

Source: Adapted from McKnight & Block, 2010

EXHIBIT 10.10	TYPES	EXAMPLES OF CAPACITIES WITHIN TYPES
Sample Capacity Inventory for Local Institutions	Historic/Arts Council Groups	Training, Personnel, Space/Facilities, Materials/Equipment
	Hospitals/Health Care Facilities	Expertise, Financial
	Libraries	Expertise, Materials, Fundraising Resources
	Local Government	Expertise, Space/Facilities, Financial
	Military facilities	Expertise, Speakers
	Older Adult Facilities	Expertise, Speakers, Space/Facilities
	Parks	Personnel, Space/Facilities, Materials/Equipment
	Police	Personnel, Authority, Financial
	Public Transportation	Expertise, Financial, Authority
	Schools	Personnel, Space/Facilities, Students, Financial

Source: McKnight & Block, 2010.

mapping tools are available on the Internet, including the U.S. Department of Housing and Urban Development (HUD) "Connecting to Success: Neighborhood Networks Asset Mapping Guide."

The process of mapping assets will vary depending on your needs, sponsor, and resources. While some circumstances may lend themselves to a thorough mapping process in a relatively short period of time, in other circumstances, the mapping process may take a year or longer. Like a community needs assessment, asset mapping provides a foundation for a community intervention, yet it is also a process that may continue while an intervention is underway. Chapter 11 will discuss the next steps for using community mapping data for an intervention.

PLANNING

A needs assessment process will bring many issues, challenges, and ideas to the forefront. The planning phase involves sorting through and prioritizing them to be able to move forward with an intervention. To make these choices, a set of criteria must be developed to provide the structure needed to select the most important issues/ideas in a fair manner. The criteria can include any or any combination of the following:

- Seriousness or frequency of an issue

- Cost of the issue, or resources needed to address the issue

- Feasibility of affecting the issue

- Readiness of the community to recognize and address the issue

- The long-term impact or benefit of addressing an issue, or in implementing an idea

Ideally, the criteria is developed in an collaborative, democratic manner with community members as well as with people that may provide technical expertise, such as in public health, health, community development, that can provide important information in the process (such as through a voting process or in a community forum). Setting the criteria to select can occur at any point in the process from the beginning to the end of the needs assessment process. After setting the criteria, a democratic process can also be used to then apply the criteria to the issues/ideas generated in the community needs assessment process to plan for an intervention (University of Kansas Work Group for Community Health and Development, 2016).

SKILLS FOR COMMUNITY-BASED PARTICIPATORY RESEARCH [EPAS 4]

The community analysis and needs assessment process offers valuable opportunities to engage in community-based participatory research. This research methodology involves engaging a wide group of people who are either direct stakeholders or who are interested in the community and/or the research. Involving community members, representatives of organizations, elected officials, and/or other researchers in the process makes the research more informed by and responsive to the community's needs.

The following key principles guide the participatory research method (Sohng, 2013):

- Seek to identify and work with communities as a whole and to strengthen the social bonds of community by engaging community members.

- Use a strengths-based approach. Identify, build on, and promote strengths and assets, as well as social structures and processes that promote community involvement in decision-making.

- Seek to collaborate with partners in all phases of the research. In particular, use community members' knowledge, share information and resources among all involved, and maintain an equitable decision-making process among the partners.

- Structure the process so members of the community and community groups have the power and ability to act on research findings.

- Seek to promote and develop the capacity of local people and organizations to create and sustain any change that may occur as a result of the research process and outcomes.

Participatory research can be used with a variety of research tools and techniques. The research process itself is a mechanism by which to enhance the well-being of communities through the inclusion of community members and organizations in all phases of the research, including the development of the research question. Using the research method to promote the community and collaborative processes increases the likelihood that the data and analysis will accurately reflect needs and that community residents will engage in action to fulfill those needs.

It is important to recognize and respect the centrality of the community experience to community experts. In acknowledging the multiple realities that are brought to bear in any community context, community-based participatory research is consistent with critical social construction. Participatory action-research empowers community members to transform their lives. Exhibit 10.11 provides an example.

The Floating Hospital (TFH), located in New York City, provides primary health care for families and children in homeless shelters. Academic researchers partnered with TFH to engage in a community-based approach to advocate for health care for homeless children. They used the strengths-based approach by identifying TFH's strengths through gathering internal agency data and client case summaries. They also used empowerment by engaging in "photovoice," by using pictures taken by clients to record the barriers to accessing education faced by homeless children. TFH enhanced its capacity by collaborating with other community agencies for data sharing. They also created advocacy briefs to provide the facts and tell client stories to be used in their advocacy. Ultimately, they were able to create the resources needed to advocate with the New York General Assembly for medical resources for homeless children so that they meet the health requirements for public education (such as vaccinations). They found that as they worked closely with the community, their capacity to advocate for the needs of homeless children was enhanced.

EXHIBIT 10.11

Community-Based Participatory Research to Advocate for Homeless Children

Source: Fetherman & Burke, 2014

CONTEMPORARY TRENDS IMPACTING COMMUNITY PRACTICE

Twenty-first century community social work practice comes with many opportunities and challenges. Social workers often intervene in low-income communities that face unique challenges with recent political, economic, and social trends, such as the following (Mondros & Staples, 2013; Ohmer & DeMasi, 2009; Putnam & Feldstein, 2003: Weil, Reisch, & Ohmer, 2013):

- *The devolution, or decentralization, of control of many federally funded programs and policies, including those that support community practice:* Increasingly, states are relying on nonprofit and for-profit organizations to deliver social services. This decentralization and cuts in funding have increased the importance of involving communities and neighborhoods in informing, designing, and delivering services and in raising local funds to pay for them. For example, some federal block grants for child welfare give state and local governments the power to allocate funds, which offers opportunities for community participation. Social workers are frequently in a position to contribute to the local-level discussions about the federal funds through their work with state and local agencies, public hearings on regulations, and legislative testimony. Social workers have also helped raise private and public funds to pay for resources in their communities.

- *The increasingly multicultural composition of society:* Hispanics are the largest minority group in the United States. The U.S. is expected to become a majority-minority in 2044, which means that the minority population (i.e., non-Whites) will be the majority of the population (U.S. Census Bureau, 2015b). The increase in minority populations in communities offers social workers the opportunity to advocate for greater inclusion, reduced conflict between races and ethnicities, participation, decreases in disparities in income and wealth, and social justice through increased attention to community issues that impact these populations such as immigration, bilingual education, and health care.

- *The increasing poverty and inequality in the fabric of our economic, social, racial, and ethnic relations:* Poverty has increased in recent decades, and despite the ending of the Great Recession with decreasing unemployment, the number of people living in poverty has remained the same as before the Great Recession (2008–2009) (Kneebone & Holmes, 2016). Income and wealth inequalities are the most extreme they have been since prior to the Great Depression due to such factors as the decline in unions, outsourcing of employment, stagnation of wages, high unemployment, and changes in tax policy (Saez, 2015). Social workers will continue to play a central role in working with and advocating for a more inclusive and responsive community for all citizens. For example, differential access to technology and the Internet is a significant barrier for many individuals and communities in their employment efforts, particularly those that are low income.

- *The widening venues and locations for community practice:* Social workers have increased opportunities to work with different types of communities, including those that organize around identity (or shared experiences), geography, and faith. For example, social workers may work with an online community of people with a similar medical diagnosis, a planning group for HIV/AIDS prevention funding, people living in a specific neighborhood, or people of various faiths. Social workers may also work in communities that are experiencing poverty for the first time, such as inner-ring and outer suburbs.

- *The increasing integration of community practice ideas and strategies into other models of practice:* For example, policy-makers are increasingly viewing elements of community practice as a part of work with individuals, families, and groups. Newer practices in services for children and families and for older adults increasingly use community-based service practice models. For example, social workers are increasingly using Assertive Community Treatment, a community-based, intensive, wrap-around case management program for intervening with individuals with severe mental illness (Slade, McCarthy, Valenstein, Visnic, & Dixon, 2012).

- *Distrust of political institutions:* Hyper-partisanship among political candidates and in national and state legislatures has created an intense atmosphere of estrangement and distrust among the American public. Social workers can engage with politicians and political groups to encourage respectful dialogue and bipartisan collaboration on social issues.

- *The decline of democratic participation and civic engagement:* The decline of social capital, including the networks, norms, and trust that facilitate collective action, is a growing concern among community practitioners. The degree to which citizens engage in public life affects community practice, including the identity and shared values in a community. Not all participation and engagement has positive effects but much of it does, and social workers can work to energize and mobilize a diverse array of individuals and groups to be engaged in public life within their communities.

Having discussed several important trends impacting community practice in the U.S., the next section will focus on the world as a community. This discussion will broaden the topic of community practice, and set the stage for Chapter 11, in which community intervention, termination, and evaluation will be explored.

THE WORLD AS A COMMUNITY

Ease of travel, communication, and economic interdependence impact social work practice in the U.S. and will certainly grow in influence in coming decades. This section discusses global interdependence (the connectedness of all nations) and its implications for domestic community social work practice.

Global Interdependence: Implications for U.S. Practice

Global interdependence influences social work practice in the U.S. in many ways, especially with regard to political, social, and technological events. Four of the primary influences are discussed as follows (Healy, 2008; Reisch, 2013):

- Due to increased migration in all parts of the world, *culturally competent skills and an understanding of the social problems* associated with refugee status and transborder issues are important for social workers in most U.S. communities. Migration occurs as a result of international events, political forces, and natural forces, such as disasters. For example, increased internal political tensions in Syria resulting from the recent widespread political upheaval in the Middle East caused almost 5 million people to seek safety and aid in neighboring countries by July 2016 (United Nations Office for the Coordination of Humanitarian Affairs, 2016).

- Using critical thinking, social workers *seek information from multiple sources,* rather than just from Western sources, about meeting common social challenges such as homelessness, poverty, violence, street children, HIV/AIDS, unemployment, increasing longevity, runaway contagious disease, and growing divisions between the "haves" and the "have-nots." Mutual inquiries and information sharing are increasingly relevant as these conditions are addressed on a worldwide basis.

- Social workers recognize the need to *build global organizations and coalitions* to work on issues that are interlinked. The actions of and activity in one country influence the social and economic well being of other countries, as well as the world's overall social health. For example, social work is involved in international groups engaged in public health initiatives that respond to: (1) natural disasters that cross country borders, (2) activities of financial institutions that impact the world economy, and 3) nuclear accidents worldwide.

- Social workers *seek new ways of using technology* to advance universal human rights. Social media and other technology have vast potential as tools for sharing agendas and materials and collaborating toward meeting basic human needs.

Approaches for a Global Community [EPAS 1]

A global perspective is gaining importance in community social work practice, as economic, demographic, and social consequences of globalization effect their practice. For example, due to global market forces, practitioners must confront widening income and wealth inequality in their community practice. The following points will be helpful in developing a global perspective and expanding your thinking as a global citizen (adapted from Ramanathan & Link, 2004, pp. 225–230).

1. *Making a personal review of global awareness:* Developing global awareness first requires an awareness of your present orientation. For example, how often do you keep up with news about other countries or about international organizations, such as the World Trade Organization (WTO)? How often do you think about economic and/or social conditions in other countries? Do you know where your clothing and shoes are made, where your food is grown, and under what conditions?

2. *Expanding knowledge of social work practice in a range of countries:* Another factor in expanding your awareness is learning about and gaining an appreciation of social work practices in other countries. What you learn about practices in other countries through cultural exchanges with their social services or by reading about their practices can inform your practice in your location. Do you, either consciously or unconsciously, consider yourself the expert and deem other countries' approaches secondary or inferior? Awareness of this issue is vitally important to your approach.

3. *Understanding "cultural humility" and respect for language:* Understanding the dynamics of culture and its implications for access to power and resources can lead to highly effective professional relationships. For example, think about the

degree to which you understand the ideas of cultures other than your own, the degree to which your language is respectful of other cultures, and whether you avoid assuming your culture is the worldwide norm. Cultural humility can help build engage and trust and fosters understanding between yourself and community members.

4. *Analyzing global policy instruments built upon consensus:* An understanding of global policy statements that apply to issues of concern to social workers around the world provides an understanding of the foundation upon which social work practice is built and build common ground. Relevant documents include the UN Convention on the Rights of Persons with Disabilities, the UN Convention on the Rights of the Child, and the UN Convention Against Torture (Oliver & Sapey, 2006; Reichert, 2007; Richards-Schuster & Pritzker, 2015).

5. *Becoming historically aware:* Understanding the historical context of U.S. policies is essential to the development of a global perspective. For example, an understanding of how U.S. policies affect the economic situations of other countries can assist in a broader understanding of immigration patterns in the U.S. Regularly accessing reputable domestic and international media sources that provide historical context for current news is one way to further your understanding.

6. *Becoming aware of privilege:* An appreciation of the privilege associated with economic power can contribute to the development of a global perspective. For

© THEGIFT777

example, awareness of your technological privilege and of issues of distributive justice, energy resources, and other dimensions related to the distribution of resources and the ethics associated with it can be illuminating. In-person exposure to domestic and international populations without the same level of access to resources you have enjoyed can assist in raising your awareness.

7. *Reviewing values and ethics:* The ability to understand the global application of the NASW *Code of Ethics* (2008) is key to a global perspective. For instance, do you respect the dignity of all the peoples of the earth, or just the dignity of people in the U.S.? Are you preoccupied with material goods? How do you reconcile this focus with the fact that global resources are finite and inequitably distributed?

8. *Evaluating local variations and uniqueness:* As a social worker, you are obliged to balance the tension between upholding universal principles that will strengthen the profession and valuing individual and local expressions of differences. The goal of social work practice is not to make everything the same, but to promote a "unified purpose" (Ramanathan & Link, 2004, p. 230).

STRAIGHT TALK ABOUT COMMUNITY PRACTICE

In addition to these forces and trends, globalization has led to deindustrialization and the outsourcing of traditional "blue-collar" as well as "white-collar" jobs. In particular, the loss of well-paying manufacturing jobs to lower-wage markets in other countries has made it more difficult for low-income populations with little formal education and training to access well-paying jobs. The corresponding economic insecurity has resulted in weaker local institutions such as churches, schools, and businesses. Areas of concentrated poverty have left increasing numbers of poor communities isolated from economic development, making it difficult for families in those communities to take advantage of mainstream social and economic opportunities. For example, it may be more difficult for people in low-income communities to access available living-wage job opportunities if the jobs are located far from the community and if transportation options are limited.

A related trend is the gentrification of metropolitan areas with rapidly growing populations. Gentrification occurs when low-income communities experience a physical renovation that results in increased property values and decreasing affordability. Property owners wishing to take advantage of increasing property values may convert their properties into high-cost housing, which can force low-income families to seek housing elsewhere, changing the social fabric of the community (Ohmer & DeMasi, 2009). These issues reflect many of the major dimensions of contemporary society that challenge all human service professions, and they also present unique and exciting opportunities for the renewal of vibrant community practice.

The American Academy of Social Work and Social Welfare Grand Challenges for Social Work Initiative identify financial capability and asset building for all as an area that the profession should address. Lack of financial capability and assets contribute to poverty and social inequality, two key concerns for the social work profession. Social workers have been involved in this work since the founding of the profession, and are today involved in related practice, policy, and research efforts. For example, social workers help families obtain resources to take care of basic needs, such as public benefits, and low-cost food and housing, as well as economic empowerment work, and financial education and coaching.

Sherraden and colleagues (2015) lay out the professional obligation to help clients achieve financial security in a number of ways:

1. *Gain financial capability*: Social workers must help clients gain financial knowledge and skills, as well as access to sound financial products and services. This involves helping people to strengthen their financial behavior, as well as to change institutions that provide financial tools.
2. *Build assets*: Financial stability is also gained with financial wealth (e.g., personal savings, retirement plans, and home and small business ownership). Social workers must be involved in helping families gain a financial foothold through building wealth that can have intergenerational effects.

How might the mandate to practice financial capability and asset building be applied to community engagement and assessment? To familiarize yourself with financial capability and asset building, visit the Grand Challenges website and read Working Paper No. 13, *Financial Capability and Asset Building for All* (Sherraden et al., 2015) at: http://aaswsw.org/wp-content/uploads/2016/01/WP13-with-cover.pdf. (See Exercise #a1 for additional exploration of engaging and assessing communities for financial capability and asset building within the context of the Brickville community.)

CONCLUSION

This chapter has introduced the concept of community as a place in which individuals and groups find identity and meaning in their various roles. Most important for social workers, community is an arena that impacts all areas of practice, and social workers in many settings engaging in generalist practice will benefit from a working knowledge of community practice. Community is the structure that supports interaction and connectedness among people over time, and it can be understood using various theories and perspectives. The characteristics of the community in which people live and grow have important implications for the resources and opportunities available to community residents. Having considered community engagement, assessment, and the global community, in the next chapter, we will examine community intervention strategies, termination, evaluation, and follow-up processes.

MAIN POINTS

- Communities play a critical role in the lives of workers and clients, even in traditional individual, family, and group practice.

- There are multiple definitions, types, functions of, and approaches to community, including traditional and postmodern approaches.

- Community engagement and assessment involves many skills and practice behaviors, including community analysis, needs assessment, community asset mapping, and community-based participatory research.

- Various factors, including the population and/or problem focus, aid in determining the assessment approach.

- Contemporary trends and globalization are changing community social work practice.

- A global perspective is imperative to contemporary community engagement and assessment.

- Understanding traditional and contemporary perspectives helps social workers view community through many different lenses.

- Skills of engagement, assessment, and intervention in community social work build on those relevant for social work practice with individuals, families, and groups. In addition, you will find the skills of participatory action-research useful as an ethnographic approach to your work.

EXERCISES

a. Case Exercises

1. Go to www.routledgesw.com/cases and click on the Brickville case (click on "Start This Case"). To familiarize yourself with the case, under the "Engage" table, review the Introduction, "You, the Social Worker," and Critical Thinking Question #1. Consider the following: your employer, the Brickville Community Development Corporation (CDC), wants to engage and assess the community about their financial capability and assets. You will start with approaching and engaging with other community institutions about this topic before engaging and assessing individual community residents. What kind of institutions would be involved in the financial capability and assets of community residents?

What kind of information might you want from the other institutions to learn about the residents' financial capability and their assets?

2. Go to www.routledgesw.com/cases and click on the Riverton case (click on "Start This Case"). Familiarize yourself with the Riverton Town Map (under "Explore This Town" case study tool), the Sociogram (case study tool), and the Interaction Matrix (case study tool). Answer the critical thinking questions on the Riverton case. What other players would you add to the interaction matrix?

3. After completing Exercise #2, consider the following case. In your position as social worker at the Alvadora Community Mental Health Center, you have observed that there are some strained connections between the center's staff and the Hispanic community it serves. You would like to learn more about the Hispanic community, both to become more culturally competent and to learn more about the needs of the community. You decide to explore the idea of a community analysis.
   a. Define the type of community you would study.
   b. Discuss the approach you might take to conduct a community analysis. What type of information would you seek? Who would you involve? With whom might you talk?

4. After completing Exercises #2 and #3, you decide to conduct a community needs assessment. Using the material in Chapter 10, create a plan for a community needs assessment of the Hispanic population in Riverton. Include the sources of data and the assessment approach that you plan to use.

5. Go to www.routledgesw.com/cases and become familiar with the Sanchez family. Review the material in the chapter that discusses the world as a global community. Identify and describe the ways in which the Sanchez family context in particular is shaped by each of the four dimensions of global interdependence. Add any other ways you think would make an impact.

6. The Chapter 10 section "Approaches for a Global Community" discusses points that could be helpful in creating a global perspective for social work practice. Apply 4 of the 8 points in the chapter to work with the Sanchez family. In your application, focus your discussion on the ways in which you can accomplish each of the tasks to create a global perspective toward the larger goal of being a culturally competent social worker.

7. Go to www.routledgesw.com/cases and become familiar with the Brickville case. Using the Brickville community redevelopment scenario, create a 10-question survey that could be used for a community needs assessment.

b. Other exercises

8. Select a community of which you are a member. Reflect on an issue that your community faces. What is the issue? How might you conduct a community analysis of your community? How might you conduct a needs assessment of your community? Create a thorough plan for each in a 1–2 page paper.

9. Select a community within which you are a member. Using the "Create Your Own Ecomap" template at www.routledgesw.com/cases, create a sociogram of your community.

10. Using Exhibit 10.6 as an example, create a scenario that begins with an individual case(s), and the need for a community needs assessment becomes apparent. Discuss the methods you would use to conduct the needs assessment in a 1–2 page paper.

11. Using Exhibit 10.5 as an example, search media sources for another real-life situation in which development threatens a community and an impact assessment could be useful in the decision-making process. In a 1–2 page paper, describe the situation and discuss how a social impact assessment could be conducted.

Social Work Practice with Communities: Intervention, Termination, and Evaluation

Passion begins with a burden and a split-second moment when you understand something like never before. That burden is on those who know. Those who don't know are at peace. Those of us who do know get disturbed and are forced to take action.

Wangari Maathai

It isn't enough to talk about peace. One must believe in it. And it isn't enough to believe in it. One must work at it.

Eleanor Roosevelt

Key Questions for Chapter 11

1. How can I use theory and perspectives to guide the development of intervention, terminations, and evaluation with communities? [EPAS 8 and 9]
2. What models can I use to intervene in communities? [EPAS 8]
3. How do I utilize evidence to practice research-informed practice and practice-informed research to guide intervention, termination, and evaluation with communities? [EPAS 4]
4. How can I apply social work values and ethics to community intervention, termination, and evaluation? [EPAS 1]

The Brickville community is in a quandary. Although the community needs redevelopment, the current proposal to completely overhaul the physical structures in the community, including razing some buildings, has stirred major controversy among current community residents, neighborhood social service providers, and sympathetic outsiders. The community has had little input into the plan, and they are fearful that many current residents would no longer be able to afford to live in the neighborhood after the redevelopment. Some do not like the plan itself, fearful that the planned changes in community real estate will change the look and character of the area. Others do not trust the developer who has proposed the redevelopment. Some residents think that, despite any drawbacks, the proposal and developer should be supported. A supporting group (Brickville Community Benefits Alliance) and an opposing group (Vision Brickville) formed and are actively engaged in community organizing to attract people and move their agendas forward.

L IKE SOCIAL WORK PRACTICE WITH INDIVIDUALS, FAMILIES, AND GROUPS, the second phase of practice with communities is engagement and assessment. We have previously covered the initial phases of engagement and assessment with communities. Intervention, termination, evaluation, and follow-up are the middle and ending phases of work with all client system levels. As noted in Chapter 10, community practice is a broad term that includes grassroots community organizing, community development, human service program development, planning and coordination, and advocacy (Weil, Gamble, & Ohmer, 2013). There are many types of community interventions, all of which are based on the data gathered and process used for community assessment. The aim of community practice interventions is to shape and create institutions and communities that respond to community needs. Community-level interventions, terminations, evaluations, and follow-up concentrate on the community level but also impact individual, family, and group change. Focusing on the community and on individuals, families, and groups requires the social worker to use many skills to begin the intervention and to facilitate the termination, evaluation, and follow-up processes.

This chapter explores community practice from the intervention plan through the termination, and evaluation and follow-up phases. In this chapter, we discuss practice models, which are based on theoretical perspectives, for community interventions, and we provide an overview of social work interventions for communities. The chapter continues with a look at the final phase of community practice—the termination process and the evaluation and follow-up processes. You will learn about the most recognized models for community intervention: Planning/Policy, community capacity development, and social advocacy, as well as the ways in which they can be mixed in practice (Rothman, 2008).

SOCIAL WORK THEORY AND MODELS FOR COMMUNITY INTERVENTION [EPAS 8 AND 9]

As we discussed in Chapter 10, theory provides a lens through which to understand and analyze communities. For example, you can apply the strengths approach to communities in general through the identification of assets and possibilities within a community, including the individuals and groups in that community. You can achieve the empowerment approach by helping the community to realize its capacity to build on its strengths (Netting, Kettner, McMurtry, & Thomas, 2017).

Community practice models, which are primarily based in the concepts and language of systems, ecological, power, change, and politics theories, guide community interventions (Netting et al., 2017). As Exhibit 11.1 notes, systems theory helps to demonstrate that planned community change reverberates throughout a community and affects units within and outside of a community. Therefore, when you choose a community intervention, you should consider the possibility that community change may affect more people than you intend. In the Brickville situation, implementing the redevelopment could affect the surrounding

THEORIES	CONTRIBUTIONS TO COMMUNITY PRACTICE	EXHIBIT 11.1
Social Systems	Reveals that changes in one community unit impact other units	*Ways in Which Theories Contribute to Community Practice*
	Indicates that changes in subunits also influence the larger community	
	Allows comparisons between the functioning of different communities	
Ecological	Sheds light on relationships among community units	
	Recognizes that community groups compete for limited resources	
	Recognizes that groups without power must adapt to community norms	
	Acknowledges the interconnections and mutual shaping of physical and social structures	
Power, Change, and Politics	Reveals the influence of external sources of resources on local communities	
	Views the community as divided into "haves" and "have-nots"	
	Focuses heavily on the "isms" such as racism	
	Acknowledges the role of power in all interpersonal transactions	

Source: Netting, et al., 2017

communities through, for example, Brickville residents moving into neighboring communities and increasing the rents in those communities or through increasing the amount of property taxes collected from Brickville residents when the redevelopment is complete.

Ecological theory's focus on competition for limited resources, which can affect the relationship among units within a community or between communities, informs community interventions. Community interventions can account for competition and limited resources. Power, change, and politics theories emphasize the ways in which external forces influence local communities. Community intervention can use the influence of external forces to increase a community's power and control over internal affairs and in relationships with other persons and institutions that possess power.

As highlighted in Chapter 10, the data from the community assessment process are the basis for community change efforts, which often use a blend of approaches. The models most common in the literature are Rothman's (2008) three models of community practice: planning/policy, community capacity development, and social advocacy. These three models, explained in the remainder of this section, have a common goal to improve social, economic, and/or environmental well-being, and they share several common elements including the following (Rothman, 2008; Weil & Gamble, 2009; Weil, Gamble, & Ohmer, 2013):

- the formulation of a change goal,

- roles for staff,

- leaders and members,

- a process of selecting issues to work on,

- a target of the change effort,

- assessment of resources needed to produce change, and

- an understanding of the role of organizations in the change process.

Planning/Policy

The **planning/policy model** of community intervention focuses on data and logic to achieve community change, using experts to assist in the process of studying problems and applying rational planning techniques. Social workers using social planning also factor in political considerations and advocacy in the intervention process, but the primary emphasis is on rational planning.

The planning/policy model can be implemented in a range of practice situations. Social workers engage in social planning efforts when they participate in efforts to envision, develop, coordinate, deliver, and improve human services. Planning is needed for all types of human services (i.e., child welfare, health, aging) and topics (i.e., gang violence, neighborhood development), and by myriad of hosts, such as local, state, or federal governments, faith-based organizations, and community councils (Sager & Weil, 2013). As one example, social workers prioritize data when they are involved in comprehensive planning, such as working with city officials to create a plan for homeless shelters or for prison facilities for the community. In these situations, data, such as U.S. Census data, local government data, or data generated by local nonprofits, are the primary considerations for making decisions. Social workers often use statistics, computer modeling, and forecasting techniques with this model (Rothman, 2008; Weil & Gamble, 2009).

Community Capacity Development

Community capacity development focuses on fostering the local community collective ability to accomplish change by building relationships and skills that help solve local problems in a cooperative manner. Participant consensus is thus the optimal decision-making process for this model. Community capacity development is consistent with the strengths-based approaches of community asset mapping (discussed later in this chapter).

The community capacity development model emphasizes building competency of community members, groups, and the community as a whole through self-help and local problem solving. Common themes within this approach include empowerment, solidarity (e.g., achieving harmonious interrelationships among diverse persons), participation in civic action within a democratic process, and the development of leadership among local leaders. For example, neighborhood associations and clubs may work to educate themselves on ways to address a trash dumping problem, or settlement houses may attempt to prevent violence and crime by assisting local citizens and leaders in organizing summer activities for youth. The work of the U.S. Peace Corps, in which international volunteers work with local communities to create a project or increase capacity in an ongoing community effort, is another example of the community capacity development model. A Peace Corps volunteer may work with local schools to develop their capacity to improve the schools' hygiene facilities and lower the rate of illness and disease. To do this, a volunteer could work with a local committee involved with the school and help them to raise money, prioritize needs, make plans, contact experts within or outside of the community, and carry out other tasks needed for the project (Rothman, 2008; Weil & Gamble, 2009).

Social Advocacy

The **social advocacy model** is based in conflict, power dependency, and resource mobilization theories of power and politics (discussed in Chapter 10). This model is both process- and task-oriented and focuses on shifting power relationships and resources to affect institutional change by applying pressure to a target (e.g., persons and/or institutions) that has created or exacerbated a problem. Through this model, beneficiaries achieve empowerment when they feel a sense of mastery in influencing community decision-making.

A helpful example of the social advocacy model is the work of Greenpeace. To seek solutions to environmental dilemmas, such as climate change, Greenpeace nonviolently confronts decision-makers and those who may influence decision-makers. The goal of their nonviolent actions is to promote public dialogue about environmental issues and to pressure decision-makers (Greenpeace, n.d.). As described in Quick Guides 35 and 36, there is a wide variety of social advocacy activities, including but not limited to testifying, protesting, striking, and walking on picket lines (Rothman, 2008; Weil & Gamble, 2009).

QUICK GUIDE 35   PROVIDING TESTIMONY

Social workers often provide testimony to legislative and planning committees at the local, state, regional, and national levels. The main purpose of testimony is to share information and ascertain public opinion. The following steps are helpful when preparing to provide testimony:

1. Learn about how legislative proposals (bills) work their way through the process in the legislature. Who has sponsored or co-sponsored the bill? To what committee(s) has your bill been assigned? What are the possible outcomes of committee work on the bill? Where would the bill go next if the committee approves the bill? Has a similar bill been introduced in the other chamber?
2. Learn about the history of the topic and bill. Has this bill been proposed before? Who sponsored it? What happened to the bill? Did the general public already vote on the topic through referendum? Has this bill already been amended?
3. Engage in research about the topic. Research existing statutes that the bill seeks to amend, revise, supplement, or delete. If possible, research the cost of the bill, if enacted.
4. Engage in research about the politics of the bill. Which individuals or what groups are working for the bill? Against the bill? What are their perspectives?
5. Research the committee membership. Who is the chair? What is his/her perspective on the topic of your bill? Who else is on the committee? What are their interests and those of their constituents? How have they voted on this topic before?
6. Determine how long your testimony should be, and, depending on time, draft a written statement that: (1) provides factual data, including cost estimates, needed to support or refute the opposition's key points; (2) analyzes the proposed changes/additions to present law; (3) discusses any new problems that attempts to solve existing problems may create; and/or (4) provides any suggestions for needed amendments.

When delivering your testimony, consider the following:

7. Use effective nonverbal communication. Dress professionally, make eye contact, and display a calm and confident demeanor.
8. Start your testimony by introducing yourself and the organization you represent. Use full titles to address committee members. At the beginning and end of your testimony, thank the committee

chair and decision-makers for allowing you to speak. State your name and background information related to the topic at hand (such as where you live, your credentials, or your connection to the topic). Clearly state your request for the outcome of the decision-making process.

9. Describe your involvement with the topic, including any helpful context or background. If the testimony is related to your employment, provide your employer's name and interest in the topic.

10. Describe how the topic affects you or your clients. Provide factual and general information, as well as anecdotes. Describe how the pending decision will positively or negatively affect you or your clients and include a description of who will benefit and who will be hurt by the decision.

11. Connect the topic to evaluation of the policy change outcomes. For example, would the proposal provide benefits for the affected? The community? What is most important in this decision?

12. End by thanking the committee again, and offer to be of further assistance. If possible, leave a copy of your written statement with the committee.

13. Convey passion for the topic you are addressing, balanced with professionalism.

14. If you are asked questions, maintain your professionalism. Do not take questions personally, but rather state facts and your position on the bill. Offer to get facts or call on someone else to help, if needed.

Remember that a vote can be the result of a particular amendment to the bill, budget projections, position of party leadership, or complex interrelationships between procedural and substantive issues—not necessarily the subject of the bill.

Source: Kleinkauf, 1981; Oregon Legislature, n.d.; Work Group for Community Health and Development at the University of Kansas, 2012.

QUICK GUIDE 36   ACTIVITIES TO PROMOTE SOCIAL CHANGE

Conduct petition drives
Conduct public hearings
Develop relationships with decision-makers
File complaints
Lobby decision-makers
Organize boycotts
Organize public demonstrations
Organize strikes
Provide testimony
Recruit and develop leaders
Register voters
Use legal action
Use media
Write letters to legislators and/or the media

Source: Bobo, Kendall, & Max, 2010; Work Group for Community Health and Development at the University of Kansas, 2012

Applying Community Practice Models to Case Examples

Exhibit 11.2 provides a case example and applies each type of model to the example.

EXHIBIT 11.2 *Applying Community Practice Models to Case Examples*	**CASE #1** In a case similar to Brickville, another city struggles with redevelopment efforts. The south side of a large Midwestern city is a low-income community populated mostly by Latino and African American populations. The other parts of the city are mainly populated with White, non-Latino, middle- and high-income families. The south side of the city has a history of oppression, including poorer quality schools and less public funding for roads and other infrastructure. In addition, it has a past history of discrimination against minority families in mortgage lending, which led to a very high rate of minorities living in rental housing rather than owning homes. Over the past half-century, real estate developers have made several half-hearted efforts to redevelop the residential and commercial parts of the community, with little success. However, several real estate developers are now working to redevelop different areas of the community, and all are requesting public funding (in addition to bank loans) for their development efforts. While some developers are working with current residents, most of them have not asked community groups or local political leaders for their input or feedback on the redevelopment plans. *The Planning/Policy Model:* Using the Planning/Policy model, the community group or local political leader would request that city planners generate data or utilize previously existing data to create a redevelopment plan for the community to which all developers would have to adhere. *The Community Capacity Development Model:* Using the Community Capacity Development model, one or more community groups from the affected area would begin a process of developing their ability to create a comprehensive community redevelopment plan that they could present to real estate developers and/or city officials. *The Social Advocacy Model:* Using the Social Advocacy model, one or more community groups from the affected area would utilize pressure tactics on a targeted decision-maker to affect the outcome of decisions about public funding for the projects, such as specific city elected or appointed officials. **CASE #2** In May 2011, Joplin, Missouri, experienced an EF-5 tornado—the highest-strength rating—that destroyed one-third of the city and killed 161 people, including one teen who had received his high school diploma that day. Homes, businesses, a hospital, and the local high school were destroyed (Shelton, 2012). Organizations and religious groups

provided tremendous resources, including basic needs (i.e., shelter, food), health services, crisis mental health services, and debris cleanup.

EXHIBIT 11.2

Continued

   The community faced the challenging task of rebuilding a large part of their area, including public institutions. To carry out this task and gain consensus among citizens regarding planning efforts, city leaders created a Citizen Advisory Recovery Team (CART) to provide a citizen voice for Joplin residents in the decisions involved in rebuilding. CART focuses on economic development, school and community facilities development, housing and neighborhood development, and infrastructure and the environment. CART membership consists of a diverse set of Joplin citizens. To gain community input into planning, a series of community meetings and open houses have been held for comments regarding a master plan for community redevelopment and the selection of a master developer. Citizens have expressed interest in developing a walkable community that includes diverse, affordable, and sustainable housing (Joplin Area CART, n.d.).

The Planning/Policy Model: By employing professional planners and other experts who are contributing their technical knowledge and expertise in the planning effort, the Joplin community is also using the Planning/Policy model.

The Community Capacity Model: The Joplin community is most clearly using the Community Capacity Development model because community members are utilizing their abilities to create a redevelopment plan with extensive community input. Involved community members are exercising and building their leadership skills by facilitating a process whereby other citizens can participate in a democratic process.

The Social Advocacy Model: The Joplin community may use the Social Advocacy model, under certain circumstances. For example, if the authorities would not seriously consider the decisions CART makes, CART may organize activities to apply pressure to targeted decision-makers.

Blending Models

While we present models here in a "pure" form, in practice they are often blended in a variety of ways (Rothman, 2008; Weil & Gamble, 2009). While the same blend occurs more than once, the first model mentioned emphasizes the blended approach:

You Can Incorporate Community Capacity Development into the Planning/Policy Model with the use of citizen input into a data-driven planning process. For example, the St. Louis, Missouri, Mental Health Board (hereafter referred to as "The Board") periodically completes a needs assessment on the mental health services of

St. Louis in order to identify the largest unmet needs. The Board then creates a multiyear plan to allocate funding to best meet those needs. Throughout the process, the Board receives feedback from mental health providers and consumers. In this way, the board mixes the two models through the strong reliance on data (Planning/Policy) and the use of citizen and provider input into the planning process (Community Capacity Development) (Rothman, 2008). In another example, data about the increase of rape on college campuses (Planning/Policy) spurred the creation of an on-campus group whose participants were taught how to identify activity that could result in sexual violence and to intervene as bystanders (Community Capacity Development) (Banyard, Moynihan, & Plante, 2007).

You Can Incorporate Social Advocacy into the Planning/Policy Model by emphasizing the use of data and logic in policy advocacy efforts. For instance, the Board can use the needs assessment and funding allocation plans to advocate for policy changes at the local, state, and/or national levels via intensive education and lobby efforts. These changes work to improve services for those with mental health challenges. In this manner, the Board uses data (Planning/Policy) and advocacy efforts (Social Advocacy) to implement community change (Rothman, 2008).

You Can Incorporate Planning/Policy into the Community Capacity Development Model (with an emphasis on the Capacity Development Model) by utilizing institutions that primarily assist communities to increase their capacity to deliver resources to their residents. For example, based on the results of a needs assessment, the Mental Health Board could work with neighborhood providers to strengthen local communities' response to mental health needs, emphasizing a local problem-solving process for working with individuals with chronic mental illness. In a second example, **Community Development Corporations** (CDCs) are resident-driven organizations that exist to provide assistance to the community. This assistance can include facilitating housing improvements throughout the community, or supporting businesses and commercial real estate efforts, and involvement in child care, community centers, and other components in the community. A board of residents, business owners, and/or local government officials govern the CDCs. The CDCs can use data-informed approaches, such as creating small business assistance programs, creating **cooperatives** (i.e., member-owned/operated businesses), or rehabilitating affordable housing in the community (Garkovich, 2011). Both examples emphasize developing the capacity of local communities (Capacity Development) using data and logic (Planning/Policy) to make decisions about the focus of community change efforts (Rothman, 2008).

You Can Incorporate Social Advocacy into the Community Capacity Development Model to encourage networks of community stakeholders to put pressure on decision-makers to improve the community. All types of communities can use this mixed approach on a wide variety of targets for policy and practice decisions. For example, a neighborhood group may learn about the plans to build a casino in their community and decide to fight it by lobbying key decision-makers, delivering petitions, and/or picketing the local government. A group of parents of children who are LGBTQ may decide to engage in an online effort to advocate for civil rights for lesbian, gay, bisexual, transgender, and questioning (LGBTQ) people in their community. Their efforts may include a sit-in at the office of a local elected official to ask for her or his support. This mixed approach emphasizes using community capacity (Community Capacity Development) with social advocacy techniques in situations where this mix will maximize the possibility for community change (Rothman, 2008).

You Can Incorporate Planning/Policy into the Social Advocacy Model to use data and logic to support advocacy efforts. This blend can best describe the efforts of many prominent social work pioneers in history, such as Jane Addams, John Dewey, Margaret Sanger, and others. These pioneers based their arguments about child labor, housing codes, food and drug safety, and other issues on data and logical arguments. Today, "think-tanks" such as the New America Foundation and others provide well-researched factual reports that social advocacy groups use to press for change. Therefore, mixing tactics that bring pressure to bear on decision-makers (Social Advocacy) with data and logic (Planning/Policy) most closely aligns with the roots of the profession (Rothman, 2008).

You Can Incorporate Community Capacity Development into the Social Advocacy Model to create strong networks of people engaged in advocacy, which can also focus on developing leadership, empowering participants, and building solidarity. This mixture is most apparent in long-term social advocacy efforts, such as the gay rights movement, the environmental movement, and the women's rights movement. This mix of pressure tactics and techniques (Social Advocacy) and developing the skills and knowledge of community members (Community Capacity Development) creates long-term aptitude for community intervention (Rothman, 2008).

These models, both in pure and mixed forms, offer ways to analyze and describe community interventions. The possibilities for interventions when mixing the models are endless. You can alter the degree of the secondary model in the mix. For example, many faith-based organizations focus on Community Capacity Development, emphasizing programming for empowerment, leadership development, and solidarity through self-help group work, and engage in only a small amount of Social Advocacy (Rothman, 2008). While there are several other conceptual frameworks for community interventions that provide helpful practice models (see for example Weil, Gamble, & Ohmer, 2013), the models described here provide a starting point for many types of community intervention. Exhibit 11.3 provides an example of mixing the models. Next we discuss intervention strategies and skills needed for intervention.

The majority of the world's leading scientists agree that global warming is a serious challenge to the long-term viability and sustainability of the planet. Therefore, global warming is the focus of community practice efforts worldwide. In 2008, Bill McKibben, a professor at Middlebury College, found 350.org, an organization that works to build political pressure to promote action that lessens global warming and climate change. Specifically, the goal of 350.org is to lower the amount of carbon dioxide in the atmosphere below 350 parts per million, the limit that scientists advocate as the maximum amount the atmosphere can absorb without leading to climate change. 350.org uses the latest scientific data about global warming from the world's leading scientists, which provides a solid evidence base for their work. 350.org encourages localities around the world—nations, cities, towns, and villages—and groups of individuals to build their community capacity by organizing individuals and groups to collaborate with them on campaigns. Local activist groups around the globe coordinate to sponsor events. For example, after the November 2012 election, 350.org began a "Do the Math Tour" in which McKibben and 350.org traveled the county to coordinate with local groups to build a movement through events that featured actors, artists, and musicians. 350.org also engages in social advocacy to both educate policy leaders by testifying to legislative committees, and to pressure them to make policy decisions that would lessen global warming. For example, the Keystone Pipeline is a proposed oil pipeline that would run from the tar fields in Canada to the Gulf of Mexico. Scientists maintain that mining the tar fields would release large amounts of carbon into the air, which would contribute to the problem of global warming. In 2011, 350.org organized protests in front of the White House to raise concern among the public about the pipeline and to put pressure on President Obama to halt plans to build the pipeline. Their work was at least partially successful: On February 24, 2015, President Obama vetoed the Keystone Pipeline. 350.org provides an example of an effort that blends two models, with their emphasis on building community capacity and social advocacy.

Source: Adapted from 350.org (n.d.)

CONTEMPORARY TRENDS AND SKILLS FOR THE MIDDLE PHASE OF COMMUNITY WORK: INTERVENTION [EPAS 8]

Community intervention is action to improve community conditions and quality of life for residents or members. This discussion will focus on the intervention strategies useful for implementing the community practice models mentioned earlier. These strategies can be useful in any of the models discussed, as they are often blended within interventions. We will discuss community social and economic development, community asset mapping, and community organizing. We will also cover the skills of conducting meetings and participating in decision-making, as these are useful skills within many community practice interventions.

© 350.org

© 350.org

Community Social and Economic Development [EPAS 1 and 8]

Community social and economic development (hereafter referred to as "community development"), also called "locality development" and "community building," is an often-ambiguous term with a variety of definitions. In this text, it is a community intervention method that seeks to maximize human potential by focusing on social relationships and the environment in order to improve the physical and social fabric of communities (Rubin & Rubin, 2008). Community development emphasizes social development through relationship-building, education, motivation for self-help, and leadership development. It encourages local participation in community efforts toward the goal of strengthening democracy at the local community level and can include efforts to revitalize institutions. Community development focused on economics includes economic development, affordable housing, employment services, and other activities. Often community social development and community economic development efforts are simultaneous and interdependent, and they can be viewed as a continuum.

Community development may include professions from many fields, including business, sociology, anthropology, psychology, and others (Gamble & Hoff, 2013). Community development work most closely aligns with the Community Capacity Development model discussed earlier, because its goal is to mobilize communities to solve problems and effectively work with institutions, rather than to engage in Social Advocacy or Planning/Policy work. However, community development work also can use a mix of models, depending on the needs at the time.

The following assumptions drive community development (Cnaan & Rothman, 2008, pp. 247–248):

- People may need to become aware of a common problem and create a desire to act in order to solve problems.

- A diverse group of people across various dimensions of diversity (i.e., race, ethnicity, socioeconomic status, etc.) adds value and authenticity to the efforts and ensures that they serve the interests of more than one group of people.

- Democratic decision-making and participatory democracy values and fosters local self-determination.

- Empowerment, or the capacity to solve problems by working with the authorities and institutions that affect the lives of community members, is a central goal of community development.

- The primary constituents of the community development social worker are community members and community organizations, rather than those who hold more power.

- Planned change is preferred to inaction that allows current conditions to continue.

Community Development Skills   The most commonly used practice skills are group work skills. Group work, covered extensively in Chapters 8 and 9, is a major part of community development work, as this type of work is often conducted in meetings. To ensure success, community development social workers must employ task group work skills including leadership; communication; problem solving; and managing group function and processes such as educating, forming groups, seeking consensus, encouraging group discussion, and focusing to solve concerns and problems common to the group. Other skills include analyzing community issues and facilitating the increase of communication among community members (Cnaan & Rothman, 2008).

As discussed in Chapter 9, promoting indigenous leadership in group work directed at community development requires the ability to distribute leadership as widely as possible. The facilitation of effective task meeting is one example of a leadership skill that social workers may use or teach to indigenous leaders. Quick Guide 37 provides an overview of the tasks involved in effective meeting facilitation. These tasks can be distributed among individuals during meetings or handled by a small group as a way to learn and exercise leadership skills.

In task groups, using decision-making processes that promote full participation is an important skill. Decision-making for groups can be handled in many ways, including the **parliamentary procedure**, or **Robert's Rules of Order**, and **consensus decision-making**. Quick Guide 38 provides an overview of Robert's Rules of Order, and Quick Guide 39 provides an overview of consensus decision-making. Both types of decision-making processes are common in task groups, depending on the context of the work. Social workers need to be familiar with decision-making processes to fully participate as individuals and to help others participate.

Recruitment of new participants is an ongoing and important community development skill. Participants involved in community development work are often volunteers, and recruitment, training, monitoring, and rewarding of volunteers is important to the success of the long-term goals. The most effective ways to recruit participants include focusing on people who are most likely to join, using a well-formed recruiting message, using multiple recruitment methods, providing orientation for new participants, and making it easy to join activities. Volunteer activities have to be calibrated to fit the skills, time, and interests of volunteers and be meaningful to them (Cnaan & Rothman, 2008).

Community Development Programs   Community economic development (CED) approaches use economic approaches to develop the capacities of low-income people and neighborhoods (Robinson & Green, 2011). Programs that fall into

QUICK GUIDE 37 ELEMENTS OF EFFECTIVE MEETINGS

STAGE	ELEMENT	NOTES
Preparation	Goals	Develop goal(s) for each meeting.
	Site	Establish a meeting site that is familiar, accessible, perceived as safe, and has parking.
	Date/Timing	Set a date and time that is convenient for the majority of (would-be) participants.
	Facilitator	The facilitator is involved in setting the agenda.
	Agenda	Include the speaker's name in each agenda item, information about the item, and a time limit. Discuss easy items first, followed by hard and then moderate decisions.
	Food	Offer food at various times, unless disruptive.
	Recruitment/Turnout	Provide oral and written meeting announcements and remind people a few days prior to the meeting.
	Meeting Roles	Assign roles ahead of time, including facilitator, note-taker, timekeeper, presenters, and greeter.
	Room Logistics	Set up chairs, AV equipment, flipchart, sign-in table, food/drink, and microphone.
	Background Materials	Prepare background materials about pending decisions and preliminary proposals to discuss.
Meeting	Timeliness	Begin and end the meeting on time.
	Welcome, Introductions	Begin with a warm welcome and introductions to set a positive tone, regardless of the turnout.
	Agenda	Review the agenda with the group and make changes as needed.
	Meeting Rules	Explain any rules, including decision-making rules.
	Discussion	Encourage discussion of various viewpoints; encourage all to speak by drawing out quieter people, limiting those who dominate, and encouraging respect for viewpoints; summarize; and bring closure to discussion.
	Focus	Bring the group back to the agenda if discussion wanders.
	Ending	Summarize meeting results, decisions, and needed follow-up. Thank people for attending.
Follow-up	Notes	Prepare and disseminate meeting notes quickly.
	Thank People	Contact people, especially new people, to thank them for their contribution to the meeting, to encourage follow-up on commitments for action, and to encourage them to attend the next meeting.

Source: Adapted from Bobo, Kendall, & Max, 2010; Minieri & Getsos, 2007

QUICK GUIDE 38   UTILIZING ROBERT'S RULES OF ORDER

Many formal groups, such as Boards of Directors, committees, and policy-making groups, use some form of a formal decision-making process. *Parliamentary procedure,* or *Robert's Rules of Order,* are often used because they are well known, help to maintain order, and allow actions to be taken in an expedient and consistent manner. Although the process can be quite complex, some groups utilize the general rules without learning the minutia. Understanding the major concepts of parliamentary procedure is a critical skill for facilitating and participating in a meeting.

Robert's Rules of Order provide a structured, democratic (majority rules) mechanism whereby formal groups can engage in efficient and fair decision-making. The following are major elements of the process:

- The use of a *motion* to introduce a proposal. Any idea for the group's consideration must be introduced as a motion (i.e., "I move that . . ."). Only one motion can be considered at a time.
- The *seconding* of a motion to move a proposal forward for discussion. A motion cannot move forward in the process unless someone other than the person who made the motion "seconds" the motion (i.e., "I second the motion"). Without a second, a motion dies and is not discussed.
- The use of *debate/discussion* to enable participants to present perspectives and ask questions about a motion. After a motion is made and seconded, the facilitator can open discussion about the motion, and group members can ask questions of the author of the motion.
- *Amendments* to reflect revisions to an original motion based on the debate/discussion. During the discussion, one or more participants may offer an amendment to clarify or narrow the motion. This amendment must be voted on before the original motion is voted on. A majority vote is required to pass an amendment.
- *Majority rules* (i.e., a minimum of 51% of members agreeing) to establish a motion as a decision.

Source: Adapted from Robert III, Honermann, & Balch, 2011

QUICK GUIDE 39   UTILIZING CONSENSUS FOR DECISION-MAKING

Real change, at the individual, family, group, community, or organizational level, comes from persons who are personally committed to a decision or direction in which they fully participated. **Consensus decision-making**, or a cooperative process in which all members develop and agree to support a decision that is in the best interests of the whole group, can be effective in situations in which the following conditions are present:

- Participants feel a genuine stake in the decision.
- Participants share a common purpose and values.
- Participants trust each other.
- Participants are willing to put the best interests of the group over personal preferences.
- Participants can share their ideas and opinions freely, without fear of ridicule.
- Enough time is available for the process.
- Participants can engage in active listening and consider different points of view.

After meeting preparation work, the process:

- Explores the issue toward the goal of developing an informed, shared understanding of the facts and the issue.

QUICK GUIDE 39   CONTINUED

- Establishes decision criteria, including such factors as interests/needs that must be met, resource constraints, and possible ramifications of decisions.
- Develops and discusses a written preliminary proposal.
- Tests for consensus, asking participants whether they can live with the proposal (original or amended), whether it meets the decision criteria, and whether it is the best decision possible.
- Reaches agreement by restating the proposed decision and ensuring that participants can support the implementation of the proposal.

Source: Adapted from Dressler, 2006

this approach include the following (Robinson & Green, 2011; Rubin & Rubin, 2008):

- *Individual Development Accounts (IDAs)*: IDAs are matched saving accounts for low-income employed persons who meet income guidelines. IDA programs involve financial education and case management. IDA funds can be spent on approved assets, such as a home, home repair, starting or expanding a small business, or secondary education.

- *Employment training and placement:* Job training programs prepare people for employment opportunities and assist participants in securing and maintaining their employment.

- *Support of small and home-based businesses:* Programs are available to assist people to start and expand small business, including training, technical assistance, support, and linkages to small business loans.

- *Financial education and credit building:* Nonprofit and for-profit organizations provide financial education to build client financial knowledge and also help people build their credit score.

- *Services to help low-income families purchase a home:* Homeownership services are available to assist families to build their credit, locate and secure a home, obtain affordable financing, avoid foreclosure, and maintain their homeownership.

- *Assistance for families:* to file their federal and state taxes and receive the Earned Income Tax Credit (EITC), which is a refundable tax credit for working, low-income families.

- *Human-rights work* (i.e., fair housing, civil rights, environmental justice, disability, and sexual orientation discrimination).

There are many examples of community social and economic development work. Youth development work often involves leadership development and relationship skills as well as job training and employment placement services (Chaskin,

EXHIBIT 11.4

Detroit, Michigan Promotes Community Social and Economic Development

The economic changes of the past few decades have brought empty boulevards, an abandoned train station, empty high-rises, shuttered storefronts, and semideserted neighborhoods to Detroit, Michigan. In striving to revitalize the local economy, the community is paying particular attention to self-reliance. One example is the reimagining of the growing amount of vacant land in the downtown area toward a new, sustainable, local food system. Community and commercial gardens are springing up on land leased from the city, providing employment and volunteer opportunities. In addition to selling produce at local farmers markets during the summer, some gardens are also installing hoop houses, in which food can be grown year-round. There are also plans for indoor tilapia and shrimp farms, tree farms, and other uses of the land that will facilitate employment and sustainability (Sands, 2015). The emergence of a local food system has been spurred by the Detroit Food Policy Council, which works to create the local policy conditions to facilitate the expansion of a "sustainable local food system that promotes food security, food justice, and food sovereignty in the city of Detroit" (Detroit Food Policy Council, 2016).

Source: Detroit Food Policy Council, 2016; Sands, 2015

2010; Wheeler & Thomas, 2011). Domestic violence services can include education, financial education, credit building, IDA services, and economic advocacy (Family Resource Center, 2016). Building community partnerships for school-based services, such as physical and mental health services, counseling, mentoring, and other programs, is an example of community development work focused primarily on social development (Poole, 2009). Work with immigrants and refugees can include community development work, including financial literacy; assistance for small business owners to start, expand, and strengthen their business; and lending for small businesses and micro business loans through a peer lending program as well as case management, translation, education, and other services (International Institute St. Louis, 2016). Some community development focuses solely on improving the physical environments of communities through efforts such as the production of affordable housing, the development of commercial space in low income communities, and/or the redevelopment of entire streets. Exhibit 11.4 provides an example of community development.

Asset-Based Community Development

We discussed community asset mapping as an assessment strategy in Chapter 10. You can use the community data you gather as part of the assessment process in the community intervention. After collecting the data, the next step is to group all of the data into categories, such as capabilities of individuals, including those marginalized within the community, associations, local institutions, physical assets, and (potential) leaders. Exhibit 11.5 provides examples of the types of information you can

EXHIBIT 11.5

Community Assets

Associations

Animal Care Groups
Anti-Crime Groups
Block Clubs
Business Organizations
Charitable Groups
Civic Events Groups
Cultural Groups
Disability/Special Needs Groups
Education Groups
Elderly Groups
Environmental Groups
Family Support Groups
Health Advocacy and Fitness
Heritage Groups
Hobby and Collectors Groups
Men's Groups
Mentoring Groups
Mutual Support Groups
Neighborhood Groups
Political Organizations
Recreation Groups
Religious Groups
Service Clubs
Social Groups
Union Groups
Veteran's Groups
Women's Groups
Youth Groups

Local Economy

Banks
Barter & Exchange
Business Associations
CDCs
Chamber of Commerce
Consumer Expenditures
Corporations & Branches
Credit Unions
For-Profit Businesses
Foundations
Institutional-Purchasing Power
and Personnel
Merchants

Physical Space

Bike Paths
Bird Watching Sites
Campsites
Duck Ponds
Fishing Spots
Forests/Forest Preserves
Gardens
Housing
Natural Habitats – Coastal, Marine, Amphibian
Parking Lots
Parks
Picnic Areas
Playgrounds
Star Gazing Sites
Streets
Transit Stops and Facilities
Vacant Land & Buildings
Walking Paths
Wildlife Center
Zoos

Individuals

Gifts, Skills, Capacities, Knowledge and Traits of:
Activists
Artists
Entrepreneurs
Ex-Offenders
Older Adults
Parents
People with Disabilities
Students
Veterans
Welfare Recipients
Youth

Institutions

Community Colleges
Fire Departments
Foundations
Hospitals
Libraries
Media
Museums
Nonprofit Organizations
Police Departments
Schools
Social Service Agencies
Universities

Source: Kretzmann & McKnight, 2005

group in each category. As a social worker, building your relationship with all of these types of assets, as well as relationships between these types of assets, is a key ingredient in a community change effort. Building strong networks among these assets will strengthen the social fabric of the community and build capacity as a whole community. For example, a social worker may be involved in establishing a network of social service providers, representatives of educational institutions, and business leaders in communities to work on local community challenges. Social workers may need to identify the self-interest of the various groups when recruiting them to become involved, such as mentioning to local businesses that strengthening their ties to organizations serving local youth also involves the possibility of expanding their pool of future labor. These efforts can result in a more self-reliant community.

As relationships are built, the ability of the community to solve problems locally increases. Social workers prompt associations and institutions to increase their contributions to community efforts. For example, social workers can facilitate and support organizations in their work to develop websites, and they can contact local newspapers and radio stations to aid the flow of useful information. The process of community asset development may involve community meetings to develop a local vision and the strategies to implement this vision. Faith communities (such as churches or synagogues), faith networks (such as ministerial alliance), associations (such as clubs or groups), or institutions (such as a local school district or large employer) can sponsor community planning processes. After the planning process, the planning group can seek outside resources, if needed, to carry out a community plan. Bringing in outside resources, such as foundations, government actors, and others, *after* creating a plan ensures that community plans are truly resident-driven. If the group brings in outside resources during the planning process, careful participatory planning must occur to ensure that citizens' knowledge and views about what is good for the community are heard and considered. The outcomes of a participatory, community-driven planning process reflect the desires of the residents (Weil, 2013).

In addition to community development work, community social work practice interventions also include community organizing. Having considered community development, our discussion now turns to community organizing as a standalone community intervention that can be integrated into community development.

Community Organizing

Community organizing is a practice skill that entails using a process to mobilize people and their resources to identify problems and advocate for change to improve the quality of life in marginalized communities (Ohmer & Brooks, 2013). Community organizing skills can be used within any of the three models of community practice mentioned earlier (planning/policy, community capacity development, and social advocacy). The target of community organizing efforts can aim at a wide variety of targets, including local, state, and federal government officials; legislators; private landlords; corporate CEOs; and officials of the global organizations. For example, in the Brickville case, the supporting and opposing groups both target public officials, who have control over the public resources needed for the budget of the redevelopment effort.

While community organizing work typically focuses on a particular change effort, such as passing a local ballot issue about sales tax, the form that community organizing takes can vary widely. Community organization can include accepting and working with the existing power relationships, or **consensus organizing**, and challenging the existing power relationship, or **direct action organizing**.

Exhibit 11.6 describes the continuum of services as framed by the degree to which people accept the existing power relationships within a community. The left side of the exhibit depicts consensus organizing. Consensus organizing involves developing strong relationships and partnerships among and between community members and stakeholders and with people and institutions that are external to the community and hold power that can facilitate community change.

External powers can include government officials, landlords who own rental property in the community, and/or private business owners. Engaging in consensus community organizing brings together community participants and uses the power structure as a partner in the change effort. Exhibit 11.7 shows the assumptions of the consensus organizing approach.

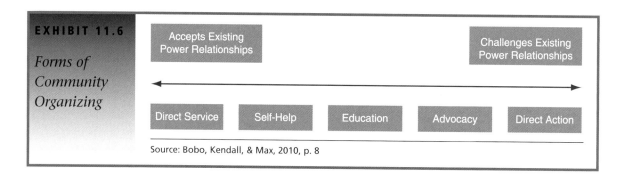

EXHIBIT 11.6 *Forms of Community Organizing*	Accepts Existing Power Relationships			Challenges Existing Power Relationships
	Direct Service	Self-Help	Education	Advocacy	Direct Action

Source: Bobo, Kendall, & Max, 2010, p. 8

EXHIBIT 11.7

Assumptions of the Consensus Organizing Approach

- Ordinary people can and should be involved in creating sustainable community change.
- It is important to identify and build on community strengths and assets, rather than deficits.
- Potential leaders are everywhere and often need recognition and support to thrive.
- The organizer must be a selfless promoter of others.
- The organizer must seek to achieve self-interest for residents and external partners.
- Powerful people and institutions want to assist with community change.

Source: Adapted from Ohmer & DeMasi, 2009

The right side of Exhibit 11.6 represents direct action community organizing, or **conflict organizing**. This form of community organizing assumes that a disadvantaged population must be organized to make demands on a target for equal treatment/resources, with the larger goal of gaining power and changing the structure of power. With conflict organizing, the power structure is not seen as a partner but more as a target of action (Ohmer & DeMasi, 2009). The targets of conflict organizing are those with power in the community to make change, such as landlords and government officials—the same people and institutions with which consensus organizers seek to create partnerships.

In the Brickville example, both sides could use consensus or conflict organizing. Using conflict organizing, both groups could organize their supporters to press public officials and the developer to demand more power in the decision-making process about the redevelopment plan. In contrast, both sides could use consensus organizing by attempting to partner with the developer and/or the public officials, and gain input through a collaborative process.

Community Organizing Skills   The three essential elements for community organizing along the continuum are empowering individuals, building and strengthening community bonds, and building progressive organizations (Rubin & Rubin, 2008). Organizers can empower individuals by (1) encouraging participation, (2) arranging tasks so individuals experience success and build their confidence to engage in public affairs, (3) organizing tasks so individuals' involvement is meaningful and builds leadership skills, and (4) recognizing and supporting their efforts (Minieri & Getsos, 2007). Building progressive organizations involves a mission to promote social equity and participatory democracy processes (Rubin & Rubin, 2008), such as Robert's Rules of Order or consensus.

People build bonds by developing a shared sense of community. When individuals work together to determine common community issues, analyze the issues, select issues on which to work, develop and implement strategies, and engage in evaluation toward a common goal, they create bonds and social networks (Rubin & Rubin, 2008). In the process of community organizing, once organizers have built relationships, they identify common challenges with a core group. As new members are continually recruited, the core group works to enact change, even of a small magnitude (Ohmer & DeMasi, 2009).

The ultimate desired outcomes of community organizing efforts frame many aspects of community practice. For example, at the conflict end of the organizing continuum, the final desired outcome is to alter the balance of power so that resources are more equitably distributed, while at the other end of the continuum, in Exhibit 11.6, strong partnerships between community residents and external power sources that result in tangible resources is the desired outcome (Ohmer & DeMasi, 2009). For example, in the Brickville case, using conflict organizing, both supporting and opposing groups could ultimately seek to change the balance of power between themselves and the developer and public officials. Using consensus

EXHIBIT 11.8	In several communities, houses of worship are the springboard for community orga-
Community Organizing to Encourage People of Faith to Vote and Facilitate the Process	nizing efforts to encourage people to vote and facilitate the electoral process. For example, community organizers are engaged in a "Rock the Muslim Vote" campaign to register Muslims to vote. They work in mosques and Islamic centers in the Los Angeles area. These efforts are encouraging Muslims to vote so their voices are amplified in political campaigns, and ultimately in community affairs (Pogash, 2016). In another example, community organizers are working in Ohio to ensure that the state law that purges infrequent voters from voting rolls does not disenfranchise African American voters. Community organizers are working in predominantly black churches to help congregants check the Secretary of State's public records to see if they are still registered to vote. If they are not still registered, they help them become registered (Yi, Rothman, & Burty, 2016, July 31)

Source: Pogash, 2016; Yi, Rothman, & Burty, 2016, July 31

organizing, the groups would seek to build strong and enduring partnerships among all of the players, and seek to gain build relationships with the powerful decision makers that will endure past the current issue of the redevelopment. This difference affects the importance of specific skills, such as analyzing the power of a target, prioritizing issues on which to work (conflict organizing), building relationships with external resources, and brokering relationships between community groups and institutions (consensus organizing) (Bobo, Kendall, & Max, 2010; Ohmer & DeMasis, 2009).

A Generalist Approach to Community Intervention [EPAS 4]

Depending on the context of the community intervention, generalist social work practitioners often integrate aspects of community organizing and community development activities into their practice. For example, in many communities, a shared identity, bonds between residents, the skills for public discourse, the ability to determine priorities, the skills to work together on common challenges, and leadership skills all must be developed for community change efforts to be possible. Social workers can play an important role in helping develop these prerequisites. Social workers who work primarily with individuals, families, and groups have opportunities to support the development of these skills and to encourage people to participate in community efforts.

There are many ways that social workers can help build the capacity of individuals to engage in community interventions. At the interpersonal level, social workers emphasize collaboration with their clients to optimize individuals' rights, strengths, and capabilities. Social workers discuss power and control with their clients to increase clients' awareness of these dynamics in their everyday lives and in community activities. Social workers can regard clients as citizens, consumers, and partners in change efforts and can use dialogue to raise client awareness about sociopolitical realities. As first suggested by educator Paulo Freire (1973), social workers educate clients about the social conditions, patterns of resource distribution, oppression, and other social and environmental factors that contribute to their situation using respectful discussion and questioning. Social workers help prepare and support people to engage in collective action.

Social workers strive to provide evidence-based interventions in community practice. Creating a body of research to inform evidence-based practice (first introduced in Chapter 4) has proven challenging due to the complexity of community interventions, the difficulties of community research, and many organizations' lack of capacity to engage in research. Yet, social workers must conduct or locate research before intervening. Quick Guide 40 lists sample resources for locating evidence on community practice interventions. Exhibit 11.9 provides research findings about the most effective community intervention activities that social workers undertake (Ohmer & Korr, 2006).

Social workers also engage in social planning efforts when they participate in proposing that elected officials or human service planning councils take action They engage by writing letters, testifying to committees, becoming a member of planning committees, and/or organizing others to lobby planning councils. As part of that process, social workers can carefully create opportunities for community members to

QUICK GUIDE 40 EXAMPLES OF PUBLIC AND PRIVATE EFFORTS TO PROMOTE EVIDENCE-BASED COMMUNITY PRACTICE

Children, Families, and Communities
1. Harvard Family Research Project, Harvard Graduate School of Education
   The Evaluation Exchange is a periodical that contains new lessons and emerging strategies for evaluating programs and policies, particularly those focused on children, families, and communities.

Community Change
2. The Aspen Institute report, *Building Knowledge about Community Change,* summarizes key learning over the past fifteen years about how to evaluate community change initiatives and how to identify strategies for enhancing the evidence base for improving conditions in poor communities. The conclusions in the report are based primarily on the experiences of a group of comprehensive community initiatives (CCIs) in the United States and the United Kingdom.

Health
3. King's Fund
   The policy paper, *Finding Out What Works,* provides information about the effectiveness of health initiatives in Britain.

QUICK GUIDE 40   CONTINUED

Early Childhood, Health Care, and Housing

4. Centers for Disease Controls and Prevention: Community Preventative Services Task Force
   The Community Guide includes systemic reviews of interventions in early childhood development programs, culturally competent health care, and housing.

Housing

5. U.S. Department of Housing and Urban Development (HUD)
   The Program Evaluation Division of HUD has done much research on housing issues, including projects such as costs of homelessness, fair housing accessibility, and comprehensive initiatives such as "Moving to Opportunity."

Mental Health in Communities

6. National Registry of Evidence-based Programs and Practices (NREPP)
   Sponsored by the Substance Abuse and Mental Health Services Administration, NREPP is an online, searchable registry of mental health and substance abuse interventions.

Neighborhood Research, Policy, and Practices

7. Economic and Social Research Council
   The Centre for Neighbourhood Research (CNR) identifies, evaluates, and synthesizes existing social science research on social, economic, and political processes relevant to neighborhood policies and practices in the UK.

Violence Prevention

8. The Center for the Study and Prevention of Violence (CSPV), University of Colorado, Boulder
   Blueprints for Violence Prevention is a project of CSPV that identifies outstanding violence and drug prevention programs that meet a high scientific standard of effectiveness.

Miscellaneous

9. The Campbell Collaboration
   This international research network prepares, maintains, and disseminates systematic reviews on a wide variety of topics related to social welfare and community practice.
10. Laura and John Arnold Foundation Evidence-Based Policy and Innovation
   This nonprofit organization provides evidence about social interventions.
11. Social Care Institute for Excellence
   This charity organization provides evidence-based practice tools and evidence about programs.
12. Society for Community Research and Action, Division 27 of the American Psychological Association (APA)
   The Society provides access to research on community interventions.
13. Society for Child and Family Policy and Practice, Division 37 of the American Psychological Association (APA)
   The Society provides information about services and service structures for children and youth.
14. Community Toolbox
   Their databases of best practices promote community health and development.

Sources: Ohmer, 2008; Thyer, 2008

EXHIBIT 11.9

Effectiveness of Community Practice

Community practice interventions are often complex, with multiple community locations, goals, and activities that make them difficult to evaluate for compliance and fidelity. Community practice interventions can have:

1. a positive impact on facilitating citizen participation, including increasing collective action and community involvement;
2. facilitate personal and collective competencies among participants, including increasing self-esteem, personal and community empowerment, leadership and political skills, and community pride and belonging;
3. a positive impact on improving the physical, social, and economic conditions of communities (i.e., creating and improving affordable housing, increasing homeownership, improving infrastructure and physical appearance, increasing income, investment, and employment, improving high school education, and reducing the sale of alcohol to and its use among young people);
4. the potential for no effect (many studies indicate that interventions do not affect the physical and economic attributes of the communities); and
5. greater likelihood of involving the community organizing efforts of older female residents, African Americans, and Hispanics (other factors that help to explain and predict citizen participation include interest in the problems the program was attempting to solve, neighborhood perceptions and relationships, and length of residency).

Community practice interventions more easily improve citizen participation and associated benefits (i.e., improving collective action and personal and political skills of participants) than they improve complex physical, social, and economic problems in poor communities. Therefore, social work strategies should simultaneously focus on developing ways to strengthen citizen participation and building the capacity of individuals.

Source: Ohmer & Korr, 2006.

participate so that their participation is meaningful and effective, rather than a token effort to "involve" residents. For example, social workers invite community residents to testify at public hearings about proposals to close schools in their neighborhood and help prepare them to testify. Social workers also seek resident involvement in neighborhood committees and work to ensure that residents can voice their opinions, participate fully in decision-making, and assist to implement decisions. Social workers also make connections between disparate situations, so that the needs of individuals are connected to broader efforts and wider structures. For example, if a social worker encounters a resident whose child has lead poisoning, the social worker may be able to link this "case" to a broader "cause" of a community problem with lead poisoning due to the old housing stock in the neighborhood and the reluctance of landlords to remediate the lead in their units. Social workers also invite residents to participate in community-wide efforts to alleviate and prevent the problem, such as lead paint screenings in schools and programs to help tenants test for lead paint in their apartments.

GLOBAL APPROACHES FOR COMMUNITY SOCIAL WORK PRACTICE

While all types of social work practice methods, including casework, group work, and family work, are used around the world, community social work practice is an intervention method that offers unique contributions. Social workers are concerned about poverty and social issues that they encounter in every country, yet large differences in the scope and severity of social issues exist. While a social worker can address poverty and social issues that she or he encounters on a small scale through individual, family, and group social work interventions and can apply a social welfare approach through offering governmental income and/or health assistance, widespread poverty and disasters in countries without social safety nets often require a community practice approach (Healy, 2008). Exhibit 11.10 provides an overview of strategies to link local social work practice with global social work practice, particularly focused on community practice. While any of the models described in this chapter may be appropriate, given a specific community context, we next turn our attention to community development and community organizing using global approaches at home and in other countries.

International Social Work Community Development

As with domestic social work community development practice, the international spectrum of social and economic development activities is broad and has many actors. Some large international organizations (e.g., the United Nations Development Programme, World Health Organization, World Bank, International Monetary Fund) and national players, such as U.S. Agency for International Development (USAID) and the U.S. Peace Corps, play important roles in community development work in developed and developing countries through funding, facilitation, oversight, and management of community development projects and programs. There are also organizations that operate from within the U.S. that support and facilitate international community development; for example, they engage in strategic planning, fundraising, and other activities that support practice outside of the U.S.

Organizations engaged in international community development work, physically located both locally and abroad, facilitate and plan small business loans, credit guarantees, the provision of primary health care, and the creation of large-scale physical projects (such as the building of dams), among other activities. Nongovernmental organizations, such as the International Red Cross, CARE, Catholic Relief Services, and Save the Children, also focus on self-sustaining development projects that have long-reaching positive effects on communities. Examples

- Concentrating on community development as a focus for practice and the incorporation of community development approaches in all social work practice.
- Extending the practice of policy advocacy to international forums.
- Developing techniques to enable the disadvantaged and oppressed to find a voice not merely in national forums, but also globally, in international solidarity.
- Making effective use of new technologies to link workers and community groups globally.
- Including global forces as a critical component of problem analysis and consciousness raising.
- Establishing social work roles and positions in international nongovernmental organizations (NGOs) and United Nations (UN) agencies.
- Incorporating a strong human rights analysis alongside more traditional social work needs-based practice.
- Seeking opportunities for social workers to develop internationalist understandings through exchange programs and international courses in schools of social work.
- Developing further analysis and research about the link between the global and the local across social work knowledge, values, and skills.

The global local web

EXHIBIT 11.10

Priorities for Social Work Practice Linking the Local and the Global

Source: Ife, 2000, pp. 62–63; Reisch, 2013

include forming local cooperatives, introducing farming techniques, and facilitating preventive health care projects and local sanitation projects (e.g., digging wells and building latrines) (Healy, 2008).

The goal of international community development projects is to reach the point at which the community can sustain them. Organizers most often employ local-level development, in which the community takes responsibility for the work. Local-level development requires and allows the persons experiencing the problem or need to plan and implement the strategies for improvement. The local-level approach requires social workers to focus on the development of relationships with community members, groups, and institutions so that development projects are truly locally determined and directed (Healy, 2008). Exhibit 11.11 provides an

EXHIBIT 11.11

Key Strategies and Programs for International Local-Level Development

- *Basic literacy courses:* Social workers can recruit and train teachers from local communities to provide basic literacy instruction that conforms to local culture, and socioeconomic realities and that responds to the desires of the local population.
- *Primary school education:* Primary school education is a key element to development. Social workers can support children seeking an education and can work with the local community to provide needed resources.
- *Basic health care:* Social workers can recruit and train staff from local communities to provide basic health care. Social workers can also be involved in education about basic hygiene, immunizations, and disease prevention efforts.
- *Adult education, basic training, and capacity building:* If a community wishes, social workers can facilitate adult basic education or training in such fields as agriculture, forestry, or marketing for small businesses.
- *Awareness-raising and empowerment:* Through informal or formal dialogue, social workers can assist individuals, families, groups, and communities to understand their life situation, whether it be oppression, exclusion, poverty, drug addiction, or something else. This understanding includes recognition of the forces that have led to and reinforce the present situation. This realization can lead to change efforts.
- *Local income-generation programs:* Social workers can be involved in education or the facilitation of programs that lead to higher income generation at the individual, family, or community level. Such programs can lead to better farming methods, increased number of or profitability of small businesses, or large community-wide industries, such as food processing plants.
- *Credit schemes and people's banks:* To overcome community members' inability to access financial credit through formal institutions, social workers can be involved in local level, small lending programs (for example, see Exhibit 11.12).
- *Community-based self-help programs:* Social workers can help facilitate a planned community response to a community need, such as developing a local program to assist the disabled, mentally ill, or AIDS orphans.
- *Leadership development:* Social workers can support existing leaders and train new ones.
- *Local organization and institution promotion and capacity building:* Social workers may be involved in helping create or promote local institutions, such as those that oversee education or community recreation.
- *Linking local organizations to government agencies and international structures:* Social workers can provide information, support, and connections between local organizations and external resources.
- *Comprehensive community development programs:* Social workers can help facilitate the integration of development efforts to create a holistic effort.

Source: Cox & Pawar, 2013, pp. 199–220

An effort to loan one Bangladeshi woman $27 dollars has evolved into a worldwide movement to help the poor escape dire poverty by providing micro-credit. Many poor small business owners lack the money to purchase needed raw goods or supplies for their business, and they depend on high-cost credit from moneylenders. The Grameen (which means "village") Bank was founded on the idea that small loans with reasonable terms would make a large difference in the lives of the poor. The bank began as a very small effort in 1983, and now has over 2,500 branches in 81,000 villages in Bangladesh, with a loan repayment rate of 96%.

The bank offers loans without collateral requirements, a credit history, or any legal instruments. The bank makes loans to a self-made group of five friends, rather than an individual. When one wants to take out a loan, the other group members must approve. Members of the group provide encouragement, support, and practical assistance to one another. The groups from each village attend weekly meetings in their village, in which they collect loan repayments, accept loan applications, and undertake activities to foster community bonds and provide education about important topics. The positive social pressure the group has exerted has facilitated a high repayment rate of the small loans. The Grameen Bank borrowers also commit to "The Sixteen Decisions," a list of values and activities that foster healthy living, communal action, and education for children.

EXHIBIT 11.12

International Community Development Case Example: Grameen Bank

overview of key strategies and programs for local-level community development. Exhibits 11.12 and 11.13 provide case examples of international community development work that implements several of the strategies and programs.

Globalization and Community Organizing in Social Work Practice [EPAS 8]

Similarities exist between community organizing efforts at the international level and efforts in the U.S. For example, regardless of the setting or context, empowering individuals, building and strengthening community bonds, and building progressive organizations are appropriate community organizing goals. Community organizing skills are similar, as they focus on a particular change effort.

Community organizing efforts, both in the U.S and abroad, are closely related to global issues; therefore, local issues must be viewed within globally interconnected systems (Reisch, 2013). For example, international migration of workers from the poorer to wealthier countries, and from countries engaged in civil conflict to those at peace has left large numbers of workers, some of whom are not documented, vulnerable to employer abuse and exploitation due to their tenuous legal status, and desperate to generate income to support themselves and their families in their home countries. A worldwide effort has ensued to build the power of immigrant workers to raise their wages and improve their working conditions by bringing together labor organizing and community organizing. These efforts mostly use direct action, or

Micro-Financing Partners in Africa (MFPA) is a U.S.-based organization that provides grants to strengthen and expand micro-financing, employment, and health programs in Africa. MFPA raises money in the U.S. through donor appeals and fundraising events. They provide funds to partner organizations working in Tanzania, Kenya, Uganda, Rwanda, and the Democratic Republic of Congo on a wide variety of projects designed to help people provide for their own needs within their families and within their communities, and promote health within their communities. They carry out their mission through four primary projects: providing funds for small business loans, providing funds for gifts of animals (such as cows) that generate income from products (such as milk), vocational skills training, and supporting cooperative ventures, such as a cooperatively owned soy farm and bakery. They have recently added a health program that promotes healthy pregnancies and births.

One example of their work is the financial support they provide for small businesses in Tanzania. A local organization organizes women into small groups of neighbors, and teaches them business skills. When they finish with their training, one woman starts a small business with loan funds, typically about $50. Business can be a wide variety of things that will sell in their local community, such as selling fried fish, tailoring, or raising rabbits. When she finishes repaying her loan from her business profits, the next woman in the group can apply for a loan. Each of the women support one another in their business, because their success means that they can apply for a loan (MicroFinancing Partners in Africa, n.d.).

conflict, organizing strategies, and activities to gain changes in public policy (Hanley & Shragge, 2009). Other global community organizing efforts focus on the domestic violence immigrants experience (Kasvin & Tashayeva, 2004), workers' rights (International Labor Rights Forum, n.d.), child welfare issues related to deportation of immigrants, global warming (350.org, n.d.), and a host of other interrelated issues in the global interconnections of systems. Due to the transnational nature of local issues, such as unemployment, environmental problems, and public health challenges, local development work must be accomplished within the framework of globalization of human challenges. For example, community development work that intends to impact the local economy must consider the global economic climate, rather than just the local market.

Community social work practice, just like social work practice with other systems levels, ends with the termination and evaluation phase. The next section will consider trends that impact this phase, as well as the skills needed to professionally master the ending phase of social work community practice.

CONTEMPORARY TRENDS AND SKILLS FOR THE ENDING PHASE OF COMMUNITY SOCIAL WORK: TERMINATION, EVALUATION, AND FOLLOW-UP

Community social work practitioners join the community in change efforts and facilitate the community leadership of the tasks required. Often, community practice accomplishments are the result of months and even years (or decades) of work and consist of many smaller change efforts. For example, social workers may engage in community development struggles to rid the community of child lead poisoning. This overarching change effort can involve tasks to change local policy regarding rental housing, work with landlords to remediate lead paint, promote local school screening for child lead poisoning, and work with the local public health clinic to create an outreach program to prevent lead poisoning and reach persons potentially affected. Each of these may have involved lengthy efforts.

Achieving the goals of community change efforts, whether smaller goals achieved in the process of working toward a larger goal or the larger goal itself, leads us to the next phase of the change effort, termination and evaluation.

Community Social Work Practice Endings

Termination in community social work practice can be more complex than termination with other clients. Community practice can involve long-term change efforts (such as Brickville's redevelopment efforts that would take many years) that are complex, with the potential involvement of many players and institutions in the process. The termination phase in community practice is often termination of the social worker from the community (if moving on to other responsibilities), of the social worker's sponsoring organization from a community change effort (if the organization can no longer participate for some reason), or termination of people or institutions from community change efforts, which may continue without them. Termination of one change effort can also occur when the community has prioritized other needs, such as a situation where the community is grappling with a natural disaster. For example, a social worker may terminate with a community lead prevention and remediation effort if lead poisoning levels drop dramatically and/or if local leadership is effectively working on the issue and no longer need the social worker's assistance.

As in terminations with other clients, endings can be emotional, particularly if the intervention has been longstanding. Building relationships is a key element to all types of community practice; therefore, the social worker's role in termination is to "help [participants] examine their accomplishments, review their experience together, and prepare for the future" (Garvin & Galinsky, 2013). Social workers may also facilitate the expression and integration of positive and negative emotions, which can include such feelings as elation and joy about successes achieved and/or such negative emotions as disappointment, rejection, abandonment, or anger, depending on the circumstances of the termination. The social worker and community participants can celebrate milestones and successes along the way toward larger goals, even if those currently involved do not see an intervention through to the final, hoped-for result.

Endings and Follow-Up in Community Practice Utilizing Strengths and Empowerment A social worker employing strengths and empowerment approaches facilitates the community process of reviewing progress toward identified goals and developing strategies for sustaining changes. In social work community practice, the social worker can invite each participant to review and reflect on her or his individual experience in the change effort, including strengths brought to the process, any change they personally experienced, and plans for contributing to the maintenance of the change(s). Engaging individual members in this process can provide closure for all involved. Like group work practice, participants can also use other participants' reflections to examine their own growth processes.

As community social work practice often involves the use of task groups, many elements of and skills needed in group work terminations may apply. For example, using a strengths-based perspective, the social worker can help the members of the group to reflect on the strengths they developed as they engaged in community change efforts. The social worker can use the group ending as an opportunity to provide feedback on the individual, group, and community changes she or he observes.

The termination process can employ a strengths perspective even when community goals are not realized. Participants can review the community and group strengths that existed at the outset of their efforts, those strengths they gained or mobilized during the process, and those strengths participants can carry with them after the formal change effort has ended. While the members (and the social worker) may be dismayed at not achieving desired goals, strategizing about ways in which participants can continue to work toward achieving the goals can, in fact, be empowering.

As in terminations with individuals, families, and groups, a key element of the termination process with communities is a focus on sustaining the gains achieved, such as community bonding, leadership skills, civic engagement, and/ or the continuation and growth of community networks and community programs. Regardless of the circumstances of the termination, a focus on community strengths and the positive outcomes of the intervention can energize community members and institutions to continue their efforts. If the termination occurs because the community intervention achieves its goal, the community can build on their successes and begin the assessment, intervention, and evaluation process anew.

Following-up involves helping to sustain any gains from the intervention. Follow-up may involve many people and institutions, particularly if the social worker (and his/her sponsoring organization) supplied many resources for the intervention. Follow-up also involves honoring any commitments made during the intervention and termination process, and welcoming any new actors into the change process. New actors, such as new community participants or institutions, may need to become involved to continue the community change efforts if professional social work resources will not be available. For example, let's consider the social worker involved in the change efforts related to lead paint discussed earlier. If the social worker was transferred to a different school and needed to terminate from the efforts, the social worker would transfer responsibilities to another leader in the effort, such as a co-worker, parent, local development organization staff member, other community resident, or a group of professionals involved in the effort, so that the change effort could continue. Following up involves ensuring that the new leaders have the resources they need to continue the efforts. However, if the local leadership was not sufficiently developed to maintain the community change effort, despite follow-up, the effort would discontinue. Exhibit 11.14 provides an example of a termination of a community organizing effort.

Evaluation of Social Work Practice with Communities [EPAS 9]

Similar to evaluation with individuals, families, and groups, evaluation of social work community practice interventions can assess the process along the way (i.e., **process evaluation**); the extent to which goals were achieved (i.e., **outcome evaluation**); and the social worker's skills in the intervention phase. Just as the community change effort was a collaborative process, so too is the evaluation. Community participation is important throughout the change effort in order to empower participants, and during the evaluation process, collaboration as an equal partner in this process leads to a feeling of ownership of the information. The evaluation process seeks to determine the value of something and differs from monitoring the intervention (Netting et al., 2017).

The evaluation process begins as an element of the intervention design, and may be predetermined by an organization, a funder, or other decision-maker. It requires social workers and community members first to determine: (1) if both the process and outcomes will be evaluated, (2) the ways in which the process and outcomes will be evaluated, and (3) the means by which data will be collected as the basis for the evaluation. Evaluation of community change efforts may include examinations of the personal, interpersonal, and community levels. Evaluation of the community effort may include an evaluation of the group work involved, which is covered extensively in Chapter 9.

Preferably, the evaluation process will include both qualitative and quantitative data to provide information about the process of community change and progress on the desired outcomes at the personal, interpersonal, and community levels. Methods may include pre- and post-measures of community functioning. These measures include, but are not limited to, the use of validated and standardized

EXHIBIT
11.14

*Termination,
Evaluation,
and Follow-Up*

Communities Facilitating Opportunity (CFO) is an organization that conducts community organizing through a federation of twenty-five local faith-based institutions. One area of their work focuses on the lack of affordable housing production in their community for over a decade. The work of the CFO leaders and members, with the support of staff members, included years of conducting research with both affected individuals, public officials, and others involved in the affordable housing production and maintenance system, holding numerous meetings with relevant public officials to demand answers to questions about the lack of quality affordable housing in their community and drawing media attention to the problem. The housing department failed time and time again to deliver on promises, despite the availability of federal funding dedicated to the production of affordable housing for the city. CFO also called attention to official city and federal audits that demonstrated a significant level of dysfunction and corruption within the city housing department. One project that they focused on was the renovation of two small houses in a working class neighborhood at a cost that exceeded twenty times the assessed value of those properties. The housing agency used many tactics to disempower citizen input, such as verbally promising to take action and not following through, and yelling and saying demeaning things to CFO leaders and members. CFO finally decided to hold a public meeting to directly address public officials in front of a large number of their constituents. They specifically invited the mayor and other local public officials to attend the meeting to directly engage the public and the leadership of their local government.

The overall goals of members for this CFO campaign were to establish: (1) an accountable city government, (2) a working program for the repair of homes, (3) a way to hold absentee landlords accountable, (4) protection from predatory mortgage lenders, and (5) a focus on building communities—not just homes. In the meeting, the group pointed out that $18 million in funds flowed annually through the city housing agency in a haphazard, nontransparent way. They offered specific policy proposals, such as establishing a $5 million fund for minor home repair to add to existing monies, targeting neighborhoods where the existing housing stock was strained. Two weeks after the public meeting, the City Manager moved all personnel out of the city housing agency to other city agencies, saying that he had concluded that the city housing agency was often controlled by outside special interests, that housing services were fragmented, and that there was no comprehensive approach for building and selling houses. A completely new staff was needed to correct these deep problems. CFO members would be involved in elements of restructuring and re-staffing the organization.

Termination: When the CFO leadership and membership recognized that at least one of the intervention goals was met, they terminated the campaign; the city was now more accountable for decisions about affordable housing production. The restructuring of the housing agency fundamentally shifted who had the power to make decisions about affordable housing in the city. As follow-up, CFO, along with its partners, monitored the rebuilding of a branch of local government that implements housing and community development. CFO action helped provide the necessary pressure to create change in the

EXHIBIT
11.14

Continued

structure of the local government. CFO decided to end its tactics designed to put pressure on the city and to instead work with the City Manager to create a new agency that would be transparent and accountable, with the hopes that new personnel could meet their other goals.

Using the strengths perspective, CFO engaged in reflection to discern group and community strengths present from the beginning and those gained through the intervention. CFO leadership and membership also engaged in a group process to review their accomplishments and to discern future movements. The CFO focused on building their strength as an organization, bonding, leadership skills, knowledge of and engagement with civic affairs and city personnel, and the continuation and growth of their network of organizations in the community.

Evaluation: Evaluation of this community practice intervention occurred both in the short-term and the long-term. Throughout the long campaign, the social worker assisted leaders to facilitate their own reflection, member reflection about the degree to which they met short-term goals, and documentation of the process. Short-term goals in this case include obtaining: meetings with involved parties and public officials; information; commitments of action; actions taken; and media coverage. Long-term efforts were evaluated over many years, and required documentation of media coverage, turnout at public meetings, and the amount and type of responsiveness of public officials and decision-makers. CFO also collected data on the housing problems over the years from the housing agency, federal agencies, and others. Evaluation also included the extent to which members realized increasing confidence, leadership skills, personal speaking skills, organizing skills, and feelings of efficacy. Methods included review of meeting minutes and other organization (i.e., internal reports); interviews with staff, CFO leadership, and members; and public documents.

Source: Speer & Christens, 2011

measures; direct observation by the social worker to document change; use of publically available data (i.e., U.S. Census data and others); administrative data from public departments such as policy, public health, child welfare, police, and others; GIS mapping (discussed in Chapter 10); and feedback from other professionals (Ohmer, 2008).

One good example of a community evaluation process comes from a community development effort in Perth, Western Australia. The aim of the evaluation was to compare the quality of life in a community that had experienced community development initiatives with the quality of life in a nearby community that had not experienced the initiatives. The residents used the Australian Unity Wellbeing Index to rate individual and neighborhood well-being. Additionally, the evaluation compared residents' well-being to national averages (Blunsdon & Davern, 2007).

STRAIGHT TALK ABOUT COMMUNITY INTERVENTION, TERMINATION, EVALUATION, AND FOLLOW-UP

Community social work practice, including the intervention, termination, and evaluation and follow-up phases, offers many rewards and challenges. One challenging aspect of some types of community social work practice is long hours at salaries less than those in individual, family, and group practice. Further, community social work practice can involve working during the day with professionals in organizations and institutions and in the evenings and on weekends with community participants. Efforts to change institutions, policies, and practices can take a long time, and there may be many setbacks along the way. Tangible rewards and successes for the work may be few and far between, which can lead to burnout (Rubin & Rubin, 2008).

The rewards include the personal satisfaction of working to change environments to better meet the needs of and to provide empowerment opportunities for individuals and communities. Many community practitioners appreciate the ability to partner with individuals, families, and groups to better their lives, while avoiding the view of persons as clients, which can involve diagnostic labels, treatment plans, and a primarily individualistic perspective. In community practice, community members are involved in making decisions that affect their lives, sometimes for the first time. Helping people gain their voices and work toward large-scale social change is work toward social justice. The variety of tasks completed, the joy of successes, and the wide autonomy and flexibility are other factors that draw and keep social workers in community practice (Rubin & Rubin, 2008).

Community practitioners must have the energy for long-term work and must be able to see value in the process and effort involved, rather than just in the outcomes. The occasional victories, even short-term or small, must be enough to sustain community practitioners. The community practitioner must celebrate small gains. She must often work diligently on short-term or immediate goals, while keeping the larger, systemic, institutional change in focus.

CONCLUSION

This chapter has presented the range of social work community practice as an important client system level for generalist practitioners. Engaging in community practice offers social workers the opportunity to influence their environments to create communities that are truly responsive to the needs of all members. Community interventions, terminations, and evaluations are complex, with a primary focus on the community, and a secondary focus on individual change. Community practice involves developing leaders, facilitating bonding among residents, and other personal and interpersonal work that provides a foundation for

A Grand Challenge for social work identified by The American Academy of Social Work and Social Welfare is reducing extreme economic inequality in the United States. Although the economy is producing more wealth than ever before, business owners are getting most of the revenue, while labor has a shrinking share. In fact, those workers at the bottom of the income distribution have seen their wages decline since 1979, and half of all workers have experienced no or little growth in their hourly wages since 2000. Heads of companies often earn hundreds of times as much income as the ordinary worker. This trend has led to increasing hardship and concentrated income poverty among lower paid workers. The median net wealth of White households is 10 to 20 times greater than the median net worth of African American and Hispanic households.

Lein, Romich, and Sherraden (2015) call for social work involvement in public policy changes to reduce extreme inequality. Community organizing has been occurring across the country to increase earnings from low-skills job through the "fight for $15," or raising the minimum wage to a new standard of $15/hour. Making part-time, shift, and variable work more humane, so that instability in hours and income and unpredictability is minimized. Expansion of the Earned Income Tax Credit (EITC), a refundable tax credit for working, low-income taxpayers, would result in some reduction of poverty and inequality. Expanding child and dependent care to enable stable employment would help working families trying to achieve a stable income and invest in assets. To familiarize yourself with the topic of reducing extreme economic inequality, visit the Grand Challenges website and read Working Paper No. 16, *Reversing Extreme Inequality* (Lein, et al., 2015) at: http://aaswsw.org/grand-challenges-initiative/12-challenges/reduce-extreme-economic-inequality/. (See Exercise #a1 to learn more about how you could become involved in community practice in your community to reduce extreme inequality.)

GRAND CHALLENGE

Reduce Extreme Economic Inequality

community change. Such complexity requires the social worker to possess skills with various clients in order to implement the community intervention and facilitate the termination and evaluation processes.

MAIN POINTS

- Community intervention uses guided community practice models, which are primarily based in the concepts and language of systems, ecological, and power, change, and politics theories.

- The three most common models of community intervention are Rothman's (2008) three models of community practice: planning/policy, community capacity development, and social advocacy. These models can be blended to best match the context of the community change effort.

- The intervention strategies of community social and economic development, community organizing, and community asset mapping aim to improve community conditions and the quality of life for community residents or members.

- Community social work practice, including community development and community organizing, makes unique contributions as an intervention method both domestically and around the globe.

- Termination in community practice can be more complex than termination with other client systems because of the potential involvement of many players and institutions in the process.

- Social work community practice evaluations and follow-up assess the process along the way, the extent to which goals are achieved, and the social worker's skills in the intervention phase.

EXERCISES

a. Case Exercises

1. To apply your learning of the Grand Challenge to reduce extreme inequality that was highlighted in this chapter, visit the Grand Challenges website and read Working Paper No. 16, *Reduce Extreme Inequality* (Lein et al., 2016) at: http://aaswsw.org/wp-content/uploads/2016/01/WP16-with-cover-2.pdf.

   Research whether there are any community interventions in your community that might reduce extreme income inequality. For example, is there an organization or coalition working to do any of the following:
   a. Raise the minimum wage in your community?
   b. Create or expand a state-EITC?
   c. Pressure employers or local or state change policy to require more predictability of income for low-wage workers?

2. Go to www.routledgesw.com/cases and review the video of the Alvadora neighborhood association meeting within the Riverton case. In groups, begin a role-play where the video ends and continue the discussion. Did the Chair of the committee vote? If not, what may have occurred? If the committee delays their vote, what additional information might be helpful to the decision-making process? Summarize the points of view. Which arguments are most persuasive? How might you vote if you were on the committee? What result would you prefer? Compare your preferences with classmates.

3. After completing Exercise #1, discuss the following questions with your classmates. What other information would you need to make a decision? If you were the Chair, what might you have done differently? What elements of Robert's

Rules of Order were used in the Alvadora video? What elements were not used? How might other elements have been used? How might that have changed the course of actions in the video?

4. Go to www.routledgesw.com/cases and become familiar with the Riverton case file, especially the "Your History" section. Choose either the planning/policy, community capacity development, or social advocacy models of community intervention described in Chapter 11 and describe a possible community intervention for Riverton to address the concerns about the coal-fired power plant. Describe a community intervention using a second model and compare and contrast the intervention with the first intervention. What are some key differences?

5. Go to www.routledgesw.com/cases and become familiar with the Riverton case file. You would like to begin to address community concerns and issues using a community social and economic development approach. What issues could you address? How would you address the issues using a community social and economic development approach?

6. Go to www.routledgesw.com/cases and become familiar with the Riverton case file. With many types of community interventions, recruiting allies from diverse groups adds to the strength of the intervention. Describe how you would recruit from various populations within Riverton to participate in a community intervention.

7. Go to www.routledgesw.com/cases and become familiar with the Brickville case. An evaluation of the youth group community empowerment effort could entail many different types of activities. Create a 5–7 question key informant interview guide that the youth group could use for evaluation purposes to gather feedback about the level of involvement and empowerment of neighborhood residents. The interviews would include faith leaders, neighborhood leaders, politicians, and professionals who serve the community through area nonprofits.

b. Other exercises

8. Choose a social issue that is important to you. Assume the role of a community developer. How would you address the issue using community development skills and techniques?

9. Choose a social issue that is important to you. Assume the role of a community organizer. How would you address the issue using community organizing skills and techniques?

10. Review the categories and examples of assets in Exhibit 11.5. List all of the types of assets present in your community (i.e., campus or neighborhood) within each of the categories.

CHAPTER 12

Social Work Practice with Organizations: Engagement, Assessment, and Planning

"Why study organizations?" There are two answers to this question. The first answer is that we have become a society of organization. Our lives are shaped by organizations, from birth to death. . . . The second is that if we want to change key aspects of our lives and/or society, we almost inevitably must change organizations.

Tolbert & Hall, 2016, pp. 1–2

Key Questions for Chapter 12

1. What competencies do I need to engage and assess organizations? [EPAS 6 and 7]
2. What are the social work behaviors that enable me to effectively engage and assess organizations? [EPAS 6 and 7]
3. How can I use evidence to engage in research-informed practice and practice-informed research to guide my engagement with and assessment of organizations? [EPAS 4]
4. How can I apply social work values and ethics to engagement with and assessment of organizations? [EPAS 1]
5. How can I determine whether an organization is culturally competent? [EPAS 2]

Organizations are the structure through which social services are delivered. For example, the RAINN organization (www.routledgesw.com//rainn/engage/components) provides vital social services to people who have experienced sexual trauma. RAINN staff and volunteers provide safe, secure, confidential services, emotional support, information, and referrals 24/7 through their website. To carry out their work, they have a wide array of collaborative partners, including local rape crisis centers, university-based evaluators, donors, and legal consultants. Learning more about this nontraditional social service agency can aid in understanding more about traditional agencies, and provides ideas of how social services agencies may be structured in the future to include more online service delivery.

INFLUENCING ORGANIZATIONS CAN RESULT IN IMPROVED services for clients. You may think of organizations as small, supportive structures that help to organize an interconnected jumble of work that needs accomplishing, or as large bureaucracies that are unresponsive to client needs or individual efforts to improve them. Organizations are "formally structured arrangements of people, tools, and resources brought together to achieve predetermined objectives through institutionalized strategies" (Barker, 2014, p. 304). Social workers work in many types and sizes of organizations and use their knowledge of organizations to promote the best interest of their clients. Although there has been considerable growth in the number of social workers choosing independent practice settings, the majority today works in agency-based organizational settings (Bureau of Labor Statistics, 2016).

This chapter focuses on the nature of organizations and social work agencies, particularly as experienced by social work practitioners. Theoretical perspectives on and dimensions of organizations will be explored. We will also discuss the engagement, assessment, and planning processes with organizations. The discussion emphasizes the social worker's interface with organizations and the ways in which organizational functions shape professional practice. The chapter will also examine the skills needed for organizational engagement, assessment, and planning and will close with a discussion about types of organizations most often used for social service delivery.

UNDERSTANDING ORGANIZATIONS

Organizations address individual, family, group, and community needs. Organizations, like other clients, can be understood through theories, models, and perspectives. Prior to moving into the change process, a theoretical understanding of organizations can assist social workers in the process of engagement, assessment, planning, intervention, termination, evaluation, and follow-up. In this next section, organizations will be described as social systems, as well as from the integration of contemporary theories of organizations.

Organization as a Social System

As discussed in earlier chapters, general systems theory posits that a system, such as an organization, is composed of intersecting components that are part of larger systems, such as the community at large and society. Organizations, therefore, acquire resources from their environments and return products or services to their environment. Understanding organizations requires understanding that organizations exchange resources with their environments (Brueggemann, 2013b). In the assessment and planning processes, which are described later in this chapter, social workers can examine the extent to which subsystems, such as funders, other organizations, or networks of organizations, meet the needs of the organization. The organization can use this information to advocate for a higher level of functioning of a subsystem, which will ultimately benefit the organization and those being served.

Contemporary Theories and Organizations

Organizational and management theory that relates to organizations of all types has a history that dates back to the late 1800s. In helping to understand organizations, today's theories emphasize (1) the role of culture in helping to understand how organizations define and pursue collective goals; (2) the idea of quality as the benchmark in organizational structures, processes, and evaluation; (3) respect for how tasks are accomplished as a factor as important as the outcomes of programs and services; and (4) recognition that there is no one correct approach to structuring organizations. Many aspects of an organization, including size, mission, clients, and staff qualifications, are important to consider when structuring an organization and developing a management style (Netting, Kettner, McMurtry, & Thomas, 2017).

Dimensions of Organizations

The characteristics and qualities that exist within social services organizations affect both service delivery to clients and the employee experience. The three most important dimensions of these differences are: (1) purpose of the organization, (2) structure of governance, and (3) the internal power relations. Let us turn to an exploration of each of these areas.

Organization Purpose

The stated purpose of an organization is the rationale for the organization's existence. While organizational objectives state the ways in which organizations work toward their goals, the purpose describes the concerns of the organization in broad terms. The three types of purposes are: (1) filling a public mandate, (2) providing a particular service, and (3) fostering social change related to an ideological concern to which the organization is committed.

Organizations Sanctioned by Law   The law sanctions organizations in several ways. First, organizations sanctioned by federal and state law ("public organizations") provide mandated social services that are widely recognized by the public. For example, adult protection services, available in all fifty states, are usually housed

© Digital Vision

within a large and visible state organization. Social workers representing these organizations are expected to act in the best interests of adults who cannot protect themselves against abuse, neglect, or exploitation; carry out the activities of daily living; or manage their own affairs. Public organizations are directly accountable to the community, as they derive the vast majority of their funding through tax revenue (i.e., federal, state, county, or local government funds).

Second, most social services are offered through nonprofit organizations designated as **501(c)3** organizations by the U.S. Internal Revenue Service (IRS). As a 501(c)3 organizations, nonprofit organizations are sanctioned by the law to meet specified public needs. Designated nonprofit organizations are exempt from paying taxes on organizational income, and donors are allowed to deduct contributions from their taxes (Holland, 2013).

Organizations with Service Goals   Organizations with service goals develop as a result of an agreed-upon need or concern and are often started by and operated by professionals. For example, youth at risk of dropping out of school are often seen gathering together in groups in blighted areas. Adolescent high school drop-outs are a high-risk population for poverty, health concerns, and criminal activity. Organizations providing youth services offer prevention services to help youth avoid dropping out, assist adolescent drop-outs in acquiring tangible resources, and provide legal assistance and referrals to addictions treatment. Service goals define the work of the organization and the social need addressed by the organization.

Organizations Arising from Social Movements Some **grassroots organizations**, which are organizations started by citizens rather than professionals, arise in response to ideological positions on particular social problems. The early development of shelters for women experiencing intimate partner violence is an example of a

---

EXHIBIT 12.1

Example of Public and Non Profit Organizations

The Area Agencies on Aging (AAA) is a network of *public* agencies across the country that provides a comprehensible and coordinated system of community-based services for older adults in localities across the U.S. Services can include nutrition programs, case management, abuse prevention programs, legal assistance, personal assistance, and other programs. The AAAs are public organizations because they are directly funded through tax dollars, and overseen by the U.S. Department of Health and Human Services.

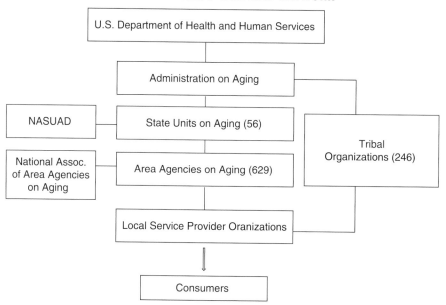

NATIONAL AGING SERVICES NETWORK

Source: National Association of Area Agencies on Aging, 2016

The Alzheimer's Association (AA) is the leading, global voluntary health organization in Alzheimer's care and support, and the largest private, nonprofit funder of Alzheimer's research. Through over 70 agencies across the country, AAs provide services such as referrals for resources, family education, support, respite care, and other services to families impacted by Alzheimer's disease. The AAs are *private* organizations because they are not directly supported through tax dollars, but rather through private funds, and are overseen by a Board of Directors.

Casa de Esperanza was started to meet the need for a culturally competent domestic violence shelter in St. Paul, Minnesota. While there were well-established domestic violence shelters in Minnesota, there was a lack of culturally appropriate services for Latina women. However, not long after it started, the vast majority of those assisted were Anglo and African American, despite the pervasive problem of family violence for Latina women. However, the board and staff knew that within the Latino community, there was a real need for education, prevention, and safe haven. In response, new programs were developed to serve the community and attract Latinas, including a Women's Empowerment program, support groups, advocacy, supportive listening, a 24-hour crisis line, a children's therapeutic program, children's advocacy, and structured daily activities, such as therapeutic dance and Spanish lessons.

Strong resistance within the Latino community to speaking openly about the problem of domestic violence existed, and the message of Casa's leaders was met with hostility and animosity. Exposing women's experience of family violence challenged the image of a happy family, and brought a private matter out into the open, potentially embarrassing family members.

The organization struggled to sort through these cultural forces, and answer important questions. While the mission statement stated that the agency existed to "eliminate oppression and its violence against women and children," many board and staff members felt a unique responsibility to work within the Latino community. This responsibility had further implications regarding expectations for bilingual and bicultural staff and publications, definitions of eligibility for services. Most significantly, should women in crisis be turned away from the shelter because they were not Latina? Receipt of public funding for the shelter required that clients be served on a "first-come, first-served basis," so no shelter or service slots could be reserved for Latinas.

In response, the organization created new programs and services to educate the community about Latino family violence, and conduct outreach to Latinas. Staff and volunteers also began to network with other Hispanic organizations to increase awareness about the problem of family violence. As the organization grew, questions about identity persisted. Were they an organization serving primarily Latinos, or a multicultural organization? The contradictions woven into the fabric of the operations needed to be addressed.

In early 1997, the Board went through a strategic planning process to grapple with their identity. Ultimately, the organization moved from being primarily a shelter to today becoming an organization that served a wide variety of needs of the Latino/a population regarding domestic violence. This affirmation created a need for a new approach to program development and operations, community relations, and an overhaul of the agency systems. Shelter services changed in duration, and were delinked from community-wide referral system, resulting in more Latina women being served. The emphasis of the organization moved away from shelter to prevention, community education and support, and policy advocacy for Latinos. For example, staff (1) offered expanded case management and referral networks to support women who live with their abusers or other family members; (2) worked to build the cultural competence of

EXHIBIT 12.2

Change the Mission?

EXHIBIT 12.2 *Continued*	other nonprofits; (3) engaged in advocating for public policies that better protected women; and (4) formed strategic alliances with other organizations to influence policy makers, judges, and law enforcement officials. To correspond with the new emphasis on the community as an agent of change, the mission was changed to "Mobilize Latinas and Latino communities to end domestic violence."
	Source: Casa De Esperanza, n.d.; Sandfort, 2005.

© Chris Fertnig

social movement, a political effort designed to change some aspect of society. A social movement is led by citizens whose commitments and energies are channeled into a political movement, and organizations are created to implement the long-term work of the social movement. A more recent example is the Black Lives Matter movement, which developed into a chapter-based national organization. As organizations are created and mature, professionals, such as social workers, are often employed. Frequently, the founders, professionals, and volunteers of such organizations are indigenous to the movement, which means they have personally experienced the oppression that is the focus of the organization. Professionals and volunteers often have extraordinary commitment to the mission of the organization (Hardina, 2013).

Structures of Governance

Organizational structure, much like family structure, refers to the ways in which members, tasks, and units relate to one another. The structure shapes the rules, or norms, of the organization. Some of the rules are explicit, such as personnel policies, and others are implicit, such as the best ways to influence the decision of an administrator. These rules, governed by organizational culture (discussed later) may be communicated openly to employees and volunteers, while others may be communicated nonverbally or through interpretation of decisions. In the next section, three kinds of organizational structures will be explored as representative of those found in many contemporary agencies: bureaucracies, project teams, and functional structures.

Bureaucracies Many human service organizations, including state and local government organizations and nonprofits, are structured as a bureaucracy; therefore, social workers benefit from knowledge about the structure of their employing organization.

German sociologist Max Weber invented the term **bureaucracy** as a conceptual type, rather than a reality, of structure. The following ten points describe the characteristics of a bureaucracy (Netting et al., 2017):

- Each position in the organization has a limited area of authority and responsibility.

- Control and responsibility are concentrated at the top of a clear hierarchy.

- The activities of the organization are documented in a central system of records.

- The organization employs highly specialized workers based on expert training.

- Staff demands require full-time commitment, and each position represents a career.

- Activities are coordinated through clearly outlined rules and procedures.

- The relationships among workers are characterized by impersonality.

- Recruitment is based on ability and relevant technical knowledge.

- The private and public lives of the organization's members are distinct.

- Promotions in the organization are made by seniority and/or achievement.

Several aspects of bureaucracy have been incorporated into the organizational experiences of many professionals, even those in smaller organizations. For example, the notion that recruitment is based on ability, rather than a relationship with other staff members, is a widely accepted idea of fairness in employment practices. On the other hand, the top-down, hierarchical authority or the impersonality of relationships among members is often an aspect of bureaucracies that challenges employees. The organizations that most often display the characteristics of bureaucracies are those embedded in large systems, such as local, state, or federal government; therefore, older adult/child protection, public health and mental health, and corrections, are fields in which bureaucratic approaches are most common.

Project Teams   In a sharp contrast with bureaucracy, **project teams** consist of a group of people who collectively work on organizational challenges or opportunities through committee or task force structures (Brueggemann, 2013b). Project teams are a flexible way to accomplish work tasks, because the committees may exercise their best collective judgment in decision-making, and the group has minimal hierarchy. Often, such groups find maintaining this structure challenging for many reasons, such as the growth of the group and limitations imposed by a higher authority. Sometimes organizations structured as bureaucracies create project teams within them to accomplish certain tasks.

For example, a group of women and men concerned about intimate partner violence may use a project team approach to develop and operate an organization that provides services to survivors of intimate partner violence. The intended services include a domestic violence shelter, therapy, and violence prevention programming. Team members may structure the organization of the shelter staff so that everyone shares the tasks of managing the agency's physical space, and identical salaries are paid to everyone. The project team structure has many positive aspects; however, the structure may be challenged by those with concerns relating to the appropriateness of some duties for those staff with higher educational degrees (e.g., the appropriateness of a person with a master's degree answering phones or vacuuming the shelter office). The project team approach can be challenged as organizations hire new workers who demand a competitive salary, or as their budget grows from funding or accountability sources (such as a Board of Directors) that require a hierarchal structure.

Functional Structures   When an agency becomes too large for a single person to administer, a layer of personnel will be added. These administrative additions are usually divided by function or area of responsibility—thus the name **functional structures**. Exhibit 12.3 shows an organizational chart that visually lays out a functional structure of the RAINN organization.

In a community agency, for example, the executive director may appoint an experienced social worker as the program director of the youth services department and appoint another as the program director of the affordable housing development unit. In this situation, the two mid-level administrative leaders would be equals and may form a management team that works directly with the executive director in larger administrative functions and decisions. Frequently, these administrative roles are added to already existing direct service roles, particularly in smaller

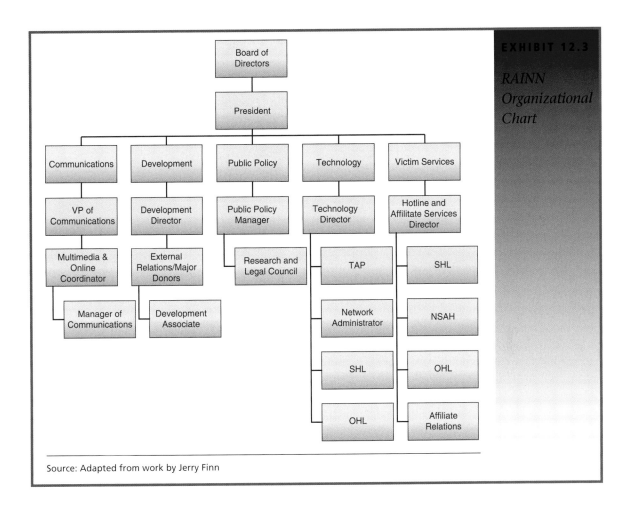

EXHIBIT 12.3

RAINN Organizational Chart

Source: Adapted from work by Jerry Finn

organizations. For example, the program director of the youth services programs would retain responsibility for actually implementing one of the programs. As the agency grows larger, the program directors may not provide the direct services due to the heavy demands of the supervisory and administrative activities.

Internal Power Relations

While organizations have overt arrangements of power, such as hierarchical arrangements of personnel, they also have unofficial power arrangements that are subtle and are unique to the organization. Chapter 3 discusses several sources of power for social workers, including agency, expert knowledge, interpersonal, and legitimate power.

Traditional Authority   Authority attributed by title or ancestry, such as someone with powerful family ties, is **traditional authority.** This type of authority is most often seen in the U.S. as based on profession, family relationships, and history or

© CandyBox Images

inheritance of money. For example, CEOs of large corporations are often related to other powerful people, such as former presidents or other CEOs, and are frequently members of the original family who started the business.

Charismatic Authority   This type of authority is an unstable dynamic in organizations. As contrasted to traditional authority, the **charismatic authority** model suggests that a captivating personality (rather than heritage, ideas, skills, or commitments) is the variable required to gain power by consensus. This form of authority is often displayed in state and national elections when, for example, entertainers and celebrities run for and win public office without previous political experience. Such authority is often present with founders of human service agencies who are successful at the necessary start-up tasks of garnering supporters, raising funds, recruiting an initial board of directors, and other tasks that involve persuasion.

Rational/Legal Authority   This authority is based on ability to achieve outcomes and, like charismatic authority, is persuasive rather than coercive. An example of a person with **rational/legal authority** is an agency staff member who is an expert in program development and program evaluation. A staff member with a particular expertise and a track record of accomplishments in the area of expertise is likely to be persuasive in an appeal to initiate new programs. Large human service agencies, particularly bureaucracies, often contain staff members with rational/legal authority because the staff is able to specialize and develop expertise. Staff in smaller organizations can also develop rational/legal authority, depending on their backgrounds, interests, opportunities, and agency needs.

In social work practice, these forms of authority can exist on a continuum (i.e., from noninfluential to very influential) and/or commingle. For example, human service organizations may have an executive director who was the founder and began the position with a great deal of charismatic authority and who developed rational/legal authority while in the position by developing expertise as an administrator. Another executive director may have initially had mainly traditional authority due to a connection with a powerful family member in human services and/or also has or developed charismatic authority due to strong persuasion skills.

Intersections among Dimensions of Organizations

Thus far, the discussion has focused on dimensions of organizations that influence practice and the social worker's experience. These dimensions, purpose, structures of governance, and internal power relations, often intersect in practice, and some dimensions are likely to be intertwined. For example, a domestic violence shelter, whose purpose reflects a social movement and ideological position, is more likely to adopt a project team rather than a bureaucratic structure. With feminist organizational roots, a domestic violence shelter is also more likely to be subject to charismatic or rational/legal authority, as social workers with strong interpersonal skills may tend to take on leadership roles even without a formal position of authority.

Understanding interconnections among these dimensions aids to understand the nature of organizations and develop a framework for examining their distinctions and impact on social workers. Ultimately, understanding possible interconnections can assist in discerning the combination of dimensions that best fit the talents and work styles of workers. For example, some social workers learn that an organization structure characterized by project team approach and rational/legal authority is the best fit for them because they would prefer to work within a more flexible organizational structure. Gaining knowledge about agency dimensions also helps to recognize the ways in which agencies in various environments can most effectively and efficiently help clients reach their goals.

Social Work Practice in Host Settings

Many social workers practice in **host settings**, such as hospitals, residential care facilities, public and private schools, and correctional facilities. Host settings are organizations in which social workers provide social services as a secondary activity. The following are examples: (1) the primary service in a school is education, yet social workers provide services to augment and support the educational goals; (2) various programs maintained by the court system, aimed at diversion or advocacy, often include social workers; and (3) housing programs and disability projects employ social workers to support the main goal of the organization. Next, we will discuss two situations with both opportunities and challenges: being a guest in a host setting, and being a member of an interprofessional team.

Guest Status Expectations and privilege accompany a **guest status** for a social worker practicing within a host setting. Professionals of other disciplines in the setting may not understand the scope of the social work role, and have inaccurate expectations—too high or too low—of the social worker. For example, a social worker in a hospital setting may find that other professionals assume that a social worker is only qualified to give referrals to clients, rather than engage in the myriad of activities for which they are qualified. At the same time, social workers may experience the privilege of working with other professionals on a team that is able to accomplish more than a social worker could independently. The experience of social worker Diane can illustrate the point.

> *Diane is a recent Bachelor's in Social Work (BSW) graduate hired to facilitate discharges in a residential psychiatric treatment center that has a positive reputation in the community. A staff psychiatrist serves as medical director, and the executive director has a graduate degree in public health. Diane is the first social worker ever employed by the center. The nursing staff had responsibility for discharge work until the number and pace of discharges outgrew their capacity to conduct discharge planning along with their other nursing duties.*
>
> *Diane is warmly welcomed by staff, who hopes that she will fill an acute organizational need. Diane is hopeful that she will gain new competencies and behaviors because she will be exposed to different perspectives and practices for treatment strategies, medication, and ethics. She knows that she will have the opportunity to observe firsthand the work of the psychiatrist, the public health administrator, nurses, and others and learn about the ways in which different professional perspectives can assist clients.*
>
> *While many of these hopes were realized, Diane also discovers that she does not have a role in decision-making about discharges; rather, the other staff expect her to simply carry out the instructions she is given. The exclusion from the decision-making process occurs because she is viewed as extraneous to the discharge (medical) decisions, rather than for any personal reason. Further, Diane has noticed a lack of professional, dignified treatment of some staff toward patients but is ambivalent about notifying officials about it. Because she is excluded from decision-making, Diane feels undervalued, and more as a guest than a valued team member.*
>
> *While she understands that the center is primarily a medical facility and medical issues take priority over other concerns, she also understands the potential value of her involvement in decision-making about discharge planning activities. She knows she has much more to contribute than she is currently allowed, and wishes to create the possibility of articulating her possible contributions in a way that will facilitate the staff's appreciation and growth, rather than engendering their resistance and resentment. Specifically, she knows that she needs to educate the staff about the complexities of discharge planning (for example, the need for day programming, employment,*

training, housing, emotional support, family support, and income support) and about the possible contributions that she could make to addressing these complexities within the decision-making process about the timing of discharge and the appropriate placement for patients. In the future, she may also want to address several practices that are inconsistent with socially just and respectful treatment.

Clearly, a guest status within an organization brings unique challenges for social workers. Some professionals with a guest status function as part of interprofessional teams (discussed in the next section), while others work side-by-side with other professionals (in multiprofessional settings). Social workers who have a guest status must exhibit effective professional behaviors concerning the education of other professions about the roles and responsibilities of social workers. Building credibility and networks of support within host organizations, a keen sense of timing, and displaying diplomacy are key skills in this process. On the other hand, social workers in host settings must also advocate for themselves and their professional obligations for client services.

Interprofessional Teams   Projects and programs that include members of several professions (e.g., health professions, public health, public administration, and social work) create **interprofessional teams.** These teams can provide an enriching and exciting atmosphere in which to practice social work. Although the social work profession emphasizes a holistic view of clients, social workers join many helping professionals in delivering services in a fragmented fashion. Many families seeking the assistance of social workers are also involved with other helping professionals, such as vocational counselors, non-social work therapists, psychologists, income maintenance specialists, physicians—including psychiatrists—and community support workers.

In an interprofessional setting, all professions carry equal power and share decision-making responsibilities—the value is in the total contribution of an integrated approach. In order to be effective, each profession must value the contribution of others. Social workers need competent collaborative skills when working with other professionals, including conflict mediation skills. A truly interprofessional setting is challenging to implement in practice. For example, in many medically oriented interprofessional teams, physicians are dominant and appear to have a privileged standpoint, while in others, you may find a social worker as the leader/facilitator of the team. The socialization of many professions can encourage narrow views to bias the perspective of the chosen profession over other perspectives. Nevertheless, even with such challenges, interprofessional settings offer vast opportunities to wrestle with the challenges of providing an integrated, highly skilled approach in the best interests of clients, as well as to explore the internal dynamics of teaming through the lens of multiple realities.

ORGANIZATIONAL ENGAGEMENT, ASSESSMENT, AND PLANNING [EPAS 4, 6, AND 7]

This section spotlights the process of organizational engagement, assessment, and planning, including the sources of data and information for the assessment. These phases are important to undertake to ensure that organizations implement their mission and serve community needs most effectively and efficiently. For example, the RAINN organization (http://routledgesw.com//rainn) engages, assesses, and plans prior to implementing an intervention (and evaluating the intervention as well). These phases set the stage for the organizational change process of intervention, termination, evaluation, and follow-up. The section closes with a discussion about integrating the information gleaned in the assessment.

Engaging the Organizations

Engagement of an organization first involves the perception of the organization as a client. An organization is comprised of many individuals and systems, yet the social worker must view the entire organization as a client in order to participate in the change process with an organization. This first step in the change process uses many of the skills needed for engagement with individuals, families, groups, and communities, namely, the active listening skills and research, evaluation, and analyzing skills discussed in previous chapters. Engagement with organizations involves working directly with all clients and staff, within the perspective of the organization.

Social workers can engage organizations for the change process as an employee, volunteer, interested citizen, or as a consultant, although most often the change process occurs with employing organizations. Social workers often see the need for organizational change, so the organization can operate more efficiently and effectively, provide a higher quality of services, and better address human needs. For example, social workers who work for a school system may identify the need to make a change in the schools and begin to engage other social workers, teachers, principals, administrators, committees, and task groups across the school district and even across districts to address a specific organizational need. Social workers may also engage organizations as part of advocacy efforts. For instance, a social worker might engage with a public agency that serves older adults to advocate for better handling of cases involving abuse, neglect, or exploitation of older adults. Social workers may also engage with a community of organizations, such as a network of homeless shelters, to work for changes across many organizations, such as to coordinate data management systems to better meet the needs of clients who are homeless, are struggling with substance abuse, and have a chronic mental illness. In all these cases, engagement skills used with other clients are necessary.

Assessment of Organizations

The overall assessment of organizations involves both research into the internal environment of the organization, or the internal mechanisms within organizations, and the external environment with which the organization receives and provides resources, such as funders, accreditation organizations, suppliers of goods and services, clients, other organizations, and others. The following assessment framework, an integration of previous frameworks, may be helpful in the assessment task (Gitterman & Germain, 2008; Netting et. al., 2017) and are more fully described in the following:

Internal Assessment

- Legal basis, mission, by-laws, and history

- Administrative structure and management style

- Program structure, programs, and services

- Organizational culture (i.e., physical surroundings, public relations, language, procedures, social justice/diversity)

- Personnel policies and procedures

- Resources (i.e., financial, technological, personnel)

External Assessment

- Relationship with funders and potential funders

- Relationship with clients

- Relationship with organizations in network (i.e., referrals and coalitions)

- Relationships with political figures

- Relationships with others (regulatory bodies, professional associations, etc.)

Assessment of an organization, similar to assessment with all clients, involves gathering data. Like community assessment, data can be gathered through observation, written documents, key informant interviews, publically available data, service statistics, previous organizational assessment (partial or full), administrative data, other data, and focus groups. Depending on the size of the organization to be assessed, a public forum and survey data may also be appropriate ways to gather data (Gitterman & Germain, 2008; Netting et al., 2017; O'Conner & Netting, 2009).

Organizations often create documents that may be helpful in the assessment process. These include organizational charts, policy and personnel manuals, procedure manuals, job descriptions, meeting minutes, and annual reports. Information from media sources and reports from other organizations can also be useful.

Elements of an Internal Assessment

The internal structures and dynamics of an organization affect many aspects of service delivery of the organization, as well as the employee experience (Grace, McClellan, & Yankey, 2009). The following section discusses the elements of an organization that can be part of an organizational assessment.

Legal Basis   Organizations must be recognized by the law to legitimately operate. The **legal basis** for public organizations is a statute or executive order, while a private organization has a legal basis in the articles of incorporation. These documents authorize an organization to officially exist, and define the parameters for their operations.

Mission Statement   Most organizations create a **mission statement**, which is a concise, broad statement of the purpose of the organization that describes a shared vision. While the statement is too broad for details, the statement identifies the client needs the organization meets, the population served, and the intended client outcomes. The details about programs, services, organizational structure, and other specifics are outlined in other documents, such as annual reports, an organizational chart (discussed later in this section), and program descriptions. The mission statement states why the organization exists and is less changeable than programs and services. Revising a mission statement is needed if an organization perceives a mismatch between the mission statement and current client needs and organization activities. For example, many child welfare agencies were founded in the early 20th century as orphanages and needed to revisit their mission statements in light of the focus in child welfare on home-based placements. Exhibit 12.4 provides an example of a mission statement.

By-laws   The way in which a nonprofit organization governs itself is described in the **by-laws**. By-laws are legal documents that describe the structure and abilities of the board of directors, such as the composition of the board, terms of the members, permanent committees, voting rights, and other matters that concern governance. The by-laws are typically brief, and the rules about them vary from state to state.

EXHIBIT 12.4 *Mission Statement, Longview Community Center*	Our mission is to enhance the quality of life of older adults, children, and families in the regional area by serving their basic needs by providing: (1) Access to education, counseling and health services; (2) Recreation and social program; (3) Daily nutritional meals.

History   Like other clients, organizations create history that defines and impacts the future of the organization. Important aspects of history include the founding of the organization, major funders, influential staff members and administrators, accomplishments, and challenging periods.

Administrative Structure and Management Style   Organizations often depict their administrative structure on an organizational chart that shows the units of the organization, and their relationship to one another. The management style of the organization can be seen in the way work is allocated, decisions are made, the nature of the supervision of employees, and how conflict is handled. Some elements of the management style will be included in written documents, while others can be learned from staff members.

Structure of Programs, Services, and Activities   Human service organizations provide programs and services and/or carry out activities to meet overall organizational goals and objectives. An assessment process would include a review of official documents where these are described, and review the extent to which the programs, services, and activities are consistent with the overall mission, goals, and objectives of the organization, as well as are based on evidence-based practice.

Organizational Culture   Organizational culture consists of many factors, including history, philosophy, styles of communication, patterns of decision-making, expectations, collective preferred personal styles of social workers, myths, behaviors, and formal and informal rules. Culture is also shaped by the purpose, structure of governance, and internal power relations. While not reflected in the mission statement or any one official document, the organizational culture is, nevertheless, an important element that shapes aspects of the agency's work and employees' experiences. For example, the extent to which social workers are expected to work overtime without financial compensation or earned time off, or if practicum students take shifts of being "on call," both represent the types of issues that are shaped by organizational culture. Exhibit 12.5 discusses the dimensions of organizational culture. Exhibit 12.6 helps you review your own organizational style.

   While the concept of organizational culture is intangible and imprecise, culture is an important dynamic of any organization. In the next section, additional dimensions that shape services will be discussed, including the legal basis, mission statement, by-laws, physical surroundings, public relations, procedures, and social justice/diversity factors.

Physical Surroundings   If organizations have a physical presence that clients see, the interior and location of an organization can provide some information about its culture to clients. An organization with dark, messy physical surroundings and/or little privacy for client interactions could be an organization with a culture that places a lower priority on the potential impact of physical surroundings on client

EXHIBIT 12.5 *Dimensions of Organizational Culture*	*Observed behavioral regularities* when people interact, including their language, customs, traditions, and rituals *Group norms* that evolve as standards and values for working together *Espoused values* that the organization is trying to achieve *Formal philosophy*, which are the board policies and ideologies that direct the work *Rules of the game*, often known as "the ropes" *Climate*, which is the physical layout and how it feels *Embedded skills*, the ability to pass along competencies to the next generation *Habits of thinking, mental models, and/or linguistic paradigms* are things taught to new members as they are socialized to the organization *Shared meanings*, which are group understandings that develop as they work together *Root metaphors or integrating symbols*, the ideas, feelings, images, and even physical layout that represent the group's artifacts *Formal rituals and celebrations*, which are ways that a group celebrates key events that reflect important values or events

Source: Schein, 2010 pp. 15–16; O'Connor & Netting, 2009

outcomes than a clean organization with bright lighting and plenty of space for private interviews. To best serve their clients, many human service agencies are located near their clients' homes, often in low- and middle-income communities. While many social workers are not employed by organizations that are housed in luxurious surroundings and/or in upscale locations, the physical atmosphere and location of an organization reflects and impacts aspects of organizational culture, and impacts employee well-being (Shier, 2012). The organizational environment is an important area to learn about the organization's culture.

Public Relations   Organizations reflect their culture in their **public relations** activities and products (Brueggemann, 2013b). Public relations is the practice of managing communication between an organization and the public. Organizations seek to gain support from a positive communication both from the public at large and from specific groups, such as funders, politicians, client populations, and even employees. Organizations can use a variety of mediums to manage their public information and image, such as websites, social media, blogs, printed materials, print newspaper articles and commentaries, radio and televisions public service announcements and appearances, and face-to-face encounters. An organization's public image gives clues about the organization's culture.

Language   The **language** used in agency settings includes the tone, range of sentiment, and degree of empathy and respect expressed. In previous chapters, we discussed postmodern ideas about the role of language and the way people create and sustain meanings based on language. Using postmodernism concepts, language

Using the key below, rate yourself on the items listed here to review your organizational style. Add other items you think are important. Be prepared to discuss this survey in class and to apply it to your field placement. What obstacles do you encounter in fulfilling these points?

EXHIBIT 12.6

Rate Your Organizational Style

☐ I offer positive feedback to my colleagues for behaviors that contribute to effective services.

☐ I involve my colleagues in seeking changes in policies and programs to improve the quality of services.

☐ I value learning about my colleagues' points of view. For example, I seek feedback that will help me to enhance my competencies and behaviors. When I have a complaint, I discuss it with the person directly involved.

☐ I involve others in arranging opportunities to discuss practice/policy issues/topics.

☐ I communicate congratulations to others regarding professional or personal vents/accomplishments.

☐ I come prepared for all types of meetings.

☐ I make positive contributions at meetings.

☐ I refrain from idle gossip at work.

☐ I make more positive than negative comments at work.

☐ _____

☐ _____

Key:0 (not at all)   **1** (a little)   **2** (a fair amount)   **3** (a great deal)   **4** (best that could be)

Source: Adapted from Gambrill, 2013

both reflects and shapes the thoughts and feelings expressed. Therefore, the language used in organizations reflects and shapes the self-perceptions of the social workers, their work, and their clients. For example, social workers' use of disrespectful language toward and about clients violates the *Code of Ethics* (NASW, 2008), displays a violation of the core commitment to respect people and treat them with dignity, and can affect other social workers through a culture of disrespect. While some organizations may attempt to justify pejorative language patterns by stating that staff members need to "blow off steam," the lack of respectful, strengths-based language can have a powerful, detrimental impact on organizational culture. In another example, the language used to describe the members of the Board of Directors or administrators can affect the perception staff has of the competence of their leaders and the value they place on their work. Describing board members as "thoughtful, informed decision-makers," even when staff do not agree with a decision, implies to clients that the organization has a culture of respect.

Procedures   A simple **procedure**, such as greeting a new client, asking them to sit down, inviting them to an office from the waiting room, or giving them paperwork, strongly impacts the quality of the experience of becoming a client and maintaining that status. Social workers must be respectful and sensitive about the explanation of the procedures concerning such matters as confidentiality, fees, appointment times, and negotiations in scheduling appointments. These aspects are relevant as a social worker's expression of respect for clients but also as clearly understood agency policy. Quick Guide 41 provides an opportunity to assess client and employee treatment regarding procedures at an organization familiar to you.

Social Justice/Diversity Factors   Aspects of social work practice that affirm social justice and support diversity can be nurtured and sustained across all client types, including organizations. Unless organizations promote social justice through policies and practices, clients may find their social workers to be "nice people" but feel victimized by unjust organizational practices. To fully promote social justice, organizations may arrange the internal administrative practices of the agency to reflect diversity, cultural competence/humility, and social justice concerns. For example, posters, magazines, and signs in the waiting area can reflect multiple languages and cultures to convey a welcoming atmosphere for clients from diverse backgrounds. Activities and services that clearly take into account cultural values, such as food at events that reflect ethnic food traditions and restrictions, and materials available in multiple languages, send a message. Activities and services can also honor history of groups and/or reflect histories of oppression for specific populations. Just as ethnically dominant white middle-class social workers struggle to become competent in working with other cultures, so must organizations assess their culture competency and the extent to which the organization works toward social justice goals. Exhibit 12.7 addresses some of the assumptions that underlie

QUICK GUIDE 41   DIGNITY ASSESSMENT AND HUMAN SERVICES GUIDE

Complete the following assessment using an organization with which you are familiar.

1. Persons seeking services from my agency are more likely to experience:

____ a poorly maintained waiting room	____ a warm and well-furnished waiting room
____ a place to sign in and be told to take a seat	____ a courteous and personal greeting
____ having their name called out and being told to "follow me" to the office	____ being personally met and invited to "follow me" to the office
____ nonverbal cues from the staff that they are a bother	____ nonverbal cues that suggest we are glad they are here
____ treatment that says "you are another case"	____ treatment that says "you are a person"

2. Persons seeking services in my agency are more likely to be:

____ treated as problems that need to be solved	____ treated as partners in a mutual process of deciding how to proceed
____ given treatment based on the medical model	____ provided treatment based on a competency model
____ seen as problems	____ seen as people with issues and needs
____ seen as needing an expert	____ seen as the expert

3. Employees within my setting are more likely to experience:

____ getting written memos about new changes	____ being asked for input about new changes
____ an expectation of independent work without much support	____ being supported in their roles
____ wishing for another job	____ joy in coming to work
____ feeling like their consumers are not important to the agency	____ feeling their consumers are important to the agency
____ feeling like they are a drain to the community	____ feeling like they are a resource to the community
____ feeling unimportant to the agency	____ feeling important to the agency
____ lack of respect for other employees	____ respect for other employees

4. My experience with the organizational culture is that:

____ respect for human diversity is ignored	____ respect for human diversity is valued
____ membership in the community is blocked to those who are different	____ membership in the community is open to all
____ social services are at best tolerated	____ social services are willingly supported

Source: Adapted from Locke, Garrison, & Winship, 1998, pp. 278–279

EXHIBIT 12.7

Basic Assumptions across Systems or Agencies for Cultural Competence [EPAS 2]

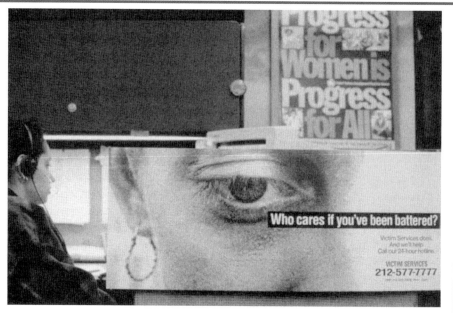

Validating client experience

Organizations that are culturally competent display the following characteristics:

- Respect the unique, culturally defined needs of various client populations.
- Acknowledge culture as a predominant force in shaping behaviors, values, and institutions
- View natural systems (i.e., family, community, faith communities, healers) as the primary mechanism of support for minority populations
- Start with the "family" as defined by each culture, as the primary and preferred point of intervention
- Acknowledge that minority people are served in varying degrees by the natural system
- Recognize that the concepts of "family," "community," etc., are different from various cultures and even for subgroups within cultures
- Believe that diversity within cultures is as important as diversity between cultures
- Function with the awareness that the dignity of the person is not guaranteed unless the dignity of his/her people is preserved
- Display understanding that minority clients are usually best served by persons who are part of or have knowledge about their culture
- Acknowledge and accept that cultural differences exist and have an impact on service delivery
- Treat clients in the context of their minority status, which creates unique mental health issues for minority individuals, including issues related to self-esteem, identity formation, isolation, and role assumptions

EXHIBIT 12.7

Continued

- Advocate for effective services on the basis that the absence of cultural competence in any part of the organization compromises the cultural competency of the entire organization
- Respect the family as indispensable to understanding the individual, because the family provides the context within which the person functions and is the primary support network of its members
- Recognize that the thought patterns of non-Western peoples, though different, are equally valid and influence the ways in which clients view problems and solutions
- Respect cultural preferences that value process rather than product, and harmony or balance within one's life rather than achievement
- Acknowledge that when working with minority clients, process is as important as product
- Recognize that taking the best of the Western and non-Western worlds enhances the capacity of all
- Recognize that minority people have to at least be bicultural, which in turn creates its own set of mental health issues such as identity conflicts resulting from assimilation
- Function with the knowledge that some behaviors are the expression of adjustments to being different
- Understand when values of minority groups are in conflict with dominant society values

Source: Adapted from Sue, Rasheed, & Rasheed, 2015

organizational practices and approaches that are critical to address in the process toward culture competency.

Personnel Policies and Procedures The size and legal basis of an organization are important factors in the creation of staff policies and procedures; small, newly created nonprofit organizations have relatively simple and concise policies and procedures. Having fewer policies and procedures lends itself to flexibility and creativity but also more uncertainty about responsibilities, processes, and scope of work. Larger, public organizations often have highly formal, complex policies and procedures, which creates a more constricted work environment, yet also provides a structure to better navigate a more multifaceted set of activities and responsibilities. Nevertheless, the development of written policies and procedures, including a plan for recruitment, selection, development, evaluation, and termination, is important. Some organizations also develop plans to address personnel changes and issues, such as to enhance staff diversity or develop career pathways for employees within the organization.

Resources (i.e., Financial, Technical, and Personnel) Other types of resources are also important to organizations. For example, the adequacy of the financial resources of organizations can be assessed through annual and monthly budgets, where income and liabilities are documented. **Technical resources** include the facilities and equipment of the organization, such as the office space, computers, software, and cell phones. **Personnel resources** include the number and capacity of current staff, including their knowledge, skills, and expertise.

Elements of an External Assessment

The external environment of organizations consists of many players. The assessment process focused on the external environment reviews the individuals, groups, organizations, and policies that impact operations. The external environment can offer opportunities and challenges for organizations, and maintaining a focus on relationships with external players is important. The following section discusses those elements external to an organization that can be considered as part of an organizational assessment.

Relationship with Funders and Potential Funders   An assessment process should uncover the sources of agency funding, as well as the nature of the relationship between the organization and each funding source. For example, the assessment process would uncover the amount and percentage of the overall budget received from each funding source. The funding sources could include government appropriations and contracts, donations, investment income, fees, fundraising events and activities, and profit-making activities. A source of funding that constitutes nearly half or more of the organization's overall budget indicates a strong relationship. Organizations that rely on a diverse source of funds have increased program and staff flexibility compared to those that rely on fewer sources.

Relationship with Clients   Human service organizations rarely have the resources to serve all people who live in their service area; therefore, organizations create client eligibility requirements for programs and services. An assessment in this area may include examining how clients are recruited and deemed eligible, the manner in which clients are treated who are not eligible for services, the degree to which clients are mandated to receive services, and which organizations are sources of referrals.

Relationship with Organizations in Service Network (i.e., Referrals and Coalitions)   Constructive, professional relationships with other organizations are imperative to a positive community perception and to the ability of the organization to function effectively. Organizations that deliver similar services often have motivation to work together to meet community needs, yet often compete for funding from similar sources. Therefore, strong relationships between similar organizations benefit the community through stronger service delivery and collective advocacy efforts. However, forming these relationships can be challenging due to competition for resources. An assessment of this aspect would uncover the nature of the relationship with similar and referring organizations, and those with whom the organization networks. Quick Guide 42 provides guidance on the types of organizational partnerships.

Relationships with Political Figures   Elected and appointed officials often carry considerable influence over public opinion about and resources for both public and private organizations. An assessment would investigate the key political figures for an organization and describe the organization's relationship with them.

QUICK GUIDE 42   GUIDE TO NONPROFIT ORGANIZATIONAL PARTNERSHIPS

A local nonprofit organization, Citizens Against Climate Change (CACC), would like to expand their influence without necessarily expanding their organization. They are exploring the idea of partnering with other organizations either locally, statewide, regionally, nationally or internationally. The forms of partnership from which they could choose are:

Task force: Task forces are temporary, flexible structures to address a community challenge to be resolved in a relatively short period of time. Membership includes representatives of all types of organizations focused on similar challenges. While the advantages include pooling of resources, ease of short-term commitment, and flexibility in structure, disadvantages include lack of organizational engagement and commitment, resources, and general trust due to the short-term nature of the arrangement.

For example, CACC could decide to create a task force with organizations to promote the creation of bike lanes on local roads.

Collaborative: Collaborative partnerships can be relatively long-term and involve sharing of resources, such as staff and funds, to engage in sustained service delivery among member organizations. Each member organization provides a unique contribution to combined work. Collaborative organizations can work closely over time and are often motivated to reduce costs, receive funding that otherwise would not be available, or fulfill unmet, complex needs. Advantages include resource sharing, expansion and improvement of services, while challenges include potential competition for similar funding opportunities and creating consensus among diverse partners.

For example, CACC could decide to create a collaborative partnership to deliver ongoing cycle safety courses and bike clubs for community members.

Coalition: Coalitions are groups formed of organizations to take joint action, such as lobbying elected officials, through collective action. While most coalitions have informal structures and fluid membership, some are formal organizations. Member organizations pool resources and devote staff and members to take action. The loose structure and fluid membership is both a strength (i.e., fairly easy to recruit like-minded organizations) and a challenge (i.e., challenge to create consensus with organizations that are diverse and do not work together regularly).

For example, CACC could decide to form or join a coalition to advocate for additional state transportation dollars to be devoted to walkable-bikeable community projects, such as sideways, bike lanes, bike corridors, and traffic-calming infrastructure improvements on side roads.

Interfaith Alliance: While faith communities are the lead organizations in Interfaith Alliances (IA), these organizational partnerships also involve other nonprofits, local groups and institutions (e.g.,

QUICK GUIDE 42   CONTINUED

public health departments, or child welfare departments). Advantages of IA include (1) faith communities offer a place of recruitment of active individuals who are motivated by their faith to take action on issues, (2) faith communities can add credibility to efforts to address societal needs, and (3) faith communities can also offer many types of resources. As with other partnerships, challenges include developing consensus among diverse groups and individuals.

For example, CACC could join an Interfaith Alliance at the local or national level to engage in advocacy about emissions standards for autos or to fund complete composting systems for food waste at schools.

Affiliation with national/international organizations: National and international organizations sponsor local chapters to work at a smaller level (e.g., state) to carry out their agenda. Local chapters benefit from affiliation by increased political influence, access to funding, and networks with similar-sized organizations across the country or world. Challenges include reaching agreement among diverse groups with varying agendas, and/or forfeiting some decision-making powers at the local level to the national/international organization.

For example, CACC could join with other, similar groups to create a chapter of Greenpeace, an international organization focused on climate change.

Social movement: Organizations can participate in social movements by joining with broad-based coalitions and national organizations dedicated to the same cause. Social movements are often the mechanism for marginalized and oppressed groups to obtain access to resources and political rights, as well as for allies to support them in their advocacy through organizational resources. Rather than a single organization, the work of a movement is carried out through partnerships of multiple organizations and coalitions to generate public support and links to decision-makers and funders.

For example, CACC could join with organizations such as the Global Campaign for Climate Action, 350. org, and other networks that are working with organizations and groups around the world to create political pressure worldwide for action on climate change.

Source: Adapted from Hardina, 2013; Netting et al., 2017

QUICK GUIDE 43   NONPROFIT ORGANIZATIONAL ASSESSMENT

Using an organization with which you are familiar, complete the following assessment:

Internal assessment:

• *Legal basis, mission, by-laws, and history*

___ The legal basis is clearly stated in appropriate documents.

___ The mission statement is current, accurate, specifies reason for existence and expected outcomes.

___ The by-laws are relevant, current, and accurately portray the needs of the organization.

• *Administrative structure and management style*

___ Fit the mission and services of the organization.

___ Transparent and structured lines/systems for decision-making exist.

___ Clear communication lines exist for dissemination of decisions.

___ Roles are clearly defined.

___ Decision-making involves broad participation as practical and appropriate.

• *Program structure, programs, and services*

___ Continual monitoring and assessment of the structure, processes, and programs occurs

___ Program evaluation data is collected, used, and linked to systematic improvements

___ Programs and services reflect evidence-based practice.

___ The need for programs and services is well-documented.

• *Organizational culture i.e., physical surroundings, public relations, language, procedures, social justice/diversity)*

___ Physical infrastructure is well-suited to current and anticipated needs.

___ Physical infrastructure enhances effectiveness.

___ Informal expectations are clearly articulated and supported by staff.

___ Communications plan and strategy is in place and updated on a frequent basis.

• *Personnel policies and procedures*

___ Recruitment, selection, orientation, supervision, training and development, performance appraisal, termination, and grievance processes identified.

___ Relationships between and among positions, and position qualifications identified.

• *Resources (i.e., financial, technological, personnel)*

___ Funding is sufficient, comes from diverse sources, fits mission, and provides insulation from market instabilities.

___ Board members embrace fundraising as a core role.

___ Board fundraising plans in place.

___ Electronic data systems sufficiently gather and report appropriate data regarding clients, staff, volunteers, program outcomes, and financial information.

___ Comprehensive, integrated system used for measuring organization's performance and progress on continual basis.

___ Programs and services are efficient, effective, and high quality.

___ Programs and services are well-defined and fully aligned with mission.

___ A system is in place to collect data about gaps in ability of existing programs to meet recipient and community-wide needs.

___ New ideas are continually offered to meet service gaps.

___ Communications carry a consistent and powerful message.

___ Marketing materials are professional, used consistently, and are current.

___ Materials are provided in multiple languages as needed, and reflect diversity.

___ Policies and procedures reflect systems that are culturally competent.

___ Diversity is characterized as an asset.

___ Organizational resources devoted to staff continuing education are sufficient.

___ Technology needs (e.g., computers, phones, etc.) are adequately met.

___ Website is sophisticated, comprehensive, interactive, and regularly maintained.

___ Positions adequately and appropriately staffed, vacancies quickly filled.

___ Staff are capable, committed, and bring complementary skills and momentum for improvement.

QUICK GUIDE 43   CONTINUED

External Assessment

• *Relationship with funders and potential funders*

___ Fundraising skills and expertise is adequate for funding needs.

___ Sustainable revenue-generating activities used.

___ System for regular communication and reporting with current funders used.

___ Feedback from current funders sought and considered.

___ System to cultivate potential funders used and continually updated.

___ Ideas for revenue diversification continually considered.

• *Relationship with clients*

___ System to actively recruit and involve clients in offering feedback is used.

___ System to actively involve clients in making decisions is used.

___ When possible, clients work collaboratively with staff in important roles, such as volunteer positions of leadership.

• *Relationship with organizations in network (i.e., referrals and partnerships)*

___ Strong, positive relationships with similar and related organizations exist.

___ Presence on relevant partnerships evident, and leadership roles appropriately taken.

___Reciprocity sought with relevant organizations.

• *Relationships with political figures*

___ Strong, high-impact, relationships using regular communication with a variety of political entities (i.e., local, state, and federal government) and community leaders exists.

___ Proactively and effectively influences policymaking at the local, state, and/or national level.

___ Participate in substantive policy discussions with opinion and political leaders.

Source: Adapted from: Netting et al., 2017; Marguerite Casey Foundation, 2012

ORGANIZATIONAL ENGAGEMENT, ASSESSMENT, AND PLANNING IN GENERALIST PRACTICE [EPAS 1, 6, AND 7]

While administrators have official roles and responsibilities, and therefore are naturally involved in the organizational change process, social workers in direct practice with individuals, families, groups, and communities, including generalist practitioners, must also be involved with the organizational change process. Both generalist practitioners and administrators are bound by the NASW *Code of Ethics* (NASW, 2008) Section 3.09 to work to improve services, to carry out their ethical obligations even if employer structures are challenging, and to act to eliminate discrimination in organizations.

What does the ethical obligation to participate in organizational change mean for social workers who are not administrators? Social workers must always learn about as many aspects of their affiliated organization as possible. Many organizational problems emerge through the experiences of clients or members of the community, and defining and documenting client or community member problems is a powerful way to make a strong case for organizational change. Social workers can engage others in identifying and documenting client problems to which the organization contributes (Gitterman & Germain, 2008). As discussed in Chapter 13, successful organizational change efforts often involve many individuals and groups.

Organizational engagement and assessment involve many of the same competencies and behaviors used with other clients. Discussed in the next section are those skills needed to effectively begin the organizational change process.

SKILLS FOR ENGAGEMENT, ASSESSMENT, AND PLANNING WITH ORGANIZATIONS

In addition to the skills previously mentioned in this chapter, (i.e., active listening, research and analysis, group facilitation, and documentation skills), integration of the data gathered in the assessment process must occur to provide direction to the next phases of the change process. One method is the **SWOT** (i.e., strengths, weaknesses, opportunities, and threats) **analysis**. In a SWOT analysis, organizational staff identify and assess both internal and external forces that impact the organization (Hardina, 2013) that can be the basis for developing the plan for intervention and change.

Another method of organizational assessment is a **force-field analysis** (FFA) (Hardina, 2013; Pippard & Bjorklunc, 2004). The FFA is a mechanism to gather and sort all of the information and data gathered in the assessment process and to provide the basis for a plan for an intervention, as will be discussed in Chapter 13.

An FFA is a method of identifying and assessing the forces that impact a decision about an issue by organizing the assessment data. To begin, a social worker would identify the forces that could impact the outcomes of change efforts, meaning constraints that work to prevent a change and advantages that will help overcome resistance to change. The forces could include influential individuals who could shape the opinion of others or who are decision-makers; organizations, committees and task forces; groups; and political parties. The technique enables a social worker to make a decision about whether to move forward with a change process, and if so, to create a plan based on an evaluation of the forces working for and against a proposed change (Hardina, 2013).

For example, the school social worker mentioned earlier has documented that LGBTQ students experience a higher number of social and academic problems in

EXHIBIT 12.8

SWOT Analysis

The Hispanic Community Development Center (HCDC), a Hispanic-serving, three-year-old nonprofit organization, wanted to increase their capacity to provide additional services to a growing Hispanic population in the community. While HCDC has been providing food, rent, and utility assistance and ESL classes for three years with one paid staff member, the Board wants to increase their capacity to provide health services to the population in response to high rates of teen pregnancy, HIV/AIDS, and poor oral health.

In their planning process, they used a Strengths, Weaknesses, Opportunities, and Threats (SWOT) analysis to analyze the factors affecting change in the organizations and the strengths and weaknesses both inside and outside of the organization. The SWOT analysis was conducted to help decide between two options: either attempting to raise funds to deliver health services themselves or partnering with an organization(s), such as the public health department, for service delivery at HCDC.

	Strengths	**Weaknesses**
Internal	• Reputation among Hispanics • History in community • Reputation among non-Hispanics • Only Hispanic-serving nonprofit • Evidence of need of health services • Diverse board with community connections	• Lack capacity to deliver health services • Lack of paid enough staff • Little experience in raising money • Little experience in partnering
External	**Opportunities** • Potential partnership with local institutions (i.e., public health department, university) • Potential coalition building with other human service organizations • Create HCDC capacity to meet growing needs	**Threats** • Other institutions may deliver services without HCDC • If deliver services, increase financial and liability risk • Partner institutions may require proof of documentation status of clients • If fail, damage reputation

Ultimately, the organization decided to attempt to raise money and deliver the health services themselves rather than partner with another organization. The primary reasons for this decision was to avoid the requirement that HCDC clients show proof of documentation status and to preserve their reputation among Hispanics in the community. The Board decided to attempt to raise funds and to request training from other health organizations.

Source: Adapted from Larson & McGuiston, 2012

middle and high school than other students. The social worker has completed an organizational assessment and would like to synthesize the information to determine whether and how to move forward. Working with a group of students who self-identify as LGBTQ, the social worker would like to engage in a change process to provide more comprehensive services to this population across the school district. After engaging and assessing the organization, the LGBTQ work group conducted an FFA to determine whether to proceed in the change process and to assist in developing an intervention plan.

As seen in Exhibit 12.9, there are many forces that support an initiative to provide more comprehensive support services to LGBTQ teens, including student leaders, student government, and high school principals. Neutral forces, including the association of principals and school counselors, could support or oppose a change process and do not yet have an opinion about the possibility. Through lobbying and education, these neutral forces could become supporters and, therefore, may become the focus of such efforts in the intervention phase. The forces that are opposed to providing support services, including several influential teachers, the parent association and others, would work against a change process. As other forces are discovered, they could be added to the analysis. The FFA is one tool to assist the LGBTQ work group in making a decision whether to proceed with their efforts, and in making an intervention plan.

The advantage of an FFA are numerous—the individuals, groups, and coalitions relevant to the issue are identified, as well as the driving and restraining forces most likely to effect the change effort. The strength of each force is assessed and ranked, and the amenability to change of each force is ranked as high, low, or uncertain. A plan for change is then created based on the information contained in the FFA. The FFA is a simple technique that can be used with groups of all sizes as a group decision-making tool that fosters creativity and critical thinking. The social worker must demonstrate keen group facilitation skills to achieve a balance of forces for and against change, to avoid the domination of a minority of the group, and to encourage the group to be specific (Pippard & Bjorklund, 2004).

SUPPORTING FORCES	NEUTRAL FORCES	OPPOSING FORCES	
Student leaders	Principal Association	Four influential teachers	**EXHIBIT 12.9**
Student government	School counselors	Parent Association	*Force Field Analysis, Assessment of Forces Impacting LGBTQ Initiative*
All high school principals	Local TV and radio station	Two student groups/clubs	
American Civil Liberties Union	Chair of the School	Three School Board members	
Three School Board members	Board		
Local activists		All middle school principals	

Planning with Organizations

Sometimes an organizational assessment process is focused on one aspect of an organization, and a decision-making person or group (such as a program director, administrator, or Board of Directors) can review the data and make a decision. At other times, an assessment process will surface many organizational issues, challenges, and ideas to the forefront. In that case, like in community assessment, the planning phase for organizations involves sorting through and prioritizing the issues to be able to move forward with an intervention. A set of criteria is needed to provide structure and fairness to the decision-making process. The criteria can include any or any combination of the following:

- Seriousness or frequency of an issue

- Cost of the issue, or resources needed to address the issue

- Feasibility of affecting the issue

- Readiness of the community to recognize and address the issue

- The long-term impact or benefit of addressing an issue, or in implementing an idea

Criteria may be set at any point in the process. Organizations may select to have some combination of administrators, staff and/or the Board of Directors set the criteria and make a decision about whether and how to move forward with an intervention by applying the criteria. After setting the criteria, a democratic process can also be used to then apply the criteria to the issues/ideas generated in the community needs assessment process to plan for an intervention (University of Kansas Work Group for Community Health and Development, 2016).

STRAIGHT TALK ABOUT PRACTICE WITHIN ORGANIZATIONS

Different types of organizations offer distinct professional rewards, opportunities, and challenges. Expectations and experiences differ from organizational setting to setting, and work style preferences that fit one type of organization may not be a match at another organization or type of organization. The following discussion will highlight several of the different types of social service organizations.

Although working for public organizations brings challenges, there are advantages unique to employment with public agencies. Compared to working within the private (i.e., nonprofit and for-profit) sector, needed services can be offered to clients with less consideration given to cost effectiveness because services may be required by law, and therefore, there are fewer demands for demonstrated outcomes than in nonprofit and for-profit organizations. In stable economic times, social workers within public agencies enjoy relative predictability and job security, with highly structured job levels and raise structures, especially in the military and federal government. Social workers in public organizations typically earn higher salaries than in some nonprofit settings (excluding hospitals) (Bureau of Labor Statistics, 2016). Many clients who served in public organizations are those without many alternatives; therefore, social workers within these agencies are implementing the historical preference of social work for working on behalf of the poor. Lastly, social workers in public organizations gain invaluable experience with a wide range of client issues and with clients with complex problems.

The number of social workers at for-profit social service agencies, such as private practices and for-profit health care systems, is projected to grow in coming years (Bureau of Labor Statistics, 2016). In contrast to public and nonprofit organizations, for-profit (or proprietary) agencies seek to produce a financial profit for their owners or shareholders. Social workers in residential care facilities, medical and psychiatric hospitals, long-term care for persons with disabilities, home health services, health maintenance organizations, substance abuse treatment centers, correctional settings, and child welfare services may be in for-profit settings.

Depending on the type of services provided, social workers in for-profit organizations may enjoy a more comfortable physical setting, more resources, use of cutting-edge interventions and treatment modalities, and higher expectations of efficiency and effectiveness than in other settings. Salaries, however, are generally similar at for-profits and nonprofits (Whitaker & Wilson, 2010). In some for-profit settings, a wide socioeconomic diversity of clients may seek services. Social workers may also enjoy the opportunities to advocate for the primary goal of client-centered human services to meet community needs, rather than a profit.

Most social service organizations are nonprofit (Holland, 2013). Advantages to working for a nonprofit organization include the following: (1) for some nonprofits, social workers generally have less need to advocate internally to maintain the historical commitment to serving the poor; (2) the funding base is often a diverse mixture of sources, including grants, contracts, memberships, fee for service, investment, donations, and events (Netting et al., 2017); (3) social work employees may enjoy more autonomy, flexibility, and creativity in service delivery due to the multitude of funding sources; and (4) social workers in faith-based nonprofit organization can implement their religious traditions and beliefs in their employment setting.

While there are other types of organizations beyond public, for-profit, and 501(c)3 nonprofit organizations (i.e., hybrid nonprofit and social enterprises, whereby nonprofit organizations engage in commercial activity (Brunell, Moray, Stevens, & Fassin, 2016), other classifications of 501(c)), these three are the central types of organizations that employ social workers. While generalities may be helpful, each setting offers a unique working environment. Social workers who explore types of organizations may gain more insight about the best fit for their preferred work style and career aspirations. Both for-profit and nonprofit organizations can engage in advocacy. Quick Guide 44 provides more details on the types of advocacy activities in which organizations engage.

QUICK GUIDE 44   ORGANIZATIONAL POLICY ADVOCACY ACTIVITIES

Complete the following tool about organizational policy advocacy activities using an organization with which you are familiar. Completing this assessment can shed light on the degree to which organizations use opportunities to engage in policy activities for the benefit of their clients and organization. Organizations that engage in few of these could consider expanding their policy advocacy activities to more opportunities, such as those listed here.

In the past, our agency has:

(Organizational Activities)

___Testified at public hearings held by the city council, state legislature, or other decision-making body.

___Participated in legislative or policy working groups with government officials.

___Engaged in nonviolent civil disobedience (i.e., deliberately broke a law to draw attention to unjust government policies, programs, or actions).

___Sent unique letters, e-mails, faxes, or texts to the city council, the mayor, local government agency directors, or senior staff members regarding legislation, government policies, government programs, or other issues that affect our clients.

___Participated in rallies, protests, vigils, and/or demonstrations to draw attention to an issue that affects our clients.

___Attempted to engage television, radio, print, or web-based media reporters to give attention to legislation, government policies, government programs, or other issues that affect our clients.

___Submitted letters to the editor or op-ed pieces to the local media regarding legislation, government policies, government programs, or other issues related to our client population.

___Helped draft legislation.

___Sponsored or cosponsored forums or other community events to educate the general public about legislation, government policies, government programs, or a social issue.

___Submitted formal comments on rules, regulations, strategic plans, or other administrative governmental documents.

___Met with the city council members, the mayor, and/or local government agency directors or senior staff to discuss legislation, government policies, government programs, or other issues that affect our clients.

___Contacted city council members, the mayor, and/or local government agency directors or senior staff to discuss legislation, government policies, government programs, or other issues that affect our client populations.

___Participated in letter-writing campaigns, "sign-on" letters, "call-in days," postcard drives, petition drives, or email drives to contact public officials about legislation, government policies, government programs, or other issues that affect our clients.

___Submitted articles in our newsletter about legislation, government policies, government programs, or other issues that affect our clients.

___Posted fact sheets, issue briefs, articles, and/or testimony about legislation, government policies, government programs, or other issues that affect our client population on our website.

___Invited council members and/or the mayor to visit our program(s) to educate them about the issues that affect our clients.

___Actively participated in coalitions related to our area of service or issue of concern. (*Actively participated means attended and gave input at coalition meetings, joined and actively participated in coalition committees, attended coalition events, etc.*)

(Direct Client Activities)

___Met with and/or distributed written information to clients to educate/inform them about legislation, government policies, government programs, or upcoming public policy activities, (e.g., meetings, public hearings).

___Solicited input from clients to inform our agency's advocacy priorities.

___Included clients when making visits to the city council, state representatives, or other decision-makers.

___Provided skill-building workshops to clients to encourage their public policy participation. *Skill building may include writing and giving testimony, writing letters, making phone calls, meeting with decision-makers, and other tactics.*

___Met with clients to help them formulate direct action strategies around issues of their choice.

___Conducted voter registration drives.

___Facilitated transportation for clients to encourage their participation in public policy activities and/or to vote at the polls.

Source: Adapted from Plitt & Shields, 2009

GRAND CHALLENGE

Promote Smart Decarceration

A focus on mass incarceration for the past several decades in the United States has resulted in the world's largest proportion of people in prison. The expansion of the criminal justice system, or mass incarceration, is a social justice issue. This challenge has been identified by the American Academy of Social Work and Social Welfare as one of the twelve Grand Challenges for Social Work.

In addition to the overwhelming financial cost, Pettus-Davis and Epperson (2016) provide an overview of this problem from a social justice perspective:

The exponential growth of incarceration in the United States is a compelling problem not only because of sheer numbers, but also because of who is most affected. The majority of the imprisoned population is made up of people of color and people suffering from poverty or behavioral health disorders. For these reasons, social workers and the American public increasingly understand mass incarceration as unaffordable (p.4).

GRAND CHALLENGE

Continued

Smart decarceration interventions build on structural and behavioral interventions that have been shown to reduce incarcerated populations. They include (1) diverting criminal offenders from prison by first implementing alternatives to incarceration, (2) reducing recidivism and thereby reduce prison populations, and (3) reinvesting criminal justice resources into treatment and prevention.

With its long history of reform efforts and focus on social justice, the social work profession is well suited to provide leadership toward promoting decarceration. Society needs to explore and evaluate a range of alternatives to transform the criminal justice system incarceration, including multidisciplinary approaches to policy and practice intervention. Social work can promote cross-sector and transdisciplinary collaboration to encourage evidence-based practice toward smart decarceration. Consider the dimensions of organizations discussed in this chapter. How can organizations be structured to promote cross-sector and transdisciplinary collaborative work? To familiarize yourself with smart decarceration, visit the Grand Challenges website and read Working Paper No. 4 (Pettus-Davis & Epperson, 2015) at http://aaswsw.org/wp-content/uploads/2015/12/WP4-with-cover.pdf. (See Exercise #a1 for additional exploration of engaging and assessing communities for financial capability and asset building within the context of the Brickville community.)

CONCLUSION

This chapter has introduced organizations as an important arena for the social work change process. Social workers in direct practice and their supervisors are uniquely informed about the impact of organizational operations on clients. Social workers may best be able to identify unmet client needs, and initiate a change process designed to meet the best interests of the client—whether that be an individual, family, group, or community. Social workers, therefore, have a mandate to engage people in the organization and external to the organization, and learn about both the internal and external environments of organizations to competently lead and participate in organizational change processes. In addition to engagement, this chapter focused on the assessment process to provide the foundation needed to initiate the change process, as well as the planning process. Organizations are an important context of generalist social work practice with all types of clients. Chapter 13 will focus on organization intervention strategies, termination, evaluation, and follow-up processes.

MAIN POINTS

- Social workers work in many types of and sizes of organizations and use their knowledge to promote the best interests of their clients.

- Organizations, like other clients, can be understood using various theories, models, and perspectives, including systems theories and contemporary organizational and management theories.

- Three main dimensions of difference between organizations are: (1) purpose of the organization, (2) structure of governance, and (3) internal power relations.

- Social workers also practice in host settings, which are organizations in which social workers provide social services as a secondary activity.

- Social workers in a variety of roles can change organizations to provide a higher quality of services.

- The overall assessment of organizations involves both a review of the internal environment of the organization, and the external environment.

- The NASW *Code of Ethics* (2008) provides direction to both generalist and advanced specialist social workers to work to improve services, carry out their ethical obligations in the work place, and to act to eliminate discrimination in organizations.

- A helpful skill in the assessment process is a force-field analysis (FFA), a tool to sort information and data gathered in the assessment process and aid in the planning process to make decisions about the change process.

- The type of organization in which a social worker is employed offers different professional rewards, opportunities, and challenges.

EXERCISES

a. Case Exercises

1. Log onto http://routledgesw.com//rainn/engage/components and read about RAINN's service components. Draft a short mission statement for RAINN.

2. Log onto www.routledgesw.com/cases and review the Sanchez family case. Imagine you were hired as a social worker approximately three months ago at a community center that serves the Sanchez family. As you have settled into your job responsibilities, you notice some tensions within the agency. Several social workers are grumbling at "the way things are around here." As you consider the reasons for your feelings of being unsettled, you decide to gather information about the organization to gain a better understanding of the dynamics. Referring back to the chapter, discuss ways in which you might obtain knowledge about each factor, and how each factor could influence the experience of staff members (one paragraph for each): purpose, structure of governance, and internal power relations.

3. After you have completed Exercise #1, you still are not sure about the dynamics that have led you to feel unsettled, and co-workers to grumble. You decide to learn more about the agency, but are not quite ready to undertake a full organizational assessment. You decide to start your mini-assessment by focusing on culture. Using the concepts described in the chapter, describe the elements of culture that exist in the center, and how you would go about learning them, to include the types of individuals you might interview, the documents you would seek, the groups you would access, and any other source of information you might use. Justify your choices.

4. Log onto www.routledgesw.com/cases. Review the Riverton case file (i.e., Your History and Your Concerns). View the community sociogram, and note all of the organizations and their relationships to one another. Develop a sociogram for an organization with which you are familiar.

5. Using the Riverton case (at www.routledgesw.com/cases), answer the Critical Thinking Question #2.

6. Using the Riverton case (at www.routledgesw.com/cases), answer the Critical Thinking Question #3 by assuming that the organization is the client. What would be your next steps after deciding that an organization in the community is the client? Which organization is the client (use the sociogram and/or town map to review the possibilities)?

7. Go to www.routledgesw.com/cases and become familiar with the Brickville case. Several events have occurred that prompt the Brickville CDC to conduct an organizational assessment. First, the Brickville CDC has been asked to join the coalition that is working for the redevelopment plan. Second, as part of the needs assessment outcomes, the youth development organization encouraged the Brickville CDC to become more politically engaged for the benefit of the neighborhood. The CDC director has stated that the organization has never taken a stance on an issue before. Olivia and her colleagues have decided to work toward organizational change and create a process whereby the Brickville CDC can take a stance on neighborhood issues. In a brief, 1-page paper, discuss the elements of an internal assessment that would need to be included to assess for political engagement. Explain the rationale for your choices.

b. Other exercises

For the following exercises, write a 1–2 page paper with your findings.

8. Choose an organization with which you are familiar. Familiarize yourself with the elements of an organizational assessment, as discussed in Chapter 12. Interview a person familiar with the organization to gather as much information as possible related to the internal and external elements of an organizational assessment. As part of the interview, ask whether the organization has completed an organizational assessment in the past and whether there are any written documents that describe the assessment that you could review.

9. Using the SWOT diagram in Exhibit 12.8 as an example, complete a SWOT diagram for an organization with which you are familiar. Briefly explain and justify the contents of your SWOT analysis.

10. Using the examples of forms of partnership in Quick Guide 42, describe the forms of partnerships that a nonprofit, "Men Against Sexual Assault," could take if they wanted to expand their influence without expanding their organization.

11. Using Exhibit 12.2 as the case (Casa De Esperanza), describe how 3 of the 10 "Dimensions of Organizational Culture," as described in Exhibit 12.5, could be implemented. That is, if Casa De Esperanza wanted to implement a culture that was friendly and welcoming to the Latino community, what would three of the ten "look like"?

Social Work Practice with Organizations: Intervention, Termination, and Evaluation

The time when you need to do something is when no one else is willing to do it, when people are saying it can't be done.

Mary Frances Berry

Key Questions for Chapter 13

1. How can I use theory and perspectives to guide the development of intervention, terminations, and evaluation with organizations? [EPAS 8 and 9]
2. What models can I use to intervene in organizations? [EPAS 8]
3. How do I utilize evidence to practice research-informed practice and practice-informed research to guide intervention, termination, and evaluation with organizations? [EPAS 4]
4. How can I apply social work values and ethics to organizations intervention, termination, and evaluation? [EPAS 1]

CONSIDER THE FOLLOWING SITUATIONS:

Toby, a tenth-grader, left Dan (the social worker)'s office having made the comment that he wished that other kids would just "leave him alone" and that he wished he "knew other kids like him." Toby, who shared with Dan that he thinks he is gay, was the third student that week to say similar things to Dan, who is struggling with a response to the needs of lesbian, gay, bisexual, transgendered, and questioning (LGBTQ) students. Dan has seen these students struggle with bullying, less social integration, and poor school performance, which they often say is due to a lack of acceptance by teachers, administrators, and peers.

Carrie, a social work case manager at a mental health service organization, is at the end at her rope. Four of the clients on her caseload, who are dual diagnosed with a chronic mental illness and a substance abuse issue, have become homeless this month due to the lack of affordable rental housing in the community. The few units that are available in the community are owned by landlords who will not rent to clients of the organization.

These are situations that may prompt organizational change that result from client needs not adequately being met by the agency, the institution, or community. Dan, for example, is realizing that his agency (i.e., the school) may not be responding adequately to the needs of one population. Carrie sees an inadequate response by the community to the housing needs of her clients, which may be worsening their mental health conditions.

Organizational change can range in size from large (e.g., changing the decision-making process within the organization) to small (e.g., changing eligibility for one program, or the working hours for staff members), and from short-term (e.g., creating a short-term project) to long-term (e.g., creating new programs). Large-scale change, such as a legal merger with another organization, can change the nature and mission of organizations. However, small-scale change can also make an important difference to the clients and community, such as offering a new program that allows people who are homeless and have chronic mental illness and substance abuse problems to live in supportive housing while clients work to reduce and eliminate substances from their lives. Both types of changes involve utilizing the change process of engagement, assessment, intervention, termination, and evaluation.

As discussed in Chapter 12, the impetus for organizational change can emerge from many sources, including administrators, direct practice staff, stakeholders, and people outside an organization. Social workers' concerns for an aspect of service, whether ineffective, wasteful, or in some other way troubling, may be the most accessible route to effect change. As frontline staff, social workers are often the first to notice that clients experience difficulty with organizational practices, and they can voice their concerns as part of the engagement, assessment, and planning processes and participate in the next parts of the change process. This chapter will focus on the change process from the perspective of direct service social workers.

After completing the engagement, assessment, and planning processes outlined in Chapter 12, the social worker, with allies who have formed a "change work group" (i.e., a committee of people who are willing to work toward organizational change), must consider possible solutions, develop a change proposal (i.e., intervention) to pursue, select an intervention strategy, and if successful, possibly be involved in the implementation of the intervention, as well as its termination and evaluation. Organizations change in much the same way as individuals. Organizations structured as bureaucracies tend to change slowly because of their complex systems. Organizations of any size with a long history can resist change because staff feel that "we have always done things this way," and change may require a great deal of effort. Organizations with a more open, flexible structure, like people who are flexible, tend to make purposeful changes easily. Based on assessments, social workers collaborating with a change work group must choose the intervention strategy to best match the organization and the context of the change.

This chapter will examine ideas social workers in change work groups can use to change policies, programs, projects, and practices within organizations. Based on the engagement, assessment, and planning phases of the change process, the next three steps—intervention, termination, and evaluation and follow-up—can help organizations to become more responsive to the individuals, families, groups, and communities they serve. First discussed are approaches, perspectives, and models for interventions with organizations. In the next section, a framework for organizational change is provided. The challenges and methods for implementing the organizational change are explored, followed by a discussion of termination and evaluation of change in organizations. The chapter ends with an overview of the challenge of maintaining a hopeful stance with clients regarding organizational change.

© gosphotodesign

APPROACHES, PERSPECTIVES, AND MODELS FOR INTERVENTIONS WITH ORGANIZATIONS [EPAS 8 AND 9]

Approaches, perspectives, and models that are grounded in theory can be used to describe organizations and inform the change process for organizations. In the following section, the organization is described using self-learning, systems, social ecology, power and politics, postmodernist, and social constructionist approaches. We will discuss each approach as well as the implications for the social worker working within an organization.

Self-Learning Model

Gambrill (2013) describes the **self-learning model** as a contemporary organizational climate that emphasizes the ability of organizations to self-correct when needed. The increasing emphasis on accountability and accessibility to clients, increasing use of information technology, and a limited resource pool lead to the ability of the organization to improve the quality of its decisions and develop new knowledge. This model maintains that organizations seek and use corrective feedback from internal and external sources by ongoing monitoring and continuously soliciting feedback from clients about their experiences with services and from other stakeholders who provide information about the external environment of the organization. This model also assumes a rational process in which all members of an organization agree on the mission, goals, and objectives of the organization and work collaboratively to achieve them. Although no organization perfectly implements its mission, goals, and objectives, the self-learning model has widespread applicability in well-focused organizations with clear goals and values committed to quality improvement. An organization that seeks feedback from many stakeholders—clients, funders, referral sources, political leaders and others—and considers this feedback when deciding whether to make change is using a self-learning model.

This model is closely related to the **ecosystems perspective**, described fully in Chapter 1 as a perspective focused on the fit between the environment and a human system. As mentioned in Chapter 1, the ecosystems perspective can relate to all clients, including work within organizations to create more responsive policies and programs (Gitterman & Germain, 2013). The model is also related to the **social ecology approach**, which assumes that the organization is continually interacting with and adapting to its environment. An organization must continue to adjust and adapt to environmental changes in order to survive and prosper. According to the social ecology approach, change efforts may emanate from changes that occur externally, which has created a need for change in some part of the organization. For example, when economic conditions force many families to seek services, different policies and procedures may be needed to adequately serve the larger number of clients with a higher level of needs. Social workers need to pay attention to changes in the organization's environment (e.g., new funding sources, a change in an area of social policy, new political support for an idea about human services) and help the organization strategize to make needed changes (Cummings & Worley, 2014).

Social workers within organizations that are using the self-learning model contribute to an organizational culture focused on receiving feedback from the internal and external environment, learning, and seeking knowledge about ways to improve their functioning and programs/services. This model is well-recognized in organizations that are involved in networks of organizations, have close relationships with their funders, and/or have a highly developed internal evaluation and feedback systems.

Systems Model

The **systems model,** also related to the ecosystems approach, recognizes an organization as a system composed of individuals, subsystems, rules, roles, and processes operating within the wider environment. Using a systems approach, change in one part of the organization can create changes in other parts of the organization. This model asserts that efforts involved in organizational maintenance and survival need to be balanced with achieving organizational goals. Thus, an administrator using this model needs to balance the resources spent fundraising with resources on strategic planning and program implementation.

An example of systems model is the idea that changing a program's eligibility requirements may result in other programs having fewer, more, or different types of prospective clients. It could also result in changes to other organizations, such as referral sources, having fewer, more, or different prospective clients. It could affect the number of staff employed, the budget of programs throughout the organization, and the outcomes of the program.

In another example, change within an organization may be pursued due to job stress, staff disagreements, and unmet social and emotional needs of employees that, unaddressed, have potential to divert workers from their commitments. Change efforts in this model are more likely to include such maintenance functions as clarification of goals, improving morale, and emphasizing better communication among employees. The systems model can clearly be seen in such activities as agency retreats, training sessions, and requests for staff feedback on redefining agency direction (Campbell, 2000). In an important respect, this approach recognizes the impact of human service work by acknowledging the stresses that accompany working within organizations, and recognizing the necessity to attend to the human side of the professionals who constitute the organization and engage in the work.

Power and Politics Model

Assuming that the organization is essentially an entity where decisions are made in a political context, the **power and politics model** emphasizes competition for resources, personal advancement, and inter- and intrapower struggles. The model asserts that the primary path to change requires strategic access to decision-makers and/or the people who have the greatest power and primary influence over decision-makers. This model is related to the **critical social construction** approach, first introduced in Chapter 1, as a postmodern approach. The approach is based in an analysis of power, which recognizes that any social group can shape its beliefs to its own benefit at the expense of other groups (Hartman, 1994). The analysis of power includes questioning the power relationships between decision makers and others, which can lead to using the power and politics model of organizational change.

The power and politics model can be used within or outside of an organization and with any size organization. For example, using it within an organization, a common tactic is to work to convince influential people that the proposed change, such as starting a new program, is both in the organization's and the individual's personal best interest. Using it outside of an organization, a common tactic is to apply pressure from outside sources, such as the media, to gain the support of influential people for a change (Pfeffer, 1992). The model reflects the reality of conflict over resources and power that can emerge in change efforts, and the necessity of consideration of the role that politics and power play in change efforts.

Postmodern Approaches

As discussed in Chapter 1, in a postmodern view of change, actions, interactions, and patterns of relationships play an important role in the change process. Interaction patterns between people and between units become stable, dominate, and occur repeatedly in a dynamic process. The language used in organizations can serve to reinforce the patterns and processes (Hasenfeld, 2000).

Recognizing the power of language, the process of making meaning through social interactions, and the potential for taking part in reshaping their world, social workers can engage with people, groups, and committees within bureaucratic organizations to influence the development of individual and organizational approaches by paying particular attention to the language used and how people make sense of the language used. There is nothing inevitable about the structures and processes that shape and guide institutions or practice—people have created them and have the ability to change them. Changes to improve the organization's functioning can occur through understanding the language, symbols, relationships, and dialogues that structure the organization, and using dialogue to explore the perceptions, values, ideologies, ideas of reality, and assumptions held by staff members, stakeholders, and decision-makers for the organization (Hasenfeld, 2000). While not an easy or quick process for change, the importance of dialogue and language cannot be overstated.

Social Constructionist Approach

A social constructionist approach to organizational change emphasizes the impact that social processes, such as dialogue, have on the perception of social reality, which impacts the prospects for change. Therefore, dialogue about an organization's problem has an impact on the perception of problems, and can be one of the most effective tools in building support for a change proposal. Using this approach during an organizational change process means paying particular attention to the way in which dialogue is approached, and how the dialogue shapes people's perceptions. Dialogue that is continuous, patient, and respectful can positively impact the view of staff about the change proposal, which can serve to break down structural barriers to organizational change.

Organizations rarely use only one approach or model in change efforts; they usually use a mixture. These approaches and models offer perspectives on change efforts, offer a lens through which change efforts can be viewed, and offer ideas to social workers involved in organizational change efforts. In the next section, we will explore a framework for intervention with organizations. We will discuss recruiting allies into a "change work group," choosing feasible solution(s), selecting a change strategy, implementing the change strategy (i.e., intervention), terminating the change effort, and evaluating the change effort and resulting program or project.

FRAMEWORK FOR ORGANIZATIONAL CHANGE

Promoting change within organizations can be challenging. Sometimes change is needed because there is an issue, but other times, it is due to an opportunity, such as new funding opportunities. Exhibit 13.1 gives examples of the origins of organizational change efforts.

| **EXHIBIT 13.1**

Origins of Organizational Change | The origins for organizational change can occur internally from staff members, administration, or members of the Board of Directors, or externally from other organizations, funders, or others. Consider the following examples:

Annie works for the Santa Clara County Social Service Agency (SSA). Years ago, she noticed that the client population was increasingly diverse, with growing numbers of Asian, Hispanics, Hawaiian/Pacific Islander, Black, and multiracial clients. At a staff meeting, she initiated a discussion about culturally competent practice, and most of the staff agreed that they did not know enough about it and needed to know more. Her supervisor agreed that this issue needed to be studied, with the possibility of educating staff, and making changes to the organization. He authorized a committee, chaired by Annie, and asked her to recruit other staff for the committee. Over many years, major organizational changes occurred as a result of committee efforts. Three separate committees composed of staff at various levels now meet on a regular basis to discuss cultural issues and promote agency-wide change. One committee consisted of representatives from separate employee committees that are organized primarily by race or ethnicity. They collaboratively discuss and make policy recommendations to the SSA |

EXHIBIT 13.1

Continued

director. The second committee includes the agency director and various managers, and makes decisions about policies. The third committee consists of representatives of department cultural committees (i.e., one each in adult and aging, families and children, etc.). This committee monitors the progress being made regarding culturally responsive policies, procedures, and training programs related to improving client services in each department, and solicits staff feedback. All three committees contribute to increased intergroup collaboration, the direct involvement of the agency director, increased capacity for employees on all levels to be heard, and increased focus on shaping policy for cultural competency.

Source: Adapted from Chun-Chow & Austin, 2008

Ethan works for The Island, an agency that does exemplary work with disadvantaged adolescents and their families. Even though Ethan loved the direct services and clinical work, he felt that he was working solely toward the goal of teens and their families adjusting to challenging community situations, rather than also encouraging them to try to improve community conditions. The surrounding community struggled with high unemployment, poor housing, underperforming public schools, and needed more responsive local politicians. In talking with his co-workers, he realized that many felt that way. He invited his co-workers to join him informally at lunch to discuss possibilities, including evidence-based programs that sought to involve clients directly with community systems. Eventually, committee members engaged in work—one team located a recent community assessment about youth and family involvement in their community, another team engaged in an organizational assessment, including speaking informally to other staff, administrators, and community leaders about the issue, while a third team researched evidence-based community programming for youth. The Island administrators eventually agreed to appoint a formal committee to work on the idea. Out of these efforts came new programming. Youth civic action teams now work out of local community centers, in partnership with The Island staff, to address community issues of concern to teen members and their peers. The goal is to assist youth to be key agents of change in activities with the potential to transform the community conditions that create problems in their lives.

Source: Adapted from Evans, Hanlin, & Prillehensky, 2007

It can be helpful to have a framework—a rough guide map—to guide such efforts. This section will discuss the need to create a change work group, develop feasible solutions, a proposal, and the selection of strategy and tactics for the intervention.

Gathering Allies and Creating a Change Work Group

Organizational change often requires the resources of more than one person. A group, informal or formal, adds credibility and power to a change effort and also allows members to share work. Even if the engagement and assessment process began with one person, social workers will want to identify supporters and allies while assisting with the change process. Volunteers will vary from passively supportive to highly active. Those who are supportive may change their involvement level throughout the process, with some people beginning as mildly supportive and, at some periods, actively joining the work, while others that may begin as active members of a change work group may lessen their work responsibilities at certain times. The key is to continually recruit allies through formal and/or informal (word of mouth) methods and change work group members throughout the change process, so that even if membership of the group changes, a change work group is always in place to support the effort. While some change processes are short-term, many are long-term and require a great deal of energy and allies (Packard, 2009).

In the ally recruitment process, social workers must raise the concerns discovered in the assessment process in staff and committee meetings and in discussions with their colleagues. When trying to garner support for a change proposal from other colleagues, social workers will want to be as explicit as possible and use real-world client examples when applicable. Statements about problems that are in clear, behavioral, and values-oriented terms are the most effective. In these discussions, the client problems must be translated into potential solutions in which the organization can participate. For example, if you think the problem is that LGBTQ adolescents in a school district need additional social and administrative support, the social worker must first consider solutions in which the organization can participate. Can each school in the district partner with the local mental health center to provide education about sexuality and gender to all students? Should the partnership provide in-school or in-home family therapy related to sexuality and adolescents in order to promote family acceptance and support? Should the partnership provide individual therapy? Should the school district provide services without organizational partners, either in-school or in-home? Should the school district engage the parent–teacher association in their efforts? Rather than provide therapy, should the school refer LGBTQ students to private therapists? Or should the school provide services more quietly, so as not to arouse opposition, by providing, but not widely marketing, support services through the counseling department? Translating the problem into potential solutions will help others understand, propose other solutions, and have input into decisions. After recruiting allies into a change work group and establishing the group dynamics—leadership, decision-making, and other aspects (see Chapter 9)—the group must generate possible solutions and select one solution to address the problem.

Considerations for the Development of Feasible Solutions for Organizational Change [EPAS 4]

The change work group, including the social worker, must ultimately develop a potential solution to the identified problem(s) that is acceptable to the decision-maker(s) and that addresses the identified client problem to the best of the organization's ability, based on the information gathered and analyzed in the engagement and assessment process. The proposed solution is a change proposal, which varies in shape, such as a formal, written document for more in-depth change proposals or an oral presentation for smaller change proposals. Decision-makers for change proposals within organizations can be colleagues (who may be able to make decisions about small changes related to organizational practices, such as changing the way the telephone is answered or email is sent), administrators, including the executive director or director, members of the board of directors, legislative bodies, or funders of the organization. Additionally, the change work group must also select a feasible solution that is based in evidence-based practice (as first defined and discussed in Chapter 4). There are several important *considerations* for selecting feasible solutions, including the following:

1. Depending on the scope of the problem, potential solutions, and size of the organization, the change work group must account for *resistance to change,* as discussed in Chapter 12 (Tolbert & Hall, 2016). According to systems theory, all organizations seek to maintain the status quo, or stability. **Inertia** can impede change by preserving a stable state that actively works against change. Change work groups must expect some opposition to change, regardless of the specifics, because change takes energy away from other pursuits (Gambrill, 2013) and individuals have preferences for stability (Tolbert & Hall, 2016).

2. Employee attitudes and behaviors impact the success of change efforts (Packard, 2013). Therefore, the amount of organizational *effort* and *risk* involved is an important consideration (Packard, 2013). Those change processes that will require considerable time, energy, and/or risk to the organization involve in-depth change and will greatly challenge the change work group. If, for example, an organization has spent significant resources on a program, the process for ending that program may take a long time. In another example, a change proposal that involves implementing activities that are new to the organization, such as a new type of therapy, may be perceived as highly risky to the financial stability and reputation of the organization. A high level of effort and risk inherent in a change proposal typically translates to a high level of challenge for the change proposal.

3. The change process may encounter *competition* for resources (e.g., financial, relationship, attention, etc.) from other change processes. The assessment process should have uncovered any other change process occurring within the organization, as well as any plans that will structure future change efforts. For example, organizations often create **strategic plans**, which are long-term formal plans for the organization's future. These plans often involve incremental, highly focused modifications to current operations that are projected to contribute to a preferred result for the organization (Austin & Solomon, 2009). A change process occurring in another part of the organization can

impact a change proposal if the organization does not have enough resources to consider or implement more than one change proposal at a time.

4. The organization must possess the *ability* to implement the change, experience a *need* for change, and the change proposal must *match with the mission and values* of the organization (Packard, 2013). The engagement, assessment, and planning processes, depending on the methods used, may have made administrators and staff aware of a possible problem or opportunity, potential solutions or options, and the possibility of an organizational change effort. If not, staff members and administrators must become aware of the problem, become dissatisfied with the current situation, and perceive that a proposed solution will alleviate the problem. In sum, the organizational system that supports the current structure that creates or exacerbates the problem must become weakened.

5. You must consider *perceived advantages and disadvantages* to the organization and staff (Packard, 2013). For example, if potential solutions will result in more work for a particular staff member or group of staff, the person(s) or unit(s) involved should be consulted before choosing a solution. Others' input may shape the change proposal itself or strengthen the support for the proposed solution; their suggestions and concerns can be considered and possibly addressed in the solution and change strategy (discussed later in this chapter). Consulting with person(s) or unit(s) may garner their support. If possible, implementing a solution should be shared widely.

6. Gathering *history* on the organization's policy-making efforts or program changes will provide helpful context to future change efforts. For example, did prior change efforts induce staff disgruntlement or staff support? Were changes perceived as coming from the top down (i.e., imposed from administrators) or from the bottom up (i.e., suggested by staff)? Long-term staff members may be helpful sources of historical information.

7. In discussions with other staff members about potential solutions, the change work group should also gather an initial impression about change ideas and the degree to which they are *understandable,* and likely be met with apathy, resistance, or support. The change work group must learn about formal and informal groupings of staff members and charismatic leaders within the organization and account for the sentiment of such "subgroups" and leaders in the change proposal.

8. Prior to developing a change proposal, the change work group must engage in *evidence-based practice* by researching the identified problem and potential solutions using evidence-based literature (Packard, 2013). This information must be integrated with the expertise of the change work group as well as the values, experiences, and expressed wishes of the client.

9. The *timing* of a proposed solution can significantly impact the proposal's reception. For example, the time in which one administrator is leaving an organization and a new administrator is arriving is a window of opportunity for some change proposals. The change work group may take advantage of

this vacuum of administrative power by proposing changes to organizational practices (possibly including a change that was not acceptable to the outgoing administrator), such as a policy that allows staff and/or clients to be part of the committee that screens and interviews candidates for administrative positions.

These considerations speak to the need for a comprehensive process to determine a solution or option. Some considerations may be more important than others, and there may be special considerations for certain organizations. Developing a change proposal involves thinking through such considerations. Your proposal may also be impacted by your chosen change strategy (discussed later in this chapter). Additionally, the proposal may evolve as you garner more information.

Change Proposal Structure   The change proposal may be in the structure of a policy, program, project, personnel, or practice, or some combination (Kettner, 2002; Netting et al., 2017). The **policy** approach involves a formal statement regarding the direction for a course of action. A policy change often involves the decision of people with high decision-making authority, such as administrators, elected officials, or a board of directors, that involves large-scale change to create new or amend existing policy. For example, a change work group in a school system that is striving to create improved services to LGBTQ students in the school district may determine that the most effective change strategy is to work toward a harassment policy that would include harassment based on sexual orientation.

A **program** approach involves the creation of or change to "structured activities, [which are] designed to achieve a set of goals and objectives" (Netting et al., 2017, p. 306). Programs are designed to provide services to clients and are long-term activities. These are often high-profile aspects of an organization because clients interact with, and know organizations for, their programs. For example, a program approach to the perceived unmet needs of LGBTQ adolescents in the school system would be to create an education program about sexual orientation for all students. **Projects** are similar to programs but are typically smaller and more flexible, can be adapted to changing needs relatively easily, and are not permanent. A demonstration project, a short-term test of an idea, can be a less controversial way of implementing change. For example, the education program described earlier could be implemented for a specific time period, such as a semester, with the possibility of extension of the program in the spring semester and the possibility of changing the program in the first semester, as needed. A change in **personnel** can address different types of problems in programs and projects. Staff members within organizations may lack the specific competencies or practice behaviors to effectively work within programs or projects, and a personnel approach is needed. A personnel approach can include additional education, internships, change in responsibilities for staff, or complete change of staff. Changes that involve personnel must be undertaken carefully, with a thorough examination to determine if such a change will better serve the client (rather than simply change office dynamics). Using the example of the unmet needs of the LGBTQ adolescents, the proposed solution may be to educate teachers to become more supportive of LGBTQ adolescents in the school. Lastly, a change for an organization can involve a **practice** approach, or the way in which organizations implement basic functions, which may or may not be formally described in written documents. For example, a subset of counselors or teachers may become the unofficial resource and support persons for LGBTQ adolescents in each school, so LGBTQ adolescents have supportive adults in each school (Netting et al., 2017). Exhibit 13.2 provides a summary of these approaches. Exhibit 13.3 provides a case example of an organization that implemented these approaches to change.

Selecting an Organizational Change Strategy [EPAS 4]

Thus far, the social worker has completed the engagement, assessment, and planning process; gathered allies; and created a change work group. Together with the change work group, the social worker has taken many factors into consideration when developing a proposed solution, including evidence-based practice, and made a decision about a specific change proposal or intervention to pursue that entails a change in the organization. The next step in the process is to determine the strategy for making a change. A **strategy** is an overall approach to a change effort. In contrast, a **tactic** refers to specific actions, or skills, taken to implement a strategy (Hardina, 2013). This section will include discussion of strategies, while the next section focuses on tactics, or specific skills, needed to implement strategies.

Change Strategies There are three basic strategies for organizational change: collaborative, campaign, or conflict (Brager, Specht, & Torczyner, 1987). A **collaborative** change is one in which the change work group and the decision-maker(s) *agree that some type of change in the organization is required,* and cooperation is needed to create a joint effort to create change in the organization. The change work group and the decision-maker(s) need to create a partnership to communicate, plan, and coordinate and share tasks to implement a change. All parties involved agree that a change is needed; therefore, the group's decisions will determine the approach (i.e., whether a policy, program, project, personnel, or practice); the ways in which the resources needed can be obtained; and other details of implementation. Choosing this strategy means that there is little opposition to a change, and the change can best be carried out collaboratively. For example, if the change work group and the school principal and administrators agree that LGBTQ adolescents need additional support and that the school should and can assume a supportive role, the change work group and administrators could partner in a change effort to determine the form that the support would take (e.g., further education of teachers, support groups, and/or education of the students) and to implement the change.

APPROACH	DEFINITION	
Policy	A formally adopted statement that reflects goals and strategies or agreements on a settled course of action.	**EXHIBIT 13.2**
Program	Prearranged sets of activities designed to achieve a set of goals and objectives.	*Approaches to Organizational Change*
Project	Similar to programs, but have a time-limited existence and are more flexible so that they can be adapted to the needs of a changing environment.	
Personnel	Persons who are in interaction within the change arena.	
Practice	The way in which organizations or individuals go about doing business. Practices are less formalized than policies and may be specific to persons or groups.	

Source: Netting, Kettner, McMurtry, & Thomas, 2017, p. 308

The local mental health organization has a long-standing program for persons with chronic mental illness who also have a substance abuse problem (i.e., clients with co-occurring disorders). In recent years, the social work case managers have noticed increasing difficulty locating affordable, decent rental housing for clients in the co-occuring disorders program. The social work case managers have convened a change work group, and they are considering a variety of change approaches, including the following:

A policy approach: The change work group may approach the administration and the board of directors to change organizational policy, so the organization can move from only providing social services to an organization that also owns and manages afford-able, supportive housing for clients.

A program approach: The change work group may propose to the administration that the organization seek to partner with local private landlords to provide the intensive, on-site case management and supportive services needed to maintain a stable living environment through a live-in care provider. The organization will guarantee that the rent and utilities will be paid on time and that the apartment will be kept clean. The live-in care provider will be the first-responder for any problems in the building that involve the client.

A project approach: This change would be the same as the program change (described earlier), but would involve a six-month trial period. During the trial period, the social worker who is overseeing the project reports weekly to the administrator, who then reports on the project monthly to the board of directors. Ongoing adjustments will be made to the project as needed. If the project is deemed successful, the board of directors may consider creating a long-term program.

A personnel approach: Using this approach, social workers will be trained to become trainers to the family members of clients about being live-in case providers to their

EXHIBIT 13.3

A Dearth of Affordable Rental Housing: A Case Example of Approaches to Change

EXHIBIT 13.3 *Continued*	family member with chronic mental health challenges. The trained live-in family members will allow clients to live with their families, and alleviate the need for rental housing.
	A practice approach: Using a practice approach, social workers will learn different approaches for assisting clients to live together in their current rental housing, so that at least two clients can live in each apartment. This will have the effect of housing more clients with the same number of rental units.

A **campaign** strategy is used when *communication can occur* between the decision-makers and the change work group, but there is *no agreement that a change is needed.* The key to this strategy is the willingness of the decision-makers to listen to arguments on behalf of a change proposal. The decision-makers may need additional information or persuasion. For example, if the change work group and the school principal and administrators do not agree that LGBTQ adolescents need additional support from the school, the change work group could choose a campaign strategy of providing additional information, developing persuasive arguments, and arranging regular communication about this topic with the principal and administrators.

The third strategy, **conflict**, can be used when *the decision-makers are opposed to a change and are unwilling to communicate with the change work group.* Due to the lack of communication, the change work group is unable to educate or persuade the decision-makers through organizational processes, and is only able to influence the decision-makers through a public conversation. This change strategy involves efforts to draw support from a wider group of supporters and often involves public conflict. The conflict strategy often involves heated and/or passionate discussion that includes negative reactions and is therefore not typically used as a first change option. For example, if the school principal and administrators do not agree that the school can take a role in providing additional support for the LGBTQ adolescents, and are unwilling to communicate with the change work group about the topic, the change work group could choose to take a conflict strategy. The group may decide to organize a march or rally to apply additional pressure to the decision-makers to begin communicating with the group. Exhibit 13.4 provides an overview of change strategies and tactics.

Contemporary Tactics and Skills for Interventions with Organizations

The skills needed for interventions with organizations are built on the skills for intervention covered in previous chapters (i.e., relationship skills in Chapter 3; intervention skills with individuals, families, groups, and communities in Chapters 3–12). In addition to basic intervention skills, social workers need specific skills for working with change processes in organizations. The following tactics, or

RELATIONSHIP OF DECISION-MAKERS AND CHANGE WORK GROUP	TACTICS	EXHIBIT 13.4

Collaboration
Decision-makers and change work group agree (or are easily convinced to agree) that change is needed, and resources must be allocated for a change.
	1. Implementation
	2. Capacity Building
	  a. Participation
	  b. Empowerment
		Strategies and Tactical Behaviors

Campaign
Decision-makers are willing to communicate with the change work group, but do not agree that a change is needed or that resources are needed for a change.
	1. Education
	2. Persuasion
	  a. Co-optation
	  b. Lobbying
	3. Mass Media Appeal	

Contest Decision-makers oppose change and/or allocation of resources and are unwilling to communicate with the change work group.	1. Bargaining and Negotiation 2. Group Actions	

Adapted from Netting, Kettner, McMurtry, & Thomas, 2017, p. 312

skills, are organized by the strategy with which they are most commonly associated. The terms tactics and skills are used interchangeably in the following section.

For collaborative change strategies:

Implementation Skills   Implementation skills are those that involve solving problems and making decisions about logistics. Examples include engaging in research about an issue, developing written materials relating to the change proposal (e.g., written proposals, fact sheets), creating and facilitating task groups and workshops, and communicating with interested parties and decision-makers (Schneider & Lester, 2001).

Capacity Building   Building the capacity of client systems has two components: (1) participation, or involving members of the client system in the change process and (2) empowerment of clients through participation in the effort. These efforts, both a process and an outcome, can improve the ability of client systems to remove real or perceived barriers to participation in change processes, and increase the likelihood of clients participating in future change processes.

   To elaborate on the earlier example of the principal and administrators agreeing that LGBTQ adolescents in the school needed additional support and that the school could take a role in providing additional support, these collaborative change skills could be used to create a new program. The change work group can use supporters and friends of LGBTQ students and LGBTQ students themselves to provide assistance with every aspect of the program, including researching, analyzing, and creating program ideas; facilitating groups; educating other students and education personnel about their unmet needs; and other tasks. Involving the LGBTQ students and student supporters in this effort can increase their competence in these skills, and potentially enable them to teach them to others in a manner appropriate to their stage of life development.

For campaign change strategy:

Education Education involves communication skills, which may include in-person meetings with individuals and groups, formal and informal presentations, written materials, and education materials designed for persons and groups influential with decision-makers. The goal of such efforts is to present different types of information to impact the perception, knowledge, attitude, and opinions of decision-makers through information.

Persuasion Convincing others to accept and support a particular view of an issue is the goal of persuasion. Skillful communication that appeals to the reasoning of the decision-makers is an essential part of persuasion. The change work group must discern the information or incentives that would be important to the decision-maker and make every effort to appeal to these. Additionally, choosing people with credibility with the decision-makers to communicate with the decision-makers also helps make persuasive argument. One form of persuasion is **co-optation**, defined as minimizing anticipated opposition by including those who would be opposed to a change effort in the change effort (Netting et al., 2017). Including the opposition in the change effort can neutralize the opposition because the opposition was part of designing the change effort and may be able to advance an interest through it. Lobbying is the use of persuasion with targeted decision-makers who are neutral or opposed to the change effort (Schneider Î Lester, 2001). Quick Guide 45 outlines specific skills needed for persuasion.

Mass Media Appeals This skill refers to the use of all types of media to influence public opinion, as well as the opinion of decision-makers, either directly or indirectly. Involved in this skill is the development and shaping of newsworthy stories that will affect viewer opinion in the hoped-for direction.

In the example of the unmet needs of LGBTQ adolescents in the school setting, these campaign skills can be applied if the change work group and school principals are able to communicate about the need for additional support, but the principals did not agree that additional support was needed and/or that the school could take a role in providing additional support. The change work group can be involved in education efforts with the principal through such efforts as holding meetings or using school media options, such as a school newspaper, to present factual information about LGBTQ adolescents and the challenges they face. The group could also

QUICK GUIDE 45   PERSUASION SKILLS

Persuasion means to convince someone to do something that they might not otherwise do through use of reason. Eight skills of persuasion are:

1. *Target your case on the other person:* Find out as much as you can about the person you wish to persuade, including their roles in organizations as well as individual characteristics. Learning about their values, priorities, goals, motivations, personality, and habits will assist to shape a reasoned argument that appeals to them.

2. *Be clear about "who," "what," and "why":* Create a reasoned argument that includes the essentials and that appeals *to the other person* (not necessarily yourself). The reasoned argument should not be constructed as a debate—there are no winners/losers.

3. *Highlight common ground:* Build your reasoned argument on interests that both sides can agree on, even if lofty (such as "freedom" or "justice").

4. *Keep it simple:* People tend to make decisions by generalizing from a limited amount of evidence. Using a few powerful arguments that provide evidence of a unifying theme, presented in simple and relevant terms, is the most effective.

5. *Appeal to "head" and "heart":* Persuasive arguments include both rational and emotional elements. Pairing case stories or anecdotes told with vivid language with compelling "hard" evidence is particularly effective.

6. *Delivery matters:* Effective verbal delivery includes the use of "I" statements, taking responsibility for your statements, projecting a positive image and adopting an active tone, showing respect to others and giving them credit, telling the truth and showing a willingness to learn from experience. Effective nonverbal behaviors include using a clear and concise tone of voice, being calm, relaxed and confident, using statements that are carefully articulated, and being attentive to the nonverbal behaviors of the other person.

7. *Use dialogue, rather than monologue:* Use active listening by asking for information, summarizing, and testing for understanding. Respond in a constructive way to comments made by the other party. Dissent and disagreement are natural and functional, in that they acknowledge differences of roles, goals, values and personal qualities out of the open.

8. *Work with challenges:* When differences arise in the conversation, one response is to ask more questions. After learning where the other party stands on the matter, ask questions to learn the basis for their position, whether they are interested in reassessing their position, and if they have any ideas for resolving the differences. If confronting the other party, it is helpful to first summarize the other party's concerns and priorities, and discuss any areas of your proposal that would address any of their concerns (i.e., common ground). It can also be helpful to offer your ideas as suggestions, rather than proposals. Above all, avoid hostile or aggressive responses.

Source: Adapted from Manning, 2012

submit op-ed articles and letters to the editor to the local community newspaper. The change work group can also engage in persuasive efforts; the group can appeal to the interests of decision-makers by describing potentially increased academic performance and decreased fighting by LGBTQ adolescents, and increased tolerance for diversity throughout the school that would result from the new program. The change work group can also use co-optation by inviting the principal or another administrator to be part of the change work group (or an advisory committee to the change work group) or by lobbying the principal and other administrators who are neutral or opposed. As part of the lobbying effort, the change work group can also use websites, blogs, and social media, as well as print media, to influence the opinion of other students, staff, parents, and district administrators about the unmet needs of LGBTQ adolescents in the hope that these populations will be persuaded to attempt to influence the principal's opinion.

For contest change strategy:

Bargaining and Negotiation   Discussing a change proposal, with the possibility of both the decision-maker and the change work group making compromises to their preferred change proposal, involves bargaining and negotiation skills. Bargaining and negotiation skills are used when both the decision-maker and the change work group understand the position of one another and understand the change proposal and when there is a sense of urgency on both sides about settling the matter. Rather than confrontation, at the core of this skill is the assumption that both sides use persuasive arguments about their position on a change proposal and that both give and receive accommodation to their preferences in the final decision. This process may involve a third party acting in the role of a mediator (Schneider & Lester, 2001).

Group Actions   Group actions include many activities designed to increase political pressure on decision-makers. These confrontational tactics cover a wide range of legal and illegal activities, including rallies, demonstrations, marches, picketing, sit-ins, vigils, blockages, strikes, slow-downs, boycotts, class action lawsuits, and civil disobedience. Several of these actions require the involvement of attorneys and other professionals, while others are possible with a skilled social worker, change work group, and/or a large group of supporters (Schneider & Lester, 2001).

Ethic and Change Tactics [EPAS 1]   The choice of tactics utilized for a change effort is influenced by a number of factors, to include the type of relationship between the decision-maker(s) and the change work group, the degree to which the sides agree on the goal, the extent of the communication, as well as social work ethics. Actions taken, particularly group actions that can involve confrontation, should be undertaken after careful thought and consideration, as well as after preparing clients involved for any possible negative consequences, such as negative publicity, fines, arrest, lost wages, or physical injury. As mentioned, when there is a moderate amount of agreement and communication between the parties, more cooperative tactics should first be attempted prior to campaign tactics, and conflict-oriented tactics are often the last set of tactics used (Netting et al., 2017). The *Code of Ethics* (NASW, 2008) should always be used as a guide for ethical decision-making.

Returning to the example of the unmet needs of LGBTQ adolescents in a school setting, if the change work group attempts tactics associated with collaborative and campaign strategies without any success, the next set of tactics utilized may be those of the contest strategy. Ultimately, the change work group wants the principal to implement a new program, and the principal has rejected the idea and is unwilling to formally communicate further about the change proposal.

In response, the change work group may consider several different actions in terms of perceived effectiveness, best estimate of any negative consequences of each, and their comfort level with each. The change work group may decide to organize a march to raise awareness of this unmet need. The march can be on public property in front of the school and can occur before or after school hours, so no school or district rules will be violated. This choice of a tactic involves several skills needed by the social worker, including using the research-based evidence about social action in general, and marches in particular, and empowerment work with LGBTQ adolescents in academic settings and integrating the research findings with the professional and client experience and preferences. The social worker may also seek to involve external organizations that specialize in advocacy and diversity issues. If this, or any subsequent actions, successfully persuades the principal and administrators to begin formally communicating again with the change work group, bargaining and negotiation between the principal and the change work group may produce a satisfactory outcome, such as a modified version of a program to be used for one year, as a project, with evaluation occurring throughout and at the end of the year. Exhibit 13.5 provides a case example of the use of strategies and tactics.

EXHIBIT 13.5

A Dearth of Affordable Housing: Strategies and Tactics

The social work case managers of a local mental health organization who work with clients who have co-occurring disorders and are experiencing challenges in locating affordable rental housing have convened a change work group. The goal of the change work group is to pursue a policy change, so the organization can develop and manage affordable rental housing. The decision-makers in this situation are the board of directors, which includes the Executive Director. The work change group is considering a variety of change approaches, including the following:

The change work group may first attempt **collaborative change strategies** with the decision-makers. If all agree that a policy change is needed so the organization can develop and manage affordable rental housing for clients, the work will involve implementation skills. The social worker and change work group may be involved in such activities as locating and presenting data regarding affordable housing development and management, creating written materials relating the policy change, creating and facilitating a task group (which includes clients), and communicating with other housing developers and managers, interested parties and decision-makers. Another tactic used is capacity building. The social worker, with the change work group, would ensure that clients would be involved in the change process, to possibly include

EXHIBIT 13.5

Continued

participating in the change work group itself or selected activities. This involvement can be considered empowerment work with the clients, in that the social workers involved with each participating client can work to build client skills related to organizational change tasks (e.g., participating in task groups and public speaking), and client self-image.

The change work group may decide to begin with **campaign change strategies,** if collaborative change strategies are unsuccessful, or if decision-makers will communicate with the change work group, but do not agree that a policy change is needed. The work change group can utilize education skills, to include conducting in-person meetings with individuals on the board of directors and others who can influence board members, such as long-term employees. The group can also provide formal presentations at the board meetings, as well as create educational materials for these meetings. In addition to education efforts using facts, the work change group must also utilize persuasion to convince the board of directors to accept and support a policy change. The work group attempts to appeal to the interests of board members, to include better meeting the needs of clients, as well as potentially raising new revenue for the organization, and increasing the status of the organization among peer organizations. The change work group carefully chooses persons with credibility to communicate with the board members, to include clients, former clients, and long-time employees. The change work group may also utilize co-optation if they invited a member of the board of directors to join the change work group in determining the exact direction and wording of the policy change proposal. Change work group members may also lobby board members about the policy change.

The change work group may decide, after unsuccessfully attempting a campaign change strategy, to utilize a **contest change strategy.** After careful thought and deliberation, the change work group may utilize a group action to raise the pressure on the members of the board of directors. For example, the change work group may decide to organize a rally, march, or a vigil, along with other similar service providers who are experiencing the same challenges with affordable rental housing. The publicity materials specifically request that organizations respond to the need for affordable rental housing for the chronically mentally ill. If board members feel there is some urgency in settling the situation, the change work group may engage in **bargaining and negotiation** with the board of directors. In this process, the two sides may agree on a policy change for the organization that looks similar to, but is the same as, the original policy change sought by the change work group.

Similar to change efforts with other client systems and levels of practice, not all change efforts are successful. Change work groups may need to change strategies or tactics, and the end result of the change process may differ from the original proposals. A proposed program may be a short-term, small project, a policy change may differ from the original intention, and an attempt to create a project may require a policy change. Some change efforts are not successful at all, and the status quo is maintained. At this point, the social worker, along with the change work group, must reassess the situation to determine next steps. The change effort may benefit from starting over at the engagement and assessment phase to determine if the identified unmet need may still be as urgent, or other data needs to be collected. Alternatively, the change effort may need to begin anew at the intervention stage, where the decision to pursue an intervention, the type of intervention, and/or the change strategy may need revisiting. An evaluation of the process so far will help determine if different directions may yield more successful results, toward the goal of better meeting the needs of the client. Overall, advocates for change at all client system levels benefit from persistence because many factors may be impacting the possibility of change, including external factors, such as a poor economy. Many change efforts take a long time, even years (Schenider & Lester, 2001). If the change process has been successful thus far, the next step is to implement the change process within the organization, as discussed in the next section.

IMPLEMENTING ORGANIZATIONAL CHANGE

If the change work group has been successful in its work to create an organizational change, the next step is to implement the organizational change. At this point, the change effort converts to administrative functions, such as a new or modified policy, program, project, personnel, or practice change. A change in one element of the organization, such as a new policy, can often impact change in another area, such as a new program, project, or even another policy change. For example, a policy change that affects the members of a committee that screens and interviews candidates for administrative positions will result in practice changes: clients will now be recruited for the committee and educated about organizational personnel procedures, interviewing techniques, and written evaluation process for interviews. Those changes that involve policy, program, or project most significantly impact organizations, and those that impact personnel and practices, while important, may not represent an in-depth change to the organization. The following discussion applies to implementing a new or modified program or project, including developing goals, objectives, and evaluation criteria and possibly using a Gantt chart to guide the time frame of activities. Implementing a new or modified program or project involves similar components.

Implementation Structure

Successful programs and projects need structure to guide implementation and for evaluation purposes, although the elements for a project may be less elaborate than those for a program due to the short-term nature of a project. The elements of a program include goals and objectives, timelines, eligibility criteria, rules and procedures, an evaluation plan, and a management information system (Hardina, Middleton,

Montana, & Simpson, 2007). **Goals** are broad statements related to an ideal state for a target, such as population or community, while **objectives** are steps toward reaching the goals. Objectives can relate to an outcome, a specific task, a process, or the means to completing a task. A **timeline** spells out in detail the activities that will carry out the goal and objectives, with specific deadlines in place. The **eligibility criteria** define the group of clients who can participate in the program, while the rules and procedures provide the structure for the day-to-day functioning of the program, such as the roles that individuals will play, the decision-making process, the responsibilities for each person involved, and the process for delivering the program. The **evaluation plan** provides the details about the instruments and/or data to be collected on a timetable and the identity of those that will collect, analyze, and report on the program data. The **management information system** is the process for collecting program data and is often a type of software or Internet-based application.

For example, if the change work group focused on the unmet needs of LGBTQ adolescents is successful in promoting a new program within the school to better educate, support, and nurture LGBTQ students, the next step is to create the elements of a program. The change work group, the school social worker, and/or administrators can create program goals and objectives, and corresponding evaluation criteria, such as the following (Hardina et al., 2007):

- *Program goal:* To enhance the academic and social functioning of LGBTQ students and their supporters in Jefferson High School.

- *Outcome objective:* By December 2018, at least one support group and three sexual orientation educational sessions will be offered to students.

- *Evaluation criteria:* Number of support groups and educational sessions offered.

- *Process objective:* By November 30, 2019, recruit at least ten students for an LGBTQ support group through one-to-one contact and advertising in the school.

- *Evaluation criteria:* Number of students recruited, number of in-person recruiting contacts made, amount of school newspaper coverage.

- *Process objective:* By October 2018, create outlines of two different curricula related to sexual orientation education for consideration by the administration.

- *Evaluation criteria:* Number of existing curricula reviewed, number of curricular outlines created.

Gantt Chart

An important component of planning program implementation is specifying activities that will implement objectives and a time frame for each of them so that

ACTIVITY	SEPT	OCT	NOV	DEC	
Produce recruitment materials and begin recruiting for support group	X				**EXHIBIT 13.6**
Locate and review at least three sexual orientation education curricular materials	X				*Gantt Chart, LGBTQ*
Create at least two outlines of a sexual orientation education curricular		X			*Support Group and*
Recruit five students		X			*Sexual*
Recruit five additional students			X		*Orientation*
Facilitate one weekly support group			X	X	*Education*
Conduct one education session			X		
Conduct two education sessions				X	

Source: Adapted from O'Connor & Netting, 2009

actions can be undertaken in a logical, sequential order. The specification of activities and a corresponding time frame can be viewed in a **Gantt chart**, as displayed in Exhibit 13.6 (O'Connor & Netting, 2009). A Gantt chart provides a visual display of the activities that must be undertaken and the time frame for the completion of each activity, which can be helpful in both implementing a program and evaluating the success of the implementation (discussed later in this chapter). The Gantt chart depicts a sample of the activities to be completed for implementation of an LGBTQ support group and sexual orientation education sessions.

In addition to the activities in the Gantt chart, client eligibility criteria, program rules and procedures, and a management information system will be created to track the program participants, as well as overall evaluation criteria for the program.

Challenges to Implementation

Due to the complexity of organizations, implementation of a change effort can be fraught with difficulty. The organization may be facing challenges imposed by external constraints, such as a scarcity of available funding for the change proposal. The challenges faced by social workers who are attempting to implement a change can include the following (Winship & Lee, 2012):

Change Participant Affects   Although the change process has been successfully approved and authorized, the staff members involved in actually implementing the change may have a significant impact. Change proposals often encounter resistance from staff members with a different perspective or philosophy or who simply have a personal conflict with a member of the change work group. Staff members may oppose the change for many reasons, including a different worldview about the potential for change in people and organization, a distrust of nonexperts (or experts), or a fear of conflict, among other reasons. If the staff member was opposed to the change initially, the staff member may covertly express her or his opposition through inaction or subversion, may simply incorrectly implement the change due to a lack of understanding or skill or may decide to implement the change with her or his unique style such that the original intent is not realized.

Generality of the Change   Changes that are major in scope, such as policy changes, tend to be worded too generally; therefore, the implementation of the change may suffer from distortion because the staff member making the change may not understand or be suited to make the intended change.

Organizational Supports   Change proposals may be adopted with low levels of commitment by the decision-makers, and the implementation consequently may suffer from inadequate financial, planning, implementation, and other types of resources. A partial implementation of a change proposal may mean that the change is unsuccessful, when a complete implementation may have resulted in a highly successful implementation. A decision-maker's perspective on change may be affected by relationships with other organizations because a change could potentially create or exacerbate competition with other organizations or unnecessarily duplicate another organization's program. This could happen while the administrator is trying to create a stronger relationship with another organization. In short, support for the implementation by the organization's decision-makers can be affected by many factors other than the merits of the change proposal. Exhibit 13.7 provides an example of the ways in which staff resources impact change efforts.

| **EXHIBIT 13.7**

Organizational Challenges of Implementing Change | The death of an infant under the supervision of the San Mateo County Human Services Agency (HAS) ultimately led to a decision to seek accreditation in all eligible agency services by the Council on Accreditation (COA). Accreditation by an outside body, such as the COA, provides an external, unbiased "stamp of approval" on an organization and is a confirmation of the highest level of professionalism of an organization. The process of seeking accreditation is a challenging, arduous, resource-laden process of organizational self-assessment toward meeting specific standards supported by documented evidence. Ultimately, the goal is to build capacity of the organization toward better organization and client outcomes.

A "change work group," the Quality Assurance and Accreditation Committee, consisted mostly of administrators, while smaller subcommittees were established of staff members. As the two-year process got underway, it was clear that some staff on the subcommittees were passive and/or resistant to the work. In general, staff were not |

EXHIBIT 13.7

Continued

highly motivated to respond to communication or meet deadlines for deliverables. Staff lacked clarity about the importance of the work, and questioned how the work involved in seeking accreditation would help clients. They were also frustrated that they were asked to work overtime to meet their regular job requirements as well as accomplish tasks needed for accreditation efforts. Some staff felt that the process devalued their many years of practice experience and reflected judgment on the quality of service they had been providing.

In response to early problems, the value of the accreditation process to client services and service outcomes was clarified. Additionally, communication systems were clarified, administrators provided more encouragement to accomplish tasks and assistance in balancing work priorities, and "tip sheets" on relevant topics were delivered to each subcommittee. Yet, even after staff better understood the importance of the work to their clients, staff were resistant to solve the problems unearthed in the process, such as a lack of formal written procedures, documentation, and evaluation in all areas required by COA. Administrators repeatedly reminded staff of the importance of the work to client outcomes, and encouraged them to take some ownership of the process as a legacy of their work at the agency. Finally, a mock site visit by COA volunteers (prior to the "real" site visit by COA evaluators) led to clarification for the staff of the inadequacies of the products produced thus far and an increased focus to complete the work as required by the COA. While challenged to finish the work within deadlines, staff then felt a higher level of camaraderie with one another and administrators, who also worked overtime during this period. Ultimately, HSA received accreditation by COA.

Source: Winship & Lee, 2012

TERMINATION, EVALUATION, AND FOLLOW-UP OF CHANGE IN ORGANIZATIONS

The next phase in the change process, termination, can apply to the change process and/or termination from the clients of the organization. Most social workers engaged in a change effort from within an organization will continue to participate in the work of the organization as an employee or a volunteer and will be engaged in follow-up activities following an intervention. In a sense, many organizations experience continual change processes, as the organization seeks to maintain programs and services that are relevant to clients' needs.

If the change process has been unsuccessful, the change work group may decide to begin anew at the assessment phase to gather more information and consider different possible unmet needs as the basis for a new intervention effort. The group may also decide to pursue a change effort based on the same unmet need, but with a different change proposal and/or a different strategy for change. Alternatively, the change work group may decide to abandon intervention efforts for now and disband. In this case, termination by the change work group from the change process may occur until the next unmet need is identified, when the change process can begin anew (possibly with a different change work group).

If the change process has been successful, the end of the change effort may occur when the change proposal has been approved by the decision-makers, or after the policy, program or project change has occurred, and an evaluation has determined that the change has positively impacted the organization. The change work group may be disbanded either after the approval or implementation and evaluation (or may stay together and begin the next organizational change effort). Follow-up effects may involve continuing to monitor the effects of a change within an organization, such as through program evaluation efforts.

When the change work group is disbanded, as with other client systems, the termination may evoke an emotional response from participants, and group termination processes may be helpful (see Chapter 9). Change work groups are one type of task group, and members may have built relationships with one another. Just as in other groups, the role of the social worker in termination is to help the group members examine and celebrate their experiences and accomplishments and discuss the ways in which their shared experiences and skills may be useful to the participants in the future (Garvin & Galinsky, 2013). Social workers may also facilitate the expression and integration of positive and negative emotion, depending on the circumstances of the termination. While change work group members are likely to experience fewer emotional responses than those of other client systems, social workers must always be attuned to the possibility of emotional reactions.

Evaluation of Social Work Practice with Organizations

Similar to evaluation with social work practice with individuals, families, groups, and communities, evaluation of social work practice with organizations is an important part of the change process. The evaluation process can focus on the change process itself, as well as the result of the change process (i.e., the new or changed policy, program, or project that resulted from the change process). The evaluation of both the change efforts and evaluation of policies, programs, and projects have similar components.

Evaluation of an advocacy effort or of a program or project begins with a decision about the measurable objectives, usually made at the beginning of a change effort. The evaluation process begins as an element of the change effort and requires a decision: (1) if both the process and outcomes will be evaluated, (2) the ways in which the process and outcomes will be evaluated, and (3) the means by which data will be collected as the basis for the evaluation. The goal of the evaluation process is to determine the *value* of something, which differs from simply monitoring an intervention (Netting et al., 2017).

Types of Evaluation For both the change process and the implementation of programs and projects, there are three types of evaluation that can be used to assess the objectives: (1) process, (2) outcome, or (3) impact evaluation. A **process evaluation** focuses on the *degree to which the effort operated well.* For example, did the change work group have a sufficient number of persons for the work involved? What methods were used to recruit persons to the change work group? If evaluating a program, a process evaluation could focus on whether sufficient resources were available for the program, the ways in which decisions were made as a group, or whether there was sufficient and timely communication between staff members implementing a program. An **outcome evaluation** focuses on *information about specific results* that the effort achieved. Questions to be answered may ask: did the work group successfully arrange meetings with decision-makers? Create educational materials? Were there any policy changes? Were new programs or projects created as a result of policy changes?

An outcome evaluation for a program focuses on the results of program efforts. For example, did support groups meet? Were educational trainings held? The objectives for the program should be reviewed, and success in their achievement should be noted. An **impact evaluation** reviews the *impact of the efforts,* such as individual or community-level behavioral changes (Edwards & Yankey, 2006). For example, in relation to advocacy efforts, is there a new decision-making process in the organization that is more participatory? In relation to a new program, are LGBTQ adolescents achieving at higher academic levels as a result? Have clients experienced behavioral changes as a result of a new policy, program, or project? Have specific changes occurred in the community, such as decreased suicides or increased involvement in community programs?

Structure of Evaluation   The structure of evaluation involves four specific concepts: inputs, activities, outputs, and outcomes. **Inputs** are those resources necessary to implement a change effort or a program. Inputs can include funding, equipment, staff, time, expertise, and other resources needed for the effort or program. **Activities** are those actions that organizations take to produce change. Activities can include attending meetings, creating flyers, interviewing clients, and conducting assessments. **Outputs** are products that emerge from the activities. Outputs are often measured by a number (e.g., number of clients served by a program, flyers produced, or hours worked). **Outcomes** are the benefits gained or changes that have occurred as a result of the activities. Outcomes may relate to behavior, skill, knowledge, attitudes, values, condition, or other attribute. In essence, the outcomes are the impact made by the change effort or program (Dudley, 2014).

Logic Model   A **logic model** is a graphic depiction of the relationship of inputs, activities, outputs, and outcomes. Logic models provide a way to demonstrate the links between resources, efforts, accomplishments, and the impacts of change efforts and programs (Hardina, 2013). They are created at the beginning of a change effort, such as creating a program or project, to understand how all of the different parts interact with one another, and are very useful for evaluation. Exhibit 13.8

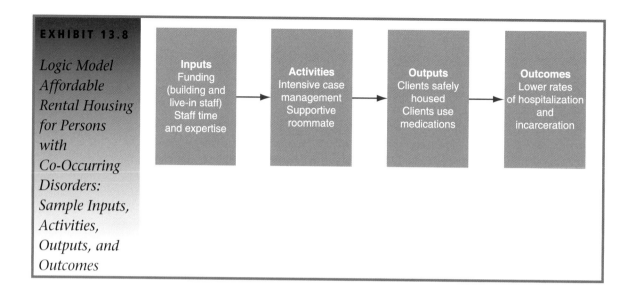

EXHIBIT 13.8

Logic Model Affordable Rental Housing for Persons with Co-Occurring Disorders: Sample Inputs, Activities, Outputs, and Outcomes

provides an example of a logic model used for a program of rental housing for dual-diagnosed clients.

In this example, funding is needed to purchase and/or renovate an apartment building (*input*), so that clients can be housed with a trained, supportive roommate and provided with intensive case management (*activities*). These activities may result in clients being housed in a decent, affordable unit, leading a more stable life, and being compliant with their medication (*output*), so that fewer clients would be homeless and/or incarcerated (*outcome*). This logic model can be useful in making a persuasive argument to a decision-maker who is interested in decreasing the number of dual diagnosed clients who are hospitalized or incarcerated. Other decision-makers may be interested in other outcomes, such as lowering levels of homelessness among persons who are dual diagnosed in the community to improve the relationship between the police force and the organization. Logic models provide a rational connection between inputs, activities, outputs, and outcomes and are often used in evaluating change efforts, programs, and projects (Hardina, 2013).

Information and Data Sources Developing and maintaining an adequate system for tracking information and data about change efforts, as well as programs and projects, is the backbone of the evaluation process. Information (hard copy and/or electronic) that may be helpful includes the following (Schneider & Lester, 2001):

- Minutes of meetings, logs of activities, sign-in sheets

- Information noting time spent on activities, appointments, assessments, client progress, activities in need of completing, and accomplishments

- Client evaluation materials, including standardized measures
- Organization strategic plans, mission, value statements, goals, objectives, and timelines
- Media coverage
- Funding sources, amounts, responsibilities, and required communications
- Information about key individuals to change efforts or programs/projects
- Government organizations related to the change effort and/or programs/projects
- Previous internal and external evaluations of advocacy efforts and programs/projects
- Records about previous internal and external advocacy efforts.

As with evaluations of community change efforts, the evaluation process ideally includes qualitative and quantitative data to provide information about the process and outcomes of organizational change. Methods may include pre- and post-measures of organizational and/or community functioning, such as validated and standardized measures, direct observation, use of publically available data (i.e., U.S. Census data and others), and feedback from other professionals.

Roles in Evaluation Generalist social work practitioners commonly contribute in several ways to the evaluation efforts. Social workers can lead and/or assist with evaluation efforts by helping maintain organizational records, submitting data for an analysis, participating in interviews and/or focus groups, or creating questions to be used in the evaluation process. Participation on evaluation teams and committees provides a way for social workers to learn about and direct the evaluation efforts, and some social workers function in the role of researchers to collect, analyze, and report on quantitative and qualitative data. Organizations benefit from well-designed and executed evaluation efforts.

STRAIGHT TALK ABOUT ORGANIZATIONAL LIFE

This chapter has highlighted both the challenging and the exhilarating aspects of social work practice with change in an organizational setting. Social workers can be tempted to view the organization as a source of challenges in practice. Sometimes organizations can be perceived as posing confounding or complex barriers to the helping process due to policies, procedures, and practice requirements.

In much the same way that some people blame their families for their challenges, some social workers point to the organization as the source of the problem when work becomes challenging or proves more difficult than expected. Shifting responsibility for challenges to organizations relieves the burden of responsibility from the social worker for a role in those organizational challenges. Social workers may not always fully understand the practice constraints inherent in organizations (such as constraints on practice by funders or regulators) and may find it easier to adopt a cynicism that eases their sense of responsibility. A related problem can occur if the social worker joins with the clients to collude about the problems of the organization as the source of the clients' challenges. In doing so, the social worker may feel temporarily relieved by engaging the client in her or his desperation with the organizational system. However, such collusion can convey a sense of hopelessness to the client, when the social worker's goal may be to convey a sense of hopefulness about the client's situation. In its most extreme implication, a hopeless stance may promote a generalized, scornful distrust of all helping efforts. The client may generalize that all helping efforts are ineptly carried out by social workers who are helpless and caught in troubled organizational structures that fail to implement their mission statements. Social workers, at times, must identify problematic agency policies or obstacles to clients. An element of empowerment practice is creating an alliance with clients, or a joint effort designed to promote more effective responses to clients. However, social workers must be able to convey an overall hopeful message to clients about their interaction with an organization.

At the same time, social workers must invest in a thorough engagement, assessment, and planning process prior to initiating in change efforts within and for an organization. For example, social workers need to understand the dynamics of bureaucracies and the slow nature of change within bureaucracies before engaging in a change effort. Social workers can be discouraged to enact change by their senior colleagues who believe that change efforts will create no effect or who are afraid of being sanctioned or fired if they attempt to create change without first building credibility.

Social workers who facilitate organizational change efforts must be well-informed, and have completed the earlier phases of the change process, knowing that every change effort will encounter resistance. In addition to understanding the organization, social workers must also understand their own strengths and weaknesses, and enlist allies to assist with the effort. However, a social worker who does not address any problematic organizational policy or practice due to fear of criticism or loss of employment is likely to have a difficult time in a social work career. Social work practice requires principled, thoughtful, and respectful risks across all settings to fully implement the work of the profession.

CONCLUSION

Organizations are structures that shape and facilitate social work practice. The change process in organizations provides an opportunity to offer improved services

In the history of the United States, some groups of people have long endured prejudice, discrimination, and exclusion from success in education and employment. A challenge for social work, identified by the American Academy of Social Work and Social Welfare, is to end racial and social injustice, dismantle inequality, and end unfair practices.

"The Grand Challenge of Promoting Equality by Addressing Social Stigma," by Goldbach, Amaro, Vega, and Walter (2015), describes the problems associated with social stigma and opportunities for social workers to end these problems. They describe stigma as "negative labeling" based on characteristics that others perceive as undesirable and distinguishing them from the rest of society. Stigma results in social disadvantage and loss of opportunities throughout life because of inequality, and leads to less favorable outcomes regarding health, academic achievement, income, wealth, and others. Stigma can be based on race and ethnicity, gender, sexual orientation, immigration status, age, ability status, health-related domains, housing status, and others.

The authors suggest a number of steps that social workers can take to reduce stigma, including examining social work's role as an agent of social control in society that has supported inequality (compared to the principles of the professions), and working to unearth unconscious biases of social workers. They also suggest engaging in employment-based training to reduce bias in service delivery, as well as active participation in public policy efforts to reduce inequality.

One effort that can be taken is at the organizational level. Organizations can make efforts to overcome stigma that is built into institutional arrangements. Stigma can result in biases built into organizations, even when they are unrecognized. Organizations can examine the assumptions built into their policies, practices, programs, personnel to determine where biases may be present that are reinforcing social stigmas. For example, unexamined biases could exist in such policies as the length of time a participant is allowed to participate in a program, the process of taking clients off waiting lists for services, or recruitment sources of programs. To consider these questions further, please familiarize yourself with Working Paper No. 18, *Promoting Equality by Addressing Social Stigma* (Goldbach et al., 2015) at http://aaswsw.org/wp-content/uploads/2016/01/W16-The-Grand-Challenge-of-Promoting-Equality-by-Addressing-Social-Stigma1-1-2.pdf. (To consider these questions further, see Exercise #a1 at the end of this chapter.)

GRAND CHALLENGE

Achieve Equal Opportunity and Justice

to clients. While the change process can be lengthy and complex, the process is an opportunity to make changes that positively impact a large number of people, including entire communities. Most organizations undergo at least modest change on a regular basis due to changes in many factors, such as funding, relationships, personnel, accreditation requirements, or accountability requirements, and staff members are in a unique position to implement the change process based on feedback and critical thinking about clients' needs as experienced by staff working directly with clients. While organizations can seem vague and too complex to change, understanding and impacting organizations is important to social work practitioners on all levels because of the significant impact on clients and practitioners. Taking an active role in shaping the organization is a significant aspect to generalist social work practice.

MAIN POINTS

- The approach of an organizational change effort will be impacted by the results of the engagement and assessment process, as well as the approach, perspective, or model utilized.

- The organizational change effort is facilitated by using a framework.

- Gathering supporters and allies into a change work group, considering important factors when choosing a change proposal, and selecting an organizational change strategy are vital steps in the intervention.

- Social workers consider social work ethics when choosing specific tactics to utilize for the change process.

- The implementation of an organizational change is facilitated by a structure, as well as consideration of challenges to implementation that can impede the implementation.

- Termination of a change effort can occur after a change proposal has been successful or after the implementation of the change.

- The evaluation phase can include evaluation of the change effort as well as evaluation of the change, such as a program or a project.

- Social workers should exercise caution about identifying organizational challenges with clients and only do so while maintaining a hopeful stance about the ability of the organization to assist the client.

EXERCISES

a. Case Exercises

1. To apply your learning of the Grand Challenge to promote equality by addressing social stigma that was highlighted in this chapter, visit the Grand Challenges website and read Working Paper No. 18 (Goldbach, Amaro, Vega, & Walter, 2015). Then, go to www.routledgesw.com/cases and become familiar with the RAINN case. Under the "Evaluate Your Results" tab, review both "The Purpose of RAINN evaluation data" and "What Data Can't Tell Us" sections. Consider whether there are any data collected that could provide hints about potential organizational bias in RAINN service delivery? Are there

any evaluation questions that cannot be answered with the data collected, yet, if it could, may shed light on some implicit bias in the organization?

2. Go to www.routledgesw.com/cases and become familiar with the Carla Washburn case, including reviewing her client history, concerns, and goals. Explore the town map and determine those organizations that may be able to assist Carla with her concerns and goals. Choose one of the organizations and consider the way(s) in which the organization may be able to assist Carla with one or more of her concerns and/or goals. Imagine that you are employed by the organization, and the assistance needed for Carla is currently not offered by the organization. Using the material from Chapter 13, describe the following:

   - The type of approach, perspective, or model with which you most closely identify
   - The way in which you would go about creating a change work group
   - Two to three possible solutions to Carla's concern or goal with which the organization could assist
   - Two to three considerations that are important to consider in deciding on the change proposal

3. Go to www.routledgesw.com/cases and become familiar with the Riverton case, including the history, concerns, and goals, as well as the town map and the interaction matrix. Imagine that you decide to work to find a solution to the problem of public intoxication by working with the organizations in the community as a "nonemployee."

   Which organizations would you approach to develop a community-wide response to this problem? What kind of changes might be needed in those organizations to better meet the unmet needs of the clients in the community? What steps might you take to facilitate the development of a change work group in these organizations? What might be some feasible solutions that organizations could implement through a partnership?

4. Go to www.routledgesw.com/cases and become familiar with the Brickville case. After an organizational assessment related to organizational engagement in political affairs, the Brickville CDC decided to move forward with a change proposal to engage more fully in local politics. The social worker, Olivia, and her colleagues formed a committee to work on the organizational change effort. For this change effort, create a goal, outcome objective, and evaluation criteria. In addition, create 2–3 process objectives and corresponding evaluation criteria for the change effort.

5. Using the Brickville case scenario described in Exercise #3, describe a policy, program, project, personnel, and practice approach to more fully engaging in local politics as an organization.

6. Go to www.routledgesw.com/cases and become familiar with the RAINN case by reviewing the RAINN Components and Ecomap. Discuss the approaches, perspectives, and models discussed in this chapter (i.e., self-learning model, social ecology approach, systems model, power and politics model, postmodern

approaches, and social constructionist approach) related to RAINN. If you were to describe RAINN using each one of these, what would you notice in particular? How would you be able to tell whether the approach, perspective, or model was relevant to RAINN?

b. Other Exercises

7. Review Exhibit 13.3. Create a different policy, program, project, personnel, or practice approach to the case than those provided.

8. Review Exhibit 13.3. Create an approach to change that mixes these approaches.

9. You are a social worker at an organization that provides treatment for adolescents who have alcohol and drug addiction issues. Yesterday, you suggested that the organization extend the service hours of the organization into the evenings and weekends so that the families of the clients would have greater access to meet with the staff, participate in treatment planning, and provide additional face-to-face support for their children. The staff was enthusiastic about the idea, and you agreed to the director's request that you compose a written proposal to be discussed at the next staff meeting.

   In your weekly meeting with your supervisor, you learn that she is upset with you. In your discussion, she is curt and states that you may not have taken into account the increased amount of work that extended service hours would entail. She states that increased service hours will have a negative impact on her life in terms of her social life and time with family members, and cost the agency additional funds. Considering the material discussed in Chapter 13, discuss the factors that may have led to this encounter in terms of creating a change proposal. Discuss possible next steps for this change process.

10. Using the two scenarios in Exhibit 13.1, create a problem statement that could be used in a change effort. The problem statement should be explicit, clear, and behavioral and should include values-oriented terms and client examples.

11. Using the case scenario in Exhibit 13.7, apply the key points in Quick Guide 45. What steps could have been taken to be more persuasive to those opposed?

REFERENCES

350.org. (n.d.). No KXL. Retrieved from http://350.org/kxl-victory/

Abramson, J. (2009). Interdisciplinary team practice. In A.R. Roberts (Ed.), *Social workers' desk reference* (2nd ed.) (pp. 44–50). New York: Oxford University Press.

Alissi, A.S. (2009). United States. In A. Gitterman & R. Salmon (Eds.), *Encyclopedia of social work with groups* (pp. 6–12). New York: Routledge.

American Academy of Social Work & Social Welfare. (2016). Grand challenges: About. Retrieved from http://aaswsw.org/grand-challenges-initiative/about/

Anderson, K.M. (2013). Assessing strengths. Identifying acts of resistance to violence and oppression. In D. Saleebey (Ed.), *The strengths perspective in social work practice* (6th ed.) (pp. 182–202). Boston: Pearson.

Anderson, K., Cowger, C., & Snively, C. (2009). Assessing strengths: Identifying acts of resistance to violence and oppression. In D. Saleebey (Ed.), *The strengths perspective in social work practice* (5th ed.) (pp. 181–200). Boston: Pearson Education, Inc.

Aotearoa New Zealand Association of Social Workers (ANZAWS). (2007). Code of ethics. Retrieved from http://anzasw.nz/summary-of-the-code-of-ethics/#1455661759310-739c7231-9145

Association for the Advancement of Social Work with Groups, Inc. (2013). Standards for social work practice with groups, second edition. Retrieved from www.aaswg.org/files/AASWG_Standards_for_Social_Work_Practice_with_Groups.pdf.

Atwood, J.D., & Genovese, F. (2006). *Therapy with single parents. A social constructionist approach.* New York: The Haworth Press.

Austin, M.J., & Solomon, J.R. (2009). Managing the planning process. In R.J. Patti (Ed.), *The handbook of human services management* (pp. 321–337). Thousand Oaks, CA: Sage Publications.

Bailey, S.J., Haynes, D.C., & Letiecq, B.L. (2013). "How can you retire when you still got a kid in school?": Economics of raising grandchildren in rural areas. *Marriage & Family Review, 49,* 671–693.

Banyard, V.L., Moynihan, M.M., & Plante, E.G. (2007). Sexual violence prevention through bystander education: An experimental evaluation. *Journal of Community Psychology, 35*(4), 463–481.

Barker, R.L. (2014). *The social work dictionary* (6th ed.). Washington, DC: NASW Press.

Barsky, A.E. (2010). *Ethics and values in social work.* New York: Oxford University Press.

Barth, R.P. (2013). Adoption: Overview. In C. Franklin (Ed.), *Encyclopedia of social work [E-reader version].* Washington, DC, and New York: National Association of Social Workers and Oxford University Press. DOI: 10.1093/acrefore/9780199975839.013.5

Bathgate, L. (2016). 5 practical points for social workers on interdisciplinary teams. *The New Social Worker, 23*(1), 14–15.

Bavelas, J., De Jong, P., Franklin, C., Froerer, A., Gingerich, W., Kim, J., Korman, H., Langer, S., Lee, M.Y., McCollum, E.E., Jordan, S.S., & Trepper, T.S. (2013). *Solution focused therapy treatment manual for working with individuals* (2nd ed.). Retrieved from www.sfbta.org/researchdownloads.html

Beaulaurier, R.L., & Taylor, S.H. (2007). Social work practice with people with disabilities in the era of disability rights. In A.E. Dell Orto & P.W. Power

(Eds.), *The psychological and social impact of illness and disability* (5th ed.) (pp. 53–74). New York: Springer Publishing.

Beck, J.S. (2011). *Cognitive therapy for challenging problems: What to do when the basics don't work*. New York: Guilford Press.

Benard, B., & Truebridge, S. (2013). A shift in thinking. Influencing social workers' beliefs about individual and family resilience in an effort to enhance well-being and success for all. In D. Saleebey (Ed.), *The strengths perspective in social work practice* (6th ed.) (pp. 203–220). Boston: Allyn & Bacon.

Berg, R.D., Landreth, G.L., & Fall, K.A. (2013). *Group counseling concepts and procedures* (5th ed.). New York: Routledge.

Berg-Weger, M. (2016). *Social work and social welfare. An invitation* (4th ed.). New York: Routledge.

Berg-Weger, M., Rubio, D.M., & Tebb, S. (2000). The caregiver well-being scale revisited. *Health and Social Work*, 25(4), 255–263.

Berman-Rossi, T., & Kelly, T.B. (2003). *Group composition, diversity, the skills of the social worker, and group development*. Presented at the Council for Social Work Education, Annual Meeting, Atlanta, GA, February.

Berzin, S.C., Singer, J., & Chan, C. (2015). *Practice innovation through technology in the digital age: A grand challenge for social work*. Working Paper No. 12, American Academy of Social Work and Social Welfare Grand Challenges for Social Work Initiative. Retrieved from http://aaswsw.org/grand-challenges-initiative/12-challenges/harness-technology-for-social-good/

Bliss, D.L. (2015). Using the social work advocacy practice model to find our voices in service of advocacy. *Human Service Organizations: Management, Leadership & Governance*, 39, 57–68.

Bloom, M., Fischer, J., & Orme, J.G. (2009). *Evaluating practice: Guidelines for the accountable professional* (6th ed.). Boston: Allyn & Bacon.

Blunsdon, B., & Davern, M. (2007). Measuring wellness through interdisciplinary community development: Linking the physical, economic and social environment. *Journal of Community Practice*, 15(1/2), 217–238.

Bobo, K., Kendall, J., & Max, S. (2010). *Organizing for social change*. Santa Ana, CA: The Forum Press.

Boland-Prom, K.W. (2009). Results of a national study of social workers sanctioned by state licensing boards. *Social Work*, 54(4), 351–360.

Bond, C., Woods, K., Humphrey, N., Symes, W., & Green, L. (2013). Practitioner review: The effectiveness of solution focused brief therapy with children and families: A systematic and critical evaluation of the literature from 1990–2010. *Journal of Child Psychology and Psychiatry*, 54(7), 707–723.

Bos, H.M.W., Knox, J.R., van Rijn-van Gelderen, L., & Gartrell, N.K. (2016). Same-sex and different-sex parent households and child health outcomes: Findings from the National Survey of Children's Health. *Journal of Developmental & Behavioral Pediatrics*, 37(3), 179–187.

Bowlby, J. (1982). *Attachment and loss: Vol. 1, Attachment* (2nd ed.). New York: Basic Books.

Brager, G., Specht, H., & Torczyner, J. (1987). *Community organizing*. New York: Columbia University Press.

Breton, M. (2006). An empowerment perspective. In C.D. Garvin, L.M. Gutiérrez, & M.J. Galinsky (Eds.), *Handbook of social work with groups* (pp. 58–75). New York: Guilford Press.

Briar-Lawson, K., & Naccarato, T. (2013). Family services. In C. Franklin (Ed.), *Encyclopedia of social work [E-reader version]*. Washington, DC, and New York: National Association of Social Workers and Oxford University Press. DOI: 10.1093/acrefore/9780199975839.013.145

Brill, C. (1998). The new NASW code of ethics can be your ally: Part I. Focus Newsletter. Retrieved from www.naswma.org/displaycommon.cfm?an=1&subarticlenbr=96

Briskman, L., & Noble, C. (1999). Social work ethics: Embracing diversity? In J. Fook & B. Pease (Eds.), *Transforming social work practice: Postmodern critical perspectives* (pp. 57–69). London: Routledge.

Brown, N.W. (2013). *Creative activities for group therapy*. New York: Routledge.

Brueggemann, W.G. (2013a). History and context for community practice in North America. In

M. Weil's (Ed.), *The handbook of community practice* (pp. 27–46). Thousand Oaks, CA: Sage Publications.

Brueggemann, W.G. (2013b). *The practice of macro social work* (4th ed.). Belmont, CA: Thomson Higher Education.

Brunell, J., Moray, N., Stevens, R., & Fassin, Y. (2016). Balancing competing logic in for-profit enterprises: A need for hybrid governance. *Journal of Social Entrepreneurship*, 1–26. DOI: 10.1080/19420676.2016.1166147

Bureau of Labor Statistics. (2016). Occupational outlook handbook, social workers. Retrieved from www.bls.gov/ooh/community-and-social-service/social-workers.htm#tab-1

Butler, C. (2009). Sexual and gender minority therapy and systemic practice. *Journal of Family Therapy*, *31*(4), 338–358.

Campbell, D. (2000). *The socially constructed organization.* London: Karnac Books.

Carter, L., & Matthieu, M. (2010). *Developing skills in the evidence based practice process*. St. Louis, MO: Washington University in St. Louis. Presented March 12, 2010.

Casa de Esperanza. (n.d.). History. Retrieved from https://www.casadeesperanza.org

Cattaneo, L.B., & Goodman, L.A. (2015). What is empowerment anyway? A model for domestic violence practice, research, and evaluation. *Psychology of Violence 5*(1), 84–94.

Chandler, S.M. (2013). The application of collaboration models to family group conferencing. *Journal of Policy Practice*, *12*(1), 3–22.

Chaskin, R.J. (2010). The Chicago School: A context for youth intervention, research and development. In R.J. Chaskin (Ed.), *Youth gangs and community intervention: Research, practice, and evidence* (pp. 3–23). New York: Columbia University Press.

Chaskin, R.J. (2013). Theories of community. In M. Weil's (Ed.), *The handbook of community practice* (pp. 105–121). Thousand Oaks, CA: Sage Publications.

Chee, L.P., Goh, E.C.L., & Kuczynski, L. (2014). Oversized loads: Child parentification in low-income families and underlying parent–child dynamics. *Families in Society: The Journal of Contemporary Social Services*, *95*(3), 204–212.

Chen, E.C., Budianto, L., & Wong, K. (2011). Professional school counselors as social justice advocates for undocumented immigrant students in group work. In A.A. Singh & C.F. Salazar (Eds.), *Social justice in group work. Practical interventions for change* (pp. 88–94). New York: Routledge.

Child, Youth, and Family (n.d.). *The Family Group Conference*. Retrieved from www.cyf.govt.nz/keeping-kids-safe/ways-we-work-with-families/family-group-conference-or-fgc.html

Chun-Chow, J., & Austin, M.J. (2008). The culturally responsive social service agency: The application of an evolving definition to a case study. *Administration in Social Work*, *32*(4), 39–64.

Cnaan, R.A., & Rothman, J. (2008). Capacity development and the building of community. In J. Rothman, J. Erlich, & J. Tropman (Eds.), *Strategies of community intervention* (7th ed.) (pp. 243–262). Peosta, Iowa: Eddie Bowers Publishing Co., Inc.

Coles, R.L. (2015). Single-father families: A review of the literature. *Journal of Family Theory & Review*, *7*(2), 144–166.

Collins, D., Jordan, C., & Coleman, H. (2013). *An introduction to family social work* (4th ed.). Belmont, CA: Brooks/Cole.

Collins, K.S., & Lazzari, M.M. (2009). Co-leadership. In A. Gitterman & R. Salmon (Eds.), *Encyclopedia of social work with groups* (pp. 299–302). New York: Routledge.

Comer, E., & Meier, A. (2011). Using evidence-based practice and intervention research with treatment groups for populations at risk. In G.L. Greif & P.H. Ephross (Eds.), *Group work with populations* (3rd ed.) (pp. 459–488). New York: Oxford University Press.

Congress, E.P. (2004). Cultural and ethical issues in working with culturally diverse patients and their families: The use of the culturagram to promote cultural competent practice in health care settings. In A. Metteri, T. Krôger, A. Pohjola, & P. Rauhala (Eds.), *Social work visions from around the globe* (pp. 249–262). Binghamton, NY: Haworth.

Congress, E.P. (2015). The culturagram. In K. Corcoran & A.R. Roberts (Eds.), *Social workers' desk reference*

(3rd ed.) (pp. 1011–1018). New York: Oxford University Press.

Corcoran, K. (2009). Using standardized tests and instruments in family assessments. In K. Corcoran & A.R. Roberts (Eds.), *Social workers' desk reference* (3rd ed.) (pp. 388–392). New York: Oxford University Press.

Corcoran, K. (2015). How clinical social workers can easily use rapid assessment tools (RATs) for mental health assessment and treatment evaluation. In K. Corcoran & A.R. Roberts (Eds.), *Social workers' desk reference* (3rd ed.) (pp. 358–364). New York: Oxford University Press.

Corcoran, K., & Fischer, J. (2013). *Measures for clinical practice and research: A sourcebook, Volume 1: Couples, families, and children* (5th ed.). New York: Oxford University Press.

Cordova, T.L. (2011). Community-based research and participatory change: A strategic, multi-method community impact assessment. *Journal of Community Practice, 19*(1), 29–47.

Council on Social Work Education (CSWE). (2012). Educational Policy and Accreditation Standards. Washington, DC: Author.

Council on Social Work Education (CSWE). (2015). Educational Policy and Accreditation Standards. Washington, DC: Author. Retrieved from www.cswe.org/File.aspx?id=81660

Cox, D. & Pawar, M. (2013). *International social work: Issues, strategies, and programs.* Thousand Oaks, CA: Sage Publications.

Cross, T.L. (2013). Cultural competence. In C. Franklin (Ed.), *Encyclopedia of social work.* Washington, DC, and New York: National Association of Social Workers and Oxford University Press.

Cross, T.L., Bazron, B.J., Dennis, K.W., & Isaacs, M.R. (1989). *Toward a culturally competent system of care.* Washington, DC: Georgetown University Development Center.

Cummings, T.G., & Worley, C.G. (2014). *Organizational development and change* (10th ed.). Mason, OH: South-Western Cengage Learning.

De Jong, P. (2009). Solution-focused therapy. In K. Corcoran & A.R. Roberts (Eds.), *Social workers' desk*

reference (3rd ed.) (pp. 268–275). New York: Oxford University Press.

De Jong, P. (2013). Interviewing. In C. Franklin (Ed.), *Encyclopedia of social work [E-reader version].* Washington, DC, and New York: National Association of Social Workers and Oxford University. DOI: 10.1093/acrefore/978019975839.013.209

De Jong, P. (2015). Solution-focused therapy. In K. Corcoran & A.R. Roberts (Eds.), *Social workers' desk reference* (3rd ed.) (pp. 268–274). New York: Oxford University Press.

De Jong, P., & Berg, I.K. (2013). *Interviewing for solutions* (4th ed.). Belmont, CA: Brooks/Cole.

De Jong, P., & Cronkright, A. (2011). Learning solution-focused interviewing skills: BSW student voices. *Journal of Teaching in Social Work, 31*, 21–37.

DeFrain, J., & Asay, S.M. (2007). Epilogue: A strengths-based conceptual framework for understanding families worldwide. In J. DeFrain & S.M. Asay (Eds.), *Strong families around the world: Strengths-based research and perspectives* (pp. 447–466). New York: Haworth Press, Inc.

DeNavas-Walt, C., & Proctor, B.D. (2015). U.S. Census Bureau, Current Population Reports, P60-252, *Income and Poverty in the United States: 2014*, U.S. Government Printing Office, Washington, DC.

deShazer, S. (1984). The death of resistance. *Family Process, 23*, 11–21.

Detroit Food Policy Council. (2016). The DFPC is. . . Retrieved from http://detroitfoodpolicycouncil.net/

Diller, J.V. (2015). *Cultural diversity: A primer for the human services* (5th ed.). Stamford, CT: Cengage Learning.

Doel, M., & Kelly, T.B. (2014). *A-Z of groups & groupwork.* New York: Palgrave Macmillan.

Dolgoff, R., Harrington, D., & Loewenberg, F.M. (2012). *Ethical decisions for social work practice.* Itasca, IL: F.E. Peacock.

Dombo, E.A. (2011). Rape: When professional values place vulnerable clients at risk. In J.C. Rothman (Ed.), *From the front lines: Student cases in social work ethics* (3rd ed.) (pp. 185–188). Boston: Allyn & Bacon.

Dominelli, L. (2014). Promoting environmental justice through green social work practice: A key challenge for practitioners and educators. *International Social Work*, *57*(4), 338–345. DOI: 10.1177/0020872814524968

Donaldson, L.P. (2004). Toward validating the therapeutic benefits of empowerment-oriented social action groups. *Social Work with Groups*, *27*(2), 159–175.

Dressler, L. (2006). *Consensus through conversation*. San Francisco, CA: Berrett-Koehler Publishers, Inc.

Dudley, J.R. (2014). *Social work evaluation: Enhancing what we do* (2nd ed.). Chicago: Lyceum Books, Inc.

Dudziak, S., & Profitt, N.J. (2012). Group work and social justice: Designing pedagogy for social change. *Social Work with Groups*, *35*, 235–252.

Dunst, C.J., & Trivette, C.M. (2009). Capacity-building family-systems intervention practices. *Journal of Family Social Work*, *12*, 119–143.

Dunst, C.J., Trivette, C.M., & Deal, A.G. (2003). *Enabling and empowering families: Principles and guidelines for practice*. Newton, MA: Brookline Books.

Dybicz, P. (2015). From person-in-environment to strengths: The promise of postmodern practice. *Journal of Social Work Education*, *51*(2), 237–249.

Early, T.J., & Newsome, W.S. (2005). Measures for assessment and accountability in practice with families from a strengths perspective. In. J. Corcoran (Ed.), *Building strength and skills. A collaborative approach to working with clients* (pp. 359–393). New York: Oxford University Press.

East, J.F., & Roll, S.J. (2015). Women, poverty and trauma: An empowerment practice approach. *Social Work*, *60*(4): 279–286.

Eaton, Y.M., & Roberts, A.R. (2009). Frontline crisis intervention. Step-by-step practice guidelines with case applications. In A.R. Roberts (Ed.), *Social workers' desk reference* (2nd ed.) (pp. 207–215). New York: Oxford University Press.

Eaton-Shull, Y.M. (2015). Crisis intervention with individuals and groups: Frameworks to guide social workers. In K. Corcoran & A.R. Roberts (Eds.), *Social workers' desk reference* (3rd ed.) (pp. 217–222). New York: Oxford University Press.

Edleson, J.L., Lindhorst, T., & Kanuha, V.K. (2015). *Ending gender-based violence: A grand challenge for social work*. Working Paper No. 10, American Academy of Social Work and Social Welfare Grand Challenges for Social Work Initiative. Retrieved from http://aaswsw.org/grand-challenges-initiative/12-challenges/stop-family-violence/

Edwards, R.L., & Yankey, J.A. (2006). *Effectively managing nonprofit organizations*. Washington, DC: NASW Press.

Ellis, R.R., & Simmons, T. (2014). Coresident grandparents and their grandchildren: 2012. Washington, DC: Current Population Reports, P20-576, U.S. Census Bureau,

Ephross, P.H. (2011). Social work with groups: Practice principles. In G.L. Grief & P.H. Ephross (Eds.), *Group work with populations at risk* (3rd ed.) (pp. 3–14). New York: Oxford University Press.

Epstein, M.H. (2004). *Behavioral and emotional rating scale: A strengths-based approach to assessment* (2nd ed.). Austin, TX: PRO-ED.

Epstein, M.H., Mooney, P., Ryser, G., & Pierce, C.D. (2004). Validity and reliability of the Behavioral and Emotional Rating Scale (2nd edition): Youth Rating Scale. *Research on Social Work Practice*, *14*(50), 358–367.

Evans, S.D., Hanlin, C.E., & Prillehensky, I. (2007). Blending ameliorative and (transformative approaches in human service organizations: A case study. *Journal of Community Psychology*, *35*(3), 329–346.

Falicov, C.J. (2013). *Latino families in therapy*. New York: Guilford Publications.

Family Resource Center. (2016). Redevelopment Opportunities for Women. Retrieved from https://www.frcmo.org/services/row/

Fetherman, D.L., & Burke, S.C. (2014). Using community-based participatory research to advocate for homeless children. *Social Work in Public Health*, *31*(1), 30–37.

Finlayson, M.L., & Cho, C.C. (2011). A profile of support group use and need among middle-aged and older adults with multiple sclerosis. *Journal of Gerontological Social Work*, *54*, 475–493.

Fischer, J., & Orme, J.G. (2013). Single-system designs. In C. Franklin (Ed.), *Encyclopedia of social work [E-reader version]*. Washington, DC, and New York: National Association of Social Workers and Oxford University Press. DOI: 10.1093/acrefore/9780199975839.013.360

Fleming, J. (2009). Social action. In A. Gitterman & R. Salmon (Eds.), *Encyclopedia of social work with groups* (pp. 275–277). New York: Routledge.

Floersch, J. (2013). Social work practice: Theoretical base. In C. Franklin (Ed.), *Encyclopedia of social work [E-reader version]*. Washington, DC, and New York: National Association of Social Workers and Oxford University Press. DOI:10.1093/acrefore/9780199975839.013.621

Fook, J., & Pease, B. (Eds.). (2016). *Transforming social work practice: Postmodern critical perspectives*. New York: Routledge.

Fortune, A.E. (2015). Terminating with clients. In K. Corcoran & A.R. Roberts (Eds.), *Social workers' desk reference* (3rd ed.) (pp. 697–704). New York: Oxford University Press.

Franklin, C., Jordan, C., & Hopson, L.M. (2015). Effective couple and family treatment. In K. Corcoran & A.R. Roberts (Eds.), *Social workers' desk reference* (3rd ed.) (pp. 438–447). New York: Oxford University Press.

Freedenthal, S. (2013). Suicide. In C. Franklin (Ed.), *Encyclopedia of social work [E-reader version]*. Washington, DC, and New York: National Association of Social Workers and Oxford University Press. DOI: 10.1093/acrefore/9780199975839.013.137

Freire, P. (1973). *Education for critical consciousness*. New York: Seabury Press.

Fruhauf, C.A., & Hayslip, B. (2013). Understanding collaborative efforts to assist grandparent caregivers: A multileveled perspective. *Journal of Family Social Work, 16*(5), 382–391.

Furman, R., Bender, K., & Rowan, D. (2014). *An experiential approach to group work* (2nd ed.). Chicago: Lyceum Books, Inc.

Gamble, D.N., & Hoff, M.D. (2013). Sustainable community development. In M. Weil (Ed.), *The handbook of community practice* (pp. 215–232). Thousand Oaks, CA: Sage Publications.

Gambrill, E. (2013). *Social work practice: A critical thinker's guide*. New York: Oxford University Press.

Garkovich, L.E. (2011). A historical view of community development. In J.W. Robinson, Jr., & G.P. Green (Eds.), *Introduction to community development* (pp. 11–34). Los Angeles, CA: Sage Publications.

Garland, J., Jones, H., & Kolodny, R. (1965). A model for stages of development in social work groups. In S. Bernstein (Ed.), *Explorations in group work: Essays in theory and practice* (pp. 12–53). Boston: Boston University School of Social Work.

Garvin, C.D. (2015). Developing goals. In K. Corcoran & A.R. Roberts (Eds.), *Social workers' desk reference* (3rd ed.) (pp. 560–565). New York: Oxford University Press.

Garvin, C.D., & Galinsky, M.J. (2013). Groups. In C. Franklin (Ed.), *Encyclopedia of social work [E-reader version]*. Washington, DC, and New York: National Association of Social Workers and Oxford University Press. DOI: 10.1093/acrefore/9780199975839.013.167

Gibson, D.M. (2013). Ambiguous roles in a stepfamily: Using maps of narrative practices to develop a new family story with adolescents and parents. *Contemporary Family Therapy, 35*, 793–805.

Gilligan, C. (1993). *In a different voice*. Cambridge, MA: Harvard University Press.

Gitterman, A., & Germain, C.B. (2008). *The life model of social work practice: Advances in theory and practice* (3rd ed). New York: Columbia Press.

Gitterman, A., & Germain, C.B. (2013). Ecological framework. In C. Franklin (Ed.), *Encyclopedia of social work [E-reader version]*. Washington, DC, and New York: National Association of Social Workers and Oxford University Press. DOI: 10.1093/acrefore/9780199975839.013.118

GLAAD. (2014). Accelerating acceptance. Retrieved from www.glaad.org/publications/glaad-accelerating-acceptance

Goldbach, J., Amaro, H., Vega, W., & Walter, M.D. (2015). *The Grand Challenge of promoting equality by addressing social stigma. Grand Challenges for Social Work Initiative*. Working Paper No. 18. Washington, DC: American Academy of Social Work and Social Welfare. Retrieved from http://aaswsw.org/

wp-content/uploads/2016/01/W16-The-Grand-Challenge-of-Promoting-Equality-by-Addressing-Social-Stigma1-1-2.pdf

Goldberg, A.E., & Allen, K.R. (2013). *LGBT-parent families. Innovations in research and implications for practice.* New York: Springer.

Gonzáles-Prendes, A.A., & Brisebois, K. (2012). Cognitive-behavioral therapy and social work values: A critical analysis. *Journal of Social Work Values & Ethics, 9*(2), 2–21.

Goodman, H. (2004). Elderly parents of adults with severe mental illness: Group work interventions. *Journal of Gerontological Social Work, 44*(1/2), 173–188.

Grace, K.S., McClellan, A., & Yankey, J.A. (2009). The nonprofit board's role in mission, planning and evaluation. Washington, DC: BoardSource.

Grady, M., & Drisko, J.W. (2014). Thorough clinical assessment: The hidden foundation of evidence-based practice. *Families in Society: The Journal of Contemporary Social Service, 95*(1), 1–10. DOI: 10.1606/1044-3894.2014.95.2

Grant, D. (2013). Clinical social work. In C. Franklin (Ed.), *Encyclopedia of social work [E-reader version].* Washington, DC, and New York: National Association of Social Workers and Oxford University Press. DOI: 10.1093/acrefore/9780199975839.013.63

Gray, M. (2011). Back to basics: A critique of the strengths perspective in social work. *Families in Society: The Journal of Contemporary Social Services, 92*(1), 5–11.

Greene, G.J., & Lee, M.Y. (2011). *Solution-oriented social work practice.* New York: Oxford University Press.

Greenpeace. (n.d.). About us. Retrieved from www.greenpeace.org/usa/what-we-do/

Gregg, B. (2012). *Human rights as a social construction.* New York: Oxford University Press.

Greif, G., & Ephross, P.H. (Eds.). (2011). *Group work with populations at risk* (3rd ed.). New York: Oxford University Press.

Grief, G.L., & Morris-Compton, D. (2011). Group work with urban African American parents in their neighborhood schools. In G.L. Grief & P.H.

Ephross (Eds.), *Group work with populations at risk* (3rd ed.) (pp. 385–398). New York: Oxford University Press.

Gumz, E., & Grant, C. (2009). Restorative justice: A systematic review of the social work literature. *Families in Society: The Journal of Contemporary Social Services, 90*(1), 119–126.

Hahn, S.A., & Scanlon, E. (2016). The integration of micro and macro practice: A qualitative study of clinical social workers' practice with domestic violence survivors. *Affilia: Journal of Women and Social Work, 31*(3), 331–343.

Hall, J.C. (2011). A narrative approach to group work with men who batter. *Social Work with Groups, 34,* 175–189.

Hamilton, B.E., Martin, J.A., Osterman, M.J.K., Curtin, S.C., & Mathews, T.J. (2015). *Births: Final data for 2014.* Hyattsville, MD: National Vital Statistics Reports, 64(12). Retrieved from www.cdc.gov/nchs/data/nvsr/nvsr64/nvsr64_12.pdf

Hanley, J., & Shragge, E. (2009). Organizing for immigrant rights. *Journal of Community Practice, 17*(1), 184–206.

Hardina, D. (2002). *Analytical skills for community organization practice.* New York: Columbia University Press.

Hardina, D. (2013). *Interpersonal social work skills for community practice.* New York: Springer.

Hardina, D., Middleton, J., Montana, S., & Simpson, R.A. (2007). *An empowering approach to managing social service organizations.* New York: Springer Publishing Company.

Hardy, K.V., & Laszloffy, T.A. (1995). The cultural genogram: Key to training culturally competent family therapists. *Journal of Marital and Family Therapy, 21,* 227–237.

Harr, C.R., Brice, T.S., Riley, K., & Moore, M. (2014). The impact of compassion fatigue and compassion satisfaction on social work students. *Journal of the Society for Social Work and Research, 5*(2), 233–251.

Harrington, D., & Dolgoff, R. (2008). Hierarchies of ethical principles for ethical decision making in social work. *Ethics and Social Welfare, 2*(2), 183–196.

Hartman, A. (1994). *Reflection & controversy: Essays on social work.* Washington, DC: NASW Press.

Hartman, A., & Laird, J. (1983). Family-centered social work practice. New York: Free Press.

Harvey, A.R. (2011). Group work with African American youth in the criminal justice system: A culturally competent model. In G.L. Grief & P.H. Ephross (Eds.), *Group work with populations at risk* (3rd ed.) (pp. 264–282). New York: Oxford University Press.

Hasenfeld, Y. (2000). Social welfare administration and organizational theory. In R.J. Patti (Ed.), *The handbook of social welfare management* (pp. 89–112). Thousand Oaks, CA: Sage Publications.

Hawkins, J.D., Jenson, J.M., Catalano, R.F., Fraser, M.W., Botvin, G.J., Shapiro, V., Bender, K.A., Brown, C.H., Beardslee, W., Brent, D., Leslie, L.K., Rotheram-Borus, M.J., Shea, P., Shih, A., Anthony, E.K., Haggerty, K.P., Gorman-Smith, D., Casey, E., Stone, S., & the Coalition for Behavioral Health. (2015). *Unleashing the power of prevention.* Working Paper No. 10, American Academy of Social Work and Social Welfare Grand Challenges for Social Work Initiative. Retrieved from http://aaswsw.org/grand-challenges-initiative/12-challenges/ensure-healthy-development-for-all-youth/

Haynes, K.S., & Mickelson, J.S. (2010). *Affecting change* (7th ed.). Boston: Pearson.

Head, J.W. (2008). *Losing the global development war.* Leiden, The Netherlands: Martinus Nijhoff Publishers.

Healy, L.M. (2008). *International social work: Professional practice in an interdependent world.* New York: Oxford University Press.

Healy, L.M. (2013). International social work: An overview. In C. Franklin (Ed.), *Encyclopedia of social work [E-reader version].* Washington, DC, and New York: National Association of Social Workers and Oxford University Press. DOI: 10.1093/acrefore/9780199975839.013.137

Healy, L.M., & Link, R.J. (2012). *Handbook of international social work: Human rights, development, and the global profession.* New York: Oxford.

Henriksen, R.C., & Maxwell, M.J. (2016). Counseling the fastest growing population in America: Those with multiple heritage backgrounds. *Journal of Mental Health Counseling, 38*(1), 1–11.

Henwood, B.F., Wenzel, S.L., Mangano, P.F., Hombs, M., Padgett, D.K., Byrne, T., Rice, E., Butts, S.C., &

Uretsky, M.C. (2015). *The grand challenge of ending homelessness.* Working Paper No. 9, American Academy of Social Work and Social Welfare Grand Challenges for Social Work Initiative. Retrieved from http://aaswsw.org/grand-challenges-initiative/12-challenges/end-homelessness/

Herbert, R.J., Gagnon, A.J., Rennick, J.E., & O'Loughlin, J.L. (2009). A systematic review of questionnaires measuring health-related empowerment. *Research and Theory for Nursing Practice: An International Journal, 23*(2), 107–132.

Hillier, A., & Culhane, D. (2013). GIS applications and administrative data to support community change. In M. Weil's (Ed.), *The handbook of community practice* (pp. 827–844). Thousand Oaks, CA: Sage Publications.

Hodge, D.R. (2005a). Social work and the House of Islam: Orienting practitioners to the beliefs and values of Muslims in the United States. *Social Work, 50*(20) 162–173.

Hodge, D.R. (2005b). Spiritual life maps: A client centered pictorial instrument for spiritual assessment, planning, and intervention. *Social Work, 50*(1), 77–87.

Hodge, D.R. (2013). Implicit spiritual assessment: An alternative approach for assessing client spirituality. *Social Work, 58*(3), 223–230.

Hodgson, J.L., Lamson, A.L., & Kolobova, I. (2016). A biopsychosocial-spiritual assessment in brief or extended couple therapy formats. In G.R. Weeks, S.T. Fife, & C.M. Person (Eds.), *Techniques for the couple therapist: Essential interventions from the experts* (pp. 213–217). New York: Routledge.

Hohman, M. (2012). *Motivational interviewing in social work practice.* New York: The Guilford Press.

Hohman, M., Pierce, P., & Barnett, E. (2015). Motivational interviewing: An evidence-based practice for improving student practice skills. *Journal of Social Work Education, 51*(2), 287–297.

Holland, T. (2013). Organizations and governance. In C. Franklin (Ed.), *Encyclopedia of social work [E-reader version].* Washington, DC, and New York: National Association of Social Workers and Oxford University Press. DOI: 10.1093/acrefore/9780199975839.013.275

Holland, T.P., & Kilpatrick, A.C. (2009). An ecological system—social constructionism approach to family practice. In A.C. Kilpatrick & T.P. Holland (Eds.), *Working with families. An integrative model by level of need* (5th ed.) (pp. 15–31). Boston: Pearson.

Hong, P.Y., & Song, I.H. (2010). Globalization of social work practice: Global and local responses to globalization. *International Social Work, 53,* 656–670.

Hudson, R.E. (2009). Empowerment model. In A. Gitterman & R. Salmon (Eds.), *Encyclopedia of social work with groups* (pp. 47–50). New York: Routledge.

Hull, G.H., & Mather, J. (2006). *Understanding generalist practice with families.* Belmont, CA: Thomson Brooks/Cole.

Human Rights Education Association (n.d.). Simplified version of the University Declaration of Human Rights. Retrieved from www.hrea.org/index.php?base_id=104&language_id=1&erc_doc_id=5211&category_id=24&category_type=3&group=

Ife, J. (2012). *Human rights and social work: Towards rights-based practice.* New York: Cambridge University Press.

Institute for Healthcare Improvement (IHI). (2016). Person-and family-centered care. Retrieved from www.ihi.org/Topics/PFCC/Pages/Overview.aspx

International Association for Social Work with Groups, Inc. (IASWG) (2015). *Standards for social work practice with groups* (2nd ed.). New York: IASWG, Inc. Retrieved from www.iaswg.org/standards

International Federation of Social Workers and the International Association of Schools of Social Work (IFSW & IASW). (2012). Statement of ethical principles. Retrieved from http://ifsw.org/policies/statement-of-ethical-principles/

International Institute St. Louis. (2016). Economic development. Retrieved from www.iistl.org/edintro.html

International Labor Rights Forum. (n.d.). Workers around the world face serious threats for democratically organizing – an internationally recognized freedom. Retrieved from www.laborrights.org/issues/right-organize-bargain

Interorganizational Committee on Guidelines and Principles for Social Impact Assessment (IOCPG). (2003). Principles and guidelines for social impact assessment in the United States. *Impact Assessment and Project Appraisal, 21*(3), 231–250.

Iowa State University Extension and Outreach. (2016). Needs assessment strategies for community groups and organizations. Retrieved from www.extension.iastate.edu/communities/assess

Jackson, K.F., & Samuels, G.M. (2011). Multiracial competence in social work: Recommendation for culturally attuned work with multiracial people. *Social Work, 56*(3), 235–245.

Jankowski, P.J., Hooper, L.M., Sandage, S.J., & Hannah, N.J. (2013). Parentification and mental health symptoms: Mediator effects of perceived unfairness and differentiation of self. *Journal of Family Therapy, 35,* 43–65.

Janzen, C., Harris, O., Jordan, C., & Franklin, C. (2006). Family treatment: Evidence-based practice with populations at risk. Belmont, CA: Thomson Brooks/ Cole.

Jenson, J.M., & Howard, M.O. (2013). Evidence-based practice. In C. Franklin (Ed.), *Encyclopedia of social work [E-reader version].* Washington, DC, and New York: National Association of Social Workers and Oxford University Press. DOI: 10.1093/acrefore/9780199975839.013.137

Johnson, S.K., von Sternberg, K., & Velasquez, M.M. (2015). Motivational interviewing. In K. Corcoran & A.R. Roberts (Eds.), *Social workers' desk reference* (3rd ed.) (pp. 684–691). New York: Oxford University Press.

Joplin Area CART. (n.d.). Joplin Area CART. Retrieved from https://www.facebook.com/JoplinAreaCART

Jordan, C., & Franklin, C. (2013). Assessment. In C. Franklin (Ed.), *Encyclopedia of social work [E-reader version].* Washington, DC, and New York: National Association of Social Workers and Oxford University Press. DOI: 10.1093/acrefore/978019997583 9.013.137

Jordan, C., Franklin, C., & Johnson, S.K. (2015). Treatment planning with families: An evidence-based approach. In K. Corcoran & A.R. Roberts (Eds.), *Social workers' desk reference* (3rd ed.) (pp. 433–438). New York: Oxford University Press.

Jung, M. (1996). Family-centered practice with single parent families. *Families in Society, 77*(9), 583–590.

Kagle, J.D. (2013). Recording. In C. Franklin (Ed.), *Encyclopedia of social work [E-reader version]*. Washington, DC, and New York: National Association of Social Workers and Oxford University Press. DOI: 10.1093/acrefore/9780199975839.013.33.

Kagle, J.D., & Kopels, S. (2008). *Social work records* (3rd ed.). Long Grove, IL: Waveland Press, Inc.

Kalyanpur, M., & Harry, B. (2012). Cultural reciprocity in special education. Building family-professional relationships. Baltimore, MD: Brookes Publishing Company.

Kasvin, N., & Tashayeva, A. (2004). Community organizing to address domestic violence in immigrant populations in the U.S.A. *Journal of Religion and Abuse, 6*(3/4), 109–112.

Kaye, M. (1980). *We speak in code: Poems & other writings*. Pittsburgh, PA: Motheroot Publications.

Kelley, P. (2013). Narratives. In C. Franklin (Ed.), *Encyclopedia of social work [E-reader version]*. Washington, DC, and New York: National Association of Social Workers and Oxford University Press. DOI: 10.1093/acrefore/9780199975839.013.259

Kelley, P., & Smith, M. (2015). Narrative therapy. In K. Corcoran & A.R. Roberts (Eds.), *Social workers' desk reference* (3rd ed.) (pp. 287–292). New York: Oxford University Press.

Kelly, M.S., Kim, J.S., & Franklin, C. (2008). Solution-focused brief therapy in schools. A 360-degree view of research and practice. New York: Oxford University Press.

Kelly, T.B., Lowndes, A., & Tolson, D. (2005). Advancing stages of group development: The case of virtual nursing community of practice groups. *Groupwork, 15*(2), 17–38.

Kemp, S.P., & Palinkas, L.A. (2016). *Strengthening the social response to the human impacts of environmental change*. Working Paper No. 5, American Academy of Social Work and Social Welfare. Retrieved from http://aaswsw.org/wp-content/uploads/2015/12/WP5-with-cover.pdf

Kettner, P.M. (2002). *Achieving excellence in the management of human service organizations*. Boston: Allyn & Bacon.

Kilpatrick, A.C. (2009). Levels of family need. In A.C. Kilpatrick & T.P. Holland (Eds.), *Working with families. An integrative model by level of need* (5th ed.) (pp. 2–14). Boston: Pearson.

Kilpatrick, A.C., & Cleveland, P. (1993). Unpublished course materials. University of Georgia School of Social Work.

Kim, A., & Barak, M.E.M. (2015). The mediating roles of leader–member exchange and perceived organizational support in the role stress–turnover intention relationship among child welfare workers: A longitudinal analysis. *Children & Youth Services Review 52*, 135–143.

Kim, H., & Hopkins, K.M. (2015). Child welfare workers' personal safety concerns and organizational commitment: The moderating role of social support. *Human Service Organizations: Management, Leadership & Governance, 39*, 101–115.

Kim, H., Ji, J, & Kao, D. (2011). Burnout and physical health among social workers: A three-year longitudinal study. *Social Work, 56*(3), 258–268.

Kim, J.S. (2013). Strengths perspective. In C. Franklin (Ed.), *Encyclopedia of social work [E-reader version]*. Washington, DC, and New York: National Association of Social Workers and Oxford University Press. DOI: 10.1093/acrefore/9780199975839.013.382

Kingsley, G.T., Coulton, C.J., & Pettit, K.L. (2014). *Strengthening communities with neighborhood data*. Washington, DC: Urban Institute.

Kisthardt, W.E. (2013). Integrating the core competencies in strengths-based, person-centered practice. In D. Saleebey (Ed.), *The strengths perspective in social work practice* (6th ed.), pp. 53–78. Boston: Allyn & Bacon.

Kleinkauf, C. (1981). A guide to giving legislative testimony. *Social Work* (July), 297–303.

Kneebone, E., & Holmes, N. (2016). U.S. concentrated poverty in the wake of the Great Recession. Washington, DC: Brookings Institution. Retrieved from www.brookings.edu/research/reports2/2016/03/31-concentrated-poverty-recession-kneebone-holmes

Knight, C. (2012). Social workers' attitudes towards engagement in self-disclosure. *Clinical Social Work Journal, 40,* 297–306.

Kohli, H.K., Huber, R., & Faul, A.C. (2010). Historical and theoretical development of culturally competent social work practice. *Journal of Teaching in Social Work, 30,* 252–271.

Koop, J.J. (2009). Solution-focused family interventions. In A.C. Kilpatrick & T.P. Holland (Eds.), *Working with families. An integrative model by level of need* (5th ed.) (pp. 147–169). Boston: Pearson.

Koren, P.E., DeChillo, N., & Friesen, B.J. (1992). Measuring empowerment in families whose children have emotional disabilities: A brief questionnaire. *Rehabilitation Psychology, 37,* 305–310.

Kresak, K.E., Gallagher, P.A., & Kelley, S.J. (2014). Grandmothers raising grandchildren with disabilities: Sources of support and family quality of life. *Journal of Early Intervention, 36*(1), 3–17.

Kretzmann, J. P. & McKnight, J. L. (1993). *Building communities from the inside out: A path toward finding and mobilizing a community's assets.* Evanston, IL: Center for Urban Affairs and Policy Research.

Kretzmann, J. P., McKnight, J., & Puntenney, D. (2005). *Discovering community power: A guide to mobilizing local assets and your organization's capacity.* Chicago, IL: Asset-Based Community Development Institute, School of Education and Social Policy, Northwestern University.

Kurland, R. (2007). Debunking the "blood theory" of social work with groups: Group workers are made and not born. *Social Work with Groups, 31*(1), 11–24.

Kurland, R., & Salmon, R. (1998). *Teaching a methods course in social work with groups.* Alexandria, VA: Council on Social Work Education.

Kurland, R., Salmon, R., Bitel, M., Goodman, H., Ludwig, K., Newmann, E.W., & Sullivan, N. (2004). The survival of social group work: *A call to action. Social Work with Groups, 27*(1), 3–16.

Larson, K., & McGuiston, C. (2012). Building capacity to improve Latino health in rural North Carolina: A case study in community-university engagement. *Journal of Community Engagement and Scholarship, 5*(1), 14–23.

Laurio, A. (2016). A grand challenge for social work: Isolation seen as a critical social problem. *NASW News, 61*(6), 7, 9.

Leahy, M.M., O'Dwyer, M., & Ryan, F. (2012). Witnessing stories: Definitional ceremonies in narrative therapy with adults who stutter. *Journal of Fluency Disorders, 37,* 234–241.

Lee, M.Y. (2015). The miracle question and scaling questions for solution-building and empowerment. In K. Corcoran & A.R. Roberts (Eds.), *Social workers' desk reference* (3rd ed.) (pp. 308–316). New York: Oxford University Press.

Lee, M.Y., & Greene, G.J. (2009). Using social constructivism in social work practice. In A.R. Roberts (Ed.), *Social workers' desk reference* (2nd ed.) (pp. 294–299). New York: Oxford University Press.

Lein, L., Romich, J.L., & Sherraden, M. (2015). *Reversing extreme inequality. Grand Challenges for Social Work Initiative.* Working Paper No. 16. Washington, DC: American Academy of Social Work and Social Welfare. Retrieved from http://aaswsw.org/wp-content/uploads/2016/01/WP16-with-cover-2.pdf

Lesser, J.G., O'Neill, M.R., Burke, K.W., Scanlon, P., Hollis, K., & Miller, R. (2004). Women supporting women: A mutual aid group fosters new connections among women in midlife. *Social Work with Groups, 27*(1), 75–88.

Levy, R. (2011). Core themes in a support group for spouses of breast cancer patients. *Social Work with Groups, 34,* 141–157.

Libal, K.R., & Harding, S. (2015). *Human rights-based community practice in the United States.* SpringerBriefs in Rights-Based Approaches to Social Work. New York: Springer.

Life Crisis Services. (n.d.) Suicide Assessment. St. Louis, MO: Author.

Locke, B., Garrison, R., & Winship, J. (1998). *Generalist social work practice: Context, story, and partnerships.* Pacific Grove, CA: Brooks/Cole.

Logan, S.L.M. (2013). Family: Overview. In C. Franklin (Ed.), *Encyclopedia of social work [E-reader version].* Washington, DC, and New York: National Association of Social Workers and Oxford

University Press. DOI: 10.1093/acrefore/9780199975839.013.545

López, L.M., & Vargas, E.M. (2011). En dos culturas: Group work with Latino immigrants and refugees. In G.L. Greif & P.H. Ephross (Eds.), *Group work with populations at risk* (3rd ed.) (pp. 144–145). New York: Oxford University Press.

Lotze, G.M., Bellin, M.H., & Oswald, D.P. (2010). Family-centered care for children with special healthcare needs: Are we moving forward? *Journal of Family Social Work, 13*, 100–113.

Lubben, J., Gironda, M., Sabbath, E., Kong, J., & Johnson, C. (2015). *Social isolation presents a grand challenge for social work*. Working Paper No. 7, American Academy of Social Work and Social Welfare Grand Challenges for Social Work Initiative. Retrieved from http://aaswsw.org/grand-challenges-initiative/12-challenges/eradicate-social-isolation/

Lum, D. (2004). *Social work practice and people of color: A process stage approach* (5th ed.). Belmont, CA: Thomson Brooks/Cole.

Lum, D. (2011). *Culturally competent practice: A framework for understanding diverse groups and justice issues.* Belmont, CA: Brooks/Cole Cengage Learning.

Lum, D. (2013). Culturally competent practice. In C. Franklin (Ed.), *Encyclopedia of social work [E-reader version]*. Washington, DC, and New York: National Association of Social Workers and Oxford University Press. DOI: 10.1093/acrefore/9780199975839.013.137

Lundahl, B.W., Kunz, C., Brownell, C., Tollefson, D., & Burke, B.L. (2010). A meta-analysis of motivational interviewing: Twenty-five years of empirical studies. *Research on Social Work Practice, 20*(2), 137–160.

Lundy, C. (2011). *Social work, social justice, and human rights: A structural approach to practice.* North York, ON: University of Toronto Press.

MacDonald, S-A. (2016). Attempting to engage in "ethical" research with homeless youth. *Intersectionalities: A Global Journal of Social Work Analysis, Research, Polity and Practice, 5*(1), 126–150.

Macgowan, M.J. (1997). A measure of engagement for social group work: The Groupwork Engagement Measure (GEM). *Journal of Social Service Research, 23*, 17–37.

Macgowan, M.J. (2000). Evaluation of a measure of engagement for group work. *Research on Social Work Practice, 10*, 348–361.

Macgowan, M.J. (2006). The group engagement measure. A review of its conceptual and empirical properties. *Journal of Groups in Addiction & Recovery, 1*(2), 33–52.

Macgowan, M.J. (2009a). Evidence-based group work. In A. Gitterman & R. Salmon (Eds.), *Encyclopedia of social work with groups* (pp. 131–136). New York: Routledge.

Macgowan, M.J. (2009b). Measurement. In A. Gitterman & R. Salmon (Eds.), *Encyclopedia of social work with groups* (pp. 142–147). New York: Routledge.

Macgowan, M.J. (2013). Group dynamics. In C. Franklin (Ed.), *Encyclopedia of social work [E-reader version]*. Washington, DC, and New York: National Association of Social Workers and Oxford University Press. DOI: 10.1093/acrefore/9780199975839.013.166

Macgowan, M.J., & Hanbidge, A.S. (2015). Best practices in social work with groups. In K. Corcoran & A.R. Roberts (Eds.), *Social workers' desk reference* (3rd ed.) (pp. 734–745). New York: Oxford University Press.

Macgowan, M.J., & Levenson, J.S. (2003). Psychometrics of the Group Engagement Measure with male sex offenders. *Small Group Research, 34*(2), 155–169.

Macgowan, M.J., & Newman, F.L. (2005). Factor structure of the Group Engagement Measure. *Social Work Research, 29*(2), 107–118.

Mackelprang, R.W., & Salsgiver, R.O. (2015). *Disability: A diversity model approach in human service practice* (3rd ed). Chicago: Lyceum Books, Inc.

Madigan, S. (2011). *Narrative therapy*. Washington, DC: The American Psychological Association.

Mallon, G.P. (2014). Lesbian, gay, bisexual, and transgender (LGBT) families and parenting. In C. Franklin (Ed.), *Encyclopedia of social work [E-reader version]*. Washington, DC, and New York: National Association of Social Workers and Oxford

University Press. DOI: 10.1093/acrefore/9780199975839.013.158

Malmstrom, T.K., & Morley, J.E. (2013). Frailty and cognition: Linking two common syndromes in older persons. *Journal of Nutrition, Health, & Aging, 17*, 723–725.

Manning, T. (2012). The art of successful persuasion: Seven skills you need to get your point across effectively. *Industrial and Commercial Training, 44*(3), 150–158.

Manning, W.D., Brown, S.L., & Stykes, J.B. (2014). Family complexity among children in the United States. *Annals of American Academic Political Social Science, 654*(1), 48–65.

Manor, O. (2009). Systemic approach. In A. Gitterman & R. Salmon (Eds.), *Encyclopedia of social work with groups* (pp. 99–101). New York: Routledge.

Maramaldi, P., Berkman, B., & Barusch, A. (2005). Assessment and the ubiquity of culture: Threats to validity in measures of health-related quality of life. *Health & Social Work, 30*(1), 27–36.

Marguerite Casey Foundation. (2012). Organizational capacity assessment tool. Retrieved from http://caseygrants.org/resources/org-capacity-assessment/

Mason, J.L. (1995). Cultural competence self-assessment questionnaire: A manual for users. Portland, OR: Portland State University, Research and Training Center on Family Support and Children's Mental Health. Retrieved from www.racialequitytools.org/ resourcefiles/mason.pdf

McCullough-Chavis, A., & Waites, C. (2008). Genograms with African American families: Considering cultural context. In C.Waites (Ed.), *Social work practice with African-American families: An intergenerational perspective* (pp. 35–54). New York: Routledge.

McGeorge, C.R., & Carlson, T.S. (2011). Deconstructing heterosexism: Becoming an LGB affirmative heterosexual couple and family therapist. *Journal of Marital and Family Therapy, 37*, 14–26. DOI: 10.1111/j.1752-0606.2009.00149.x

McGoldrick, M. (2015). Using genograms to map family patterns. In K. Corcoran & A.R. Roberts (Eds.), *Social workers' desk reference* (3rd ed.)

(pp. 413–426). New York: Oxford University Press.

McGoldrick, M., Gerson, R., & Petry, S. (2008). *Genograms assessment and intervention* (3rd ed.). New York: W.W. Norton & Company.

McGowan, B.G., & Walsh, E.M. (2012). Writing in family and child welfare. In W. Green and B.L. Simon (Eds.), *The Columbia guide to social work writing* (pp. 215–231). New York: Columbia University Press.

McKnight, J.L., & Block, P. (2010). *The abundant community: Awakening the power of families and neighborhoods.* San Francisco, CA: Berrett-Koehler Publishers.

McKnight, J.L., & Kretzman, J.P. (1996). *Mapping community capacity.* Evanston, IL: Institute for Policy Research. Retrieved from www.racialequity-tools.org/resourcefiles/mcknight.pdf

McLaughlin, B., Ryder, D., & Taylor, M.F. (2016). The effectiveness of interventions for grandparent caregivers: A systematic review. *Marriage & Family Review,* 1–23. DOI: 10.1080/01494929.2016.1177631

McWhirter, P.T., Robbins, R., Vaughn, K., Youngbull, N., Burks, D., Willmon-Haque, S., Schuetz, S., Brandes, J.A., & Nael, A.Z.O. (2011). Honoring the ways of American Indian women: A group therapy intervention. In A.A. Singh & C.F. Salazar (Eds.), *Social justice in group work. Practical interventions for change* (pp. 73–81). New York: Routledge.

Meyer, C. (1993). *Assessment in social work practice.* New York: Columbia University Press.

MicroFinancing Partners in Africa. (n.d.). About us. Retrieved from http://microfinancingafrica.org/about-us/#Our-History

Middleman, R.R., & Wood, G.G. (1990). *Skills for direct practice in social work.* New York: Columbia University Press.

Miley, K.K., O'Melia, M.W., & DuBois, B.L. (2016). *Generalist social work practice: An empowering approach* (8th ed.). Boston: Pearson Allyn & Bacon.

Miller, C.C. (2014). The divorce surge is over, but the myth lives on. *New York Times.* Retrieved from www.nytimes.com/2014/12/02/upshot/the-divorce-surge-is-over-but-the-myth-lives-on.

html?smid=fb-nytimes&smtyp=cur&bicmp=AD&
bicmlukp=WT.mc_id&bicmst=1409232722000&b
icmet=1419773522000&_r=4&abt=0002&abg=0

Miller, L. (2012). *Counselling skills for social work*. London, Thousand Oaks, CA: Sage Publications.

Miller, W.R., & Rollnick, S. (2013). *Motivational interviewing: Helping people change* (3rd ed.). New York: The Guilford Press.

Minieri, J., & Getsos, P. (2007). *Tools for radical democracy*. San Francisco, CA: Jossey Bass.

Minuchin, P., Colapinto, J., & Minuchin, S. (2007). *Working with families of the poor* (2nd ed.). New York: The Guilford Press.

Minuchin, S. (1974). *Families & family therapy*. Cambridge, MA: Harvard University Press.

Missouri Department of Social Services. (n.d.) Family Intervention Plan. Jefferson City, MO: Author.

Mondros, J., & Staples, L. (2013). Community organization. In C. Franklin (Ed.), *Encyclopedia of social work [E-reader version]*. Washington, DC, and New York: National Association of Social Workers and Oxford University Press. DOI: 10.1093/acrefore/9780199975839.013.74

Morgan, A. (2000). *What is narrative therapy?* Adelaide, South Australia: Dulwich Centre Publications.

Morrow-Howell, N., Gonzales, E., Matz-Costa, C., & Greenfield, E.A. (2015). *Increasing productive engagement in later life*. Working Paper No. 8, American Academy of Social Work and Social Welfare Grand Challenges for Social Work Initiative. Retrieved from http://aaswsw.org/grand-challenges-initiative/12-challenges/advance-long-and-productive-lives/

Moxley, D. (2013). Interdisciplinarity. In C. Franklin (Ed.), *Encyclopedia of social work [E-reader version]*. Washington, DC, and New York: National Association of Social Workers and Oxford University Press. DOI: 10.1093/acrefore/9780199975839.013.200

Mulroy, E. (2013). Community needs assessment. In C. Franklin (Ed.), *Encyclopedia of social work [E-reader version]*. Washington, DC, and New York: National Association of Social Workers and Oxford University Press. DOI: 10.1093/acrefore/9780199975839.013.73

Musick, K., & Meier, Ann. (2009). Are both parents always better than one? Parental conflict and young adult well-being. *Rural New York Minute, 28*, 1.

Myerhoff, B. (1982). Life history among the elderly: Performance, visibility and remembering. In J. Ruby (Ed.), *A crack in the mirror: Reflexive perspectives in anthropology* (pp. 99–117). Philadelphia: University of Pennsylvania Press.

Nakhaima, J.M., & Dicks, B.H. (2012). A role for the religious community in family counseling. *Alliance for Strong Families and Communities*. Retrieved from: www.alliance1.org/sites/default/files/fis/PPF/PDFs/nakhaima_76_6.pdf

National Alliance on Mental Illness. (NAMI). (2013). Cognitive behavior therapy (CBT). Retrieved from www.nami.org

National Association of Area Agencies on Aging. (2016). About n4a. Retrieved from www.n4a.org/about

National Association of Cognitive-Behavioral Therapists (NACBT). (n.d.). Cognitive behavioral therapy. Retrieved from www.nacbt.org/whatiscbt.aspx

National Association of Social Workers (NASW). (2007). *Indicators for the achievement of the NASW Standards for cultural competence in social work*. Washington, DC: NASW. Retrieved from www.socialworkers.org/practice/standards/NASWCulturalStandardsIndicators2006.pdf

National Association of Social Workers (NASW). (2008). Code of ethics. Washington, DC: NASW. Retrieved from https://www.socialworkers.org/pubs/code/code.asp

National Association of Social Workers (NASW). (2013a) *NASW guidelines for social worker safety in the workplace*. Washington, DC: NASW.

National Association of Social Workers (NASW). (2013b). *Standards for social work case management*. Washington, DC: NASW.

National Association of Social Workers (NASW). (2015a). *Indicators for the achievement of the NASW Standards for Cultural Competence in Social Work Practice*. Washington, DC: NASW. Retrieved from www.socialworkers.org/practice/standards/index.asp

National Association of Social Workers (NASW). (2015b). *Cultural and linguistic competence in the social work profession. Social work speaks: National Association of Social Workers policy statements*. Washington, DC: NASW Press.

National Association of Social Workers (NASW). (2015c). *Professional self-care and social work. Social work speaks: National Association of Social Workers policy statements*. Washington, DC: NASW Press.

National Association of Social Workers (NASW). (2015d). *Standards and indicators for cultural competence in social work practice*. Washington, DC: Author. Retrieved from www.socialworkers.org/practice/standards/PRA-BRO-253150-CC-Standards.pdf

National Center for Cultural Competence. (n.d.). Definitions of cultural competence. Retrieved from www.ncccurricula.info/culturalcompetence.html

Netting, F.E., Kettner, P.M., & McMurtry, S.L., & Thomas, L. (2017). *Social work macro practice*. Boston: Pearson Allyn & Bacon.

New York Times. (2015, Nov. 17). Block by block: Jackson Heights. *New York Times*. Retrieved from www.nytimes.com/2015/11/17/realestate/block-by-block-jackson-heights.html

Newhill, C.E. (1995). Client violence toward social workers: A practice and policy concern. *Social Work, 40*, 631–636.

Nichols, M.P. (2014). *The essentials of family therapy* (6th ed.). Boston: Pearson.

Nilsson, P. (2014). Are compassion and empathy bad for professional social workers? *Advances in Social Work, 15*(2), 294–305.

O'Connor, M.K., & Netting, F.E. (2009). *Organization practice: A guide to understanding human service organizations*. Hoboken, NJ: Wiley.

Obama, Barack. (2008, Feb. 5). Speech of February 5, 2008 [transcript]. *New York Times*. Retrieved from www.nytimes.com/2008/02/05/us/politics/05text-obama.html?_r=1

Ohmer, M.L. (2008). Assessing and developing the evidence base of macro practice: Interventions with a community and neighborhood focus. *Journal of Evidence-Based Social Work, 5*(3/4), 519–547.

Ohmer, M.L., & Brooks, F. (2013). The practice of community organizing. In M. Weil (Ed.), *The handbook of community practice* (pp. 233–248). Thousand Oaks, CA: Sage Publications.

Ohmer, M.L., & DeMasi, K. (2009). *Consensus organizing: A community development workbook*. Thousand Oaks, CA: Sage Publications.

Ohmer, M.L., & Korr, W.S. (2006). The effectiveness of community practice interventions: A review of the literature. *Research on Social Work Practice, 16*(2), 132–145.

Ohmer, M.L., Sobek, J.L., Teixeira, S.N., Wallace, J.M., & Shapiro, V.B. (2013). Community-based research: Rationale, methods, roles, and considerations for community practice. In M. Weil's (Ed.), *The handbook of community practice* (pp. 791–807). Thousand Oaks, CA: Sage Publications.

Oliver, M., & Sapey, B. (2006). *Social work with disabled people*. New York: Palgrave Macmillan.

Oregon Legislature. (n.d.). How to testify before a legislative committee. Retrieved from www.leg.state.or.us/comm/testify.html/

Packard, T. (2009). Leadership and performance in human services organizations. In R.J. Patti (Ed.), *The handbook of social welfare management* (pp. 143–164). Thousand Oaks, CA: Sage Publications.

Packard, T. (2013). Organizational change in human service organizations. In C. Franklin (Ed.), *Encyclopedia of social work [E-reader version]*. Washington, DC, and New York: National Association of Social Workers and Oxford University Press. DOI: 0.1093/acrefore/9780199975839.013.272

Paniagua, F.A. (2014). *Assessing and treating culturally diverse clients* (4th ed.). Los Angeles, CA: Sage Publications.

Papell, C.P., & Rothman, B. (1962). Social group work models: Possession and heritage. *Journal of Education for Social Work, 2*(2), 66–77.

Papero, D.V. (2015). Bowen family systems theory. In K. Corcoran & A.R. Roberts (Eds.), *Social workers' desk reference* (3rd ed.) (pp. 456–462). New York: Oxford University Press.

Paris, R., & DeVoe, E.R. (2013). Human needs: Family. In C. Franklin (Ed.), *Encyclopedia of social work*

[E-reader version]. Washington, DC, and New York: National Association of Social Workers and Oxford University Press. DOI: 10.1093/acrefore/9780199975839.013.555

Parsons, R.J., & East, J. (2013). Empowerment practice. In C. Franklin (Ed.), *Encyclopedia of social work [E-reader version]*. Washington, DC, and New York: National Association of Social Workers and Oxford University Press. DOI: 10.1093/acrefore/9780199975839.013.128

Payne, M., & Askeland, G.A. (2008). *Globalization and international social work: Postmodern change and challenge*. Burlington, VT: Ashgate Publishing Company.

Peterson, Z. (2002). More than a mirror: The ethics of therapist self-disclosure. *Psychotherapy: Theory, Research, Practice, and Training*, 39, 21–31.

Pettus-Davis, C. & Epperson, M. W. (2015). *Smart decarceration: A grand challenge for social work*. Working Paper No. 16, American Academy of Social Work and Social Welfare Grand Challenges for Social Work Initiative. Retrieved from http://aaswsw.org/wp-content/uploads/2015/12/WP4-with-cover.pdf

Pew Research Center. (2015). U.S. foreign-born population trends. In *Modern wave brings 59 million to U.S., driving population growth and change through 2065: Views of immigration's impact on U.S. society mixed*. Retrieved from www.pewhispanic.org/2015/09/28/chapter-5-u-s-foreign-born-population-trends/#fn-23157-24

Pfeffer, J. (1992). *Managing with power and politics: Influence in organizations*. Boston: Harvard Business School Press.

Pippard, J.L., & Bjorklund, R.W. (2004). Identifying essential techniques for social work community practice. *Journal of Community Practice*, 11(4), 101–116.

Plitt, D.L., & Shields, J. (2009). Development of the Policy Advocacy Behavior Scale: Initial reliability and validity. *Research on Social Work Practice*, 19(1), 83–92.

Pogash, C. (2016, June 1). Unsettling U.S. political climate galvanizes Muslims to vote. *New York Times*. Retrieved from www.nytimes.com/2016/06/02/us/unsettling-political-climate-galvanizes-muslims-to-vote.html

Poole, D.L. (2009). Community partnerships for school-based services. In A. Roberts (Ed.), *Social workers desk reference* (pp. 907–912). New York: Oxford University Press.

Pope, N.D., Rollins, L., Chaumba, J., & Risler, E. (2011). Evidence-based practice knowledge and utilization among social workers. *Journal of Evidence-Based Social Work*, 8, 349–368.

Potocky, M. (2013). Asylum-seekers, refugees, and immigrants in the United States. In C. Franklin (Ed.), *Encyclopedia of social work [E-reader version]*. Washington, DC, and New York: National Association of Social Workers and Oxford University Press. DOI: 10.1093/acrefore/9780199975839.013.193

Putnam, R.D., & Feldstein, L.M. (2003). *Better together: Restoring the American community*. New York: Simon & Schuster.

Ramanathan, C.S., & Link, R.J. (2004). *All our futures: Principles and resources for social work practice in a global era*. Belmont, CA: Brooks/Cole.

Randall, A.C., & DeAngelis, D. (2013). Licensing. In C. Franklin (Ed.), *Encyclopedia of social work [E-reader version]*. Washington, DC, and New York: National Association of Social Workers and Oxford University Press. DOI: 10.1093/acrefore/9780199975839.013.225

Rapp, C.A., & Goscha, R.J. (2012). *The strengths model: A recovery-oriented approach to mental health services*. New York: Oxford University Press.

Rasheed, M.N., & Rasheed, J.M. (2013). Family: Practice interventions. In C. Franklin (Ed.), *Encyclopedia of social work [E-reader version]*. Washington, DC, and New York: National Association of Social Workers and Oxford University Press. DOI: 10.1093/acrefore/9780199975839.013.546

Reamer, F.G. (2013a). Ethics and values. In C. Franklin (Ed.), *Encyclopedia of social work [E-reader version]*. Washington, DC, and New York: National Association of Social Workers and Oxford University. DOI: 10.1093/acrefore/9780199975839.013.134

Reamer, F.G. (2013b). *Social work values and ethics* (4th ed.). New York: Columbia University Press.

Reamer, F.G. (2013c). Social work malpractice, liability, and risk management. In C. Franklin (Ed.),

Encyclopedia of social work [E-reader version]. Washington, DC, and New York: National Association of Social Workers and Oxford University. DOI: 10.1093/acrefore/9780199975839.013.977

Reichert, E. (2007). *Challenges in human rights: A social work perspective.* New York: Columbia University Press.

Reichert, E. (2011). *Social work and human rights: A foundation for policy and practice.* New York: Columbia Press.

Reid, K.E. (1997). *Social work practice with groups: A clinical perspective* (2nd ed.). Pacific Grove, CA: Brooks/Cole.

Reid, K.E. (2002). Clinical social work with groups. In A.R. Roberts & G.J. Greene (Eds.), *Social Workers' Desk Reference* (2nd ed.) (pp. 432–436). New York: Oxford University Press.

Reisch, M. (2013). Community practice challenges in the global economy. In M. Weil (Ed.), *The handbook of community practice* (pp. 47–71). Thousand Oaks, CA: Sage Publications.

Richards-Schuster, K., & Pritzker, S. (2015). Strengthening youth participation in civic engagement: Applying the Convention on the Rights of the Child to social work practice. *Children and Youth Services Review 57*, 90–97.

Ringel, S. (2005). Group work with Asian-American immigrants: A cross-cultural perspective. In G.L. Greif & P.H. Ephross (Eds.), *Group work with populations at risk* (2nd ed.) (pp. 181–194). New York: Oxford University Press.

Robert III, H., Honemann, D.H., & Balch, T.J. (2011). *Robert's rules of order newly revised.* Philadelphia, PA: Da Capo Press.

Roberts, A.R. (2013). Crisis interventions. In C. Franklin (Ed.), *Encyclopedia of social work [E-reader version].* Washington, DC, and New York: National Association of Social Workers and Oxford University Press. DOI: 10.1093/acrefore/9780199975839.013.137

Roberts-DeGennaro, M. (2013). Case management. In C. Franklin (Ed.), *Encyclopedia of social work [E-reader version].* Washington, DC, and New York: National Association of Social Workers and

Oxford University Press. DOI: 10.1093/acrefore/9780199975839.013.42

Robinson, J.W., & Green, G.P. (2011) *Introduction to community development: Theory, practice, and service-learning.* Thousand Oaks, CA: Sage Publications.

Roche, S.E., & Wood, G.G. (2005). A narrative principle for feminist social work with survivors of male violence. *Affilia, 20*(4), 465–475.

Rogers, C. (1957). The necessary and sufficient conditions of therapeutic personality change. *Journal of Consulting Psychology, 22*, 95–103.

Romano, M., & Peters, L. (2015). Evaluating the mechanisms of change in motivational interviewing in the treatment of mental health problems: A review and meta-analysis. *Clinical Psychology Review, 38*, 1–12.

Roscoe, K.D., & Madoc-Jones, L. (2009). Critical social work practice: A narrative approach. *International Journal of Narrative Practice, 1*, 9–18.

Roscoe, K.D., Carson, A.M., & Madoc-Jones, L. (2011). Narrative social work: Conversations between theory and practice. *Journal of Social Work Practice, 25*(1), 47–61.

Rostoky, S.S., & Riggle, E.D.B. (2011). Marriage equality for same-sex couples: Counseling psychologists as social change agents. *The Counseling Psychologist, 39*(7), 956–972.

Rothman, J.C. (2008). Multi modes of community intervention. In J. Rothman, J. Erlich, & J. Tropman (Eds.), *Strategies of community intervention* (7th ed.) (pp.141–170). Peosta, Iowa: Eddie Bowers Publishing Co., Inc.

Rothman, J.C. (2009). An overview of case management. In A.R. Roberts (Ed.), *Social workers' desk reference* (2nd ed.) (pp. 751–755). New York: Oxford University Press.

Rothman, J.C. (2015). Developing therapeutic contracts with clients. In K. Corcoran & A.R. Roberts (Eds.), *Social workers' desk reference* (3rd ed.) (pp. 553–559). New York: Oxford University Press.

Royse, D., Staton-Tindall, M., Badger, K., & Webster, J.M. (2009). *Needs assessment.* New York: Oxford University Press.

Rubin, H.J., & Rubin, I.S. (2008). *Community organizing and development.* Boston: Pearson Allyn & Bacon.

Saez, E. (2015). *The evolution of top incomes in the United States (updated with 2014 preliminary estimates).* University of California, Berkeley, Working Paper. Retrieved from http://eml.berkeley.edu/~saez/saez-UStopincomes-2012.pdf

Safe Connections. (n.d.) Group Assessment Screening. St. Louis, MO: Author.

Sager, J.S., & Weil, M. (2013). Larger-scale social planning: Planning for services and communities. In M. Weil (Ed.), *The handbook of community practice* (pp. 299–325). Thousand Oaks, CA: Sage Publications.

Saint Louis University Pius XII Library (n.d.). Research guides. Retrieved from http://libguides.slu.edu/index.php

Saleebey, D. (2009). *The strengths perspective in social work practice* (6th ed.) Boston: Pearson.

Saleebey, D. (2013). *The strengths perspective in social work practice* (6th ed.). Boston: Allyn & Bacon.

Samudio, M. (2015). Doing family therapy as a new social worker: The dos and don'ts. *The New Social Worker, 22*(1), 6–7.

Samuels, C.A. (2016). Number of U.S. students in special education tickets upwards. *Education Week.* Retrieved from www.edweek.org/ew/articles/2016/04/20/number-of-us-students-in-special-education.html

Sandfort, J. (2005). Casa de Esperanza. *Nonprofit Management & Leadership, 15*(3), 371–382.

Sands, D. (2015). Looking back on a decade of growth in Detroit's urban ag movement. *Model D.* Retrieved from www.modelmedia.com/features/10-years-urban-ag-091415.aspx

Schein, E.H. (2010). *Organizational culture and leadership.* San Francisco, CA: Jossey-Bass.

Scheuler, L., Diuof, K., Nevels, E., & Hughes, N. (2014). Empowering families in difficult times: The women's economic stability initiative. *Affilia, 29*(3), 353–367.

Schiller, L.Y. (1995). Stages of development in women's groups: A relational model. In R. Kurland & R. Salmon (Eds.), *Group work practice in a troubled society: Problems and opportunities* (pp. 117–138). New York: The Haworth Press.

Schiller, L.Y. (1997). Rethinking stages of group development in women's groups: Implications for practice. *Social Work with Groups, 20*(3), 3–19.

Schiller, L.Y. (2003). Women's group development from a relational model and a new look at facilitator influence on group development. In. M.B. Cohen & A. Mullender (Eds.), *Gender and group work* (pp. 16–31). New York: Routledge.

Schiller, L.Y. (2007). Not for women only: Applying the relational model of group development with vulnerable populations. *Social Work with Groups, 30*(2), 11–26.

Schneider, R.L., & Lester, L. (2001). *Social work advocacy.* Belmont, CA: Brooks/Cole.

Schwartz, W. (1961). The social worker in the group. *The Social Welfare Forum,* 146–177.

Sebold, J. (2011). Families and couples: A practical guide for facilitating change. In G.J. Greene and M.Y. Lee (Eds.), *Solution-oriented social work practice* (pp. 209–236). New York: Oxford University Press.

Seligman, M., & Darling, R.B. (2007). *Ordinary families, special children: A systems approach to childhood disability* (3rd ed.). New York: The Guilford Press.

Shakya, H.B., Usita, P.M., Eisenberg, C., Weston, J., & Liles, S. (2012). Family well-being concerns of grandparents in skipped generation families. *Journal of Gerontological Social Work, 55,* 39–54.

Shebib, B. (2015). *Choices: Interviewing and counseling skills for Canadians.* New York: Pearson Canada.

Shelton, M. (2012, May 7). Tornado recovery offers Joplin students new lessons. NPR. Retrieved from www.npr.org/2012/05/07/151950143/tornado-recovery-offers-joplin-students-new-lessons

Sherraden, M.S., Huang, J., Jacobson Frey, J., Birkenmaier, J.M., Callahan, C., Clancy, M., & Sherrden, M. (2015). *Financial capability and asset building for all. American Academy of Social Work and Social Welfare.* Retrieved from http://aaswsw.org/wp-content/uploads/2016/01/WP13-with-cover.pdf

Shier, M.L. (2012). Work-related factors that impact social work practitioners' subjective well-being: Well-being in the workplace. *Journal of Social Work, 12*(6), 402–421.

Shulman, L. (2009). Group work phases of helping: Preliminary phase. In A. Gitterman & R. Salmon (Eds.), *Encyclopedia of social work with groups* (pp. 109–111). New York: Routledge.

Shulman, L. (2011). *Dynamics and skills of group counseling*. Boston: Cengage Learning.

Shulman, L. (2015). Developing successful relationships: The therapeutic and group alliances. In K. Corcoran & A.R. Roberts (Eds.), *Social workers' desk reference* (3rd ed.) (pp. 623–629). New York: Oxford University Press.

Siebold, C. (2007). Everytime we say goodbye: Forced termination revisited, a commentary. *Clinical Social Work Journal*, 35(2), 91–95.

Simon, B. (1990). Re-thinking empowerment. *Journal of Progressive Human Services*. 1(1), 29.

Sims, P.A. (2003). Working with metaphor. *American Journal of Psychotherapy*, 57(4), 528–536

Singh, A.A., & Salazar, C.F. (2011). Conclusion: Six Considerations for Social Justice Group Work. In A.A. Singh & C.F. Salazar (Eds.), *Social justice in group work* (pp. 213–222). Practical interventions for change. New York: Routledge.

Slade, E.P., McCarthy, J.F., Valenstein, M., Visnic, S., & Dixon, L.B. (2013). Cost savings from assertive community treatment services in an era of declining psychiatric inpatient use. *Health Services Research*, 48(1), 195–217.

Sohng, W.S.L. (2013). Community-based participatory research. In C. Franklin (Ed.), *Encyclopedia of social work [E-reader version]*. Washington, DC, and New York: National Association of Social Workers and Oxford University Press. DOI: 10.1093/acrefore/9780199975839.013.69

Sormanti, M. (2012). Writing for and about clinical practice. In W. Green and B.L. Simon (Eds.), *The Columbia guide to social work writing* (pp. 114–132). New York: Columbia University Press.

Sowers, K.M., & Rowe, W.S. (2009). International perspectives on social work practice. In A.R. Roberts (Ed.), *Social workers' desk reference* (2nd ed.) (pp. 863–868). New York: Oxford University Press.

Specht, H. (1990). Social work and the popular psychotherapies. *Social Service Review*, 64, 345–357.

Specht, H., & Courtney, M.E. (1994). *Unfaithful angels: How social work has abandoned its mission*. New York: The Free Press.

Speer, P.W., & Christens, B.D. (2011). Local community organizing and change: Altering policy in the housing and community development system in Kansas City. *Journal of Community & Applied Social Psychology*, 22(5), 414–427.

St. Anthony's Medical Center. (2010). Family Intervention and Planning. St. Louis, MO: Author.

Stamm, B.H. (2010). *The concise ProQOL manual* (2nd ed.). Pocatello, ID: ProQOL.org.

Steger, M.B. (2009). *Globalization*. New York: Sterling Publishing.

Steinberg, D.M. (2014). *A mutual-aid model for social work with groups* (3rd ed). New York: Routledge.

Strand, V., Carten, A., Connolly, D., Gelman, S.R., & Vaughn, P.B. (2009). A cross system initiative supporting child welfare workforce professionalization and stabilization. A task group in action. In C.S. Cohen, M.H. Phillips, & M. Hanson (Eds.), *Strength and diversity in social work with groups* (pp. 41–53). New York: Routledge.

Streeter, C.L. (2013). Community: Overview. In C. Franklin (Ed.), *Encyclopedia of social work [E-reader version]*. Washington, DC, and New York: National Association of Social Workers and Oxford University Press. DOI: 10.1093/acrefore/9780199975839.013.531

Strom-Gottfried, K.J. (2000). Ensuring ethical practice: An examination of NASW Code violations, 1986–97. *Social Work*, 45(3), 251–261.

Strom-Gottfried, K.J. (2003). Managing risk through ethical practice: Ethical dilemmas in rural social work. Presentation at the National Association of Social Workers Vermont chapter, Essex, VT.

Strom-Gottfried, K.J. (2008). *The ethics of practice with minors*. Chicago: Lyceum Books, Inc.

Substance Abuse and Mental Health Services Administration's National Registry of Evidence-based Programs and Practices. (2012). Solution-focused group therapy. Retrieved from http://legacy.nreppadmin.net/ViewIntervention.aspx?id=281

Sue, D.W., Rasheed, M.N., & Rasheed, J.M. (2015). *Multicultural social work practice: A competency-based approach to diversity and social justice.* Hoboken, NJ: John Wiley & Sons.

Supreme Court of the United States. (2015). *Obergefel et al. v. Hodges, Director, Ohio Department of Health, et al.* Retrieved from http://webcache.googleusercontent.com/ search?q=cache:W5B8IhdnXt8J:www.supremecourt.gov/opinions/14pdf/14-556_3204.pdf+&cd =2&hl=en&ct=clnk&gl=us

Tariq, S.H., Tumosa, N., Chibnall, J.T., Perry, M.H., & Morley, J.E. (2006). Comparison of the Saint Louis University mental status examination and the mini-mental state examination for detecting dementia and mild neurocognitive disorder—a pilot study. *American Journal of Geriatric Psychiatry, 14*, 900–910.

Tatian, P., Leopold, J., Oo, E., Joseph, G., MacDonald, G., Nichols, A., Woluchem, M., Zhang, S., & Abazajian, K. (2016). *Affordable housing needs assessment for the District of Columbia Phase II.* Washington, DC: Urban Institute.

Tay, D., & Jordan, J. (2015). Metaphor and the notion of control in trauma talk. *Text & Talk, 35*(4), 553–573. DOI: 10.1515/text-2015-0009

Tebb, S.C. (1995). An aid to empowerment: A caregiver well-being scale. *Health and Social Work, 20*(2), 87–92.

Tebb, S.C., Berg-Weger, M., & Rubio, D.M. (2013). The Caregiver Well-Being Scale: Developing a short-form rapid assessment instrument. *Health and Social Work 38*(4), 222–230. DOI: 10.1093/hsw/ hlt019

Tervalon, M., & Murray-Garcia, J. (1998). Cultural humility versus cultural competence: A critical distinction in defining physician training outcomes in multicultural education. *Journal of Health Care for the Poor and Underserved, 9*(2), 117–125.

Thompson, L.J., & West, D. (2013). Professional development in the contemporary educational context: Encouraging practice wisdom. *Social Work Education, 21*(1), 118–133.

Thyer, B.A. (2008). Evidence-based macro practice: Addressing the challenges and opportunities. *Journal of Evidence-based Social Work,* (3/4), 453–472.

Thyer, B.A. (2015). Evidence-based practice, science, and social work. An overview. In K. Corcoran & A.R. Roberts (Eds.), *Social workers' desk reference* (3rd ed.) (pp. 1193–1197). New York: Oxford University Press.

Tobert, P.S., & Hall, R.J. (2016). *Organizations: Structures, processes, and outcomes.* New York: Routledge.

Tomasello, N.M., Manning, A.R., & Dulmus, C.N. (2010). Family-centered early intervention for infants and toddlers with disabilities. *Journal of Family Social Work, 13,* 163–172.

Toseland, R.W., & Horton, H. (2013). Group work. In C. Franklin (Ed.), *Encyclopedia of social work [E-reader version].* Washington, DC, and New York: National Association of Social Workers and Oxford University Press. DOI: 10.1093/acrefore/ 9780199975839.013.168

Turner, H. (2011). Concepts for effective facilitation of open groups. *Social Work with Groups, 34,* 146–156.

U.S. Census Bureau. (2014a). Characteristics of same-sex couple households. 2014 American Community Survey 1-year data file. Retrieved from www.census.gov/hhes/samesex/files/ssex-tables-2014.xlsx

U.S. Census Bureau. (2014b). Poverty status in the past 12 months of families. 2010–2014 American Community Survey 5-year estimates. Retrieved from http://factfinder.census.gov/faces/tableservices/jsf/pages/productview.xhtml?src=bkmk

U.S. Census Bureau. (2015a). Current Population Survey, 2015 Annual Social and Economic Supplement. Retrieved from https://www.census. gov/hhes/families/data/cps2015FG.html

U.S. Census Bureau. (2015b). New Census Bureau report analyses U. S. population projections. CB15-TPS.16. Retrieved from www.census.gov/ newsroom/press-releases/2015/cb15-tps16.html

Uken, A., Lee, M.Y., & Sebold, J. (2013). The Plumas Project: Solution-focused treatment of domestic violence offenders. In P. De Jong & I.K. Berg (Eds.), *Interviewing for solutions* (4th ed.) (pp. 333–345). Belmont, CA: Brooks/Cole.

United Nations Office for the Coordination of Humanitarian Affairs. (2016). Syrian Arab Republic. Retrieved from www.unocha.org/syria

United Nations Office of the High Commissioner for Human Rights. (2016). What are human rights? Retrieved from www.ohchr.org/EN/Issues/Pages/WhatareHumanRights.aspx

University of Kansas Work Group for Community Health and Development. (2016). Community Toolbox. Retrieved from http://ctb.ku.edu/en/table-of-contents

Van Hook, M.P. (2014). *Social work practice with families: A resiliency-based approach*. Chicago: Lyceum Books.

Van Soest, D. (2013). Oppression. In C. Franklin (Ed.), *Encyclopedia of social work [E-reader version]*. Washington, DC, and New York: National Association of Social Workers and Oxford University Press. DOI: 10.1093/acrefore/9780199975839.013.271

Van Treuren, R.R. (1993). Self-perception in family systems: A diagrammatic technique. In C. Meyer (Ed.), *Assessment in social work practice* (p. 119). New York: Columbia University Press.

Van Wormer, K. (2009). Restorative justice as social justice for victims of gendered violence: A standpoint feminist perspective. *Social Work, 54*(2), 107–116.

Vinter, R.D. (1974). Program activities: An analysis of their effects on participant behavior. In P. Glassner, R. Sarri, & R. Vinter (Eds.), *Individual change through small groups* (pp. 233–243). New York: The Free Press.

Vodde, R., & Giddings, M.M. (1997). The propriety of affiliation with clients beyond the professional role: Nonsexual dual relationships. *Arete, 22*(1), 58–79.

Wagaman, M.A., Geiger, J.M., Shockley, C., & Segal, E.A. (2015). The role of empathy in burnout, compassion satisfaction, and secondary traumatic stress among social workers. *Social Work, 60*(3), 201–209.

Wagner, E.F. (2013). Motivational interviewing. In C. Franklin (Ed.), *Encyclopedia of social work [E-reader version]*. Washington, DC, and New York: National Association of Social Workers and Oxford University Press. DOI: 10.1093/acrefore/9780199975839.013.252

Wahab, S. (2005). Motivational interviewing and social work practice. *Journal of Social Work, 5*(1), 45–60.

Walker, L. (2013). Solution-focused reentry and transition planning for imprisoned people. In P. De Jong & I.K. Berg (Eds.), *Interviewing for solutions* (4th ed.) (pp. 318–328). Belmont, CA: Brooks/Cole.

Walsh, J., & Manuel, J. (2015). Clinical case management. In K. Corcoran & A.R. Roberts (Eds.), *Social workers' desk reference* (3rd ed.) (pp. 820–824). New York: Oxford University Press.

Walters, K.L., Spencer, M.S, Smukler, M., Allen, H.L., Andrews, C., Browne, T., Maramaldi, P., Wheeler, D. P., Zebrack, B., & Uehara, E. (2016). *Health equity: Eradicating health inequalities for future generations*. Working Paper No. 19, American Academy of Social Work. Retrieved from http://aaswsw.org/wp-content/uploads/2016/01/WP19-with-cover2.pdf

Walz, T., & Ritchie, H. (2000). Gandhian principles in social work practice: Ethics revisited. *Social Work, 45*(3), 213–222.

Warde, B. (2012). The Cultural Genogram: Enhancing the cultural competency of social work students. *Social Work Education, 31*(5), 570–586.

Weick, A. (1999). Guilty knowledge. *Families in Society, 80*(4), 327–332.

Weick, A., Kreider, J., & Chamberlain, R. (2009). Key dimensions of the strengths perspective in case management, clinical practice, and community practice. In D. Saleebey (Ed.), *The strengths perspective in social work practice* (5th ed.) (pp. 108–121). Boston: Pearson.

Weil, M. (2013). Community-based social planning. In M. Weil (Ed.), *The handbook of community practice* (pp. 265–298). Thousand Oaks, CA: Sage Publications.

Weil, M., & Gamble, D.N. (2009). Community practice model for the twenty-first century. In Roberts (Ed.), *Social workers' desk reference* (pp. 882–892). New York: Oxford University Press, Inc.

Weil, M., & Ohmer, M.L. (2013). Applying practice theories in community work. In M. Weil's (Ed.), *The handbook of community practice* (pp. 123–161). Thousand Oaks, CA: Sage Publications.

Weil, M., Gamble, D.N., & Ohmer, M L. (2013). Evolution, models, and the changing context of community practice. In M. Weil (Ed.), *The handbook of community practice* (pp. 167–193). Thousand Oaks, CA: Sage Publications.

Weil, M., Reisch, M., & Ohmer, M.L. (2013). Introduction: Contexts and challenges for 21st century communities. In M. Weil's (Ed.), *The handbook of community practice* (pp. 3–26). Thousand Oaks, CA: Sage Publications.

Weisman, D., & Zornado, J.L. (2013). *Professional writing for social work practice*. New York: Springer Publishing Company.

West Virginia Board of Social Work Examiners. (n.d.). Level D: LICSW: (Licensed Independent Social Worker) license. Retrieved from www.wvsocial-workboard.org/licensinginfo/regular/licswlicense.htm

Wharton, T.C., & Bolland, K.A. (2012). Practitioner perspectives of evidence-based practice. *Families in Society: The Journal of Contemporary Social Services, 93*(3), 157–164.

Wheeler, W., & Thomas, A.M. (2011). Engaging youth in community development. In J.W. Robinson Jr., & G.P. Green (Eds.), *Introduction to community development: Theory, practice and service-learning* (pp. 209–227). Los Angeles, CA: Sage Publications.

Whitaker, T., & Wilson, M. (2010). *National Association of Social Workers 2009 compensation and benefit study: Summary of key compensation findings*. Washington, DC: NASW.

White, M. (2007). MAPS of narrative practice. NY: WW Norton and Co.

Williams, N.R. (2009). Narrative family interventions. In A.C. Kilpatrick & T.P. Holland (Eds.), *Working with families. An integrative model by level of need* (5th ed.) (pp. 199–223). Boston: Pearson.

Winship, K., & Lee, S.T. (2012). Using evidence-based accreditation standards to promote continuous quality improvement: The experience of San Mateo County Human Services Agency. *Journal of Evidence-based Social Work, 9*(1–2), 68–86.

Wise, J.B. (2005). *Empowerment practice with families in distress*. New York: Columbia University Press.

Wood, G.G., & Roche, S.E. (2001). Representing selves, reconstructing lives: Feminist group work with women survivors of male violence. *Social Work with Groups, 23*(4), 5–23.

Wood, G.G., & Tully, C.T. (2006). *The structural approach to direct practice in social work: A social constructionist Perspective* (3rd ed.). New York: Columbia University Press.

Work Group for Community Health and Development at the University of Kansas. (2012). The Community Tool Box. Retrieved from http://ctb.ku.edu/en/tablecontents/chapter_1033.aspx

World Health Organization. (2012). Global democracy deficit. Retrieved from http://www.who.int/trade/glossary/story037/en/index/html

Yalom, I.D., & Leszcz, M. (2005). *The theory and practice of group psychotherapy* (5th ed.). New York: Basic Books.

Yeager, K.R., & Roberts, A.R. (2015). *Crisis intervention handbook: Assessment, treatment, and research* (4th ed.) (pp. 183–213). New York: Oxford University Press.

Yee Lee, M. (2013). Solution-focused brief therapy. In C. Franklin (Ed.), *Encyclopedia of social work [E-reader version]*. Washington, DC, and New York: National Association of Social Workers and Oxford University Press. DOI: 10.1093/acrefore/9780199975839.013.1039

Yi, H., Rothman, M., & Burty, C. (2016, July 31). Inside Ohio's fight over voting rules. PBS News Hour. Retrieved from www.pbs.org/newshour/bb/inside-ohios-fight-voting-rules/

Young, S. (2013). Solutions for bullying in primary schools. In P. De Jong & I.K. Berg (Eds.), *Interviewing for solutions* (4th ed.) (pp. 308–318). Belmont, CA: Brooks/Cole.

Zandee-Amas, R.R. (2013). A good groups runs itself—and other myths. *The New Social Worker, 20*(1), 10–11.

Zeleznikow, L., & Zeleznikow, J. (2015). Supporting blended families to remain intact: A case study. *Journal of Divorce & Remarriage, 56*(4), 317–335.

Zelnick, J.R., Slayter, E., Flanzbaum, B., Butler, N.G., Domingo, B., Perlstein, J., & Trust, C. (2013). Part of the job? Workplace violence in Massachusetts social service agencies. *Health & Social Work, 38*(2), 75–85.

Zur, O., & Lazarus, A.A. (2002). Six arguments against dual relationships and their rebuttals. In A.A. Lararus & O. Zur (Eds.), *Dual relationships and psychotherapy* (p. 3–24). New York: Springer.

CREDITS

Ex 5.1: Adapted from The structural approach to direct practice in social work: A social constructionist perspective (3rd ed.), by G.G. Wood and C.T. Tully. Copyright 2006, Columbia University Press. Reprinted with permission.

Photo 5-B: © Adam Gregor

Photo 5-C: © monkeybusinessimages/Thinkstock

Photo 6-A: © Harry Hu, courtesy of Shutterstock® images

QG 16: Sormanti, M. (2012). Writing for and about clinical practice. In W. Green and B. L. Simon, The Columbia guide to social work writing (pp. 114–132). NY: Columbia University Press.

Photo 6-B: Comstock Images/Thinkstock

Photo 6-D: © Rob Hainer

Ex 6.3: From Culture in special education, by M. Kalyanpur and B. Harry. Copyright 1999, Paul H. Brookes. Reprinted with permission.

Ex 6.4: Van Hook, M.P. (2008). Social work practice with families: A resiliency-based approach. Chicago: Lyceum Books.

Ex 6.5: Van Hook, M.P. (2008). Social work practice with families: A resiliency-based approach. Chicago: Lyceum Books.

Ex 6.6: From Self-perception in family systems: A diagrammatic technique, by R.R. Van Treuren. In assessment in social work practice, by C. Meyer. Copyright 1993, Columbia University Press. Reprinted with permission.

QG 18: Warde, B. (2012). The Cultural Genogram: Enhancing the cultural competency of social work students. Social Work Education, 31(5), 570–586. Used by permission.

Ex 6.7: From The Culturagram, by E. P. Congress. In Social Workers' desk reference (2nd ed.), by A.R. Roberts. Copyright 2009, Oxford Press. Reprinted with permission.

QG 19: Adapted from St. Anthony's Medical Center, St. Louis, Missouri. Reprinted with permission.

Ex 7.1: From Hull/Mather. Understanding Generalist Practice with Families, 1E. © 2006 Wadsworth, a part of Cengage Learning, Inc. Reproduced by permission. www.cengage.com/permissions

Ex 7.2: Sebold, J. (2011). Families and couples: A practical guide for facilitating change. In G. J. Greene and M. Y. Lee, Solution-oriented social work practice (pp. 209–236). NY: Oxford University Press.

Photo 7-A: © Lisa F. Young

Ex 7.3: Adapted from St. Anthony's Medical Center, St. Louis, Missouri. Reprinted with permission.

Ex 7.4: Adapted from St. Anthony's Medical Center, St. Louis, Missouri; Missouri Department of Social Services.

QG 22: From Enabling and empowering families: principles and guidelines for practice, by C.J. Dunst, C.M. Trivette and A.G. Deal. Copyright 2003, Brookline Books. Reprinted with permission.

QG 23: From Enabling and empowering families: principles and guidelines for practice, by C.J. Dunst, C.M. Trivette and A.G. Deal. Copyright 2003, Brookline Books. Reprinted with permission.

Photo 7-B: © Lisa F. Young

Photo 7-C: © monkeybusinessimages/Thinkstock

Photo 8-A: © SerrNovik/Thinkstock

Photo 8-B: © Blaj Gabriel

Ex 8.6: From Teaching a methods course in social work with groups, by R. Kurland and R. Salmon. Copyright 1998, Council on Social Work Education.

Ex 8.7: Kurland, R. & Salmon, R. (1998). Teaching a methods course in social work with groups. Alexandria, VA: Council on Social Work Education.

Photo 8-C: © Yuri Arcurs

Ex 8.8: Adapted from St. Anthony's Medical Center, St. Louis, Missouri. Reprinted with permission.

Ex 8.9: Adapted from Women's Support and Community Services, St. Louis, Missouri.

Photo 9-A: © Design Pics/Don Hammond/Thinkstock

Photo 9-B: © Glynnis Jones

QG 27: From Group Composition, diversity, the skills of the social worker, and group development, by T. Berman-Rossi and T.B. Kelly. Presented at the Council for Social Work Education Annual Meeting, Atlanta, February. Copyright 2003. Reprinted with permission.

Photo 9-C: © Blaj Gabriel

Ex 9.1: Comer, E. & Meier, A. (2011). Using evidence-based practice and intervention research with treatment groups for populations at risk. In G.L. Greif & P.H. Ephross (Eds.) Group work with populations at risk (3rd ed.) (pp. 459–488). New York: Oxford University Press

Ex 9.2: Greif, G. & Ephross, P.H. (Eds.). (2011). Group work with populations at risk (3rd ed.). New York: Oxford University Press.

QG 28: Berg, R.D., Landreth, G.L., & Fall, K.A. (2013). Group counseling concepts and procedures (5th ed.). New York: Routledge.

Photo 9-D: © vm

Photo 9-E: © Yuri Arcurs

QG 30: Berg, R.D., Landreth, G.L., & Fall, K.A. (2013). Group counseling concepts and procedures (5th ed.). New York: Routledge.

Ex 9.7: Berg, R.D., Landreth, G.L., & Fall, K.A. (2013). Group counseling concepts and procedures (5th ed.). New York: Routledge.

Photo 10-A: © vm

Ex 10.2: Adapted from Center of Organizational and Social Research, Saint Louis University.

Ex 10.3: Royse, D., Staton-Tindall, M., Badger, K., & Webster, J.M. (2009). Needs assessment. New York: Oxford University Press.

Photo 10-B: © CREATISTA

Ex 10.4: City of Seattle, Washington. (2012). A Community Assessment of Need for Housing and Services for Homeless Individuals and Families in the Lake City Neighborhood. Retrieved from http://seattle.gov/reales-tate/pdfs/Needs_Assessment_data_report.pdf

Ex 10.8: Kretzmann, J. P. & McKnight, J. L. (1993). Building communities from the inside out: A part toward finding and mobilizing a community's assets. Evanston, IL: Center for Urban Affairs and Policy Research. Used by permission.

Ex 10.9: McKnight, J. L., & Block, P. (2010). The abundant community: Awakening the power of families and neighborhoods. San Francisco, CA: Berrett-Koehler Publishers.

Ex 10.10: McKnight, J. L., & Block, P. (2010). The abundant community: Awakening the power of families and neighborhoods. San Francisco, CA: Berrett-Koehler Publishers.

Photo 10-C: © THEGIFT777

Ex 11.1: Netting, F. E., Kettner, P. M., McMurtry, S. L., & Thomas, L. (2011). Social work macro practice. Boston: Pearson Allyn & Bacon.

Ex 11.3: Source: 350.org

Photo 11-A: © 350.org

Photo 11-B: © 350.org

QG 36 & 37: Adapted from Organizing for social change, by K. Bobo, J. Kendall, and S. Max. Copyright 2010, The Forum Press. Reprinted with permission.

QG 38: Adapted from New Robert's Rules of Order by L. Rozakis. Copyright 1996, Smithmark Reference.

QG 39: Adapted from Consensus through conversation, by L. Dressler. Copyright 2006, Berrett-Koehler Publishers, Inc. All rights reserved. www.bkconnection.com

Ex 11.5: Kretzmann, J. P. & McKnight, J. L. (2005). Discovering community power: A guide to mobilizing local assets and your organization's capacity. Evanston, IL: Asset-Based Community Development (ABCD) Institute. Used by permission.

Ex 11.7: Ohmer, M.L. & DeMasi, K. (2009). Consensus organizing: A community development workbook. Thousand Oaks, CA: Sage Publications, Inc.

Ex 11.9: Ohmer, M.L. & Korr, W.S. (2006). The effectiveness of community practice interventions: A review of the literature. Research on Social Work Practice, 16(2),132–145. Used by permission.

Ex 11.10: From Localized needs and a globalized economy, by J. Ife in Social work and globalization (Special Issue), Canadian Social Work, 2(1). Copyright 2000.

Ex 11.11: From International social work: Issues, strategies and programs by D. Cox and M. Pawar. Copyright 2006, Sage Publications, Inc. Reprinted with permission.

Ex 11.14: Speer, P. W. & Christens, B. D. (2011). Local community organizing and change: Altering policy in the housing and community development system in Kansas City. Journal of Community & Applied Social Psychology, 22(5), 414–427. Used by permission.

Photo 12-A: © Digital Vision

Ex 12.1: National Association of Area Agencies on Aging. (2012). National aging services network. Retrieved from http://www.n4a.org/about-n4a/join/

Photo 12-B: © Chris Fertnig

Photo 12-C: © CandyBox Images

Ex 12.6: Gambrill, E. (2012). Social work practice: A critical thinkers guide. New York: Oxford University Press.

QG 41: From Locke/Garrison/Winship. Generalist Social Work Practice, 1E. © 1998 Wadsworth, a part of Cengage Learning, Inc. Reproduced by permission. www.Cengage.com/permissions

Ex 12.8: Larson, K., & McGuiston, C. (2012). Building capacity to improve Latino health in rural North Carolina: A case study in community-university engagement. Journal of Community Engagement and Scholarship, 5(1), 14–23.

QG 44: Plitt, D. L. & Shields, J. (2009). Development of the Policy Advocacy Behavior Scale: Initial reliability and validity. Research on Social Work Practice, 19(1), 83–92. Reprinted by permission.

Photo 13-A: © gosphotodesign

Ex 13.1: Evans, S. D., Hanlin, C. E., & Prillehensky, I. (2007). Blending Ameliorative and transformative approaches in human service organizations: A case study. Journal of Community Psychology, 35(3), 329–346. Used by permission.

Ex 13.2: Netting, F. E., Kettner, P. M., McMurtry, S. L., & Thomas, M. L. (2012). Social work macro practice. Boston: Pearson Allyn & Bacon.

Ex 13.4: Netting, F. E., Kettner, P. M., McMurtry, S. L., & Thomas, M. L. (2012). Social work macro practice. Boston: Pearson Allyn & Bacon.

QG 45: Manning, T. (2012). The art of successful persuasion: Seven skills you need to get your point across effectively.

Ex 13.6: O'Connor, M. K., & Netting, F. E. (2009). Organization practice: A guide to understanding human service organizations. Hoboken, NJ: John Wiley and Sons.

Ex 13.7: Winship, K. & Lee, S. T. (2012). Using evidence-based accreditation standards to promote Continuous Quality Improvement: The experience of San Mateo County Human Services Agency. Journal of Evidence-based Social Work, 9(1–2), 68–86.

GLOSSARY / INDEX

Alphabetization is word-by-word.
Locators in *italics* refer to figures, tables, and exhibits.

Taylor & Francis eBooks

Helping you to choose the right eBooks for your Library

Add Routledge titles to your library's digital collection today. Taylor and Francis ebooks contains over 50,000 titles in the Humanities, Social Sciences, Behavioural Sciences, Built Environment and Law.

Choose from a range of subject packages or create your own!

Benefits for you

>> Free MARC records
>> COUNTER-compliant usage statistics
>> Flexible purchase and pricing options
>> All titles DRM-free.

REQUEST YOUR FREE INSTITUTIONAL TRIAL TODAY

Free Trials Available
We offer free trials to qualifying academic, corporate and government customers.

Benefits for your user

>> Off-site, anytime access via Athens or referring URL
>> Print or copy pages or chapters
>> Full content search
>> Bookmark, highlight and annotate text
>> Access to thousands of pages of quality research at the click of a button.

eCollections – Choose from over 30 subject eCollections, including:

Archaeology	Language Learning
Architecture	Law
Asian Studies	Literature
Business & Management	Media & Communication
Classical Studies	Middle East Studies
Construction	Music
Creative & Media Arts	Philosophy
Criminology & Criminal Justice	Planning
Economics	Politics
Education	Psychology & Mental Health
Energy	Religion
Engineering	Security
English Language & Linguistics	Social Work
Environment & Sustainability	Sociology
Geography	Sport
Health Studies	Theatre & Performance
History	Tourism, Hospitality & Events

For more information, pricing enquiries or to order a free trial, please contact your local sales team:
www.tandfebooks.com/page/sales